terra australis 22

Terra Australis reports the results of archaeological and related research within the south and east of Asia, though mainly Australia, New Guinea and island Melanesia — lands that remained *terra australis incognita* to generations of prehistorians. Its subject is the settlement of the diverse environments in this isolated quarter of the globe by peoples who have maintained their discrete and traditional ways of life into the recent recorded or remembered past and at times into the observable present.

Since the beginning of the series, the basic colour on the spine and cover has distinguished the regional distribution of topics as follows: ochre for Australia, green for New Guinea, red for South-East Asia and blue for the Pacific Islands. From 2001, issues with a gold spine will include conference proceedings, edited papers and monographs which in topic or desired format do not fit easily within the original arrangements. All volumes are numbered within the same series.

List of volumes in *Terra Australis*

Volume 1: Burrill Lake and Currarong: coastal sites in southern New South Wales. R.J. Lampert (1971)
Volume 2: Ol Tumbuna: archaeological excavations in the eastern central Highlands, Papua New Guinea. J.P. White (1972)
Volume 3: New Guinea Stone Age Trade: the geography and ecology of traffic in the interior. I. Hughes (1977)
Volume 4: Recent Prehistory in Southeast Papua. B. Egloff (1979)
Volume 5: The Great Kartan Mystery. R. Lampert (1981)
Volume 6: Early Man in North Queensland: art and archaeology in the Laura area. A. Rosenfeld, D. Horton and J. Winter (1981)
Volume 7: The Alligator Rivers: prehistory and ecology in western Arnhem Land. C. Schrire (1982)
Volume 8: Hunter Hill, Hunter Island: archaeological investigations of a prehistoric Tasmanian site. S. Bowdler (1984)
Volume 9: Coastal South-west Tasmania: the prehistory of Louisa Bay and Maatsuyker Island. R. Vanderwal and D. Horton (1984)
Volume 10: The Emergence of Mailu. G. Irwin (1985)
Volume 11: Archaeology in Eastern Timor, 1966–67. I. Glover (1986)
Volume 12: Early Tongan Prehistory: the Lapita period on Tongatapu and its relationships. J. Poulsen (1987)
Volume 13: Coobool Creek. P. Brown (1989)
Volume 14: 30,000 Years of Aboriginal Occupation: Kimberley, North-west Australia. S. O'Connor (1999)
Volume 15: Lapita Interaction. G. Summerhayes (2000)
Volume 16: The Prehistory of Buka: a stepping stone island in the northern Solomons. S. Wickler (2001)
Volume 17: The Archaeology of Lapita Dispersal in Oceania. G.R. Clark, A.J. Anderson and T. Vunidilo (2001)
Volume 18: An Archaeology of West Polynesian prehistory. A. Smith (2002)
Volume 19: Phytolith and starch research in the Australian-Pacific-Asian regions: the state of the art. D. Hart and L. Wallis (2003)
Volume 20: The Sea People: late-Holocene maritime specialisation in the Whitsunday Islands, central Queensland. B. Barker (2004)
Volume 21: What's changing: population size or land-use patterns? The archaeology of Upper Mangrove Creek, Sydney Basin. V. Attenbrow (2004)
Volume 22: The Archaeology of the Aru Islands, Eastern Indonesia. S. O'Connor, M. Spriggs and P. Veth (2005)

terra australis 22

The Archaeology of the Aru Islands, Eastern Indonesia

EDITED BY

S. O'Connor, M. Spriggs and P. Veth

The Australian National University
Canberra ACT 0200 Australia
Email: anuepress@anu.edu.au
Web: http://epress.anu.edu.au

NNational Library of Australia Cataloguing-in-Publication entry

The Archaeology of the Aru Islands, Eastern Indonesia.

Bibliography.

ISBN 978 1 74076 113 0 (pbk).
ISBN 978 1 921313 04 2 (web).

1. Archaeological surveying — Indonesia — Aru Islands. 2. Excavations (Archaeology) — Indonesia — Aru Islands. 3. Aru Islands (Indonesia) — Antiquities. 4. Aru Islands (Indonesia) — Civilization. I. O'Connor, Sue. II. Spriggs, Matthew, 1954- . III. Veth, Peter Marius. IV. Australian National University. Research School of Pacific and Asian Studies. (Series : Terra Australis; 22).

959.801

Cover: Contemporary pottery vessel forms from Batu Lei, South east Aru.

Back cover map: *Hollandia Nova.* Thevenot 1663 by courtesy of the National Library of Australia.
Reprinted with permission of the National Library of Australia.

Series Editor: Sue O'Connor

Typesetting and design: Emily Brissenden

Acknowledgements

The principal investigators from the Australian side would like to thank their respective Departments and Institutions: The Division (later Department) of Archaeology and Natural History of the Research School of Pacific and Asian Studies, and the Department (later School) of Archaeology and Anthropology, Faculty of Arts, at The Australian National University (ANU) in Canberra, and the Department of Anthropology at James Cook University in Townsville. We acknowledge the financial assistance provided by the Australian Research Council and the support for radiocarbon dating of materials provided by the Centre for Archaeological Research (CAR) at ANU, and by the Australian Institute of Nuclear Science and Engineering (AINSE) for AMS dating at the Lucas Heights Facility of the Australian Nuclear Science and Technology Organisation (ANSTO). Matthew Spriggs would like to thank St John's College, Cambridge, United Kingdom, for an Overseas Visiting Scholarship from October 2001 to March 2002, during which much of his contribution to this volume was written.

The interest and co-operation of Dr Hasan Anbari and Dr Truman Simanjuntak of Puslit Arkenas made this project possible. Mrs Dewi Soenarijadi of Lembaga Ilmu Pertahuan Indonesia (LIPI) was also instrumental in providing permission for the research. We should also like to thank our Indonesian co-workers Ako Jatmiko, Husni Mohammad and Aliza Diniasti Saleh of Puslit Arkenas; Widya Nayati of Gajah Mada University; and Djoko Witjaksono (a Master's student of The Australian National University). In Jakarta we also acknowledge the hospitality and assistance of James Batley of the Australian Embassy.

In Ambon we were encouraged and aided by a number of officers of Universitas Pattimura including the Rektor and the late Albert Nikijuluw. We were also helped by Drs Frans Rijoly, Curator of the Siwa Lima Museum, and by Mrs da Lima of Sumber Budi Travel.

In the field in Aru we acknowledge the interest and support of the Camat of Kepulauan Aru, the various Kepala Desa and Adat officials of the villages we visited, and the guides and field crews who accompanied us. In 1995 Peter Paul Rahaor of Universitas Pattimura acted as our translator. Hospitality and discussions on the linguistics of Aru were also provided by Jock Hughes and family, and Rick Nevins and family of Summer Institute of Linguistics (SIL). Staff of the Hotel Fany were always very welcoming and of great help in our work, and we would also especially like to acknowledge Jhonny Limbers of Dobo and the crew of his fishing boat for transport and logistic support. Among the individuals who assisted us in Aru were the Kepala Desa of Afara, Batu Lei, Beimun, Dosi, Durjela, Jambu Air, Jirlay, Longgar, Papakulah Besar, Samang, Silibatabata, Ujir, Wakua, Wangil, and Wokam; and Abdullah (Batu Lei), Jimmy Leifurfaten (Papakulah Besar), Domingus, Isaac, Octavianus and Panus Manila (Dosi), Anton Ohoiwirin (Wokam), Simon Sirlay (Jirlay), Budi Siswanto (Police Chief at Dobo), Michael Tafuran, and Martinus Waitau (Dosi), and the large teams involved in the excavations of Liang Lemdubu, Liang Nabulei Lisa and Wangil (some 35 individuals in all). Brendan Corrigan assisted in the field during part of the excavation of Liang Lemdubu in 1996, and Kelvin Gale helped out at the Liang Nabulei Lisa excavation the following year. Specialist analyses were carried out by a large number of researchers in Australia and other countries. In many cases their contribution has been significant enough to warrant authorship on the papers. Assistance is only acknowledged here where the collaboration has not resulted in authorship. In Australia we were assisted with dating a variety of materials by Rainer Grün, Linda Ayliffe, Tom Higham (in New Zealand and the UK), Ewan Lawson, Ugo Zoppi, Quan Hua and Abaz Alimanovic. Donald Pate attempted an isotopic analysis of bone from Lemdubu woman; Anthony Barham described the sediments from Liang Lemdubu (Chapter 9, Appendix 9.1), Jim Fox gave advice on historical research; Katherine Szabó is responsible for the pottery illustrations; William Dickinson carried out the thin-section analysis on the pottery and his reports are included in full in Chapter 6, Appendix 6.1; Gillian Atkin carried out the pollen preparation, Dominique O'Dea the identifications, and Doreen Bowdery checked the cave sediment samples for phytoliths. Adrian and Anne Veth translated the Dutch and German texts. Dr Pat Woolley (La Trobe University) and Dr Ric How (Western Australian Museum) provided unpublished information on the modern mammal fauna of the Aru Islands. Dr Tim Flannery and Mr Walter Boles, both from the Australian Museum, assisted with some of the taxonomic determinations. John Stanic from the Queensland Museum is thanked for identifications of the landsnails in Liang Lemdubu. Kay Dancey and Anthony Bright from ANU Cartography produced most of the figures for this volume.

If we have left anyone out we apologise profusely.

Contents

1

The Aru Islands In Perspective: A General Introduction

Matthew Spriggs[1], Sue O'Connor[1] and Peter Veth[2]

1. Department of Archaeology and Natural History, Research School of Pacific and Asian Studies, The Australian National University, Canberra, ACT, Australia
2. Research Unit, Australian Institute of Aboriginal and Torres Strait Islander Studies, Canberra, ACT, Australia

> I realise my position as the first European who has ever lived for months together in the Aru Islands, a place which I had hoped rather than expected ever to visit. I think how many besides myself have longed to reach these almost fairy realms, and to see with their own eyes the many wonderful and beautiful things which I am daily encountering ...
>
> *Wallace 1869:450*

Prologue: In the Footsteps of Wallace

Alfred Russell Wallace arrived at the sand-spit settlement of Dobo in the Aru Islands (Fig. 1.1) on January 8, 1857, having travelled from the Kei Islands by local sailing *perahu* on a journey which had taken 30 hours. The following day he set off to explore the small island of Wamar, to which that sand-spit was connected, but soon lost the path to the village of Wamma and had to turn back. But not before he 'had taken about thirty species of butterflies, more than I had ever captured in a day since leaving the prolific banks of the Amazon, and among them were many most rare and beautiful insects, hitherto only known from a few specimens from New Guinea' (1869:433). Apart from a day trip to nearby Wokam Island, Wallace was held up in his travels by bad weather and pirate raids on coastal shipping. This gave him time to observe daily life in Dobo and the differences in appearance and behaviour of the 'Malay' traders and the 'Papuan' indigenous population of the group: 'So far as I have yet seen, the Malay and Papuan appear to be as widely separated as any two human races that exist, being distinguished by physical, mental and moral characteristics, all of the most marked and striking kind' (1869:439).

On March 13 he was finally able to transfer to the larger island of Wokam. Negotiating a berth in a house already occupied by a dozen men, women and children, Wallace remarked: 'I felt that degree of satisfaction and enjoyment which I always experience when, after much trouble and delay, I am on the point of beginning work in a new locality' (1869:445). Even though he was a couple of months too early to find the various birds of paradise in their best plumage, he was quietly ecstatic over a specimen of the King Bird of Paradise, and over other bird species he was able to collect. His two week stay allowed him to observe the local economy:

> The Aru men have no regular supply, no staff of life, such as bread, rice, mandiocca, maize, or sago, which are the daily food of a large proportion of mankind. They have, however, many sorts of vegetables, plantains, yams, sweet potatoes, and raw sago; and they chew up vast quantities of sugar-cane, as well as betel nuts, gambir, and tobacco. Those who live on the coast have plenty of fish; but when inland, as we are here, they only go to the sea occasionally, and then bring home cockles and other shell-fish by the boatload. Now and then they get wild pig or kangaroo, but too rarely to form anything like a regular part of their diet, which is essentially vegetable (Wallace 1869:452).

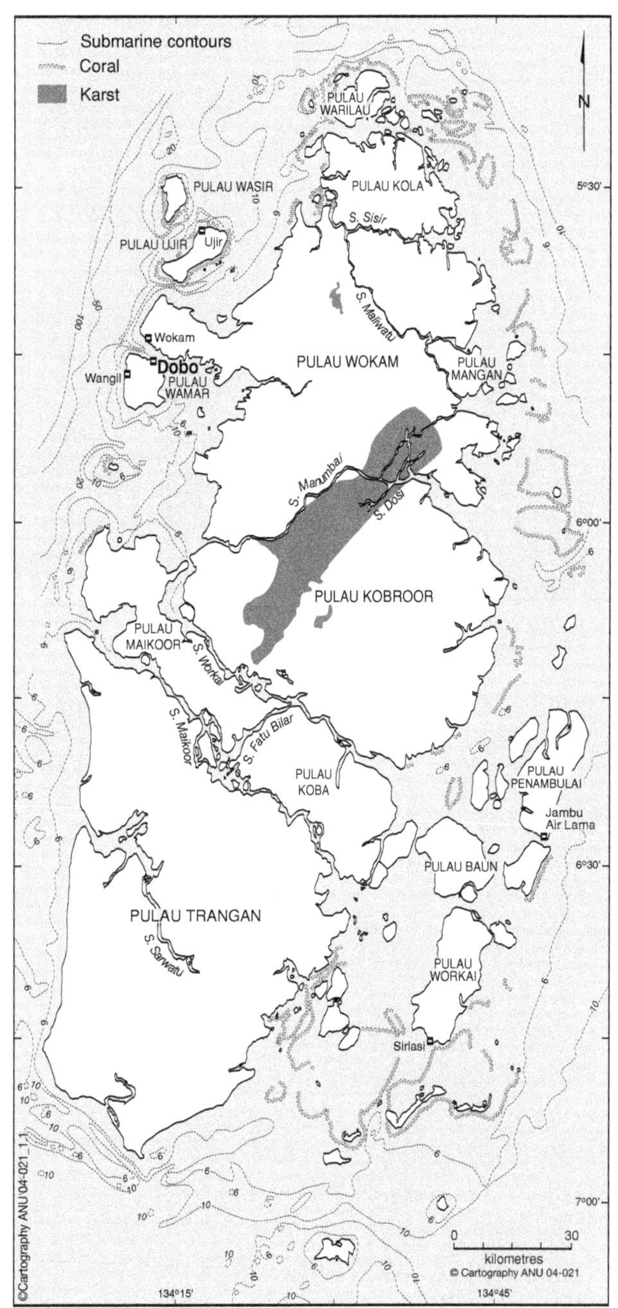

Figure 1.1 Map of Aru showing main islands, *sungai* (rivers) and towns

Once Wallace (1869:454) got his anthropometric eye in, he noticed that there was considerable variation in appearance among the indigenous inhabitants of Aru.

> Many of the natives, though equally dark with the others, have little of the Papuan physiognomy, but have more delicate features of the European type, with more glossy, curling hair. These at first quite puzzled me, for they have no more resemblance to Malay than to Papuan, and the darkness of skin and hair would forbid the idea of Dutch admixture. Listening to their conversation, however, I detected some words that were familiar to me … This cleared up the difficulty. I at once understood that some early Portuguese traders had penetrated to these islands, and mixed with the natives …

At the end of March, Wallace shifted to the area of Wanumbai on the island of Kobroor (not Maykor as he called it), after an abortive attempt to reach the village of Watelai (Batulei) on the east coast of Aru. He stayed at Wanumbai for six weeks, much of his time spent laid up with ulcerated feet from insect bites, but had good collecting and was sorry to leave (Fig. 1.2). Our collecting experience in the same area nearly 140 years later was similar, though we were after different kinds of specimens. The cave site of Liang Lemdubu is situated in the same area as that where Wallace stayed (see Chapter 9, this volume).

Figure 1.2 Small hut on *sungai*, probably very similar to the one in which Wallace would have stayed

Wallace headed back to Dobo and watched the traders packing up before they headed back to Sulawesi and points west, with the shifting wind of that season. He had time to wonder at the price of European goods in this out of the way port:

> One of the most surprising things connected with Aru was the excessive cheapness of all articles of European or native manufacture. We were here two thousand miles beyond Singapore and Batavia, which are themselves emporiums of the 'far East', in a place unvisited by, and almost unknown to, European traders; everything reached us through at least two or three hands, often many more ... (Wallace 1869:478–9).

We were equally bemused to find that the same was true in 1995 when we first set foot in Dobo, but by then the cheap goods were all Japanese or Chinese rather than European.

Wallace left the Aru group on July 2 with the Malay traders. His enthusiastic summary of achievements demonstrates that Aru was a seminal experience in his visit to the East Indies and in his career as a naturalist:

> I brought away with me more than nine thousand specimens of natural objects, of about sixteen hundred distinct species. I had made the acquaintance of a strange and little known race of men; I had become familiar with the traders of the far East; I had revelled in the delights of exploring a new fauna and flora, one of the most remarkable and most beautiful and least-known in the world; and I had succeeded in the main object for which I had undertaken the journey — namely to obtain fine specimens of the magnificent Birds of Paradise and to be enabled to observe them in their native forests. By this success I was stimulated to continue my researches in the Moluccas and New Guinea for nearly five years longer, and it is still the

portion of my travels to which I look back with the most complete satisfaction (Wallace 1869:486).

In the same year he penned a brief account (Wallace 1857) that would be the forerunner to one of the most important scientific texts ever published, which appeared the following year in February 1858 (Wallace 1858) (see Bastin 1986:xxii). Together with that of Charles Darwin (1859), it formed the basis for modern evolutionary thought. The first edition of Wallace's major work on the region, *The Malay Archipelago*, from which the above quotations come, was published in March 1869 some 11 years later.

At various points in the book, Wallace suggests on the basis of the distribution of animals and birds, that Aru had once been joined to New Guinea, although his explanation of its separation did not consider sea level rise (see for instance Wallace 1869:489–92). Earlier (1869:20–1), he tipped the hat to George Windsor Earl, who had first contrasted the shallow continental shelves of what he called 'the Great Asiatic Bank' with 'the Great Australian Bank', corresponding respectively to what archaeologists would now generally call Sunda-land, and the continent of Sahul, incorporating Australia, New Guinea, Aru and Tasmania (Earl 1845; see Ballard 1993 for discussion). It was precisely the position of Aru, as once a series of low hills on the edge of a continent, which attracted our archaeological team to explore it as a potential early landfall for Pleistocene seafarers out of Asia.

The Aru Islands

Much of the following account is taken from Healey (1995, 1996). The Aru Islands archipelago centres on about 6 degrees south Latitude, 134 degrees 30 minutes east Longitude, and is part of the *Kabupaten* (Regency) Maluku Tenggara in Maluku Province of Indonesia. New Guinea is some 150km to the north across a shallow sea; central Arnhem Land in Australia is some 550km to the south; and the Kei Islands lie across a deep ocean trench some 120km to the west. There are six low-lying islands of significant size — Kola, Wokam, Kobroor, Maikor, Koba and Trangan — and many smaller ones, comprising about 180 islands in total. The archipelago stretches about 180km north to south, and is 80km east to west at its widest, with a total area of about 8225km^2 (van Balgooy 1996). It has a low dissected terrain including chains of low hills with the highest point only some 240m above sea level, and extensive areas of coastal and inland swamp (van Balgooy 1996).

The bedrock consists of a variety of raised marine deposits (Fig. 1.3), with the harder limestone substrates displaying sinkhole caves and abandoned underground river channels. The northern islands are rainforest-covered, giving way in the south to drier savannah with *Pandanus* palms on Trangan. Much of the coast and the tidal channels or *sungai* (river in Malay) between islands are fringed with mangroves. The channels, which in some of their upper reaches are true rivers, are the most remarkable feature of the topography, allowing rapid penetration by boat well into the interior of the various islands, and the availability of estuarine shellfish and other 'marine' resources far from the coast as conventionally defined. The *sungai* also form the access routes via which goods such as forest products and pots are moved in canoes or small boats and traded between villages (Fig. 1.4).

The fauna, described in detail in Chapter 3, is basically Australian and Papuan, which bears witness to the land connection to Australia and New Guinea surmised by Wallace. This includes three species of birds of paradise common on the New Guinea mainland, and a variety of marsupial species.

The people of Aru live in 122 mostly coastal villages and the town of Dobo — the only town of significant size. The population reached 62,893 in 1998, comprising 32,048 males and 32,299 females in 12,713 families (Hidayat 1998). The majority of the 15,000 or so residents who are not indigenous to the archipelago live at Dobo and at the fishing port of Benjina. Raw population density outside Dobo is close to five people per square kilometre of total land. The population is said to be predominantly Christian: 90% Protestant, six per cent Catholic, and four per cent Muslim (Dolcemascolo 1996). However, our impression was that the percentage of Muslims must be considerably higher than this, so perhaps Dolcemascolo's figures relate only to the indigenous population. The commercial economy is dominated by fishing and pearl-farming, and is run almost exclusively by non-Aruese. The indigenous Aru Islanders work for these enterprises, and gain a further source of monetary income from the sale of marine and forest resources.

Figure 1.3 Island in *sungai* showing bedding in uplifted marine sedimentary rock

Figure 1.4 A mobile hunter sells or trades his catch of deer and cassowary from his canoe on the *sungai*

The village subsistence economy relies on processing the extensive stands of 'wild' and planted sago palms, and the swidden agriculture of bananas, cassava and maize (Figs 1.5, 1.6). Hunting and collecting of forest resources are also important (Figs 1.7, 1.8), as is fishing (Fig. 1.9). The dry season from May to December can result in seasonal water shortages, water being particularly critical for sago processing. Malaria is a common cause of death and the population, almost completely bereft of modern medical facilities, is also subject to high levels of hookworm and tuberculosis (Dolcemascolo 1996).

The earliest direct historical reference to Aru is in the *Suma Oriental of Tomo Pires* dating from 1512–15, from information collected at Melaka (Courtesao 1944:209). Subsequently, the Portuguese must have at least circumnavigated the archipelago by about 1530, as it appears on maps from that time (see Chapter 5, this volume, for information on historical sources for Aru). Apart from the construction of occasional forts such as that at Wokam from the mid-17th century onwards, there was little attempt by the Dutch to establish a significant presence on Aru until well into the 19th century (see Chapter 4). Islam may have been introduced in the late 15th century, and Christianity came in with the Dutch in the 17th and 18th centuries. While much of the population was not converted to Christianity until the 20th century, it is untrue that Christian missionaries did not have any success until the 1920s as claimed by Dolcemascolo (1996:82).

Figure 1.5 Sago processing

Figure 1.6 Slashing and burning for swidden agriculture on Sungai Papakulah near Benjina

Figure 1.7 Hunters and local villagers with catch of Rusa deer

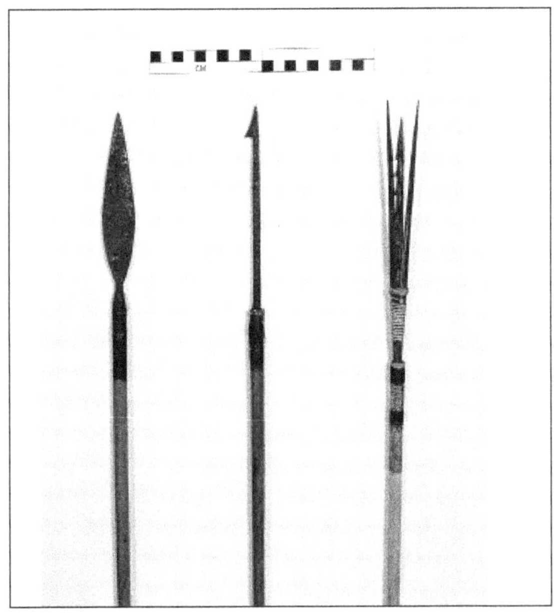

Figure 1.8 Three arrows collected by authors from a hunter at the village of Papakulah Besar

Figure 1.9 Fishtrap made of wood and brush in *sungai*

As we have seen earlier, Wallace (1869) along with other travellers and savants have left us with some detailed accounts of the islanders from the later 19th and early 20th centuries. Prominent among these accounts is Riedel (1886), von Hoevell (1890) and Merton (1910). Kolff (1840) is an extremely important account from an 1826 visit to the group when the Dutch government was trying to re-establish control. The fifth article of his personal instructions was: 'you will inquire as to what remains of the forts erected by the East India Company on the islands, especially those of Arru, Tenimber, and Kessa, noting down with correctness the particulars you may obtain concerning them, subjoining your own observations on their positions and other points' (1840:31). He was an astute observer and provides several important notes on sites which we later visited as part of our reconnaissance surveys of Aru. These are integrated into our own site descriptions in Chapters 4 and 5. Von Rosenberg's account (1867) of his 1865 visit was similarly useful for its descriptions of sites we visited.

Modern ethnographic studies are limited. The most comprehensive to date are: Spyer's (2000) ethnographic study of the Aruese today in the context of the historical imprint of the archipelago's trading past, based on her earlier thesis (Spyer 1992); Healey's (1995) account of trapping methods and their place in the traditional and contemporary economy of Jirlay village, and his more general account (1996) of Jirlay; Dolcemascolo's (1996) study of Wokam village; and economic studies by Universitas Pattimura researchers referred to by Healey and Dolcemascolo. The languages have been researched in recent times by Summer Institute of Linguistics workers, with 12 distinct languages known (Hughes 1987). All of them are Austronesian languages of the Central Malayo-Polynesian grouping, but may have traces of a non-Austronesian substrate which requires further detailed study (Jock Hughes, pers. comm. 1996).

Aru in Perspective: Research Questions in Maluku Archaeology

Sustained archaeological research started late in Maluku compared to regions to the east and west. The first archaeological survey in the region was conducted by Danny Miller and Matthew Spriggs in 1975 in Ambon, Haruku, Saparua, West Seram, Banda, and Kei Kecil (see Spriggs 1990 for a summary). Scientific excavations began only in 1990–91 with Peter Bellwood and his colleagues in Halmahera, Gebe and Morotai (Bellwood 1992, 1998a, 1998b; Bellwood et al. 1993, 1998; Irwin et al. 1999) and Wilhelm Solheim on Halmahera (Solheim 1998). In a paper given at the First Maluku Studies Conference in 1986, Spriggs sketched what was then known about Maluku archaeology and how it fitted into the regional picture (Spriggs 1990). Since that time research has been undertaken in northern Maluku, as already noted, and further archaeological work has been conducted on Ambon, Buru and Seram in Maluku Tengah by a joint Indonesian–University of Hawaii team (Latinis 1999, 2000; Stark 1996; Stark and Latinis 1992, 1996), and on Banda by Peter Lape (2000a, 2000b). Significant archaeological research began in southeastern Maluku with our project in the Aru Islands in 1995 — as documented in this volume — after some earlier exploratory work on Kei Kecil (Ballard 1988, 1992; Spriggs and Miller 1988). Initial reports of our work have already appeared as O'Connor et al. (2002a), Spriggs et al. (1998), and Veth et al. (1998a, 1998b, 2000). The first palaeoenvironmental studies in Maluku were carried out in waters off Halmahera (Barmawidjaja et al. 1993; van der Kaars 1991), and on Obi in northern Maluku by Geoff Hope of The Australian National University (pers. comm. 2003). Such work, using pollen analysis and other techniques, will prove vital for establishing the nature of human use of the environment over time, particularly with questions in mind about the change from hunting and gathering economies to agriculture, and the date of any such change (see Chapter 2, this volume).

Results bearing on the archaeology of the region have also come from the re-awakening of archaeological research in New Guinea (see for instance Denham et al. 2003; Pasveer 2004; Pasveer et al. 2002; papers in Bartstra 1998, and in Denham and Ballard 2003), and particularly the Bismarcks and Solomons in the last two decades (summarized in Allen and Gosden 1991; Spriggs 1997). It is instructive to examine Maluku, as a group of islands immediately to the west of the large island of New Guinea, in the light of the mass of research that has taken place in the islands immediately east of New Guinea. There are a series of similar challenges facing the human inhabitants of both these island areas and, when research is able to resume in Maluku, comparisons and contrasts in their archaeologies will be important in assessing how humans have been able to adjust to these challenges.

In starting research in northern Maluku in 1990, Bellwood identified four major questions to be investigated at the initial stage of research (Bellwood et al. 1993:20):

1) The date and source of initial Pleistocene settlement;
2) The role played by the region in the Austronesian settlement of the Pacific;
3) The nature of the interaction between the two major ethnolinguistic population groups of the region — Papuan (or Non-Austronesian) and Austronesian — during the past 4000 years; and
4) The history of the spice trade with China, India and the West.

The program of research of Bellwood's team has mainly come up with information on the first three topics. They are all pertinent to research anywhere in the archipelago, as we shall see.

Another topic which has proved important in the archaeology of the Bismarcks and Solomons, and for which information is also available in Maluku research, is the nature of the economic system of the region's earliest inhabitants and changes in this economy through time. The origins and development of an agricultural and/or arboricultural economy are pertinent here (most recently see Latinis 2000). Let us look at these five topics in more detail as background to the particular research questions we set out to answer in Aru.

The Date and Source of Initial Pleistocene Settlement

During Pleistocene low sea levels, Sunda was the southernmost extension of the Afro-Eurasian-American continent, comprising Sumatra, Java, Bali, Borneo, Palawan and the now drowned shelf in between. Sahul formed a large continent comprising New Guinea and Australia, including the present islands of the Aru group. Wallacea is a series of island stepping stones between these two extensive land areas. Wallacea includes the islands of the lesser Sundas, much of Maluku including the Kei and Tanimbar islands, Nusa Tenggara, Sulawesi and the Philippines. The zoogeography of the two regions — the placental / marsupial divide — supports this history of isolation.

Movement beyond Sundaland, out into the Wallacean islands and on to Sahul required maritime technology and had to await the advent of anatomically modern humans. Middle Pleistocene cultural deposits in Flores have been documented (Morwood et al. 1998, 1999) but are not conclusively related to modern human voyaging. *Homo erectus* is postulated to be the hominid responsible. *Homo floresiensis,* a diminutive species thought to be descended from *Homo erectus* (Brown et al. 2004), is believed by the excavators of Liang Bua on Flores to be the creator of the cultural assemblage deposited in that cave from 95,000–74,000 years through to about 12,000 BP (Morwood et al. 2004). Others are less convinced and suggest that the artifacts in question were made by modern humans, whose own occupation of the island most certainly overlapped for a considerable period with that of *H. floresiensis* (Lahr and Foley 2004). It must be said, however, that if the stone artifacts from 95,000 to 74,000 year levels are made by the same species as those in the 38,000 to 12,000 BP levels, then that species would be unlikely to be *Homo sapiens* if it really did arrive in the region only 65,000 to 50,000 years ago.

No publications on the Flores cave site have appeared so far with dates for *Homo sapiens* which are earlier or even as early as the Australian sites. Indeed, a central problem is that there are still no dates for modern human occupation in Island Southeast Asia beyond the Sunda shelf as old as the earliest dates obtained for occupation in Australia based on applying Optically Stimulated Luminescence (OSL). Sundaland sites such as Lang Rongrien in southern Thailand and Niah Cave in Sarawak have dates in excess of 40,000 years BP and therefore are up against the so called 'radiocarbon barrier' (Chappell et al. 1996). Dates from the Wallacean Islands are more recent, but only radiocarbon and Uranium-Thorium dating have been undertaken apart from the recent work on the Flores assemblages. The present oldest sites dating to 35–30,000 BP are thus unlikely to represent earliest colonization. Bellwood's team obtained a date of 37,500 BP on marine shell from within a rubble and sediment layer (Layer 2) in Tanjung Pinang rockshelter in southern Morotai, but the shell is thought to be natural and derived from the cave walls, and the deposit at this depth is culturally sterile (Bellwood et al. 1998:237–45). From Gebe Island, at the site of Golo Cave, a more obviously cultural deposit has provided a date of 31,000 BP (Bellwood et al. 1998:249), and from other sites on that island and on Halmahera there are continuous sequences covering the last 15,000 years or more of human occupation (Bellwood et al. 1998; Irwin et al. 1999). Also from within Wallacea are dates of 28,000 BP from Leang Burung 1 cave in southeast Sulawesi (Glover 1981) — although the basal levels remain undated — and, most recently, 35–30,000 BP dates from caves in East Timor (O'Connor et al. 2002b; Spriggs et al. 2003). The site of Labarisu cave on Buru, excavated by Stark (1996), may also date to this early period.

The suggested date of human settlement of the then-continent of Sahul, comprising present day Australia, Tasmania, New Guinea and the Aru Islands, has recently been pushed back to about 55,000 to 65,000 years ago by the use of new dating techniques at sites in both northern and southern Australia (Roberts et al. 1990, 1994; Thorne et al. 2000) although there is vigorous debate about these claims (e.g. O'Connell and Allen 2004; O'Connor and Chappell 2003). Occupation of what is now northeastern New Guinea is documented for at least 40,000 years (Chappell et al.

1994; Groube et al. 1986). The islands to the east of New Guinea were also first settled at least 40,000 years ago (Allen 1994:341; Allen et al. 1988; Leavesley and Chappell 2004; Leavesley et al. 2002; Pavlides and Gosden 1994). The sea crossings from New Guinea to New Britain and New Ireland and onwards to the main Solomons chain (the latter settled by at least 29,000 BP: Wickler and Spriggs 1988) were no greater distance than those traversed in passing from Southeast Asia to Sahul. Manus Island in the Admiralties, however, requires an open ocean voyage out of sight of land to reach it. It is some 200km from the nearest significant land and was settled at sometime prior to 21,000 BP (Fredericksen et al. 1993; Spriggs, ongoing research). Although we do not know what kind of watercraft were used at this time, the Manus case suggests a sophisticated boat technology capable of successfully delivering colonists across long stretches of open ocean.

One of the two likely routes of colonization into Sahul (Fig. 1.10; Birdsell 1977) passes through Maluku via Sula, splitting to form a northern route via Halmahera to the Bird's Head, with alternative southern routes via Buru and Seram either directly from Seram across to the Bomberai Peninsula area of present day New Guinea, or via Kei across to Aru, which in the Pleistocene was a series of low hills on the edge of the Sahul continent. The second main hypothesized early colonization route ran along the Lesser Sundas to Timor and then either directly across to present-day Australia, or again via Maluku through Wetar, Babar and Tanimbar to make a landfall south of Aru (Fig. 1.10). The Manus evidence for advanced boat technology in the Pleistocene does raise the possibility of direct settlement of the Australian part of Sahul from a jumping-off point in the Lesser Sunda Islands which bypasses Maluku, but it is quite possible that Maluku was reached and explored at about the same time. An up to 55,000-year history for at least some parts of Maluku is therefore a real possibility.

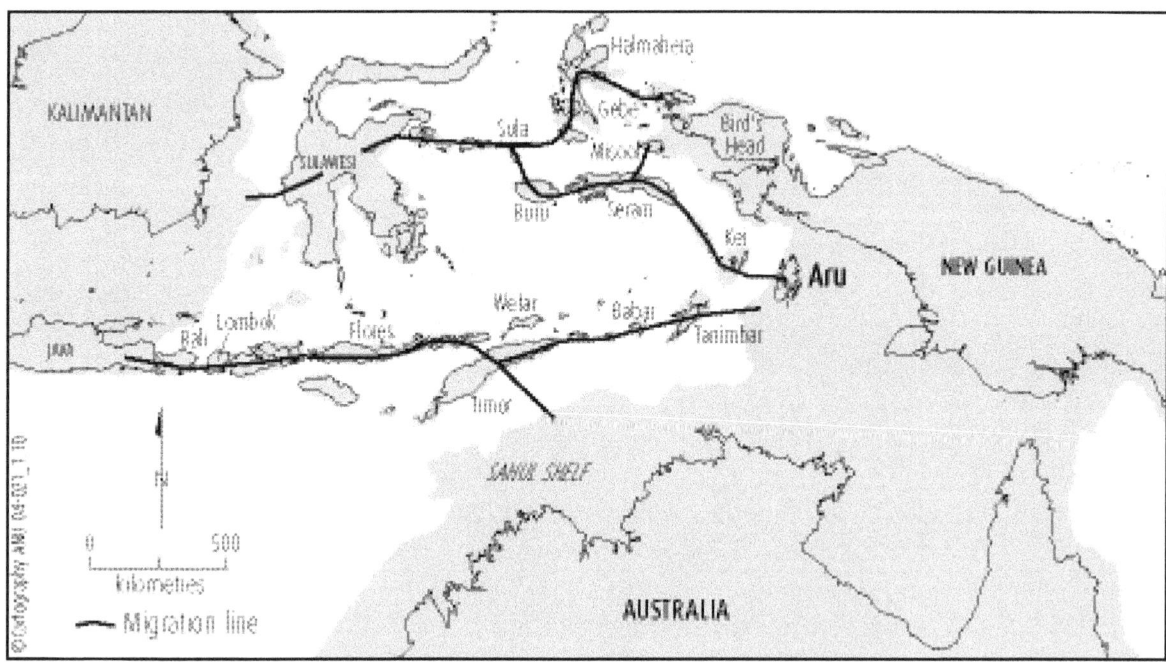

Figure 1.10 Birdsell's proposed colonizing routes through Island Southeast Asia and into Sahul

Economic Changes in the Pleistocene and Early Holocene

Human impact on the environment of the wider region did not start with agriculture (Hope and Golson 1995), and early signs of forest disturbance may point to the kind of 'hunter-horticulturalism' suggested at least for the area to the east, in New Guinea and the Bismarcks and

Solomons (Guddemi 1992). This is seen as an economy beyond simple hunting and gathering which incorporated low intensity gardening and tree cropping, and deliberate movement of plants and animals across water gaps to more impoverished environments. The antiquity of this kind of economy in New Guinea and Island Melanesia goes back at least 20,000 years and probably a lot longer (Gosden 1995; Spriggs 1996a).

From at least 20,000 years ago, the economy in the Bismarcks and Solomons incorporated features such as long-distance exchange of the valued stone obsidian, and the transport of nut-tree species and 'wild' animals from the New Guinea mainland into the forests of the Bismarcks, which were naturally poor in food species.

Advances in analyses of the residues often found on stone and other artefacts mean that the plant food part of ancient diets can now be investigated in much greater detail. Initial results from the northern Solomons suggest that people were exploiting and possibly planting root vegetables such as taro (*Colocasia* sp.) at least 28,000 years ago (Loy et al. 1992). Maluku is clearly within the natural range of a variety of important food plants, including sago. Indeed, the region is implicated in the domestication of some of these plants as part of a putative New Guinea centre of plant domestication (Yen 1991, 1995). Important among the early exploited trees of New Guinea and Island Melanesia are *kenari* trees, various species of the genus *Canarium*. Their human use (and transport between islands) is attested from before 13,000 BP. It is interesting that among the artefacts from early Holocene levels at Tanjung Pinang in southern Morotai, and at Um Kapat Papo on Gebe, were nut-cracking stones identified by people from the area as being for opening *kenari* nuts (Bellwood et al. 1998:242, 247).

This is not the only evidence that Maluku had an early economy of the same type as found in Melanesia. The most important of the animal species transported from New Guinea to the Bismarcks is the cuscus, *Phalanger orientalis*. Later introductions in the Pleistocene and early Holocene include a wallaby, *Thylogale browni*, the bandicoot *Echymipera kalubu*, and a bush rat, *Rattus praetor*. An introduction of unknown antiquity to New Britain but not to the other areas of Island Melanesia is the large flightless bird, the cassowary. The sugar glider, *Petaurus breviceps*, also occurs on New Britain and may have been introduced (see Flannery 1995a, 1995b for a general description of New Guinea and Southwest Pacific [including Maluku] mammals and their distribution).

In the Aru Islands there are many marsupial species of New Guinea origin, but we must remember that until about 11,500 years ago Aru was not an island group but part of the Sahul continent incorporating New Guinea and Australia. These animals therefore more likely represent New Guinea species stranded by rising sea levels at the end of the Pleistocene, and not human introductions across water. In fact, the archaeological faunal assemblage from the lower levels of Lemdubu Cave contains a higher diversity of mammal species than the upper levels, suggesting a depletion of fauna following sea level rise and insulation (see Chapter 9, this volume).

From archaeological research carried out in East Timor, we do have evidence for the early introduction of wild animals to the islands west of New Guinea. There are of course two possible directions of introduction in this case: from New Guinea, and from further west in Southeast Asia. Later introductions of wild animals to Timor, such as the civet cat, deer, macaque monkey, and *Rattus exulans*, certainly came from the west. But the earliest example of an animal introduction there was the same cuscus as found in the Bismarcks, *Phalanger orientalis*, first recognized in Timor in deposits dating to about 6000 years ago (Glover 1986), and recently recovered from caves in the east end of the island in deposits dating to 9000 BP (Aplin and O'Connor, ongoing research). Its presence on several islands in Maluku (Kei, Banda, Leti, Gorom, Seram, Ambon-Lease, Buru and Sula) is almost certainly because of human introduction at some period in the past.

A second New Guinea cuscus, *Spilocuscus maculatus*, is also present on several Maluku islands including Kei, Banda, Seram, Ambon and Buru. At some point it was even spread further afield to Salayer Island, off the south coast of Sulawesi (Flannery 1995a, 1995b). Although we lack the archaeological evidence it seems reasonable to hypothesize that this species was a human introduction to Maluku.

To the east of New Guinea a cuscus was introduced to the Mussau Group about 3300 years ago. A New Guinea bandicoot, *Echymipera rufescens,* is found on Kei, and words for what appears to be the same species have been collected from languages in Ambon, Seram, Leti-Moa and Damar (Blust 1993:251), so it may be more widespread in the islands. A related species of bandicoot was introduced to Manus, east of New Guinea, about 13,000 years ago, again suggesting that the present distribution of *rufescens* is humanly-assisted. Two rat species found today in Kei (*Uromys caudimaculatus* and *Hydromys chrysogaster*) are less likely to be human introductions from New Guinea, as rats are known to disperse across water by natural means such as drifting on logs. The cassowary, found on Seram, is not known to disperse naturally across water gaps and presumably represents a human introduction at a presently unknown time. Hints of the picture we are likely to find in the region were given by the results of the first seasons of excavations in northern Maluku. At Gua Siti Nafisah at Nusliko on southern Halmahera, Bellwood et al. (1993) and Flannery et al. (1995) report bones of two locally extinct marsupial species in pre-pottery levels dating to between 5120 and 3410 BP. They are a species of *Dorcopsis* wallaby (*Dorcopsis muelleri mysoliae*) and a bandicoot (cf. *Echymipera rufescens*). Also found was an endemic species of cuscus, *Phalanger ornatus,* which is still present on the island today. The *Dorcopsis* wallaby survived to be deposited into a midden with pottery that dates to about 1870 BP, and the bandicoot may have disappeared earlier at about 3000 BP. The initial interpretation was that the wallaby and bandicoot were probably endemic species rather than human introductions (Flannery et al. 1995). While still the case in relation to the bandicoot, Flannery et al. (1998) have more recently suggested the likelihood of human introduction for the *Dorcopsis* from Misool Island, via Gebe.

On Gebe, the same species of *Dorcopsis* wallaby first occurs in the archaeological record between 10,000 and 8500 BP and most probably represents a human introduction from Misool, which before 10,500 BP was part of the mainland of Sahul (Flannery et al. 1998). The Halmahera bandicoot species does not appear to have reached Gebe. The *Dorcopsis* had become extinct on the island by 1500 BP (Bellwood 1998b).

The sugar glider, *Petaurus breviceps,* is present on Halmahera today but has not been found in any of the archaeological sites, suggesting that it may be a comparatively recent introduction from New Guinea.

Local extinction of wild fauna after settlement by pottery-using Neolithic groups, as is documented for Halmahera and Gebe, is also a feature of the sites in the Bismarcks and Solomons to the east of New Guinea. There, endemic species of bush rats and several species of birds became extinct with the advent of the first pottery using cultures. The reasons given include competition with introduced domestic animals — particularly the dog — and rats such as *Rattus exulans* and *Rattus praetor*. The latter originated from the Asian mainland and was also a presumably pre-3500 BP introduction to Maluku. Hunting pressure, habitat destruction and, in the case of the birds, possible avian diseases introduced with the domestic chicken, are other likely causes of extinctions (Steadman 1997). Austronesian occupation of the empty islands of the western and eastern Pacific resulted in major environmental devastation and faunal extinctions (Steadman 1995).

The Role Played by the Region in the Austronesian Settlement of the Pacific

The 'package' which is known as the Island Southeast Asian Neolithic, is associated with the appearance of pottery, a fully agricultural economy, and domestic animals such as the pig, the dog and the chicken, and is thought by many researchers to be co-associated with the spread of Austronesian (AN) languages into this region (Bellwood 1997). The sudden appearance of the package within archaeological site contexts, coupled with the linguistic evidence, has been interpreted as evidence for the rapid spread of an immigrant group (or groups). The colonization of the western and eastern Pacific was finally accomplished by speakers of AN languages taking with them an attenuated version of the economic suite by which they are distinguished in Island Southeast Asia. Its eastern expression in Island Melanesia and Western Polynesia is the Lapita culture which has a narrow spread of colonization dates from 3300 to 3000 BP across its range from the Bismarck Archipelago to Tonga and Samoa (Spriggs 1999). Ironically, the timing and nature of Austronesian impact is better understood archaeologically in the previously occupied regions of Island Melanesia and on the previously unoccupied islands of the Pacific, than for the donor area of Island Southeast Asia.

Bellwood has argued that the earliest Neolithic sites are found in Taiwan and dated at between 6000–5000 BP and that the subsequent spread of this culture through the southern Philippines, Borneo, Sulawesi and eastern Indonesia occurred *after* 4000 BP (Bellwood 1997:219). In view of the dates to the west and east of Maluku for the spread of Neolithic culture the expected age in the region should be between about 4000 and 3500 BP. If Bellwood is correct in his view of the Neolithic spread, the entire expansion beyond Taiwan through to the Western Pacific may have taken only 500 years. Such an extremely rapid rate would have implications for the demography of the migration and the interaction with indigenous groups along the way. Aside from the excavations of Bellwood and his colleagues in the northern Moluccan islands, there has been little excavation carried out in the immediate region which might clarify the situation.

An assemblage of classic Neolithic type with pottery has been found by Bellwood and his colleagues at Uattamdi on Kayoa Island off Halmahera, with clear links to contemporary assemblages from Sulawesi, Eastern Timor and the Bismarck Archipelago. Neolithic dates in Maluku do not yet go back beyond about 3300 BP, but this is to be expected at this early stage of research (cf. Bellwood et al. 1993:32). What is more surprising though is that Uattamdi is the only northern Maluku pottery site of this period, pottery occurring elsewhere in the area only from about 2000 BP, and being of common Indonesian Metal Age type (Bellwood 1998b).

Another site dating to this period was found by Lape on the island of Ay in the Banda Group (Lape 2000a:215–29, 2000b:141). Two dates were obtained on mammal bone of about 3200 BP associated with pig and fish bone, chert, obsidian of unknown source and pottery — including a red-slipped sherd with an incised decoration of a classic Lapita motif zone marker. Undecorated red-slipped pottery continued below the dated layers. Clearly it is a site with great potential for elucidating the early Neolithic of central and south Maluku, although the reliance on bone as a dating medium means that the age must be considered provisional.

According to Blust (1993), Central Malayo-Polynesian (CMP) Austronesian languages spread rapidly through Maluku and the Lesser Sundas from a primary dispersal point in northern Maluku soon after the break-up of Central-Eastern Malayo-Polynesian (Proto C-EMP), the language ancestral to CMP and Eastern Malayo-Polynesian (EMP). Pawley (1999:125) suggests that this split took place around 4000 BP. Recalculating his figure on the basis of revised dating of the break-up of the Oceanic group to 3200 BP rather than 3500 BP would suggest a slightly later date of about 3700 BP for the split. EMP includes the ancestor of the Austronesian languages spoken in South Halmahera and West New Guinea (the SHWNG group) and the Oceanic group which includes all the other Austronesian languages of New Guinea, Island Melanesia, Polynesia and most of the Micronesian languages. Northern Maluku is thus the key area for the dispersal of Austronesian languages across the region, and also by extension for the spread of Neolithic culture. Blust suggests that CMP languages later spread from Tanimbar to the Bomberai Peninsula of New Guinea (1993:278).

The spread of this Neolithic culture is interpreted to represent an immigrant group with a fully agricultural economy and domestic animals such as the pig, the dog and the chicken (Spriggs 1996b). The main variety of domestic pig in Maluku, New Guinea and the Pacific appears to be a hybrid between *Sus scrofa vittatus* (naturally distributed in Malaya and Western Indonesia) and the endemic Sulawesi species, *Sus celebensis*. The hybridisation appears to have occurred in northern Maluku (Groves 1981:65–6). While earlier pig remains have been claimed from New Guinea, the weight of evidence now suggests that its introduction there occurred in association with the Austronesian expansion (Hedges et al. 1995). No definitely *in situ* pig remains have been found in the pre-pottery levels at the northern Maluku sites. The dog, the chicken, the commensal rat *Rattus exulans* and later animal introductions such as goat and deer, also came from the west.

There is evidence, however, of reciprocal influences from further to the east during this period of expansion, and also of an additional strand in the history of agriculture in the region. Evidence for the independent development of horticulture in the New Guinea Highlands between 9000 and 7000 years ago (Golson 1977) has recently been much strengthened by the research of Denham and his colleagues (Denham et al. 2003). It seems possible, therefore, that horticulture first reached the Aru Islands from the east rather than the west (cf. Spriggs 1996a, 2003). This hypothesis receives support from recent genetic and palaeobotanical research which show that some important domesticates that were previously believed to have a Southeast Asian origin — such as *Eumusa* section bananas, some *Dioscorea* yams and *Saccharum* sugarcane — have a New Guinea origin and likely diffused from there to Southeast Asia during the early to mid-Holocene after which hybridization with local varieties occurred (De Langhe and de Maret 1999:380; Lebot 1999:621–2). Based on the importance of forest and tree crops in Maluku (especially the sago palm, *Metroxylon sagu*), Latinis and Stark (1998; cf. Latinis 2000) have argued the need to incorporate more flexible models of mobility and subsistence in our modelling of early horticulture. In view of the proximity of the Aru Islands to the New Guinea mainland and Aru's biogeographical suitability for growing the same root and tree crops as grown in New Guinea, it seems possible that when Austronesian speakers arrived in the Aru Islands they discovered hunter-horticulturalists growing a range of root and tree crops, combined with exploitation of wild and cultivated sago stands, much as people were in the recent past in Aru.

We have already noted the humanly-assisted movement of animal species from New Guinea into Wallacea during the late Pleistocene or early Holocene period. The most tangible evidence of similar contacts during the Neolithic is the presence of obsidian sourced to the Talasea region of New Britain found in a site in Sabah dated to 3000 BP (Bellwood and Koon 1989; Chia 2001). The situation as regards the Lapita pottery design system of the Bismarck Archipelago is at present not so clear. Similar designs have been found on Island Southeast Asian Neolithic pottery, most recently on a Banda Island sherd as discussed above, but are nowhere clearly earlier than in the Bismarcks. Spriggs (1989:607) raised the possibility that the design system diffused back from the Bismarcks along the original route of settlement from Southeast Asia. These cross-overs (and potential cross-overs) are markers of what is increasingly appearing as not just a simple one way colonization 'out of Asia', as had earlier been thought, but rather a series of complex two-way interactions, both in the Pleistocene and the Holocene. For a recent review of the Island Southeast Asian Neolithic see Spriggs (2003).

Austronesian — Non Austronesian Interaction

Non-Austronesian (NAN) languages of the Maluku region include some on the islands near Timor, which are immediately derived from there, and the languages of northern Halmahera and Morotai. They are thought to be related to languages of Western New Guinea. Whether they represent ancient language stocks present in pre-Austronesian times throughout Maluku or are the result of more recent population movements from further east is unknown. For an extensive discussion of the linguistic evidence for northern Maluku see Bellwood (1998b). Archaeological research elsewhere in Maluku is at too early a stage to try and compare it with the picture from linguistics. Possible NAN substrates or later connections between the Austronesian languages of Kei and Aru with the Asmat-Kororo family of the NAN Central and South New Guinea Stock have been suggested (Collins 1982; Jock Hughes pers. comm. 1996).

Wallace distinguished between Malays and Papuans as two populations present in different parts of Island Southeast Asia (Wallace 1869:584–98). He saw the boundary between these groups as occurring within Wallacea:

> If we draw a line, commencing to the east of the Philippine Islands, thence along the western coast of Gilolo [Halmahera], through the island of Bouru, and curving round the west end of Flores, then bending back by Sandalwood Island [Sumba] to take in Rotti, we shall divide the Archipelago into two portions, the races of which have strongly marked distinctive peculiarities. This line will separate the Malayan and all the Asiatic races, from the Papuans and all that inhabit the Pacific; and though along the line of junction intermigration and commixture have taken place, yet the division is on the whole almost as well defined and strongly contrasted, as is the corresponding zoological division of the Archipelago, into an Indo-Malayan and Austro-Malayan region (Wallace 1869:592).

He noted Aru, along with Kei and of course New Guinea itself, as being 'inhabited almost exclusively by the typical Papuans' (Wallace 1869:591). In the light of recent genetic work showing that many distinctive Polynesian markers originate not in Taiwan as might be expected, but within southern Wallacea (Hurles et al. 2002; Oppenheimer and Richards 2001; Richards et al. 1998), Wallace seems particularly perspicacious in linking Polynesians more directly to 'Papuan' populations in this region than to the Malays (1869:593). The implications of this have recently been discussed by Spriggs (2003).

The implication would be that in large part the present populations of Aru descend from its Pleistocene settlers and that language shift to Austronesian languages, rather than a major in-migration of Neolithic farmers en route from Taiwan ('Malays' in Wallace's terminology) has been the main local mechanism which explains their current linguistic affiliation. The inland populations of Aru in particular may well have retained a primarily pre-Austronesian hunter-horticultural lifestyle until it was somewhat transformed by World System demands for forest products within the last 2000 and particularly the last 200 years.

The History of the Spice Trade

Until recently the earliest evidence of the international trade in Maluku spices came from Han Chinese and Indian sources of about 2000 years ago (Andaya 1993b:1–2), and hints from the spread of metal from mainland Southeast Asia through the islands as far as areas either side of Maluku, starting 2300–2100 years ago. The sudden appearance of metal and, a few hundred years later, the distribution of Dongson bronze drums originating in northern Vietnam and southern China and found as far as Maluku and the Bird's Head of New Guinea, have been interpreted as marking the beginning of the spice trade (Spriggs and Miller 1988; see also Kempers 1988; Swadling 1996). The northern Maluku evidence for widespread adoption of pottery of general Indonesian Metal Age style from 2000 BP, would fit in with this interpretation.

Dramatic claims from Syria have extended the dating for the spice trade back another 1500 years. The evidence comes from the ancient city of Terqa (modern Ashara) on the Middle Euphrates, a halfway station between Ebla and Akkad. Excavation of a residential quarter of the city dating to about 3710–3550 BP (1760–1600 BC) revealed an area destroyed by fire. In the storage area of one house were a series of jars and other clay vessels. One of them contained well-preserved spices including what has been claimed by the excavators to be a clove (Bucellati and Kelly-Bucellati 1977:116; Bucellati and Kelly-Bucellati 1977–1978:77–79). The clove, *Eugenia aromatica,* if it is such, can only have come from Maluku.

The dating of this evidence is from a period not long after the initial Neolithic Austronesian settlement of the region is inferred to have taken place. Perhaps part of the reason for the Austronesian expansion was to do with the extension of trading networks that were already at this time on an Old World scale? At the time, the connections of the Austronesian sphere ran north through the Philippines, Taiwan, and into South China. Cloves could potentially have moved along the ancient caravan routes north of the Himalayas to their Syrian destination.

So, at least, it seemed to Spriggs when he presented a paper in 1994 at the Third Maluku Studies Conference (later published in revised form as Spriggs 1998). Pam Swadling independently considered the implications of the Syrian finds in her book on the birds of paradise trade in Eastern Indonesia and New Guinea (Swadling 1996). Other early discoverers of the relevance of the Terqa finds to Maluku, and the first to get into print on it, were Taylor and Aragon (1991). The problem is that other Near Eastern specialists and palaeobotanists do not accept the original identification of the clove from Terqa, and believe it to be some other unrelated species (Carl Lamberg-Karlovsky, pers. comm. 1996). On the basis of the Terqa clove and early claimed pottery, betel nut and pigs from northern New Guinea, Swadling (1996:51–3, 269) has claimed that there was an early period of contact linking New Guinea and Asia dating from about 6000–5000 BP. She posits an association with the spread of Austronesian languages and claims an 'almost simultaneous introduction of pottery across Island Southeast Asia as far as New Guinea about 5000 years ago' (1996:51). The dating of pigs and pottery in northern New Guinea has been challenged (Spriggs 1996b), and the latest ideas on the spread of pottery through Island Southeast Asia and into the Pacific would put it as reaching Maluku only some 4000–3500 BP (see above).

Swadling's (1996) claims for an important role for bird of paradise feathers in the later exchange systems associated with the spread of early metal in the region are far more persuasive. Such birds occur in Maluku only in the Aru Islands, but the long-standing connections between northern Maluku and New Guinea provide the conduit through which such feathers probably first entered the world market. Whether the spices or the feathers entered the exchange networks first, or together, is at present unknown, but Swadling's book is an important corrective to earlier spice-centred views of regional trade. It is obvious that the more recent history of Maluku, including the archaeology of the Portuguese and Dutch colonial period, is closely bound up with the spice trade and the efforts of world powers to access and control it (Andaya 1993b), but the importance of other forest and marine products should not be underestimated.

How far south and east such trade connections went in this region in the recent past is attested by the Macassan trepangers and their contacts with Aboriginal groups along the northern coast of Australia from the seventeenth to the early twentieth centuries (Clarke 2000; Fox 2000), and also by some interesting linguistic material from southern New Guinea. This suggests a period of long-range interaction between the Non-Austronesian languages of northern Maluku, specifically Ternate and/or Tidore, and communities along the southern coast of New Guinea in the Gulf of Papua, to the east of Torres Strait (Donohue 1995:226–7; Voorhoeve 1982). The contact was also probably quite late, however, and was associated with the trade in birds of paradise plumes (Swadling 1998). It may be attested by stories in the Gulf of an attempted introduction of Islam — thus dating the connection to the period subsequent to the late fifteenth century AD (our interpretation of Laba 1996; cf. Wagner 1996:294). An additional clue may be the references in oral traditions in the Gulf to the place-name Adiri 'at the extreme western border of the world' (Wagner 1996:288, quoting Landtman 1917), which we take to refer to Tidore. Swadling (1996:154–65) prefers to see the contact in the Gulf as having been with traders from Seram Laut between 1645 and 1790, who were denied by the Dutch their traditional trade with the Aru Islands. She points to some linguistic connections but did not seem to be aware of Voorhoeve's (1982) publication. Tidore had traditional relations with Seram Laut, and Tidorese-speaking agents appear to have been based in the area (Andaya 1993a, cf. 1993b), but the strength of these connections is disputed by Ellen (1993).

Directions for Aru Research

When the Joint Indonesia-Australian archaeological team first set out for the Aru Islands in 1995 we thus anticipated finding archaeological evidence relating to several theoretical issues in Southeast Asian archaeology which also have parallels in other parts of the world. Such issues include:

1) the nature and rate of maritime colonization and island settlement by early *H. sapiens sapiens* in the Pleistocene, and the subsequent impact of such settlement on the 'pristine' landscapes of previously unoccupied islands;
2) the extent of inter-island connectivity or isolation and contact and exchange in the Pleistocene and early Holocene as demonstrated by the evidence relating to the translocation of animal species, plants and exotic stone;
3) the impetus for the development and/or adoption of agriculture by pre-agricultural communities or hunter-horticulturalists;
4) the interaction between indigenous groups and incoming Austronesian settlers and/or traders; and
5) the involvement of Aru as a supplier of bird of paradise feathers and other forest and marine products to world markets over the last 2000 years or so.

Aru was part of a continuous landbridge to both Australia and New Guinea for at least the first 40,000 years of occupation of Sahul by *H. sapiens sapiens*. Approximately 14,000 years ago rising seas began to encircle the island group, separating it from Australia and by 11,500 years BP it was completely separated from New Guinea (see Chapter 2, this volume).

As noted earlier, the presence on Aru of numerous marsupials and the cassowary attest to this shared history. While the waters to the east of the Aru Islands are relatively shallow, reflecting the previous landbridge with New Guinea and northwest Australia, the continental shelf to the west slopes steeply with the 100m isobath located as little as 10km away. Due to their optimal position, the Aru Islands have the potential to register a multitude of maritime colonizing events through time. It has already been mentioned that the Aru Islands and their now-inundated Pleistocene coastal plains are located on two of the major colonizing routes into Sahul, as proposed by Birdsell (1977) (Fig. 1.10). The key point is that branches of both the postulated primary northern and southern colonizing routes pass through, or close to, the Aru Islands. This feature, combined with the fact that they are positioned right on the edge of the Sahul Shelf, make them prime targets for investigating initial and subsequent maritime colonizations.

The narrow water corridor which separated the southeastern Moluccan islands of Kei and Tanimbar from the Aru Islands throughout the last 50,000 years and more, make this one of the most likely routes of colonization (Birdsell 1977; Irwin 1992). The steeply shelving off-shore profile in this region also makes Aru one of the most *discoverable* first jumping-off points into Sahul where evidence of early coastal settlement might be preserved. Such proximity would also have facilitated two-way voyaging in this region, both before and after Aru was separated from the rest of Sahul approximately 11,500 years ago.

The Aru Islands also have the advantage of being composed in part of limestone, with a substantial belt of karst located near the central western coast (see Fig. 1.1). Rockshelters and caves occur in the karst and the alkaline environment has the potential to provide excellent faunal and botanical preservation. We expected to be able to track extinction and faunal introduction events from such sites.

We also anticipated that Aru would provide coastal midden sites of mid-Holocene to recent age, which would cover the period of the introduction of, or transition to, agriculture, and provide pottery and other artefactual sequences which could be linked to sites elsewhere in the region. Such base camp and/or village locations might also provide evidence for interaction between the Aru Islanders and exogenous groups, such as traders in search of forest or marine products.

Finally, following some of the early travellers' reports of Aru, we expected to find evidence of the attempts by the Dutch to establish control of the archipelago in the form of forts and other structures, which might be amenable to historical and archaeological research.

Our research was sponsored by the National Research Centre for Archaeology in Jakarta (Pusat Penelitian Arkeologi Nasional, also known as PPAN or Puslit Arkenas) as the 'Joint Indonesia–Australian Archaeological Project: Prehistory of the Aru Islands'. Co-operation with the National Research Centre was formalized in a Memorandum of Understanding (MOU) signed on October 8, 1996, which concluded at the end of 1999 after the fieldwork was completed. All finds from the field seasons have now been lodged with the National Research Centre after being taken out of Indonesia for analysis as part of the MOU. In Maluku the research was sponsored by Universitas Pattimura in Ambon.

Our team reached Dobo on December 1, 1995, having travelled over night by ferry from Tual in Kei Kecil. It consisted of Spriggs, Veth and Ako Jatmiko from Puslit Arkenas (Jakarta). Further trips to Aru were made in 1996 and 1997. The 1996 team consisted of O'Connor, Spriggs and Veth, Husni Mohammad from Puslit Arkenas (Branch Menado), and Widya Nayati, a lecturer in the Department of Archaeology at Gajah Mada University, Yogyakarta. The 1997 field team consisted of Geoff Hope from Australian National University, O'Connor, Veth, and Aliza Diniasti Saleh from Puslit Arkenas (Jakarta).

The research was funded by a Small Australian Resesarch Council (ARC) Grant to Veth for 1995, and a Large ARC Grant to Veth, Spriggs and O'Connor for the period 1996–98. This monograph presents the results of these three seasons of fieldwork. Further research, extending coverage also to Kei and Tanimbar, had been planned to commence in 2000 and was funded by a further Large ARC Grant to Spriggs, Veth and O'Connor, but had to be abandoned owing to the deepening political and humanitarian crisis in Maluku. The research focus and the grant were then shifted to East Timor.

References

Allen, J. 1994. Radiocarbon determinations, luminescence dating and Australian archaeology. *Antiquity* 68:339–43.

Allen, J., C. Gosden, R. Jones, and J.P. White. 1988. Pleistocene dates for the human occupation of New Ireland, northern Melanesia. *Nature* 331:707–9.

Allen, J. and C. Gosden (eds). 1991. *Report of the Lapita Homeland Project.* Canberra: Department of Prehistory, Research School of Pacific and Asian Studies, Australian National University. *Occasional Papers in Prehistory* 20.

Andaya, L. 1993a. Centers and peripheries in Maluku. *Cakalele: Maluku Studies Research Journal* 4:1–21.

Andaya, L. 1993b. *The World of Maluku: Eastern Indonesia in the Early Modern Period.* Honolulu: University of Hawai'i Press.

van Balgooy, M.M.J. 1996. Vegetation sketch of the Aru Islands. In H.P. Nooteboom (ed.), *The Aru Archipelago: Plants, Animals, People and Conservation,* pp. 1–14. Amsterdam: Nederlandse Commissie Voor Internationale Natuurbescherming. *Mededelingan* 30.

Ballard, C. 1988. Dudumahan: a rock art site on Kai Kecil, southeast Moluccas. *Bulletin of the Indo-Pacific Prehistory Association* 8:139–61.

Ballard, C. 1992. Painted rock art sites in western Melanesia: locational evidence for an 'Austronesian' tradition. In J. McDonald and I. Haskovec (eds), *State of the Art: Regional Rock Art Studies in Australia and Melanesia*, pp. 94–106. Melbourne: Australian Rock Art Association. *AURA Publication* 6.

Ballard, C. 1993. Stimulating minds to fantasy? A critical etymology for Sahul. In M.A. Smith, M. Spriggs, and B. Fankhauser (eds), *Sahul in Review: Pleistocene Archaeology in Australia, New Guinea and Island Melanesia*, pp. 17–23. Canberra: Department of Prehistory, Research School of Pacific and Asian Studies, Australian National University. *Occasional Papers in Prehistory* 24.

Barmawidjaja, B.M., E.J. Rohling, W.A. van der Kaars, C. Vergnaud Grazzini, and W.J. Zachariasse. 1993. Glacial conditions in the northern Molucca sea region, Indonesia. *Palaeogeography, Palaeoclimatology and Palaeoecology* 101:147–67.

Bartstra, G.-J. (ed.). 1998. *Bird's Head Approaches: Irian Jaya Studies, A Programme For Interdisciplinary Research*. Rotterdam: A.A. Balkema. *Modern Quaternary Studies in Southeast Asia* 15.

Bastin, J. 1986 Introduction. In A.R. Wallace, *The Malay Archipelago*, pp. vii–xxvii. Singapore: Oxford University Press.

Bellwood, P. 1992. New discoveries in Southeast Asia relevant for Melanesia (especially Lapita) prehistory. In J.-C. Galipaud (ed.), *Poterie Lapita et Peuplement: Actes du Colloque Lapita, Noumea, Nouvelle-Caledonie, Janvier 1992*, pp. 49–96. Noumea: ORSTOM.

Bellwood, P. 1997. *Prehistory of the Indo-Malaysian Archipelago*. 2nd Edition. Honolulu: University of Hawaii Press.

Bellwood, P. 1998a. The archaeology of Papuan and Austronesian prehistory in the northern Moluccas, eastern Indonesia. In R. Blench and M. Spriggs (eds), *Archaeology and Language II: Correlating Archaeological and Linguistic Hypotheses*, pp. 128–40. London: Routledge.

Bellwood, P. 1998b. From bird's head to bird's eye view: long term structures and trends in Indo-Pacific prehistory. In J. Miedema, C. Odé, and R.A.C. Dam (eds), *Perspectives on the Bird's Head of Irian Jaya, Indonesia: Proceedings of the Conference, Leiden, 13–17 October 1997*, pp. 951–75. Amsterdam: Rodopi.

Bellwood, P. and P. Koon. 1989. 'Lapita colonists leave boats unburned!' The question of Lapita links with island Southeast Asia. *Antiquity* 63:613–622.

Bellwood, P., A. Waluyo, Gunadi, G. Nitihaminoto, and G. Irwin. 1993. Archaeological research in the northern Moluccas: interim results, 1991 field season. *Bulletin of the Indo-Pacific Prehistory Association* 13:20–33.

Bellwood, P., G. Nitihaminoto, G. Irwin, Gunadi, A. Waluyo, and D. Tanudirjo. 1998. 35,000 years of prehistory in the northern Moluccas. In G.-J. Bartstra (ed.), *Bird's Head Approaches: Irian Jaya Studies, A Programme for Interdisciplinary Research*, pp. 233–75. Rotterdam: A.A. Balkema. *Modern Quaternary Studies in Southeast Asia* 15.

Birdsell, J.B. 1977. The recalibration of a paradigm for the first peopling of Greater Australia. In J. Allen, J. Golson, and R. Jones (eds), *Sunda and Sahul: Prehistoric Studies in Southeast Asia, Melanesia and Australia*, pp. 113–67. London: Academic Press.

Blust, R. 1993. Central and Central Eastern Malayo-Polynesian. *Oceanic Linguistics* 32(2):241–93.

Brown, P., T. Sutikna, M.J. Morwood, R.P. Seojono, Jatmiko, E.W. Saptomo, and R.A. Due. 2004. A new small-bodied hominin from the Late Pleistocene of Flores, Indonesia. *Nature* 431:1055–61.

Buccellati, G. and M. Kelly-Buccellati. 1977. Terqa preliminary reports 1: general introduction and the stratigraphic record of the first two seasons. *Syro-Mesopotamian Studies* 1(3).

Buccellati, G. and M. Kelly-Buccellati. 1977–1978. The Terqa archaeological project: first preliminary report. *Les Annales Archeologiques Arabes Syriennes: Revue d'Archeologie et D'Histoire* 27/28:71–96.

Chappell, J., A. Omura, M. McCullough, T. Esat, Y. Ota, and J. Pandolfi. 1994. Revised late Quaternary sea levels between 70 and 30 ka from coral terraces at Huon Peninsula. In Y. Ota (ed.), *Study on Coral Reef Terraces of the Huon Peninsula, Papua New Guinea: Establishment of Quaternary Sea Level and Tectonic History*, pp. 155–65. Yokohama: Department of Geography, Yokohama National University.

Chappell, J., J. Head, and J. Magee. 1996. Beyond the radiocarbon limit in Australian archaeology and Quaternary research. *Antiquity* 70:543–52.

Chia, S. 2001 The Prehistory of Bukit Tengkorak, Sabah, Malaysia. *Journal of Southeast Asian Archaeology* 21: 136–159.

Clarke, A. 2000. The 'Moormans Trowsers': Macassan and Aboriginal interactions and the changing fabric of indigenous social life. *Modern Quaternary Research in Southeast Asia* 16:315–35.

Collins, J.T. 1982. Linguistic research in Maluku: a report of recent field work. *Oceanic Linguistics* 31(1&2):73–150.

Courtesao, A. (trans. and ed.). 1944. *The Suma Oriental of Tomo Pires*. London: Hakluyt Society. 2 volumes.

Darwin, C. 1964[1859]. *On the Origin of Species*. A Facsimile of the First Edition. Cambridge, Mass.: Harvard University Press.

Denham, T. and C. Ballard (eds). 2003. Perspectives on prehistoric agriculture in the New Guinea highlands: a tribute to Jack Golson. *Archaeology in Oceania* 38(3).

Denham, T.P., S.G. Haberle, C. Lentfer, R. Fullagar, J. Field, M. Therin, N. Porch, and B. Winsborough. 2003. Origins of agriculture at Kuk Swamp in the highlands of New Guinea. *Science* 301:189–93.

Dolcemascolo, G. 1996. Foreign encounters in an Aruese landscape. *Cakalele: Maluku Research Journal* 7:79–92.

Donohue, M. 1995. Barking up the wrong tree: chasing an Oceanic dog west to Indonesia. In C. Baak, M. Bakker, and D. van der Meij (eds), *Tales from a Concave World: Liber Amicorum Bert Voorhoeve*, pp. 216–45. Leiden: Department of Languages and Cultures of Southeast Asia and Oceania, Leiden University.

Earl, G.W. 1845. On the physical structure and arrangement of the islands of the Indian Archipelago. *Journal of the Royal Geographical Society* XV:358–65.

Ellen, R. 1993. Faded images of old Tidore in contemporary southeast Seram: a view from the periphery. *Cakalele: Maluku Research Journal* 4:23–37.

Flannery, T.F. 1995a. *Mammals of the South-West Pacific and Moluccan Islands.* Sydney: Australian Museum/Reed Books.

Flannery, T.F. 1995b. *Mammals of New Guinea* (revised edition). Sydney: Reed Books.

Flannery, T.F., P. Bellwood, J.P. White, A. Moore, Boeadi, and G. Nitihaminoto. 1995. Fossil marsupials (Macropodidae, Perocytidae) and other mammals of Holocene age from Halmahera, north Moluccas, Indonesia. *Alcheringa* 19:17–25.

Flannery, T.F., P. Bellwood, J.P. White, T. Ennis, G. Irwin, K. Schubert, and S. Balasubramaniam. 1998. Mammals from Holocene archaeological deposits on Gebe and Morotai Islands, northern Moluccas, Indonesia. *Australian Mammalogy* 20(3):391–400.

Fox, J.J. 2000. Maritime communities in the Timor and Arafura region: some historical and anthropological perspectives. *Modern Quaternary Research in Southeast Asia* 16:337–56.

Fredericksen, C., M. Spriggs, and W. Ambrose. 1993. Pamwak rockshelter: a Pleistocene rock shelter on Manus Island, PNG. In M. Smith, M. Spriggs, and B. Fankhauser (eds), *Sahul in Review: Pleistocene Archaeology in Australia, New Guinea and Island Melanesia*, pp. 144–52. Canberra: Department of Prehistory, Research School of Pacific and Asian Studies, Australian National University. *Occasional Papers in Prehistory* 24.

Glover, I. 1981. Leang Burung 2: an Upper Palaeolithic rock shelter in south Sulawesi, Indonesia. *Modern Quaternary Research in Southeast Asia* 6:1–38.

Glover, I. 1986. *Archaeology in East Timor 1966–67.* Canberra: Department of Prehistory, Research School of Pacific Studies, Australian National University. *Terra Australis* 11.

Golson, J. 1977. No room at the top: agricultural intensification in the New Guinea Highlands. In J. Allen, J. Golson, and R. Jones (eds), *Sunda and Sahul: Prehistoric Studies in Southeast Asia, Melanesia and Australia*, pp. 601–38. London: Academic Press.

Gosden, C. 1995. Arboriculture and agriculture in coastal Papua New Guinea. *Antiquity* 69:807–17. *Special Issue* 265.

Groube, L.M., J. Chappell, J. Muke, and D. Price. 1986. A 40,000 year-old human occupation site at Huon Peninsula, Papua New Guinea. *Nature* 324:453–55.

Groves, C.P. 1981. *Ancestors for the Pigs: Taxonomy and Phylogeny of the Genus Sus.* Canberra: Department of Prehistory, Research School of Pacific Studies, Australian National University. *Technical Bulletin* 3.

Guddemi, P. 1992. When horticulturalists are like hunter-gatherers: the Sawiyano of Papua New Guinea. *Ethnology* 31(4):303–14.

Healey, C. 1995. Traps and trapping in the Aru Islands. *Cakalele: Maluku Research Journal* 6:51–65.

Healey, C. 1996. Aru connections: outback Indonesia in the modern world. In D. Mearns and C. Healey (eds), *Remaking Maluku: Social Transformation in Eastern Indonesia*, pp. 14–26. Darwin: Centre for Southeast Asian Studies, NTU. *Special Monograph* 1.

Hedges, R.E.M., R.A. Housley, C.R. Bronk, and G.J. van Klinken. 1995. Radiocarbon dates from the Oxford AMS system: archaeometry datelist 20. *Archaeometry* 37:417–30.

Hidayat, H. 1998. Forest management by the local peoples in Aru District, southeast Maluku, in *A Step Toward Forest Conservation Strategy(1) — Interim Report.* Unpublished report to IGES, Forest Conservation Project. URL: http://www.iges.or.jp/en/fc/phase1/ir98-3-9.PDF

von Hoevell, G.W.W.C., Baron. 1890. De Aroe-eilanden, geographisch, ethnographisch en commercieel. *Tijdschrift van het Koninglijk Nederlandsch Aardrijkskundig Genootschap, Leiden* 33:57–102.

Hope, G. and J. Golson. 1995. Late Quaternary change in the mountains of New Guinea. *Antiquity* 69:818–30.

Hughes, J. 1987. The languages of Kei, Tanimbar and Aru: a lexicostatistic classification. In S. Dardjowidjojo (ed.), *Miscellaneous Studies of Indonesian and other Languages of Indonesia, part IX. Nusa* 27:71–111.

Hurles, M.E., J. Nicholson, E. Bosch, C. Renfrew, B.C. Sykes, and M.A. Jobling. 2002. Y chromosomal evidence for the origins of Oceanic-speaking peoples. *Genetics* 160:289–303.

Irwin, G. 1992. *The Prehistoric Exploration and Colonization of the Pacific.* Cambridge: Cambridge University Press.

Irwin, G., P. Bellwood, G. Nitihaminoto, D. Tanudirjo, and L. Siswanto. 1999. Prehistoric relations between Island Southeast Asia and Oceania: recent archaeological investigations in the northern Moluccas. In J.-C. Galipaud and I. Lilley (eds), *The Pacific from 5000-2000 BP: Colonization and Transformations*, pp. 363–74. Paris: IRD.

van der Kaars, W.A. 1991. Palynology of eastern Indonesian marine piston-cores. *Palaeogeography, Palaeoclimatology and Palaeoecology* 85:239–302.

Kempers, A.J.B. 1988. *The Kettledrums of Southeast Asia: A Bronze Age World and its Aftermath.* Rotterdam: A.A. Balkema. *Modern Quaternary Research in Southeast Asia* 10 (for 1986–7).

Kolff, D.H. 1840. *Voyages of the Dutch Brig of War 'Dourga' through the Southern and Little Known Parts of the Moluccan Archipelago...during the Years 1825 and 1826.* London: James Madden.

Laba, B. 1996. Oral traditions about early trade by Indonesians in southwest Papua New Guinea. In P. Swadling, *Plumes from Paradise: Trade Cycles in Outer Southeast Asia and Their Impact on New Guinea and Nearby Islands Until 1920*, pp. 299–307. Port Moresby: Papuan New Guinean National Museum in association with Robert Brown and Associates (Queensland).

Lahr, M.M. and R. Foley. 2004. Human evolution writ small. *Nature* 431:1043–4.

Landtmann, G. 1917. *The Folk-Tales of the Kiwai Papuans.* Helsingfors: Finnish Society of Literature. *Acta Societatis Scientiarum Fennicae* 47.

de Langhe, E. and P. de Maret. 1999. Tracking the banana: its significance in early agriculture. In C. Gosden and J. Hather (eds), *The Prehistory of Food*, pp. 377–96. London: Routledge.

Lape, P.V. 2000a. Contact and Conflict in the Banda Islands, Eastern Indonesia, 11th to 17th Centuries. Unpublished PhD thesis, Brown University, Rhode Island.

Lape, P.V. 2000b. Political dynamics and religious change in the late pre-colonial Banda Islands, Eastern Indonesia. *World Archaeology* 32(1):138–55.

Latinis, D.K. 1999. Subsistence System Diversification in Southeast Asia and the Pacific: Where does Maluku fit? Unpublished PhD thesis, University of Hawai'i at Manoa, Honolulu.

Latinis, D.K. 2000. The development of subsistence system models for Island Southeast Asia and Near Oceania: the nature and role of arboriculture and arboreal-based economies. *World Archaeology* 32(1):41–67.

Latinis, D.K. and K. Stark 1998. Subsistence, arboriculture and prehistory in Maluku. In S. Pannell and F. von Benda-Beckmann (eds), *Old World Places, New World Problems: Exploring Issues of Resource Management in Eastern Indonesia*, pp. 34–65. Canberra: Centre for Resource and Environmental Studies, The Australian National University.

Leavesley, M.G., M.I. Bird, L.K. Fifield, P.A. Hausladen, G.M. Santos, and M.L. di Tada. 2002. Buang Merabak: early evidence for human occupation in the Bismarck Archipelago, Papua New Guinea. *Australian Archaeology* 54:55–7.

Leavesley, M.G. and J. Chappell. 2004. Buang Merabak: additional early radiocarbon evidence of the colonisation of the Bismarck Archipelago, Papua New Guinea. *Antiquity* 78(301). URL:http://antiquity.ac.uk/ProjGall/leavesley/index.html

Lebot, V. 1999. Biomolecular evidence for plant domestication in Sahul. *Genetic Resources and Crop Evolution* 46:619–28.

Loy, T.H., M. Spriggs, and S. Wickler. 1992. Direct evidence for human use of plants 28,000 years ago: starch residues on stone artefacts from the Northern Solomon Islands. *Antiquity* 66:898–912.

Merton, H. 1910. *Forschungsreise in den Sudostlichen Molukken (Aru-und Kei Inseln).* Frankfurt, A.M.: Senckenbergischen Naturforschenden Gesellschaft.

Morwood, M.J., P. O'Sullivan, F. Aziz, and A. Raza. 1998. Fission track age of stone tools and fossils on the east Indonesian island of Flores. *Nature* 392:173–6.

Morwood, M.J., F. Aziz, P. O'Sullivan, Nasruddin, D.R. Hobbs, and A. Raza. 1999. Archaeological and palaeontological research in central Flores, East Indonesia: results of fieldwork 1997–98. *Antiquity* 73:273–86.

Morwood, M.J., R.P. Seojono, R.G. Roberts, T. Sutikna, C.S.M. Turney, K.E. Westaway, W.J. Rink, J.-x. Zhao, G.D. van den Bergh, R.A. Due, D.R. Hobbs, M.W. Moore, M.I. Bird, and L.K. Fifield. 2004. Archaeology and age of a new hominin from Flores in Eastern Indonesia. *Nature* 431:1087–91.

O'Connell, J.F. and J. Allen. 2004. Dating the colonization of Sahul (Pleistocene Australia-New Guinea): a review of recent research. *Journal of Archaeological Science* 34:835–53.

O'Connor, S., K. Aplin, M. Spriggs, P. Veth, and L.A. Ayliffe. 2002a. From savannah to rainforest: changing environments and human occupation at Liang Lemdubu, the Aru Islands, Maluku, Indonesia. In A.P. Kershaw, B. David, N. Tapper, D. Penny, and J. Brown (eds), *Bridging Wallace's Line: The Environmental and Cultural History and Dynamics of the Southeast Asian–Australian Region*, pp. 279–306. Reiskirchen: Catena Verlag. *Advances in GeoEcology* 34.

O'Connor, S., M. Spriggs, and P. Veth. 2002b. Excavation at Lene Hara cave establishes occupation in East Timor at least 30,000 to 35,000 years ago. *Antiquity* 76:45–50.

O'Connor, S. and J. Chappell. 2003. Colonization and coastal subsistence in Australia and Papua New Guinea: different timing, different modes. In C. Sand (ed.), *Pacific Archaeology: Assessments and Prospects. Proceedings of the International Conference for the 50th Anniversary of the First Lapita Excavation (July 1952), Koné-Nouméa 2002*, pp. 15–32. Nouméa: Départment Archéologie, Service des Musées et du Patrimoine de Nouvelle-Calédonie. *Le Cahiers de l'Archéologie en Nouvelle-Calédonie* 15.

Oppenheimer, S. and M. Richards. 2001. Fast trains, slow boats, and the ancestry of the Polynesian Islanders. *Science Progress* 84(3):157–81.

Pasveer, J.M. 2004. *The Djief Hunters: 26,000 Years of Rainforest Exploitation on the Bird's Head of Papua Indonesia.* Lisse: A.A. Balkema. *Modern Quaternary Research in Southeast Asia* 17.

Pasveer, J.M., S.J. Clarke, and G.H. Miller. 2002. Late Pleistocene human occupation of inland rainforest, Bird's Head, Papua. *Archaeology in Oceania* 37:92–5.

Pavlides, C. and C. Gosden. 1994. 35,000 year-old sites in the rainforests of West New Britain, Papua New Guinea. *Antiquity* 68:604–10.

Pawley, A. 1999. Chasing rainbows: implications of the rapid dispersal of Austronesian languages for subgrouping and reconstruction. In E. Zeitoun and P.J.-K. Li (eds), *Selected Papers from the Eighth International Conference on Austronesian Linguistics*, pp. 95–138. Taipei: Academia Sinica.

Richards, M., S. Oppenheimer, and B. Sykes. 1998. MtDNA suggests Polynesian origins in eastern Indonesia. *American Journal of Human Genetics* 63:1234–6.

Riedel, J.G.F. 1886. *De Sluik- en Kroesharige Rassen Tusschen Selebes en Papua.* 's-Gravenhage: Martinus Nijhoff.

Roberts, R.G., R. Jones, and M.A. Smith. 1990. Thermoluminescence dating of a 50,000 year old human occupation site in northern Australia. *Nature* 345:153–6.

Roberts, R.G., R. Jones, N.A. Spooner, M.J. Head, A.S. Murray, and M.A. Smith. 1994. The human colonization of Australia: optical dates of 53,000 and 60,000 bracket human arrival at Deaf Adder Gorge, Northern Territory. *Quaternary Science Reviews* 13:575–83.

von Rosenberg, C.B.H. 1867. *Reis Naar de Zuidoostereilanden Gedaan in 1865 op last der Regering van Nederlandsch-Indie.* 's-Gravenhage: Martinus Nijhoff.

Solheim, W.G. III. 1998. Preliminary report on Makbon archaeology, the Bird's Head, Irian Jaya. In G.-J. Bartstra (ed.), *Bird's Head Approaches: Irian Jaya Studies, A Programme for Interdisciplinary Research*, pp. 29–40. Rotterdam: A.A. Balkema. *Modern Quaternary Studies in Southeast Asia* 15.

Spriggs, M. 1989. The dating of the Southeast Asian Neolithic: an attempt at chronometric hygiene and linguistic correlation. *Antiquity* 63:587–612.

Spriggs, M. 1990. Archaeological and ethnoarchaeological research in Maluku, 1975 and 1977: an unfinished story. *Cakalele: Maluku Research Journal* 1:47–60.

Spriggs, M. 1996a. Early agriculture and what went before in Island Melanesia: continuity or intrusion? In D. Harris (ed.), *The Origins and Spread of Agriculture and Pastoralism in Eurasia*, pp. 524–37. London: UCL Press.

Spriggs, M. 1996b. What is Southeast Asian about Lapita? In T. Akazawa and E. Szathmary (eds), *Prehistoric Mongoloid Dispersals*, pp. 324–48. Oxford: Clarendon Press.

Spriggs, M. 1997. *The Island Melanesians.* Oxford: Blackwell.

Spriggs, M. 1998. Research questions in Maluku archaeology. *Cakalele: Maluku Research Journal* 9(2):51–64.

Spriggs, M. 1999. Archaeological dates and linguistic sub-groups in the settlement of the Island Southeast Asian-Pacific region. *Bulletin of the Indo-Pacific Prehistory Association* 18:17–24.

Spriggs, M. 2003. Chronology of the Neolithic transition in Island Southeast Asia and the Western Pacific: a view from 2003. *The Review of Archaeology* 24(2):57–74.

Spriggs, M. and D. Miller. 1988. A previously unreported bronze kettledrum from the Kai Islands, Eastern Indonesia. *Bulletin of the Indo-Pacific Prehistory Association* 8:79–89.

Spriggs, M., P. Veth, and S. O'Connor. 1998. In the footsteps of Wallace: the first two seasons of archaeological research in the Aru Islands, Maluku. *Cakalele: Maluku Studies Research Journal* 9(2):63–80.

Spriggs, M., S. O'Connor, and P. Veth. 2003. Vestiges of early pre-agricultural economy in the landscape of East Timor - recent research. In A. Karlstrom and A. Kallen (eds), *Fishbones and Glittering Emblems: Southeast Asian Archaeology 2002*, pp. 49–58. Stockholm: Museum of Far Eastern Antiquities.

Spyer, P. 1992. The Memory of Trade: Circulation, Autochthony, and the Past in the Aru Islands (Eastern Indonesia). Unpublished PhD thesis, Department of Anthropology, The University of Chicago, Chicago.

Spyer, P. 2000. *The Memory of Trade: Modernity's Entanglements on an Eastern Indonesian Island.* Durham and London: Duke University Press.

Stark, K. 1996. Alternative Rainforest Economies of Maluku, Indonesia: A Reply to the "Wild Yam" Hypothesis from the Archaeological Record. Unpublished PhD thesis, University of Hawai'i at Manoa, Honolulu.

Stark, K. and K. Latinis. 1992. Research report: the archaeology of sago economies in central Maluku. *Cakalele: Maluku Research Journal* 3:69–86.

Stark, K. and K. Latinis. 1996. The response of early Ambonese foragers to the Maluku spice trade: the archaeological evidence. *Cakalele: Maluku Research Journal* 7:51–67.

Steadman, D. 1995. Prehistoric extinctions of Pacific Island birds: biodiversity meets zooarchaeology. *Science* 267:1123–30.

Steadman, D. 1997. Extinctions of Polynesian birds: reciprocal impacts of birds and people. In P.V. Kirch and T.L. Hunt (eds), *Historical Ecology in the Pacific Islands: Prehistoric Environmental and Landscape Change*, pp. 51–79. New Haven: Yale University Press.

Swadling, P. 1996. *Plumes From Paradise: Trade Cycles in Outer Southeast Asia and Their Impact on New Guinea and Nearby Islands Until 1920*. Port Moresby: Papua New Guinean National Museum in association with Robert Brown and Associates (Queensland).

Taylor, P.M. and L.V. Aragon. 1991. *Beyond the Java Sea: Art of Indonesia's Outer Islands*. Washington D.C.: Smithsonian Institution; New York: H.N. Abrams.

Thorne, A., R. Grun, G. Mortimer, N.A. Spooner, J.J. Simpson, M. McCulloch, L. Taylor, and D. Curnoe. 2000. Australia's oldest human remains: age of the Lake Mungo 3 skeleton. *Journal of Human Evolution* 36:591–612.

Veth, P., M. Spriggs, A. Jatmiko, and S. O'Connor. 1998a. Bridging Sunda and Sahul: the archaeological significance of the Aru Islands, southern Moluccas. In G.-J. Bartstra (ed.), *Bird's Head Approaches: Irian Jaya Studies, A Programme for Interdisciplinary Research*, pp. 157–77. Rotterdam: A.A. Balkema. *Modern Quaternary Studies in Southeast Asia* 15.

Veth, P., M. Spriggs, and S. O'Connor. 1998b. After Wallace: preliminary results of the first season's excavation of Liang Lemdubu, Aru Islands, Maluku. In M. Klokke and T. de Bruijn (eds), *Southeast Asian Archaeology 1996: Proceedings of the 6th International Conference of the European Association of Southeast Asian Archaeologists*, pp. 75–86. Hull: Centre for Southeast Asian Studies, University of Hull.

Veth, P., S. O'Connor, M. Spriggs, W. Nayati, A. Jatmiko, and H. Mohammed. 2000. The mystery of the Ujir site: insights into the early historic maritime settlement of the Aru Islands, Maluku. *Bulletin of the Australian Institute for Maritime Archaeology* 24:125–32.

Voorhoeve, C.L. 1982. The Halmahera connection: a case for prehistoric traffic through Torres Strait. In A. Halim, L. Carrington, and S.A. Wurm (eds), *Papers from the Third International Conference on Austronesian Linguistics, Tracking the Travellers*, pp. 217–239. Canberra: Department of Linguistics, Research School of Pacific Studies, Australian National University. *Pacific Linguistics* C-75.

Wagner, R. 1996. Mysteries of origin: early traders and heroes in the Trans Fly. In P. Swadling, *Plumes From Paradise: Trade Cycles in Outer Southeast Asia and Their Impact on New Guinea and Nearby Islands Until 1920*, pp. 285–298. Port Moresby: Papua New Guniean National Museum in association with Robert Brown and Associates (Queensland).

Wallace, A.R. 1857. On the natural history of the Aru Islands. *Annals and Magazine of Natural History* (Series 2) 20:473–85.

Wallace, A.R. 1858. On the tendency of varieties to depart indefinitely from the original type. *Proceedings of the Linnaean Society of London, Zoology* 3:53–62.

Wallace, A.R. 1869. *The Malay Archipelago: The Land of the Orang-Utan and the Bird of Paradise. A Narrative of Travel, with Studies of Man and Nature*. London: MacMillan.

Wickler, S. and M. Spriggs. 1988. Pleistocene human occupation of the Solomon Islands, Melanesia. *Antiquity* 62(237):703–6.

Yen, D.E. 1991. Polynesian cultigens and cultivars: the questions of origin. In P.A. Cox and S.A. Banack (eds), *Islands, Plants and Polynesians: an Introduction to Polynesian Ethnobotany*, pp. 67–95. Portland: Dioscorides Press.

Yen, D.E. 1995. The development of Sahul agriculture with Australia as bystander. *Antiquity* 69 (special number 265):831–47.

2

Environmental Change in the Aru Islands

Geoffrey Hope[1] and Ken Aplin[2]

1. Archaeology and Natural History, Research School of Pacific and Asian Studies, The Australian National University, Canberra, ACT, Australia
2. Sustainable Ecosystems, CSIRO, GPO Box 284, Canberra, ACT 2601, Australia

Introduction

The Aru archipelago has attracted scientific interest over the past two centuries because of its position as a 'lifeboat' of the former Torresian plain of the continent of Sahul. Yet despite a lengthy visit by Wallace (1857, 1869; see Chapter 1, this volume), and subsequent studies of birds and other biota (e.g. van Balgooy and Nooteboom 1995; Monk et al. 1997; Flannery 1995), and geomorphology (Verstappen 1959), virtually no comprehensive environmental studies have been published with the exception of Nooteboom (1996). Although remoteness has been blamed for this state of affairs, the islands have experienced more than two centuries of reasonable communications and significant business activity based on pearling, bird of paradise feathers, and most recently timber extraction and commercial fishing. The islands have failed to attract comprehensive scientific work despite being known to western science, perhaps because New Guinea became accessible. For example, the large British Ornithological Union expedition called in at Dobo in 1910 as the last western outpost before tackling the New Guinean coast (Wollaston 1912), but made no studies on Aru.

This chapter reviews what is known of the Aru natural environments, and provides a background to the archaeology by deducing the past environments and palaeoclimates from regional studies such as marine palynology (van der Kaars et al. 1997), reconstruction of past shorelines from bathymetry and isostatic modelling (e.g. Voris 2000; Yokoyama et al. 2001a), and limited local data. The major discovery by the present research team, of faunal change in the past that reflects climate change, is dealt with in detail in Chapters 7 and 9. These findings are summarized here and set in a regional context.

The Aru Region

Topography and regional setting

The Aru Islands lie on the western edge of the shallow seas of Torres Strait, around 7°S and 134°E (see Chapter 1, Fig. 1.1). The group is quite discrete, for their nearest neighbours are the Kei Islands of the Banda outer arc, 130km to the west, and New Guinea 110km to the north. To the south, the shelf is deeper (60–80m) until Croker Island in northern Australia is reached (510km). The archipelago consists of about 80 islands greater than 40ha, and a further 80 that are smaller, totalling ca. 8225km^2 (van Balgooy 1996). The islands lie very close to one another. The seven largest, with a combined land area of 7050km^2, are separated only by narrow channels and are effectively one land mass. The highest point on the islands is 241m altitude on Kobroor, but the other large islands generally reach only 50–100m altitude, becoming lower to the south. The sea around the islands is shallow, generally less than 20m in depth, and a slight submarine ridge connects them eastwards to Yos Sudarso (Prinz Hendrik) Island in New Guinea.

A very significant aspect of the Aru islands is that they lie within a region of macro-tides that extends from the northwest Australian coast. Open water spring tides have a range of 1.5m (British Admiralty 1998) but can vary in closed estuaries to considerably more depending on the lunar cycle and prevailing winds, resulting in a very variable shoreline environment.

Geology and geomorphology

Torres Strait and the southern plains of West Papua and Papua New Guinea are a submerged extension of the Australian continental plate, which has enjoyed relative stability since the Proterozoic. Sediments in the Northern Territory are around 500–700 million years in age but include gently folded sandstones. Granites, rhyodacites, shales, and quartzites are also common and occur in southern Papua. Some basins occur in the east and reflect Cretaceous or earlier sea ways. The shelf is mantled by late Neogene and Quaternary sediments a few hundred metres in thickness. The Aru Islands are uplifted Pliocene and Quaternary marly limestone, siltstone and sandstone sediments, that are domed up as a high point on the shelf (Gregory et al. 1924; Verstappen 1959). They are mostly horizontal or gently dipping beds of similar lithology to the modern shelf sediments forming in shallow seas. Corals are rare in the limestones and this matches the situation in shallow areas around the group, where coral reefs are quite restricted but shell beds and calcareous sandy muds are common (Verstappen 1959). Some bedding horizons onshore are marked by lines of scallop and oyster shells. The bedding is consistent with Verstappen's interpretation of a large geanticline: a gently arched structure over 100km across. Older cratonic bedrock may not be far down, since coarse quartz, mica and feldspar have been seen on the southeast part of Pulau Trangan (Verstappen 1959).

There is a low drainage density due to the absorption of surface water by the marls, although seasonal stream ways are common and some flowing water occurs from springs. Dry or internally draining valleys are found in the raised karst, but on lowland plains clays and silts mantle some hills and valleys, allowing surface flow and shallow streamlines in heavy rain. Lakes are rare except for a few small karst hollows on Kobroor and Trangan Islands. Van Balgooy (1996) also notes the occurrence of permanent and seasonal ponds and swamps on Trangan Island. Springs occur along the cliffed coast and interior gorges.

The Aru Islands are famous for the *sungai*, a series of about eight major channels that traverse the islands or penetrate deeply into them (see Chapter 1, Fig. 1.2). These waterways are like rivers, but are flooded by the sea. The channels are 100–300m wide, and incised 20–100m deep in gorges through the hills. They are usually 10–20m deep, but in places are scoured out to well below the level of the sea floor. The three largest — Sungai Manumbai, S. Workai, and S. Maikoor — separate

Wokam, Kobroor, Koba and Trangan Islands, and are up to 50km in length with side channels and connections. The high tidal range causes rapid flow in both directions twice a day, providing an obvious mechanism for maintaining the channels. In places the limestone cliffs are notched at high water level, indicating that solution is active. The width and depth of the channels varies greatly. At low tide the main channels remain water filled but side channels drain, exposing kilometres of mangrove muds or rocky solution surfaces with sharp edges. Extremely high tides sometimes leave a band of open scald land behind the dense mangrove forest in the zone of daily flooding.

Verstappen (1959) discusses the various theories for formation of these channels. He concludes that they are the result of solution along joint cracks that are concentrated in NNW–SSE and NNE–SSW directions, symmetrical to the north-south axis of the group. The jointing may be the result of relatively recent or even continuing shear planes on the geanticlinal upwarp. Once the joints had enlarged and captured local drainage they cut down by flow and solution to the level of the shelf. On being flooded by rising sea level they were scoured out and cut by active tidal flows. During low sea levels they may have been a series of freshwater lakes and streamways, fed by active springs.

Away from the steep banks of the *sungai* the islands have gentle slopes, although steep scarps and low ridges occur. Soils are shallow on the limestone, and ridges of rock are common under the forest. Karstic landforms are not very common, as the limestone is porous and solution general. However, numerous dolines and lines of collapsed tunnel caves occur. These tunnel caves, mostly seen on Kobroor Island, are often located near the top of ridgelines, with thin roofs. They must represent a former underground drainage that is now abandoned due to general surface lowering and the development of deeper drainage.

The coastline is generally steep with low (5–10m) cliffed or steep sections, which on the west coast often lie behind calcareous sand beaches or mud flats. These cliffs are the result of marine erosion during the earliest period of sea level rise, following which progradation has led to a generally low energy coastline, invaded in many areas by mangroves or protected by offshore reefs and mud flats.

Climate

The islands lie in the extreme east of the Indian ocean but are sheltered by the islands to the southwest around Timor and Nusa Tenggara. For most of the year surface water flows to the northwest under the influence of the southeast trade winds, and warm Torres Strait water derived from the Coral Sea inflow surrounds the islands. A warm current also flows below surface drift to the south and west to form the unusual Leeuwin current of the Western Australian coast. During the northwest monsoon, from November to March, large rainfall systems pass eastwards and surface currents in Torres Strait are reversed. At this time rainfall is heavy and there are widespread thunderstorms. Rainfall data is scanty for the archipelago; the rainfall maps of Monk et al. (1997) suggest that the rainfall is about 2000mm per annum on the western coast of Trangan Island, rising east and north to possibly 3000mm in the interior of Kobroor. Dobo has an annual rainfall of 2078mm (van Balgooy 1996), and probably lies in a slight rainshadow (Table 2.1).

Table 2.1 Dobo rainfall (from van Balgooy 1996)

MONTH	JAN	FEB	MAR	APR	MAY	JUN	JUL	AUG	SEPT	OCT	NOV	DEC
mm	272	229	200	153	154	116	63	78	115	164	243	234
Rain days	15.3	15.6	14.8	13.9	12.9	12.0	9.1	6.8	7.5	8.9	11.8	14.8

Much of Aru is more southerly than the Kei Islands where rainfall is better studied. On Kei Kecil the rainfall is estimated to be only 1400mm at the southern tip and hence it is possible that the rainfall of southern Aru has been overestimated. There is a marked gradient in seasonality, the southern part experiencing a pronounced dry season each year of about 4 months with monthly rainfall less than 100mm, while the northern half has a less pronounced winter minimum. In comparison to more southerly islands such as Tanimbar, Timor and Sumba, Aru has a moist climate with a relatively modest water deficit, comparable with southern New Guinea and the tip of Cape York, Australia. The islands lie generally north of the tropical cyclone zone but have experienced very occasional high winds. For example, a cyclone formed off northwest Aru in April 1920 and travelled between Aru and Kei (Monk et al. 1997). Temperatures are slightly cooler in May–August and the diurnal fluctuations greater, with an estimated mean of 28.5°C. The islands are affected by El Niño fluctuations, and were in a state of pronounced drought when visited in the 1997–98 very severe ENSO event. However, local thunderstorms provided some relief and the forest was not greatly stressed.

Vegetation

The formational boundary between closed tropical forest and more open savannah woodlands and sclerophyll forest runs across the group. Despite active logging, the botany is still incompletely known and no quantitative surveys are available, but descriptions have been given by van Balgooy and Nooteboom (1995) and van Balgooy (1996). The latter predicts that over 2000 species of plants may be present. The natural vegetation of the northern islands (Wokam, Kobroor and Koba) consists of tall forest about 40–60m in height, with emergents to 60m such as dipterocarps, *Pometia pinnata* (Sapindaceae), *Alstonia scholaris* (Apocynaceae), and *Syzygium* (Myrtaceae) and *Ficus* species (Moraceae). Van Balgooy (1996) notes several species as important in the main canopy, namely *Canarium* spp., *Flindersia amboinensis, Dillenia pteropoda, Instia bijuga* (merbau), *Maranthes corymbosa,* and *Podocarpus* spp. Smaller trees include species of *Elaeocarpus, Diospyros, Cryptocarya, Litsea, Myristica, Rauwolfia, Kibara, Gardenia, Fagraea, Antidesma,* and *Macaranga*. Van Balgooy and Nooteboom (1995) suggest that the flora is remarkably rich, incorporating both west Malesian and Australo–Papuan taxa, and hence more diverse than that occurring in other Maluku islands. They also found very marked patchiness, with species common in one location but rare or lacking in another.

Although the forests are rich rainforest, they are relatively open in the understorey and canopy gaps are numerous. On limestone, dry forest floor conditions prevail, so that ferns and epiphytes are less common than in other rainforest areas. Walking is thus relatively easy and numerous small tracks run between clearings, making access from the *sungai* good for hunting. Secondary forest, with tell-tale regrowth trees such as *Acalypha, Glochidion,* and *Macaranga,* is quite widespread along major tracks and around sago palm areas.

The savannah on Trangan Island is an open woodland to about 15–20m in height, dominated by a wide array of myrtaceous shrubs and trees. Examples are *Melaleuca leucadendron, M. caja-putih, Lophostemon suaveolens, Asteromyrtus symphiocarpa, Xanthostemon brassii,* and *Syzygium* species (spp.). *Banksia dentata, Acacia mangium, Pandanus* spp., and *Timonius timon* are also found but are not ubiquitous. The undergrowth includes numerous shrubs and hummock graminoids such as *Lomandra banksii,* and parasitic epiphytes and climbers are common, for example *Hydnophytum, Myrmecodia,* and *Cladomyza stellata*. Grasses, principally *Eriachne squarrosa, E. triseta, Eragrostis lasioclada,* and *Digitaria fuscescens,* form an open bunch cover. During the rainy season moisture-loving sedges, restiads such as *Leptocarpus* spp., *Xyris bancana* and *X. oligantha,* and pitcher plants (*Nepenthes* spp.) do well, and a herb layer of *Drosera, Leschenaultia filiformis, Centrolepis banksii, Wahlenbergia marginata* and *Mitrasacme pygmaea* becomes common in waterlogged areas (van Balgooy 1996). During the dry season fires are very common but the savannah species are adapted to resprout and recover.

Van Balgooy (1996) found patches of rainforest along watercourses and in fire sheltered rises on Trangan Island. The gallery rainforests grow well due to the permanent flow of streams on Trangan, which has less limestone than the northern islands. *Ficus, Syzygium, Alloxylon brachycarpum,* and *Dubouzetia galorei* are common here, and sago palm (*Metroxylon sagu*) occurs naturally or is planted. He also records huge buttressed *Melaleuca leucodendron* trees within rain forest on Kobroor Island. However, these former patches of savannah in the rainforest are not regenerating and must represent old openings in the forest.

There are also areas of stunted forests or shrublands 5–10m in height on areas of bare limestone pavement. This heath of poor soils or *kerangas* (in Malay) supports *Ilex, Vavea, Glochidion, Acronychia* and *Diospyros* shrubs, and the epacridaceous *Dracaena angustifolia*. In addition there are coastal forests of *Barringtonia asiatica* and *Calophyllum inophyllum*, with coconuts, *Hibiscus tiliaceus, Terminalia catappa*, and *Casuarina equisetifolia*. Shrubs include the boraginaceous *Tournefortia argentea* and *Scaevola sericea*. The other major coastal formation is widespread mangroves, such as *Rhizophora apiculata, R. stylosa, Ceriops tagal*, and *Bruguiera cylindrica. Avicennia officinalis, Sonneratia caseolaris, Xylocarpus granatum* and *Camptostemon schultzii* are also widespread. There is a high diversity of mangrove taxa, van Balgooy (1996) noting seventeen species, forming communities described by Gylstra (1996). Rearwards of mangroves are limited areas of swamp forest with sago palm and *Barringtonia* sp. above a ground layer of sedges and mangrove fern.

The savannah formation has strong relationships with southern Papua and northern Australia, especially Cape York. Curiously, *Eucalyptus* is absent (despite being on Timor and at similar latitudes in southern New Guinea) but the species of *Melaleuca* in Aru are widespread in northern Australia, where they occur as the dominants of a major open forest community of seasonally flooded plains. *Asteromyrtus symphiocarpa* and probably several other species are found in Aru and on Cape York, possibly representing a remnant of a savannah that once occupied the land now flooded by Torres Strait.

The change from savannah to closed rainforest on Trangan Island marks the modern position of a major biome boundary that occurs also in southern New Guinea around Merauke, Daru and Port Moresby, and on eastern Cape York. Relatively few deciduous tree species occur in the transitional rainforest, although substantial leaf fall does occur in many rainforest species during the dry season. The rainforest includes many taxa found only in New Guinea such as the dipterocarps *Anisoptera thurifera* and *Hopea iriana* but some (e.g. *Celtis philippinensis, Diospyros* sp.) extend to northern Australia or to the west. The coastal vegetation is far more cosmopolitan, with some strand species such as *Scaevola sericea* extending to the furthest edge of the Pacific.

Fauna

The contemporary vertebrate fauna of the Aru Islands is quite diverse and contains a high proportion of typically Australo-Papuan groups such as marsupials (e.g. wallabies, possums and a bandicoot), birds of paradise, and cassowaries. In contrast, the faunas of nearby oceanic Moluccan islands (e.g. the Kei Islands) are far less diverse, being particularly depauperate in both mammals and reptiles, and containing far fewer Australo–Papuan elements. This very clearly reflects the location of the Aru Islands on the continental shelf and its former landbridge connection with southern New Guinea.

All of the mammal, bird and reptile species found on the Aru Islands today are also present in southern New Guinea. However, the archaeological record contains evidence of a more diverse vertebrate fauna during late Pleistocene times. As discussed in more detail by Aplin and Pasveer (Chapter 3, this volume), the late Pleistocene mammalian fauna of the Aru Islands shows evidence of strong biogeographic continuity with the contemporary fauna of the Trans-Fly region of southern New Guinea. The Trans-Fly area was identified by Flannery (1995) as part of a broader zoogeographic province that he labelled the 'Austral Province'. This province also includes several extensive tracts of savannah woodland in southeast Papua New Guinea, most notably around Port Moresby and Popondetta. Today, the Aru Islands make up part of Flannery's 'Tumbunan Province', which otherwise includes the extensive tracts of rainforest on New Guinea and its major satellite islands.

As noted above, the boundary between closed tropical forest and more open savannah woodlands and sclerophyll forest runs across Trangan Island, in the south of the group. The fauna of the savannah habitats on Trangan has not been surveyed to any extent and it is possible that additional mammal species may persist there.

Conservation

The Aru Islands contain 66,487ha of nature conservation forest, 217,866ha of limited production forest, and 457,991ha of conservation forest (Hidayat 2000). Forest degradation is occurring on the islands, for example on Wokam and Maikor Islands. The main causes are the lack of control by forest administrators over the exploitation of forests by companies. One logging company is working in Aru — P.T. Budhi Nyata — on a concession of 98,000ha of forest. This company employed 312 workers in 1998, some of whom are locals, but the majority of workers come from outside the Aru Islands. Many species of trees are logged, including kayu Besi *(Eusideroxylon zwageri)*, kayu Kenari (*Canarium amboinense),* kayu Gofasa (*Vitex cofassus),* kayu Merah (*Eugenia rumphii),* and kayu Bawang (*Dysoxylum euphlebium).* In addition, local people cut kayu Burung, kayu Dompet, kayu Nyato, and kayu Gofasa for house-building and furniture-making.

With changes to the Forestry law in 1967, communal rights (*hak ulayat*) to forest in the Outer Islands ceased to be recognized by the government, leading to some land conflicts in Aru between local people and logging concessionaires. In this conflict, the government usually takes the side of, and maintains relations with, the logging companies, since it receives benefits (stumpage fees, or replanting fees) from the owners of concessions (Hidayat 2000). In practice, about 15km^2 around villages can be utilized by local people for forest products for their daily needs, such as housing material, furniture, fishing tools, etc. New conservation laws, intended to protect the bird life and other protected species, have also been introduced, but Aru remains a centre for smuggling of parrots and bird of paradise (Monk et al. 1997).

Change Since The Late Pleistocene

Torresian plain to islands

Situated on the Australian continental plate, the Aru Islands have enjoyed a high degree of stability by comparison with the tectonically active plate boundary provinces to the north and west. Any uplift or downwarping has been slow and of low magnitude. The land mass has experienced continuing tropical weathering and gradual erosion for probably all of the Pleistocene. This has led to mature landforms with inverted topographies, in which the old stream ways (indicated by caves) are sometimes preserved in crestal positions. The most obvious environmental changes are associated with the changes in sea level caused by change in the global ice volume (Chappell et al. 1996; Yokoyama et al. 2001b). Because the surrounding shelf is between 40–60m deep, the islands become low hills on a vast plain at times of lowered sea levels (Voris 2000).

Yokoyama et al. (2001a) illustrate the Torresian plain at five time periods. Their shorelines are reconstructed from a consideration of the global sea level change modified by hydro-isostatic effects. These reflect the sinking of the crust when loaded by water as sea level rises, and on such a huge shelf the effect is significant (Fig. 2.1). At the lowest sea level (–115m), the Aru Islands lie 20km from the western end of the shelf but are directly connected to New Guinea, although a large river draining the whole southern slopes of the mountain range of Papua, possibly flowed westward between the low hills and the mountains to the north. A broad shallow bay lay 70km south. As the sea level rises, the shoreline of this bay creeps eastward although little change is evident at 16,000 BP, despite a rapid rise after 17,000 BP to –90m. By 12,000 BP (–42m) the embayment is expanding rapidly northward and southward, and the sea is flooding up the northern valley as well. Aru, however, is still the western end of a broad peninsula to Papua, and the connection south from there to Australia is intact. Within another 1500 years (–25m) though, these connections are lost, and by 9000 years ago (–16m) Aru is a single island about twice as large as present, with a western coast close to the present but a broad plain extending out on the east.

One aspect that is still unknown is how tidal regimes may have changed with changing land extent. Tidal range may have been less until a broad expanse of sea way had formed in the Holocene. Thus the *sungai* may have changed in character as the sea level rose and their modern flow regime became established. When sea levels were depressed they must have acted as freshwater streams with probable flows to the west. As they are deeper than the surrounding plain they may have also provided chains of permanent freshwater lakes fed by springs in the limestone.

The modern shoreline is reached before 6000 BP, at which time the *sungai* separate the modern islands from each other. Global sea level may have fallen by 1–2m since then, but this has probably been offset by

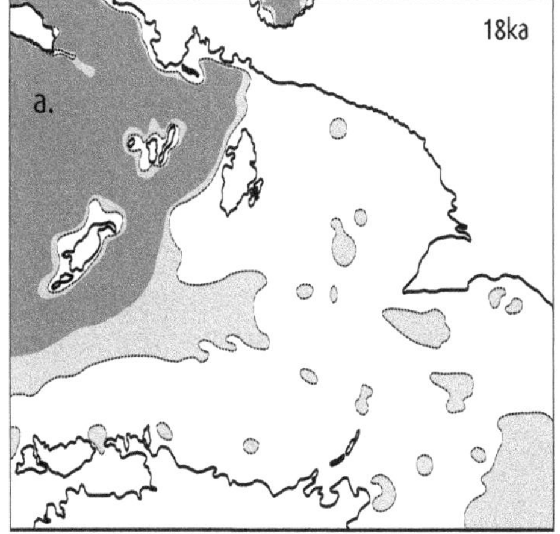

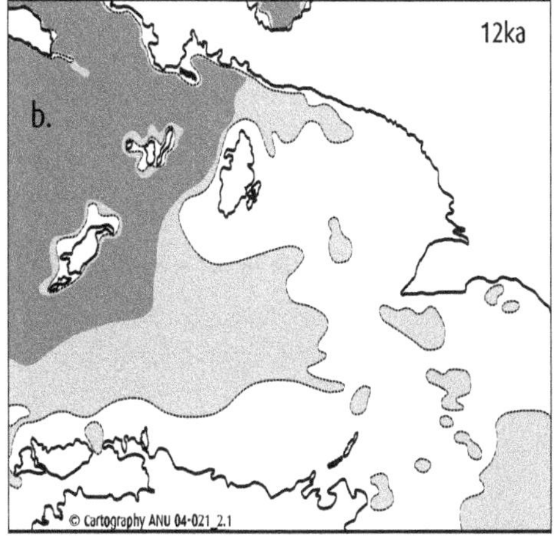

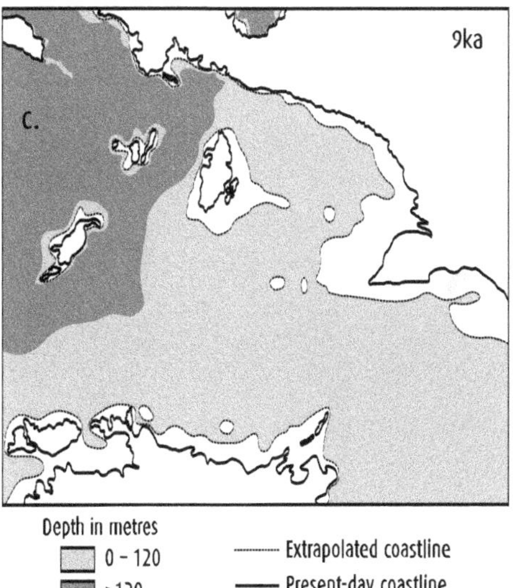

Figure 2.1 Palaeo-shoreline maps for the western Arafura shelf: LGM at 18,000 BP, 12,000 BP and 9000 BP. Bathymetric contours indicated by changes in shading at depths 0–120m and >120m. Adapted from data in Yokoyama et al. (2001a)

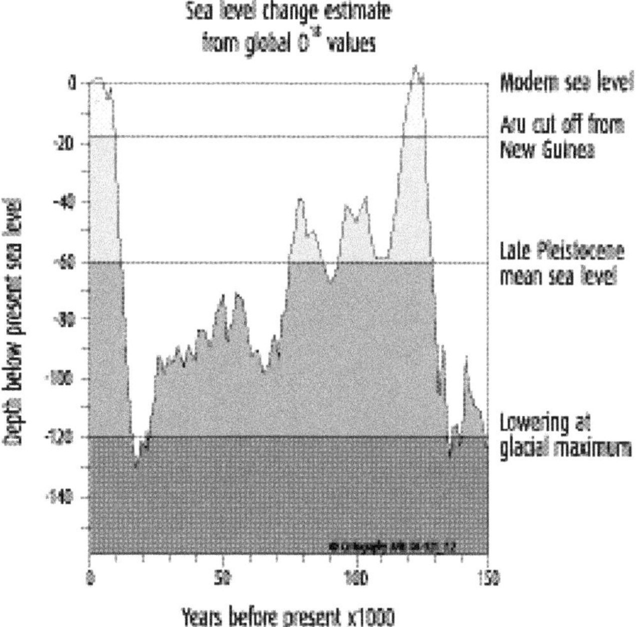

Figure 2.2 Sea level fluctuations of the last 150,000 years, based on the oxygen isotope record of Martinson et al. (1987). Connections between Aru and New Guinea are severed at ca. –18m

sinking of the outer shelf. Aru may be subsiding slightly, but early Holocene coastal features such as cliffed coastlines and beach ridges are preserved up to 1km inland, suggesting relatively stable conditions in the last 6000 years.

The global sea levels of the last 150,000 years can be reconstructed from foraminiferal oxygen isotope values (Martinson et al. 1987; Fig. 2.2). The reconstructed sea level shows that Aru has been a hilly promontory for about 80% of that time, becoming an island only during interglacial periods. Recent work (Chivas et al. 2000) on the Torresian plain has demonstrated the presence of numerous hardened layers of calcrete and ferricrete (limestone and iron concretions) within the upper Quaternary marine sediments. These represent the subaerial surfaces at times of the lowered sea level, when the sediments were welded by soil forming processes under semi arid conditions.

Non-anthropogenic Quaternary deposits

Sites for pollen analysis were sought in Aru by the present research team, but the karstic ponds encountered drained internally and were not suitable sites for long term sedimentation, being filled by red mud or having little sediment. Small lakes are shown on the map in the interior of Kobroor but could not be reached. Pollen was not preserved in the middens nor in other cave-fill sequences at Liang Nabulei Lisa or Liang Lemdubu. However, mid-Holocene sequences based on estuarine sediments are plentiful, consisting of peaty clays, sands, and mangrove muds. An infilled embayment on the west coast of Wamar Island was cored to see if a Holocene section was present, that could provide an environmental history to match to the archaeological sequence found in the Wangil midden (Chapter 6, this volume). The Wangil Core site (Lat: 5°47'S, Long: 134°08'E; Fig. 2.3) is in a small valley infilled by clays from surrounding slopes about 0.9m above modern high water (assessed by levelling to the beach HWM). The site is in open woodland of *Pandanus* over sedge-grassland at present, but 100m down the valley is an area of dense sago swamp, and beyond that mangroves are situated behind a low coastal sand barrier and flooded by a small estuarine stream. To the west and north of the core site is a steep low ridge of mudstone on which Wangil midden is found. The footslopes of the ridge are currently gardened.

Stratigraphy and dating

The valley plain about 25m south of the base of the ridge was augered with a bucket auger through silty clay to about 85cm. Below this, organic rich clays and silts were soft enough to be cored by D section auger to 250cm, where gravelly sand or rock was encountered (Table 2.2). Samples were collected at 10cm intervals for pollen analysis, and organic materials from 60cm and 240cm for dating.

Estuarine infill commenced as the rising sea level flooded the shallow valley about 7750 cal BP. The dates on organic matter show that the bulk of the section infilled rapidly with estuarine muds at a rate of ca. 20cm/100yr, but since around 6850 cal BP sediment has accumulated at only 1cm/100yr under intermittently dry conditions. This abrupt slowing of sedimentation mirrors the well-dated sections from macro-tidal northern Australia, where onshore sediment transport brought the estuary to an equilibrium with high tide levels within a few millennia of the flooding event (Woodroffe et al. 1985).

Pollen analysis and vegetation history

Pollen samples were taken at 10cm intervals down the core, and 2ml suspended and treated with dilute HCl to remove carbonates. The samples were washed on 8 micron mesh to remove clay, and then treated by standard acetolysis methods. Pollen was not abundant and the pollen diagram has been prepared with total counts of between 120 and 250 (Fig. 2.4). A CONISS analysis of the common pollen types divides the diagram into four zones, with the following inferred chronology as calibrated years BP at 2 sigma, assuming the two sedimentation rates were constant and allowing for stratigraphic imprecision in the zone boundary levels (Table 2.3).

Figure 2.3 Wangil: The authors taking a core behind a beach ridge at Wangil, Dobu Island (altitude 1m). The site is a former mangrove swamp that has gradually filled up with mud until a seasonally flooded forest invaded. At 58cm mangroves give way to disturbed forest. The large Wangil midden site (see Chapter 6, this volume) occurs on the adjacent ridge. Photo Sue O'Connor

Zone WGL 4. This zone contains moderate levels of Rhizophoraceae which confirms that the lower sediments are estuarine. Except for an unknown tricolporate, possibly another mangrove, or gallery forest trees, the other components are sparse or intermittent. *Neonauclea,* a tropical savannah tree, has a peak but is likely to be a component of forest as grass, and surprisingly *Casuarina,* are absent. The site may have been an open quiet estuary at this time, with a fringing band of mangroves that filtered out dryland pollen. A succession is apparent as *Rhizophora* pollen increases towards the top of the zone, and occasional grains of *Barringtonia* and sago palm may reflect a swamp forest inland of the mangroves. Charcoal is at very low levels.

Zone WGL 3. Mangrove pollen increases to a maximum in this zone, which may reflect the development of a closed mangrove

Table 2.2 Wangil Core: stratigraphy and dating

DEPTH (CM)	SEDIMENT
0–5	Fibrous peat with roots
5–29	Black organic-rich clay
29–52	Brown clay with an orange mottle and root cracks filled with fine sand and black silts
52–59	White silts with scattered orange nodules
59–88	Mottled yellow-brown silty clay with scattered organic lenses. Organic material at 60cm gave an AMS age of 6030±40 BP (OS-35221)
88–240	Grey fine sandy silts with wood and gastropod shells below 100cm. Wood fragments at 240cm gave an AMS age of 6890±60 BP (OS-35318)
240–>255	Coarse sandy gravel with coral fragments

Table 2.3 Wangil Core: zones and inferred chronology (cal BP, 2 sigma) from CONISS analysis

ZONE	INTERVAL (CM)	TOP	BASE
WGL 1	0–15	Modern	2075–1350
WGL 2	15–58	2075–1350	6950–6750
WGL 3	58–130	6950–6750	7325–7100
WGL 4	130–240	7325–7100	7800–7725

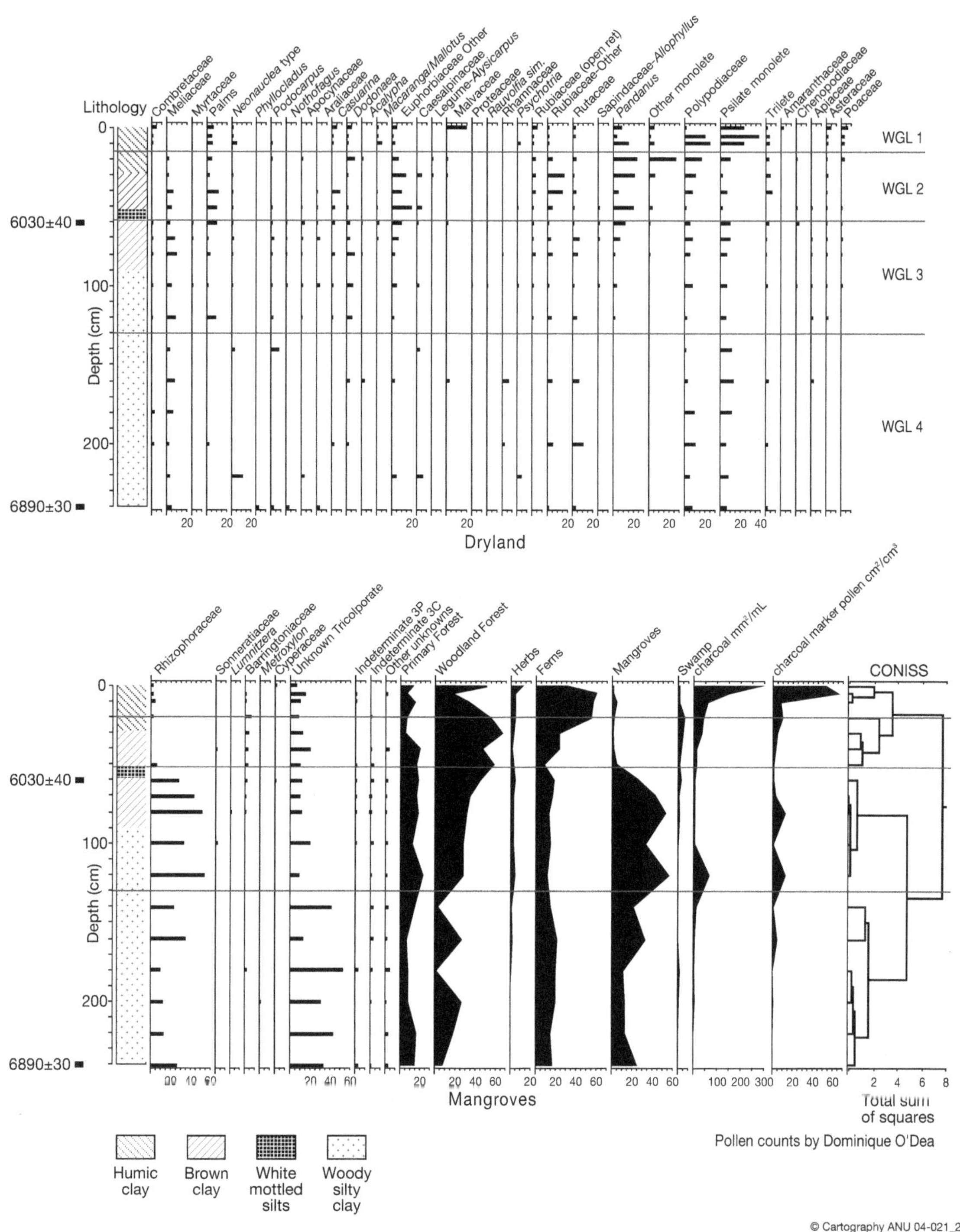

Figure 2.4 Wangil: pollen diagram from core. Pollen sum is total pollen and spores

forest on site as water depth became less. A decline commences at 70cm, near the top of the zone. The unknown tricolporate grains decrease but remain a significant component to the top of the diagram, suggesting that they have a dryland source. Their decrease coincides with an increase in tree and shrub pollen so that the input from a mixed forest including the unknown may have remained steady, but diversity increased. Charcoal has a peak at the base of the zone but is not important above that. However, some disturbance is indicated by an increase in secondary taxa such as *Dodonaea, Casuarina, Macaranga,* and other Euphorbiaceae. More open conditions are indicated by the first traces of grass and Asteraceae pollen, and an increase in *Pandanus*.

Zone WGL 2. The rapid decline in mangrove pollen to very low levels is achieved at the start of this zone, and subsequent Rhizophoraceae may be the result of the re-working of older sediments. This change is a succession to dry land, borne out by the stratigraphy and the consistent presence of *Barringtonia,* which prefers wet non-saline sites. The pollen of *Pandanus* palms and disturbance taxa such as *Casuarina, Dodonea,* and Euphorbiaceae, reach their maximum in this zone, but Meliaceae and Rubiaceae (possibly representing less disturbed forest) decline above 40cm. Weed indicators such as some ferns, grass and daisies become more common in the upper 40cm. This change correlates with a distinct increase in charcoal, so that increased disturbance by fire and clearing seem likely at an inferred age of 4400–3600 cal BP.

Zone WGL 1. This zone is probably less than 1000 years old and may even represent the changing land use of colonial times. Since the surface organic sediments typically accumulate more quickly, the long term average used to infer the age of the Zone 2–1 boundary is a maximum. The zone is typified by considerable increases in ferns and a wide range of shrubs and herbs including some plants associated with gardening, such as possible *Terminalia,* palms, *Pandanus,* grass and Asteraceae. A single peak of Malvaceae (possibly *Hibiscus*) and Chenopodiaceae occurs only in the top 5cm. However, some secondary trees such as Euphorbiaceae are reduced, implying more extensive clearance. Charcoal reaches its highest levels. This zone thus reflects modern levels of disturbance and utilization of the catchment, with very common burning off.

This mid-Holocene sequence reflects a normal process of rapid infill of the heads of embayments, by species that are widespread to the present. The presence of some anthropogenic disturbance throughout seems likely but forest decline and clearance becomes more obvious around 4000–3000 years ago. Similar sequences might be expected around the coast of the archipelago, although the rate of estuarine infill and possibly the degree of disturbance could vary considerably.

Environmental implications of vertebrate faunal change

The two cave sites of Liang Nabulei Lisa and Liang Lemdubu together provide a more or less continuous record of vertebrate faunal change from around 28,000 years ago to the present (see Chapters 7 and 9, this volume, for details of site location and dating). The major changes can be summarized as follows:

Phase I (ca. 28,000–ca. 20,000 cal BP)

This period is recorded in Lemdubu Spits 31–19. The vertebrate fauna from this period makes it is clear that the dominant vegetation community in the vicinity of the site was relatively dry and open, probably savannah woodland with grassy understorey. This supported a range of species, today found in savannah woodland and grasslands of the Trans-Fly and across northern Australia. However, the presence in the same levels of many species found today in rainforest or dense gallery forest also points to the presence in the area of substantial patches of wetter, denser vegetation. These communities presumably occupied topographic lows in the karst landscape, including the major drainage features.

Exactly how much of the area was occupied by each of these vegetation communities is difficult to judge. However, the fact that the two largest of the obligate rainforest animals are recorded only sporadically through this period suggests either that the wetter forest communities were of insufficient size and continuity to support viable populations of larger animals, or that these patches were subject to early and intense hunting pressure such that the larger animals were rapidly extirpated. If the latter process took place, then it left no archaeological signature.

Phase II (ca. 20,000–ca. 12,000 cal BP)

The earlier part of this period is recorded in Lemdubu, and in both sites from 16,000 cal BP onwards. In Lemdubu, this phase is characterized by an increase in the relative abundance of the dry community taxa and a corresponding fall in those taxa associated with wetter, denser habitats. Although the transition point between this phase and the last is set at the boundary between Spits 18 and 19, the transition between the two phases is really a gradual one, with different taxa most likely responding to common stimuli at different times and rates. However, the overall impression is that rainforest patches probably declined in both extent and quality through this period. This may have occurred as a result of climatic deterioration or through increasing pressure on these habitats as a consequence of hunting and/or general exploitation of forest products. The timing of this change, which corresponds with the peak of the last glaciation, perhaps lends weight in favour of a climatic explanation.

Occupation of Nabulei Lisa probably commenced around 16,000 cal BP. The fauna from this period (Spits 43–33) points to the presence of substantial areas of open habitat in the vicinity of the site, but with sufficient areas of rainforest to support large mammals such as a *Dorcopsis* wallaby. The most likely scenario is that patches of dense evergreen or semi-evergreen rainforest were present near Nabulei Lisa, most likely in sheltered contexts along watercourses including the major *sungai* channels. Drier, more open habitats presumably dominated on more elevated and exposed sites away from the channels; these drier habitats are recorded in the Lemdubu fauna from this period.

Nabulei Lisa provides little evidence of the exploitation of freshwater resources such as crabs and economically useful molluscs during this period. This raises the possibility that the major *sungai* were seasonally dry, to the extent that these aquatic organisms were unable to establish viable, long-term populations. The apparent absence of cassowaries in the local area during the earlier part of this period (below Spit 35 in Nabulei Lisa) might also be taken as an indicator that conditions were drier in comparison with subsequent periods.

Phase III (ca. 12,000–10,200 cal BP)

This phase is recorded in Nabulei Lisa Spits 32–26. At Lemdubu, this phase through to the recent phase is represented by a compressed sequence at the top of the site. The vertebrate fauna from this period in Nabulei Lisa documents a continuation of open savannah habitats in the area around the site. However, other changes in the fauna suggest a possible expansion of rainforest habitats, perhaps indicating some climatic amelioration. In addition, evidence of the more regular exploitation of aquatic resources suggests that the *sungai* may have supported larger bodies of permanent water at this time. At the same time, small quantities of typical estuarine and marine organisms were making their way to the site, marking the progressive inundation of the continental shelf.

Phase IV (ca. 7700–6100 cal BP)

This phase is recorded in Nabulei Lisa Spits 25–10. It is characterized mainly by the loss of the savannah and grassland-dwelling mammals — a clear signal that open habitats have either disappeared entirely or else become reduced to small remnants of insufficient size to support viable populations. In general terms, the local environment may have resembled that found around the site today but with a slightly more diverse mammal fauna. The brief appearance of freshwater turtle in the lower part of this period is further evidence that the major *sungai* supported at least a seasonally productive stream or wetland habitat. However, such conditions were evidently short-lived, and the dramatic increase in marine and estuarine shell above Spit 20, and simultaneous change in the crab fauna, clearly reflect the local establishment of estuarine conditions with associated mangrove communities in the *sungai* at that time. The crab fauna also suggests that marine conditions were established in the *sungai* from Spit 15 onwards.

Phase V (ca. 1000 cal BP–modern)
This phase is recorded in Nabulei Lisa Spits 9–1. It is also recorded in the upper four spits in Lemdubu. The major faunal changes include the appearance of several introduced mammals (pig, dog and deer), an increase in the exploitation of fish, and a relative decline in the exploitation of terrestrial mammals and reptiles. Bats show a slight increase in relative abundance during this period. Cassowary bone and eggshell reappear during this period. The terrestrial mammals found in these levels are the same as those found on the islands today and are typical of closed rainforest habitats.

Unfortunately, the archaeological remains are too sparse to build a detailed picture of environmental changes during this interesting, final phase of occupation. Accordingly, it is unclear whether the sites were being used as remote hunting camps subject to occasional visits, or alternatively, whether the area around the sites was subject to cultivation.

Discussion

Aru is a remarkable outpost of the northern Arafura shelf, which provides a rare record of the changing terrestrial environments of the shelf as sea extent varied. From the point of view of origins, it has to be regarded as a continental island to New Guinea as it has direct connections to southern Papua for over 80% of the last million years, and its northerly position means that it has shared a warm tropical environment of less seasonality than northern Australia. The faunal changes found at Liang Lemdubu on Kobroor Island are the only direct evidence for climate fluctuations that have yet been found (see Chapters 7 and 9, this volume), but these results can be supplemented by regional studies of more detailed and longer term data.

Regional climate change

Several lines of evidence suggest that during glacial periods, conditions in Torresia — the biogeographic province between northern Australia and southern New Guinea — were much drier and slightly cooler than present (Walker 1972). The soils preserved on the Arafura plain to the south and east are indicative of dry and possibly seasonal conditions (Chivas et al. 2001). This is supported by evidence of the vegetation around Lake Carpentaria — a large, partly saline lake that formed on the eastern side of the plain (Torgersen et al. 1988; Chivas et al. 2001). Conditions were mostly treeless and the pollen of Chenopodiaceae, probably from desert steppe shrublands of saltbush, is common. It is assumed that the rainfall gradient between New Guinea and northern Australia was shifted northward (van der Kaars 1991), but in fact there are few precise records of this change. Patches of isolated eucalypt savannah occur north of Port Moresby and Merauke and may represent former northward retreat of the savannah-rainforest boundary. The long terrestrial record from the Atherton Tablelands of Queensland (Kershaw 1994; Kershaw et al. 2002) records cooler montane rainforest until about 35,000 years ago, when eucalypt woodlands start to increase. Lowland rainforest recovers the site about 8000 years ago. Kershaw considers that rainfall may have fallen to 35% of its modern total, but this represents an eastwards shift in the savannah-rainforest boundary of only a few kilometres, as there is a steep rainfall gradient in the area.

Other long records in the region come from marine cores. Van der Kaars (1991) studied pollen and charcoal in cores from the Banda Sea and north of Australia and obtained vegetation records extending back to before the last glacial maximum (LGM). The most complete record is from the Lombok Rise and it was subsequently analysed further (Wang et al. 1999). At the same latitude (5°46′S) as Aru, but 680km to the west, van der Kaars et al. (2000) obtained a 175,000 year record. These records have been reviewed by Kershaw et al. (2002), and long climatic change indices have been calculated. Both spectra have high levels of fern spores and mangrove pollen during interglacial stages. During glacials, the spectra are dominated by grass with increases in *Eucalyptus*. This indicates that pollen was being derived by the southeast Trade winds from the Australian continental mass. Pollen from New Guinea is a minor component only, and lowland forest signals are low as well. Kershaw et al. (2002) suggest that this is due to cooler conditions which restricted the warm rainforests. This is supported by increased lower montane rainforest pollen from *Lithocarpus* and other lower montane trees. Upper montane taxa, such as *Nothofagus* and *Phyllocladus* are rare but increase markedly during the shift from glacial to interglacial, which Kershaw et al. (2002) suggest may be evidence for an increase in area of the upper montane zone in the Holocene. This is supported by pollen cores from northern New Guinea (Hope 1996). The data are interpreted as indicating temperatures 4–6°C cooler than present at the last glacial maximum. This estimate agrees with that of Hope (2001) from a site in Sulawesi, but contrasts with an analysis of oxygen isotopes from foraminifera from the northern Banda sea off Halmahera. Here, Barmawidjaja et al. (1993) found little shift in sea temperature, even though the pollen signature showed a lowering of the lower montane boundary.

Kershaw (1994) infers rainfalls of only 30% of modern at the time of the lowest sea level on the Atherton Plateau, but his sites lie on very steep rainfall gradients. Van der Kaars (1991) suggests that rainfall boundaries were displaced about 200km northwards across Torres Strait, implying that rainfall would have resembled that in the Darwin area today. However, since Aru lies outside cyclone tracks, the change would not be as extreme and summer rainfall was probably more reliable than Darwin, despite a longer dry season.

The major change associated with the end of the LGM was a rapid rise in sea level about 16,500 BP, followed by a rapid rise in temperature around 14,000 BP (van der Kaars et al. 2000). This date accords well with the appearance of obligate rainforest mammals at Liang Lemdubu, and so it is probably associated with increasing moisture as a warm shallow sea approached from the south. Change continues until ca. 9500 BP with fluctuations in rainforests across the Holocene-Pleistocene boundary in New Guinea. It is likely that rainfall steadily increased as Torres Strait flooded, with modern temperatures and rainfall being established in the early Holocene, about 9000 years ago. This is borne out by the loss of savannah fauna at Liang Lemdubu (Chapter 7), which must reflect the southwards movement of the boundary of closed forest. In north Queensland, Kershaw (1994) found that closed forest was more extensive between 7500 and ca. 4000 BP than at present. This mid-Holocene extension possibly also occurred on Aru, and may possibly have been the result of more reliable climates rather than higher temperatures and rainfall (Hope et al. 2004).

In the Pleistocene, Aru would have been a notable feature on the otherwise monotonous open savannah of the Arafura plain. Even though rainforest was restricted, it probably occurred along the gorges of the *sungai* as these would have been spring fed and a source of permanent water during the dry season. The greater landscape variety and biotic diversity of these low hills must have been attractive to humans venturing inland from the coast. As the sea spread rapidly across the plain, the embayments cut off the peninsular from the west, south and north, and rainforests spread out from more restricted sites. The length of coastline rapidly increased, and maritime peoples would have been gradually concentrated along the Aru ridge. Within a single lifetime, coastal retreat of 20–50km would have been apparent when the sea was around 30–50m below present. Once sea level had stabilized, coastal habitats continued to adjust with the rapid development of sand spits, reefs and mangroves between ca. 7000 and 5000 years ago.

References

van Balgooy, M.M.J. 1996. Vegetation sketch of the Aru Islands. In H.P. Nooteboom (ed.), *The Aru Archipelago: Plants, Animals, People and Conservation*, pp. 1–14. Amsterdam: Nederlandse Commissie Voor Internationale Natuurbescherming. *Mededelingan* 30.

van Balgooy, M.M.J. and H.P. Nooteboom. 1995. Report on the Botany of the Aru Islands. Leiden: Rijksherbarium. 12pp.

Barmawidjaja, B.M., E.J. Rohling, W.A. van der Kaars, C. Vergnaud Grazzini, and W.J. Zachariasse. 1993. Glacial conditions in the northern Molluca Sea region (Indonesia). *Palaeogeography, Palaeoclimatology, Palaeoecology* 101:147–67.

British Admiralty. 1998. Admiralty Tide Tables Vol. III Pacific Ocean and Adjacent Seas (including Tidal Stream Tables). British Admiralty Bureau.

Chappell, J.M.A., A. Omura, T. Esat, M. McCulloch, J. Pandolfi, Y. Ota, and B. Pillans. 1996. Reconciliation of late Quaternary sea levels derived from coral terraces at Huon peninsula with deep sea oxygen isotope records. *Earth and Planetary Science Letters* 141:227–36.

Chivas, A.R., A. García, S. van der Kaars, M. Couapel, J.J.S. Holt, J.M. Reeves, D.J. Wheeler, A.D. Switzer, C.V. Murray-Wallace, D. Banerjee, D.M. Price, S.X. Wang, G. Pearson, N.T. Edgar, L. Beaufort, P. De Deckker, E. Lawson, and C.B. Cecil. 2000. Sea-level and environmental changes since the last interglacial in the Gulf of Carpentaria, Australia: an overview. *Quaternary International* 83–85:19–46.

Flannery, T. 1995. *Mammals of the South-West Pacific and Moluccan Islands*. Sydney: Australian Museum/Reed Books.

Gregory, J.W., L.R. Cox, and E.D. Currie. 1924. The geology of the Aru islands. *Geological Magazine* 61:52–72.

Gylstra, M.L.D. 1996. The use of remote sensing and GIS for classification of mangrove ecosystems on Aru. In H.P. Nooteboom (ed.), *The Aru Archipelago: Plants, Animals, People and Conservation*, pp. 15–34. Amsterdam: Nederlandse Commissie Voor Internationale Natuurbescherming. *Mededelingan* 30.

Hidayat, H. 2000. Forest Management by the Local Peoples in Aru District, Southeast Maluku. Unpublished Manuscript, LIPI 154-63. URL: http://iges.or.jp/en/fc/phase1.

Hope G.S. 2001. Environmental change in the Late Pleistocene and later Holocene at Wanda Site, Soroako, South Sulawesi, Indonesia. *Journal of Palaeogeography, Palaeoclimatology, Palaeoecology* 17:129–45.

Hope, G.S. 1996. Quaternary change and historical biogeography of Pacific Islands. In A. Keast and S.E. Miller (eds), *The Origin and Evolution of Pacific Island Biotas, New Guinea to Eastern Polynesia: Patterns and Process*, pp. 165–90. Amsterdam: SPB Publishing.

Hope, G.S., X. Sun, P-M. Liew, A.P. Kershaw, W.A. van der Kaars, H. Takahara, M. McGlone, L.E. Heusser, and N. Miyoshi. 2004. History of vegetation and habitat change from the PEP II transect. *Quaternary International* 118–119:103–26.

van der Kaars, W.A. 1991. Palynology of eastern Indonesian marine piston-cores: a late Quaternary vegetational and climatic record for Australasia. *Palaeogeography, Palaeoclimatology, Palaeoecology* 85:239–302.

van der Kaars, W.A. 1997. Marine and terrestrial pollen records of the last glacial cycle from the Indonesian region: Bandung Basin and Banda Sea. *Palaeoclimates: Data and Modelling* 4:1–11.

van der Kaars, W.A., X. Wang, P. Kershaw, F. Guichard, and D.A. Setiabudi. 2000. A late Quaternary palaeoecological record from the Banda Sea, Indonesia: patterns of vegetation, climate and biomass burning in Indonesia and northern Australia. *Palaeogeography, Palaeoclimatology, Palaeoecology* 155:135–53.

Kershaw, A.P. 1994. Pleistocene vegetation of the humid tropics of northeastern Queensland, Australia. *Palaeogeography, Palaeoclimatology, Palaeoecology* 109:399–412.

Kershaw, A.P., S. van der Kaars, P. Moss, and X. Wang. 2002. Quaternary records of vegetation, biomass burning, climate and possible human impact in the Indonesian–Northern Australian region. In A.P. Kershaw, B. David, N. Tapper, D. Penny, and J. Brown (eds), *Bridging Wallace's Line: The Environmental and Cultural History and Dynamics of the Southeast Asian–Australian Region*, pp. 97–118. Reiskirchen: Catena Verlag. *Advances in GeoEcology* 34.

Martinson, D.G., N.G. Pisias, J.D. Hays, J. Imbrie, T.C. Moore, and N.J. Shackleton. 1987. Age dating and orbital theory of the Ice Ages: development of a high resolution 0–300,000-year chronostratigraphy. *Quaternary Research* 27:1–29.

Monk, K.A., Y. De Fretes, and G. Reksodiharjo-Lilley. 1997. *The Ecology of Nusa Tenggara and Maluku*. Hong Kong & Cambridge: Periplus and Cambridge University Press. *Ecology of Indonesia Series* 5.

Nooteboom, H.P. (ed.). 1996. *The Aru Archipelago: Plants, Animals, People and Conservation*. Amsterdam: Nederlandse Commissie Voor Internationale Natuurbescherming. *Mededelingan* 30.

Torgersen, T., J. Luly, P. De Deckker, M. Jones, D.E. Searle, A.L Chivas, and W.J. Ullman. 1988. Late Quaternary environments of the Carpentaria basin, Australia. *Palaeogeography, Palaeoclimatology, Palaeoecology* 67:245–61.

Verstappen, H.Th. 1959. Geomorphology and crustal movements of the Aru Islands in relation to the Pleistocene drainage of the Sahul shelf. *American Journal of Science* 257:491–502.

Voris, H.K. 2000. Maps of Pleistocene sea levels in Southeast Asia: shorelines, river systems and time durations. *Journal of Biogeography* 27:1153–67.

Walker, D. (ed.). 1972. *Bridge and Barrier: The Natural and Cultural History of Torres Strait*. Canberra: Department of Biogeography and Geomorphology, Research School of Pacific Studies, The Australian National University.

Wallace, A.R. 1857. On the natural history of the Aru Islands. *Annals and Magazine of Natural History* (Series 2) 20:473–85.

Wallace, A.R. 1869. *The Malay Archipelago: The Land of the Orang-utan and the Bird of Paradise. A Narrative of Travel with Studies of Man and Nature*. London: MacMillan.

Wang, X., S. van der Kaars, A.P. Kershaw, M. Bird, and F. Jansen. 1999. A record of fire, vegetation and climate through the last 3 glacial cycles from Lombok Ridge core G6–4, eastern Indian Ocean, Indonesia. *Palaeogeography, Palaeoclimatology, Palaeoecology* 147:241–56.

Wollaston, A.F.R. 1912. *Pygmies and Papuans*. London: Smith Elder.

Woodroffe, C.D., J.M.A. Chappell, B.G. Thom, and E. Wallensky. 1985. Stratigraphy of the South Alligator tidal river and plains, Northern Territory. In K.S. Bardsley, J.D.S. Davie, and C.D. Woodroffe (eds), *Coasts and Tidal Wetlands of the Australian Monsoon Region*, pp. 17–42. Darwin: Australian National University North Australia Research Unit. *Mangrove Monograph* 1.

Yokoyama, Y., A. Purcell, K. Lambeck, and P. Johnston. 2001a. Shore-line reconstruction around Australia during the Last Glacial Maximum and Late Glacial Stage. *Quaternary International* 83–85:9–18.

Yokoyama, Y., P. De Deckker, K. Lambeck, P. Johnston, and L.K. Fifield. 2001b. Sea-level at the Last Glacial Maximum: evidence from northwestern Australia to constrain ice volumes for Oxygen isotope Stage 2. *Palaeogeography, Palaeoclimatology, Palaeoecology* 165:281–97.

3

Mammals and Other Vertebrates from Late Quaternary Archaeological Sites on Pulau Kobroor, Aru Islands, Eastern Indonesia

Ken Aplin[1] and Juliette Pasveer[2]

1. Sustainable Ecosystems, CSIRO, GPO Box 284, Canberra, ACT 2601, Australia
2. Archaeology and Natural History, Research School of Pacific and Asian Studies, The Australian National University, Canberra, ACT, Australia

Introduction

Excavations in each of Liang Lemdubu and Liang Nabulei Lisa, limestone caves on Pulau Kobroor, Aru Islands, produced substantial quantities of bone and other vertebrate faunal remains. Together, these provide a rich record of the late Pleistocene to Holocene vertebrate fauna of Pulau Kobroor, important new information on local environmental conditions through the period of human occupation of the sites, and some insights into the economic activities that were undertaken from each site.

In this chapter we provide a systematic review of the prehistoric vertebrate fauna, giving justification in support of the more controversial determinations and providing a brief commentary on the likely ecological associations of each taxon. This information is provided as background for archaeological and palaeoecological interpretation of the faunal sequences and associated cultural remains from Liang Nabulei Lisa and Liang Lemdubu, elaborated in two companion chapters in this volume (Chapters 7 and 9). An earlier paper by O'Connor et al. (2002) gave a brief summary and preliminary interpretation of the vertebrate faunal remains from Liang Lemdubu.

Contemporary Vertebrate Fauna of the Aru Islands

Knowledge of the contemporary vertebrate fauna of the Aru Island group is surprisingly incomplete. Despite the early attention given to the island group by biological explorers such as Alfred Russell Wallace (1857), Hermann von Rosenberg (1867) and Orlando Beccari (1873), the focus of subsequent biological effort shifted to the main island of New Guinea and to major island groups to the east. During the last half-century, relatively few biologists have visited the islands and none for more than a few weeks.

Szalay (1995) compiled a species list for the terrestrial mammal fauna, based mainly on the historical records. Van Strien (1996) summarized the routes taken by each of the historical collectors and provided an updated species list that includes material collected in recent decades by several Australian biologists (most notably, Drs R.A. How and D.J. Kitchener of the Western Australian Museum, and Dr P. Woolley of La Trobe University). Woolley in 1992 collected two samples on Kobroor from 'kitchen middens and hunters', coming from the villages of Jilkai and Namara (see Appendix 3.1 for details of localities and content). These consist primarily of lower jaws and resemble 'trophy' collections from elsewhere in Melanesia.

An updated list of the extant mammal fauna is given in Table 3.1, with species listed separately for each of the major and several of the smaller islands. Taxonomic differences from previous lists are chiefly due to recent generic changes among murid rodents, along with some revised identifications (see below). The combined list for all islands includes 10 marsupials, five native rodents and 15 bats. Seven introduced mammals are recorded from feral populations.

The avifauna of the Aru Islands is more completely known, in part from the efforts of numerous amateur ornithologists. No attempt has been made to tabulate this element of the fauna.

The herpetofauna remains poorly documented. The classic works of van Kampen (1923) on amphibians and de Rooij (1915, 1917) on reptiles remain the major sources of information for this region.

The ichthyofauna of the Aru Islands was last reviewed comprehensively by Weber (1911).

The Archaeological Vertebrate Fauna

The great bulk of the archaeological remains comes from a relatively small number of mammal and reptile species. However, a total of 29 mammal species are represented, together with an unknown number of reptiles, frogs, and birds. We focus here on the mammal species which are most readily identified from fragmentary remains. Future study of the bird, reptile and frog remains might prove rewarding.

Modern reference specimens are identified by the following prefixes: 'AM' (Australian Museum, Sydney); and 'CM' (Australian National Wildlife Collection, CSIRO Division of Sustainable Ecosystems, Canberra).

Family Tachyglossidae

Tachyglossus aculeatus (Shaw and Nodder 1792) Short-beaked Echidna

Current status: No historical or contemporary records.

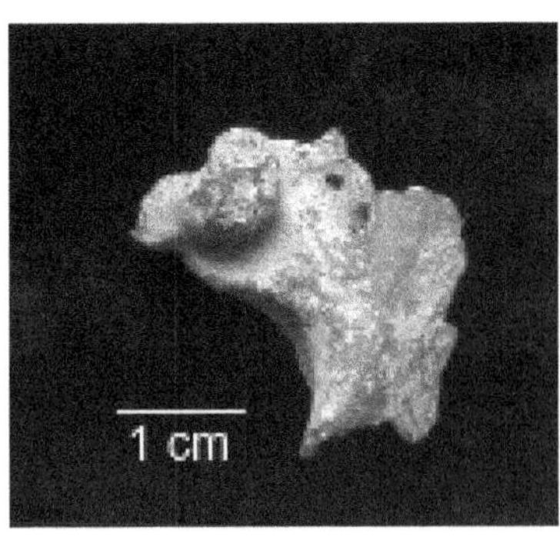

Figure 3.1 Liang Lemdubu: partial humerus of *Tachyglossus aculeatus* from Spit 9

Referred material: This taxon is consistently represented between Spits 5 and 25 in Lemdubu (see Fig. 3.1). Only one specimen was identified in the Nabulei Lisa fauna: a distal tibia in Spit 35.

Wider distribution and habitat associations: The Short-beaked Echidna is known from scattered records in lowland to mid-montane New Guinea and from all major regions of Australia. Although most New Guinean records come from open or drier habitats, the species is present in all major habitats in Australia and is reported from lowland and lower montane rainforest localities in Papua New Guinea.

Table 3.1 List of mammal species recorded as living animals on each of the major islands in the Aru Group, compiled from the following sources: Flannery (1995b), Van Strien (1996), Kitchener (n.d.) and Woolley (Appendix 3.1; pers.comm.). Species believed to be present as a result of deliberate or accidental human introduction are indicated with an (I)

TAXON	WARILAU	WAMAR	WOKAM (W)	KOBROOR (K)	WORK	MAIKOOR	TRANGAN	KOBA	PENAMBULAI	WORKAN	UNKNOWN
DASYURIDAE											
Murexia longicauda				+							
Myoictis wallacei					+						+
Sminthopsis virginiae											+
PERORYCTIDAE											
Echymipera rufescens			+	+							+
PHALANGERIDAE											
Phalanger gymnotis			+	+							
Phalanger mimicus				+							+
Spilocuscus maculatus		+	+	+		+	+				+
PETAURIDAE											
Dactylopsila trivirgata			+	+							+
Petaurus breviceps		+									+
MACROPODIDAE											
Thylogale brunii		+	+				+				
MURIDAE											
Hydromys chrysogaster		+	+								
Melomys rufescens			+								
Mus musculus (I)		+					+				
Paramelomys naso			+								
Paramelomys platyops											
Rattus leucopus			+								
Rattus rattus (I)		+	+								
Uromys caudimaculatus				+							+
SORICIDAE											
Crocidura maxi (I)			+								
Suncus murinus (I)			+								
VIVERRIDAE											
Paradoxurus hermaphroditus (I)											+
SUIDAE											
Sus scrofa (I)											
CERVIDAE											
Cervus timorensis (I)		+	+	+							
PTEROPODIDAE											
Dobsonia moluccensis			+	+							
Macroglossus minimus		+	+	+							
Nyctimene albiventer			+								
Pteropus macrotis			+								
Pteropus melanopogon			+	+							
Syconycteris australis			+	+							
HIPPOSIDERIDAE											
Hipposideros ater					+						
Hipposideros cervinus				+			+				
Hipposideros diadema				+							
RHINOLOPHIDAE											
Rhinolophus euryotis											
VESPERTILIONIDAE											
Miniopterus australis				+							
Miniopterus schreibersii											+
Pipistrellus javanicus											+
Pipistrellus papuanus											+
EMBALLONURIDE											
Emballonura nigrescens				+							

Family Dasyuridae (Marsupial mice and native cats)

Dasyurus albopunctatus (Schlegel 1880) New Guinea Quoll

Current status: There are no historical of contemporary records of this or any other species of *Dasyurus* on the Aru Islands.

Figure 3.2 Liang Lemdubu: partial dentary of *Dasyurus albopunctatus* from Spit 27

Referred material: Two partial lower jaws (see Fig. 3.2) and a proximal femur from the lower levels of the Lemdubu deposit (Spits 27 and 37) represent a species of *Dasyurus*. An edentulous lower jaw from Spit 37 of Nabulei Lisa is also referred to the same taxon. The lower jaws were compared directly with specimens of *D. albopunctatus* from various localities in Papua New Guinea and Indonesian Papua, and to published accounts only of *D. spartacus* (Van Dyck 1988). They are referred to *D. albopunctatus* on account of the shorter toothrow, relatively reduced metaconids, and crowded premolars. They differ most convincingly from *Dasyurus spartacus* in the proportions of the toothrow: this taxon has a proportionally longer, more spaced out premolar row, reflecting its more elongate rostrum. The illustrated specimen from Spit 27 (Fig. 3.2) has a molar row of 16.9mm; the premolar row measures 6.1mm.

Wider distribution and habitat association: *Dasyurus albopunctatus* is recorded from across a wide altitudinal range and diverse habitats on the main island of New Guinea (Flannery 1995a). *Dasyurus spartacus* is known only from the Morehead region of the Fly Plains of Papua New Guinea, a region of low mixed savannah (Waithman 1979; Van Dyck 1988), although Flannery (1995a) notes unconfirmed reports of the species from similar habitats in Wasur National Park, Indonesian Papua. Given the strong evidence for savannah habitats on the Aru Islands during late Pleistocene times, it is somewhat surprising to find that *D. albopunctatus* was present throughout this period.

Myoictis wallacei (Gray 1858) Aru Island Three-striped Dasyure

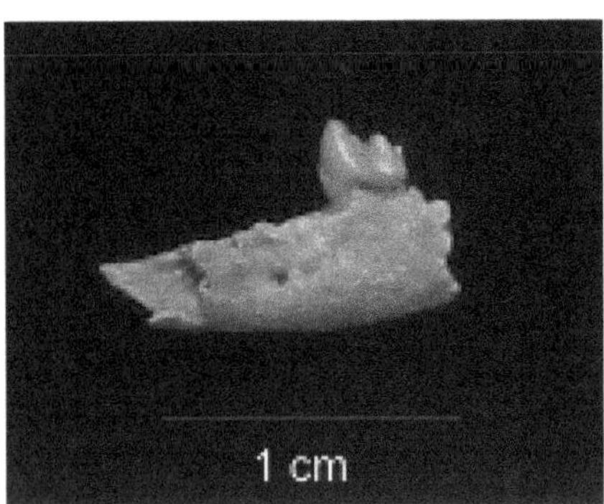

Figure 3.3 Liang Lemdubu: partial dentary of *Myoictis wallacei* from Spit 27

Current status: There are historical records of this species on Kobroor. More recently, Dr P. Woolley collected two specimens on Kobroor and Wokam. Recognition of *M. wallacei* as a distinct species follows the impending revision of this genus by Woolley and her colleagues.

Referred material: This species is represented by two lower jaws retaining single molars. A specimen from Spit 27 of Lemdubu has an unworn M_1 that displays the typical reduced para- and metaconids of a dasyurine (Fig. 3.3).

Wider distribution and habitat association: All members of this genus are associated with closed forest types.

Sminthopsis virginiae (Tarragon 1847) Red-cheeked Dunnart

Current status: This species is still known from the Aru Island group only from the type series of *Sminthopsis rufigenis* that Thomas (1922) collected from an unspecified locality.

Referred material: This species is not definitely represented in the archaeological faunas. However, several dentary fragments lacking teeth (e.g. from Lemdubu Spit 5 and Nabulei Lisa Spit 32) are smaller than *M. wallacei* and might belong to *Sminthopsis virginiae*.

Wider distribution and habitat association: In northern Australia this species inhabits grassland and savannah woodland habitats (Woolley 1995).

Family Peroryctidae (New Guinean Bandicoots)

Echymipera spp.

Current status: *Echymipera rufescens* (Peters and Doria 1875) has been recorded on several occasions from each of Wokam and Kobroor. Van Strien (1996) includes *E. kalubu* (Lesson 1828) in lists of taxa collected by each of Bik, Wallace, von Rosenberg and Kowalevsky. However, the subsequent taxonomic listing includes only *E. rufescens*, making it likely that the other entries are an oversight. A third member of this group, *E. echinista* (Menzies 1990), is recorded from two localities in the Fly-Strickland region of Papua New Guinea.

Referred material: This genus is represented in both sites by moderate numbers of fragmented jaws and teeth, and other cranial and postcranial remains. Further comparative study is needed to resolve final identifications of this material; in the interim, the following observations are warranted.

Among the more complete dentaries, several specimens are very close in size and morphology to a modern series of *E. rufescens* from Kobroor (CM29405-406, 29409, 29411, 29413). However, until direct comparisons have been made also with *E. echinista*, it is not possible to provide a confident allocation of this material to either taxon. The best preserved dentaries come from Spits 15 and 19 in Lemdubu but two well-preserved calcanea from Spits 1 and 4 are also referred to this species based on a close match to CM29506, a skeletal specimen of *E. rufescens* that is labelled as coming from 'West New Guinea'. As reported by Flannery (1990) for other samples of this species, the modern Aru Island sample of *E. rufescens* shows only slight sexual dimorphism in overall cranial size and relative premolar size.

Several dentary fragments appear to be too small to belong to the same taxon. These include two clearly adult specimens in which the molar alveolae are positioned well forward of the anterior root of the coronoid process. Other specimens also display a more crowded premolar series than occurs in *E. rufescens*. These specimens most likely represent *E. kalubu*, which possesses smaller molar teeth, a more slender lower jaw and a less elongate rostrum (hence more crowded premolar series) than either *E. rufescens* or *E. echinista* (Menzies 1990). All three *Echymipera* species are recorded from the Trans-Fly region, along with a fourth bandicoot with Australian affinities, *Isoodon macrourus* (see below).

Wider distribution and habitat association: *Echymipera rufescens* is widely distributed in lowland New Guinea and also on the Kei Islands, and is found locally on Cape York Peninsula, Australia. In New Guinea, *Echymipera rufescens* is primarily a rainforest inhabitant (Flannery 1995a). On Cape York Peninsula its distribution is centred on patches of closed forest. However, it also utilizes 'adjacent heath and eucalypt-woodland and low-layered open forest' (Gordon 1995a). The endemic New Guinean *Echymipera kalubu* is widespread in low to mid-montane rainforests but it also inhabits anthropogenic grassland and woody regrowth. It is recorded on the Fly Plateau as *E. oriomo* (Tate and Archbold 1935). The few capture records for *E. echinista* indicate an association with lowland rainforest either as a dominant community or as gallery forest.

Peroryctes sp. A previously unknown peroryctid

The most remarkable element of the Aru archaeological fauna is a previously unknown peroryctid bandicoot species (Figs 3.4 and 3.5). The preserved material of this taxon includes

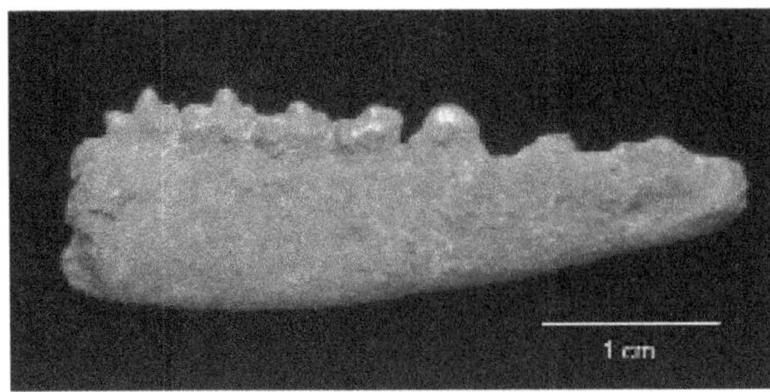

Figure 3.4 Liang Lemdubu: partial dentary of an unknown bandicoot species (*Peroryctes* sp.) from Spit 21. This individual is probably a female, based on the lack of premolar hypertrophy

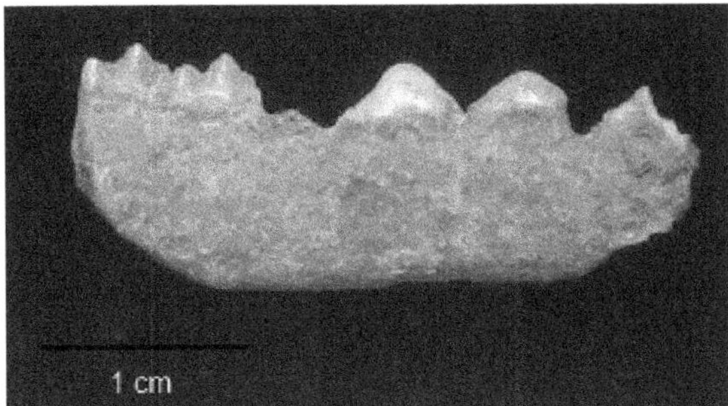

Figure 3.5 Liang Lemdubu: partial dentary of an unknown bandicoot species (*Peroryctes* sp.) from Spit 21. This individual shows marked premolar hypertrophy and is probably a male

several relatively complete dentaries with all postcanine teeth intact (eg Figure 3.4) and two partial maxillae, one with P^3–M^4 in a moderate state of wear, and the other with P^3–M^4 in a virtually unworn condition. Additionally, through a process of elimination of *I. macrourus* and *Echymipera* spp., it has been possible to allocate isolated petrosal elements and calcanea to this taxon. The cranio-dental and postcranial material suggests an animal with a body size somewhat exceeding that of *E. rufescens*. The sample of dentaries shows a strongly bimodal variability in premolar size relative to the molar teeth; this is interpreted as a manifestation of sexual dimorphism in the taxon.

The fossil taxon is most similar in dental morphology to species of *Peroryctes* but shows unusual features of upper molar morphology that preclude referral to this or any other previously recorded genus of bandicoot. It further differs from the altitudinally wide-spread *P. raffrayana* (Milne-Edwards, 1878) in its extreme premolar hypertrophy of putative male specimens. Sexual dimorphism in pre-molar size does occur in several species of peroryctid bandicoots, most notably *Peroryctes broadbenti* (Ramsay, 1879) of southeastern Papua New Guinea and *Echymipera clara* Stein, 1932 of the northern lowlands, but these taxa differ in other important respects from the fossil taxon.

The unknown taxon is moderately abundant in the Liang Lemdubu fauna, being second only to *Isoodon macrourus* in number of referred specimens. It is consistently present through the Liang Lemdubu sequence, with examples in all spits between 25 and 18, and isolated specimens in higher levels (Spits 14 and 6). All of the bandicoot material is more fragmented in Nabulei Lisa; however, dentary fragments and pedal elements in Spits 40 to 33 are referred to the new taxon with a high level of confidence.

Family Peramelidae (Australian Bandicoots)

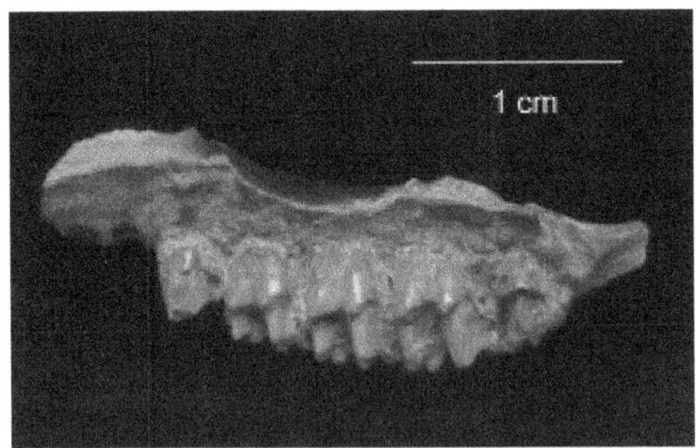

Figure 3.6 Liang Lemdubu: partial maxilla of *Isoodon macrourus* from Spit 23

Isoodon macrourus (Gould 1842) Northern Brown Bandicoot

Current status: No historical or contemporary records.

Referred material: Well-represented in the lower levels of both sites (Fig. 3.6). The reduced abundance of this species in the uppermost levels of Lemdubu and its absence in the upper half of Nabulei Lisa are consistent with the notion that it is locally extinct, at least on Kobroor.

Wider distribution and habitat association: Found in the Morehead region of the Trans-Fly and in the monsoonal woodlands and grassland habitats of southeastern New Guinea (Flannery 1995a). *Isoodon macrourus* is also widely distributed in northern and eastern Australia, where it occupies a wide variety of open and closed habitats (Gordon 1995b).

Family Phalangeridae (Cuscuses)

Phalanger gymnotis (Peters and Doria 1875) Ground Cuscus

Current status: The type specimen of *Phalangista gymnotis* Peters and Doria, 1875 was collected by Beccari at Jabulenga on Wokam. Subsequent examples were collected by Frost and Woolley on Kobroor (see Appendix 3.1).

Referred material: Consistently present through both sequences but often highly fragmented. A specimen showing the diagnostic large third premolar is illustrated in Figure 3.7.

Wider distribution and habitat association: The endemic New Guinean *P. gymnotis* has a broad altitudinal range on mainland New Guinea but it has not been recorded outside of rainforest habitats. There are no contemporary records from the Trans-Fly region.

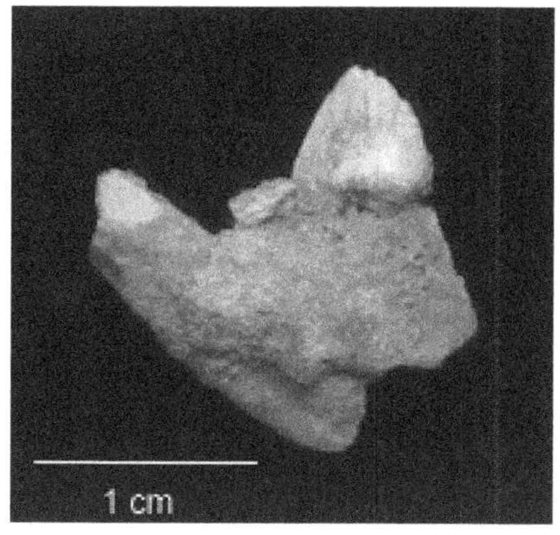

Figure 3.7 Liang Lemdubu: partial dentary of *Phalanger gymnotis* from Spit 25

Phalanger mimicus (Thomas 1922) Southwestern Common Cuscus

Current status: Only certainly recorded from Kobroor, but probably widespread in the island group.

Referred material: Consistently present through both sequences with some well-preserved examples (see Fig. 3.8).

Wider distribution and habitat association: This species was reported by O'Connor et al. (2002) under the name *Phalanger intercastellanus* (Thomas 1895). Subsequent to submission of that article, the lowland cuscuses of New Guinea and Australia were revised by Norris and Musser (2001), who additionally distinguish *P. mimicus*, a smaller-toothed species that is found from the Trans-Fly area west to the Mimika River on the New Guinean mainland. Although Norris and Musser (2001) did not include Aru Islands material in their study, trophy specimens collected by Woolley on Kobroor (see Appendix 3.1) are consistent with their description of *P. mimicus* and with Cape York examples of this species (e.g. CM787-788 from Iron Range). On the Trans-Fly, this species occupies a mosaic of rainforest and savannah habitat. In Australia, it is largely confined to rainforests, although Winter and Leung (1995a:269) note that the species (as *P. intercastellanus*) will 'penetrate the acacia fringes of rainforest'. The Mimika River animals were presumably obtained from lowland rainforest.

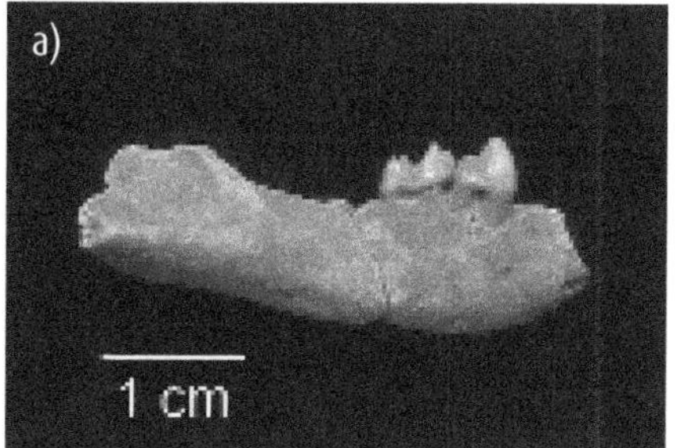

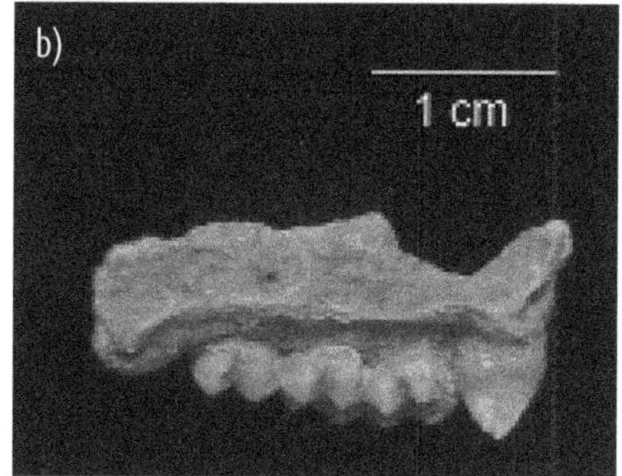

Figure 3.8 Liang Lemdubu: a) partial dentary and b) maxilla of *Phalanger mimicus*, both from Spit 20

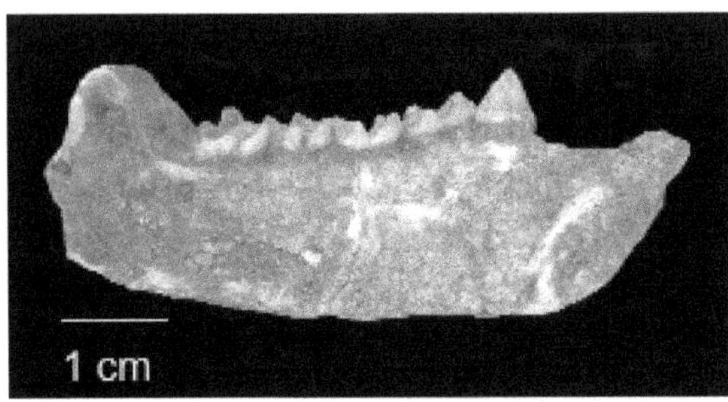

Figure 3.9 Liang Lemdubu: partial dentary of *Spilocuscus maculatus* from Spit 19.

Spilocuscus maculatus (Desmarest 1818) Common Spotted Cuscus

Current status: According to van Strien (1996), *S. maculatus* is 'probably the mammal most commonly collected in Aru, though all the recorded specimens were taken almost 90 years and more ago'. It is recorded from many large and small islands.

Referred material: *Spilocuscus maculatus* is represented by excellent material (Fig. 3.9). The sample is characterized by the small size of the teeth and jaws, in which regard they are consistent with Australian populations of this species.

Wider distribution and habitat association: *Spilocuscus maculatus* is more or less ubiquitous in lowland New Guinea and on all satellite islands. On mainland New Guinea it is generally associated with lowland to mid-montane rainforest habitats (Flannery 1995a). However, *S. maculatus* is also recorded from numerous localities in the Trans-Fly region where it occupies the mosaic of savannah and rainforest habitats (Waithman 1979). In Australia it has been observed 'in freshwater and saline mangroves, in larger paperbarks in thin riparian forest strips and in open forest up to half a kilometer from the nearest rainforest' (Winter and Leung 1995b:266).

Family Petauridae (Gliders and Striped Possums)

Dactylopsila trivirgata (Gray 1858) Striped Possum

Current status: The type specimen of *Dactylopsila trivirgata* (Gray 1858) was collected by Wallace and presumably comes from Wokam or Kobroor. Subsequent records confirm the presence of the species on both islands. Van Strien (1996) remarks that this species 'is not particularly rare in collections' and notes seven specimens in collections. Three additional specimens are held by the Western Australian Museum, collected by How and Kitchener. Woolley also collected one specimen on Kobroor (Appendix 3.1).

Referred material: O'Connor et al. (2002) reported that *Dactylopsila trivirgata* was absent from the Lemdubu fauna and this prompted their suggestion that it may have been a recent introduction to the Aru Islands. However, subsequent work on the Lemdubu collection led to the recognition of an incisor fragment from Spit 1. More significantly, better preserved specimens from Nabulei Lisa confirm a long prehistoric occurrence of *D. trivirgata* on Kobroor. Despite these new findings, the fact remains that this taxon is poorly represented in both sites compared to other, similar sized mammals (e.g. *Phalanger* spp. and bandicoots). Given the broad ecological tolerance of this species (see below), environmental factors including human disturbance seem unlikely to be responsible for its archaeological rarity. Across New Guinea, *Dactylopsila* spp. are generally regarded as desirable food items and they are well-represented in a number of archaeological faunas (White 1972; Aplin et al. 1999).

Wider distribution and habitat association: Widespread on New Guinea, from lowland to lower montane elevations; also found on Cape York Peninsula. In New Guinea the species is usually thought of as a denizen of lowland rainforest and hill forest. However, it is also recorded from numerous localities across the Trans-Fly where it presumably occupies gallery forest or savannah woodland. It is also recorded from secondary forests and old gardens, and therefore is moderately tolerant of human presence.

Family Macropodidae (Kangaroos and wallabies)

Macropus agilis (Gould 1842) Agile Wallaby

Current status: No historical or contemporary records. However, this species may persist on one or more of the poorly surveyed southeastern islands of the Aru group, where there is suitable open wooded habitat.

Referred material: Abundant archaeological remains from the earliest levels in both sites (Fig. 3.10). This species is represented up to Spit 27 in Nabulei Lisa, corresponding to around 10,200 BP, after which time it probably became locally extinct. Dental measurements of the Lemdubu sample shows no indication of changes in tooth size through the sequence (Fig. 3.11).

Wider distribution and habitat association: *Macropus agilis* is found in the savannah woodlands of the Trans-Fly and of southeastern New Guinea. It is also widespread across northern Australia. Throughout its range *M. agilis* is associated with open wooded habitats and grassy understorey. The species has been intensively hunted in coastal Papua both during prehistoric times and historically, and its numbers have declined in some areas as a consequence (Flannery 1995a).

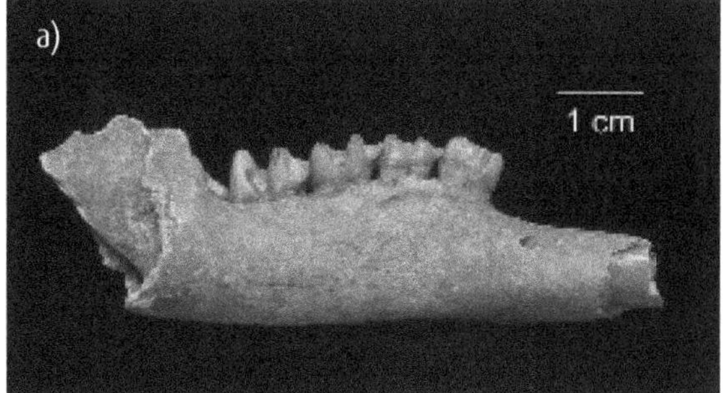

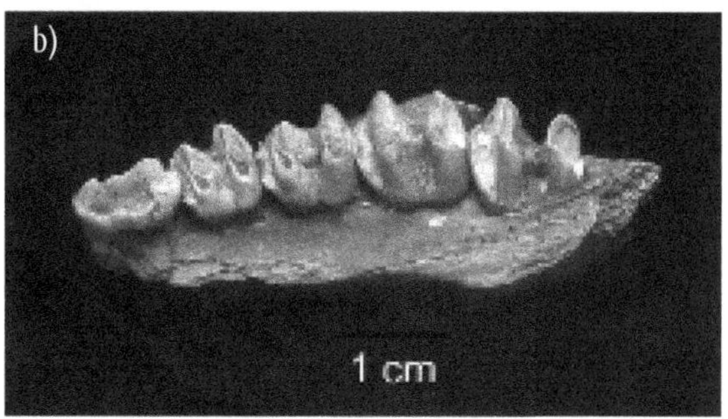

Figure 3.10 Liang Lemdubu: a) partial dentary and b) maxilla of *Macropus agilis* from Spits 22 and 20, respectively

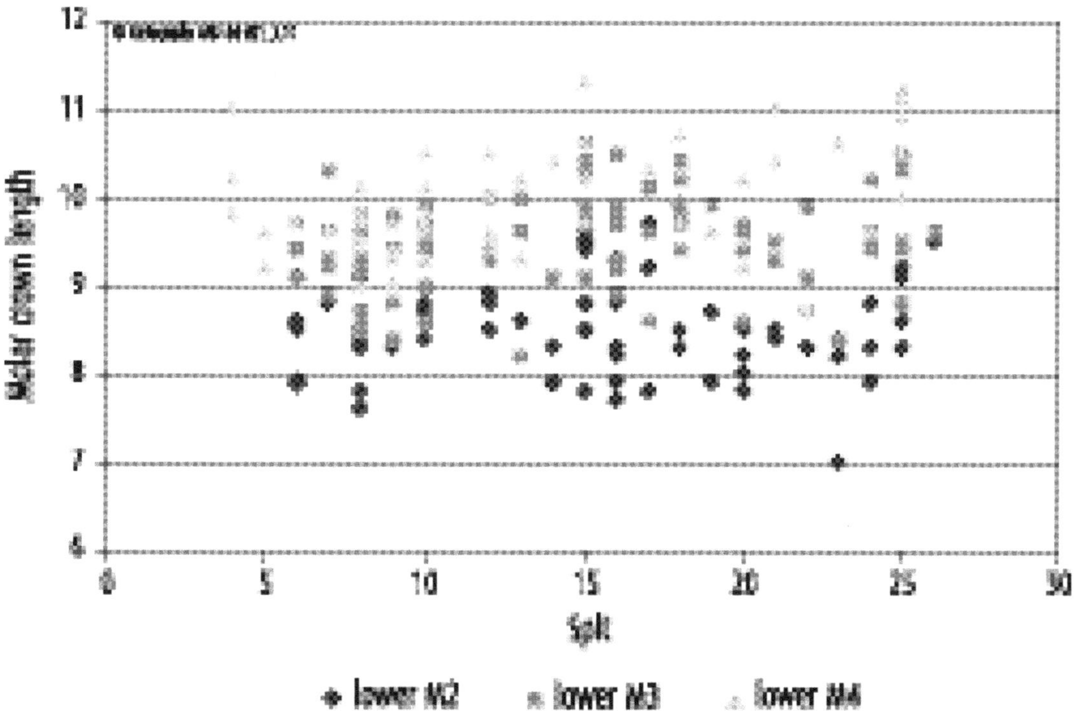

Figure 3.11 Liang Lemdubu: graph showing lower molar lengths of specimens of *Macropus agilis* from each level in the sequence. Values are plotted with different symbols for each of the second, third and fourth molars. The graph illustrates the fact that this species underwent no change in dental dimensions through the period 27,000–10,000 BP

Dorcopsis sp. Forest Wallaby

Current status: No historical or contemporary records.

Referred material: Fragmentary remains of this taxon include one heavily worn premolar from near the base of Lemdubu, and several molars and postcranial elements from the lower half of the Nabulei Lisa deposit. Unfortunately, the remains are too incomplete to identify the species involved. Today, the adjacent southern coastal lowlands of Indonesian Papua support populations of *D. muelleri*. However, another possible candidate is *D. luctuosa* that occurs west at least to the Trans-Fly region.

Wider distribution and habitat association: All species of *Dorcopsis* inhabit deep, closed forest habitats (Flannery 1995a), yet little detailed information is available on their ecology. In general, they are shy and secretive animals, intolerant of human presence.

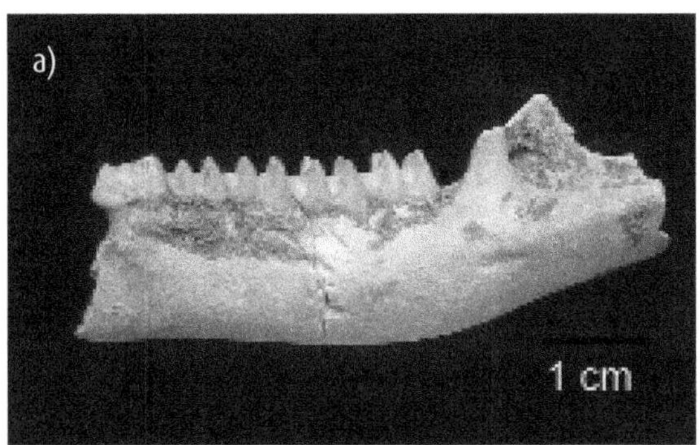

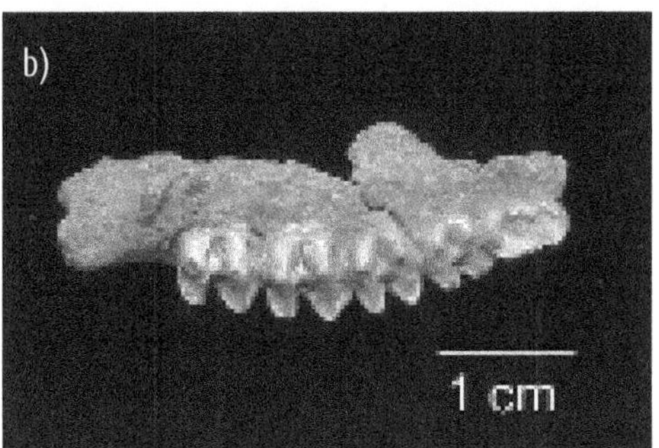

Figure 3.12 Liang Lemdubu: a) partial dentary and b) maxilla of *Thylogale brunii*, both from Spit 21

Thylogale brunii (Schreber 1778) Dusky Pademelon

Current status: *Didelphis brunii*, described from a captive animal seen in a menagerie on Java (Schreber 1778), is widely believed to refer to the 'true kangaroo' observed by Wallace and subsequently collected on Wokam, Kobroor, Wamar and Terangan (Van Strien 1996). The number of specimens in museum collections and in Woolley's 'kitchen midden' samples (see Appendix 3.1) suggests that this species can be locally abundant.

Referred material: Well-preserved remains from Lemdubu (see Fig. 3.12) compare closely with modern examples from the islands and from adjacent parts of the mainland.

Wider distribution and habitat association: The endemic New Guinean *T. brunii* is reported to occur in dense monsoonal rainforest in the Morehead area (Waithman 1979). In the recent past, it was apparently present in grassland/ savannah habitats around Post Moresby (Flannery 1995a).

Thylogale stigmatica (Gould 1860) Red-legged Pademelon

Current status: No historical or contemporary records.

Referred material: This taxon is represented by abundant well-preserved material in both sites (Fig. 3.13). As reported previously in O'Connor et al. (2002), the large Lemdubu sample of this taxon shows a greater size variation than would normally be observed within a single population. The majority of specimens compare closely in size and morphology with north Queensland specimens of *Thylogale stigmatica*. Unfortunately, no material of the New Guinean race, *T. s. oriomo* (Tate and Archbold 1935), is available in Australia for direct comparisons. However, Tate and Archbold (1935) comment that *oriomo* is comparable in size to north Queensland *stigmatica*. As it was not possible to allocate many of the less complete specimens to either the larger or smaller form of *T. stigmatica*, the two groups are not distinguished in the analysis.

Wider distribution and habitat association: In Australia, *T. stigmatica* seems to prefer rainforest but it also occurs in wet sclerophyll and drier vine thicket communities (Johnson and Vernes 1995). Tate and Archbold (1935) described the species' habitat on the Oriomo Plateau of Papua New Guinea as 'mixed grasslands and gallery woods', while Waithman (1979:320) reports it to be uncommon in 'low-mixed savannah or woodland near swamps' in the Morehead area.

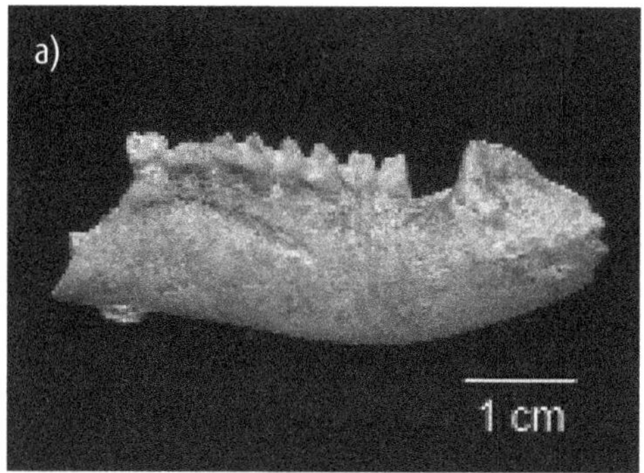

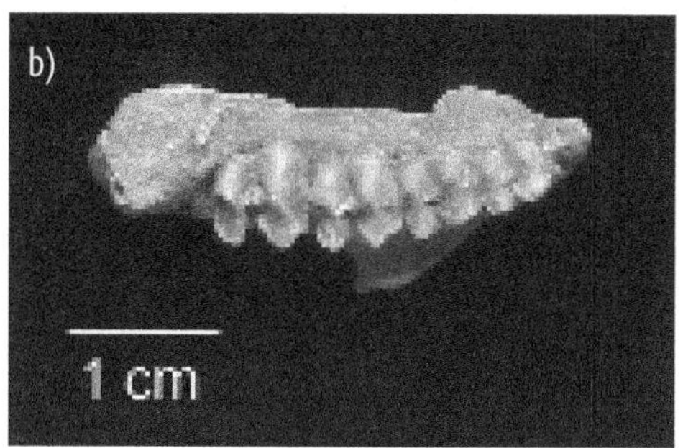

Figure 3.13 Liang Lemdubu: a) partial dentary and b) maxilla of *Thylogale stigmatica*, from Spits 22 and 12, respectively

Family Muridae (Rats and mice)

Melomys sp. cf. *M. burtoni* (Ramsay 1887)
Grassland Melomys

Current status: There are no historical or contemporary records of a small *Melomys* in the Aru Islands.

Referred material: Two specimens (both mandibles with molar teeth) from the lower levels of Lemdubu represent a small species of *Melomys*. These specimens were listed by O'Connor et al. (2002) as *M. lutillus*. With M_1 lengths of 5.5 and 5.7mm, this taxon is considerably smaller than *M. rufescens* (Alston 1877), the only species of this genus recorded in the modern fauna (Kitchener and Maryanto 1995; Van Strien 1996). The Lemdubu specimens were compared with examples of *M. burtoni* (Ramsay 1887) from localities in the Northern Territory Australia, and two specimens (CM29320, CM29336) referrable to the form *muscalis* (Thomas 1913) from the vicinity of Wipim on the Oriomo River, Trans-Fly region of Papua. The archaeological specimens are an excellent match with the northern Australian specimens, but differ from the Oriomo specimens in having narrower molars and a more elongate anterior cusp complex. Menzies (1996) was uncertain whether *muscalis* of the Trans-Fly region should be associated with the New Guinean taxon *M. littoralis* or with *M. burtoni* of northern Australia. Musser and Carleton (1993) included *littoralis* within *burtoni* but these authors now favour separation of these taxa, with placement of *muscalis* under *burtoni* (Musser pers. comm. 2004). Our limited observations on this group suggest that *muscalis* is distinct from *burtoni* and also point to the possibility that a form close to *burtoni* may persist in suitable habitats on the Aru Islands.

Wider distribution and habitat association: Across its range *M. burtoni* is associated with grassland habitats, including anthropogenic grassland patches within forested regions.

Parahydromys asper (Thomas, 1906) Waterside Rat

Current status: There are no historical or contemporary records of this species in the Aru Islands.

Referred material: A maxillary fragment from Spit 28 in Liang Lemdubu with an unworn M^1 probably represents this taxon (see Figure 3.14). The M^1 measures 7.0 mm in length and is substantially larger the M^1 of modern specimens of *Hydromys chrysogaster* Geoffroy, 1804 from the Aru and Kai Islands (M^1 length in four specimens is 5.65 to 5.9; K. Helgan, pers. comm.). These taxa are otherwise similar in cheek tooth morphology.

Wider distribution and habitat association: Widely distributed along the central cordillera of New Guinea, across a known altitudinal range of 700–2,000 m. It is also recorded from montane

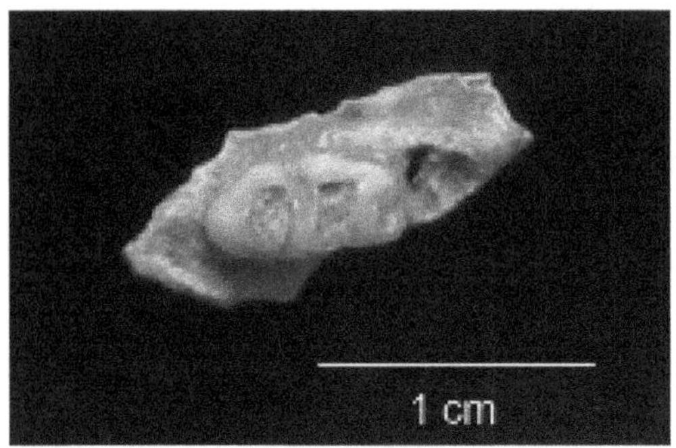

Figure 3.14 Liang Lemdubu: partial maxilla of *Parahydromys asper* from Spit 28

habitats in the Arfak and Torricelli Mountains. Aplin et al. (1999) reported a mid-Holocene sub-fossil from the Ayamaru Plateau on the Bird's Head Peninsula, at an elevation of c. 350 m.

Paramelomys naso (Thomas 1911) Long-nosed Melomys

Current status: Flannery (1995b) reported a specimen collected by Dr P. Woolley from Wokam as an example of *P. lorentzii* (Jentink 1907). Van Strien (1996) repeated this attribution. The correct allocation of the specimen to *P. naso* was reported by Menzies (1996).

Referred material: Two specimens from Lemdubu are tentatively referred to this species. A well-preserved maxilla with relatively unworn molars from Spit 26 has an M^1 that measures 4.4mm in length and 2.3mm in width. These dimensions are an exact match with the holotype of *P. naso*, as reported by Tate (1951). The taxon is considerably larger toothed than other possible candidate species including *P. platyops* (Thomas 1906), *P. moncktoni* (Thomas 1904) and *P. lorentzii*, all which are recorded from localities along the southern lowlands of New Guinea.

Wider distribution and habitat association: This poorly known species is otherwise recorded from a few localities in the lowlands and foothills of southwest New Guinea. All mainland records come from areas of lowland rainforest habitat.

Pogonomys sp. Tree-mouse

Current status: No historical or contemporary records.

Referred material: A species of *Pogonomys* is represented by a total of 19 tooth-bearing specimens from Lemdubu. These are evenly spread within the sequence from Spits 30 to 13. The molar teeth in these specimens are slightly smaller than those of north Queensland *Pogonomys*, which are usually identified as *Pogonomys mollipillosus* (Winter and Whitford 1995). The type specimen of *Pogomonys mollipilosus* that Peters and Doria (1881) collected at Katau on the lower Fly River, often has been associated with montane populations of the larger *Pogonomys* (eg, *P. loriae* Thomas 1897; *P. dryas* Thomas 1904). However, Musser (pers. comm. 2004) instead suggests an affiliation with *P. macrourus* (Milne-Edwards 1877), a taxon that is widespread through the lowland and mid-montane forests of New Guinea. The lack of taxonomic resolution within this group hinders any attempt to more precisely identify the Aru Island fossil sample.

Wider distribution and habitat association: All *Pogonomys* species are associated with rainforest habitats. They are highly arboreal animals but live communally in burrows dug in the forest floor or into the banks of small watercourses.

Pseudomys sp. cf. *P. gracilicaudatus* 'species group'

Current status: There are no historical of contemporary records of any member of this species group on the Aru Islands or anywhere on the New Guinean mainland.

Referred material: Two specimens only from Lemdubu derived from Spit 17 (a left dentary with M_1), and a mixed sample that combined material from Spits 21 and 23 (an unworn right M^1). The M^1 is a three-rooted tooth that measures 2.6mm by 1.8mm. The relatively simple cusp pattern of this tooth and the presence of only three roots identifies it as a member of the largely Australian assemblage of 'conilurins'. Within this group, it compares most favourably with members of the *P. gracilicaudatus* species group, both in size and in overall cusp pattern (including the presence of a well-developed anterior cingular cuspule). The two members of this group — *P. gracilicaudatus*

(Gould 1845) of eastern Australia and *P. nanus* (Gould 1858) of northern Australia — not only overlap in size but also appear to be indistinguishable from each other in cusp arrangement. The Lemdubu specimen differs from both of these taxa in many small details including the more discrete and angular nature of cusps t1 and t4, the smaller size of cusp t1 relative to cusp t4, and the more posterior placement of these cusps relative to the central row of cusps.

Another taxon that begs comparison on morphological and biogeographic criteria is *P. desertor* (Troughton 1932). However, the degree of morphological fit with this taxon is much less satisfactory, as the M^1 of *P. desertor* lacks a prominent anterior cingular cuspule (it sometimes has a low bulge or ridge), and has less prominent anterior buccal crests on cusps t6 and t9. There is also a general resemblance between the Lemdubu specimen and members of the *P. delicatulus* species group. However, all members of this group are considerably smaller in tooth size.

Wider distribution and habitat association: *Pseudomys nanus* is widely distributed across mainland northern Australia, from the Pilbara coastline to the Barkly Tableland in northwest Queensland. It is recorded from the Sir Edward Pellew Island group in the Gulf of Carpentaria. A variety of habitats are occupied but these usually feature tussock grasses as a major component of the understorey (Robinson 1995). *Pseudomys gracilicaudatus* is restricted to the eastern seaboard of Australia, north to the vicinity of Townsville (Watts and Aslin 1981); it occupies moister habitats including coastal heath and wetter forests.

Rattus sordidus (Gould 1858) Canefield Rat

Current status: Not recorded in the contemporary fauna.

Referred material: A member of this species group is represented in Lemdubu by abundant, well-preserved remains, distributed more or less continuously between Spits 28 and 11. Several maxillae clearly show the deeply invasive anterior palatal foramen that distinguishes members of the *Rattus sordidus* group from all other native New Guinean *Rattus*. The molars are substantially larger than in examples of *R. colletti* from the Northern Territory, and slightly smaller than examples of *R. villossisimus* from the same area. They are a very close match to specimens of *R. sordidus aramia* (Troughton 1937) from localities in the Oriomo River area (e.g. CM29345, CM29350).

Wider distribution and habitat association: The closest populations are found on the Trans-Fly region of New Guinea and in Queensland on the Sir Edward Pellew Islands in the Gulf of Carpentaria. In New Guinea this species is associated with grassland and savannah woodland habitats (Flannery 1995a).

Uromys caudimaculatus (Krefft 1867) Mottled-tailed Giant Rat

Current status: Collected in the Aru Islands on several occasions, including the holotype of *Uromys aruensis* (Gray 1873), purchased by A.B. Meyer in 1870 from an unspecified locality. Subsequently recorded on Kobroor by Dr P. Woolley (Appendix 3.1) and others.

Referred material: This species is represented in both sites. Comparisons were made with Australian and New Guinean specimens of *U. caudimaculatus* and with examples of *Xenuromys barbatus*. Diagnostic remains from Lemdubu include a maxilla with M^2 from Spit 22, and unworn upper and lower first molars from Spit 1.

Wider distribution and habitat association: This species is widespread in lowland to mid-montane habitats in New Guinea and it is also found on Cape York Peninsula. It also occurs on the Kei Islands. On mainland New Guinea it occurs in both primary rainforest and associated secondary forests, and in areas of mixed rainforest and savannah, such as the Trans-Fly.

Family Suidae (Pigs)

Sus scrofa (Linnaeus 1758) Domestic Pig

Current status: Established as a feral animal on all major islands of the Aru group (Van Strien 1996).

Referred material: Fragmentary bones and teeth of pigs are confined to the uppermost levels of both sites.

Wider distribution and habitat association: Feral pigs are highly adaptable and can utilize a wide variety of both densely forested and more open habitats.

Family Cervidae (Deer)

Cervus timorensis (Quoy and Gaimard 1830) Rusa Deer

Current status: Feral populations are probably found on all of the major islands. Healey (1995:56) suggested that Rusa Deer may have been introduced by the Portuguese. However, Wallace does not mention this species at all, and it is unlikely that he would have failed to notice this species if it was abundant and as important a hunted animal then, as it is today. Van Strien (1996) reviewed the known history of introductions and mentioned museum specimens from Wokam and Wamar Islands and sight records from Ujir and Wasir.

Referred material: Deer remains are restricted to Spit 1 of Nabulei Lisa. Although no definite deer remains were found in Lemdubu, the upper few spits contain quantities of highly fragmented bone from pig- or deer-sized mammals, that might easily include some bone from this taxon.

Wider distribution and habitat association: In the Morehead region of Papua New Guinea this species is said to occur 'mainly on the grassland strips bordering the rivers' (Waithman 1979:325).

Family Canidae (Dogs)

Canis familiaris (Linnaeus 1758) Domestic Dog

Current status: There is no information on the status of feral dog populations in the Aru Island group. However, dogs are ubiquitous around human habitation areas.

Referred material: Dog remains are restricted to Spit 1 in Nabulei Lisa and Spit 2 in Lemdubu. The material is very fragmentary and provides no useful morphological information.

Wider distribution and habitat association: Waithman (1979) reported that domestic dogs were starting to become feral by the early 1970s in the Morehead region of Papua New Guinea, preying mainly on Rusa Deer.

Family Pteropodidae (Flying Foxes and Fruit Bats)

Dobsonia spp. Bare-backed Fruit-bats

Current status: *Dobsonia moluccensis* (Quoy and Gaimard 1830) was recorded by Anderson (1912) for the Aru Islands, based on specimens in the British Museum and in Leiden. Bergmans and Sarbini (1985) questioned the origin of these specimens and questioned the occurrence of the genus in the Aru Group. This doubt is maintained by Flannery (1995a) who does not record any *Dobsonia* species from Aru. The Western Australian Museum expeditions to the Kei and Aru Islands obtained *Dobsonia* in both island groups. These are tentatively identified as *D. moluccensis,* pending more detailed study. Van Strien (1996) reported specimens from Kobroor in several collections. One example is present in the 'kitchen midden' sample collected by Woolley on Kobroor (Appendix 3.1).

Referred material: Both sites produced the remains of megachiropteran bats, most often in a highly fragmented state. Fortunately, *Dobsonia* spp. possess a distinctive dental morphology that allows most isolated teeth to be distinguished from other comparable-sized pteropodids including species of *Pteropus*. The dentary of *Dobsonia* spp. is also distinctive in having closely adpressed canines with reduced and anteriorly displaced incisors. From examination of all dentary fragments and isolated molars, it appears that the great bulk of the megachiropteran material from both sites is referrable to a large species of *Dobsonia,* here tentatively identified as *D. moluccensis*. However, a small number of isolated canine teeth and edentulous jaw fragments appear to represent a second, much smaller *Dobsonia* species. The most likely candidate is *D. viridis* (Heude 1896) which is recorded from the nearby Kei Islands (Flannery 1995b).

Wider distribution and habitat association: *Dobsonia moluccensis* is otherwise restricted to the Seram and Buru Island groups in the Central Moluccas. Apart from the fact that it is a cave roosting bat, little is known of its biology. *Dobsonia viridis* has a similar distribution but even less is known of its habits. Most, though not all, species of *Dobsonia* roost in caves.

Pteropus sp. cf. *P. macrotis* (Peters 1867) Big-eared Flying Fox

Current status: The only record in the Aru Group is the holotype of *Pteropus acrotis* (Peters 1867) collected by von Rosenberg in 1865.

Referred material: An isolated tooth from Lemdubu Spit 15 shows its closest match with posterior post-canine teeth of specimens of this species from mainland New Guinea. This record requires confirmation.

Wider distribution and habitat association: This species is recorded from widely scattered localities in lowland New Guinea (Flannery 1995a), and from Salawatti Island to the west of the main island (Flannery 1995b). Waithman (1979:320) reported it as common in the Morehead region where it was obtained by shooting 'mainly from low mixed savannah and the gardens of natives'.

Pteropus sp. cf. *P. melanopogon* (Peters 1867) Black-bearded Flying Fox

Current status: This species has been collected in the Aru Islands on two occasions, at 'Wonumbai' (this is probably 'Manumbai'; see Flannery 1995b:269) on Kobroor and on Wokam.

Referred material: A single edentulous lower jaw fragment from Lemdubu Spit 10 represents a very large pteropodid, consistent in size with *P. melanopogon*. However, various other large *Pteropus* are recorded from the adjacent mainland of Nw Guinea, including *P. alecto* (Temminck 1837), *P. conspicillatus* (Gould 1858), and *P. neohobernicus* (Peters 1876), and any one of them might have occurred in the vicinity of Lemdubu during the late Pleistocene.

Wider distribution and habitat association: The wider range of *P. melanopogon* includes the Kei Islands, and the Seram and Buru groups of the Central Moluccas.

Family Hipposideridae (Horseshoe-bats)

Hipposideros diadema (Geoffroy 1813) Diadem Horseshoe-bat

Current status: Van Strien (1996) reported one historical specimen collected by von Rosenberg, and other collected more recently by Mark van der Wal on Kobroor.

Referred material: A dentary with well-preserved $M_{1\text{-}3}$ from Lemdubu Spit 23 provides the only prehistoric evidence of this taxon. This species is easily recognized by its large size relative to all other hipposiderids in the Australia–New Guinea region.

Wider distribution and habitat association: The nearest records of this widely distributed species are in the Kei Islands (Flannery 1995b) and along the southern lowlands of Indonesian Papua (Flannery 1995a). *Hipposideros diadema* is often encountered roosting in caves (Flannery 1995a) but a variety of other roosting sites are used in areas that lack caves.

Family Molossidae (Insectivorous Bats)

Chaerephon sp. cf. C. jobensis (Miller 1902) Northern Mastiff-bat

Current status: There are no historical or contemporary records of any molossid bat from the Aru Islands.

Referred material: A total of eight dentaries from Nabulei Lisa, several retaining one or more teeth, are tentatively referred to this species. They give a very close match in size and morphology to reference specimens (e.g. CM2175, CM7606) from localities in the Northern Territory. Key points of similarity include the tightly compressed lower molar trigonids, the broad talonid of M_3 and the V-shaped ectolophid crests. The presence of these specimens in the deposit presumably reflects the use of the cave as a roost site.

Wider distribution and habitat association: The nearest modern records of this species are from the Morehead area of Papua New Guinea (Flannery 1995a), and Seram in the Central Moluccas (Flannery 1995b). Waithman (1979:323) reported that the Morehead specimens (as *Tadarida jobensis*) 'were collected from holes in the trunks of coconut palms by local villagers'. Australian populations generally roost in hollow trees and buildings. However, some cave roosting populations are known (Richards 1995).

Non-mammalian vertebrates

None of the reptile, bird or fish material has been subject to close scrutiny. The abundant snake material in both sites is clearly dominated by the remains of pythons (Family Boidae), with much smaller numbers of colubroid snakes (e.g. Lemdubu Spits 10 and 14). Two python species are recorded from the Aru Islands, *Morelia amethystinus* and *M. viridis*. These attain maximum lengths of two and eight meters, respectively. The lizard material includes vertebrae and cranial elements of moderately large varanids, as well as vertebrae and dentigerous elements referable to the families Agamidae and Scincidae. A scincid dentary fragment from Spit 26 in Lemdubu has the characteristic pebble-like teeth of a member of the *Egernia–Tiliqua* assemblage of skinks. Judging from its size and morphology, it most likely represents *Tiliqua gigas*, a species which occurs on the Aru Islands today (de Rooij 1915). Two species of *Varanus* are recorded from the contemporary Aru Islands: the Mangrove Monitor, *V. salvator*, and the Black Tree Monitor, *V. beccarii* (de Rooij 1915; De Lisle 1996), both of which are arboreal and semi-aquatic, with head and body lengths well under one metre. The latter taxon is endemic to the Aru Islands.

A single osseous scute of a crocodile from Nabulei Lisa Spit 15 is the only evidence of this group in either site.

Small quantities of turtle carapace and associated bones were recovered from Spits 19 to 26 in Nabulei Lisa, and several levels in Lemdubu. These are referrable to the freshwater turtle family Cheluidae, several species of which are probably found on the Aru Islands today.

A small number of frog bones are also present in both sites. Variation in ilial morphology indicates that two or more taxa are represented.

Casuarius spp., the cassowaries, are represented in several levels of both sites. The better preserved material includes a partial vertebra from Spit 1 of Lemdubu. It also includes two pedal phalanges (Fig. 3.15) from Spits 20 and 21 that were mentioned by O'Connor et al. (2002) as potentially derived from a large macropodid species. This error occurred because Aplin previously compared the fossil specimens with reference skeletons of the Emu (*Dromaius novaehollandae*) as a surrogate for a cassowary. More recently, the fossil specimens were compared with a modern specimen of *Casuarius casuarius* in the collection of the Queensland Museum. This process now leaves us in no doubt that the two fossil bones are both second phalanges from the third digit of a large species of *Casuarius*. Additional highly fragmented material coming from various levels in Lemdubu is almost certainly derived from this taxon.

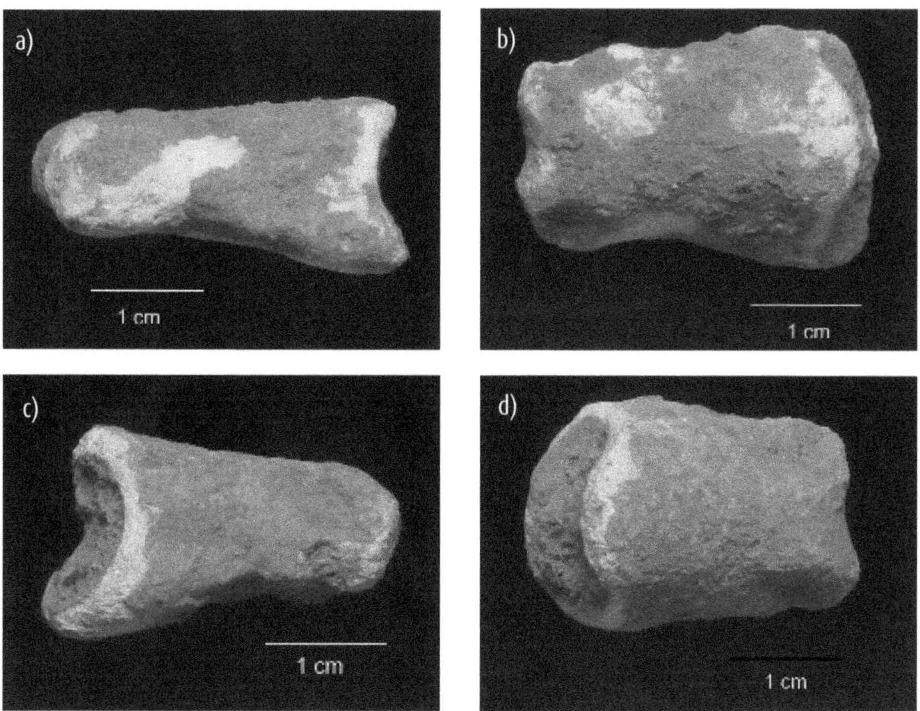

Figure 3.15 Liang Lemdubu: medial phalanges of *Casuarius* sp. cf. *C. casuarius* from Spits 20 (a–b), and Spit 21 (c–d). These specimens were previously reported as belonging to a large macropodid

Smaller birds are also represented by fragmentary remains in many levels. A lack of comprehensive reference material hinders attempts to identify material from sites in this area (Aplin et al. 1999).

The fish remains in Lemdubu are mostly derived from small to medium-sized fish and are badly fragmented. Other than for some fragmentary head shields of an ariid (freshwater to estuarine) catfish, very few potentially diagnostic elements are represented in this site. Fish remains are more abundant in Nabulei Lisa, especially in the upper half of the sequence, with representatives of the families Plotosidae, Labridae and Lutjanidae. More precise identification of this material has not yet been attempted.

Discussion

The archaeological fauna includes several mammal species not previously recorded from the Aru Islands, but it also lacks several species that are present today (summarized in Table 3.2). The major additions are the macropodids (*Macropus agilis, Thylogale stigmatica* and *Dorcopsis* sp.), the bandicoots (*Isoodon macrourus* and *Echymipera kalubu* — tentatively identified), the Short-Nosed Echidna (*Tachyglossus aculeatus*), a Native Cat (*Dasyurus albopunctatus*), several rodents (*Pogonomys* sp., *Melomys* sp. cf. *M. burtoni, Rattus sordidus, Pseudomys* sp., *Parahydromys asper*), at least one megachiropteran bat (*Dobsonia* sp. – small species), and one microchiropteran bat (*Chaerephon* sp. cf. *C. jobensis*). An important point to make is that the majority of these taxa are large and conspicuous mammals that are unlikely to have been missed by the various collectors to the Aru Islands.

In contrast, the contemporary species that are missing from the archaeological faunas are predominantly small-bodied species such as insectivorous bats (eight species), small megachiropteran bats (three species), small to medium sized rodents (five species), and small marsupials (two species — *Murexia longicaudata* and *Petaurus breviceps*). The largest of the unrecorded mammal species, the

Table 3.2 Composite list of mammal species recorded from both modern and archaeological contexts on the Aru Islands

SPECIES	COMMON NAME	MODERN	ARCHAEOLOGICAL
TACHYGLOSSIDAE	(Echidnas)		
Tachyglossus aculeatus	Short-beaked Echidna	-	+
DASYURIDAE	(Marsupial mice and native cats)		
Dasyurus albopunctatus	New Guinea Quoll	-	+
Murexia longicauda	Short-furred Dasyure	+	-
Myoictis melas	Three-striped Dasyure	+	+
Sminthopsis virginiae	Red-cheeked Dunnart	+	-
PERORYCTIDAE	(New Guinean Bandicoots)		
Echymipera sp. cf. *E. kalubu*	Common Echymipera	-	+?
Echymipera rufescens	Long-nosed Echymipera	+	+
Peroryctes sp.	Previously unknown peroryctid	-	+
PERAMELIDAE	(Australian Bandicoots)		
Isoodon macrourus	Northern Brown Bandicoot	-	+
PHALANGERIDAE	(Cuscuses)		
Phalanger gymnotis	Ground Cuscus	+	+
Phalanger mimicus	Southwestern Common Cuscus	+	+
Spilocuscus maculatus	Common Spotted Cuscus	+	+
PETAURIDAE	(Gliders and Striped Possums)		
Dactylopsila trivirgata	Striped Possum	+	+
Petaurus breviceps	Sugar Glider	+	-
MACROPODIDAE	(Kangaroos and wallabies)		
Macropus agilis	Agile Wallaby	-	+
Thylogale brunii	Dusky Pademelon	+	+
Thylogale stigmatica	Red-legged Pademelon	-	+
Dorcopsis sp.	Forest Wallaby	-	+
MURIDAE	(Rats and mice)		
Hydromys chrysogaster	Common Water Rat	+	-
Melomys rufescens	Black-tailed Melomys	+	-
Melomys sp. cf. *M. burtoni*	Grassland Melomys	-	+
Parahydromys asper	Riverside Rat	-	+
Paramelomys naso	Long-nosed Melomys	+	+
Paramelomys platyops	Lowland Melomys	+	-
Pogonomys sp.	Tree-mouse	-	+
Pseudomys sp. cf. *P. nanus*	Chestnut mouse	-	+
Rattus leucopus	Cape York Rat	+	-
Rattus sordidus	Cane field Rat	-	+
Rattus rattus (I)	Black Rat	+	-
Uromys caudimaculatus	Mottled-tailed Giant Rat	+	+
SORICIDAE	(Shrews)		
Crocidura maxi (I)	Crocidura	+	-
Suncus murinus (I)	House Shrew	+	-
VIVERRIDAE	(Civets etc.)		
Paradoxurus hermaphroditus (I)	Palm Civet	+	-
SUIDAE	(Pigs)		
Sus scrofa (I)	Domestic Pig	+	+
CERVIDAE	(Deer)		
Cervus timorensis (I)	Rusa Deer	+	+
PTEROPODIDAE	(Flying Foxes and Fruit Bats)		
Dobsonia moluccensis	Bare-backed Fruit-bat	+	+
Dobsonia sp. (small species)		-	+
Macroglossus minimus	Northern Blossum-bat	+	-
Nyctimene albiventer	Common Tube-nosed Bat	+	-
Pteropus macrotis	Big-eared Flying Fox	+	+?
Pteropus melanopogon	Black-bearded Flying Fox	+	+?
Syconycteris australis	Common Blossum-bat	+	-
HIPPOSIDERIDAE	(Horseshoe-bats)		
Hipposideros ater	Dusky Horseshoe-bat	+	-
Hipposideros cervinus	Fawn Horseshoe-bat	+	-
Hipposideros diadema	Diadem Horseshoe-bat	+	+

continued over

Table 3.2 Continued

SPECIES	COMMON NAME	MODERN	ARCHAEOLOGICAL
RHINOLOPHIDAE	(Horseshoe-bats)		
Rhinolophus euryotis	New Guinea Horseshoe-bat	+	-
VESPERTILIONIDAE	(Insectivorous Bats)		
Miniopterus australis	Little Bentwing-bat	+	-
Miniopterus schreibersii	Common Bentwing-bat	+	-
Pipistrellus javanicus	Javan Pipistrelle	+	-
Pipistrellus papuanus	Papuan Pipistrelle	+	-
MOLOSSIDAE			
Chaerephon sp. cf. *C. jobensis*		-	+
EMBALLONURIDAE			
Emballonura nigrescens	Lesser Sheathtail-bat	+	-

Palm Civet (*Paradoxurus hermaphroditus*), is clearly an exotic element in the modern fauna. The fact of its absence from the deposits is a good indication of just how recently its introduction occurred. The same argument can be applied in the case of the Rusa Deer, *Cervus timorensis*, the remains of which are confined to the uppermost levels of both sites. In contrast, pig remains extend further into both deposits, although these too are confined to relatively recent contexts. Taken conversely, these results also give cause for confidence in regard to the stratigraphic integrity of both sites.

The species recorded only from the prehistoric context fall into two clear groups – those whose apparent decline or extinction on the islands probably occurred as a consequence of environmental change; and those whose decline or extinction is more difficult to explain in such terms. Taxa in the first group are *Macropus agilis*, *Isoodon macrourus*, *Rattus sordidus*, *Melomys* sp. cf *M. burtoni*, *Pseudomys* sp. cf *P. nanus* and *Parahydromys asper*. With the exception of *P. asper*, all of these taxa are found today in grassland or savannah habitats. Their former presence on the Aru Island constitutes strong evidence for considerably drier and more open conditions on the dissected Aru 'plateau' during late Pleistocene times. The available habitat for these species presumably shrank during and after the period of sea level rise, when warmer wetter conditions over the newly created Aru Islands favoured expansion of wetter, more closed forest types. *Parahydromys asper*, in contrast, is only recorded as a living animal from rainforest habitat at low to mid-montane elevations. We are unable to provide a satisfactory reason for its occurrence on the Aru Islands during late Pleistocene times, virtually at sea level and in the context of a predominantly open country fauna.

The second group includes several taxa that seem to be ecologically well-suited to the contemporary Aru environment. The two obvious examples are *Dorcopsis* sp. and *Dasyurus albopunctatus*, both of which are widely associated with lowland rainforest habitat on the New Guinea mainland. Other taxa that might also fit this profile are *Thylogale stigmatica* and *Tachyglossus aculeatus*, both of which are known to occupy lowland rainforest habitats in at least some part of their total geographic ranges. Why did these species decline and ultimately disappear from the Aru Islands? The answer to this question is almost certainly complex and may well be different in each case. Each of *T. stigmatica* and *Dorcopsis* sp. may have suffered from direct competition with *T. brunii* in an environment characterized by a progressive loss of heterogeneity. Hunting pressure might also have played a role, especially in the case of *Dorcopsis* sp. and *T. aculeatus*. Decline of the native predator, *D. albopunctatus*, is difficult to understand, except perhaps in terms of some general biogeographic principle of simplification in island faunas. However, such statements are unsatisfactory unless they invoke actual ecological mechanisms.

Biogeographic relationships of the prehistoric Aru Island vertebrate fauna

The late Pleistocene mammalian fauna of the Aru Islands shows evidence of strong biogeographic continuity with the contemporary fauna of the Trans-Fly region of southern New Guinea. This continuity is demonstrated by the fact that all but one of the additional mammal species recorded from the prehistoric Aru island context are part of the contemporary fauna of the Trans-Fly area of southern New Guinea. The sole exception is the native rodent *Pseudomys* sp. cf. *P. gracilicaudatus* 'species group'. This species is widely distributed across northern Australia but previously has not been recorded in New Guinea or on any of its satellite islands. Surviving populations of this taxon should perhaps be sought in the Trans-Fly region or elsewhere in southeastern New Guinea, wherever savannah habitat is found.

The Trans-Fly area was identified by Flannery (1995a) as one part of a broader zoogeographic province that he labelled the 'Austral Province'. This province also includes several extensive tracts of savannah woodland in southeast Papua New Guinea, most notably around Port Moresby and Popondetta. Today, the Aru Islands lie far to the west of the boundaries of this province and instead, make up part of Flannery's 'Tumbunan Province'. However, during late Pleistocene times, the Austral Province clearly expanded to occupy a much larger area that included the Aru 'plateau', then situated on the edge of the exposed Sahul shelf. How much further west and north it extended is not known for sure. However, it is worth noting that a broadly contemporaneous archaeological fauna from Toé Cave, on the Ayamaru Plateau in the central Bird's Head, shows no indication of more open, savannah conditions or of any Austral faunistic influence (Pasveer and Aplin 1998; Pasveer 2004). Instead, the Toé Cave fauna documents a downward extension of montane forest faunal elements onto the lowland Ayamaru Plateau, an environmental change that might have resulted from more persistent cloud-lie over this area, perhaps coupled with a slight decrease in ambient temperature (Pasveer and Aplin 1998).

Although the late Pleistocene fauna of the Aru 'plateau' was certainly dominated by Austral faunal elements, it also contained a number of uncharacteristic elements that hint at biogeographic connections with Tumbunan New Guinea. These include such characteristic lowland rainforest elements as *Dorcopsis* sp., *Dasyurus albopunctatus*, *Echymipera rufescens*, *Phalanger gymnotis*, *Paramelomys naso*, and *Pogonomys* sp. At a local environmental level, these elements are taken as evidence for a complex mosaic of wetter, closed and drier, more open habitats (see Chapter 9, this volume). In a broader biogeographic context, the complex admixture of open and closed, and wet and dry faunal elements, suggests that the Aru Islands are positioned close to a major faunistic boundary and thus, experienced repeated episodes of faunistic change related to Pleistocene glacial cycles.

The discovery of a distinctive new kind of bandicoot in the Aru Islands archaeological assemblages gives further emphasis to the fact that our knowledge of the small to medium mammal diversity of late Pleistocene New Guinea remains very incomplete.

Acknowledgements

Dr Pat Woolley (La Trobe University) and Dr Ric How (Western Australian Museum) provided unpublished information on the modern mammal fauna of the Aru Islands. Dr Tim Flannery and Mr. Walter Boles (both Australian Museum) advised on some taxonomic determinations. Kristofer Helgen (University of Adelaide) read and made helpful comments on the manuscript.

References

Aplin, K.P., J.M. Pasveer, and W.E. Boles. 1999. Late Quaternary vertebrates from the Bird's Head Peninsula, Irian Jaya, Indonesia, including descriptions of two previously unknown marsupial species. *Records of the Western Australian Museum*, Supplement 57:351–87.

Bergmans, W. and S. Sarbini. 1985. Fruit bats of the genus *Dobsonia* Palmer, 1898 from the islands of Biak, Owi, Numfoor and Yapen, Irian Jaya (Mammalia, Megachiroptera). *Beaufortia* 34:181–9.

van Dyck, S.M. 1988. The Bronze Quoll, *Dasyurus spartacus* (Marsupialia: Dasyuridae), a new species from the savannas of Papua New Guinea. *Australian Mammalogy* 11:145–56.

Flannery, T.F. 1990. *Echymipera davidi*, a new species of Perameliformes (Marsupialia) from Kiriwina Island, Papua New Guinea, with notes on the systematics of the genus *Echymipera*. In J.H. Seebeck, P.R. Brown, R.L. Wallis, and C.M. Kemper (eds), *Bandicoots and Bilbies*, pp. 29–35. Sydney: Surrey Beatty and Sons Pty. Ltd.

Flannery, T.F. 1995a. *Mammals of New Guinea* (revised edition). Sydney: Reed Books.

Flannery, T.F. 1995b. *Mammals of the South-West Pacific and Moluccan Islands*. Sydney: Australian Museum/Reed Books.

Gordon, G. 1995a. Rufous Spiny Bandicoot, *Echymipera rufescens*. In R. Strahan (ed.), *The Mammals of Australia*, pp. 191–2. Sydney: Reed Books.

Gordon, G. 1995b. Northern Brown Bandicoot, *Isoodon macrourus*. In R. Strahan (ed.), *The Mammals of Australia*, pp. 174–5. Sydney: Reed Books.

Healey, C. 1995. Traps and trapping in the Aru Islands. *Cakalele: Maluku Research Journal* 6:51–65.

Johnson, P.M. and K.A. Vernes. 1995. Red-legged Pademelon, *Thylogale stigmatica*. In R. Strahan (ed.), *The Mammals of Australia*, pp. 397–9. Sydney: Reed Books.

van Kampen, P.N. 1923. *The Amphibia of the Indo-Australian Archipelago*. Leiden: E.J. Brill.

Kitchener, D.J. n.d. Report on Phase X of a Study of the Vertebrate Fauna of Nusa Tenggara and the Moluccas, Indonesia. Ambon, Banda, Aru and Kai Islands. Unpublished Report.

Kitchener, D.J. and I. Maryanto. 1995. A new species of *Melomys* (Rodentia, Muridae) from Yamdema Island, Tanimbar group, Eastern Indonesia. *Records of the Western Australian Museum* 17:43–50.

de Lisle, H.F. 1996. *The Natural History of Monitor Lizards*. Malabar, Florida: Krieger.

Menzies, J.I. 1990. Notes on Spiny Bandicoots, *Echymipera* spp. (Marsupialia; Peramelidae) from New Guinea and description of a new species. *Science in New Guinea* 16:86–98.

Menzies, J.I. 1996. A systematic revision of *Melomys* (Rodentia: Muridae) of New Guinea. *Australian Journal of Zoology* 44:367–426.

Musser, G.G. and M.D. Carleton. 1993. Muridae. In D.E. Wilson and D.M. Reeder (eds), *Mammal Species of the World: A Taxonomic and Geographic Reference*. Washington D.C.: Smithsonian Institution Press.

Norris, C.A. and G.G. Musser. 2001. Systematic revision within the *Phalanger orinetalis* complex (Diprotodontia, Phalangeridae): a third species of lowland gray cuscus from New Guinea and Australia. *American Museum Novitates* 3356:20.

O'Connor, S., K. Aplin, M. Spriggs, P. Veth, and L.A. Ayliffe. 2002. From savannah to rainforest: changing environments and human occupation at Liang Lemdubu, the Aru Islands, Maluku, Indonesia. In A.P. Kershaw, B. David, N. Tapper, D. Penny, and J. Brown (eds), *Bridging Wallace's Line: The Environmental and Cultural History and Dynamics of the Southeast Asian–Australian Region*, pp. 279–306. Reiskirchen: Catena Verlag. *Advances in GeoEcology* 34.

Pasveer, J.M. 2004. *The Djief Hunters: 26,000 Years of Rainforest Exploitation on the Bird's Head of Papua Indonesia*. Lisse: A.A. Balkema. *Modern Quaternary Research in Southeast Asia* 17.

Pasveer, J.M. and K.P. Aplin. 1998. Late Pleistocene to Recent faunal succession and environmental change in lowland New Guinea: evidence from the Bird's Head of Irian Jaya, Indonesia. In J. Miedema, C. Odé, and R.A.C. Dam (eds), *Perspectives on the Bird's Head of Irian Jaya, Indonesia: Proceedings of the Conference, Leiden, 13–17 October 1997*, pp. 891–930. Amsterdam: Rodopi.

Richards, G.C. 1995. Northern Freetail-bat, *Chaerephon jobensis*. In R. Strahan (ed.), *The Mammals of Australia*, pp. 479–80. Sydney: Reed Books.

Robinson, A.C. 1995. Western Chestnut Mouse, *Pseudomys nanus*. In R. Strahan (ed.), *The Mammals of Australia*, pp. 609–10. Sydney: Reed Books.

de Rooij, N. 1915. *The Reptiles of the Indo–Australian Archipelago. I. Lacertilia, Chelodina, Emydosauria*. Leiden: E.J. Brill.

de Rooij, N. 1917. *The Reptiles of the Indo–Australian Archipelago. II. Ophidia*. Leiden: E.J. Brill.

von Rosenberg, C.B.H. 1867. *Reis Naar de Zuidoostereilander Gedaan in 1865 op last der Regering van Nederlandsch–Indie*. 's-Gravenhage: Martinus Nijhoff.

van Strien, N.J. 1996. Mammals of the Aru Islands. In H.P. Nooteboom (ed.), *The Aru Archipelago: Plants, Animals, People and Conservation*, pp. 87–106. Amsterdam: Nederlandse Commissie Voor Internationale Natuurbescherming. *Mededelingan* 30.

Szalay, A. 1995. Annotated faunal list for the south-west Pacific and Moluccan Islands. In T.F. Flannery, *Mammals of the South-West Pacific and Moluccan Islands*, pp. 409–23. Sydney: Reed Books.

Tate, G.H.H. 1951. Results of the Archbold Expeditions. No. 65. The rodents of Australia and New Guinea. *Bulletin of the American Museum of Natural History* 97:185–430.

Tate, G.H.H. and R. Archbold. 1935. Results of the Archbold Expeditions. No. 4. An apparently new race of wallabies from southern New Guinea. *American Museum Novitates* 804:1–2.

Wallace, A.R. 1857. On the natural history of the Aru Islands. *Annals and Magazine of Natural History* (Series 2) 20:473–85.

Waithman, J. 1979. A report on a collection of mammals from southwest Papua, 1972–1973. *Australian Zoologist* 20:313–26.

Watts, C.H.S. and H.J. Aslin. 1981. *The Rodents of Australia.* Sydney: Angus and Robertson.

Weber, M. 1911. *Die Fische der Aru- und Kei-Inseln. Ein Beitrag sur Zoogeographie dieser Inseln.* Sonderabdruck aus den Abhandlungen der Senckenbergischen Naturforschenden Gesellschaft Bd 34:1–49.

White, J.P. 1972. *Ol Tumbuna: Archaeological Excavations in the Eastern Central Highlands, Papua New Guinea.* Canberra: Department of Prehistory, Research School of Pacific Studies, Australian National University. *Terra Australis* 2.

Winter, J.W. and L. K.-P. Leung, 1995a. Southern Common Cuscus, *Phalanger intercastellanus.* In R. Strahan (ed.), *The Mammals of Australia,* pp. 268–70. Sydney: Reed Books.

Winter, J.W. and L. K.-P. Leung. 1995b. Common spotted cuscus, *Spilocuscus maculatus.* In R. Strahan (ed.), *The Mammals of Australia,* pp. 266–7. Sydney: Reed Books.

Winter, J.W. and D. Whitford. 1995. Prehensile-tailed rat, *Pogonomys mollipilosus.* In R. Strahan (ed.), *The Mammals of Australia,* pp. 643–5. Sydney: Reed Books.

Woolley, P.A. 1995. Red-cheeked dunnart, *Sminthopsis virginae.* In R. Strahan (ed.), *The Mammals of Australia,* p. 156. Sydney: Reed Books.

Appendix 3.1: 'Kitchen midden and hunter' samples collected in October-November 1992 by Dr P. Woolley on Kobroor Island

JILKAI VILLAGE	5° 54′ S 134° 22′ E
Echymipera rufescens	3 individuals
Phalanger mimicus	1 individual
Spilocuscus maculatus	1 individual
Thylogale brunii	9 individuals
Varanus sp. cf. *V. salvator*	1 individual
NAMARA	6° 03′ S 134° 22′ E
Phalanger gymnotis	4 individuals
Phalanger mimicus	1 individual
Spilocuscus maculatus	2 individuals
Thylogale brunii	4 individuals
Dobsonia moluccensis	1 individual
Pteropus sp. cf. *P. melanopogon*	1 individual

4

Three Seasons of Archaeological Survey in the Aru Islands, 1995–97

Matthew Spriggs[1], Peter Veth[2], Sue O'Connor[1], Husni Mohammad[3], Ako Jatmiko[4], Widya Nayati[5], Aliza Diniasti Saleh[4], and Djoko Witjaksono[6]

1. Archaeology and Natural History, Research School of Pacific and Asian Studies, The Australian National University, Canberra, ACT, Australia
2. Research Unit, Australian Institute of Aboriginal and Torres Strait Islander Studies, Canberra, ACT, Australia
3. Puslit Arkenas, Branch Menado, Indonesia
4. Puslit Arkenas, Jakarta, Indonesia
5. Department of Archaeology, Gajah Mada University, Yogyakarta, Indonesia
6. Museum Negeri Ronggowarsito, Jalan Abdulrahman Saleh, Semarang, Central Java, Indonesia

Introduction

Armed with the set of questions and issues discussed in Chapter 1, we arrived in Aru in 1995 and began a reconnaissance survey, which was continued in a more targeted way in 1996 and 1997. In each year, a considerable amount of time was spent liaising with *kepala desa* (village leaders, Bahasa Indonesian) and communities, towards a thorough explanation of our objectives and in order to identify any known sites. After travelling to the various islands from the *kecamatan* (district capital), Dobo, the general strategy was to carry out formal discussions and interviews, address *adat* (customary law) issues, and then carry out surveys and site inspections with community representatives.

Initial reconnaissance surveys in 1995 were focussed on the northwest islands as these lay closest to the edge of the Continental Shelf. As discussed in Chapter 1, we had hoped they might provide stratified sites with old and continuous occupation sequences, perhaps going back to the earliest period of human occupation of Aru. These islands comprised Kobroor, Wamar, Wokam, Ujir and Wasir (Fig. 4.1). Most of the geological formations surveyed on these islands were found to be unsuitable for cave or rockshelter formation. Where caves were found, they were either post-transgression sea caves of recent origin in soft sedimentary rock or contained running water and thus were unsuitable for human occupation. Our initial strategy to target cave sites on the northwestern islands closest to the edge of the Continental Shelf, in the hope of finding evidence of Pleistocene occupation, thus proved unsuccessful.

Suitable caves in this part of Aru appear to be restricted to the karst formations, which mainly occur in the interior of the larger islands and are away from early shorelines. In 1995 only one cave with clear excavation potential was located. This was Liang Lemdubu (Site 9), the focus

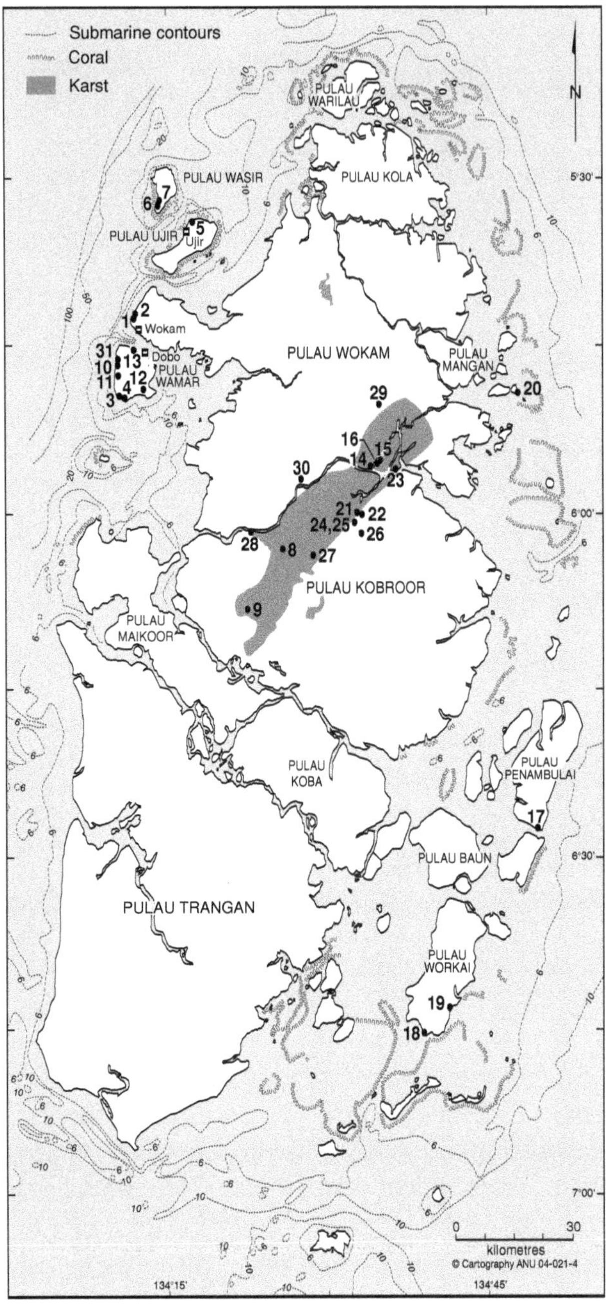

Figure 4.1 Map of the Aru Islands showing the location of all sites mentioned in the text and areas of karst. Bathymetric contours are shown in metres and illustrate the steep declination to the west (original northwestern coastline of Sahul) and the shallow declination to the north and west where the islands were once joined to Greater Australia.

of excavation in 1996. In 1996 efforts were made to find further suitable cave sites, and this resulted in the identification of Liang Nabulei Lisa (Site 22), which formed the main focus of excavation in 1997. Surveys in 1995 and 1996 also concentrated on finding midden sites likely to have mid- to late Holocene sequences. We hoped to examine the transition to agriculture and develop pottery sequences on the basis of excavation of such sites. The site with the greatest excavation potential was judged to be the Wangil midden (Site 10), located in 1995. This was excavated in 1997. The 1997 survey extended our coverage of cave sites in the Nabulei Lisa area, but did not produce any with the archaeological potential of that site. We were thus not diverted from our plan to excavate Liang Nabulei Lisa to fill in the later parts of the Aru cultural sequence. Early to mid-Holocene deposits had not been found in Liang Lemdubu during the 1996 excavations, and Liang Nabulei Lisa was targeted in order to fill this gap.

Sites found in all years are numbered in sequence from 1 to 31. The site descriptions given here replace those in previous publications (Spriggs et al. 1998; Veth et al. 1998).

The 1995 Reconnaissance Survey of Aru

The joint Australian-Indonesian survey team in 1995 consisted of Veth and Spriggs, and Ako Jatmiko (Puslit Arkenas). Thirteen sites were recorded on the five islands in 1995. These included two caves with cultural deposits (Sites 8 and 9); three further caves of primarily religious significance (Sites 4, 6 and 7); five midden complexes, at least three of them with associated pottery (Sites 3, 10 to 13); a substantial fortified settlement at Ujir, possibly with an associated shipwreck (Site 5); and an early Dutch fort and nearby stone church (Sites 1 and 2). Bad weather prevented more detailed examination of the Wangil (Site 10) and Durjela (Site 11) middens, and only passing observations were made of the other surface sites. We were taken to many other cave sites on Wasir, and near Wokam and Semang villages on Wokam Island, but none showed any signs of human use and they were mostly the mouths of underground stream systems.

Sites 1 and 2 - Kota Lama Wokam

Wokam Island (5° 42.465'S, 134°12.877'E). The first fort on the site would have been built during the mid to late 17th century. It is known locally as Kota Lama Wokam (Wokam old village). It is under the custodianship of the Education Department and is occasionally visited by tourists. The fort is adjacent to the beach and commands the entrance to the channel between Wokam and Wamar Islands (Fig. 4.2). The coral block walls are in generally good condition, and measure approximately 50 by 35m with the longest axis parallel to the beach. There are remains of corner bastions, and attached to and projecting four metres out from the western, sea-facing wall is a rectangular blockhouse, 10m in its greatest dimension (Fig. 4.3). There is a small entrance on the seaward side adjacent to the blockhouse and another blocked entrance on the landward side.

Figure 4.2 Site 1 — Kota Lama Wokam: Dutch Fort, view of rampart looking southwest

Figure 4.3 Site 1 — Kota Lama Wokam: entrance to Wokam Fort, view facing west

Among the internal structures is a stone-walled building in the southern half of the fort, with five internal rooms and with its external walls well-preserved. Foundations of another stone building are also visible in the southern half of the fort. In the northeast corner is a stone-lined well. Coconuts have been planted within the walls. There is an entrance on the seaside immediately south of the blockhouse and a blocked larger entrance opposite it in the east, inland side with door slots preserved. Porcelain and bottle glass sherds are found inside the fort and there are dumps of porcelain and bottle glass outside the fort to the east, and between the fort and the church.

South of the fort are the remains of a stone church (Site 2), with its walls remaining to the full height in some places. The church has three windows on each side and a small door to the seaward side as well as a larger one at the inland, eastern end (Fig. 4.4). The pottery illustrated in Figure 4.5 was collected from outside the walls at the east end of the church. The present site of Wokam village is immediately south of the church site.

Valentijn (1862[1722]:III:36–8) described Wokam as the main village in the Aru Islands and noted that around 1700 AD there were a sergeant, a corporal, and 10 or 12 soldiers stationed in the fort. Merton (1910:163) claimed that the Aru forts were abandoned in the 18th century because of local uprisings. Wright (1958:18–9) may have been referring to this fort when he noted that a fort in Aru had to be abandoned in 1792 because of such attacks. Kolff (1840) gives a very interesting account of this fort and church from his 1826 visit. At that time the main village of Wokam was north of the fort. His description suggests that the fort was rebuilt some time after his visit:

Figure 4.4 Site 2 — Kota Lama Wokam: remains of church

> This fort, which is now in a state of great dilapidation — patches of a wall, which was once three feet thick and twenty feet high, alone remaining — formed a square with bastions at the corners; but of the latter nothing was now visible, some posts having been erected in their place, on which several lelahs [guns] were mounted. The house of the Orang Kaya, which stands in the centre, is the only part in good repair. The natives were very desirous of having a

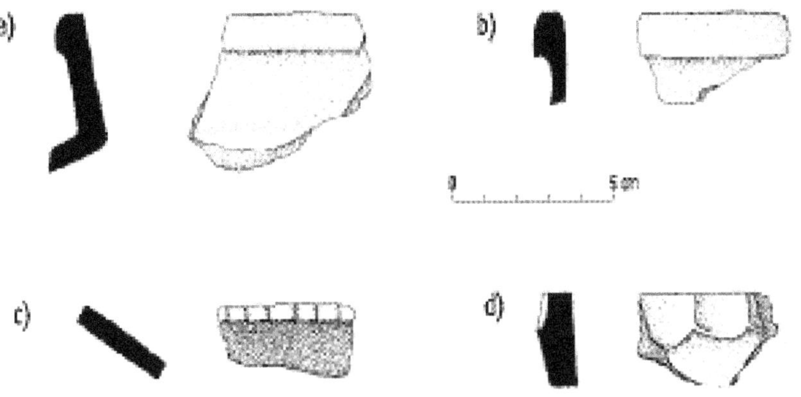

Figure 4.5 Site 2 — Kota Lama Wokam: pottery rim sherds from outside east end of church

> Dutch garrison again among them, in which they would willingly set to work and put the fort into complete order (Kolff 1840:192–3).

During his visit, the stone church was actively in use:

> The church, situated on the south side of the village, is a handsome and strong stone building, and although the doors and windows are wanting, it is otherwise kept carefully in order. On each side of the entrance are benches and reading desks for the men, while a number of old-fashioned carved chairs, certainly a century and a half old, were placed in the centre for the women. Here and there gravestones might be perceived, the inscriptions of which had become illegible. Their dead are not now interred in or near the church, but are deposited in an enclosed cemetery, some distance to the north-east of the fort. The tombstones here are ornamented in different ways, and it is strong proof of the good disposition of these people, that the tombs of the officers of the late East India Company, who have died here, are kept in as good order as those of their own chiefs and forefathers ... (Kolff 1840:189–90).

Von Rosenberg (1867) adds further interesting details of the fort and church from his 1865 visit. The attack on the fort, and its abandonment by the Dutch, is given there as occurring in 1808 on the basis of a gold-knobbed cane given to the then-Orang Kaya of Ujir for his assistance to the fort commander who fled to that village during the attack. An inscription on the cane gives the date. Von Rosenberg's (1867:14) account of Wokam village is worth giving in detail:

> The fourteen houses built high above the ground occupy two sides of an open square in the middle of which the [house of the] Orang kaya stands. The south side of this square is occupied by a stone church of which the brightly white-washed walls make a sharp contrast with the dark ground of the forest. Because of the absence of the Orang kaya I had to stay in the village chief's house. In the morning I visited the ruins of a large fort of the Company, which we had already passed when entering the village. Judging by the ruins in the middle of the village it must have been an enormous structure which in these far remote regions bears witness to the power and greatness of the East Indies Company. A square wall of more than 100 ells surrounded it all, a tower-like bastion, two gates and parts of the base of walls towards the sea still remain ... An inscription carved in stone, which stood above the eastern gate, cannot now be found anywhere. Nobody seemed to know the historical particulars surrounding this fort; that it was deserted in 1808 and most probably had also been destroyed.

This account suggests that some rebuilding of the fort took place after 1865, as the sea walls were fully extant when we visited in the 1990s.

Site 3 — Karkur

Wamar Island (5° 49.685'S, 134° 13.190'E). South of Durjela on a walking track close to the shoreline, we visited an old village site in a cassava garden accompanied by the *kepala desa* of Durjela (Fig. 4.6). The site was marked by marine shell, earthenware pottery — some red-slipped (Fig. 4.7) — a stoneware *tempayan* (large waterjar) sherd and an iron knife. The site probably dates at least in part to the last few centuries and is 200m north of Liang di Karkur. Immediately behind the site are low hills 10–15m high and it was not clear whether the midden had been deposited *in situ* or dumped downslope.

Site 4 — Liang di Karkur

Wamar Island (6° 3.40'S, 134° 26.22'E). A small cave less than 200m from Site 3, at about two metres above sea level and only 10m from the beach. It was probably formed by wave action and the substrate is a soft marine sedimentary rock. The cave mouth is 2.5m wide, and it extends back about 4.5m. Because of recent washed-in soil the ceiling is very low and the cave has to be crawled

Figure 4.6 Site 3 — Karkur

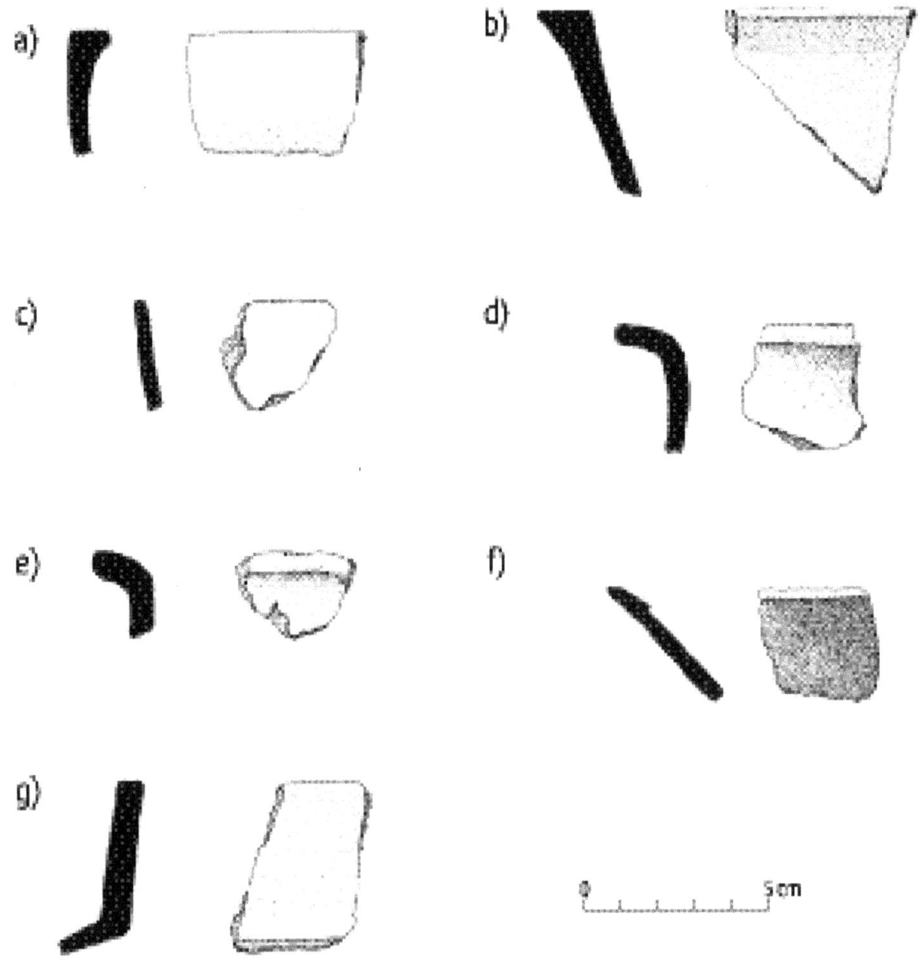

Figure 4.7 Site 3 — Karkur: pottery rim forms

into. The cave is used in *adat* (custom or tradition) ceremonies and food and drink offerings have been left at its mouth. Until recently the cave may well have been reached by high wave action and so probably has very little excavation potential.

Site 5 — Ujir

Ujir Island (5° 34.465′S, 134° 18.080′E). This early pre-colonial trading settlement and its historical context are described and illustrated in detail in Chapter 5.

Site 6 — Liang Belnarnar

Wasir Island (5° 32.534′S, 134° 15.214′E). A sacred cave owned by the people of Ujir. It is immediately behind the beach and faces southwest. It is 12m wide at the mouth and is some 25m deep in a soft marine sedimentary rock. The original owner of the cave was said to be buried inside and there is a stone table in the interior of the cave with offerings on it. The white sand floor and its low height above sea level — less than two metres — suggest that it has no excavation potential. The cave is very low and can only be entered by squatting. Names, some in Arabic script, have been carved in the soft marine sedimentary rock above the mouth.

Site 7 — Liang Batul Bakar

Wasir Island (5° 29.646′S, 134° 15.2055′E). Another sacred cave owned by the people of Ujir. It is a solution cave in limestone about two metres above the forest floor in a 4.5m high cliff and some 45m behind the beach. It is wet and there is no room for habitation. The cave is three metres wide, four metres deep and about 1.3m to ceiling height. Some broken porcelain was seen on the floor, presumably old offerings. There is a stone table inside and a stalagmite is said to be a person turned to stone. The cave has no excavation potential.

Site 8 — Liang Lisaibam

Kobroor Island (6° 3.47′S, 134° 26.21′E). This limestone tunnel cave resembles a smaller version of Liang Lemdubu (Site 9) (Figs 4.8, 4.9). The site was located in 1995 but was revisited in 1997 in company with the landowner, Simon Sirlay, from Jirlay village, and the photographs were taken at that time.

It is located only 300m from the nearest *sungai* and is 18.5m in length, 6.7 to 7.3m in width and 1.9 to 2.5m in ceiling height. The cave floor has been cut through by a later channel to create a two metre wide trench that has infilled with sediments at the southern end (Fig. 4.10). The sediment infill in the deep channel appears in places to be up to one metre deep and may have some excavation potential, but there is evidence of considerable disturbance to the surface of the deposit (Fig. 4.10). The cave is aligned roughly east–west, with an eastern entrance facing 110°, and the west entrance facing 240°. It has well-developed shell deposits at its entrances containing the mangrove species *Geloina* sp. (approx. 95%), *Terebralia* sp. (four per cent), *Anadara* sp. and other species (approximately one per cent), as well as earthenware pottery and Chinese porcelain sherds. Some deer bone was also present. The most remarkable feature of the cave is the plethora of engravings on most of its walls. Motifs include abstract geometrics, anthropomorphs and stylised feet/hands, naturalistic representations including

Figure 4.8 Site 8 — Liang Lisaibam: showing tunnel form of cave

Figure 4.9 Site 8 — Liang Lisaibam: close up of midden scatter at entrance

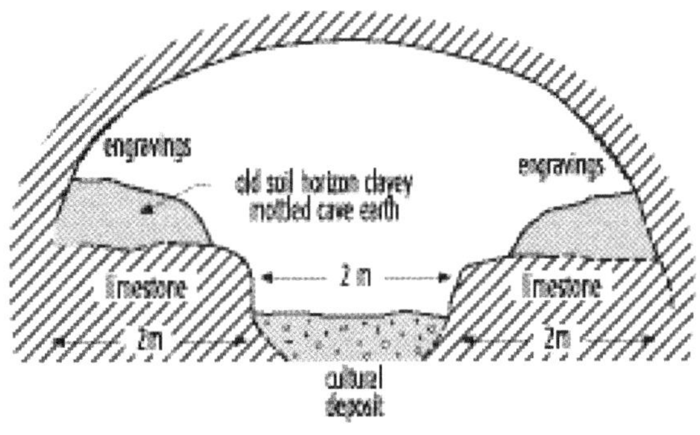

Figure 4.10 Site 8 — Liang Lisaibam: section showing channel in central floor area with deposit fill.

marine craft (specifically *perahu* [boat] and a modern *Pelni*-line steamship), and crocodiles/lizards (Figs 4.11–4.15). While many of the engravings are clearly very recent — dates of 1925 and 1972 were seen — some of the art could be older, and the engraved 'branching tree' motif near the entrance has Dongson stylistic parallels and also resembles the 'tree of life' symbol common in Island Southeast Asian woven fabric designs. The 'star' motif with the radiating lines (Fig. 4.16) is ubiquitous in the painted rock art of Island Southeast Asia (O'Connor 2003). The art in Liang Lisaibam would repay detailed recording.

Site 9 — Liang Lemdubu

Kobroor Island (6° 9.13'S, 134° 22.28'E). This site was seen as having the greatest potential to yield a long cultural sequence and was test excavated in 1996 with spectacular results. It is described and illustrated in detail in Chapter 9.

Site 10 — Wangil Midden

Wamar Island (5° 46.024'S, 134° 11.63'E). This was ascertained in 1995 and 1996 as having the greatest potential of the open midden sites located in those two seasons, and so was targeted for excavation in 1997. It is described and illustrated in Chapter 6.

Figure 4.11 Site 8 — Liang Lisaibam: overview of engravings, geometrics, anthropomorphs, and feet

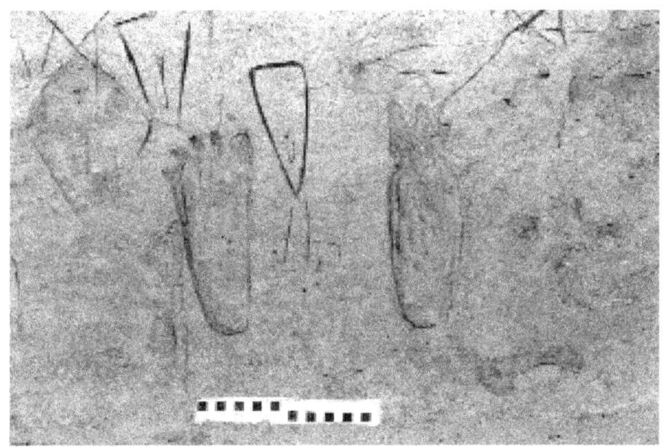

Figure 4.12 Site 8 — Liang Lisaibam: engravings, enlargement of feet and triangular incision at bottom right of Fig. 4.11

Figure 4.13 Site 8 — Liang Lisaibam: engraving of Pelni ship and letters

Figure 4.14 Site 8 — Liang Lisaibam: engraving of crocodile/lizard form

Figure 4.15 Site 8 — Liang Lisaibam: older weathered engravings including 'vulva' and 'branching tree'

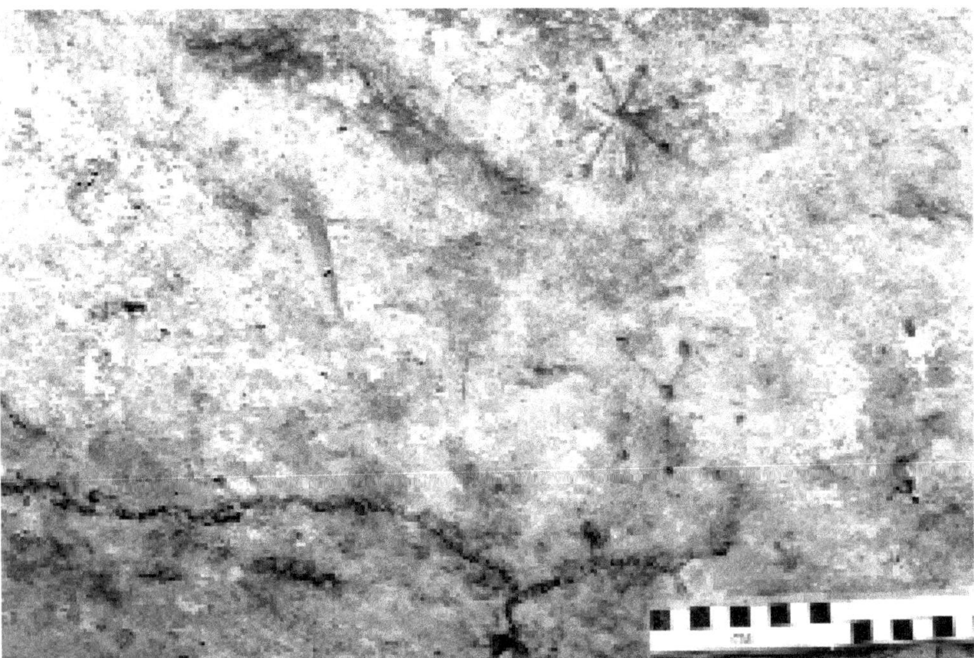

Figure 4.16 Site 8 — Liang Lisaibam: older weathered 'star' motif

Site 11 — Durjela

Wamar Island (5° 46.026'S, 134° 11.63'E). Shell midden mounds were observed among the houses of Durjela village and appeared to predate the current village.

Site 12 — unnamed complex

Wamar Island (no GPS available but approximate latitude and longitude based on field map location are 5° 49.35'S, 134° 12.71'E). Near the south coast of Wamar, along a vehicle track to the Pertamina oil complex and along a secondary vehicle track from it to Dibelakang Wamar village, were observed multiple shell midden exposures associated with fossil beach ridge systems (Fig. 4.17). Clearly there has been significant coastal progradation over time in this area. The area would repay further study as having the potential to provide a sequence of sites associated with beach deposits of different ages postdating mid-Holocene sea level stabilization.

Figure 4.17 Site 12 — shell midden exposures on Wamar Island

Site 13 — Fany Hotel Sports Field

Wamar Island (5° 45′37.6′S, 134° 13′22.1′E). This site consists of shell midden deposits exposed in the main football field adjacent to the Fany Hotel in Dobo town, near the beachside memorial to the Battle of the Aru Sea. The area has been flattened by bulldozing and so the surface may be partly disturbed. No pottery was observed in the exposed areas at this site in 1995 but some sherds were recovered from an auger hole excavated in a naturally higher area, probably an old beach ridge, near the goalpost at the Fany Hotel end of the pitch, during the 1997 field season (Fig. 4.18).

Figure 4.18 Site 13 — Fany Hotel Sports Field Midden: Geoff Hope augering (O'Connor to left of Hope and Kelvin Gale to his right). The memorial statue to the Battle of the Aru Sea can be seen in the central rear of the frame with the exposed mud/sand flats at low tide in the distance

The auger revealed that the underlying stratigraphy consisted of the following: 0–5cm, black sandy topsoil; 5–30cm, grey medium sand with abundant shell midden; 30–35cm, very coarse calcareous sand still with some midden shell (*Geloina* sp. only); 35–50cm, sterile yellow-grey coarse sand; and 50–65cm plus, pale orange coarse sand of the underlying beach ridge. The midden consisted of *Geloina* sp., *Terebralia* sp. and *Anadara* sp. as well as small quantities of crab and fish bone. The few pottery sherds were in the top 10cm of the grey medium sand unit.

The sands, which were finer-grained with depth are a typical beach ridge, but the modern shoreline is fine sandy silt. To build the beachridges that are here, the channel may have been deeper, and hence even the surface may be greater than 2000 years old. Inland of the beach ridge spit is a sago swamp ca. 1.5m below the sand plain, but only in a thin deposit onto limestone. The sands mantle the northern shoreline and extend out as a spit in Dobo Town. They are a source of freshwater from wells, although surrounded by saline flats.

The 1996 Reconnaissance Survey of Central and Southeastern Aru

The 1996 survey team consisted of O'Connor, Spriggs, Veth, Mohammad, and Nayati. A further 10 sites were located during a week of survey along Sungai Manumbai and some of its branches, and on islands off the east coast of the 'mainland' of Aru, using a local 15m motor vessel as our base and transport. The smaller islands visited were Penambulai, Workai (or Barakai), and Batu Lei, although a very short period of time was spent in each location. We were told of many more sites than we had time to visit during the 1996 season, including a second Dutch fort near Dosi village on Wokam Island at Namalau Kota. We were able to visit four cave sites (Sites 14, 15, 16, and 22), and six former village sites (Sites 17–21, and 23). Sites 14, 15, and 16 were in lands controlled by Wakua village, on both sides of Sungai Manumbai, while Liang Nabulei Lisa (Site 22) was on Dosi village lands on Kobroor Island. As this cave site clearly had the greatest excavation potential of those visited in 1996 and 1997, it was the second cave targeted for excavation (see Chapter 7). The village sites were identified by informants from Jambu Air (Barakan Island), Afara and Beimun (Workai or Barakai Island), Batu Lei, and Dosi (Wokam Island).

Site 14 — Liatai

Kobroor Island (5° 56.121'S, 134° 34.250'E). A limestone cave about three metres above the high tide mark adjacent to Sungai Manumbai. It is about two metres wide at the mouth and does not exceed this width inside, running back about 15m. A small hearth was found just inside the entrance but no other cultural remains were seen. The site does not have good excavation potential.

Site 15 — Elan 1

Wokam Island (5° 355.612'S, 134° 35.079'E; called 'Elan' by the local informants). This limestone cave is on the same side of the *sungai* as 'Elan 2'. Elan is the Dobel language word for eagle, a bird associated with the origin myths of some of the caves we recorded. It is in a cliff face about 20m above the *sungai* and goes through from one side of a headland to the other in a series of chambers. It is currently used for collecting birds' nests. Some shells are present at the main entrance, but what cultural deposit there is seems to be extensively disturbed by animal burrows. The site has little archaeological potential.

Site 16 — Elan 2

Wokam Island (5° 55.855'S, 134° 35.168'E; also called 'Elan' by the local informants, and therefore designated 'Elan 2'). A limestone cave which seemed to have excavation potential. It is a large cave of several chambers that may have more than one entrance, located about 20m above a mangrove swamp along a branch *sungai*. The entrance is quite small but this appears to be because of possibly recent stalagmitic growth. There are excavatable sediments, at least near the cave mouth. The cave had several chambers but observations were cut short when we disturbed a substantial colony of large cave bats.

Site 17 — Jambu Air Lama

Penambulai Island (6° 28.115'S, 134° 49.796'E). This is a village site on the south coast of Penambulai Island, across the channel from the present village of Jambu Air, and ancestral to it (Fig. 4.19). We were told that it was abandoned because of an outbreak of disease, which on the basis of the porcelain and glass bottle assemblage may have occurred within the first half of the 19th century. The people then dispersed to several smaller settlements. Active erosion of a maximum five metre high sand cliff is depositing large amounts of midden material in the intertidal zone along several hundred metres of beach between a small *sungai* and an area of mangrove swamp. In section the midden is about 25cm thick in the cliff-face (Fig. 4.20). Behind the eroding cliff-face are some areas of low midden mounds.

The assemblage consists of large amounts of Dutch and Chinese porcelain sherds, earthenware (similar to that produced in the Batu Lei area up to the present) (Fig. 4.21), and Dutch square liquor bottles of early 19th century type. Makers' marks on the bottles included 'NI' for 'Nederlands Indie', a cockerel, and crossed anchors with the inscription 'VAN CHARENT & C AND D[OUB]EL ANKER'. The midden consisted of mangrove shellfish such as *Geloina* sp., *Terebralia* sp., and *Telescopium* sp., and occasional dugong bones. Some volcanic cobbles, possibly ballast, were present and included a large flaked cobble. The density of material suggests a rich trading centre associated with the extensive reef system between this island and the 'mainland' of Aru. Jambu Air, Waka and Lola villages form a single language group.

Figure 4.19 Site 17 — Jambu Air Lama: eroding sand cliffs with shell and pottery exposed in section

Figure 4.20 Site 17 — Jambu Air Lama: close-up of eroding section of site

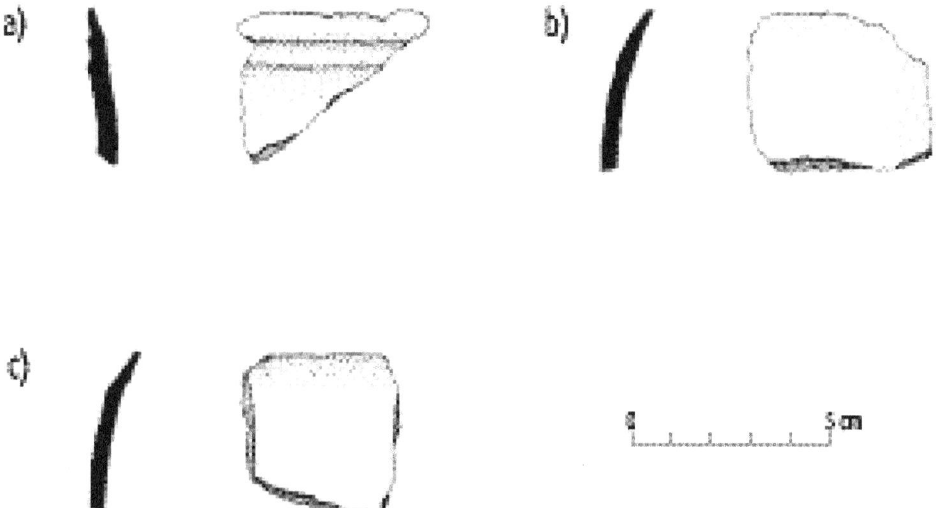

Figure 4.21 Site 17 — Jambu Air Lama: pottery rims

Site 18 — Sirlasi

Workai (or Barakai) Island (no GPS available but approximate latitude and longitude based on field map location are 6° 46.6′S, 134° 38.5′E). This is the ancestral village site of the inhabitants of Afara and Longgar on Workai Island, and of Gomo Gomo Island (cf. Spyer 2000:20). Together they form a single language group, separate from the language of the Jambu Air people. We were told that it was an uncertain supply of fresh water which forced the abandonment of this settlement. Again, an early 19th century date seems likely on the basis of the ceramic and glass bottle assemblages which are very similar to that from Jambu Air Lama. One bottle had a round lozenge with maker's mark 'JOHN ALBERTY VIEUX COGNAC 1815 BORDEAUX', and others included potentially datable inscriptions and motifs. Among such on square bottles were 'NI', the crossed anchor motif as at Site 17, 'JH HENKES' with a long-footed wading bird motif, 'P HADEWIKERS & Co' on the base and 'DE VALK' at the top with the motif of a bird on a branch, and 'ROTTERDAM INTERNATIONALE CA' (rest broken off) with a coat of arms motif flanked by lions. One of the round bottle bases has part of a label 'NHAVN', presumably 'KØBENHAVN'.

The site is on a peninsula, above low, limestone cliffs, and has views to sea on three sides. It looks out over an extremely large area of reef flat and so controls an extremely rich marine environment. The core of the site is an area of dense midden at its southern end, with midden mounds up to three metres in height. There seemed to be a wider range of earthenware rim forms at this site than at Site 17, although the fabric was similar (Fig. 4.22). The shell species present were also similar. Notable finds included porcelain sherds and at least one piece of earthenware which had been flaked into round discs, perhaps as counters for a game, and also a stone pestle decorated with incised designs on its sides, and a stone flake. A similar, though smaller, type of settlement to Jambu Air Lama seems to be indicated by the remains.

Workai Island was already famous by 1824 as a source of trepang and black pearls and Kolff (1840) gives a detailed account of the preparation and trade in these commodities as witnessed by A.J. Bik in 1824 (see Spyer 2000:295). Sirlasi is probably the site he refers to as 'Old Affara':

> Among the chief villages on Vorkay, are Old and New Affara, Longa, Uri and Goor, before the last of which lies a great pearl bank. The natives informed me it was exhausted, and that they had not fished it for two years ... (Kolff 1840:177)

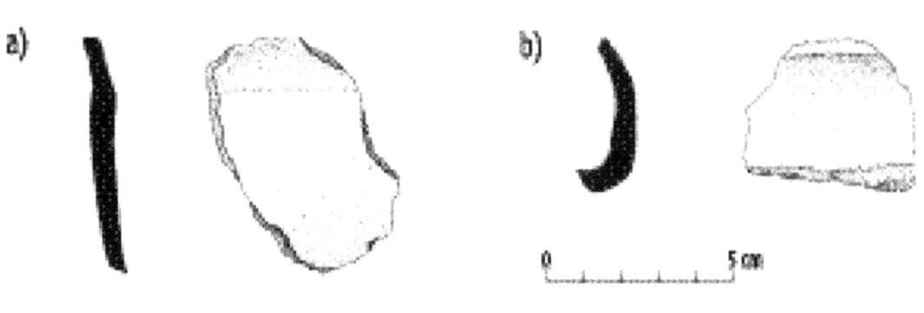

Figure 4.22 Site 18 — Sirlasi: earthenware sherds

Site 19 — Tanjung Goljurong

Workai (or Barakai) Island (6° 44.614'S, 134° 42.553'E). This village site is situated on an extensive headland surrounded by vast shoal reef flats on the east coast of Workai, north from Beimun. According to Spyer (2000:20) the Beimun people claim it as the site of their ancestral village of Wonusomor (*Seltimor* in Malay), and their stories stress its impressive size as a 'city'.

This site appears to have been abandoned earlier than Sites 18 and 19, as it had small amounts of porcelain but no bottle glass. The earthenware assemblage is considerable in size and similar to the previous sites including a number of decorated perforated rims. The dense shell midden deposit at this site appears to be up to 1.5m in depth.

Site 20 — Wangang

Batu Lei Island (no GPS available but approximate latitude and longitude based on field map location are 5° 49.2'S, 134° 47.7'E). This village site is a few hundred metres south of the present village of Batu Lei, on the island of that name. The villagers were reticent to give us information about the history of the site, or details of any other sites in this area in the absence of the *kepala desa*. Wangang is situated on low, limestone cliffs adjacent to a small embayment. Although not examined *in situ*, large quantities of ceramics and bottles, both square and round, were clearly visible in the intertidal silt below the cliffs. It also contained quantities of earthenware similar to contemporary Batu Lei pottery (Fig. 4.23). The site is currently under coconuts and showed signs of having been recently gardened (Fig. 4.24).

A fairly sparse scatter of material over a limited area of the headland may not do justice to the size or importance of the site when the material dumped over the cliff is taken into account. The site was abandoned sometime after 1926 as a man of 70 years whom we met had been born there. It contained some early 20th century Dutch ceramics as well as earlier Dutch and Chinese porcelain. Several pieces of Dutch porcelain had the name 'Petrus Regout and Co, Maastricht, Made in Holland', and in one case had what appeared to be writing in Thai script below. One piece from this company also included the date 1836. Contemporary pottery making in Batu Lei village is discussed in Chapter 6.

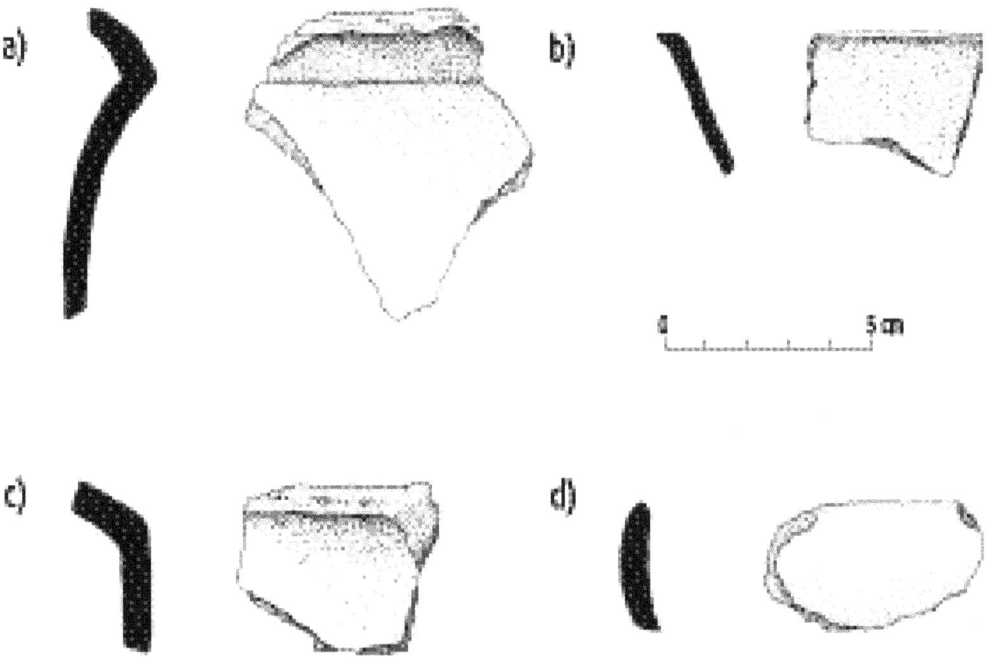

Figure 4.23 Site 20 — Wangang: pottery rims

Site 21 — Nyanyapati

Kobroor Island (no GPS available but approximate latitude and longitude based on field map location are 6° 0.00'S, 134° 32.7'E). This is a former settlement site located close to and on the other side of Sungai Nyanyafafi from Liang Nabulei Lisa (Site 22). It is an ancestral site for one of the Dosi village families. Houses there would have had to be of stilt construction, given the rough limestone surface and the tidal range in the area. Such houses can be seen today close to the site. Only occasional sherds of porcelain were seen in the area, including blue and white Chinese trade ware (Fig. 4.25), and 20th century Dutch and Indonesian types. It appeared to represent only a hamlet-sized interior settlement.

Figure 4.24 Site 20 — Wangang: pottery and shell exposed in area which has been previously cleared and gardened

Site 22 — Liang Nabulei Lisa

Kobroor Island (6° 00.112'S, 134° 33.627'E). This massive tunnel cave was excavated in 1997. See Chapter 7 for a description of the cave, its excavation, and the cultural assemblage. We were told of other caves in this area, away from the *sungai*, with which it could be usefully compared, and some of these were visited in 1997 (see below for sites 24, 25 and 26).

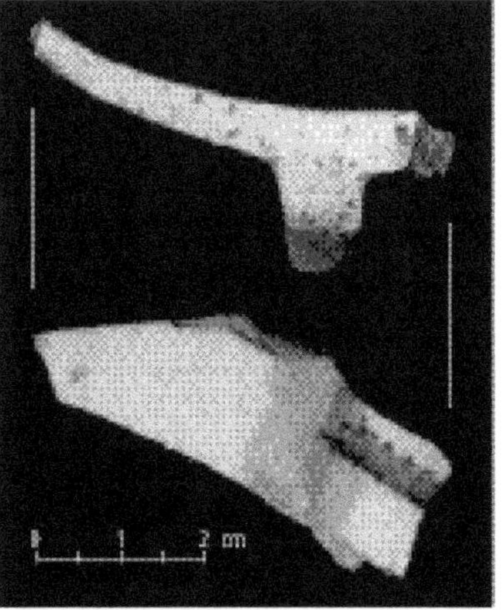

Figure 4.25 Site 21 — Nyanyapati: first *kota lama*, Chinese blue and white porcelain

Site 23 — Dosi Namalau

Wokam Island (5° 56.367'S, 134° 36.502'E). This is a large village site apparently abandoned about 1945 when several families came together to form the present village of Dosi. It is situated on the north bank of Sungai Manumbai (Fig. 4.26). Its location is significant as it is one of the few places along the *sungai* east of Papakulah Besar where limestone fingers down to the shore and larger vessels can anchor directly adjacent to the land. Steps have been cut into the limestone at this point to give access to the site, which is on the side of a limestone hill perhaps some 50m above the *sungai*. On the sides of the hill, which appears to have been artificially terraced, is a dense scatter of mangrove shellfish, porcelain, earthenware and occasional pieces of metal cooking pots and other artefacts (Fig. 4.27). There does not appear to be any deep cultural deposit and the site may be comparatively recent in age. A small-capacity spring of drinking water is located on the side of the hill.

The 1997 Reconnaissance Survey

Survey in 1997 targeted further interior cave sites in the Sungai Manumbai area, prior to choosing to excavate Liang Nabulei Lisa (Site 22) as the most prospective of those visited. In addition, an examination of the vicinity of the Wangil Midden (Site 10) on Wamar Island prior to excavation there, located a 17th century Dutch fort. The survey and excavation team in 1997, in addition to O'Connor and Veth, consisted of Geoff Hope (Research School of Pacific and Asian Studies, ANU), Aliza Diniasti Saleh and Djoko Witjaksono (Puslit Arkenas), and Kelvin Gale (then of James Cook University, Townsville). A further seven cave and/or rockshelter sites were recorded during the 1997 season. In addition, the midden near the Hotel Fany on Wamar (Site 13) was sampled by auguring and Liang Lisaibam (Site 8) was revisited and the rock art photographed. For convenience the additional information obtained from these two sites is integrated within the original site descriptions of the 1995 season.

Figure 4.26 Site 23 — Dosi Namalau: the steps of the old kota lama (centre left just above the sungai)

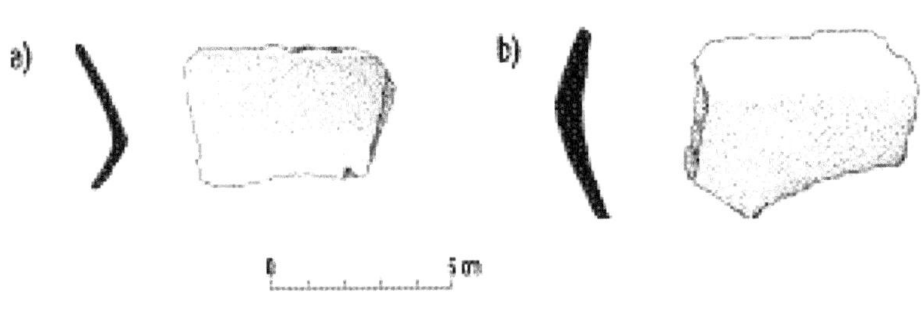

Figure 4.27 Site 23 — Dosi Namalau: rim and carination

Site 24 — Lisa Karar

Kobroor Island (no GPS available but approximate latitude and longitude based on field map location are 6° 01.6'S, 134° 32.4'E). The cave is in a broad ridge about 1.5km south of Liang Nabulei Lisa, above the extreme limit of mangrove growth. This is another former underground river channel forming a tunnel cave, similar to Liang Lemdubu (Site 9) and

Liang Nabulei Lisa (Site 22). It is oriented north-south and is approximately 50m long with its widest point near the southern entrance of some 14m. Its width decreases to nine metres in the middle, 7–8m in the northern quarter, and approximately 6–7m wide near the northern entrance. The height of the cave is about eight metres and remains relatively consistent throughout. At both the northern and southern ends talus slopes probably formed by roof collapse drop about 20 degrees and approximately eight metres into the cave. The useable floor space or potential 'living area' within the cave is only about 18 by eight metres. There could be a substantial depth of sediment here, trapped by the roof collapses at the entrances. The cave roof is only a few metres thick.

Surface midden consists of abundant and sizeable *Geloina* sp. and *Terebralia* sp. shell, as well as pig and deer bone. The bones show evidence of having been chewed by murids. Potsherds on the surface are similar to those seen at Liang Nabulei Lisa. Modern use appears to be as a temporary camp when hunting or sago processing in the vicinity, and when collecting birds' nests in the cave. The floor consists of dusty, dry cave earth. Recent hearths occur at the northern entrance. Wooden platforms associated with this latter activity are found on the cave floor. Further disturbance has been caused by wild pig wallowing, with individual wallows being about 1.5 by one metre and some 30cm deep.

Site 25 — Lisa Sadum

Kobroor Island (no GPS available but approximate latitude and longitude based on field map location are 6° 01.6'S, 134° 32.4'E). A smaller cave with a single entrance facing north, 10m west of Site 24. It is approximately 10m long and eight eight metres wide, with a domed ceiling to a height of 3.5m. The potential living floor is gravelly and sloping. It measures about 6×4m. There are perched stalactites joined by flowstone to the wall about one metre above the present floor. They suggest that the floor level has dropped about one metre, possibly because of solution of the underlying basal sediments (cf. Glover 1979 for a similar process affecting limestone caves in Sulawesi), or alternatively as a result of erosion of the cave floor. The surface sediments on the cave floor are gullied and cracked indicating that water enters in the wet season. The sediments are unlikely to have much depth as there are indications that they are continually washing out.

Pottery, shell midden (*Geloina* sp. and *Terebralia* sp.), landsnail and bone are present on the floor and in a large (dry) splash pool which has created a lag deposit of calcium carbonate encrusted midden materials.

Site 26 — Arkwai Sala

Kobroor Island (no GPS available but approximate latitude and longitude based on field map location are 6° 01.8'S, 134° 33.3'E). This cave occurs adjacent to a dry channel and is a cut-off cave on the edge of a ridge, hence younger than the ridge crest caves. It is thus more related to modern hydrology. The cave is approximately two kilometres south of Liang Nabulei Lisa. This is another former underground river channel forming a tunnel cave, but in this case has a sinuous rather than straight course (Fig. 4.28). It is about 45m long, five metres wide at its south entrance and perhaps a metre wider at its northern entrance. About half of the width of the south entrance is blocked by stalactites and flowstone — the flowstone emanating from just below the ceiling and covering all but a small area of the floor. The cave ceiling is smooth and

Figure 4.28 Site 26 — Arkwai Sala: the cave

Figure 4.29 Site 26 — Arkwai Sala: the art

approximately 3.5 to four metres in height. The cave floor consists of bedrock and there is thus no excavation potential. A modern hearth is found near the northern entrance and it is at this end of the cave that recent rock drawings are found, some dated 1925, 1965 and 1988. The drawings are mostly executed in charcoal and depict soldiers, boats, men with bows and arrows, birds, deer, and dogs (Fig. 4.29). As with the engravings at Liang Lisaibam (Site 8), it would appear that the charcoal drawings at Arkwai Sala were executed over a considerable time period and include both contemporary and more traditional subjects.

Site 27 — Tengum Lisa

Kobroor Island (6° 04.08'S, 134°28.77'E). This is another tunnel cave four kilometres from a *sungai* and at 60m altitude (Fig. 4.30). It is formed in the side of a north-south sloping ridge and has two branch entrances at the south end, joining to form a single chamber inside with a single northern entrance. The southern entrances are both about one metre wide while the northern entrance is about four metres wide, the width of the main chamber. The cave is 15m long and ceiling height is about 1.7m. It has a dry cave earth floor, littered with large quantities of recent habitation debris from its use as a hunting camp. Associated with several recent hearths are meat-smoking racks, and the northern entrance ceiling is fire-blackened. Glass bottles and cut-down plastic water bottles litter the floor, along with *Geloina* sp. shell, pig tusks, pig and deer bones. No surface pottery was seen. The deposit appears to have good excavation potential.

Figure 4.30 Site 27 — Tengum Lisa

Although the floor area is much smaller than at caves such as Lemdubu and Nabulei Lisa, Tengum Lisa would make an interesting comparison as a functionally-specific hunting bivouac.

Tengum Lisa is located about 400m from a permanent waterhole in a doline, called *tengum*, and the proximity of freshwater obviously attracts game to this locale. A recently constructed hunting hide adjacent to the doline, which we were told was constructed to hunt birds of paradise, attests to this (Fig. 4.31).

Figure 4.31 Site 27 — Tengum Lisa: bird of paradise hunting hide near waterhole in doline

Site 28 — Silu Bata Bata

Kobroor Island (6° 01.21′S, 134° 23.55′E). Silu Bata Bata is a burial shelter on the edge of the karst formation, owned by the people of Silu Bata Bata village which is directly across Sungai Manumbai on Wokam Island (Fig. 4.32). It is formed by a shallow overhang, perhaps originally cut by the *sungai* itself. At high tide the cave is about 1.5m above the water level. Inside are about 40 or 50 skulls as well as neat piles of long bones. Extensive grave goods include *Trochus* sp. shell armbands, Chinese trade porcelains, Dutch VOC-era ceramics, brass

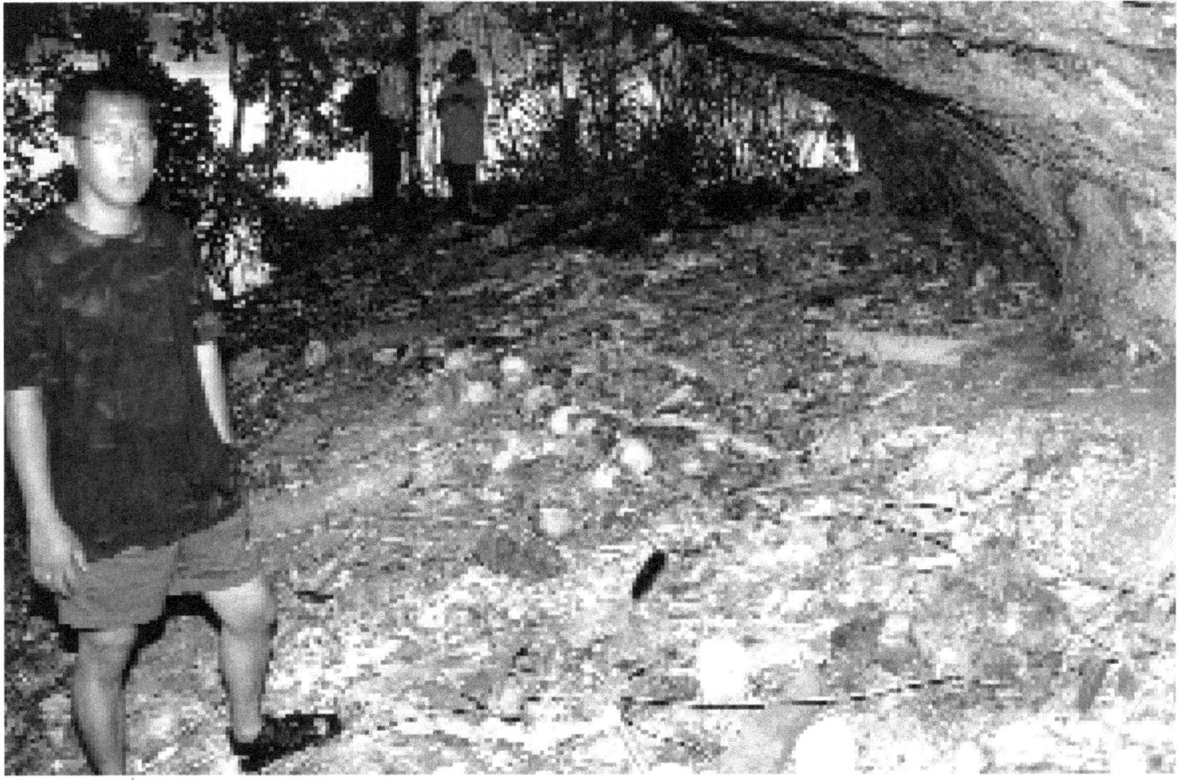

Figure 4.32 Site 28 — Silu Bata Bata: burial shelter with decayed remains of boat coffins and human skulls littering surface

Figure 4.33 Site 28 — Silu Bata Bata: close-up of imported ceramic grave goods

ladles and plates, local earthenware pots, and pearl buttons (Fig. 4.33). Some of the burials are in wooden canoe coffins. The present inhabitants of the village said that these burials were already here when they settled the area. Only minimal limestone rubble and silts cover an otherwise stony floor indicating that the cave has no excavation potential.

Site 29 — Gorangai Gua

Wokam Island (5° 50.48'S, 134° 35.64'E). A rockshelter at 100m altitude, about an hour's walk from the nearest navigable *sungai* — Sungai Juaju (off Sungai Bauwtu) — and on Wakua village land. The name translates in Wakua as 'men who live in the forest'. The cliff face here is eight metres high, and ceiling height at the entrance is about two metres. The shelter mouth faces 220° and is about 12m across. The shelter goes back six metres into the cliff. The front of the cave consists of a fine loose grey sediment and is covered in dried palm leaves used for sleeping on, placed around a hearth. The back of the cave has a firmer cave earth deposit. The shelter is used as a hunting camp today but the owner did not know anything about the people who had left *Geloina* sp. and *Terebralia* sp. shells on the floor. Animal bone on the surface included the ulna of a small wallaby, of a type targeted by hunters in this area. The area of deposit immediately behind the dripline has some excavation potential. The site lies within a closed valley with a periodically flooded doline about 200m to the east. We were told that this doline holds water even during dry periods.

The site area is a closed forest of medium height and the topography is more hilly than Kobroor Island. A dense canopy of *Elaeocapus*, Sapindaceae and Myrtaceae occurs here but the forest is open underneath with thick leaf litter. The understorey consists of scattered palms and cycads and is relatively easy to walk through.

Site 30 — Djara Leang

Wokam Island (5° 57.30'S, 134° 26.00'E). A limestone cave, 24m from the dripline to the back wall. The cave is close to Sungai Manumbai. The entrance faces southwest 230°, but the main axis of the cave runs southeast to northwest. The cave has a length of 24m from the dripline to the back wall, and a maximum width of six metres. A talus deposit slopes gently from the dripline at the entrance into the cave for a length of 19m, and is covered with roof-fall and broken stalactites. The surface sediment is dark grey-brown with little cultural material evident. A few *Geloina coaxans* and *Terebralia* sp. shells, and one fragment of bone were observed, but no pottery was seen on the surface. Cracking of the surface indicates a wet-dry cycle, with the cave being regularly inundated. Andrerias Jelon, *kepala desa* of Wakua, said that the cave was used during World War II to store village valuables such as brass gongs and elephant ivory. It shows no sign of recent use and has little excavation potential because of regular flooding and its dark and wet environment, making it unsuitable for occupation.

Site 31 — Yansen

Wamar Island (5° 46.02'S, 134° 11.63'E). This is the site of a Dutch fort on a headland of this name to the north of the Wangil midden (Site 10) (Fig. 4.34). It is identified by the local inhabitants as a Dutch fort and is probably the third such fort in Aru mentioned by Merton (1910:163) as being at Wangil, the other two being at Wokam (Site 1) and Dosi (not visited). Merton claims that these 17th century forts were abandoned because of local uprisings during the 18th century and were not re-occupied. The name is derived from the probable Dutch name of this fort, Janszoon, named after Willem Janszoon, captain of the *Duyfken* and first European to set foot on Australia. The fort or blockhouse consists of a 15 by 10m rectangular structure. Also present round the headland were partly-buried coral block wall footings about 0.5m wide, the robbed remains of the enclosing wall of the fort. The headland is covered by a scatter of Chinese and Dutch trade porcelains and also some red-slipped local earthenware, as well as shell midden. Later use is shown by several dugout positions — probably Japanese gun emplacements from World War II — and two Japanese graves. The graves are made of coral blocks covered with plaster. The plaster on one had nearly all disappeared, but the other had recently had Japanese characters scratched into it. Local tradition asserts that these are Japanese war graves.

Figure 4.34 Site 31 — Yansen: view of the Yansen headland on which we located the remains of the Dutch fort. Photo taken looking north from near the Wangil midden

Conclusions

Our work on the islands of the northwest, closest to the edge of the continental shelf, has indicated that suitable caves and rockshelters do not exist in this part of Aru. Caves with excavation potential were only located within the interior limestone karst country, and even there they are relatively uncommon. We were lucky in choosing to excavate two sites with complementary sequences covering much of the last 30,000 years of occupation of the Aru interior.

Coastal midden sites are relatively common in some areas and have the potential to produce mid-Holocene to recent cultural sequences. This potential was not fully realized within this project because of time constraints. The main excavated midden site at Wangil (Site 10) yielded deposits dating back over 700 years in the portion which we excavated. However, the preliminary data derived from auguring of the Fany oval suggest that mid-Holocene sediments are to be found on the sandspit forming the Dobo peninsula. This spit precedes the silting up of the old valleys and formation of the present low-energy coastline. The midden deposits in the Fany oval are likely to be of mid-Holocene age and further study of such deposits would no doubt be productive.

The location of large, pre-1850 village sites in the extensive reef systems on the east coast of Aru suggests a much greater involvement of this area with the wider world than is commonly appreciated. At least two of the sites — Jambu Air Lama and Sirlasi (Sites 17 and 18) — appear to represent major entrepots or distribution centres for traded marine products. Ujir in the northwest of the group appears to have had a similar function, perhaps more in relation to forest products, and possibly starting somewhat earlier in the period prior to Dutch penetration of the region (see Chapter 5, this volume).

We visited two of the three historically-known Dutch forts. It is likely that further work at all three sites would reveal much about the early interaction between the indigenous Aru population and the colonial power as Aru became ever more enmeshed into the world system of trade.

References

Glover, I.G. 1979. The effects of sink action on archaeological deposits in caves: an Indonesian example. *World Archaeology* 10(3):302–17.

Kolff, D.H. 1840. *Voyages of the Dutch Brig of War 'Dourga' through the Southern and Little Known Parts of the Moluccan Archipelago ... during the Years 1825 and 1826.* London: James Madden.

Merton, H. 1910. *Forschungsreise in den Sudostlichen Molukken (Aru-und Kei Inseln).* Frankfurt A.M.: Senckenbergischen Naturforschenden Gesellschaft. English translation by A. and A. Veth (1998), James Cook University, Townsville.

O'Connor, S. 2003. Report of nine new painted rock art sites in East Timor in the context of the western Pacific region. *Asian Perspectives* 42(1):96–128.

von Rosenberg, C.B.H. 1867. *Reis Naar de Zuidoostereilander Gedaan in 1865 op last der Regering van Nederlandsch-Indie.* 's-Gravenhage: Martinus Nijhoff.

Spriggs, M., P. Veth, and S. O'Connor. 1998. In the footsteps of Wallace: the first two seasons of archaeological research in the Aru Islands, Maluku. *Cakalele: Maluku Studies Research Journal* 9(2):63–80.

Spyer, P. 2000. *The Memory of Trade: Modernity's Entanglements on an Eastern Indonesian Island.* Durham and London: Duke University Press.

Valentijn, F. 1862[1722]. *Oud en Nieuw Ost-Indien: met Aanteekeningen, Volledige Inhoudsregisters, Chronologische Lijsten, enz.* Volume III. 's-Gravenhage: H.C. Susan.

Veth, P., M. Spriggs, A. Jatmiko, and S. O'Connor. 1998. Bridging Sunda and Sahul: the archaeological significance of the Aru Islands, Maluku. *Modern Quaternary Research in Southeast Asia* 15:157–77.

Wright, H.R.C. 1958. The Moluccan spice monopoly, 1770-1824. *Journal of the Malay Branch of the Royal Asiatic Society* 31(1).

5

The Ujir Site: An Early Historic Maritime Settlement in Northwestern Aru

Peter Veth[1], Sue O'Connor[2], Matthew Spriggs[2], Widya Nayati[3], Ako Jatmiko[4] and Husni Mohammad[5]

1. Research Unit, Australian Institute of Aboriginal and Torres Strait Islander Studies, Canberra, ACT, Australia
2. Archaeology and Natural History, Research School of Pacific and Asian Studies, The Australian National University, Canberra, ACT, Australia
3. Department of Archaeology, Gajah Mada University, Yogyakarta, Indonesia
4. Puslit Arkenas, Jakarta, Indonesia
5. Puslit Arkenas, Branch Menado, Indonesia

Introduction

This chapter is an expansion of Veth et al. (2000) and includes additional information. During archaeological reconnaissance of the western coasts of the Aru Islands in 1995 a remarkable complex of major stone ruins was located near the contemporary village of Ujir (Fig. 5.1). Initial inspection of the settlement revealed a considerable number of stone structures covering what appeared to be several architectural phases. The structures are heavily overgrown by secondary rainforest and are located directly adjacent to a *sungai* or tidal channel, forming a deep natural harbour.

Despite the claim of local villagers that the settlement was a *benteng portuguese* or Portuguese fort, the majority of the structures appeared to be of non-European origin. However, two heavily concreted cannons and an anchor of European origin have been found near the settlement. Their original provenance and relationship to the built structures were unclear.

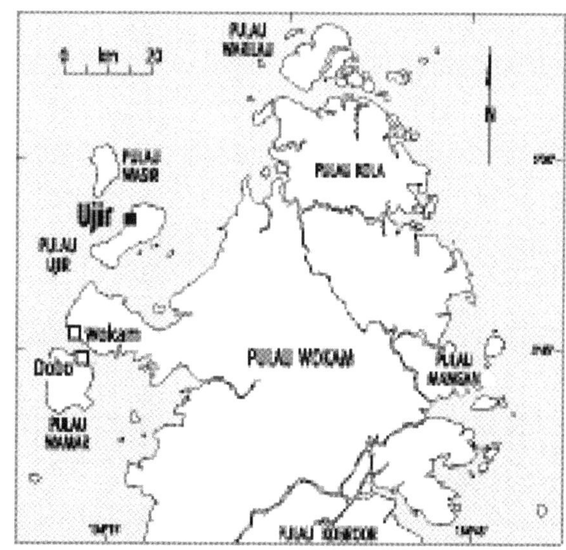

Figure 5.1 The village site of Ujir on Pulau Ujir on the northwest coast

A mystery presented itself. The only other major historic stone buildings in the Aru Islands were well documented, and comprised three mid-17th century Dutch V.O.C. forts at Wangil, Wokam and Dosi (see for instance Merton 1910; Valentijn 1862[1722]), yet here was a major settlement of significantly greater areal extent than the documented Dutch forts. We

Figure 5.2

Figure 5.3

Figure 5.4

Figures 5.2 to 5.4 Ujir: coral block walls and columns showing plasterwork with non-figurative designs in relief

originally thought it was previously unrecorded, but upon our return from the field we found that others too had pondered over these mystery structures and their origin.

A Summary Description of the Structures

Further visits to the site in 1996 and 1997 revealed that the Ujir settlement (labelled Site 5 in our reconnaissance surveys) covered many hectares. To plan the structures accurately would involve clearing dense vegetation and secondary forest. As many of the strangler roots are actually growing through the walls this presents a major conservation problem, as removal of the vegetation would destabilise the structures. Even a survey of the structures would be a major undertaking. Here we simply aim to provide a preliminary description of the extent of the site and the architectural affinities of Ujir.

The structures are all made from coral blocks, some with walls preserved to heights of up to three metres, which were plastered. The plaster bears non-figurative designs in relief (Figs 5.2–5.4). Some of the structures comprise long continuous walls of over 20m length (where still extant), whereas others are square to rectangular in plan and approximately four metres across. Several have small windows of semi-circular form, with plaster relief designs embellishing both the inside and outside (Figs 5.5, 5.6). A number of these rooms, or chambers, are flanked by square columns topped by chamfered edges, and what appear to be truncated spires. In an earlier paper (Spriggs et al. 1998) we stated that the chambers lacked entrance doorways and must have been entered via the roof. Our reconnaissance in 1997 revealed that some chambers have narrow doorway entrances.

Near the settlement, a number of large stone-walled grave enclosures with headstones were recorded. These are also built from cut coral blocks and are plastered (Fig. 5.7). They are typical of the so-called historic long graves associated with Islamic men of high status (James Fox pers. comm.) The relationship of the graves to the settlement is not certain, however.

The most prominent and best preserved of the structures is perched on the edge of the *sungai* at the inland (east) edge of the site. It is a large rectangular stone building with buttressing and arched windows, sitting on a stone revetment wall. The arched windows of the original structure have subsequently been infilled with coral boulders (Fig. 5.8). Iron lintels are exposed in the arched windows and plate impressions were noted on the apex of the window, probably indicating where china plates formed part of the ornamentation around the windows at some time. The local villagers refer to this building as a *mesjid* or mosque, and suggested that it had been built later than the other structures in the area. It appears that its use as a mosque is a re-use of a structure that may have originally been a fortified position. We were told in Ujir that the mosque was destroyed by Allied bombing in World War II.

Figure 5.5

Figure 5.6

Figures 5.5 and 5.6 Ujir: coral block structures with semi-circular windows displaying plaster relief designs embellishing both the inside and the outside

Figure 5.7 Ujir: Islamic long grave with headstones and walls made from plastered coral blocks

Figure 5.8 Ujir: details of infilled arched window at previous fortification

Figure 5.9 Natural tidal creek that may have been artificially extended. The banks of the channel are covered in shell midden and Chinese and Dutch ceramics

To the west of this structure is a natural tidal creek, separating it from the other remains of the settlement (Fig. 5.9). The creek appears to have been artificially extended landward to create a deep water channel or seawater moat at high tide. This is referred to by the local villagers as *Fuabil*. The upper banks of this channel are covered with shell midden of approximately 10-15cm in thickness, comprising mainly mangrove species such as *Terebralia* sp. and *Anadara* sp. Earthenware pottery sherds appear to be eroding from at least the upper portion of the shell lens. Neither Chinese nor European porcelain were recorded in the shell midden, and it is possible that the midden predates the appearance of such ceramics. In the intertidal zone at the mouth of the creek and extending around to the mosque along the shore of the *sungai* is a substantial amount of Chinese, Dutch and what might be Middle Eastern trade ceramics, earthenware pottery, as well as square-based glass bottles. In addition, occasional metal fragments and a gun flint were found adjacent to the mosque.

Figure 5.10 Ujir: weathered cannon found lying in the intertidal zone

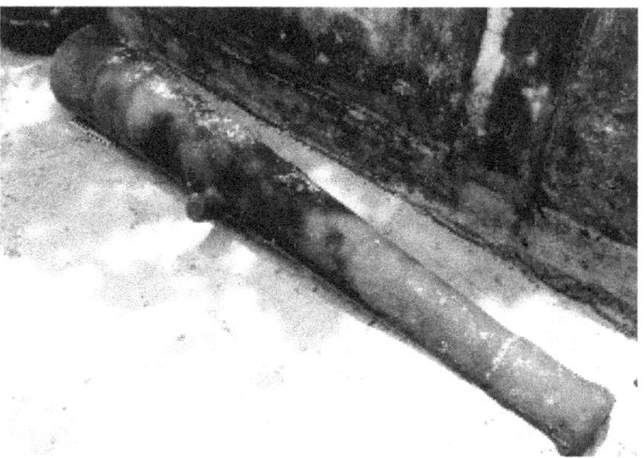

Figure 5.11 Ujir: view of the cannon which has been relocated to the contemporary mosque from the previous fortification

The cannons were recovered by villagers from near the mosque. One heavily corroded cannon still rests in the sand at the edge of the *sungai*, while the other has been relocated to outside the modern mosque in the village of Ujir (Figs 5.10, 5.11). Insignia are not visible on the heavily concreted cannons but they are consistent with 16th or 17th century ordnance of European origin. A large stone mortar also lies in the intertidal zone next to the mosque.

A large section of the steep earthen embankment along the edge of the *sungai*, west of the inlet, is reinforced by large cut coral blocks. The villagers refer to this as *yan vallender*, which they gloss as the Dutch steps, from *belanda*, referring to Europeans such as the Dutch as 'Hollanders'.

Historic Sources Relating to Ujir

It is possible that the fortified structure represents a previously unknown Portuguese or Dutch fort. But the problem with this interpretation is that there is little evidence for any Portuguese activity in the Aru archipelago, and the Dutch period of influence seems well documented. The Portuguese were never successful in establishing either fort or factory in the Banda Group (Villiers 1981:740) and so can probably be ruled out as candidates.

Before and during the period of Portuguese presence in the region, the people of Banda controlled most of the trade with Aru and nearby island groups (Villiers 1981, 1990), purchasing sago, birds of paradise, and parrots in return for cloth. The sourcing of the red-slipped pottery found in the Wangil midden to Banda (see Chapter 6, this volume) would suggest that this trade link was of pre-colonial antiquity, and that pottery as well as cloth went from Banda to Aru. Some gold is also said to have come from Aru (Markham 1911:85), but its ultimate origin must have been from West New Guinea, perhaps through another trade route via the Gorom and Seram-Laut islands at the eastern end of Seram down to Aru (Goodman 1998; Villiers 1981:742).

The first Portuguese voyage to the Moluccan region occurred in 1512, but there is no evidence that they visited Aru directly. Claims to the contrary (repeated by Spyer 1992:58) result from a mistranslation of the description of that voyage (Courtesao 1944:lxxxiii, footnote 1). Galvao's account of the voyage (cited by Wood 1922:69) mentions that the products of 'Arus' consisted of ' ... delicate birds which are of great estimation because of their feathers'. As Courtesao points out (*ibid.*) this passage is not describing Abreu's voyage, but the trading voyages of the Javanese. Spyer (2000:82, 87) reports an oral history tradition of the 'Portugis' as the 'first comers' to Aru. However, she recognizes that in Indonesia the term 'Portugis' is used as a generic label to describe all 'first comers' prior to the Dutch, regardless of their nationality (Spyer 2002:303).

The *Suma Oriental* of Tomo Pires, written in 1512–15 from information obtained in Melaka, has this to say of Aru:

> The *nore* parrots [lories] come from the island of Papua. Those which are prized more than any others come from the islands called Aru (*Ilhas Daru*), birds which they bring over dead, called birds of paradise (*passaros de Deus*), and they say they come from heaven, and that they do not know how they are bred; and the Turks and Persians use them for making panaches [plumes for hats] — they are very suitable for this purpose. The Bengalees buy them. They are good merchandise, and only a few come (Cortesao 1944:209).

Villiers reports (1981:741) that the Portuguese often referred to the birds as *passaros de Banda*, believing that they died in the Banda Islands. Portuguese knowledge of Aru was largely indirect as implied by the attribution of birds of paradise to Banda, but its presence on maps in roughly its correct position by 1530–36 shows that they had probably at least sailed around it by that time. It is labelled 'Arrum' on the so-called Dauphin Chart of that period (Collingridge 1906:32–3; Wood 1922:115), as 'Arru' on the Desceliers map of 1550 (Collingridge 1906:68–9), and as 'Aruu' on Mercator's 1569 map (Wood 1922:91).

Earlier in the 14th century the Majapahit kingdom of Java extended its influence to the Moluccas to obtain regular spices. The sphere of influence and dominance of trade claimed by the Indonesian kingdom of Majapahit in 1365 is given in the *Negarakertagama* poem, written in the old Javanese by the poet Prapanca. Both Ambwan (Ambon) and Moloko (the Northern Moluccas) are mentioned. Contact with Java stimulated the development of a number of sultanates, such as Ternate in the northern Moluccas (Reid 1995:315; Swadling 1996:23). While the influence exerted by this Kingdom in southeast Maluku is unknown, outside influence in the form of Islam had spread to the region by the third quarter of the 15th century, through the trade contacts between the Bandanese, Javanese, and Malay traders (Ellen 1990; Lape 2000a; Villiers 1981:731).

The Islamic-influenced structures of Ujir would appear to be testimony to this trade relationship — the settlement probably being based around the production of sago and the supply of birds of paradise. Obviously, systematic recording and excavation is now required to test this proposition.

In 1623 the Governor of Ambon dispatched two ships under Jan Carstensz to sign a treaty of friendship with the *orang kaya* or merchant-aristocrats of prominent villages on the west coast of Aru (Spyer 1992:58, 60, 63). The most important were Ujir, Wamar, Wokam and Maikoor. From then on, these villages played a prominent role acting as mediators in local disputes in the archipelago, and as representatives of the Dutch rulers during periods of indirect rule when there was no official colonial presence in Aru. By the early 19th century, the archipelago had been divided into four districts under the rule of these villages. Spyer (1992:63) notes that:

> The main thrust of the 1623 treaty was an effort to revive the ancient trade between Banda and Aru which had come to a halt during the extermination wars in Banda in the first quarter of the sixteenth [sic — should be seventeenth] century ... The renewal of this trade under a VOC monopoly would have enabled the Dutch to cut down on the high costs of transporting foodstuffs from Java to Banda through the import of sago and other garden produce from the Aru Islands.

She also reports on a subsequent agreement of 1645 for these same villages to trade exclusively with Dutch-controlled Banda (Spyer 1992:62; see also Loth 1998:67 on Banda trade). Perhaps the fortified structure was Dutch-inspired rather than Dutch-built.

Kolff's 1826 visit to Ujir, called by him Wadia, provides the first direct reference to the ruins we have been able to find. The village may have been bigger then than it is now, as he reports structures also on the left bank of the *sungai*:

> After entering the creek we passed a temple and a number of tombs, and soon arrived at the village, which lies about a cable's length and a half from the mouth. The houses, which stand separated from each other, are erected on both sides of the river, but by far the greater number are to be found on the right hand side, the dwelling of the Orang Kaya forming a conspicuous object among them (Kolff 1840:206).

Kolff reported on the trade in birds of paradise from the village, noted sago and yams as productions of the island, and that the inhabitants obtained rice from Macassans, and from Kei and Goram traders who picked it up from Banda. He continues:

> During our stay here I examined the neighbourhood of the village, and met with some former strongholds, the remains of which proved that they must have been extensive. We also found the traces of a long street, enclosed with walls, running east and west through the village, together with the ruins of many stone houses. The natives could give us no clear information concerning them (Kolff 1840:216).

Kolff also offers some support for our interpretation of the structure later used as a mosque as being Dutch-inspired rather than of Dutch origin. He reported on a dispute between Ujir and a village called 'Fannabel' on the northeast side of Wokam Island. The Orang Tua of Fannabel was said to have 'possessed a stone building, defended by cannon' (Kolff 1840:213), which may have been of a similar type.

Further clues to the antiquity and importance of Ujir come from the treatise on the Aru Islands by van Hoevell (1890) and from the German zoologist Merton (1910). During a trip to the Aru Islands in 1888 Baron van Hoevell (1890:8) noted that the stone mosque of Ujir could be seen from the estuary (*sungai*). Of interest is his observation that Ujir had the most substantial fortified walling of any of the 'indigenous' communities and that there appeared to be extensive walls/ structures from an earlier time period.

Similar observations were made by Merton (1910:166) on his visit to the settlement in 1908, when he noted (translated into English by A. and A. Veth):

> When we entered the Ujir *sungai*, we had before us a wonderful landscape, more beautiful than we had ever seen here. A wide *sungai*, which was framed by mangroves and coco-palms, and in the foreground some overhanging casuarinas, was actually nothing new for us and yet the landscape had something strange. On one bank on a jutting out rock stood a rectangular building constructed from stone; its palm leaf roof was finished step-like. That was the mosque of Ujir ... When we went ashore, everything also made an unusual impression. At a small jetty we got out; from here a well kept road led to the village, past Moslem graves, which had been made partly of stone and partly of wood. The village itself was surrounded by stone walls; often the plots of land belonging to a house were also bordered by walls from the neighbouring

> one ... Ujir consists of many houses, and is one of the largest places of the Aru Islands ... In the village itself in various places were the remainders of stone foundations. On the bank there was another second jetty with stone railings. All that seems to indicate a higher culture, which must have gained a firm footing here for quite some time. Probably the East India Company had obtained a firm footing here for some time. Unfortunately I could find out nothing at all from the less than friendly population.

The link with the VOC of course is just Merton's speculation and we have seen no documents which support this. It is interesting that his report is similar to Kolff's in suggesting that the villagers either did not know or were unwilling to indicate an origin for the structures. Our experience was somewhat similar.

In terms of the age and origins of the extensive ruins at Ujir with Islamic-inspired architecture it is worth considering the likely role of the Aru Islands in the wider trading systems associated with commodities such as birds of paradise and spices, which historical sources date back to at least 2000 years ago (Swadling 1996). The central role of the Bandas as a trading entrepot for these valuable commodities is well documented (Meilink-Roelofsz 1962; Villiers 1981). Lape (2000b, 2002) similarly documents a site in Banda (BN1), the construction of which was dated to the 16th century but which does not appear to be European built, or even inspired, and which may have been part of general defensive orientation as conflicts became more a part of trading, as there was more orientation of traders to Islam.

Conclusions

On the basis of architectural construction, the nature of the decorative plasterwork and the presence of 'long graves', the ruins of Ujir are clearly non-European, whilst the large rectangular building is possibly an early Dutch, or at least Dutch-inspired, fort which was later modified by the Ujir villagers to serve as a mosque, the structure noted by Merton as operating in 1908 and almost certainly that referred to as a 'temple' by Kolff during his 1826 visit (1840:206).

To what extent the clearly non-European settlement overlaps in time with the supposed fort is uncertain. The historic sources for trade in other parts of the Moluccas, however, suggest that the original settlement could have been established by the late 15th century. Whoever made the structures, it is clear that a settlement of this permanence and extent implies an involvement in regional, if not global, trading systems. The degree of Aru's involvement in these early trading systems has probably been historically neglected, due in part to the dominance of the north Moluccan and Bandanese trade-polities of the 15th and 16th centuries.

The discoveries at Ujir hint that a more complex picture of wider trading relationships within the Moluccas, before the presence of Europeans, waits to be unfolded.

References

Collingridge, G. 1906. *The First Discovery of Australia and New Guinea.* Sydney: William Brooks.

Courtesao, A. (trans. and ed.). 1944. *The Suma Oriental of Tomo Pires.* London: Hakluyt Society. Second Series LXXXIX, volume 1.

Ellen, R.F. 1990. Trade, environment, and the reproduction of local systems in the Moluccas. In E. Moran (ed.), *The Ecosystems Approach in Anthropology,* pp. 191–228. Ann Arbor: University of Michigan Press.

Goodman, T. 1998. The sosolot exchange network of eastern Indonesia during the seventeenth and eighteenth centuries. In J. Miedema, C. Odé, and R.A.C. Dam (eds), *Perspectives on the Bird's Head of Irian Jaya, Indonesia: Proceedings of the Conference, Leiden, 13–17 October 1997,* pp. 421–54. Amsterdam: Rodopi.

von Hoevell, G.W.W.C., Baron. 1890. De Aroe-eilanden, geographisch, ethnographisch en commercieel. *Tijdschrift van het Koninglijk Nederlandsch Aardrijkskundig Genootschap, Leiden* 33:57–102.

Kolff, D.H. 1840. *Voyages of the Dutch Brig of War 'Dourga' through the Southern and Little Known Parts of the Moluccan Archipelago... during the Years 1825 and 1826.* London: James Madden.

Lape, P. V. 2000a. Political dynamics and religious change in the late pre-colonial Banda Islands, eastern Indonesia. *World Archaeology* 32(1):138–55.

Lape, P.V. 2000b. Contact and Conflict in the Banda Islands, Eastern Indonesia, 11th to 17th Centuries. Unpublished PhD thesis, Brown University, Rhode Island.

Lape, P.V. 2002. Historic maps and archaeology as a means of understanding late pre-colonial settlement in the Banda Islands, Indonesia. *Asian Perspectives* 41:43–70.

Loth, V. 1998. Fragrant gold and food provision: resource management and agriculture in seventeenth century Banda. In S. Pannell and F. Von Benda-Beckmann (eds), *Old World Places, New World Problems: Exploring Issues of Resource Management in Eastern Indonesia,* pp. 66–93. Canberra: Australian National University.

Markham, Sir C. (trans. and ed.). 1911. *Narrative of the Voyage to Malucos or Spice Islands by the Fleet under the Orders of the Commander Garcia Jofre de Loaysa, in Early Spanish Voyages to the Straits of Magellan.* London: Hakluyt Society, Second Series XXVII.

Meilink-Roelofsz, M.A.P. 1962. *Asian Trade and European Influence Between 1500 and 1630.* The Hague: Martinus Nijhoff.

Merton, H. 1910. *Forschungsreise in den Sudostlichen Molukken (Aru-und Kei Inslen).* Frankfurt, A.M.: Senckenbergischen Naturforschenden Gesellschaft. English translation by A. and A. Veth (1998), James Cook University, Townsville.

Reid, A. 1995. Continuity and change in the Austronesian transition to Islam and Christianity. In P. Bellwood, J.J. Fox, and D. Tryon (eds), *The Austronesians: Historical and Comparative Perspectives,* pp. 314–31. Canberra: Department of Anthropology.

Spriggs, M., P. Veth, and S. O'Connor. 1998. In the footsteps of Wallace: the first two seasons of archaeological research in the Aru Islands, Maluku. *Cakalele: Maluku Studies Research Journal* 9(2):63–80.

Spyer, P. 1992. The Memory of Trade: Circulation, Autochthony, and the Past in the Aru Islands (Eastern Indonesia). Unpublished PhD thesis, Department of Anthropology, The University of Chicago, Chicago.

Spyer, P. 2000. *The Memory of Trade: Modernity's Entanglements on an Eastern Indonesian Island.* Durham & London: Duke University Press.

Swadling, P. 1996. *Plumes From Paradise: Trade Cycles in Outer Southeast Asia and Their Impact on New Guinea and Nearby Islands Until 1920.* Port Moresby: Papua New Guniea National Museum in association with Robert Brown and Associates (Queensland).

Valentijn, F. 1862[1722]. *Oud en Nieuw Ost-Indien: met Aanteekeningen, Volledige Inhoudsregisters, Chronologische Lijsten, enz.* Volume III. 's-Gravenhage: H.C. Susan.

Veth, P., S. O'Connor, M. Spriggs, W. Nayati, A. Jatmiko, and H. Mohammad. 2000. The mystery of the Ujir site: insights into early historic settlement in the Aru Islands, Maluku. *The Bulletin of the Australian Institute for Maritime Archaeology* 24:125–32.

Villiers, J. 1981. Trade and society in the Banda Islands in the sixteenth century. *Modern Asian Studies* 15 (4):723–50.

Villiers, J. 1990. The cash-crop economy and state formation in the Spice Islands in the fifteenth and sixteenth centuries. In J. Kathirithamby-Wells and J. Villiers (eds), *The Southeast Asian Port and Polity: Rise and Demise,* pp. 83–105. Singapore: Singapore University Press.

Wood, G.A. 1922. *The Discovery of Australia.* London: Macmillan.

6

Wangil Midden: a Late Prehistoric Site, With Remarks on Ethnographic Pottery Making

Peter Veth[1], Matthew Spriggs[2], Sue O'Connor[2], and Aliza Diniasti Saleh[3]

1. Research Unit, Australian Institute of Aboriginal and Torres Strait Islander Studies, Acton, Canberra, ACT, Australia
2. Department of Archaeology and Natural History, Research School of Pacific and Asian Studies, The Australian National University, Canberra, ACT, Australia
3. Puslit Arkenas, Jakarta, Indonesia

Introduction

During our surveys around the Aru Islands from 1995–97 we noted a number of mounded and linear middens, some of considerable extent (see Chapter 4, this volume). Only one of these coastal sites, an extensive mounded midden on the northwestern littoral of Wamar Island (Figs 6.1–6.3), was excavated. It is located approximately one kilometre from the modern village of Wangil. This paper documents the test pitting and analysis of the Wangil midden.

Many of the coastal middens recorded in the Aru group (Chapter 4, this volume) were noted to contain both plain and decorated pottery, and this raised the possibility of characterizing and dating assemblages from the Neolithic through to the historic period. This had been identified as one of the major research aims of the Aru Project (see Chapter 1, this volume; Spriggs 1998).

It was clear from the presence of imported ceramics that many of these sometimes extensive coastal middens were quite recent. This was demonstrated in several cases by the presence of glass bottles eroding from the deposits that could be dated to the 18th and 19th centuries, possibly attesting to a colonial-era trade in prized marine commodities such as pearl shell. Previous survey had located midden complexes along the northwestern coastline and at various localities along the central east and southeastern sectors of the island group (see Chapter 4, this volume). Surface scatters of shellfish were less commonly sighted than buried linear and mounded forms, presumably due to the better preservation of the latter due to their greater inherent mass and resistance to the leaching of calcium carbonate in the tropics.

The island of Wamar had yielded evidence from survey of the presence of potentially older coastal midden deposits than seen elsewhere in the island group, some of which appeared on initial inspection to lack pottery and perhaps represent mid-Holocene 'Mesolithic' sites. Others, particularly in the Wangil area, seemed to have the possibility to provide a long pottery sequence for an area predicted to have a 4000–3500 year old local ceramic tradition on the basis of comparison with areas to the north and southwest (Bellwood 1997:Chapter 7). Examination of the Dobo to Durjela vehicle track during our 1995 survey revealed that construction of the track had disturbed several shell middens in this area (Site 10, see Chapter 4, this volume). Small-scale sand quarry areas had exposed red-slipped and other decorated sherds that superficially at least resembled those found in Neolithic and Metal Age contexts elsewhere in Island Southeast Asia (Bellwood 1997:224–34, 297). These sherds are illustrated and described later in this chapter.

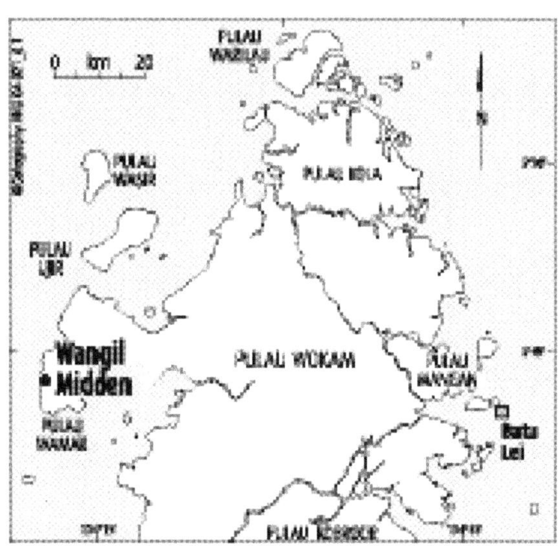

Figure 6.1 Wangil Midden: the site's location on the west coast, and the modern pottery making village of Batu Lei on the island of the same name on the east coast

In 1997, the potential of the Wangil midden sites was explored through excavation by Veth and Diniasti. The cave site of Liang Lemdubu had been excavated in the previous year. At that site only a very small number of non-diagnostic pottery sherds had been recovered from the uppermost two spits, dating to the last two thousand years (see Chapter 9, this volume). The general dearth of pottery in the upper spits of this intensively occupied site (apart from whole specimens of Chinese tradeware at an *adat* shrine on the surface) suggested that — not unpredictably — very different patterns of pottery usage and discard had occurred between the coastal midden sites and the interior caves. The excavation of Wangil, therefore, provided data for the first step of a comparison of pottery assemblages for an area whose late Holocene archaeology was *terra incognita*. At the

Figure 6.2 Wangil Midden: southern view of the midden

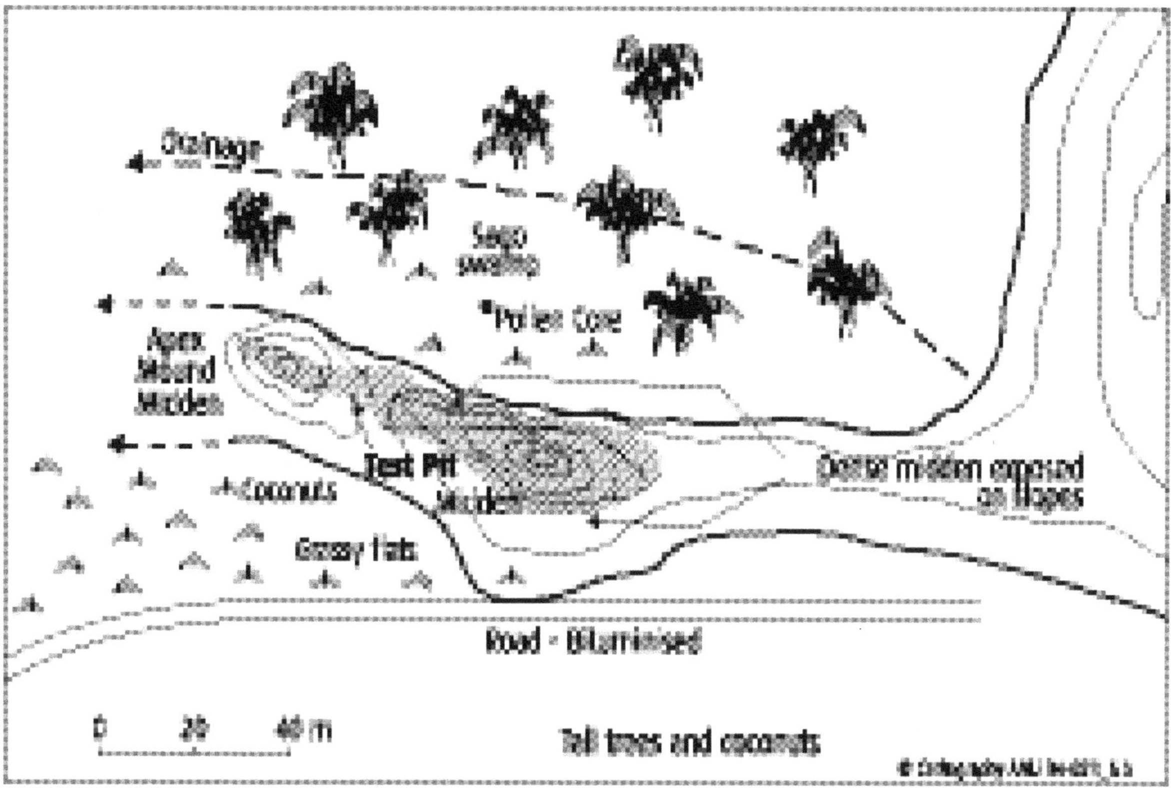

Figure 6.3 Wangil Midden: plan of the midden

same time that Wangil was being investigated, a further pottery assemblage was being recovered in the upper levels of Nabulei Lisa cave in the interior of Aru. It will be dealt with in the report on that site (Chapter 7, this volume).

Historical Records on Wangil and on Pottery Production in Aru

Of all the naturalists and explorers who visited the Aru Islands by the late 19th century, it is only the records of German naturalist Hugo Merton (1910) that provide specific details on the village of Wangil and of local pottery making traditions. Merton traveled through the Aru group between October 1907 and August 1908.

He describes the village of Wangil as one of two large villages on the west side of Wamar Island (also Warmar), the other being Durjela:

> Almost all the huts of Wangil stood at ground level and in rows. It especially occurred to us that every hut was surrounded by a small garden and every property was surrounded by a fence. In the middle of the village is the main street, from which side streets branch off to both right and left sides (Merton 1910:21, 87, translation by A. and A. Veth, and following).

A *Patti* (hereditary leader) had his residence at Wangil. These conditions were still in place when the team worked on the midden site in 1997.

Merton (1910:42, 163) records three centres of pottery production in the Aru Islands during his lengthy journey: at Watulai (Batu Lei) on the east coast (Figs 6.1, 6.4); at Maikoor on the southwest coast; and at the site of Samang, on the island of Wokam to the north of Wamar. At the latter, a pit had been dug as a source of clay for pottery production. Merton purchased various kinds of pots from the inhabitants of Samang, mentioning water jars, sago ovens, meat pots and clay hearth supports. All but the meat pots — which came from Batu Lei — were manufactured in

Samang. There are in fact several more pottery making villages than have been previously recorded (Jock Hughes, pers. comm. 1996; cf. Ellen and Glover 1974:353).

Merton (1910:115) describes the production of pottery at Maikoor (Maekoor village) in some detail:

> Only the women and girls occupy themselves with it. The potter's wheel is here, as on all neighbouring groups of islands, unknown. The vessels are made in the following primitive method. A lump of loam-coloured clay is first kneaded by hand, or with a pounder, then superficially rounded, and after that hollowed out by hand; once this has been roughly achieved to a certain point, then the mass is beaten for some time by a rounded stone [anvil] and by a paddle for beating simultaneously from the outside and inside, until the whole wall of the vessel, which is continually turned about in the process, has gradually become evenly thin and firm. It is surprising how the vessels turn out to be quite regular, with this of itself so primitive procedure. When they are sufficiently dried and smoothed on the outside with fine sand, they are then placed on a brushwood fire in order to be finished. It is not surprising that with such a primitive method these products turn out to be very uneven and many a vessel is destroyed in the process. Various kinds of pottery are produced here: water containers with narrow necks, vessels with wider mouths as cooking vessels, and sago ovens of various sizes. These consist of a square box which contains a number of rectangular compartments. Each compartment has the shape of a sago loaf. Two handles on both sides of the sago ovens serve to take it off the fire at the right moment. The distinctive sirih [lime] containers are also made of pottery. They are the only vessels which are decorated, at the most with simple linear ornaments; on the water jars and cooking pots small impressions are made by the finger-nail on the lip of the vessel rim or on the neck.

Figure 6.4 The village of Batu Lei on the east coast

Figure 6.5 Pottery production at Batu Lei showing sand temper, clay and paddle

Finally, Merton documents the similarity of some pottery vessels in the Aru group to containers made in Java of brass and concludes '... one has to assume that these served the Aruese only as a model ... ' (Merton 1910:42). The majority of pots he describes as made in Aru appear to belong to the common Eastern Indonesian ethnographic types (Ellen and Glover 1974; Gasser 1969).

The Maikoor manufacturing technique as described by Merton consists of impact from a solid lump, finished with paddle and anvil. In Batu Lei on 13 November 1996 we witnessed a pottery making demonstration — by no means the ideal method of observing such techniques. The information as collected at Batu Lei and given here represents an extremely superficial study and is only presented in the absence of any more detailed studies known to us. The method used was similar to that described for Maikoor. The clay is apparently obtained from another island, and the sand temper is assumed to be from beach deposits (Figs 6.5, 6.6). The pot forms being made in Batu Lei included an open bowl probably for mixing sago paste or *pepeda,* a restricted orifice water container with a hollowed base, an ashtray or *asbak* which looked more like a lamp with a handle, mortars and pestles (*cobe dan muntu*), and sago ovens or *forna* (Fig. 6.7). The pots are decorated with a red pigment painted decoration (Figs 6.6, 6.7). Water jars, bowls, and mortar and pestle sets sell for 2000 rupiah, and the *asbak* form for 1500 rupiah. There seem to be about four to seven potters in the village, but only two were said to be regularly involved in pot making. We were told that until recently the industry was on a larger scale but was by 1996 in serious decline. This might explain why no-one had come that year to Papakulah Besar and Kepala Sungai to sell pots, as people remarked in those two places.

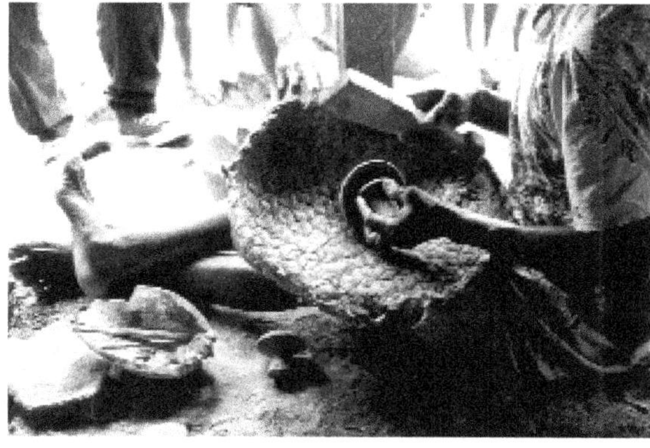

Figure 6.6 Pottery production at Batu Lei showing baler shell with pigment for painting pottery

Figure 6.7 Contemporary Batu Lei pottery vessel forms

As at Maikoor, the technique as observed by us in the manufacture of a mortar was impact from a solid lump, with paddle and anvil finishing (Fig. 6.5). The potter had two wooden paddles of different thickness and the anvils were themselves of baked clay rather than stone. The clay and sand were mixed using salt water, with sand continuing to be added to the mix when some cracking of the base of the pot appeared during manufacture. The mineral paint is mixed with salt water and painted on with a stick. The pots are said to be dried in the sun for two or three hours before they are painted and then fired. Some of the pots of the woman we observed were further decorated with lip notching.

The firing area was adjacent to the village playing field in an area exposed to the wind. Coconut leaves were noted to have been used as fuel in the firing. Water jars are said to be tested for leaks post-firing and then caulked traditionally by rubbing with mangrove fruit. We were told that soap is now used!

Pétrequin and Pétrequin (1999) present a general overview of pottery production techniques in the Eastern Indonesian and New Guinea regions. Their Figure 1 gives a graphic representation of pottery production at Kumul, a village on an island just north of Batu Lei and in the same language group. Techniques are clearly similar to Batu Lei. They also illustrate pottery produced at Barakai, an island south of Batu Lei and in a different language group (1999:Fig. 6).

Physical Setting of the Site and Method of Excavation

The area chosen for excavation at Wangil is located 135m inland on a north-south oriented ridge parallel to the coast and rising southwards (Figs 6.2, 6.3). The geology of the area consists of an uplifted arenaceous limestone mantle overlying older muddy sands of shallow marine origin. However, the ridge lacks any limestone debris and consists of sandy clays, so it may represent the eroded remnant of a former valley fill or fan. A sand ridge plain of medium coralline sand extends westwards 100m to the top of a gentle beach. This area supports a coastal forest of *Barringtonia asiatica, Hibiscus tiliaceus,* and *Calophylum inophyllum,* with scattered coconuts above a scrub of

Figure 6.8 Wangil Midden: view of test pit during excavation

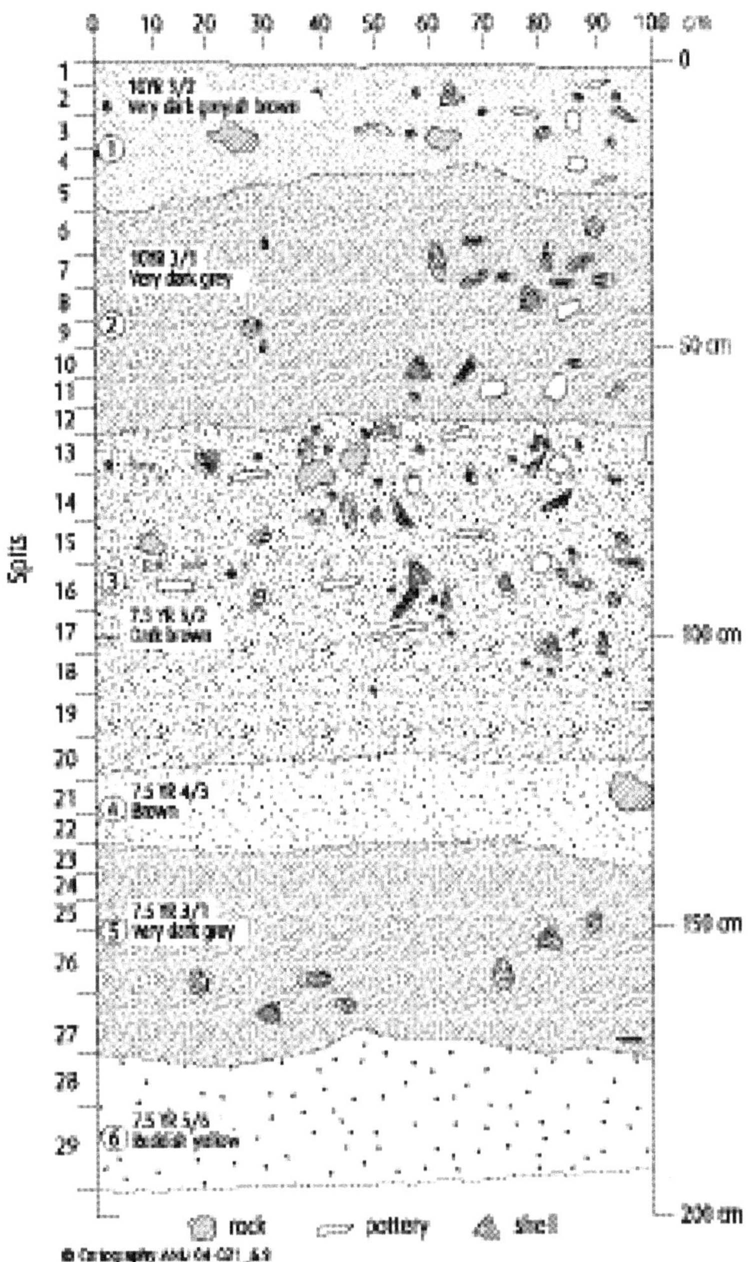

Figure 6.9 Wangil Midden: north section of the test pit

Argusia argenteum and *Scaevola sericea*. The ridge has steep, possibly wave-cut sides and an open low woodland of *Macaranga* sp. and other secondary shrubs. It falls inland to a swampy plain at +0.85m above high water with scattered *Pandanus* and secondary scrub, and groves of sago palm (*Metroxylon sagu*) (see Fig. 6.3).

The mound is approximately eight metres above the current high water mark. A bitumen road follows the coastal base of the ridge and has cut into the earliest of the sand ridges. It is from here that the sand quarry assemblage was collected.

Shell midden is exposed on the central and upper slopes of the ridge, containing a variety of marine shellfish, plain and undecorated pottery, and broken quartzite pebbles and cobbles. A coconut grove and garden plots are sited on the mound and these expose midden where disturbance has been most recent. The major exposure of midden measures over 110m in length north-south, and some 30m in width east-west (Fig. 6.3).

The low beach ridges to the west of the uplifted limestone ridge and mound area, where the cultural deposit is located, are thought to have formed as a result of progradation beginning in the mid-Holocene. At the time of sea level stabilization the uplifted ridge may have been an isthmus flanked by open sea on one side and a tidal lagoon with mangrove stands on the other. Subsequent infilling of the mouth of the palaeolagoon would have shifted the basin towards a freshwater regime with the subsequent establishment of sago (see below).

Cuttings through the edge of the ridge and mound from the construction of the road, and erosional rills and gullies on the slopes, indicated that the cultural deposit was likely to have significant depth. A $1m^2$ test pit was located on the northern slope of a minor saddle on the ridge (Figs 6.3, 6.8). The GPS location is 5° 46.024'S, 134° 11.63'E. It was located so as to sample deposits which did not appear to have been seriously disturbed through gardening activity, and where the density of surface pottery was highest for the upper portions of the mound. This test pit reached sterile deposits at almost two metres below surface level, confirming the appreciable depth of deposit at this point (Figs 6.9, 6.10). While the site is referred to as a midden, the shell, other faunal material and pottery are fairly sparsely distributed in a sediment matrix.

Figure 6.10 Wangil Midden: the $1m^2$ test pit

The surface deposit of the test pit was characterized by very dark grayish brown clays (10YR 3/2, Munsell® Soil Colour Charts) with loose particles of charcoal, rootlets of grass and coconut husk (Fig. 6.9). Plain pottery fragments and sherds of Chinese glazed ware were present in addition to several vertebrae from a large pelagic fish and valves of the mud whelk *Anadara granosa.*

Deposits were removed in five centimetre spits unless features or stratigraphic changes were noted; the average depth of spits increased in the lower layers largely due to the large size of included pottery fragments and due to the extreme compaction of the clays. All recoveries were processed through a nest of 2.5mm and five millimetre sieves. Volumetric records were noted for each removal and spit so that corrected volumes could be calculated to compare cultural residues in a meaningful fashion. Records of Munsell colours were recorded *in situ.* A column sample was made on the southern face of the test pit at the end of the excavation, to retrieve solid sub-samples. Oriented sub-samples were also taken on this face at two centimetre intervals so that palynological analysis could be carried out. A 250cm core was also taken by Hope within the adjacent sago swamp, 30m northwest of the midden excavation (see Chapter 2 this volume; Fig. 6.3).

Summary Description of Test Pit and Stratigraphy

The test pit recovered midden to nearly two metrese depth below surface level, containing mainly marine shellfish and plain and decorated pottery. The stratigraphy for the northern section is shown in Figure 6.9. Other fauna were rare, with only turtle carapace and portions of dugong rib recovered from Spits 3 and 13, and pig elements from several spits between Spits 1 and 19. A pig mandible with teeth intact was recovered from Spit 17 (these are accessioned with Puslit Arkenas Arkeologi Nasional in Jakarta, as is the decorated pottery).

Layer 1 (Spits 1–5) comprises very dark grayish brown clays (10YR 3/2) and contained copious quantities of shellfish and pottery fragments, including sections of rims, handles and bases (Fig. 6.9). The turtle and dugong elements come from this layer. The density of pottery decreases at the base of this layer.

Layer 2 (Spits 6–12) comprises a very dark gray clay (10YR 3/1) with a lower density of cultural residues.

Layer 3 (Spits 13–20) is dark brown (7.5YR 3/2) and has a high density of both shellfish and pottery (Fig. 6.9). The pig elements were recovered from this layer. Decorated pottery was recovered from Spits 16–20, and is described below. The density of cultural material decreased markedly towards the base of this layer.

Layer 4 (Spits 21–22) is an extremely clayey brown (7.5YR 4/3) strata with very little pottery or shellfish in its lower portion.

Layer 5 is a very dark gray clay (7.5YR 3/1) containing negligible economic shellfish but still appreciable quantities of pottery, including some decorated specimens.

Layer 6 (Spits 28–29) comprised reddish yellow clays (7.5YR 5/6), which become culturally sterile by the base of the excavation at two metres depth. Marine fauna and undecorated pottery are only present in very small quantities in the upper part of the layer.

Dating the Cultural Assemblages

Dates were obtained from three *in situ* samples of charcoal and one of marine shell, and aimed to sample the boundary between Layers 2 and 3, the base of Layer 3, and the lowest assemblage of pottery and shellfish reliably assigned to Layer 4. Samples Wk-6097 and OZE232 reliably bracket the majority of the decorated pottery recovered from the site in Layer 3, while sample OZE233 provides a conservative date for first deposition of pottery and economic shellfish at this locality. The dates from Layers 3 and 4 (OZE232 and OZE233) are vertically separated by only approximately 10cm of deposit, and statistically overlap to represent essentially the same date. The dates were calibrated using CALIB REV4.4.2 (Stuiver and Reimer 1998) and are presented at the maximum probability distribution at 2 sigma.

Table 6.1 Wangil Midden: uncalibrated and calibrated (CALIB REV4.4.2) results for dated samples of charcoal and shell recovered from the test excavation (na = information not available)

LAB CODE	LAYER	SPIT	MATERIAL	$\delta^{13}C$	CONVENTIONAL ^{14}C	CALIBRATED ^{14}C
Wk-6097	2	13	Charcoal	-28.2	450±90 BP	644-307
OZE232	3	20	Charcoal	-25.0	735±60 BP	786-556
OZE233	4	24	Charcoal	-25.0	725±60 BP	760-554
ANU-11111	Base of 4	28	Marine shell	na	1080±70 BP	1167-771

The location of the dates against spits on Figure 6.9 indicates that the rate of deposition was rapid at this locality following first occupation — possibly due to clearing, firing and slope instability — and most of the deposit between Layers 4 and 2 accumulated over a few hundred years. The majority of decorated pottery recovered from the site, and indeed the greatest volume of all pottery recovered also falls within this period.

Environmental Data

Pollen was not preserved in the silty sands of the Wangil midden. However, the swampy area inland of the midden was augered and produced a pollen sequence. The augered area is a plain about 0.9m above modern high water. The augered section (described in detail in Chapter 2, this volume) revealed peat overlying swampy loams with mottled brown clays in the upper 85cm, giving way to black sandy silts with wood and gastropods down to 240cm. Mangrove pollen increases from 240–160cm, remains at a maximum to 70cm and then declines rapidly, suggesting a succession from an open inlet at the base through tidally flooded mangrove that silted up and became dry land. This is supported by the presence of estuarine shell below 85cm. Dates on organic matter show that this estuarine phase accumulated rapidly, reaching modern sea level about 6000 years ago at 60cm, after which sediment build-up under seasonal swamp conditions has been very slow.

Summary of Artefacts and Economic Fauna

Artefacts comprised mainly undecorated pottery, with a minor component of decorated sherds (see below). Small sherds of Chinese ceramics were recovered from Spits 1, 2, and 15. Economic fauna comprised mainly marine shellfish and these are discussed below. Portions of dugong rib bones were recovered from Spits 3 and 13. Terrestrial faunal remains were extremely sparse comprising pig elements in Spits 1, 4, 5, 12, 13, 15, 17, and 19.

All pottery recovered from the excavation was weighed at the time and corrections then carried out for volumetric differences between spits (see Table 6.2). There are major variations in the patterning and rate of discard of ceramics between spits and through time that are not obviously attributable to the nature of vessel parts represented, e.g. heavy bases or sago ovens versus walls of thinner vessels. Similar variations in the quantity of economic shellfish discarded through time were also noted (see Table 6.3).

While acknowledging the small size of the excavation this variability does suggest that different patterns of occupation and discard have obtained through time on at least this portion of the site. This stands in contrast to the uniformity in depositional patterns and homogeneity often seen in mono-specific shell mound middens from non-agricultural groups (e.g. Veitch 1996).

Table 6.2 Wangil Midden: weights (g) of undecorated and weights (g) and (no.) of decorated pottery by spit (total (g) rounded)

SPIT	UNDECORATED (g)	DECORATED (g) and (no.)	TOTAL (g)
1	605	-	605
2	1892	36.2 (3)	1928
3	1480	-	1480
4	1075	29.0 (1)	1104
5	80	-	80
6	-	-	-
7	215	34.6 (2)	250
8	155	15.7 (3)	171
9	95	-	95
10	245	-	245
11	170	-	170
12	400	-	400
13	620	-	620
14	2025	28.7 (3)	2054
15	940	23.8 (1)	964
16	1125	192.3 (13)	1317
17	880	55.7 (3)	936
18	600	10.8 (1)	611
19	160	-	160
20	440	-	615
21	780	-	780
22	550	484.1 (3)	1034
23	45	-	45
24	325	-	325
25	320	-	320
26	220	14.9 (2)	235
27	90	-	90
28	150	-	150

The vast majority of fragments are not stylistically diagnostic — coming from the walls of cooking vessels and (likely) water jars. Numerous sub-rounded, cubed fragments appear to be from broken sago ovens, and their degree of breakage suggests they may have served a subsequent function as heat retainers in open hearth fires. The assumed sago oven fragments occur only in the upper 12 spits. They thus all post-date Wk-6097 calibrated to 644–307 BP, and may suggest a post-European contact date for the introduction of clay sago moulds to Aru.

Decorated pottery fragments were present in small numbers throughout the site in Spits 2, 4, 7, 8, 14, 15, 16, 17, 18, 22, and 26 (Table 6.2) and are discussed and illustrated below.

The variety of gastropods and bivalves represented in Table 6.3 illustrates exploitation of a wide variety of habitats including littoral sand and mudflats, coral reef/shallow water embayments, and mangrove mudflat systems. All habitats are located within several hundred metres of the site.

Most shellfish species are registered in all six layers, although only in very small weights and in highly fragmented form in the lower two. The highest figures for NISP and weights in most species were obtained from layers one and three. *Tridacna* sp. typically occurs in very low numbers, usually being processed and discarded on reef flats while the *Lambis lambis* shows typical breakage patterns created from the extraction of flesh after roasting (cf. Bird et al. 2002).

Table 6.3 Wangil Midden: number of individual specimens identified (NISP), and weight (g) by spit for economic shell species recovered from the test excavation

SPITS	*ANADARA GRANOSA*		*GELOINA COAXANS*		*TEREBRALIA PALUSTRIS*		*LAMBIS LAMBIS*		*TELESCOPIUM TELESCOPIUM*		*ANADARA TRAPEZIA*		*TRIDACNA SP.*		ANADARA FRAGMENTS	OTHER FRAGMENTS
	NISP	g	NISP	g	NISP	g	NISP	g	NISP	g	NISP	g	NISP	g	g	g
1	125	1190	18	100	9	25	7	260	15	180	14	55	0	0	65	530
2	370	3410	44	250	33	180	3	100	48	700	22	95	1	110	100	1370
3	90	680	29	200	32	125	3	150	27	500	7	25	2	100	80	370
4	40	215	7	50	13	45	2	140	17	240	11	120	0	0	10	300
5	3	15	1	10	1	5	1	20	6	25	1	10	0	0	0	40
6	4	20	4	15	6	15	0	0	3	10	5	15	0	0	10	25
7	24	24	4	50	3	10	3	60	4	50	11	80	0	0	5	180
8	3	15	5	25	4	15	0	0	3	25	9	25	0	0	5	15
9	2	10	2	10	0	0	0	0	3	25	3	10	0	0	0	90
10	10	50	4	15	3	10	1	10	2	10	5	20	0	0	5	420
11	12	75	0	0	0	0	0	0	3	25	7	50	0	0	0	180
12	12	100	0	0	0	0	0	0	7	40	5	20	1	60	5	240
13	64	340	29	150	11	25	0	0	26	260	8	80	2	10	10	570
14	150	1090	37	230	25	110	7	150	42	650	22	130	0	0	155	1850
15	111	770	13	95	13	55	5	140	28	270	25	140	0	0	10	710
16	235	1820	41	350	53	240	9	280	46	680	54	380	0	0	100	1520
17	129	940	44	300	29	220	4	110	60	400	53	360	2	25	130	690
18	51	340	10	90	9	50	4	90	12	150	28	230	1	220	50	390
19	21	120	3	15	10	75	0	0	7	90	14	140	0	0	5	90
20	35	260	7	60	36	200	3	50	7	25	18	220	0	0	20	250
21	11	50	0	0	9	30	2	50	5	60	4	40	0	0	50	60
22	5	50	1	5	2	10	1	20	4	20	9	25	0	0	10	50
23	Only negligible weights were recorded for shellfish from this spit and below															

Fluctuations in the density of the different species through time in the six layers are broadly consistent between each other (and the pottery weights) and are likely to reflect levels of activity rather than changes in habitat or other environmental factors. There is a clear deterioration in the condition of shellfish in Layers 5 and 6 with all but the most robust portions being heavily etched and having a moist and friable appearance. This seems likely to be due to the effect of water movement causing dissolution of the shell in this lower part of the site.

Description of the Decorated Pottery Assemblage

We have illustrated the majority of decorated sherds from the test pit excavation at Wangil and from the nearby disturbed sand quarry area so that future research will be able to fit them into a more definite schema (Figs 6.11–6.15). Although the material from the test pit dates to the last millennium, this is not necessarily the case with the sample from the quarry area. It could be somewhat earlier and is considered separately below.

Within the Aru group, comparison is only possible with the Nabulei Lisa pottery assemblage. Aside from the semi-complete broken vessels collected from the surface (see Chapter 7, Figs 7.26–7.28), the Nabulei Lisa pottery consisted of a small number of undecorated and largely undiagnostic sherds confined to the top eight spits, to a depth of approximately 18cm. Based on the dates from Spit 5 of 780±50 (ANU-1092), Spit 10 of Modern (ANU-10919), and Spit 11 of 2530±60 (OZF249), it is assumed that the pottery in Nabulei Lisa all dates to the last 1000 years (see Chapter 7, this volume). The maximum number of sherds in any single spit was eight — in Spit 1. Only three small, undiagnostic, earthenware sherds were recovered from Test Pit C at Liang Lemdubu, all from the upper two spits.

Sherds from the Wangil test pit comprised several vessel types. Fragments of clay sago ovens were the most easily identifiable, and were recovered from the upper 12 spits. There were also unrestricted vessels that were probably cooking pots or sago paste (*pepeda*) bowls. Restricted orifice vessels, sometimes carinated, were also probably used for cooking but the presence of flat bases and handles in the uppermost spit might suggest some functioned as water storage jars. There was also a shallow bowl — or more likely a lid — with curvilinear incision, two parallel incised lines bordering punctation, and a post-firing drill-hole (WM-22-3; Figs 6.14, 6.15). Imported Chinese ceramics made up the rest of the collection.

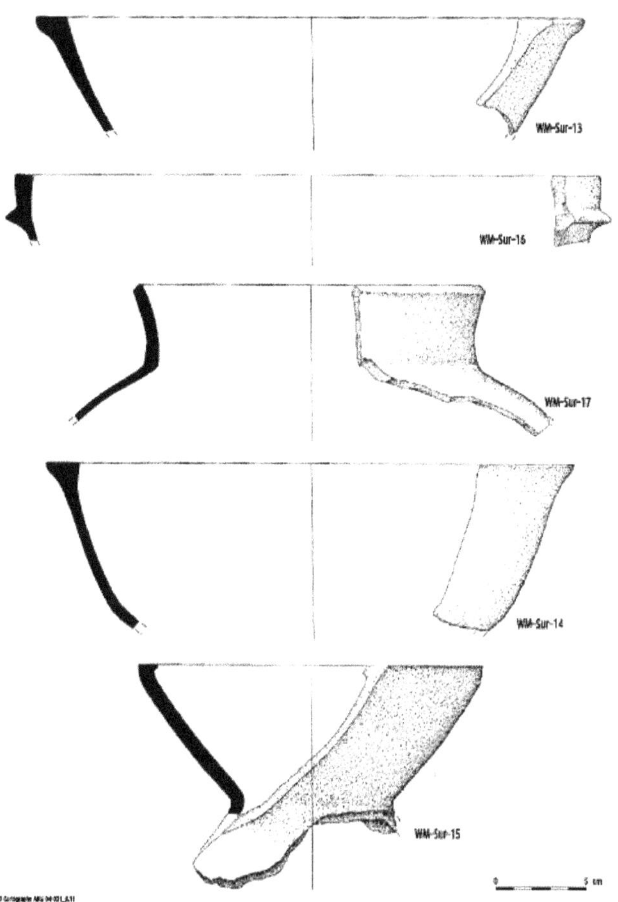

Figure 6.11 Wangil Midden: vessel forms among the surface collected pottery, including open bowls (WM-Sur-13, WM-Sur-14, WM-Sur-16 – one with red slip), a red-slipped open bowl with stand (WM-Sur-15), and a red-slipped globular pot with out-curving neck (see Table 6.4 for details)

Most of the decoration consists of linear and curvilinear incision, simple rectilinear motifs being less common. Decoration generally occurs just below the rim and above the carination or change of direction where this is present. One rim of a restricted vessel from Spit 22 (WM-22-2) has what seems to be an applied 'collar' around the restriction, and a distinctive scalloped and partly notched lip (Figs 6.14, 6.15). There are two other examples of notching on the lip from Spit 26 (WM-26-1 and WM-26-1, Fig. 6.14), the remainder of the rim sherds being plain. The absence of lip notching in the upper spits of the site may purely be a question of sample size. Merton's 1907–08 description of pottery manufacture at Maikoor (quoted above) and our own observations at Batu Lei in 1996, showed that lip notching has certainly been practiced over the past 100 years. A single sherd from Spit 16 has a probable suspension hole through an applied band, but its orientation is unclear. Several other sherds have holes bored through them, again possibly for suspension. A plain rim, red-slipped bowl form, also from Spit 16, has an applied notched band along the carination, 3–4cm below the lip (WM-16-1, Fig. 6.13). The only other piece with applied decoration (from Spit 2) has a plain external ridge added of a form found in central Moluccan late prehistoric pottery and known as a 'ridge-rim' (Spriggs 1990). One red-slipped neck sherd has fingernail impressions along the exterior corner point (WM-17-2, Fig. 6.14), and one carinated sherd from Spit 18 has a row of 'stick' or single tool impressions above the carination (WM-18-1, Fig. 6.14). Several incised sherds have impressed dots or punctation as part of the design (see Figs 6.13, 6.14). There seems to be no relation between sherd thickness and type of decoration. Sherds of two vessels of very different thickness — one from Spit 7 and the other from Spit 22 — bear very similar complex incised motifs. There is nothing in the vessel forms or

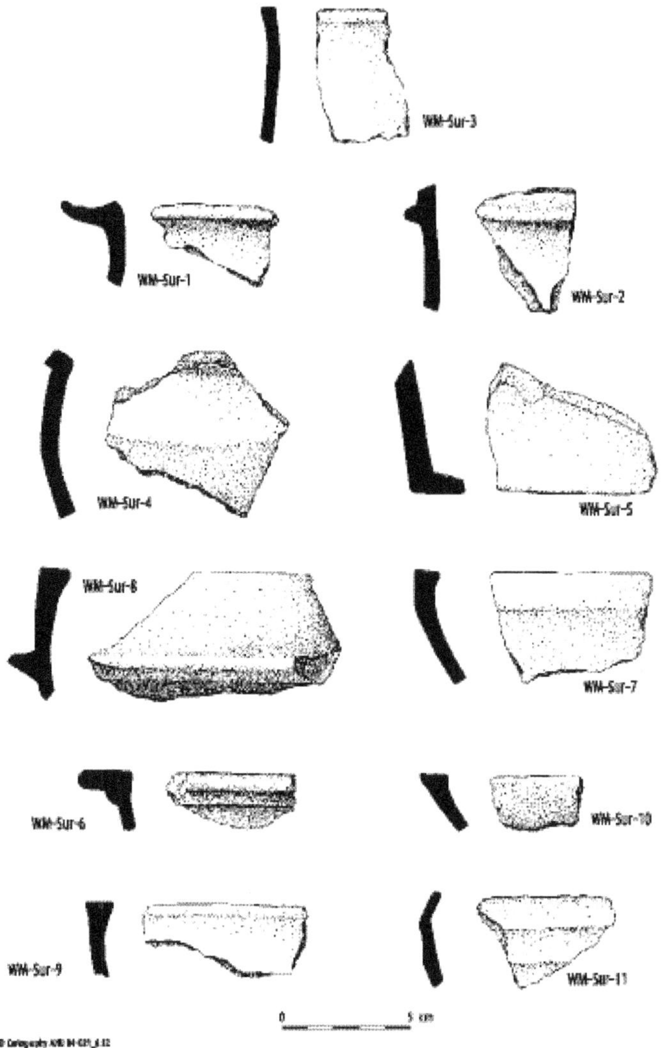

Figure 6.12 Wangil Midden: diagnostic and decorated pottery sherds among the surface collection, including rims from restricted neck vessels (WM-Sur-3, WM-Sur-1); a rim from a restricted bowl and a body sherd with ridged flanges (WM-Sur-2, WM-Sur-8); a necked shoulder from an everted globular pot (WM-Sur-4); part of a flat-based vessel (WM-Sur-5); rims from plain and carinated open bowls (WM-Sur-7, WM-Sur-10); a parallel rim with raised ridge (WM-Sur-6); and two rims from restricted bowls (WM-Sur-9, WM-Sur-11 – the latter with raised ridges) (see Table 6.4 for details)

decoration to suggest anything other than a relatively recent age for their production. Red-slipped pottery is mainly found in the surface deposits at Wangil, including the disturbed quarry site, but two red-slipped pieces (WM-17-1 and WM-22-1) were also recovered from Spits 17 and 22 of the excavation (Figs 6.14, 6.15).

One potentially distorting factor in any discussion of Aru pottery decoration is that we do not know how long the painted decoration on the modern pottery of the group could be expected to last once buried or exposed on the surface. Observations in 1975 by Spriggs of surface-collected pottery from the Kei Islands, suggested that the painted decoration ubiquitous on modern pottery there does not last long once exposed following breakage and discard. Conditions in the Aru Islands might be comparable and so many plain sherds excavated at Wangil or other sites, or those that display only lip notching, may have once been painted. The painted decoration on the Nabulei Lisa pottery is only apparent on the sherds recovered from the surface. With the exception of painted decoration, however, the pottery from the excavation looks very similar to that from the surface (in terms of temper and vessel form), so it seems likely that painted decoration simply does not survive burial. This is obviously an issue that needs further research.

The sherds from the sand quarry area, as mentioned earlier, included some red-slipped vessels which superficially resemble some from the Neolithic and Early Metal Age assemblages elsewhere in Eastern Indonesia. If we compare them with the material from the test pit, there is certainly the possibility that they date to a period earlier than the last millennium.

The diagnostic sherds from Nabulei Lisa are illustrated and discussed in Chapter 7. Vessel forms included a series of restricted orifice cooking pots, usually with plain lips and lacking incised decoration on the body. The collar form was distinctive and different from the Wangil examples. Some strongly restricted orifice vessels were most probably water jars, one of which was decorated with a complex rectilinear painted design in red. This resembles ethnographically recorded decoration. The larger size of several surface sherds at Nabulei Lisa makes it easier to reconstruct vessel form and this inhibits direct comparisons with Wangil. Clearly, however, the curvilinear incised decoration favoured at Wangil in the last thousand years is missing at Nabulei Lisa. This might imply temporal differences — with a general tendency in Island Southeast Asia for pottery to become more highly decorated over time — but it might also represent stylistic differences between pottery production centres in the Aru group, or simply be due to a more limited range of pottery vessels being employed in the cave site. Nabulei Lisa is much closer to Batu Lei than to Samang or Maikoor, and so its pottery probably comes from a different source than that at Wangil.

Most of the pottery at Nabulei Lisa, both from the surface and from the excavation resembles the Batu Lei pottery in having a coarse calcareous and quartz sand temper, and in being low fired. In contrast, the Wangil decorated pottery is much more variable in the vessel form, types of decoration, and fabric composition. The difference is likely to reflect the different site types which we have sampled. Nabulei Lisa is a cave site and while close to the *sungai* it was probably used predominantly as a hunting or stop over camp whilst visiting gardens. It is not likely therefore to have the range in pottery vessels that one might expect at a village site on the coast.

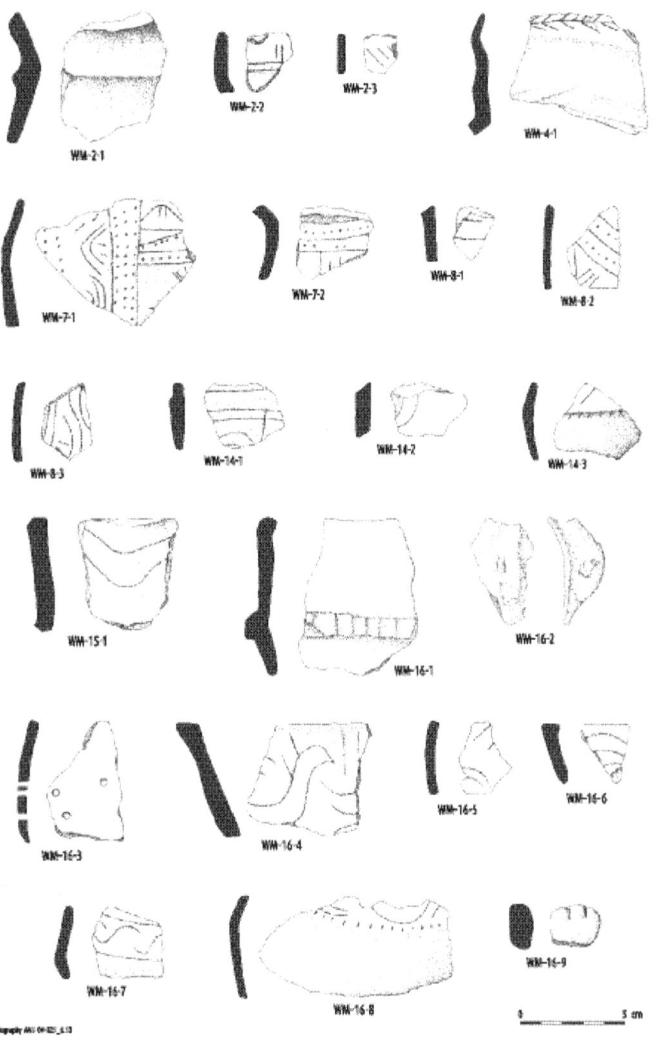

Figure 6.13 Wangil Midden: decorated pottery sherds from the excavation, including techniques such as linear and curvilinear incision (WM-2-2, WM-2-3, WM-4-1, WM-8-1, WM-8-3, WM-14-1, WM-14-2, WM-15-1, WM-16-4, WM-16-5, WM-16-6, WM-16-7); linear and curvilinear incision with punctation (WM-7-1, WM-7-2, WM-8-2, WM-16-8); a raised ridge (WM-2-1); notching or fingernail pinch along the carination (WM-14-3); an applied relief band with spaced notching along the carination (WM-16-1); a handle with pierced hole (WM-16-2); multiple pierced holes (WM-16-3); and a possible lug handle or rim with linear incised notching (WM-16-9) (see Table 6.4 for details)

Initial separation into different fabric groups was accomplished using a binocular microscope at low level magnification (×10) and aimed at discriminating the maximum number of 'potential types'. This megascopic examination discriminated nine potential temper types. Examples from each type group were then sent for petrographic analysis to Prof. William Dickinson at the University of Arizona (see Appendix 6.1 for his full description). After further megascopic examination, Dickinson selected 25 sherds comprising examples of each of the temper types from Wangil and Nabulei Lisa for detailed petrographic analysis, and these were compared against each other and with temper and clay samples collected from the modern pottery making center at Batu Lei. Eighteen sherds were examined from Wangil. Dickinson concluded that all of the Nabulei Lisa sherds (described in Chaper 7, this volume), and nine of the Wangil sherds, are quartz-calcite tempers that are generically similar to the Batu Lei sand

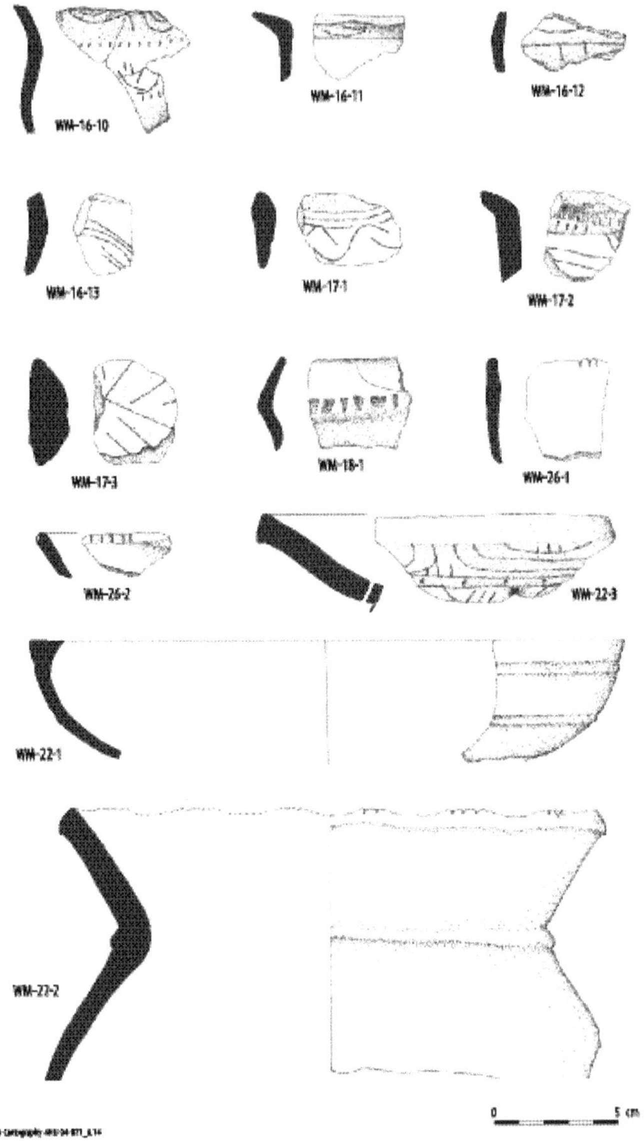

Figure 6.14 Wangil Midden: decorated pottery from Spit 22 of the excavation, including techniques such as linear and curvilinear incision on neck and body sherds and a carination (WM-16-11, WM-16-12, WM-16-13, WM-17-1, WM-17-3); linear and curvilinear incision with punctation (WM-16-10); linear incision with fingernail impressions (WM-17-2); single tool impressions (WM-18-1); linear incised lip notching (WM-26-1, WM-26-2); linear and curvilinear incision with punctation and a drilled hole (WM-22-3); grooves (WM-22-1); and a scalloped and incised lip (WM-22-2) (see Table 6.4 for details)

(megascopic temper groups 1–5) and are almost certainly indigenous to Aru (WRD-212). The quartz-calcite ratio varies, as does the temper texture, but Dickinson believes it is unlikely that the variations are geologically very significant. Six of the Wangil quartz-calcite tempered sherds contained a much siltier paste than the Nabulei Lisa specimens, indicating that the two related ceramic suites were not identical. In addition, the Wangil sample contained eight sherds, including three with red-slip, that were very different, having a volcanic sand temper and a paste that could not be derived from the Aru Islands (megascopic temper groups 6, 8 and 9). With the exception of the red-slipped sherd from Spit 22, the exotic specimens were all from the surface of the Wangil test pit. Dickinson compared the exotic Aru temper with sherds from Halmahera and Banda (WRD-237, -238, -220) and found that while some of the Halmahera tempers were mineralogically similar to the exotic Aru sherds, some of the Banda tempers were 'visually identical texturally and statistically indistinguishable mineralogically from tempers in the exotic Aru sherds'. The 'pastes in the Banda sherds also contain vitroclastic glass shards of volcanic ash that are indistinguishable from those in the pastes of exotic Aru sherds'.

Dickinson concludes that the combined petrographic match of temper and paste between indigenous Banda sherds and exotic Aru sherds leaves no reasonable doubt that the exotic Aru sherds derive from wares brought to Aru from Banda, and not from Halmahera (Appendix 6.1, WRD-238).

A single sherd collected from the surface of Wangil, WM-Sur-5 (megascopic temper type 7; WRD-212), contained an unusual subangular quartz-feldspar sand temper. Dickinson concludes that this temper is not related to either the 'indigenous quartz-calcite temper' group or the 'exotic volcanic sand temper' group. He suggests that this temper is unlike the other Aru sherds in that it almost certainly derives from an imported ware, but its origin is indeterminate. Dickinson's full reports on the Aru, Halmahera and Banda sherds are contained in Appendix 6.1.

Figure 6.15 Wangil Midden: decorated pottery sherds from the excavation, including the fragment of an everted globular pot with a scalloped and incised lip (WM-22-2); the red-slipped open bowl fragment with exterior grooves (WM-22-1); and the possible lid fragment with linear and curvilinear incision, punctation, and a drilled hole (WM-22-3) (see illustrated sherds and Table 6.4 for details)

Wider stylistic comparisons of the Wangil test pit material did not prove enlightening. We have reviewed all the published material on surface-collected pottery, or that dated to the last 2000 years from Maluku, Timor, Papua (former Irian Jaya) and Sulawesi — the references are too numerous to list here — and can find no close parallels to the incised decoration other than in rectilinear motifs so simple as to be almost ubiquitous. This is of course to be expected for this time period in the region, as discussed by Pétrequin and Pétrequin (1999:73–4). First of all they note the presence of a number of different methods to produce what is basically the same vessel type, but which on typological grounds might be divided into several stylistic 'provinces' based on variants in form. They note that 'if the same typologist used a detailed comparison of pottery decoration the number of small stylistic provinces would grow: virtually every production area possesses specific decorative techniques and processes which allow one, usually at first glance, to differentiate each production centre from its neighbours' (translation by Spriggs).

The painted designs on ethnographic pottery from Aru, however, would clearly bear comparison with that from the neighbouring island group of Kei, and more distantly with the painted pottery of Timor (see Pétrequin and Pétrequin 1999:fig. 6), but such a comparison is beyond the scope of this study. The time depth of painted decoration on Aru, Kei and Timor pottery is itself unknown, at least in part because of the taphonomic problems of paint preservation on sherds over time referred to above.

The technological study by the Pétrequins suggests that the current pottery manufacturing techniques in Kei, Aru and Timor represent the diffusion of techniques from further west during the Metal Age of the early first millennium AD (1999:fig.17c). The current dates available for pottery in the Aru Islands, discussed above, do not contradict this suggestion. Their idea of further diffusion of pottery technology perhaps from Aru itself into the Papuan Gulf of present-day Papua

Table 6.4 Wangil Midden: description of illustrated sherds

NUMBER	SHERD TYPE	VESSEL FORM	RIM DATA					DECORATION DATA		FABRIC ANALYSIS
			DIRECTION	RIM PROFILE	LIP PROFILE	EXTRA RIM FEATURES	RIM DIAMETER	LOCATION	TECHNIQUE	
WM-Sur-1	rim	restricted neck vessel	right-angle everted	gradual convergent	pointed					2
WM-Sur-2	body							1) outer surface 2) interior & exterior	1) ridged flange 2) red slip	6
WM-Sur-3	rim	restricted neck vessel	out-curving	abruptly divergent	flat	symmetrically thickened interior & exterior				1
WM-Sur-4	neck/shoulder	restricted neck w/ globular body						exterior	red slip	2
WM-Sur-5	base	flat-based vessel								7
WM-Sur-6	rim		right-angle everted	parallel	rounded			1) exterior corner point 2) exterior	1) raised ridge 2) remnant red slip/ paint?	6
WM-Sur-7	rim/ carination	open bowl	direct	abruptly divergent	flat	asymmetrically thickened interior				8
WM-Sur-8	rim	restricted bowl	incurving	abruptly divergent	flat	asymmetrically thickened interior		1) exterior point of vertical tangency 2) interior & exterior	1) ridged flange 2) red slip	6
WM-Sur-9	rim	restricted bowl	incurving	abruptly divergent	flat	symmetrically thickened interior & exterior		interior & exterior	red slip	6
WM-Sur-10	rim	open bowl	direct	abruptly divergent	flat	asymmetrically thickened interior				9
WM-Sur-11	rim	restricted bowl	inverted	gradual convergent	rounded	asymmetrically thickened interior		exterior corner point and neck	two raised ridges separated by a channel	1
WM-Sur-12	body (4 joined)							interior & exterior	red slip	8
WM-Sur-13	rim	open bowl	direct	abrupt divergent	flat	asymmetrically thickened exterior	30cm			8
WM-Sur-14	rim	open bowl	direct	abrupt divergent	flat	asymmetrically thickened interior & exterior	29cm	interior & exterior	red slip	6
WM-Sur-15	rim/ body									
stand	open bowl w/ restricted stand		direct	abrupt divergent	ridged	asymmetrically thickened interior	19cm	interior & exterior	red slip	8
WM-Sur-16	rim	open bowl	direct	gradual divergent	flat	asymmetrically thickened interior	32cm	exterior point of vertical tangency	ridged flange	6
WM-Sur-17	rim/ neck/ shoulder		out-curving globular pot	out-curving	parallel	flat	19cm	interior & exterior	red slip	2
WM-2-1	neck	restricted neck vessel (everted)						exterior corner point	raised ridge	1
WM-2-2	body							exterior	linear incision	1

continued over

Table 6.4 continued

NUMBER	SHERD TYPE	VESSEL FORM	RIM DATA					DECORATION DATA		FABRIC ANALYSIS
			DIRECTION	RIM PROFILE	LIP PROFILE	EXTRA RIM FEATURES	RIM DIAMETER	LOCATION	TECHNIQUE	
WM-2-3	body							exterior	linear incision	1
WM-4-1	body							exterior	linear incision	3
WM-7-1	shoulder	globular vessel						exterior	linear and curvilinear incision; punctation	1
WM-7-2	neck	restricted neck vessel (out-curving)						outer surface	linear incision; punctation	1
WM-8-1	body							exterior	linear incision	5
WM-8-2	body							exterior	linear and curvilinear incision; punctation	5
WM-8-3	body							exterior	linear and curvilinear incision	5
WM-14-1	carination	carinated vessel						exterior	linear and curvilinear incision	1
WM-14-2	body							exterior	curvilinear incision	1
WM-14-3	carination	carinated vessel						1) above & below carination 2) exterior corner point	1) linear incision 2) notching/fingernail pinch?	2
WM-15-1	rim	restricted neck vessel	direct	parallel	flat/ scalloped			exterior	curvilinear incision	1
WM-16-1	rim/carination	unrestricted carinated vessel		direct	abrupt divergent rounded	asymmetrically thickened interior		1) exterior corner point 2) interior & below carination	1) applied band w/ spaced notching 2) red slip	1
WM-16-2	handle	pierced hole								1
WM-16-3	body							spaced over surface	multiple pierced holes (3 complete)	1
WM-16-4	rim	unrestricted vessel	direct	gradual divergent	flat	asymmetrically thickened exterior		exterior	linear and curvilinear incision	1
WM-16-5	body							exterior	linear and curvilinear incision	1
WM-16-6	rim		direct	abrupt divergent	flat	asymmetrically thickened interior		exterior	curvilinear incision	1
	(3 joined)	globular pot							punctation	

continued over

Table 6.4 continued

NUMBER	SHERD TYPE	VESSEL FORM	RIM DATA					DECORATION DATA		FABRIC ANALYSIS
			DIRECTION	RIM PROFILE	LIP PROFILE	EXTRA RIM FEATURES	RIM DIAMETER	LOCATION	TECHNIQUE	
WM-16-7	carination	carinated vessel						exterior above carination	linear and curvilinear incision	1
WM-16-8	carination/ shoulder	carinated vessel						exterior above carination	curvilinear incision; punctation	1
WM-16-9	rim/lug/handle?							one edge	linear notching	1
WM-16-10	neck/shoulder	out-curving	(out-curving)					exterior	linear and curvilinear incision;	1
WM-16-11	neck	restricted neck vessel	(everted)					exterior	linear and incision	1
WM-16-12	carination	carinated vessel						above & below carination	linear and curvilinear incision	1
WM-16-13	body							exterior	curvilinear incision	1
WM-17-1	neck							exterior	linear and curvilinear incision; red slip	4
WM-17-2	neck	restricted neck vessel	(everted)					1) exterior below corner point 2) exterior corner point 3) interior & exterior	1) linear incision 2) fingernail impressions 3) red slip	1
WM-17-3	body							exterior	linear incision	1
WM-18-1	rim/ neck/ carination	restricted vessel	incurving	gradual convergent	pointed			exterior corner point	spaced single tool impressions	1
WM-22-1	rim	open bowl	direct	abrupt divergent	flat w/shallow central groove	asymmetrically thickened interior	24cm	1) exterior 2) interior & exterior	1) two sets of double grooves 2) red slip	9
WM-22-2	rim/ neck	everted globular pot	everted	gradual convergent	flat w/ rounded edge	collared rim	21.5cm	1) lip 2) exterior corner point	1) scalloped and incised 2) raised ridge	1
WM-22-3	lid?			gradual divergent	flat		22cm	exterior	linear and curvilinear incision; punctation; post-firing drilled hole	2
WM-26-1	rim	restricted vessel	direct	abruptly divergent	flat	asymmetrically thickened interior		lip exterior	linear incised notching	2
WM-26-2	rim	open bowl?	direct	parallel	flat			lip exterior	linear incised notching	2

New Guinea (Yule Island and the Port Moresby region) is even more speculative, but is supported by some other lines of evidence indicating connections between the two regions over the last several hundred years at least (discussed in Chapter 1), related to the birds of paradise trade. Detailed technological studies of Aru and other archaeological pottery assemblages to identify details of manufacturing techniques will be required for the ideas of the Pétrequins to be given any more than speculative time depth. Will the earliest pottery of the region turn out to have been constructed using quite different potting techniques as their model would seem to require? Their suggestion is that, given the difficulty of learning the particular techniques now practiced in Aru and the other areas mentioned — which are unlikely to be acquired by simple imitation — a direct migration of potters from further west in Indonesia would be required (1999:97).

Interpretation of the Sequence Within the Aru Islands

The Wangil midden is an extensive mounded structure perched on an isthmus, flanked by marine coast on one side and a sago swamp formed within a palaeolagoon on the other. Large volumes of marine shellfish attest to systematic exploitation of a variety of proximal habitats including coral reef and flats, sand and mudflats, and mangroves.

Substantial volumes of pottery occur on the site with a minor component consisting of decorated ware. Historical and ethnographic accounts document several centres of pottery production in the Aru group, the closest being Samang on Pulau Wokam to the north. Fragments of broken sago ovens were extremely common on the site, most likely reflecting the importance of this staple food, the proximity of sago stands, and the likely role of this product as an export from the Aru Islands in supporting the forced labourers of the Banda spice production centre (Spyer 2000; Veth et al. 2000; Chapter 5, this volume). This trade relationship receives substantive support from the analysis of the red-slipped and other earthenware sherds in the Wangil midden which contained an exotic volcanic temper and paste. Dickinson's analysis, discussed above, leaves no doubt that these sherds derive from wares brought from Banda to Aru. Although most of the exotic sherds were from the surface, one was obtained from Spit 22, attesting to the longevity of this relationship over the last 700 years. Historically, Wangil was noted to be one of the largest villages on the west coast with an early Dutch garrison established there in the course of the 17th century (see Chapter 5, this volume).

Dates from the test pit illustrate occupation during the last millenium with the majority of decorated ware bracketed by dates of approximately 800 BP and 300 BP, at the extremes. The Wangil pottery is consistent with the regional ethnographic pattern that displays great variability of decoration within a few major production traditions (cf. Pétrequin and Pétrequin 1999:73–4). The site is used for gardening today and also the casual processing and discard of a limited range of shellfish. There are no obvious changes in the proportions or species of economic shellfish through time to suggest major changes in the use of the site or local habitats over the last millennium. During three seasons of survey and recording, the most common midden forms encountered are buried linear middens often situated near historic village sites, such as at Wangil. Where older shorelines have been augered and middens detected, such as in front of the Fany Hotel in the nearby town of Dobo, they are likely to be mid-late Holocene in age, although no dates have been obtained to verify this (see Chapter 4, this volume). This pattern is very likely to be a product of various factors, among which is certainly sampling. Other important factors could be coastal progradation, poor preservation on coarse sands due to leaching in the tropical climate, and the combined cultural effects of gardening and mining for lime.

References

Bird, D.W., J.L. Richardson, P. Veth, and A. Barham. 2002. Explaining shellfishing variability in middens on the Meriam Islands, Torres Strait, Australia. *Journal of Archaeological Science* 29:457–69.

Bellwood, P. 1997. *Prehistory of the Indo-Malaysian Archipelago*. Honolulu: University of Hawai'i Press.

Ellen, R.F. and I.C. Glover. 1974. Pottery manufacture and trade in the Central Moluccas, Indonesia: the modern situation and the historical implications. *Man* (N.S.) 9:353–79.

Gasser, S.A. 1969. Das Töpferhandwerk von Indonesien. *Basler Beitrage Ethnologie* 7. Basel: Pharos-Verlag, Hans Rudolph Schwabe.

Merton, H. 1910. *Forschungsreise in den Sudostlichen Molukken (Aru-und Kei Inslen)*. Frankfurt, A.M.: Senckenbergischen Naturforschenden Gesellschaft. English translation by A. and A. Veth (1998), James Cook University, Townsville.

Pétrequin, P. and A.M. Pétrequin. 1999. La poterie en Nouvelle-Guinée: savoir-faire et transmission des techniques. *Journal de la Société des Océanistes* 108:71–101.

Spriggs, M. 1990. Archaeological and ethnoarchaeological research in Maluku 1975 and 1977: an unfinished story. *Cakalele: Maluku Studies Research Journal*. 1(1–2):51–65.

Spriggs, M. 1998. Research questions in Maluku archaeology. *Cakalele: Maluku Studies Research Journal* 9(2):49–62.

Spyer, P. 2000. *The Memory of Trade: Modernity's Entanglements on an Eastern Indonesian Island*. Durham: Duke University Press.

Veitch, B. 1996. Evidence for mid-Holocene change in the Mitchell Plateau, Northwest Kimberley, Western Australia. In P. Veth and P. Hiscock (eds), *Archaeology of Northern Australia: Regional Perspectives*, pp. 66–89. St Lucia: Anthropology Museum of the University of Queensland. *Tempus* 4.

Veth, P., S. O'Connor, M. Spriggs, D. Witjaksono, and A. Diniasti. 2000. The mystery of the Ujir Site: insights into early historic settlement in the Aru Islands, Maluku. *The Bulletin of the Australian Institute for Maritime Archaeology* 24:125–32.

Appendix 6.1: Petrography of Temper Sands in Prehistoric Potsherds from the Aru Islands, South of West Irian Near the Shelf Edge of the Arafura Sea

William R. Dickinson

Petrographic Report WRD-212 (23 April 2002)

From a collection of prehistoric potsherds from the Aru Islands sent for study by Sue O'Connor of the Australian National University, 25 were examined petrographically in thin section. The sherds derive from the Nabulei Lisa cave site (sherd prefix NL-) on Aru and the Wangil mounded midden site (sherd prefix WM-) on Wammar.

The Aru ceramic suite includes sherds containing three distinct kinds of temper:

1) quartz-calcite temper (n=16) inferred to be indigenous to the Aru Islands;
2) volcanic sand temper (n=8) inferred to be exotic to the Aru Islands; and
3) quartz-feldspar temper (n=1) in one anomalous sherd (WM-Su-5).

The exotic temper is imbedded in an unusual ash-rich paste, and occurs only in sherds judged typologically to be imports to the Aru Islands from elsewhere, probably Indonesian islands lying farther west.

Geologic Setting

The Aru Islands lie near the shelf edge of the Arafura Sea south of West Irian, and expose only Neogene marine shelf strata deposited in shallow water (Hamilton 1979). As the Aru Islands are part of the Australia–New Guinea continental block, which formed the contiguous Sahul landmass during Pleistocene glaciations, Aru sedimentary assemblages are presumably of continental derivation.

Quartz-Calcite Temper

The majority of the sectioned sherds (n=16) contain generically similar hybrid sand tempers composed of quartz-rich terrigenous detritus mixed with calcareous grains of reef detritus. The sherds include all those grouped megascopically as temper types 1–5 at both Nabulei Lisa (n=7) and Wangil (n=9). A majority of the Wangil sherds (n=6) contain much siltier paste than any of the Nabulei Lisa sherds, indicating that the two related ceramic suites are not identical. Proportions of terrigenous and calcareous grains vary widely (Table 212-1), but the quartz-calcite aggregates represent the type of sand expected for the Aru Islands. As the more calcareous of the tempers closely resemble the hybrid beach sand used as temper today at Batu Lei in the Aru Islands (Table 212-1), the gradational spectrum of quartz-calcite tempers is interpreted as indigenous to the Aru Islands, and the sherds containing them as local wares. Determination of the quartz/feldspar ratio in the terrigenous fraction of the quartz-calcite tempers awaits the preparation of stained thin sections, but quartz grains appear to be dominant, as expected for sand of ultimately continental derivation.

Table 212-1: approximate relative proportions of calcareous and terrigenous grains in quartz-calcite tempers of indigenous Aru sherds and modern Batu Lei temper sand

A. Calcareous grains predominant, with terrigenous grains rare but present [includes all Wangil (WM-) sherds with silty paste containing quartzose detritus]:

Batu Lei sand, WM-15-1, WM-16-11, WM-16-13, WM-17-1, WM-22-3, WM-Su-17

B. Calcareous grains dominant, but with terrigenous grains present in significant amounts (post-burial leaching has corroded many calcareous grains in WM-Su-1):

NL-A-5C, NL-Su-1, NL-Su-6, NL-Su-11, WM-Su-1

C. Calcareous and terrigenous grains present in subequal proportions (post-burial leaching has corroded many calcareous grains in NL-A-5F and WM-4-1, and removed a significant percentage from WM-4-1):

NL-A-4, NL-A-5B, NL-A-5F, WM-4-1, WM-8-3

Among the quartz-calcite tempers, there seems no systematic correlation in detail between megascopic temper type and microscopic appearance. Megascopic discrimination among quartz-calcite tempers partly encounters the difficulty that post-burial leaching of calcareous grains from sherds may reduce the apparent ratio of calcareous to terrigenous grains unless the small sand-sized vacuoles left after dissolution of calcareous sand grains are correctly identified (Table 212-1). This problem has been encountered irregularly but quite widely in sherd suites studied from both Micronesia and Melanesia. Although ratios of calcareous to terrigenous grains may be significant for understanding the nature of tempers used at different sites within the Aru Islands, confident assessment of local variations will prove difficult for intrinsic geologic reasons as well. For example, all the sectioned sherds with predominantly calcareous tempers derive from Wangil, yet sectioned Wangil sherds also include examples of both classes of more terrigenous quartz-calcite temper (Table 212-1); it is unclear how one might distinguish between local temper variability on Wammar and ceramic transfer from Nabulei Lisa or elsewhere within the Aru Islands.

Volcanic Sand Temper

Eight sherds (three with red slips) from Wangil [megascopic temper types 6 & 8–9] contain similar volcanic sand tempers (Table 212-2) wholly different mineralogically from the indigenous quartz-calcite tempers. The pastes in the sherds are also quite different, and to the best of my knowledge are unique among Oceanian sherd suites in containing a high proportion of fresh volcanic glass shards derived from unconsolidated silicic ash deposits. As there is no indication that any volcanic rocks or ash deposits are exposed within the Aru Islands, importation from elsewhere seems assured on the basis of the petrographic character of paste and temper.

The ash particles imbedded in clay paste are isotropic volcanic glass, pale brown or tan to colourless in thin section, with the curvilinear, forked, and branching shapes that are characteristic of glass shards formed by explosive disintegration of vesiculating rhyodacitic or other comparably viscous magmas. In effect, the thin shards represent disrupted vesicle (gas bubble) walls derived from expanding pumice. Proportions of fine ash and clay are difficult to estimate optically, but glass shards consistently appear to form 15%–20% of the clay bodies. This is a significant fraction but evidently not enough to spoil the plasticity of the clay. Although the shards are extremely thin (<0.05mm), they reach lengths ~0.25mm, and their vitroclastic form is unmistakable in thin section.

The occurrence of fresh volcanic glass within a clay body derived from products of rock weathering is difficult to explain. Such intimate mixture of fine ash with clay could probably not be achieved by forcefully kneading ash and clay together without damaging the fragile glass shards,

Table 212-2. Frequency percentages of grain types in volcanic sand tempers of exotic Aru sherds (prefix WM-) based on areal grain counts of n grains in thin section [megascopic temper type in brackets].

SHERD ⇒	SUR-7 n=155 [#8]	SUR-8[1] n=190 [#6]	SUR-9 n=145 [#6	SUR-10 n=130 [#9]	SUR-14 n=80 [#6]	SUR-15[1] n=205 [#8]	SUR-16 n=235 [#6]	22-1[1] n=100 [#9]	MEAN[2]
GRN TYPE[3]									
qtz	tr	tr	-	-	-	tr	-	-	tr
plg	37	33	31	41	36	33	37	42	36±4
cpx	5	7	4	5	4	6	9	7	6±2
opa	12	15	22	6	14	4	6	4	10±6
gls	42	44	40	43	45	52	46	45	45±3
mic	4	1	3	5	1	5	2	1	3±2

1 sherds with visible red slips

2 average and standard deviation

3 qtz, quartz; plg, plagioclase feldspar; cpx, clinopyoxene; opa, opaque iron oxides; gls, vitric (glassy) volcanic rock fragments with vesicular internal structure; mic, microlitic (and rare felsitic) volcanic rock fragments

but no breakage of the delicately formed shard shapes is evident. Weathered ash, converted partly to clay, is an unlikely source because glass shards should weather at least as readily as any other constituents of volcanic ash. The most likely source is an alluvial deposit in which clayey sediment and reworked fine ash jointly settled quietly from slackwater. The observed intimate admixture of the two disparate components of the paste could not be achieved by sprinkling ash carefully into clay during preparation of the clay bodies because there are no compositional gradients of ash content visible as banding or any other domains of more irregular shape.

Temper sand grains imbedded in the ash-bearing clay pastes contrast markedly in grain size with any paste constituents, and were doubtless added manually to clay bodies. The sands are closely similar and mineralogically simple aggregates (Table 212-2), derived exclusively from volcanic sources, composed mainly of vitric volcanic rock fragments of microvesicular (pumiceous) volcanic glass together with mineral grains of plagioclase feldspar (dominant) and clinopyroxene (subordinate) inferred to derive from sand-sized phenocrysts in the pumiceous volcanic source rock. Evident abrasion of subrounded rock fragments, coupled with lesser abrasion of the harder mineral grains, which tend to be subangular, suggests that the source of the temper was reworked volcanic ash of coarser grain size than the glass shards imbedded in the clay pastes. Both paste and temper could have been derived from different parts or layers of the same reworked ash forming a blanket over the landscape near an active volcano. Generic association of the mineral grains, pumice, and ash is indicated by mineral grains with pumiceous volcanic glass adhering to their edges, and by some pumiceous rock fragments that contain plagioclase microphenocrysts. Varying proportions of opaque iron oxide grains of high specific gravity probably reflect different degrees of sedimentological placering during transport and deposition of the reworked ash. Small numbers of microlitic volcanic rock fragments with tiny microlites of untwinned plagioclase imbedded in volcanic glass may represent detrital contributions from volcanic rocks older than the ash eruptions. Traces of quartz in some of the volcanic sand tempers suggest dacitic rather than andesitic ash, as expected for explosive eruptions.

Grain type frequencies in the volcanic sand tempers are statistically distinguishable only with respect to the variable content of opaque iron oxide grains. Standard deviations of mean grain frequencies (Table 212-2) are otherwise comparable to standard deviations of counting error for the grain populations (n=80-235) present within each sherd. Grain populations visible in each sherd depend partly on the sizes of the sherds and partly on the proportions of temper and paste. A preliminary megascopic temper classification was based partly upon paste color, which is in turn dependent partly on firing conditions and partly on subsequent sherd weathering, and partly upon average sizes of temper grains, which vary but in no systematic way relative to temper compositions. Megascopic temper types 8–9 tend to be more abundant relative to paste, and somewhat coarser grained, with megascopic temper type 6 sparser and finer grained, but sherd WM-Su-16 of the latter group falls microscopically within the former group. In my view, attempts to discriminate among the volcanic sand tempers are unlikely to point to any significant compositional differences, and may simply reflect habits or tastes of individual potters working with the same or closely related raw materials.

Anomalous Temper

The temper sand (megascopic temper type 7) in sherd WM-Su-5 of unusual appearance is an angular to subangular quartz-feldspar sand, including both plagioclase and K-feldspar, lacking any ferromagnesian grains, but containing a minor proportion of polycrystalline/polymineralic felsitic to microgranitic lithic fragments probably derived from intrusive igneous rocks. The origin of the temper is indeterminate, but it does not appear to be related to either the indigenous (quartz-calcite) or exotic (volcanic sand) tempers that are prevalent in Aru sherds. Derivation from a continental island is likely, but no specific candidates can be suggested from what is observed in just the one sherd. The temper is so unlike those in other Aru sherds that some adventitious introduction to Aru should be entertained as a possibility, but as I am unaware of the occurrence of the sherd, further speculation on my part would be fruitless.

Temper Sources

Beach sands within the Aru Islands appear to represent an adequate and attractive source for the indigenous quartz-calcite tempers, and require no further discussion. There is no firm basis for further discussion of the anomalous temper in one unusual sherd.

Search for the origin of the exotic sherds with ash-bearing paste and volcanic sand temper can be guided by the distribution of active volcanism within Indonesia (Neumann van Padang 1951; Simkin et al. 1968; Hamilton 1978), with special focus on explosive volcanism. The closest volcanic centers lie along the Banda island arc in the Banda Sea to the west of the Aru Islands, but the tiny islands on which they occur are unlikely sites for significant cultural development. Next closest are multiple volcanic centers on Halmahera and nearby smaller islands well to the northwest of the Aru Islands (Hall et al. 1988). The Sangihe island arc (Morrice et al. 1983), extending off the northern arm of Sulawesi across the Molucca Sea to the west of Halmahera is even more distant, and consists of islands as small as those in the Banda Sea.

Essentially all the volcanic centers of Indonesia are dominated by andesitic and basaltic eruptives more mafic than the silicic ash in the exotic Aru sherd pastes, but some explosive dacitic eruptions can be inferred for many of the larger composite stratocones. From that perspective, as well as its position as a large landmass in comparative proximity to the Aru Islands, Halmahera seems the most attractive target to investigate as a potential source for the exotic sherds.

References

Hall, R., M.G. Audley-Charles, F.T. Banner, S. Hidayat, and S.L. Tobing. 1988. Late Palaeogene-Quaternary geology of Halmahera, eastern Indonesia: initiation of a volcanic arc. *Geological Society of London Journal* 145:577–90.

Hamilton, W. 1979. Tectonics of the Indonesian region. *U.S. Geological Survey Professional Paper* 1078:345.

Morrice, M.G., P.A. Jezek, J.B. Gill, D.J. Whitford, and M. Monoarfa. 1983. An introduction to the Sangihe arc: volcanism accompanying arc-arc collision in the Molucca Sea, Indonesia. *Journal of Volcanology and Geothermal Research* 19:135–65.

Neumann van Padang, M. 1951. Catalogue of the active volcanoes of the world including solfatara fields; Part I, Indonesia, p.271. Napoli: International Volcanological Association.

Simkin, T., L. Siebert, L. McClelland, D. Bridge, C. Newhall, and latter J.H. 1968. *Volcanoes of the World*, p. 232. Washington (DC): Smithsonian Institution.

Petrography of Additional Aru Sherds

Petrographic Report WRD-221 (25 Oct. 2002)

Four additional sherds from the Aru Islands were passed to me by Matthew Spriggs in Noumea in August (2002). With reference to my previous report on 25 Aru sherds (*Petro Rpt WRD-212*), two of the additional sherds appear to be indigenous Aru wares, whereas the other two contain typical exotic temper imbedded in clay paste rich in glass shards of volcanic ash.

Indigenous Sherds

The two indigenous sherds are 77-1 from Papakulah (thin body sherd with whitened interior surface and pale gray exterior surface with protruding calcareous grains), and 77-2 from Jurlay (thin body sherd with blackened exterior surface and brownish interior surface with scattered visible calcareous grains). Sherd 77-1 contains predominantly calcareous temper (Type A temper of Table 212-1), although quartz silt is present in the clay paste. Sherd 77-2 contains hybrid quartz-calcareous temper, with calcareous grains more abundant than quartz (Type B temper of Table 212-1). Both these sherds appear to fit within the spectrum of indigenous Aru wares.

Exotic Sherds

The two exotic sherds, both with red slips that were possibly wiped before firing, are 77-3 from Karkur (rim sherd containing flashing dark ferromagnesian temper grains visible megascopically), and 77-4 from Wangil Midden (rim sherd with hard glossy slip possibly polished after firing). In both (as is the case for the typical exotic Aru sherds examined previously), abundant vitroclastic glass shards of volcanic ash are imbedded in the clay pastes. The frequency counts of temper grain types (Table 221-1) fit within the spectrum of typical Aru exotic wares (Table 212-2).

Summary

Examination of the four additional Aru sherds confirms the results of my previous study of Aru tempers, and shows that both indigenous and exotic Aru wares are consistently of the same types.

Table 221-1: frequency percentages of grain types in two exotic Aru sherds from Karkur (77-3) and Wangil Midden (77-4) based on areal counts of n grains in thin section; 'previous mean' (Table 212-1) refers to mean composition of eight sherds examined previously (Petro Rpt WRD-212); 'new mean' refers to mean composition of the ten sherds counted to date (Petro Rpt WRD-212 + Petro Rpt WRD-221)

SHERD fi	77-3 (n=222)	77-4 (n=211)	PREVIOUS MEAN [N=8]	NEW MEAN [N=10]
GRAIN TYPE				
qtz	tr	tr	tr	tr
plg	42	39	36±4	37±4
cpx	6	9	6±2	6±2
opa	8	10	10±6	10±5
gls	43	40	45±3	44±3
mic	1	2	3±2	3±2

Evaluation of Aru-Banda Temper and Paste Match

Petrographic Report WRD-238 (15 June 2004)

Initial petrographic study of Aru sherds (*Petro Rpt WRD-212* of 23 April 2003) indicated the presence of an indigenous quartz-calcite temper type (derived from the Aru Islands) in two-thirds of the sherds examined in thin section, but also of an exotic volcanic sand temper type (derived from elsewhere) in the other one-third of the sherds examined. The exotic sherds contain tiny vitroclastic shards of volcanic glass (eruptive ash) imbedded in the clay pastes. This distinctive paste constituent had not previously been detected in any other Oceanian sherd suites. Further study of an additional four Aru sherds revealed the same two types of temper and paste in two sherds each (*Petro Rpt WRD-221* of 25 Oct. 2003).

A search for the origin of the exotic Aru sherds led to examination of five sherds from Halmahera (*Petro Rpt WRD-220* of 17 July 2003 as revised 15 June 2004). One of the Halmahera sherds, from Pulau Kumo, proved to contain vitroclastic ash in its paste. Moreover, the Pulau Kumo temper, although much finer grained than the tempers in exotic Aru sherds, has a mineralogical composition closely comparable to the latter. These fortuitous similarities suggested the hypothesis that the exotic Aru sherds may have come from somewhere in northern Halmahera.

Subsequently, however, examination of sherds from Banda (*Petro Rpt WRD-237* of 15 June 2004) indicates that selected Banda tempers (n=4) are visually identical texturally and statistically indistinguishable mineralogically from tempers in the exotic Aru sherds. Pastes in the Banda sherds also contain vitroclastic glass shards of volcanic ash that are indistinguishable from those in the pastes of exotic Aru sherds.

The combined petrographic match of temper and paste between indigenous Banda sherds and exotic Aru sherds leaves no reasonable doubt that the exotic Aru sherds derive from wares brought to Aru from Banda, and not from Halmahera. The suggestive similarities between Aru sherds and the Pulau Kumo sherd from Halmahera carry little or no weight in the face of the conclusive and combined temper-paste matches between Aru and Banda sherds.

The search for the origin of the exotic Aru sherds, including erroneous consideration of Halmahera as a possibility for a year or so, is an apt reminder that only exact temper matches constitute robust evidence for ceramic transfer from one island to another.

Comparison of Aru and Halmahera Sherds

Petrographic Report WRD-220 (17 July 2002)[Revised 15 June 2004]

In an effort to trace the possible origin of exotic Aru sherds (*Petro Rpt WRD-212)*, Sue O'Connor sent me five sherds (numbered by me as 74-1 thru 74-5) collected by Peter Bellwood on Halmahera and neighboring islets:

74-1 & 74-2: Makian Island west of Halmahera
74-3: Vattandi on Kayoa Island west of Halmahera
74-4: Pulau Kumo near Tobele on north Halmahera
74-5: Umera Island (?) near Halmahera

I cannot locate either Kayoa or Umera on any maps available to me, but Makian is an active volcano (six historic eruptions, AD 1646–1890) of the Quaternary Halmahera volcanic arc. I presume that Pulau Kumo and Tobele are on the north arm of Halmahera where the Halmahera arc (several active volcanoes including major edifices at Dukono, Ibu, Gamkonora from north to south) extends to the north of the offshore volcanic islands lying west of Halmahera (including Ternate, Tidore, Makian from north to south).

Tempers in the sherds from the offshore islands (74-1, 2, 3, 5) are volcanic sands, well sorted and variably abraded, of probable beach origin. Temper is more abundant relative to clay paste than in the exotic Aru sherds, and there are no particles of volcanic ash (glass shards) imbedded in the pastes. Major grain types in each are the following (in approximate decreasing order of abundance, but quantitative petrography has not yet been attempted in the absence of apparent need to generate detailed data): plagioclase feldspar, volcanic rock fragments (varied internal textures), clinopyroxene, opaques, hornblende. The sherds from the islands near Halmahera afford no attractive grounds for a match with the exotic Aru sherds.

The sherd (74-4) from Pulau Kumo near Tobele on north Halmahera is much more promising, not an identical match but with close genetic affinities. One intriguing similarity is the presence of the same kind of glass shards (volcanic ash) imbedded in the clay paste. As this constituent has not been observed in ~2000 Pacific island sherds, except for the exotic Aru sherds and the Pulau Kumo sherd, its presence is compatible with an origin for the exotic Aru sherds somewhere near Tobele on Halmahera. Additional data may show that many Indonesian ceramic suites (none examined personally to date) have analogous 'ash-in-paste' character, in which case the occurrence of glass shards in the pastes of the exotic Aru and the indigenous Pulau Kumo sherds may not alone be definitive of a close relationship.

The temper in the Pulau Kumo sherd is a distinctly finer grained sand than the tempers in the exotic Aru sherds, but a frequency count of 600 temper grains in the Pulau Kumo sherd shows that its mineralogical composition is statistically indistinguishable from the mean composition of the tempers in the exotic Aru sherds (Table 220-1). The standard deviation of the mean for each of five salient mineralogical constituents in eight Aru sherds overlaps with the standard deviation of the inherent counting error for the same constituents in the Pulau Kumo sherd. This congruence in composition, despite the difference in the coarseness of the tempers, when coupled with the unusual 'ash-in-paste' character of the both the exotic Aru sherds and the Pulau Kumo sherd, suggests the strong possibility that the exotic Aru wares were derived from Halmahera. Especially notable is the similarity of the volcanic rock fragments, which in both cases are dominantly silicic volcanic glass, in part pumiceous (microvesicular) with ragged margins suggestive of volcanic tephra and with internal textures (arrangement of glass and vesicles) that are visually indistinguishable.

Despite the similarities, however, between the Pulau Kumo sherd and exotic Aru sherds, additional work (in 2004) has shown that clay pastes in sherds from the volcanic island of Banda in the Banda Sea also contain vitroclastic ash visually indistinguishable from the ash in exotic Aru sherds. Moreover, the textures of indigenous Banda tempers and exotic Aru tempers are closely comparable (unlike the much finer grained temper sand in the Pulau Kumo sherd), and the mineralogical composition of the Banda temper is an even closer match for the temper in exotic Aru sherds than the Pulau Kumo temper. For these reasons, origin of the exotic Aru sherds on Banda, rather than Halmahera, seems the more robust inference.

Table 220-1: comparative compositions (grain frequency percentages) of temper sands in Pulau Kumo sherd from Halmahera and exotic Aru sherds (N=8; data from *Petro Rpt WRD-212*) where VRF=volcanic rock fragments

GRAIN TYPE	PULAU KUMO SHERD (74-4) (± COUNTING ERROR, CE[1])	EXOTIC ARU SHERDS (± STANDARD DEVIATION SD[2])
plagioclase feldspar	40±2	36±4
clinopyroxene	6±1	6±2
opaque iron oxides	8±1	10±6
microlitic VRF	4±1	3±2
vitric (glassy) VRF	43±2	45±2

1 $CE = [p(100-p)/n]^{1/2}$ where p is observed percentage and n is total grain count (n=600)

2 SD is standard deviation of the mean for eight frequency counts (*Petro Rpt WRD-212*)

Petrography of Sand Tempers in Sherds From Banda Naira and Ay in the Banda Islands of Eastern Indonesia

Petrographic Report WRD-237 (15 June 2004)

Ten sherds from the Banda Islands sent by Peter Lape were examined petrographically in thin section with two aims in mind: (1) to establish the nature of Banda temper sands; and (2) to test whether exotic sherds in the Aru Islands to the east were possibly derived from Banda rather than Halmahera (as had previously been thought, but only provisionally without a robust temper match). Table 237-1 indicates the provenience of the Banda sherds examined in thin section.

Temper Overview

A contemporary sherd (#OUW) from Ouw (Ouh) village on Saparua in the Lease Islands well north of Banda contains as temper a calcareous sand composed of globular foraminiferal tests that are hollow, and the vacuoles within the temper grains have in many cases been enlarged by leaching that has removed the thin calcareous walls of the tests (whether partial dissolution occurred during firing or later is impossible for me to determine). The temper is indistinguishable from the tempering materials from Ouw provided previously by Matthew Spriggs (*Petro Rpt WRD-223*): raw and cleaned modern tempering sand, a modern sherd, and a prehistoric sherd. As no additional provenance information can be gleaned from the Ouw sherd, its temper is not discussed further here.

Table 237-1: Provenance of Banda sherds examined in thin section

ISLAND	THIN SECTION LABEL	SHERD LABEL (AND DEPTH), LOCALE ON ISLAND
Ay	PAS	surface sherd near clay sources
	PA-1	PA-1-1 (100–110 cm), coast near south end
	PA-2A	PA-2-2 (100–125 cm), north coast
	PA-2B	PA-2-2 (125–150 cm), north coast
	PA-9	PA-9-1 (0–50 cm), near northeast tip
Banda Naira	BN-1	BN-1-4 (170–180 cm), north coast
	BN-4A	BN-4-1 (190–200 cm), south coast
	BN-4B	BN-4-2 (220–230 cm), south coast
	BN-4C	BN-4-2 (235–250 cm), south coast
Saparua	OUW	Ouw village, Saparua (Lease Islands)

Sherd #PA-1 from the calcareous islet of Ay is riddled with voluminous vacuoles that probably represent sites originally occupied by calcareous grains removed by leaching after burial (a common phenomenon in Oceanian sherd suites). The vacuoles are clearly visible megascopically as multiple closely spaced pits on the sherd surface. Tiny angular grains of plagioclase feldspar mineral grains, volcanic lithic fragments, opaque iron oxide grains, and clinopyroxene mineral grains are also present (in that approximate order of relative abundance). The terrigenous detritus may be natural temper imbedded within the clay body, perhaps as pyroclastic debris, but the comparable size of the terrigenous grains to the vacuoles left by removal of calcareous grains suggests instead that both calcareous and terrigenous detritus are components of a fine coastal sand added manually as temper to a clay body lacking aplastic impurities. The fine grain size and angular nature of the terrigenous debris leaves open the possibility that it was reworked from pyroclastic deposits on Ay, and mixed with calcareous detritus on local beaches. In either case, the paucity of terrigenous grains and the fine grain size of the temper make detailed analysis unrewarding, and the temper is not discussed further here (generically, however, it is similar to other pyroxene-bearing but hornblende-free temper sands in sherds from Ay and Banda Naira).

Most (n=6) of the other sherds from both Banda Naira (n=3) and Ay (n=3) contain as temper related pyroxene-bearing (but hornblende-free) feldspathic sands in which the dominant volcanic lithic fragments are composed of pumiceous felsic glass. This temper type is interpreted as indigenous to Banda, and variants are indistinguishable, texturally and compositionally, from the tempers in exotic sherds from Aru and Gorom.

Two sherds, one each from Ay and Banda Naira, contain hornblende-bearing volcanic temper sands that are both mineralogically and texturally unlike the pyroxene-bearing indigenous tempers, and may document ceramic transfer of exotic wares to Banda from some other volcanic island (Manuk to the south along the Banda chain being the closest geographically).

Indigenous Temper Type

The most abundant temper type in the Banda sherds is pyroxene-bearing feldspathic sand (Table 237-2) imbedded in clay pastes that contain a significant component of volcanic ash in the form of curvilinear and branching vitroclastic shards of felsic volcanic glass. Most abundant among the sand grains of the tempers are pumiceous glassy volcanic lithic fragments probably derived from volcanic source rocks closely related petrologically to the pyroclastic debris within the clay pastes. The tempers are appropriate in mineralogical composition for derivation from the volcanic assemblage of Banda, and the volcanic ash in the clay pastes was presumably derived from pyroclastic blankets that mantle islands of Banda. Much of the volcanic sand used for temper may well have been reworked from coarse ash deposits, but the moderately sorted and abraded (subangular to subrounded) character of the temper sands suggests that they were collected from stream deposits.

The indigenous Banda tempers in two sherds excavated from Ay (Table 237-2) are more feldspathic than the others, but contain the same grain types in different proportions and probably also derive from a volcanic island of Banda. Although they are not included in the calculation of the mean Banda temper composition (Table 237-3), they appear to represent but an end member of a gradational temper spectrum without sharp breaks. There seems little likelihood that volcanic aggregates of medium to coarse sand size occur on the calcareous islet of Ay, and all three Ay sherds containing the Banda temper type are inferred to reflect transport of finished wares (or temper sands) from a Banda volcanic island to Ay.

The four, less feldspathic indigenous Banda tempers, are texturally and compositionally indistinguishable from tempers in exotic sherds from Giri Gajah and Ondor on Gorom and from Wangil Midden and Karkur in the Aru Islands (Table 237-3). The exotic Aru-Gorom sherds also contain vitroclastic volcanic ash imbedded in their clay pastes. With both paste and temper so similar, prehistoric ceramic transfer from Banda to Gorom and Aru seems a robust conclusion to reach. Although one sherd from a Halmahera ceramic assemblage studied for comparative purposes contains volcanic ash in its paste and a temper sand compositionally similar to the exotic tempers in Aru-Gorom sherds (*Petro Rpt WRD-220*), the texture of the temper sand in the Halmahera sherd is quite different. By contrast, the temper match between indigenous Banda and exotic Aru-Gorom sherds seems exact and conclusive. No temper match between indigenous and exotic sherds anywhere in Pacific Oceania is any more robust.

Exotic Temper Type

The hornblende-bearing temper sands (Table 237-4) are placer aggregates that could not have been derived from concentration of ferromagnesian minerals from detritus like the feldspathic indigenous sands because the latter lack any hornblende mineral grains at all. One of the exotic temper sands (BN-4C) is a well sorted subrounded aggregate, whereas the other (PA-9) is only

Table 237-2: frequency percentages of grain types in the indigenous pyroxene-bearing tempers of Banda sherds based on counts of *n* sand grains in thin section (especially feldspathic tempers of PA-2A/PA-2B not included in mean composition of Table 237-3)

GRAIN TYPE	BN-1 (*n*=235)	BN-4A (*n*=180)	BN-4B (*n*=185)	PAS (*n*=200)	PA-2A (*n*=105)	PA-2B (*n*=445)
quartz	tr	tr	tr	1	0	0
plagioclase	33	29	43	33	57	48
clinopyroxene	2	4	5	6	10	6
opaque Fe oxide	5	9	7	8	1	2
vitric (glassy) VRF	59	56	42	51	29	40
microlitic VRF	1	2	3	1	3	4

Table 237-3: comparative compositions of selected indigenous Banda tempers (Table 237-2) and of exotic tempers in sherds from Aru (*Petro Rpts WRD-212, 221*) and Gorom (*Petro Rpt WRD-232*) based on average percentages for *N* thin sections (± is SD)

GRAIN TYPE	BANDA (*N*=4)	GOROM (*N*=7)	ARU (*N*=10)
Quartz mineral grains	tr	tr	tr
Plagioclase mineral grains	35±5	34±6	37±4
Clinopyroxene mineral grains	4±1	4±1	6±2
Opaque iron oxide grains	7±2	10±4	10±5
Vitric volcanic lithic fragments	52±6	50±3	44±3
Microlitic volcanic lithic fragments	2±1	2±1	3±2

Table 237-4: frequency percentages of grain types in the exotic hornblende-bearing tempers of Banda sherds based on counts of 400 sand grains in each thin section

GRAIN TYPE	BN-4C	PA-9	AVERAGE
plagioclase feldspar	47	42	45
clinopyroxene	7	11	9
hornblende	29	37	33
opaque Fe oxides	16	2	9
volcanic lithics	1	8	4

moderately sorted and subangular, but both are probably beach sands, as judged both from their placer character and from the presence in both sherds of vacuoles that appear to represent sites where calcareous grains of hybrid beach sand have been leached from the sherds by post-depositional dissolution (but no calcareous grains remain). No discernible volcanic ash is present in the clay paste of either sherd, and this is an additional mark of distinction from the sherds interpreted as indigenous to Banda.

The origin of the sherds containing exotic hornblende-bearing tempers is indeterminate with present information, but their mineralogy is so different from the tempers thought to be indigenous to Banda that derivation from some other island is inferred. A source along the Banda chain of volcanic islands is the most attractive postulate geographically, but the Banda arc erupts mostly pyroxene andesite and the abundant hornblende in the exotic temper is accordingly anomalous. Conceivably, the sherds may reflect ceramic transfer to Banda from much farther afield. Search should be made for the nearest volcano erupting hornblende andesite, but my knowledge of the comparative volcanology of Indonesia is inadequate to that task and published literature available to me is not enlightening on that point.

Summary of Temper Relations

A majority of the Banda sherds contain plagioclase-rich and pyroxene-bearing temper sands (hornblende-free) that are inferred to be indigenous to Banda, and are imbedded in clay pastes that contain a significant component of vitroclastic volcanic ash presumably derived from ash blankets that mantle Banda. In thin section, the indigenous sherds are visually indistinguishable from exotic sherds recovered previously on Gorom and Aru, and comparison of the texture and mineralogical composition of the indigenous Banda temper type with tempers in the exotic Gorom-Aru sherds shows the three temper suites to be statistically indistinguishable. Ceramic transfer from Banda to both Gorom and Aru accordingly seems a robust inference. Subordinate Banda sherds containing hornblende-rich placer tempers are unlikely to derive from Banda, but apparently reflect ceramic transfer to Banda from elsewhere, either another volcanic island along the Banda chain or farther afield within Indonesia.

7

Liang Nabulei Lisa: A Late Pleistocene and Holocene Sequence from the Aru Islands

Sue O'Connor[1], Ken Aplin[2], Juliette Pasveer[1] and Geoff Hope[1]

1. Department of Archaeology and Natural History, Research School of Pacific and Asian Studies, The Australian National University, Canberra, ACT, Australia
2. Sustainable Ecosystems, CSIRO, GPO Box 284, Canberra, ACT 2601, Australia

Introduction

The excavation at Liang Nabulei Lisa began on 24 November 1997, approximately one year after the Liang Lemdubu excavation was carried out (see Chapter 4, this volume). The site was selected for excavation as it was located close to a stream-fed *sungai*, had abundant cultural material on the surface and appeared to have some depth of deposit. The Lemdubu excavation had recovered a Pleistocene sequence dating from ca. 27,000 years ago through to the historic period, but the early to mid-Holocene were not represented. It was hoped that Nabulei Lisa would complement the Lemdubu sequence by providing a full Holocene sequence.

Liang Nabulei Lisa is only about 50m inland from the landward end of the southern arm of Sungai Dosi, a tributary of the western end of Sungai Manumbai (Fig. 7.1). It lies near the crest of a low but steep limestone ridge on the eastern side of the tidal *sungai*, and at about 30m altitude. The *sungai* is fringed by mangroves and *Barringtonia* on muds, while the rocky slopes around the cave support a low and not very dense forest in which figs, *Eugenia*, *Litsea* legumes, and *Fagraea* are common, with many palms and large climbers evident. A more varied rainforest occupies the lower areas between ridges although this has been disturbed by cutting and shifting cultivation. Like Lemdubu, Nabulei Lisa is a tunnel cave left stranded near the crest of a ridge, with a collapsed section on the ridge that results in it having two entrances: one northwest and one southeast facing (Figs 7.2–7.4). The cave is capacious and very dry but only a restricted area close to the northwest facing entrance would be useful for habitation. The southeast entrance rises quite steeply to a height of about eight metres above the cave floor, is extremely rocky, and is partially blocked by large boulders of roof-fall and flowstone/stalagmite formations. Extensive stalactite and stalagmite formations occur in the central and southern areas of the cave (Figs 7.2–7.4). A 3–5m wide potential living floor of soft cave earth, interrupted by scattered stalagmite bases, extends along the northeastern wall for about 18m (Fig. 7.2). This surface has dense patches of marine shell scattered about.

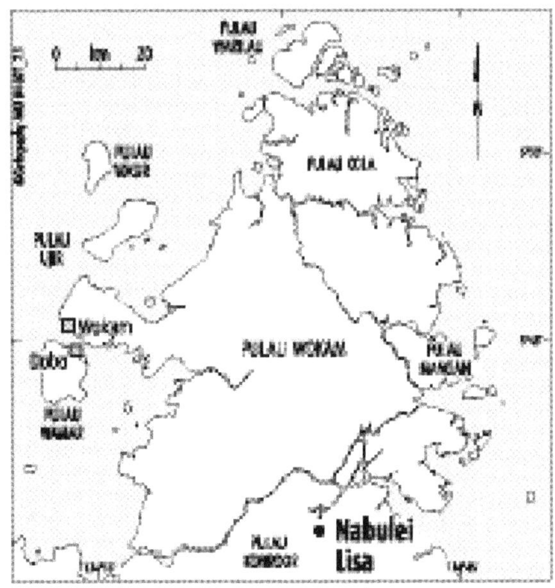

Figure 7.1 Liang Nabulei Lisa: location of the site

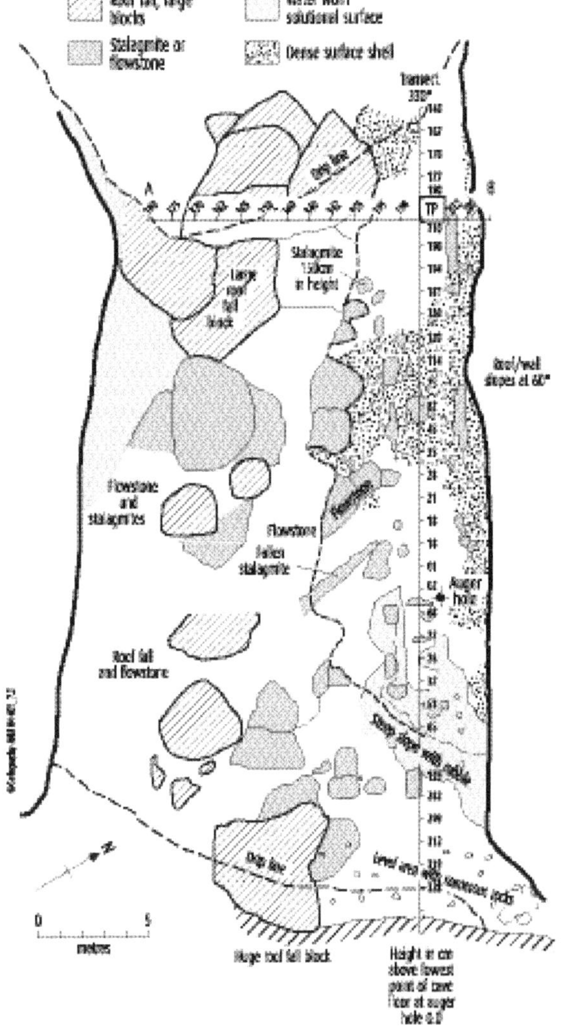

Figure 7.2 Liang Nabulei Lisa: plan of cave showing position of Test Pit A, auger hole, concentrations of cultural material and position of cave section A-B

Figue 7.3 Liang Nabulei Lisa: view looking to northwest entrance

Figure 7.4 Liang Nabulei Lisa: view into cave looking to southeast entrance

Excavation and Stratigraphy

A 1m^2 excavation, Test Pit A, was positioned at the north entrance of the cave approximately two metres inside the dripline (Figs 7.2, 7.5–7.7). The cave walls in this area were stained black from smoke indicating that repeated fires had been lit, and loose ashy sediment containing shell was exposed on the surface.

Figure 7.5 Liang Nabulei Lisa: view of Test Pit A, facing northern wall, showing east section

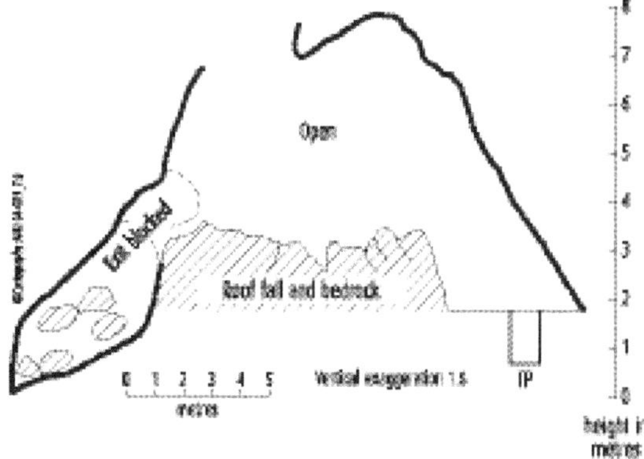

Figure 7.6 Liang Nabulei Lisa: section A–B across northwest entrance of cave through Test Pit A

Cultural material is abundant along the east wall of the shelter (Fig. 7.2). It is possible that it banked up in this area as a result of people deliberately moving sharp shells and bones away from the more centrally positioned domestic living space.

Excavation was undertaken in approximate two centimetres spits or excavation units, although in reality spit depths varied between 1.5 and four centimetres. Excavation followed visible changes in the stratigraphy where such were evident. Spit depths for the southeast corner of Test Pit A are shown in the section diagram (Fig. 7.8), and all other depth readings are given in Appendix 7.1. Each spit was levelled in using a dumpy and staff. Depth levels were recorded for the corners and a central point in the excavation square. Each bucket removed from an excavation unit was weighed and the weight recorded separately. Rocks discarded were recorded and their volumes estimated. All excavated material was wet sieved at the cave to remove larger fragments of limestone/flowstone and was then re-bagged for further sorting. A <2mm mesh was used for wet sieving, ensuring excellent recovery of small bones, lithics, and macrofloral material. Final sorting was not carried out in the field as even after wet sieving the shell in the upper spits was comminuted and friable. Final sorting was undertaken in Dobo where all material was washed until clean in freshwater, dried and sorted.

Little visible change in the sediment with depth was apparent. Four layers have been distinguished on the basis of slight changes in the colour of the sediments. In some cases these coincide with changes in the distribution and/or abundance of cultural material. The layers are shown on the section in Figure 7.8.

Layer 1 consists of the thin surface topsoil and is equivalent to Spit 1. It was composed of a very fine silt with a minor component of sand (10YR 5/2). In places the top sediments were mottled with pockets of loose ash.

Layer 2 is an ash-rich layer comprising Spits 2–4 (10YR 6/1–5/1) (Fig. 7.8). Aside from the ash lenses there was little to distinguish this layer from Layer 1 above or 3 below. Little bone was recorded in these spits and most shell was extremely burnt and friable and fell apart when trowelled. Much of the bone from this layer was burnt.

Layer 3 (10YR 5/2-4/2 Greyish Brown to Dark Greyish Brown) occurs immediately below the ash layer and includes Spits 5–22. The sediment appears to be texturally similar to the topsoil but with significantly less ash. Bone and shell in this layer are well preserved.

south

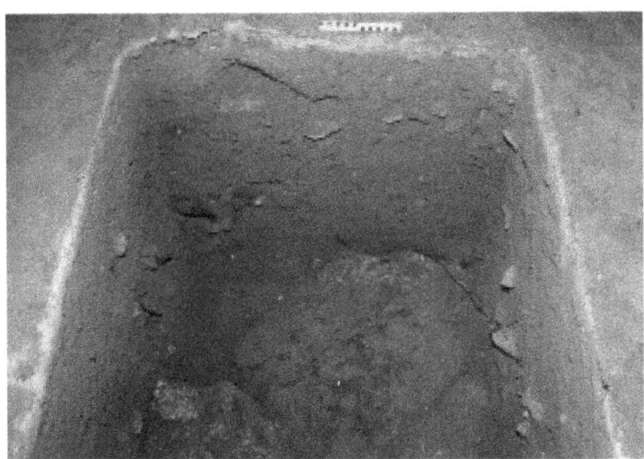

west

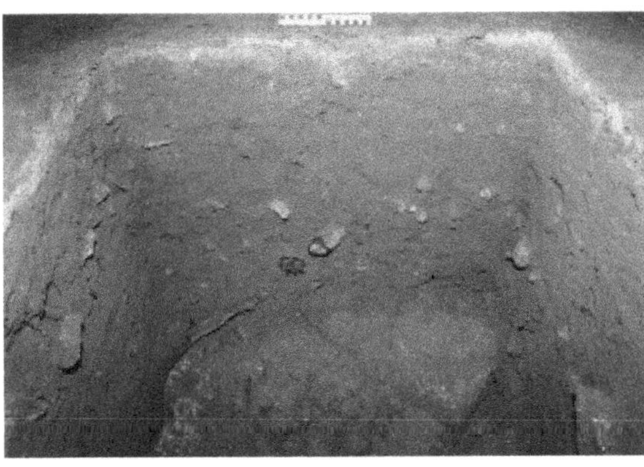

north

Figure 7.7 Liang Nabulei Lisa: south, west, and north sections of the excavation

Layer 4 begins at Spit 23 and continues to the base of the excavation. The sediment in Layer 4 is a richer Dark Greyish Brown (10YR 4/2), and roots and small rocks become more prevalent (Fig. 7.8). There is no obvious change in sediment texture although the sediment was much moister at this depth. Layer 4 coincides with a change in cultural material and this may account for the difference in sediment colour. Shell decreases from over 500g in Spit 20 to less than 20g in Spit 23. Approximately coinciding with the decrease in shell is a massive increase in the quantity of bone recovered.

The excavation was discontinued at a maximum depth of 1.25m (Fig. 7.8). This depth was reached only in the central part of the south face of the pit. Bone was still present but the excavation area was reduced to a crack between rocks and further removals were not possible without enlarging the excavation. Spit 43 was the final spit excavated and both Spit 42 and 43 were very small removals from the restricted area in this part of the square (see Fig. 7.8). Depths of all spits and volumes of removals are provided in Appendix 7.1. The rock underlying the deposit and which forms a floor over most of the square was exposed on the cave surface for some time prior to deposition of sediment, as it has the distinctive pitting which results from water dripping from the roof. Whether it comprised the cave floor or part of a large boulder could not be determined.

Coinciding with the excavation of Test Pit A, an auger probe was carried out at the deepest point in the internal chamber of the cave about 15m in from the excavation (Fig. 7.2). This was done to test the depth of deposit in this area and whether there was any difference in the type or quantity of cultural material in the deeper reaches of the cave. Although the surface is about two meteres lower than the entrance, the depth of deposit, 135cm, is similar. The upper 40cm consisted of grey-orange silts with occasional pieces of shell but no charcoal. Below this is 57cm of brown cave earth above 25cm of pale grey calcareous silt from which a single *Anadara* shell was recovered. The basal 13cm of brown mottled silt had rotted rock fragments and sat on limestone rubble, probably roof-fall. The probe contains no evidence of direct occupation, and the shells detected were probably discards from the living area at the front of the cave. This indicates that the area of dense occupation deposit is much smaller than the liveable area of the cave.

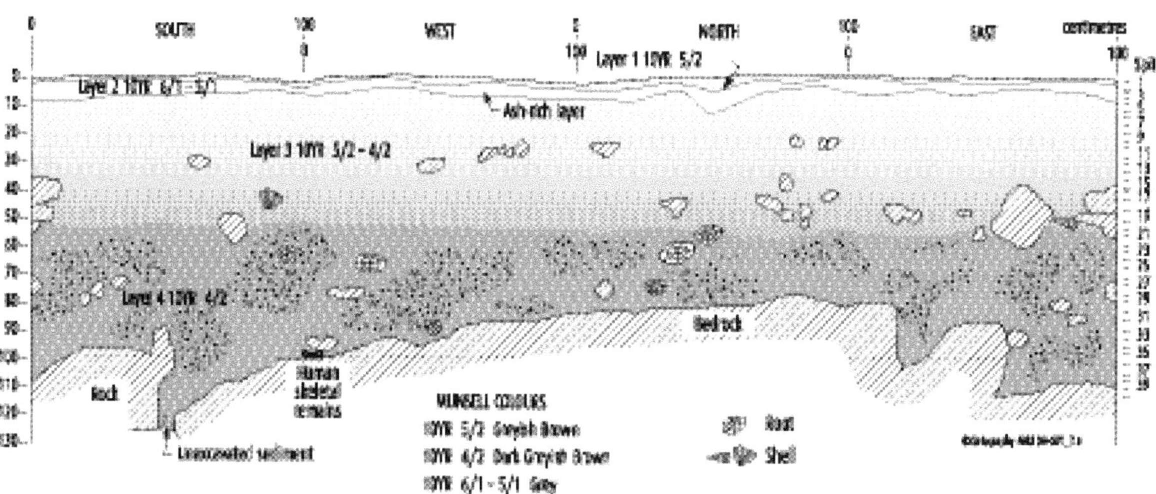

Figure 7.8 Liang Nabulei Lisa: Test Pit A sections with spit depths shown for southeast corner

Dating the Liang Nabulei Lisa Sequence

As at Lemdubu, charcoal was only preserved in the upper part of the deposit (Table 7.1 and 7.2). A variety of materials and experimental techniques have been used to date the Nabulei Lisa sequence.

Sufficient charcoal was available in the upper 10 spits to obtain conventional radiocarbon dates on this material. The charcoal sample from Spit 3 (ANU-10918) was assayed as modern. Spit 5 returned a date of 780±150 BP (ANU-10921), Spit 8 of 260±190 BP (ANU-10920) and Spit 10 of modern (ANU-10919). The dates from Spits 5, 8 and 10 are inverted and possibly indicate some

Table 7.1 Liang Nabulei Lisa: radiocarbon dates.

LAB. CODE	SPIT	DEPTH (CM)	SAMPLE TYPE	δ13C	CONVENTIONAL AGE (YEARS BP, ± 1σ)	CALIBRATED AGE (cal years BP)[1]
ANU-10918	3	10.0	Charcoal	-28.2	Modern	Modern
ANU-10921	5	13.0	Charcoal	-27.3	780±150	512–1045
ANU-10920	8	19.0	Charcoal	-30.1	260±190	0–548
ANU-10919	10	27.5	Charcoal	-28.2	Modern	Modern
OZF249	11	30.5	*Casuarius* eggshell	-13.6	2530±60	2362–2751
ANU-10906	12	33.0	*Terebralia* sp.	-5.2	5900±60	6192–6429
ANU-10905	23	61.0	*Terebralia* sp.	-5.0	6970±160	7167–7754
OZF250	25	68.5	*Casuarius* eggshell	-16.1	9310±80	10,243–10,689
OZF030	26	71.0	*Celtis* sp. seed	-25.4	8420±50	9431–9550
OZD696	26	71.0	*Celtis* sp. seed	-20.4	9320±60	10,279–10,688
AA-32849	26	71.0	*Casuarius* eggshell	-16.0	10,460±75	11,960–12,833
ANU-10907	26	71.0	*Nerita* shell	na	4410±60	4411–4773
OZD697	28	76.0	*Celtis* sp. seed	-18.1	9630±60	10,746–11,172
OZD698	28	76.0	*Hyridella misoolensis* shell	-10.0	9750±60	10,793–11,255
OZD699	31	84.0	*Hyridella misoolensis* shell	-26.9	9870±70	11,164–11,553
OZD700	31	84.0	*Celtis* sp. seed	-27.0	9450±60	10,503–11,068
OZF848	32	86.0	*Casuarius* eggshell	-15.9	10,340±60	11,767–12,782
OZF518	34	93.0	*Casuarius* eggshell	-13.6	13,130±80	14,817–16,292
OZD702	36	99.0	*Celtis* sp. seed	-15.6	9850±60	11,162–11,548
OZF362	41	115.0	*Celtis* sp. seed	-14.9	7140±50	7839–8107

[1] Calibrated ages at maximum – minimum intercepts ± 2σ range, na = not available.

Table 7.2 Liang Nabulei Lisa: weights (g) of cultural material from all spits

CONV. AGE BP	SPIT	STONE ARTEFACTS	POTTERY	BONE	CHARCOAL	*CELTIS* SEEDS	CASSOWARY EGGSHELL	MARINE/ ESTUARINE SHELL	TOTAL WT. (KG) SEDIMENT
	1		10.1	26.5	29.0			130.7	24.5
	2		23.3	0.0	1.4			475.6	26.6
Modern	3		16.9	4.2	2.6			693.7	31.3
	4		12.2	28.9				718.3	29.2
	5		17.0	55.9	1.9			1129.4	33.0
	6		9.0	13.8				1160.3	34.3
	7	8.0	12.2	14.4				528.5	29.1
	8	17.4	14.9	25.7	0.7			773.3	30.7
	9	3.3		17.7			1.0	633.8	31.7
Modern	10	29.3		21.9	0.6			938.1	31.8
2530±60	11			23.4			1.5	906.7	34.5
5900±60	12	8.8		19.5			1.9	874.8	25.2
	13			14.2				629.4	28.3
	14	2.5		25.1			1.0	556.6	27.0
	15			23.0				735.9	33.0
	16	2.3		33.1				741.0	30.9
	17			15.5				312.0	33.4
	18			43.5				685.1	27.4
	19			45.3			1.4	646.9	35.6
	20			42.7				519.8	44.9
	21	2.8		37.7		3.5	0.8	90.4	33.9
	22	22.1		35.6		10.7		60.1	37.8
6970±160	23	15.2		63.1				17.4	34.2
	24	5.2		55.6				19.5	34.8
9310±80	25	9.2		77.9			0.4	26.7	36.8
9320±60	26	1.2		68.8		7.7	0.8	39.8	37.1
	27			54.9			0.9	19.6	31.0
9750±60	28	0.1		140.3		5.0	1.2	14.3	33.5
	29	1.1		93.3		3.2	0.5	17.5	33.3
	30	4.9		153.1		7.4		6.4	52.4
9870±70	31	7.8		157.5		1.2		1.4	36.4
10,340±60	32	33.8		170.0			0.4	3.4	35.2
	33	3.0		211.4				-	19.0
13,130±80	34	12.7		254.3			0.4	0.5	18.5
	35	3.5		265.4				0.4	18.5
	36			188.2		0.1			12.5
	37	0.3		180.3					13.5
	38	0.8		250.4					10.9
	39			128.6					4.6
	40			138.8					4.6
	41			93.1					3.5
	42			74.4					3.4
	43			9.0					3.5

degree of disturbance within the upper 25cm of loose ashy deposit. However, for reasons outlined below disturbance is generally thought to be minimal and localized.

Spit 11 was dated on *Casuarius* eggshell to 2530±60 BP (OZF249) and immediately below this a mangrove gastropod *Terebralia* sp. returned an age of 5900±60 BP (ANU-10906). Details about the use of *Casuarius* eggshell as a dating material are provided in Chapter 13. The result on a *Terebralia* sp. from Spit 23 was 6970±160 BP (ANU-10905), suggesting that the deposit between Spits 23 and 12 accumulated rather rapidly.

Four dates were obtained for Spit 26. The original date on *Nerita* sp. shell returned an age of 4410±60 (ANU-10907). This date was obviously at odds with the dates returned from samples in Spits 11 (OZF249), 12 (ANU-10906), 23 (ANU-10905), and 25 (OZF250) which were significantly older. A *Celtis philippinensis* seed (OZF030) from the same spit was submitted to the ANSTO laboratory. Unfortunately, this sample was given the wrong pretreatment. *Celtis* is predominantly composed of primary aragonite. The sample OZF030 was treated to remove the inorganic component so was effectively destroyed. A small organic fraction remained and this was dated and returned an age of 8420±50 BP. This explains why the $\delta^{13}C$ values for this sample are close to –25 permil rather than the usual –14 permil for the inorganic component. Another *Celtis* sample was processed by ANSTO to replace OZF030. This sample (OZD696) was assayed at 9320±60 BP, which is statistically the same date as the *Casuarius* eggshell sample in Spit 25 (OZF250, 9310±80 BP).

A *Casuarius* eggshell fragment was then dated from Spit 26 (AA-32849). This sample returned a slightly older date of 10,460±75. Two samples were dated from Spit 28 — one freshwater bivalve *Hyridella misoolensis* (OZD698) and a *Celtis* seed (OZD697) — returning ages of 9750±60 and 9630±60 BP respectively. Spit 31 was also dated using a *Hyridella* valve (OZD699) and a *Celtis* seed (OZD700) for comparison, and again the results are in good agreement (9870±70 BP and 9450±60 BP respectively). *Hyridella* is a freshwater mussel and potentially subject to contamination from 'old carbon', however, the dates on these samples are in correct stratigraphic order and in accord with the other dated sample materials from the same and adjacent spits. Although the two valves from Spits 28 and 31 produced a statistically overlapping date, there is no chance that they were derived from the same individual as both were left valves. The major difference in the δ^{13} C values for the *Hyridella* valves has not been explained by the laboratory.

With the exception of the *Nerita* shell sample (ANU-10907) and the *Celtis* seed (OZF030) that is dated on the organic component, the dates give some confidence that Spits 25–31 were deposited between 10,200 and 12,000 cal BP.

The age estimates on the *Casuarius* eggshells from Spits 32 (10,340±60 BP, OZF848) and 34 (13,130±80, OZF518) indicate these spits were deposited in the terminal Pleistocene. These results are obviously at odds with the much younger results on the *Celtis* seed samples from Spit 36 (OZD702) of 9850±60 BP, or Spit 41 (OZF362) of 7150±50 BP.

Research by Wang et al. (1997:339) suggests that *Celtis* derive atmospheric CO^2 during a single growing season and provided that no diagenesis occurs subsequently, they should make a highly reliable dating material. The results of Wang et al.'s study indicate that diagenesis can be easily detected by XRD analysis. Unfortunately, the Aru *Celtis* seeds were not subjected to XRD analysis prior to dating. Although the small literature on *Celtis* as a dating material suggests that individual samples from selected environments when tested showed no evidence of diagensis, recent XRD analyses on the species *Celtis philippinensis* from archaeological contexts in the Kimberley region of northern Australia, have demonstrated significant replacement of aragonite with carbonate. For this reason, and for others to do with changes in the faunal composition in the lower part of the sequence (discussed in detail below), the Pleistocene dates below Spit 32 are thought to better estimate the true age of the deposit than the early Holocene ages obtained on the *Celtis* seeds.

In summary, the lower part of Layer 4, from Spits 41–32 is thought to have accumulated in the terminal Pleistocene between 16,200 and 12,000 cal BP. Spits 31–25 built up fairly rapidly between 12,000 and 10,200 cal BP. The dates would suggest slow deposition or at least minimal accumulation of deposit between Spits 25 and 23, followed again by rapid deposition of sediment and shell in Spits 23–12, probably following the establishment of estuarine conditions between 7700 and 6100 cal BP. There is scant evidence for use of this area of the Nabulei Lisa cave from 6000 cal BP until approximately a thousand years before present, bracketed by the dates between Spits 10 and 3.

The Liang Nabulei Lisa Cultural Sequence

During excavation and on-site sorting it was obvious that the material in the upper four spits was heavily burnt. Marine/estuarine shellfish was concentrated between Spit 20 to the surface. Vertebrate faunal material was present in all levels but was much less abundant than at Lemdubu, especially in the upper part of the sequence. Introduced species such as deer, pig and dog were found only in the upper spits. The vertebrate fauna in Nabulei Lisa show changes in species composition through time that document environmental changes in the vicinity of the site. Stone artefacts occurred below Spit 6 but were fewer in number and even less diverse than at Lemdubu. Pottery was found on the surface and down to Spit 8. Only the surface pottery was painted but this may be due to poor preservation of paints in buried contexts. Aside from the robust seeds of *Celtis philippinensis*, no plant material was preserved, so we have no indication of the nature of plant foods or their contribution to the diet of the Nabulei Lisa occupants. Fragments of human skeletal material representing at least three individuals were found in Layer 4 (Spits 23 to 41) and are discussed in detail in the following chapter.

Weights per spit for each class of cultural materials are presented in Table 7.2. As there was significant variation in the quantity of sediment removed in different spits (e.g. lower excavated spits were very small removals between rocks), the weights of cultural materials have been adjusted to compensate for differences in the amount of sediment removed in Table 7.3.

Organic Remains

Marine/estuarine and freshwater molluscs

All shellfish identifications were carried out at Puslit Arkenas in Jakarta and only weight of shellfish by species was obtained. Examples of different shell types were returned to Australia and identifications were made using the ANH comparative collection; these specimens were then returned to Jakarta. Species represented include the gastropods *Terebralia palustris* and unidentified members of the family Neritidae, and the bivalves *Geloina coaxans* and *Anadara* sp. (see Table 7.4). A few individuals of freshwater species such as the mussel *Hyridella misoolensis* were recovered in Spits 28 and 31. With the exception of the freshwater species all shellfish in the deposit at Nabulei Lisa could probably be obtained from the *sungai* adjacent to the site today. Live specimens of *Geloina coaxans* and *Terebralia palustris* were collected from the *sungai* to the east of the site at the time of the excavation.

Marine/estuarine molluscs occur down to Spit 31, but less than two grams are found below Spit 29. These taxa are most abundant between Spit 20 and the surface. Beneath Spit 20 they decrease dramatically, from 500g in Spit 20 to less than 100g of total shell in Spit 21 (Table 7.4, Fig. 7.9a). This decrease in quantity of shell with depth is unlikely to be due to preservation. The date of 7,060±140 BP was obtained from Spit 23 on a *Terebralia palustris* shell. If a marine reservoir correction of 450 years is applied, it suggests a date for Spit 23 of ca. 6600 BP. This would suggest that the change from freshwater to estuarine/tidal conditions occurred around Spit 20/21 (Fig.

Table 7.3 Liang Nabulei Lisa: distribution and weights (g) of cultural material through the sequence, adjusted for differences in the weight (kg) of sediment per spit

CONV. AGE BP	SPIT	STONE ARTEFACTS	POTTERY	BONE	CHARCOAL	CELTIS SEEDS	CASSOWARY EGGSHELL	MARINE/ ESTUARINE SHELL	TOTAL WT. OF EXCAVATED DEPOSIT
	1		56.6	21.6	62.1			279.5	24.5
	2		0.0	45.9	2.7			936.9	26.6
Modern	3		7.1	28.4	4.4			1161.3	31.3
	4		51.8	21.9				1289.0	29.2
	5		88.8	27.1	3.1			1793.4	33.0
	6		21.0	13.8				1772.7	34.3
	7	14.4	25.9	21.9				951.7	29.1
	8	29.7	4.4	25.5	1.2			1319.8	30.7
	9	5.5		29.2			1.7	1047.7	31.7
Modern	10	48.3		36.0	1.0			1545.8	31.8
2530±60	11			35.5			2.2	1377.1	34.5
5900±60	12	18.3		40.6			4.0	1819.0	25.2
	13			26.4				1165.4	28.3
	14	4.9		48.8			1.9	1080.3	27.0
	15			36.5				1168.5	33.0
	16	3.9		56.2				1256.6	30.9
	17			24.2				489.5	33.4
	18			83.2				1310.2	27.4
	19			66.7			2.1	952.2	35.6
	20			49.9				606.6	44.9
	21	4.3		58.2		5.3	1.2	139.7	33.9
	22	30.6		49.3			14.9	83.3	37.8
6970±160	23	23.3		96.7				26.7	34.2
	24	7.8		83.7				29.4	34.8
9310±80	25	13.1		110.9			0.6	38.0	36.8
9320±60	26	1.7		97.2		10.9	1.1	56.2	37.1
	27			92.7			1.5	33.1	31.0
9750±60	28	0.1		219.5		7.8	1.9	22.4	33.5
	29	1.7		146.7		5.0	0.8	27.5	33.3
	30	4.9		153.1		7.4		6.4	52.4
9870±70	31	11.2		226.8		1.7		2.0	36.4
10,340±60	32	50.3		253.1			0.6	5.1	35.2
	33	8.1		583.1					19.0
13,130±80	34	36.0		720.2			1.2	1.4	18.5
	35	9.9		751.8				1.1	18.5
	36			788.9		0.5			12.5
	37	1.2		699.8					13.5
	38	3.9		1203.6					10.9
	39			1464.6					4.6
	40			1580.2					4.6
	41			1393.4					3.5
	42			1146.2					3.4
	43			134.3					3.5

Table 7.4 Liang Nabulei Lisa: marine and estuarine shellfish weights by spit (g); 1.17g of *Hyridella misoolensis* (= 1 L valve from Spit 28) and 0.86g (= 1 L valve from Spit 31)

DATE	SPIT	*ANADARA* SP.	*GELOINA COAXANS*	*TEREBRALIA PALUSTRIS*	*NERITA* SP.	UNIDENTIFIED	TOTAL SHELL
	1	13.0	10.9	39.3	3.0	64.5	130.7
	2	26.5	51.1	261.9	13.2	122.9	475.6
Modern	3	37.0	181.1	319.2	15.7	140.7	693.7
	4	33.9	216.1	344.4	10.1	113.8	718.3
	5	49.8	603.8	420.7	33.4	21.7	1129.4
	6	49.4	571.2	492.8	31.6	15.3	1160.3
	7	19.6	153.9	197.7	14.9	142.4	528.5
	8	13.1	375.9	353.3	21.9	9.1	773.3
	9	3.3	169.9	321.7	34.4	104.5	633.8
Modern	10	3.6	178.9	383.4	67.2	305.0	938.1
2530±60	11		238.5	445.5	90.0	132.7	906.7
5900±60	12	10.0	182.0	559.0	85.5	38.3	874.8
	13	11.3	123.7	310.0	76.6	107.8	629.4
	14		72.7	314.6	73.1	96.2	556.6
	15	3.0	186.1	404.0	122.6	20.2	735.9
	16	1.4	150.9	427.9	126.1	34.7	741.0
	17		47.8	168.9	57.3	38.0	312.0
	18	14.0	104.6	429.8	97.3	39.4	685.1
	19		86.0	403.1	116.2	41.6	646.9
	20		121.0	283.4	93.6	21.8	519.8
	21		41.7	30.8	11.0	6.9	90.4
	22		28.3	16.5	10.9	4.4	60.1
6970±160	23		7.7	3.4	0.7	5.6	17.4
	24		9.1	5.4	3.3	1.7	19.5
9310±80	25		8.9	10.4	2.4	5.0	26.7
9320±60	26		16.0	18.4		5.4	39.8
	27		9.5	3.4	0.2	6.5	19.6
9750±60	28		8.1	1.0	0.6	4.6	14.3
	29		10.7	4.2		2.6	17.5
	30					6.4	6.4
9870±70	31		1.2				1.2
10,340±60	32					3.3	3.3
	33						
13,130±80	34					0.5	0.5
	35					0.4	0.4

7.9a). The gastropod *Terebralia palustris* dominates the shell assemblage between Spit 20 and the surface (Fig. 7.9b). *Terebralia* are mangrove-dwelling and their dominance between Spits 20 to 9 indicates that mangroves rapidly colonized the *sungai* once tidal conditions established, and then persisted throughout the Holocene. *Geloina coaxans* are filter-feeding bivalves found in sediments on the fringes of mangroves; this taxon is also abundant in the above upper part of the sequence. The small fragment of *Geloina* in Spit 31 may have been brought to the site from some distance away or may result from minor disturbance and vertical movement. The bivalve *Anadara* sp., whose habitat includes sand/mud flats, was recovered chiefly between Spit 8 and the surface (Table 7.4, Fig. 7.9b). This species may have colonized the *sungai* only after estuarine conditions stabilized and some infilling and siltation took place. The Neritidae occupy diverse habitats (including marine, brackish and freshwater); without species identifications, it is not possible to extract environmental information from their distribution. However, the fact that their distribution tracks that of *Terebralia* and *Geloina* so closely suggests that they are probably marine/estuarine species.

No marine/estuarine shellfish were positively identified below Spit 31, and the unidentified shell at this depth is probably from freshwater species. Two fragments of *Hyridella misoolensis* were identified in Spit 28 (1.17g) and three fragments in Spit 31 (0.86g); in each case the fragments were used to date these spits. *Hyridella misoolensis* is a bottom-dwelling, filter-feeding bivalve. It occurs in still or running water and can be found in seasonally still lakes or rivers with a firm silty bottom (Walker, nd).

A single individual *Terebra subulata* — a marine gastropod found on open sandy substrates — was recovered from Spit 28. It has a circular hole drilled opposite the opercular opening and is likely to be an ornamental addition to the assemblage rather than food refuse (Fig. 7.10). It is even possible that it is associated with the secondary burial of the child found between Spits 29 and 35 (see Chapter 8, this volume).

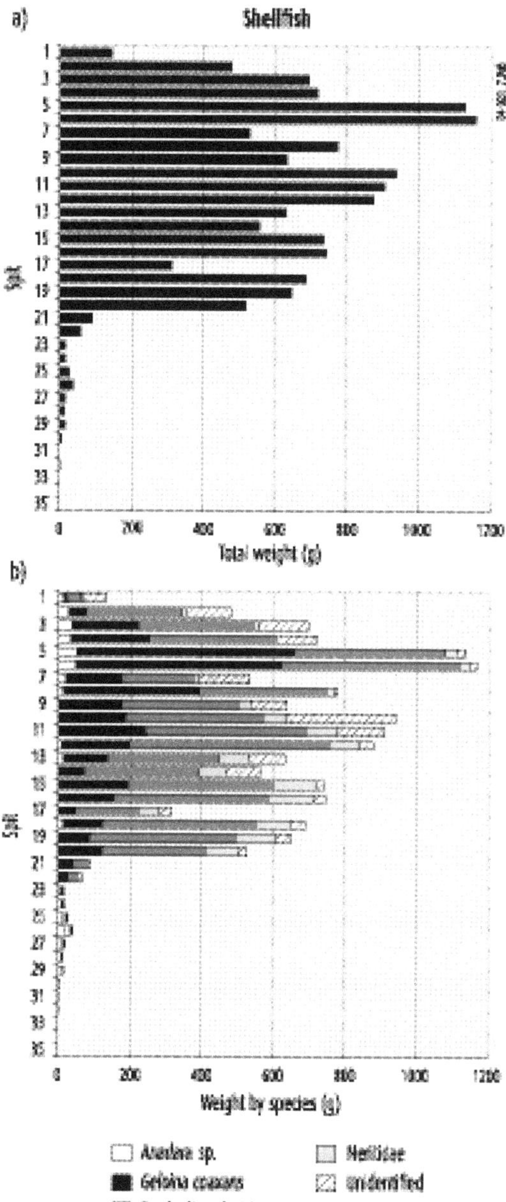

Figure 7.9 Liang Nabulei Lisa: a) total shellfish raw weights (g) b) raw weights of different species of marine/estuarine shellfish

Vertebrate fauna

Nabulei Lisa produced much smaller quantities of faunal remains than Lemdubu and the vertebrate material is more heavily burned and fragmented. Despite these limitations, the assemblage has yielded a remarkably detailed picture of environmental changes in the vicinity of the site and some insights into the nature of human responses to these changes.

Analytical methods

A preliminary examination of the Nabulei Lisa fauna revealed that the samples from the lower levels are dominated by remains of macropodids (wallabies) and snakes, comparable in fact to the greater part of the Lemdubu sequence (O'Connor et al. 2002; and see Chapter 9, this volume). In contrast, the upper levels of Nabulei Lisa were found to contain a more diverse and balanced fauna as well as the remains of introduced animals (e.g. pig and deer), again paralleling a change observed in the uppermost levels of Lemdubu. In the light of these initial impressions, it was decided to focus on the distribution of the various species through the stratigraphic column, and on the quantification of changes in relative abundance among the major species. The critical requirements were therefore:

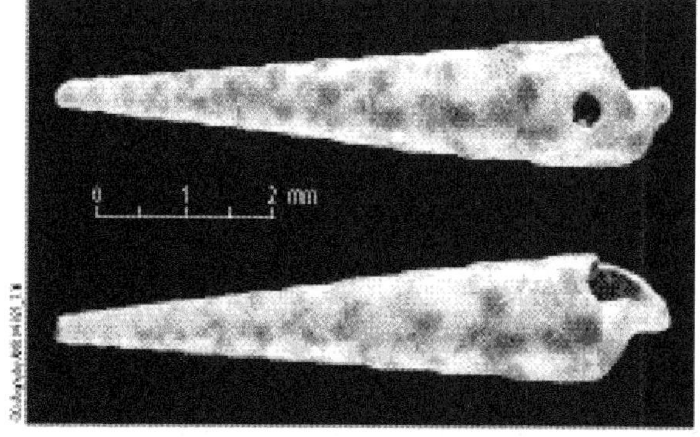

Figure 7.10 Liang Nabulei Lisa: shell of *Terebra subulata* with hole drilled opposite opercular opening, probably used for personal decoration

1) to determine the range of species present;
2) to establish the pattern of distribution of each species through the sequence; and
3) to estimate the relative abundance of the major species, both within each unit (interspecific) and through the sequence (intraspecific).

Prior to detailed analysis of the vertebrate fauna, all samples were washed in a fine-mesh sieve and air dried. Artefacts produced on bone as a raw material were separated from the remaining bone material at this stage; these are reported in Chapter 11.

An initial sort of each sample produced the following categories:

— reptile bone (lizards, snakes, turtles, crocodilians)
— bird bone
— fish bone
— cranial and all recognisable post-cranial remains of various mammalian families other than Macropodidae
— cranio-dental and pedal (foot) bones of macropodids
— avian eggshell
— crustacean exoskeleton
— 'unidentified' bone.

For most samples, the 'unidentified' category includes a large proportion of macropodid bone fragments representing all body parts other than cranio-dental and pedal remains, along with a small proportion of genuinely non-diagnostic bone fragments. The decision to not isolate all of the macropodid remains was based on time considerations, especially in regard to the parallel analysis of the much larger Lemdubu vertebrate faunal assemblage.

Remains of each major taxon were then examined in turn to identify the individual taxa. As a rule, mammalian remains were identified to generic or species level, while remains of other groups were identified to family or higher level and then assigned to a size category (e.g. small fish, large bird). For macropodids, species level identifications were made on cranial and dental remains, and from two of the most diagnostic foot bones, the calcaneum and astragalus. No special effort was made to identify the genera or species of reptile or bird remains, except where the conclusion was obvious (e.g. cassowary, crocodile). Lack of suitable reference material seriously hinders precise taxonomic allocation of the majority of Papuan birds and reptiles.

The 'unidentified' bone was further sorted into the following four burning categories, drawing on previous classifications by Ubelaker (1978), Shipman et al. (1984) and Pearce & Luff (1994):

1) Unburnt (bone is pale, yellow to light brown and porous);
2) Lightly burnt (bone is light brown to dark brown and more dense in texture; this is usually the result of cooking of the bone inside a fleshed carcass rather than direct contact with flames);
3) Burnt (bone is very dark brown or dark grey to black and very dense, usually resulting from direct contact with flame); and
4) Calcined (bone is grey to white, very dense and sometimes crazed or warped; all organic material has been lost, resulting in shrinkage and increased brittleness).

Each burning category was weighed separately.

For each identified taxon, the allocated bone fragments were first sorted according to the four burning categories. Each category was then counted (NISP) and weighed separately. This procedure allows us to calculate the total weight of each burning category for each spit (by summing identified taxa + unidentified). It also allows us to compare the intensity of burning of bone from each of the major taxa. For the various macropodid species, separate counts and weights were made on teeth or tooth-bearing elements, other cranial pieces, and calcanea and astragali. The remains of pythons

(Boidae) and other large reptiles were counted in two classes: vertebrae and cranial — the latter including tooth bearing elements. Raw bone weights and NISP data for all identified specimens is shown in Appendix 7.2.

Crustacean exoskeleton and avian eggshell were weighed as single samples without reference to burning condition.

Because the abundance of each of the major animal groups has been calculated in slightly different ways, it is not possible to directly equate the relative abundance of each taxon with any measure of economic importance. However, the fact that the same methods were applied consistently through the sequence (and also for the analysis of the Lemdubu fauna) means that proportional increases or decreases in any particular taxon can be treated as indicators of economic and/or environmental change, although perhaps not necessarily equally scaled from group to group.

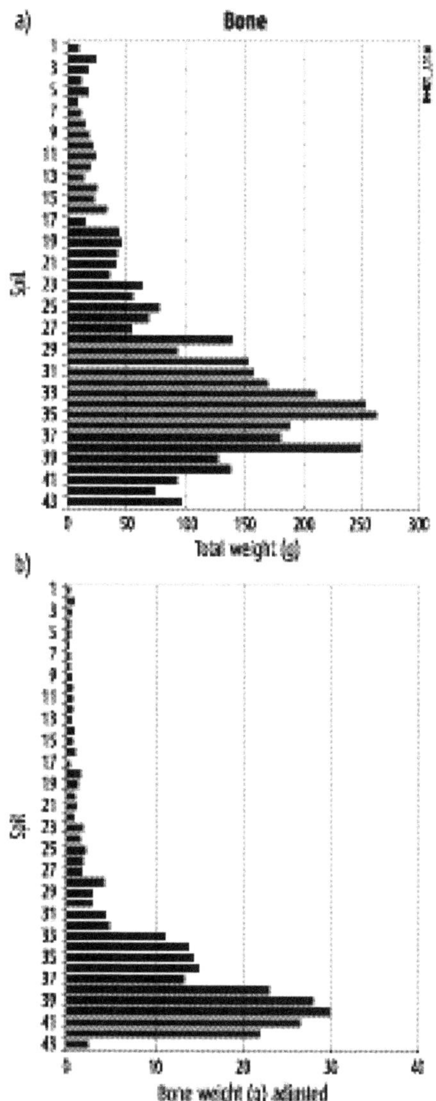

Figure 7.11 Liang Nabulei Lisa: a) total bone weight (g) and b) adjusted bone weight through the sequence (bone weight/excavated deposit weight)

Vertical distribution and preservational state of bone

The vertical distribution of bone based on raw weights is shown in Figure 7.11a, and 7.11b shows bone weights adjusted for weight of excavated sediment by spit (Table 7.3). Bone is sparse in Spits 1–17. There is a minor increase in bone quantities between Spits 18 and 23 and another slight increase between Spits 28 and 32. Below Spit 32 bone quantities increase dramatically, with a further increase to maximum levels between Spits 38 to 42. The lowermost spit produced a small quantity of bone.

The proportion of bone in each burning class varies markedly through the sequence (Fig. 7.12). Three main zones can be distinguished. Bone from the uppermost Spits 1–3 shows a high proportion of burning, with calcined bone alone accounting for more than 50% of the total bone in these levels. Between Spits 4-32 there is a marked decline in the proportion of burning; unburnt bone makes up around 50–60% of the total remains, with occasional excursions above and below these values. Calcined bone usually makes up less than 20% of the remains in these levels. Below Spit 32 even less of the bone shows any evidence of burning, with unburnt bone making up 70–85% of the total remains. This corresponds with the zone of highest bone concentrations in the sequence.

Faunal assemblages characterized by a high proportion of calcined bone are often a product of intense post-depositional destruction or degradation in environments where all but the most resistant remains have disappeared. To explore this possibility in the case of the upper levels of Nabulei Lisa, we examined the unburnt bone from each level for obvious signs of post-depositional destruction or degradation, such as tooth marks, root marks, surface pitting or rounding of fracture edges. Although a small proportion of bone fragments showed surface damage consistent with root and tooth marks, these are not concentrated in any particular part of the sequence. Overall, the bone appears well-preserved throughout the sequence and there is little indication that much material has been lost following burial of the assemblage. However, there are good grounds to suggest that the more intense burning of the faunal remains in Spits 1–3 may have caused a higher rate of destruction of bone than occurred during earlier times.

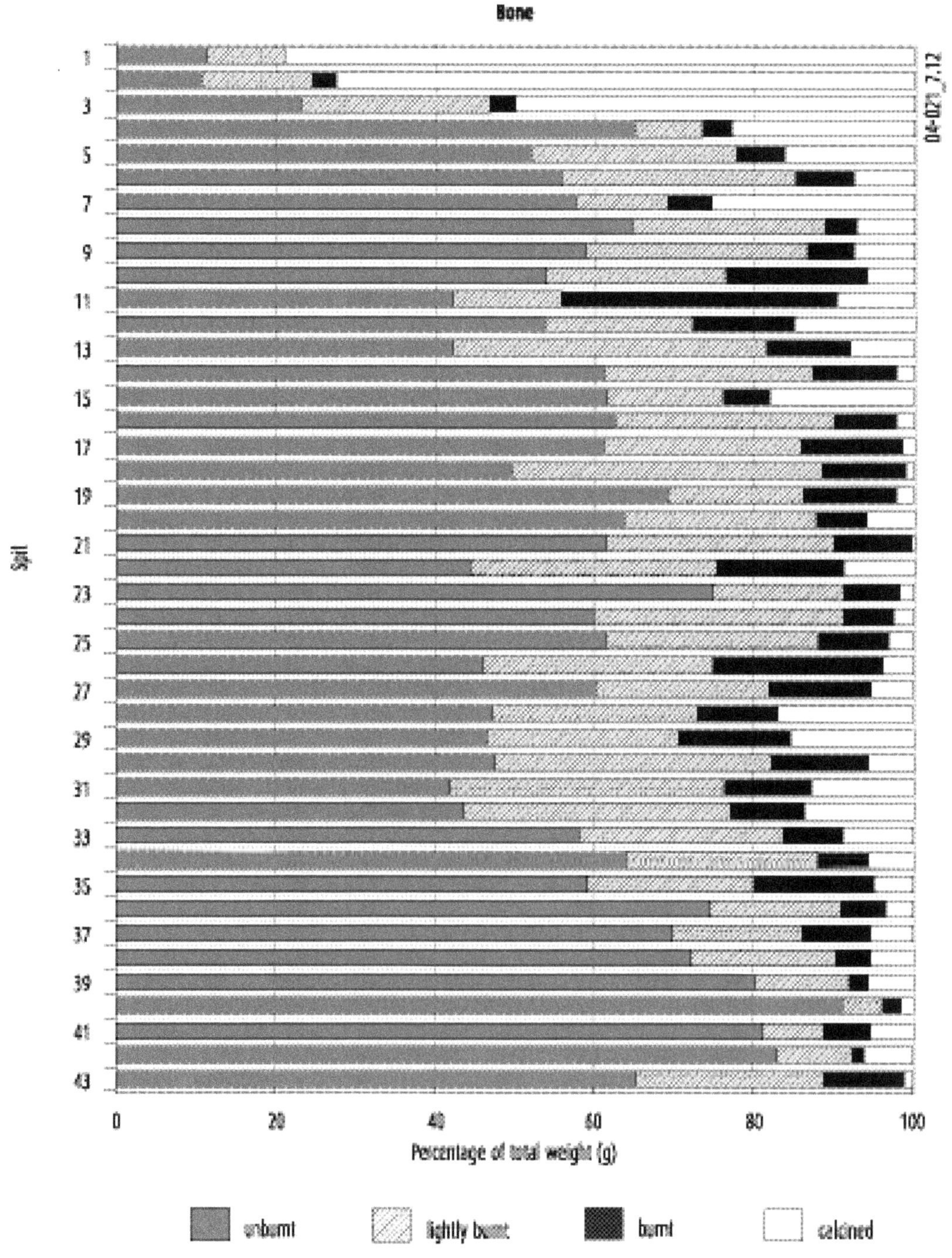

Figure 7.12 Liang Nabulei Lisa: changes in the burning composition of the bone assemblage through time, based on weight of remains in each burning category

Origin of the remains

The relative paucity of small mammal remains through the sequence (see Fig. 7.13), and the preponderance of medium- to large-bodied animals such as macropodids, boid snakes and phalangers (Fig. 7.13; Appendix 7.2), suggests that the Nabulei Lisa fauna is predominantly derived from human activity. This conclusion is supported by the scarcity of tooth marks on the remains and by the lack of rounding of fracture edges on all but a few specimens. Some of the smaller mammal remains, including the occasional bones of smaller rodents and bats, might be derived from other

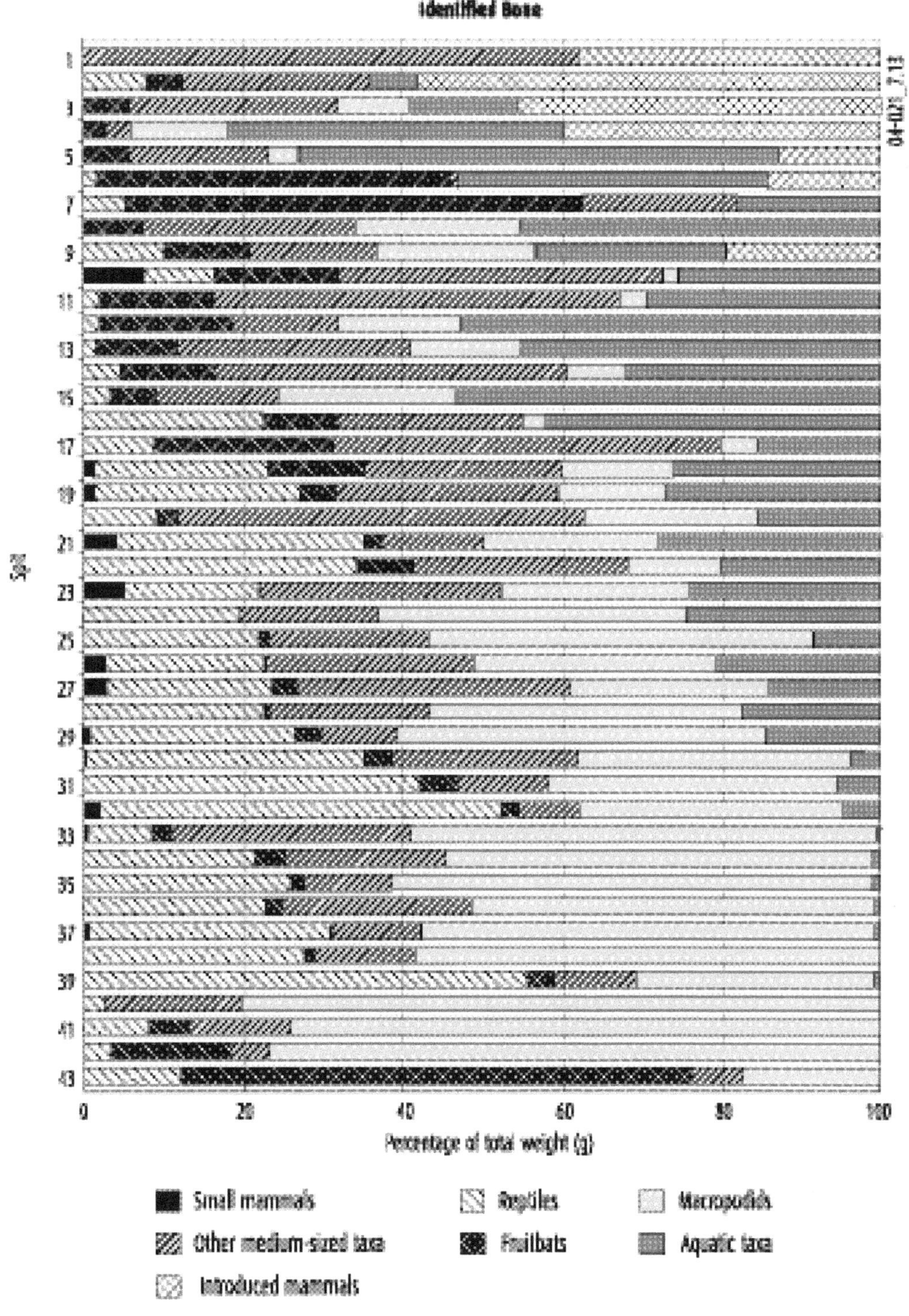

Figure 7.13 Liang Nabulei Lisa: changing proportional representation of major vertebrate groups through time, based on the weight of identified remains of each group

sources including the regurgitated pellets of predatory birds roosting in the cave. However, as these are scattered through the sequence, they do not influence the overall composition of the fauna. Bones of very small microchiropteran bats might be from natural deaths in the cave.

Species distributions

The archaeological fauna includes many of the mammal species that are present on the Aru Islands today, but also contains several species that have never been recorded as living animals. The major additions are three macropodids (*Macropus agilis, Thylogale stigmatica* and *Dorcopsis* sp.), two bandicoots (*Isoodon macrourus* and *Echymipera kalubu*), and the Short-beaked Echidna (*Tachyglossus aculeatus*). Other additions are a Native Cat (*Dasyurus albopunctatus*), several small rodents (*Rattus sordidus, Pogonomys* sp., *Pseudomys* sp., and *Melomys* sp. cf *M. burtoni*), and several bats (*Chaerephon* sp. cf *C. jobensis* and a small *Dobsonia* sp.). The basis of these taxonomic determinations is discussed in Chapter 3 (this volume).

Four species of macropodids are recorded in the archaeological fauna, compared with a single species (*Thylogale brunii*) recorded for the islands today. The additions are a mixed bunch and include *Macropus agilis*, a true grassland/ savannah wallaby, *Dorcopsis* sp. an inhabitant of dense rainforest, and *Thylogale stigmatica*, an inhabitant of rainforest margins and wet gallery forests. The *Macropus* and *Thylogale* species were reported earlier from Liang Lemdubu (O'Connor et al. 2002), but *Dorcopsis* sp. is an entirely new record for the islands.

As reported previously in O'Connor et al. (2002) for the Liang Lemdubu fauna (see also Chapter 9, this volume), the archaeological *Thylogale* remains are divisible into two or three taxa. One of these is clearly referrable to the extant Aru species *Thylogale brunii*. The remaining specimens as a group compare most closely to modern reference specimens of *T. stigmatica*. However, the sample shows a greater size variation than would normally be observed within a single population and may include two closely related taxa. Because it was not possible to allocate many of the less complete specimens to either the larger or smaller form of *T. stigmatica*, the two groups are not distinguished in the analysis.

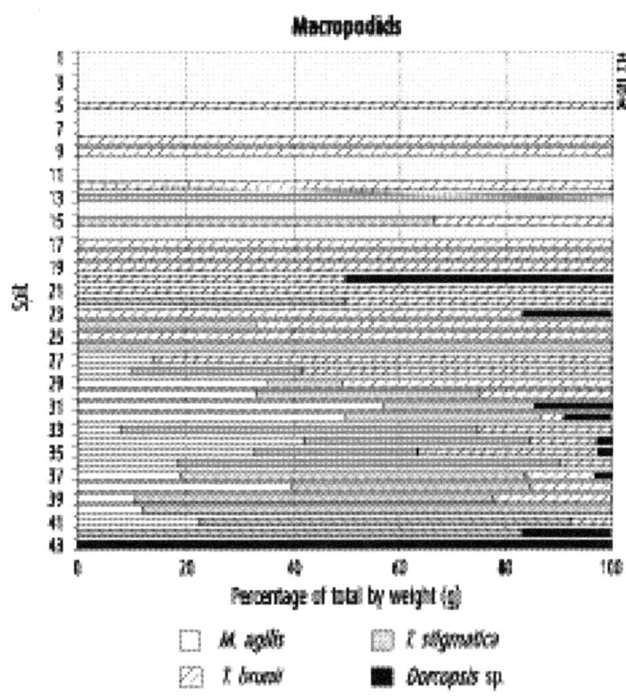

Figure 7.14 Liang Nabulei Lisa: distribution of different wallaby species through the sequence

Each of the four macropodids shows a contrasting distribution within the sequence (Fig. 7.14). The two *Thylogale* species together make up the greater part of the macropodid remains throughout the sequence. *Thylogale brunii* is dominant above Spit 30, but poorly represented below that level (Fig. 7.15a). It is the only macropodid found above Spit 12, an observation that is consistent with the persistence of this species on Pulau Kobroor until the present day. *Thylogale stigmatica* is consistently well represented below Spit 30 but occurs sporadically up to a final occurrence in Spit 12 (Fig. 7.15b). *Macropus agilis* makes up a significant proportion of all macropodid remains in Spits 27–41 but is absent above Spit 27 (Fig. 7.15c). *Dorcopsis* sp. occurs in low but consistent quantities in the lower part of the deposit, up to Spit 31 (Fig. 7.15d). A single example was recovered above this level, coming from Spit 23.

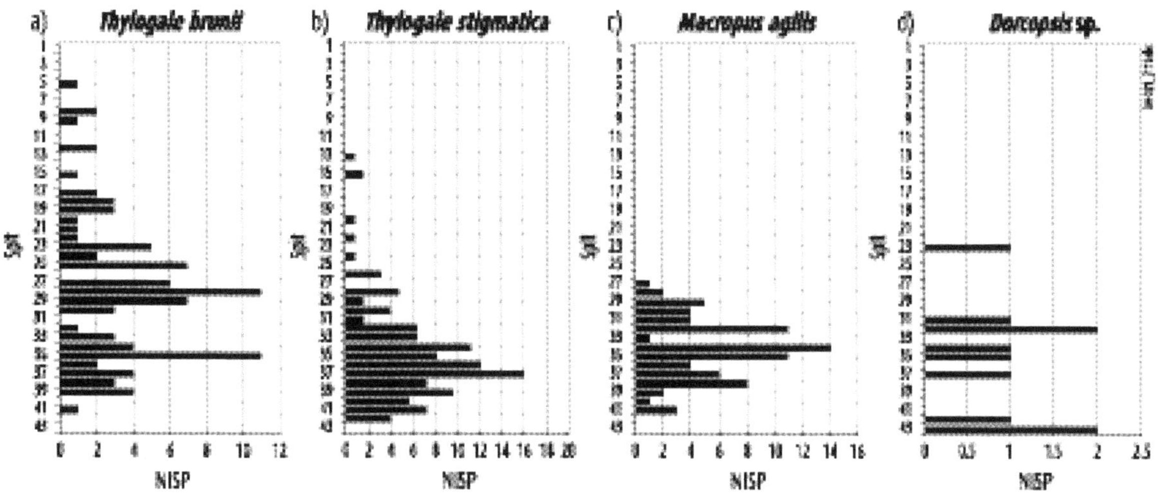

Figure 7.15 Liang Nabulei Lisa: distribution of a) *Thylogale brunii* b) *Thylogale stigmatica* c) *Macropus agilis* and d) *Dorcopsis* sp. through the sequence

To be more certain on the stratigraphic ranges of the various macropodids, the 'unidentified' material from the higher levels was subjected to special scrutiny. No post-cranial remains of *Macropus agilis* were identified in any sample above Spit 27. From Spits 26–11, the unidentified category is dominated by the remains of small macropodids, consistent in size with one or other of the two *Thylogale* species. In contrast, the bulk of the 'unidentified' category from Spits 1–10 appeared to be made up of highly fragmented remains of larger mammals (presumably pig and deer), together with remains of smaller mammals (e.g. possums, bats). Small macropodids clearly make up a smaller proportion of this category than is true for any of the lower levels.

The *Dorcopsis* remains from Nabulei Lisa are too fragmentary to identify the species involved (see Chapter 3, this volume). There are two principal candidates: *D. muelleri* that occurs on the adjacent southern coastal lowlands of Indonesian Papua; and *D. luctuosa* that occurs in southeastern New Guinea but with modern records in the Trans-Fly region (Groves and Flannery 1989; Flannery 1995b). All species of *Dorcopsis* inhabit deep closed forest habitats (Flannery 1995a), yet little detailed information is available on their ecology. In general, they are shy and secretive animals, intolerant of human presence. Today, they most often fall prey to hunting dogs but they can also be captured by hand or in nets (Flannery 1995b). Although a species of *Dorcopsis* has not been recorded in the contemporary Aru fauna, the possibility cannot be ruled out that they persist somewhere within the island group, perhaps in areas of dense forest far from areas of human habitation.

The ecology of the various New Guinean *Thylogale* species is unfortunately not well known. The endemic New Guinean *T. brunii* is reported to occur in dense monsoonal rainforest in the Morehead area (Waithman 1979). In the recent past, it was apparently present in grassland/savannah habitats around Post Moresby (Flannery 1995a). In Australia, *T. stigmatica* prefers rainforest habitat but it also occurs in wet sclerophyll and vine forest. Tate and Archbold (1935) described this species from 'mixed grasslands and gallery woods' on the Oriomo Plateau of Papua New Guinea, while Waithman (1979) reports it to be uncommon in low mixed savannah and woodland near swamps in the Morehead area. Where the two species occur together in the Trans-Fly region, it would thus seem that *T. brunii* tends to dominate in the core rainforest habitats, perhaps causing *T. stigmatica* to occupy the rainforest margins.

At least three species of bandicoots are represented in the Nabulei Lisa assemblage, compared with a single species in the modern fauna (Fig. 7.16a). The sole surviving taxon, *Echymipera rufescens*, is well-represented in the lower part of the deposit but has its most recent definite occurrence in Spit 21 (Fig. 7.16b). Small numbers of unallocated bandicoot remains occur above this level. *Echymipera kalubu* is tentatively identified from Spits 10, 16, 20 and 35. This species is more confidently identified in the Lemdubu fauna (Chapter 9, this volume). Both species of *Echymipera* occur today in lowland rainforest habitats on the New Guinea mainland. However, *E. kalubu* appears to have broader ecological tolerance than *E. rufescens*, as it extends to higher elevations and also occurs in anthropogenic grassland. The third species of bandicoot is *Isoodon macrourus*, a species that is broadly associated with savannah grassland habitat in New Guinea and northern Australia (Flannery 1995a). This species is confined to Spits 26–38 within the sequence; it reaches peak abundance in Spit 34 (Fig. 7.16c). An enigmatic, fourth bandicoot taxon, recognized in the Lemdubu fauna, is represented in the lower levels of Nabulei Lisa, with dentary fragments and pedal elements in Spits 40 to 33.

Four species of possums are represented in the assemblage. All are part of the contemporary fauna of the Aru Islands. The Spotted Cuscus, *Spilocuscus maculatus*, is present in approximately half of all excavated spits, with no obvious change in absolute abundance from bottom to top (Fig. 7.17a). Two smaller cuscuses, *Phalanger gymnotis* and *P. intercastellanus*, also occur sporadically through the sequence and in almost equal numbers throughout (Fig. 7.17b). Relative to the total quantity of faunal remains, all three cuscus species are proportionally better represented in the upper half of the sequence. The Striped Possum, *Dactylopsila trivirgata*, is poorly represented by comparison, with single fragments in each of Spits 20, 28, 30 and 31. All four species are indicative of forest habitats. *Phalanger gymnotis* has not been recorded outside of rainforest habitats. The remaining species are more adaptable and occur today in a variety of forest types including riparian forests and relatively open woodlands. The scarcity of *Dactylopsila trivirgata* in Nabulei Lisa and Lemdubu (Chapter 9) appears to contrast with its current status as one of the more commonly collected native mammals on both Wokam and Kobroor Islands (see Chapter 3).

The only dasyurid species that is positively identified in the Nabulei Lisa fauna (Spit 37) is *Dasyurus albopunctatus*, an inhabitant of rainforest. A second, smaller species is represented by very incomplete remains in Spit 32.

The Nabulei Lisa fauna produced very little in the way of rodent remains and the majority of these are derived from large murids (Fig. 7.18). The few diagnostic specimens are all referrable to *Uromys caudimaculatus*, a highly adaptable species that occurs across a variety of habitat types.

Bat remains are present in virtually all samples and it was generally possible to separate these into megachiropterans and microchiropterans based on size and morphology (Fig. 7.19a and b) Megachiropteran bat remains were found throughout the deposit but never in especially large

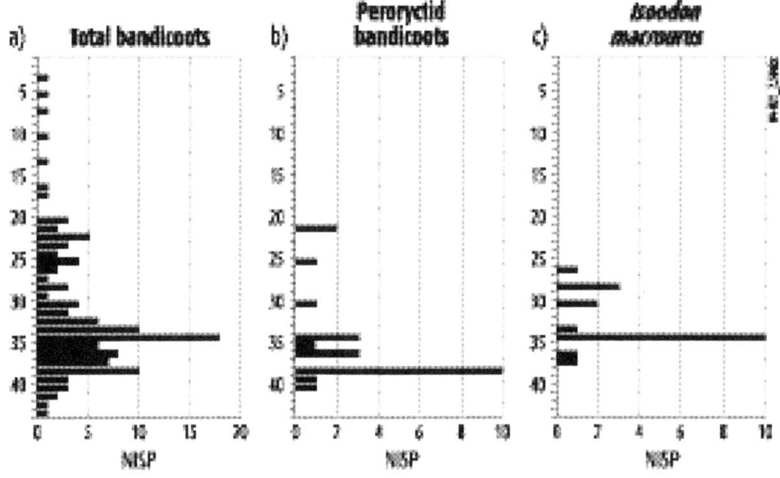

Figure 7.16 Liang Nabulei Lisa: distribution of a) all bandicoot species b) peroryctid bandicoots (*Echymipera* spp. and *Peroryctes* spp.) and c) Isoodon macrourus through the sequence

numbers (Fig. 7.19a). Most of the identifiable elements consist of isolated teeth and partial lower jaws. Fortunately, species of *Dobsonia* share a distinctive dental morphology that allows members of this genus to be distinguished from other comparable-sized pteropodids including species of *Pteropus*. All dentary fragments and isolated molars in the Nabulei Lisa assemblage appear to belong to a large species of *Dobsonia*, tentatively identified as *D. moluccensis*. These come from various levels in the excavation, from the very base (Spit 43) up to Spit 7 near the surface. No specimens were found of the second, much smaller *Dobsonia* species that occurs in Lemdubu. Microchiropteran remains are concentrated in two parts of the sequence, in Spits 28–43 and in Spits 2–18 (Fig. 7.19b). A total of eight lower jaws are present and all clearly represent a single taxon which is tentatively identified as *Chaerephon* sp. cf. C. *jobensis*, a molossid bat that is known to sometimes roost in caves. These small animals are more likely to represent the result of natural deaths in the cave rather than human food refuse. The gap in their occurrence may represent a period when the cave was abandoned by the bat colony, perhaps in response to human activity.

The remains of introduced mammal species are confined to the upper part of the sequence (Fig. 7.13). Pig bone occurs in Spits 2–6 and appears again in Spit 9; all of these occurrences presumably date to within the last 1000 years. In contrast, deer and dog remains are restricted to Spit 1. The Rusa Deer, *Cervus timorensis*, may be a recent introduction to the Aru Islands. Healey (1995:56) suggested that Rusa Deer may have been introduced by the Portuguese. However, Wallace does not mention this species at all, and it is unlikely that he would have failed to notice it if it was abundant and as important a hunted animal then, as it is today. Van Strien (1996) also favours a more recent date of introduction, during the early years of Dutch administration. No other introduced mammals are recorded in the archaeological fauna. One notable absence from the record is the Palm Civet *Paradoxurus hermaphroditus*, which is present in Aru today.

Snakes are consistently well-represented throughout the greater part of the sequence; in

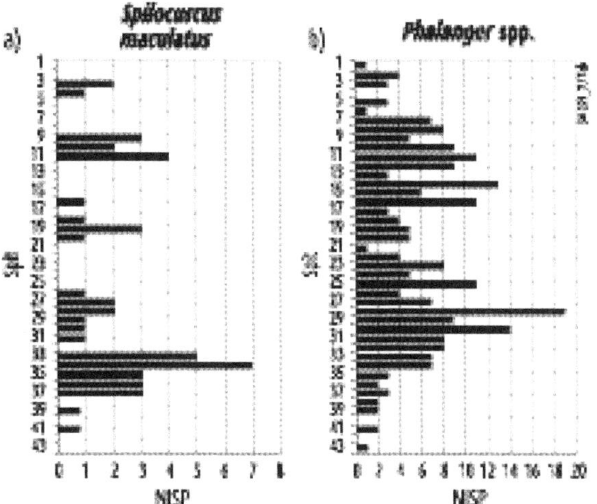

Figure 7.17 Liang Nabulei Lisa: distribution of possum species a) *Spilocuscus maculatus* and b) *Phalanger* spp. through the sequence

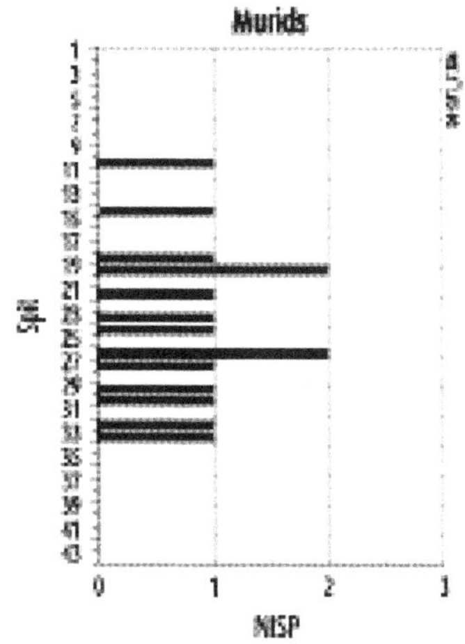

Figure 7.18 Liang Nabulei Lisa: distribution of murids through the sequence

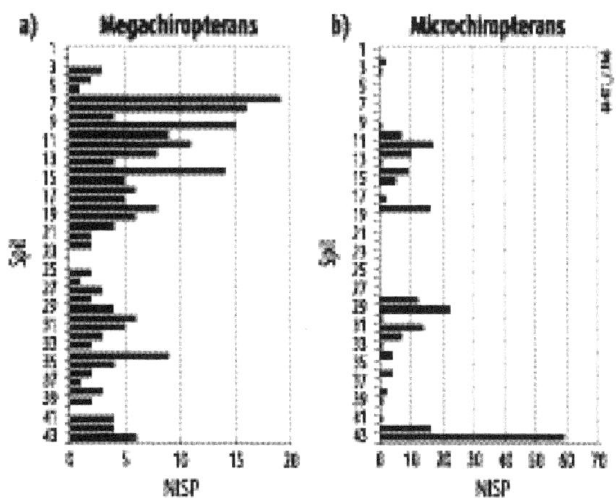

Figure 7.19 Liang Nabulei Lisa: distribution of a) megachiropterans and b) microchiropterans bats through the sequence

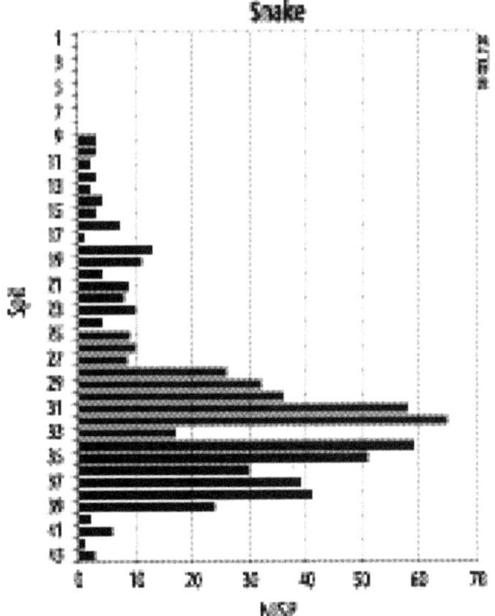

Figure 7.20 Liang Nabulei Lisa: distribution of boid snakes through the sequence

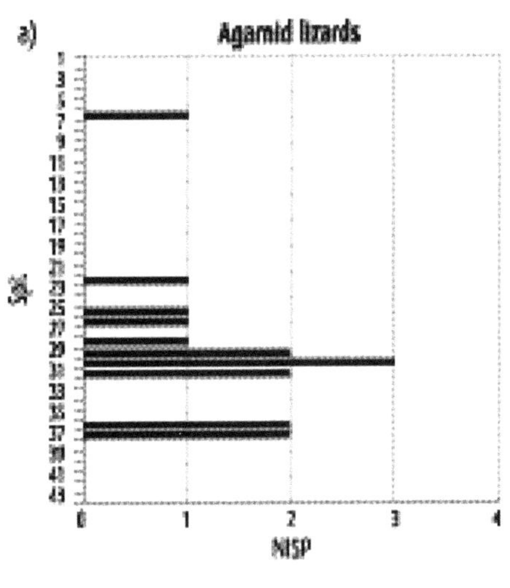

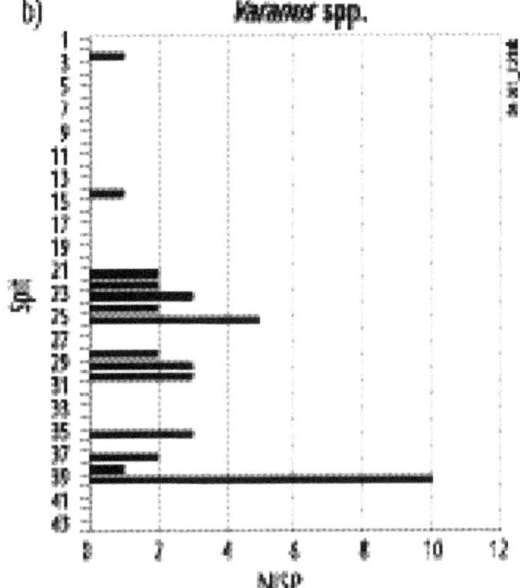

Figure 7.21 Liang Nabulei Lisa: distribution of a) Agamid and b) *Varanus* spp. lizards through the sequence

most spits they account for around 5–10% of all bone (Fig. 7.13). However, snakes are absent above Spit 9 (Fig. 7.20). Almost all of the snake remains come from moderately large snakes belonging to the Family Boidae (pythons), with rare examples referrable to the Family Colubridae. In view of the high meat weight to bone ratio of these large pythons, they must have made a regular and important contribution to the diet.

Other reptile groups are less well-represented in the site. These include two families of lizards, the Agamidae (dragons) and Varanidae (monitors); remains of both groups occur sporadically through the deposit (Fig. 7.21a and b). The remains of freshwater turtles (family Cheluidae) are confined to a narrow band of the deposit, between Spits 19–26 (Fig. 7.22). Freshwater turtles are presumably indicative of at least seasonal wetland or riverine habitat in the vicinity of the site, prior to the establishment of estuarine conditions.

No definite cassowary bone was recovered from Nabulei Lisa, however, eggshell fragments occur between Spits 9–34. Cassowaries are not known to lay eggs in caves, hence it is reasonable to assume that any eggshell in the deposit results from eggs brought into the site by people as food. Three species of cassowary are found in New Guinea (*C. unappendiculatus*, *C. bennetti*, and *C. casuarius*), but only *C. casuarius* is found in northern Australia and in the Aru Islands today (see Chapter 13, this volume). *Casuarius casuarius* is actively hunted in the Aru Islands today and the eggs collected for food. No information is available on the breeding times of *C. casuarius* in Aru. In north Queensland breeding 'occurs mostly in the dry season from about June to October' coinciding 'with the average maximum availability of fruit in the forest' (Crome 1975:9, 13). If the archaeological eggshell is from *C. casuarius* then the eggshell fragments presumably demonstrate use of the site in the dry season.

The absence of eggshell fragments above Spit 9 and below Spit 35 is difficult to explain solely in terms of sample sizes. Intense burning and destruction of the remains in Spits 1–3 might help explain this absence for the uppermost levels, but this argument would not hold for Spits 4–8 or for the lower levels. The absence of eggshell below

Spit 35 is especially difficult to explain when it is remembered that the highest concentrations of bone were recovered from these levels.

The fish remains are derived mostly from small- to medium-sized fish and make a regular and sizable contribution throughout (Fig. 7.23). However, the collection also includes some larger, obviously marine taxa, especially in the upper half of the sequence. Identification of this material has not yet been attempted.

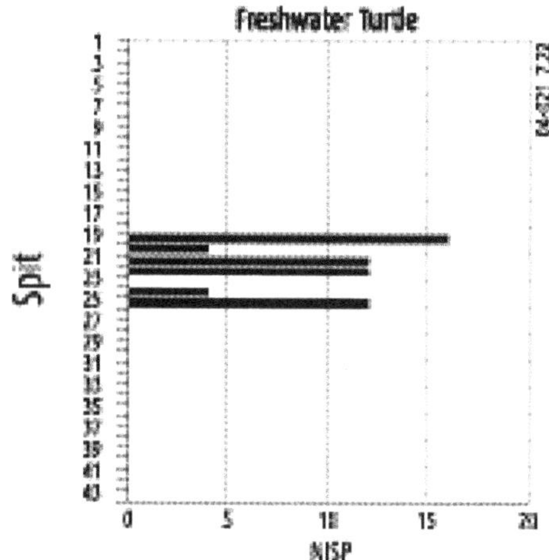

Figure 7.22 Liang Nabulei Lisa: distribution of freshwater turtles (family Cheluidae) through the sequence

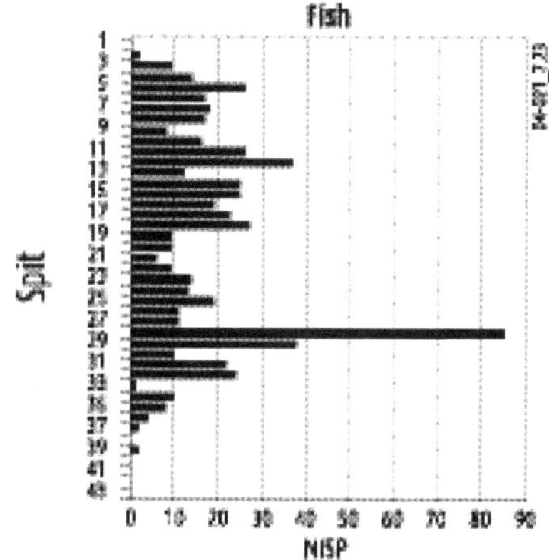

Figure 7.23 Liang Nabulei Lisa: distribution of fish through the sequence

Crustacean exoskeleton

Crustacean exoskeleton was found in small quantities down to Spit 32 but the largest quantities occur in Spits 3–20 (Fig. 7.24a). Most of the sample consists of fragments of chelae. Three different morphological types were noted, differing in the overall form of the chelae (short, robust versus elongate, gracile), the style of ornamentation and the presence of distinct pores. Examples of each type were shown to Dr Diana Jones of the Western Australian Museum. She identified them as belonging to two families, Xanthidae (the more robust elements) and Portunidae (the more gracile groups). Xanthid crabs are typically associated with marine, higher energy environments such as rocky shorelines. Among the portunids, she further distinguished the specimens with distinct pores from those lacking such structures and advised that these represent ecotypes: those taxa with pores are indicative of faster flowing freshwater stream conditions, and those without pores are associated with muddier water conditions and exposed muddy substrate. The samples were subsequently divided into these three groups — xanthid, portunid A (with pores), and portunid B (without pores) — and a count made of the number of fragments in each group.

Changes in the representation of each group of crustaceans through the deposit is shown in Figure 7.24b. The pattern is remarkably strong, with evidence for progressive replacement of a freshwater crab community, first by an estuarine, and then finally by a fully marine community. The major phases in the transition are represented by: Spits 32–22, during which period the freshwater portunids are dominant and xanthids make an occasional appearance; Spits 20–11, characterized by a mixed assemblage of estuarine portunids and xanthids; and Spits 10–2 when xanthids dominate. The major transition at Spit 20 corresponds exactly to the time when marine and estuarine shell increase dramatically in abundance. The absence of any crab remains below Spit 32 is of some interest, especially given the increased abundance of vertebrate bone below this level. One obvious possibility is that the occupants of the site simply could not be bothered with hunting for crabs during the early period of occupation of the site. However, it is also possible that the *sungai* channel did not contain sufficient water throughout the year during this period (16,200–12,000 cal BP) to support viable long-term populations of the particular portunid crab

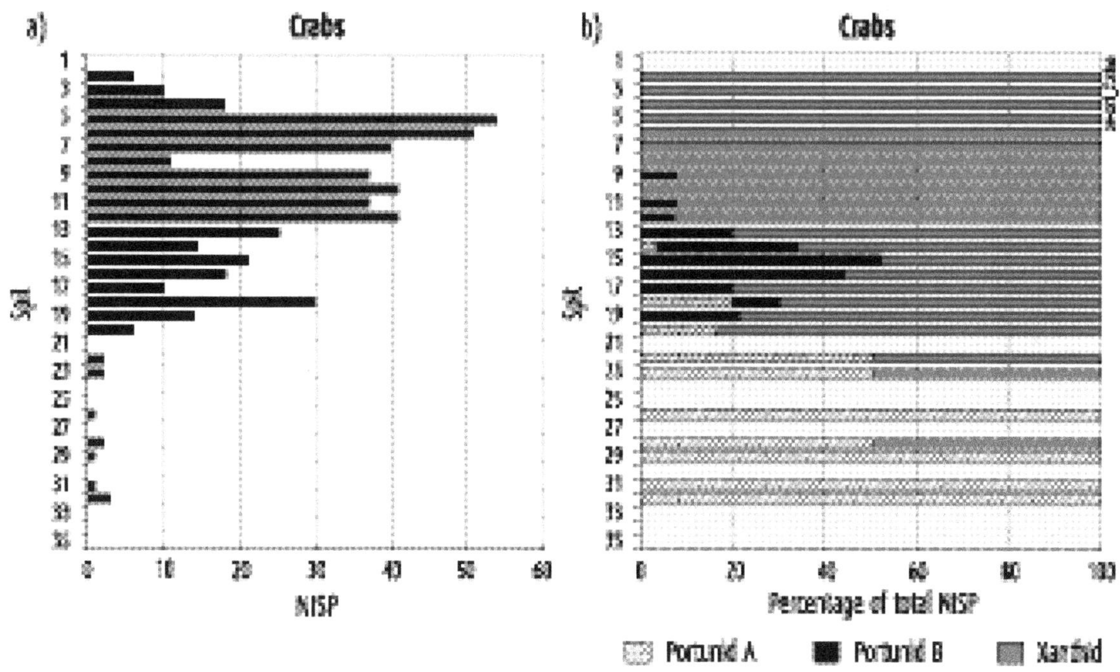

Figure 7.24 Liang Nabulei Lisa: Distribution of a) total crustacean remains and b) three major crustacean groups through the sequence

species. The scarcity of freshwater mollusc remains in the lower part of the deposit may also point to conditions that were at least seasonally unsuitable for establishment of a full freshwater stream community.

Plant material

Seeds of *Celtis philippinensis* were the only plant material preserved. They are confined to the lower part of the excavation, with most examples coming from Spits 21–31 and one specimen only below this level (from Spit 36; Table 7.2). Being composed primarily of inorganic material, *Celtis* seeds are very robust so it is unlikely that poor preservation conditions are responsible for their absence in the upper and lowermost spits. It may be significant that their major appearance in Spit 31 corresponds with the first appearance of crab remains and that their disappearance coincides with the major increase in marine and estuarine shell and crab species in Spit 20. A possible scenario is that *Celtis* trees grew along the freshwater stream below the site for a few thousand years in the early Holocene but ceased to grow in this area when tidal conditions established. Their absence from the same area during the earlier period might be a further indication of seasonally dry conditions in the *sungai* channel at this time.

Palaeoenvironmental Interpretation

The combined mollusc, crustacean, and vertebrate faunal analysis provides a remarkably detailed picture of environmental changes in the vicinity of Liang Nabulei Lisa over the past 16,000 years. The sequence of changes is most conveniently described as a succession of four time periods. However, the exact delineation of these periods should be regarded as somewhat arbitrary.

Spits 43–33 (16,200–12,000 cal BP)

The earliest phase of occupation of the site is characterized by higher absolute quantities of vertebrate faunal remains and by the predominance of macropodid and snake remains. Other groups of mammals including bandicoots, possums, and bats are all represented, but in small numbers. This period is further characterized by the presence of all four macropodid species including *Macropus agilis* and *Dorcopsis* sp., and by the dominance of *Thylogale stigmatica* over the other species. The bandicoot *Isoodon macrourus* is also well-represented. Fish remains are rare through this period and there is no evidence for exploitation of crabs or freshwater molluscs, perhaps because these groups were unavailable locally.

The occurrence of *Macropus agilis* and *I. macrourus* in these levels points to the presence of substantial areas of open habitat in the vicinity of the site. This was most likely some form of savannah woodland with grassy understorey. The lowland evergreen rainforest environment around the site today certainly does not provide a suitable habitat for either of these species. In this context, the simultaneous presence in these levels of a suite of typical lowland 'rainforest' species — including *Dorcopsis* sp., *Echymipera rufescens* and *Phalanger gymnotis* — is intriguing, and surely points to a mosaic of wet and dry habitats around the site. This conclusion is further supported by the presence of two species of *Thylogale* wallabies in these levels, both of which show a preference for forest edge habitats, typically the interface between rainforest and more open habitats. In the immediate context of Nabulei Lisa, the most likely scenario is that patches of dense evergreen or semi-evergreen rainforest were present in sheltered contexts along watercourses, including the major *sungai* channels. Drier, more open habitats presumably dominated on more elevated and exposed sites away from the channels.

The very limited evidence for exploitation of freshwater resources during this period raises the possibility that the major *sungai* channels were seasonally dry to the extent that crabs and economically useful molluscs were unable to establish viable, long-term populations. The apparent absence of cassowaries in the local area during the earlier part of this period (below Spit 35) might also be taken as an indicator of relatively dry conditions compared with subsequent periods. Despite these indications, the site appears to have been used more intensively during this period than at any time subsequently, at least if the quantity of vertebrate faunal remains is taken as a measure of activity.

Spits 32–26 (12,000–10,200 cal BP)

This period is characterized by greater diversity and more evenness of representation in the vertebrate assemblage. Macropodids and snakes remain important but there is a proportional increase in the quantities of fish, phalangerid possums and bandicoots. At the species level, this period is characterized by the decline or disappearance of *Dorcopsis* sp. (one record only at Spit 23), and by an increase in the proportional representation of *T. brunii*. *Macropus agilis* and *I. macrourus* are present through this period but make their last appearance together in Spit 26. Small quantities of freshwater crab and mollusc remains are present through this period. Marine and estuarine shell both make their first appearance, albeit in small quantities, in Spit 29. The total quantity of faunal remains is lower through this part of the deposit. However, cassowary eggshell is present in most levels.

The presence of both *M. agilis* and *I. macrourus* through this period documents a continuation of open savannah habitats in the area around the site. The apparent decline of *Dorcopsis* sp. could be taken as evidence for a reduction in area or suitability of wetter forest types from the preceding period, perhaps as a result of increasing aridity. However, other changes in the fauna suggest the opposite scenario of wetter conditions with a possible expansion of rainforest habitats. Most compelling in this regard are the increased importance of *Thylogale brunii*, a species that appears to thrive today in rainforest habitats in the Aru Islands, and the evidence for exploitation of freshwater crabs and molluscs during this period. The evidence for cassowaries in the local area might also point to larger areas of dense forest habitat. Given these contrary indications, we feel that a more likely interpretation for the decline of *Dorcopsis* sp. at this time is that it fell victim to some combination of over-hunting and interspecific competition, perhaps due to the greater tolerance of the *Thylogale* species to human disturbance.

The molluscan and crab remains give a clear and consistent picture of local freshwater conditions in the *sungai* channel through this period, but with coastal conditions sufficiently nearby that small quantities of typical estuarine and marine organisms were making their way to the site.

Spits 25–10 (ca. 7700–6100 cal BP)

This period is characterized mainly by the absence of *Macropus agilis* and *Isoodon macrourus*. Otherwise, it continues the same trend of progressive decline in the relative importance of macropodids and corresponding increases in the representation of phalangerids, bats and fish. *Thylogale stigmatica* occurs sporadically up to Spit 12.

The loss of the savannah and grassland dwelling mammals by the start of this period is a clear signal that these open habitats have either disappeared entirely, or else become reduced to small remnants of insufficient size to support viable populations even of the bandicoot. In general terms, the local environment may have resembled that found around the site today but with a slightly more diverse mammal fauna that included *T. stigmatica*. The eventual loss of this species rather than *T. brunii* may have been largely a result of chance factors; both species are probably capable of occupying continuous rainforest habitat in addition to the preferred forest edges. However, it is also possible that *T. brunii* had a slight competitive edge that allowed it to become increasingly dominant as closed forest gradually became more continuous.

The brief appearance of freshwater turtle in the lower part of this period (Spits 19–26) is further evidence that the major *sungai* channel supported at least a seasonally productive stream or wetland habitat. However, such conditions were evidently short-lived and the dramatic increase in marine and estuarine shell above Spit 20, and simultaneous change in the crab fauna, clearly reflect the local establishment of estuarine conditions with associated mangrove communities in the *sungai* at that time. The mollusc fauna does not seem to record the eventual change from estuarine to marine conditions in the *sungai*. In contrast, the crab fauna shows a very suggestive decline in estuarine species and corresponding rise of true marine species from Spit 15 onwards.

Spits 1–9 (ca. 1000 cal BP–modern)

This period is characterized by the appearance of several introduced mammals (pig, dog and deer) and by a decline in the relative abundance of macropodids, phalangerids, snakes and fish. Bats show a slight increase in relative abundance during this period. *Thylogale brunii* is the only macropodid identified from these levels.

Unfortunately, the archaeological remains from this period are too sparse to build a detailed picture of faunal exploitation during this interesting, final phase of occupation. Accordingly, it is unclear whether the site was being used as a remote hunting camp subject to occasional visits, or alternatively, whether the area around the site was subject to cultivation as it is today.

Human Skeletal Material

A small quantity of human skeletal material was recovered from Liang Nabulei Lisa. Some was recognized during excavation and removed and bagged separately, and other fragments were recognized during sorting of the faunal material. A full description of this material is presented in the following chapter.

Bone Artefacts

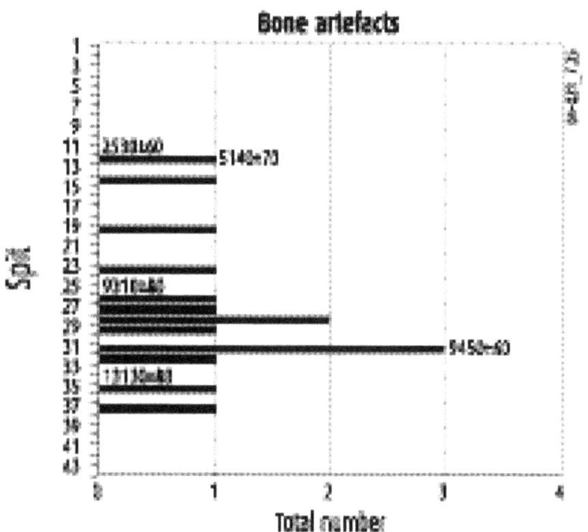

Figure 7.25 Liang Nabulei Lisa: distribution of bone artefacts through the sequence

Bone artefacts were recovered from Liang Nabulei Lisa, distributed more or less evenly between Spits 12–37 (Fig. 7.25). The artefacts are described in detail and illustrated by Pasveer in Chapter 11 (this volume). There are a total of fifteen specimens, with peak occurrences in Spit 28 and Spit 31 (see Fig. 11.1). This distribution indicates that most of the bone artefacts (n=11) date between 9000 and 13,000 BP. The Nabulei Lisa bone artefacts are difficult to categorise as they are highly variable in shape, including unipoints, spatulae forms and a single bipoint. A total of 80% are produced on shaft fragments and a large number are made on lightly burnt bone which may indicate that the raw material was deliberately prepared by lightly 'cooking' it prior to manufacture. Interestingly, while some complete points were recovered most of the bone artefacts at Nabulei Lisa are represented by fragments. This suggests that they result from repair or maintenance activities taking place on site rather than from the primary manufacture, as no broken or incomplete specimens from the early stages of production were found.

Stone Artefacts

Stone artefacts were sparse throughout, with only 42 recovered in total. No stone artefacts at all occur in Spits 1–6. As these spits fall within the last thousand years, and in view of how poorly represented stone artefacts are throughout, their absence is hardly surprising as we may presume that metal would have been used for many activities by this time. No stone artefacts occur below Spit 35, however, the volume of deposit drops off sharply at this point so the absence is probably a sample size effect. The assemblage is composed almost exclusively of small unretouched flakes of chert and limestone. There is a change in raw material proportions at Spit 30. Above Spit 30, stone artefacts are predominantly made of limestone. Below Spit 30, 80% of artefacts are made on chert and 20% on limestone. Although with such small artefact numbers this change may not appear very significant, it does parallel a similar change at Lemdubu (Chapter 9, this volume). In Lemdubu chert accounts for between 30–56% of raw material in the upper spits, 2–5, in Spit 6 it accounts for 60% of all raw material, and below Spit 9 it accounts for 80–90%. As at Lemdubu, the changeover from chert to limestone appears to occur at the Pleistocene/Holocene interface. Attributes of the artefact assemblages from both caves such as technology of manufacture and weathering are discussed in detail in Chapter 10 (this volume).

Pottery

Several broken pottery vessels with intact rims were recovered from the surface of Liang Nabulei Lisa as well as a number of more fragmented sherds (Figs 7.26–7.30) Some of the surface pottery was painted with red designs, reminiscent of the contemporary pottery produced at Batu Lei in the

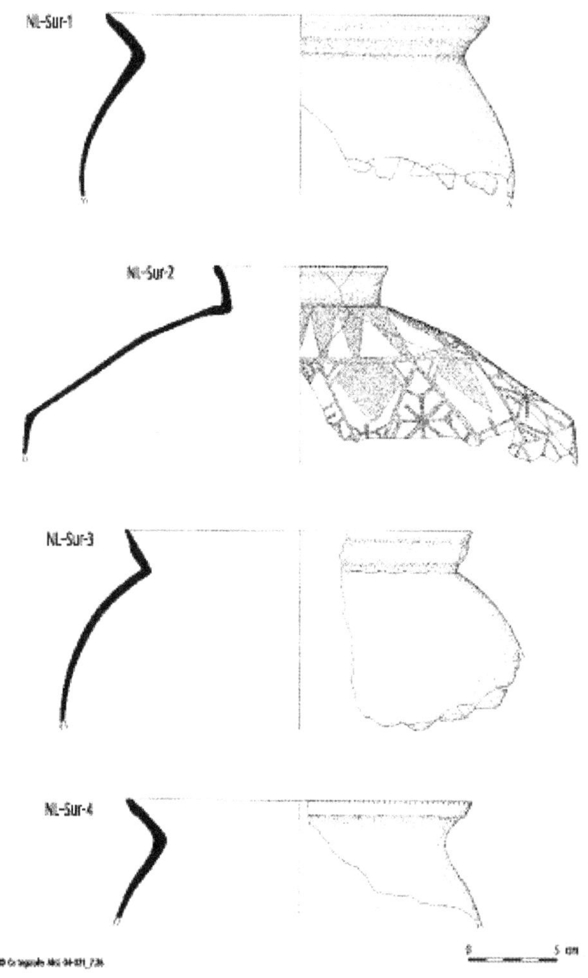

Figure 7.26 Liang Nabulei Lisa: vessel forms among the surface collected pottery, including everted globular pots with raised ridges on the rim exterior (NL-Sur-1, NL-Sur-3); a strongly restricted, everted and carinated jar — possibly a water jar — with a red painted rectilinear design (NL-Sur-2); and an out-curving globular pot with lip notching on a collared rim (NL-Sur-4)

south east (NL-Sur-2, Fig. 7.26). The method of manufacture of the Batu Lei pottery is discussed and illustrated in Chapter 6 (this volume). Aside from the broken vessels collected from the surface, the Nabulei Lisa pottery consisted of a small number of undecorated and largely undiagnostic sherds confined to the top eight spits of the excavation: a depth of approximately 18cm below the surface (Table 7.5). Based on the date from Spit 11 of 2530±60 (OZF249), at a depth of approximately 25cm, it is assumed that the pottery in Nabulei Lisa all dates to the last 1000 years. As might be expected in a cave site, pottery is not abundant in the excavation. The maximum number of sherds in any single spit was eight — in Spit 1. Weights are presented in Table 7.2. With the exception of painted decoration, the sherds recovered from the excavation look similar in all respects to the surface pottery (i.e. in terms of vessel form and temper), and to the ethnographic examples, so it seems likely that painted decoration simply does not survive burial. Two conjoinable fragments of Chinese blue and white porcelain, comprising a small section of the rim and body, were recovered from Spit 3 (NL-A-3, shown conjoined in Fig. 7.30), and a rim and body section of a small porcelain bowl with a pale green glaze was recovered from the surface (NL-Sur-16, Fig. 7.29).

There is considerably less variety in the Nabulei Lisa earthenware pottery assemblage than in that recovered from the Wangil test excavation (see Chapter 4, this volume) in terms of vessel form, types of decoration, and fabric. Vessel forms at Nabulei Lisa included a series of restricted orifice cooking pots, usually with plain lips, and apart from one rim/ neck sherd (NL-A-6) lacking incised decoration on the body. The collar form (Figs 7.27–7.28) was distinctive and different from the Wangil examples. Some strongly restricted orifice vessels were most probably water jars, one of which was decorated with a complex rectilinear painted design in red (NL-Sur-2, Fig. 7.26). This resembles ethnographically recorded decoration (see Batu Lei pottery Fig. 6.7, Chapter 6, this volume). One slightly restricted bowl form with a strongly everted notched lip (NL-A-6) may be paralleled at Wangil where some broken examples of similar rims occur. Clearly, however, the curvilinear incised decoration favoured at Wangil in the last thousand years is absent at Nabulei Lisa. In addition, no examples of the fine, burnished, red-slipped pottery found at Wangil were recovered at Nabulei Lisa. Five temper 'types' were identified in the macroscopic fabric examination of the Nabulei Lisa assemblage whereas nine types were recognized at Wangil. Based on this initial separation, 25 sherds from Nabulei Lisa were sent to William R. Dickinson for thin-

Table 7.5 Liang Nabulei Lisa: surface and excavated pottery sherd descriptions

NUMBER	SHERD TYPE	VESSEL FORM	RIM DATA					DECORATION DATA		FABRIC ANALYSIS
			DIRECTION	RIM PROFILE	LIP PROFILE	EXTRA RIM FEATURES	RIM DIAMETER	LOCATION	TECHNIQUE	
NL-Sur-1	rim/ neck/ shoulder	everted globular pot	everted	gradual convergent	rounded		22cm	rim exterior	raised ridge	1B
NL-Sur-2	rim/ neck/ carination	strongly restricted, everted, carinated jar (shouldered-ware)	everted	parallel	rounded		10cm	1) lip 2) body below collar (above & below carination)	1) notching 2) red paint	1
NL-Sur-3	rim/ neck/ shoulder	everted globular pot	everted	gradual convergent	rounded	asymmetrically thickened exterior	20cm	rim exterior	raised ridge	1
NL-Sur-4	rim/ neck	out-curving globular pot	out-curving	abrupt convergent	rounded	asymmetrically thickened exterior (collared rim)	20cm	lip	notching	1
NL-Sur-5	rim/ neck/ shoulder	everted globular pot	everted	gradual convergent	pointed		23cm	interior & exterior	red slip	1
NL-Sur-6	rim/ neck	everted globular pot (shouldered-ware)	everted	abrupt convergent		asymmetrically thickened exterior; channelled neck/ body convergence				1B
NL-Sur-7	rim/ neck	everted restricted neck vessel	everted convergent	gradual rounded			28cm			1
NL-Sur-8	rim/ neck/ shoulder	everted globular pot (shouldered-ware)	everted	parallel	rounded	asymmetrically thickened exterior (collared rim); channelled neck/ body convergence	16cm			1
NL-Sur-9	rim/ neck	everted globular pot (shouldered-ware)	everted	gradual convergent	flat	asymmetrically thickened exterior; channelled neck/ body convergence	20cm	1) neck 2) body	1) wiped lines 2) red slip	1
NL-Sur-10	rim/ neck/ carination	everted carinated jar	everted	gradual convergent	pointed		20cm	lip	notching	1
NL-Sur-11	rim/ neck	everted restricted neck vessel	everted	abrupt convergent	pointed	asymmetrically thickened exterior (collared rim)	20cm	exterior	black paint?	1B
NL-Sur-12	rim/ neck	out-curving restricted neck vessel		out-curving	parallel	rounded		28cm		1
NL-Sur-13	body									1
NL-Sur-14	rim/ neck	everted globular pot (shouldered -ware)	everted	gradual divergent	rounded	asymmetrically thickened exterior (collared rim); channelled neck/ body convergence	18cm	exterior	red slip	1
NL-Sur-16	rim	open bowl	direct	abrupt convergent	rounded		14cm	interior & exterior	pale green glaze	porcelain
NL-Sur-18	rim/ neck	everted restricted neck vessel	everted	gradual convergent	pointed	asymmetrically thickened exterior	12cm	rim exterior	raised ridge w/ a channel on either side	1

continued over

Table 7.5 Liang Nabulei Lisa: surface and excavated pottery sherd descriptions

NUMBER	SHERD TYPE	VESSEL FORM	RIM DATA					DECORATION DATA		FABRIC ANALYSIS
			DIRECTION	RIM PROFILE	LIP PROFILE	EXTRA RIM FEATURES	RIM DIAMETER	LOCATION	TECHNIQUE	
NL-A-1a	body									1
NL-A-1b	body									1
NL-A-1c	body									1
NL-A-1d	body									1
NL-A-1e	body									1
NL-A-1f	body									1
NL-A-1g	body									1
NL-A-1h	body									1
NL-A-3	rim/ body	open bowl	slight out-curving	gradual convergent	rounded			interior & exterior	blue and white paint/ glaze	porcelain
NL-A-3a	body									1
NL-A-3b	body									1
NL-A-4a	body									1
NL-A-4b	body									1
NL-A-4c	body									1
NL-A-4d	body									1
NL-A-4e	body									1C
NL-A-5a	body									1
NL-A-5b	body									1C
NL-A-5c	body									1B
NL-A-5d	body									1
NL-A-5e	body									1
NL-A-5f	body									1C
NL-A-6	rim/ neck	everted restricted neck vessel	everted	parallel	flat		14cm	1) lip 2) exterior lip 3) exterior neck corner point	1) linear incised notching 2) groove 3) linear incision	1
NL-A-6a	body									1
NL-A-7a	body									1
NL-A-7b	body									1
NL-A-7c	body									1
NL-A-7d	rim									1
NL-A-8	neck/ shoulder	everted globular pot	everted				10cm (at neck)	exterior	red slip	1
NL-A-8a	rim			parallel	flat					1
NL-A-8b	rim									1

sectioning and petrographic analysis. He examined them all and then selected seven representing the above macroscopic groups for detailed analysis. He concluded that the Nabulei Lisa tempers were all 'quartz-calcite which were generically very similar to the Batu Lei sand and presumably indigenous to Aru.' The sand samples referred to had been collected in 1998 from the contemporary pottery making village. These were identified as Temper Type 1. The quartz-calcite Nabulei Lisa sherds could be further subdivided into two classes:

1) Temper Type 1B. Calcareous grains dominant, but with terrigenous grains present in significant amounts. NL-Sur-1 (Nabulei Lisa-Surface), NL-Sur-6, NL-Sur-11, and NL-A-5C fall into this class; and
2) Temper Type 1C. Calcareous and terrigenous grains present in subequal proportions (post-burial leaching has corroded many calcareous grains in NL-A-5F). NL-A-4, NL-A-5B, and NL-A-5F fall into this class.

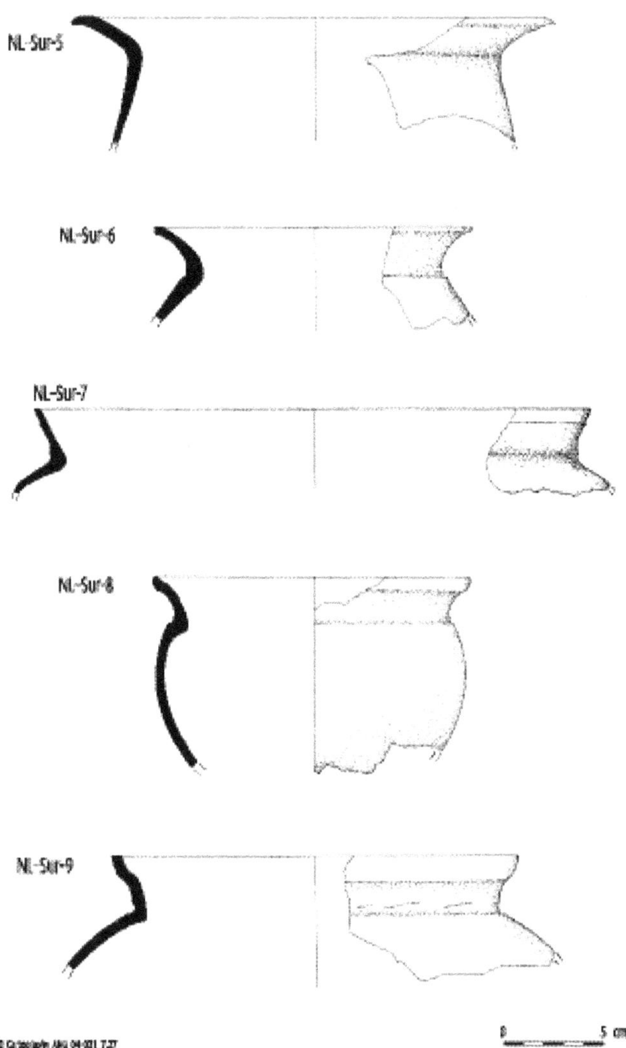

Figure 7.27 Liang Nabulei Lisa: vessel forms among the surface collected pottery, including plain everted globular pots (NL-Sur-5, NL-Sur-7 — the former with red slip); and everted globular pots with shoulders (NL-Sur-6, NL-Sur-8, NL-Sur-9 — the latter with red slip)

Pottery sherds from Nabulei Lisa that were not petrographically analysed have been identified in Table 7.5 simply as temper 'Type 1', while the thin-sectioned sherds are identified as Types 1B and 1C.

The restricted range of pots at Nabulei Lisa and the similarities with the contemporary Batu Lei pottery may be due to:

1) The difference in sample size. Far fewer sherds were recovered from Nabulei Lisa;
2) Stylistic change through time. There is a general tendency in Island Southeast Asia for pottery to become more highly decorated over time. However, this is unlikely to account for the differences between the two assemblages. The Nabulei Lisa and Wangil assemblages are more or less contemporaneous;
3) Difference in site type/function. While it is located close to the *sungai*, being a cave site Nabulei Lisa was probably used predominantly as a hunting camp or casual stop-over whilst visiting gardens. Simply for this reason it is not likely to have the range of pottery found at a permanent village settlement on the coast;
4) Stylistic differences between pottery production centres in the Aru group. Nabulei Lisa is geographically closer to Batu Lei, than to the pottery producing centres of Samang and Maekoor (see Chapter 6, this volume), and so its indigenous pottery probably comes from a different source than that at Wangil.

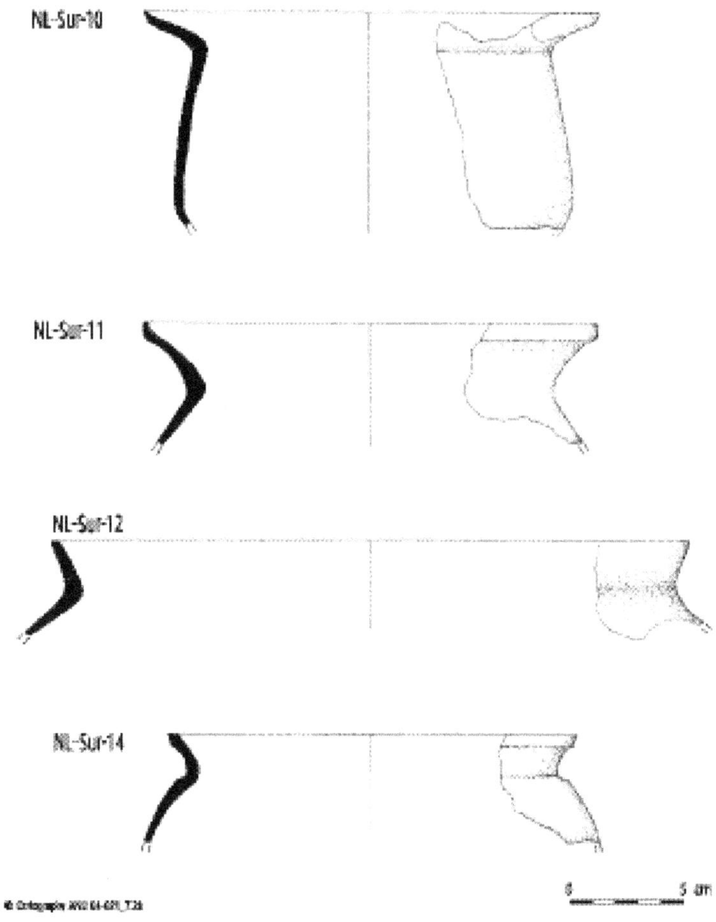

Figure 7.28 Liang Nabulei Lisa: vessel forms among the surface collected pottery, including an everted carinated jar with lip notching (NL-Sur-10); everted and out-curving, restricted neck vessels (probably globular pots) (NL-Sur-11, NL-Sur-12); and a shouldered, everted globular pot with red slip (NL-Sur-14)

Conclusions

Liang Nabulei Lisa provides a detailed cultural sequence that bridges the terminal Pleistocene to mid-Holocene. The site perfectly complements the record from Liang Lemdubu, where most of the deposit accumulated in the period from ca. 28,000 BP to the beginning of the Holocene. The placement of Liang Nabulei Lisa close to the major *sungai* channel also provides a wealth of detailed information of the changes that occurred within the aquatic to marine realm during the marine transgression, thereby providing a part of the overall archaeological picture that is missing from the Liang Lemdubu record.

The faunal sequence indicates that between 16,000 and 11,000 cal BP savannah/ grassland environments were accessible to hunters using Liang Nabulei Lisa. As in the Lemdubu cave, Agile Wallaby (*Macropus agilis*) was an important game species during this time, but it disappears in Spit 28 around the beginning of the Holocene, providing further support that more open conditions prevailed widely in the Aru Islands prior to about 10,000 BP. A freshwater stream probably flowed along the same channel where the tidal *sungai* is today, although there are indications in the crab remains that it may have been dry or at least seasonal in the early period of site occupation represented by the cultural material below Spit 31. Patches of rainforest thicket are likely to have been present along this channel from which the hunters of Liang Nabulei Lisa could exploit a range of closed forest dwelling animals. Freshwater shellfish and crabs were exploited from the stream. The beginning of the Holocene brought wetter conditions to the newly formed coastal regions of southern New Guinea, including the Aru Islands. The almost immediate loss of savannah-dependent species at the beginning of the Holocene tracks the expected changes in vegetation well. With the Holocene rise in sea level, tidal conditions were established, and the succession from freshwater to brackish to marine/estuarine conditions is reflected clearly in changes in the species composition of the crabs and shellfish.

The upper 6000 years attest to use of the cave when it was proximal to the tidal *sungai* and estuarine marine conditions prevailed. During this time the economic emphasis seems to have switched to the immediate resources of the *sungai*, supplemented by hunting of small to medium game species from the surrounding forest. Prior to this time, freshwater fish and shellfish were exploited but in small numbers, and the emphasis was on hunting of medium to large game species. Evidence for the introduction of domestic animals such as pig and dog, and by proxy the introduction of an agricultural economy into the Aru Islands, appears only in the last thousand years of the Liang Nabulei Lisa sequence. Pottery is also confined to the uppermost levels of the site dating within the last thousand years, and a restricted range of vessels are represented. This may reflect the limited range of activities that are carried out at cave sites rather than provide an accurate reflection of the date of the introduction of horticulture and pottery production in Aru (see Chapter 6, this volume).

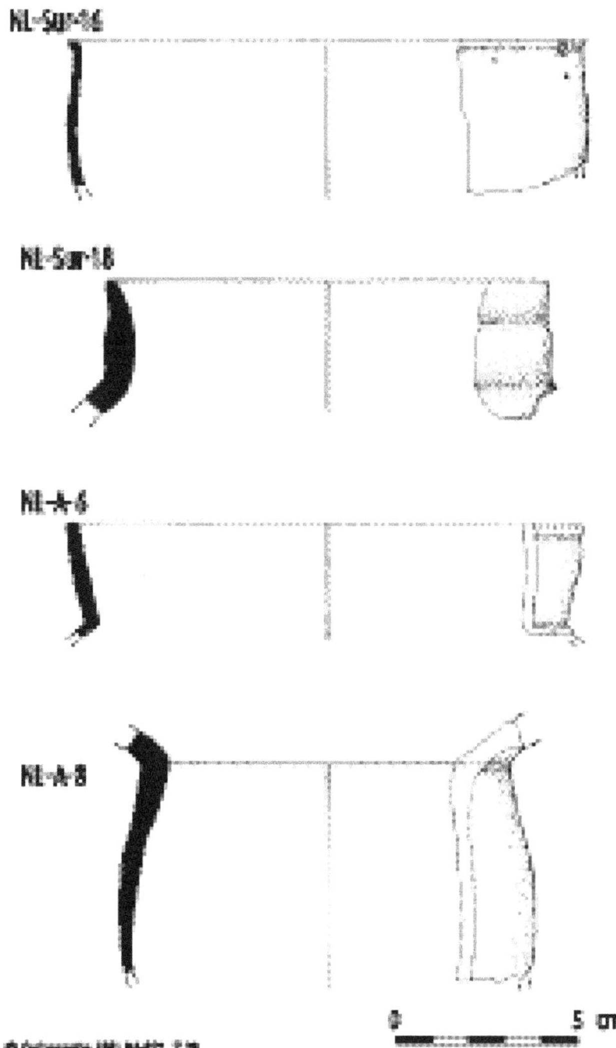

Figure 7.29 Liang Nabulei Lisa: diagnostic and decorated pottery sherds from the surface collection and excavation, including the rim of an open porcelain bowl with pale green glaze (NL-Sur-16); a rim sherd with an exterior raised ridge (NL-Sur-18); an everted rim sherd with incised linear notching on the lip and linear incision on the exterior neck corner point (NL-A-6); and a neck/shoulder sherd from a red-slipped, everted globular pot (NL-A-8)

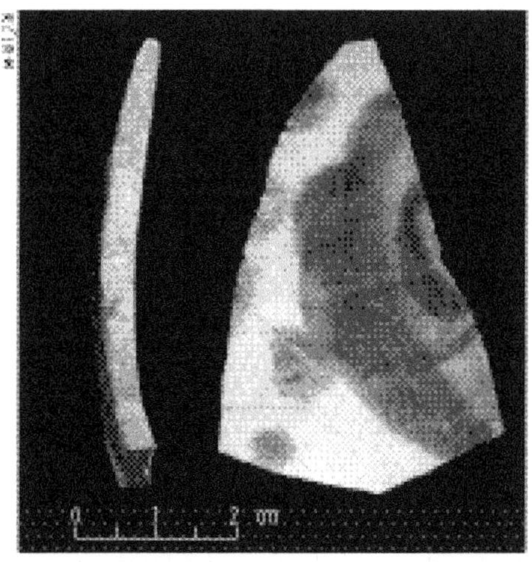

Figure 7.30 Liang Nabulei Lisa: rim and body section of a Chinese blue and white tradeware bowl from Spit 3 (NL-A-3)

References

Crome, F.H.J. 1975. Some observations on the biology of the cassowary in northern Queensland. *Emu* 76:8–14.

Flannery, T.F. 1995a. *Mammals of New Guinea* (revised edition). Sydney: Reed Books.

Flannery, T.F. 1995b. *Mammals of the South-West Pacific and Moluccan Islands*. Sydney: Australian Museum/Reed Books.

Groves, C.P. and T. F. Flannery. 1989. Revision of the genus *Dorcopsis* (Macropodidae: Marsupialia). In G. Grigg, P. Jarman, and I. Hume (eds), *Kangaroos, Wallabies and Rat-kangaroos*, pp. 117–128. Volume 1. Chipping Norton, NSW: Surrey Beatty & Sons.

Healey, H. 1995. Traps and trapping in the Aru Islands. *Cakalele: Maluku Research Journal* 6:51–65.

O'Connor, S., K. Aplin, M. Spriggs, P. Veth, and L.A. Ayliffe. 2002. From savannah to rainforest: changing environments and human occupation at Liang Lemdubu, the Aru Islands, Maluku, Indonesia. In A.P. Kershaw, B. David, N. Tapper, D. Penny, and J. Brown (eds), *Bridging Wallace's Line: The Environmental and Cultural History and Dynamics of the Southeast Asian-Australian Region*, pp. 279–306. Reiskirchen: Catena Verlag. *Advances in GeoEcology* 34.

Pearce, J. and R. Luff. 1994. The taphonomy of cooked bone. In R. Luff and P. Rowley-Conwy (eds), *Whither Environmental Archaeology? Oxbow Monograph* 38:51–6. Oxford: Oxbow Books.

Shipman, P., G. Foster, and M. Schoeninger. 1984. Burnt bones and teeth: an experimental study of color, morphology, crystal structure and shrinkage. Journal of Archaeological Science 11:307–25.

van Strien, N.J. 1996. Mammals of the Aru Islands. In H.P. Nooteboom (ed.), *The Aru Archipelago: Plants, Animals, People and Conservation*, pp.87–106. Amsterdam: Nederlandse Commissie Voor Internationale Natuurbescherming. *Mededelingan* 30.

Tate, G.H.H. and R. Archbold. 1935. Results of the Archbold Expeditions. No. 4. An apparently new race of wallabies from southern New Guinea. *American Museum Novitates* 804:1–2.

Ubelaker, D.H. 1978. *Human Skeletal Remains*. Chicago: Aldine Publishing Co.

Waithman, J. 1979. A report on a collection of mammals from southwest Papua, 1972–1973. *Australian Zoologist* 20:313–26.

Walker, K. The Freshwater Mussels (Hyriidae, Unionidae) of Australasia. URL: http://www.lucidcentral.com/keys/lwrrdc/public/Aquatics/aemoll/html/KEY_TO_S.htm

Wang, Y., A. Hope Jahren, and R. Amundson. 1997. Potential for ^{14}C dating of biogenic carbonate in Hackberry (Celtis) endocarps. *Quaternary Research* 47:337–43.

Appendix 7.1

Liang Nabulei Lisa: Depths (cm) of Excavation Units (Spits) and Weight (kg) of Sediment and Rocks by Spit

SPIT	NW DEPTH	NE DEPTH	SW DEPTH	SE DEPTH	CENTRAL DEPTH	SEDIMENT WT.	ROCKS WT.
1	1.5	2.0	1.0	3.0	2.5	24.3	0.2
2	1.5	2.5	2.5	1.0	2.5	26.6	0.0
3	2.0	2.5	2.0	3.5	5.0	31.3	0.0
4	3.5	2.0	2.0	2.0	0.5	29.3	0.0
5	2.0	3.0	3.0	3.0	2.5	33.0	0.0
6	3.5	3.0	3.0	2.5	3.0	34.1	0.2
7	1.5	2.5	3.0	2.0	2.5	29.1	0.0
8	2.0	2.0	2.0	3.0	3.0	30.7	0.0
9	3.0	3.0	3.5	2.5	3.0	31.8	0.0
10	3.0	3.0	2.0	2.5	3.0	28.7	3.1
11	2.0	2.5	3.5	3.5	3.0	32.0	2.5
12	2.0	2.5	2.0	2.0	2.5	24.4	0.8
13	3.0	2.5	2.0	3.0	1.5	25.3	3.0
14	2.5	1.5	2.0	2.5	2.5	23.6	3.4
15	4.0	2.5	3.5	2.5	1.5	30.4	2.6
16	2.0	3.0	3.0	1.5	3.0	28.3	2.6
17	3.0	1.5	2.5	2.0	1.5	28.7	4.7
18	2.0	rock nr	2.5	4.0	3.5	25.9	1.5
19	3.3	rock nr	2.2	3.5	3.7	32.9	2.7
20	2.7	10.0	3.8	3.5	2.3	34.4	10.5
21	2.4	2.7	1.5	1.8	2.8	27.1	6.8
22	1.6	2.8	3.5	3.7	3.2	32.0	5.8
23	3.5	4.5	3.0	2.0	2.5	30.0	4.2
24	2.5	2.0	3.0	2.5	3.0	31.3	3.5
25	3.5	4.5	3.5	3.0	4.5	31.9	4.9
26	1.5	0.5	2.5	3.5	2.5	28.8	8.3
27	4.0	3.0	3.0	2.0	1.5	27.3	3.7
28	3.0	1.5	3.0	3.5	3.5	29.0	4.5
29	2.0	4.0	1.0	1.0	3.0	27.3	6.0
30	4.0	2.5	4.5	4.5	4.0	39.4	13.0
31	0.0	2.0	3.0	2.8	1.0	27.8	8.6
32	4.2	3.3	2.8	3.4	2.2	31.7	3.5
33	3.3	4.2	2.2	2.8	3.8	17.7	1.3
34	3.5	3.0	3.0	3.0	3.0	18.5	0.0
35	3.0	3.5	1.5	2.0	2.5	16.0	2.5
36	3.8	5.2	3.5	3.8	3.5	12.5	0.0
37	3.7	0	3.5	3.7	3.5	13.5	0.0
38	rock nr	5.1	2.3	1.5	3.3	10.9	0.0
39	rock nr	rock nr	rock nr	3.0	3.2	4.6	0.0
40	rock nr	rock nr	rock nr	2.5	3.0	4.6	0.0
41	rock nr	rock nr	rock nr	rock nr	3.0	3.5	0.0
42	rock nr	rock nr	rock nr	rock nr	4.0	3.4	0.0
43	rock nr	rock nr	rock nr	rock nr	6.0	3.5	0.0

NB: nr = no reading recorded

Appendix 7.2

Liang Nabulei Lisa: Faunal Data

NISP Data for all Identified Faunal Specimens by Spit

SPIT	*DASYURUS ALBOPUNCTATUS*	CF *SMINTHOPSIS* SP.	*ISOODON MACROURUS*	PERORYCTIDAE	UNIDENTIFIED BANDICOOT	*DORCOPSIS* SP.	*THYLOGALE STIGMATICA*	*THYLOGALE BRUNII*	*MACROPUS AGILIS*	*SPILOCUSCUS MACULATUS*	*PHALANGER GYMNOTIS*	*PHALANGER MIMICUS*	*PHALANGER* SP.	*DACTYLOPSILA TRIVIRGATA*	*UROMYS CAUDIMACULATUS*	SMALL MURID	PTEROPODIDAE	MICROCHIROPTERA	SUIDAE	CERVIDAE	CANIDAE	FROG	BIRD	CROCODILE	CHELUID TURTLE	BOIDAE	COLUBROIDEA	UNIDENTIFIED SNAKE	VARANIDAE	AGAMIDAE	ARIIDAE	PLOTOSIDAE	LUTJANIDAE	LABRIDAE	UNIDENTIFIED FISH	PORTUNIDAE TYPE A	PORTUNIDAE TYPE B	XANTHIDAE
1	0	0	0	0	0	0	0	0	0	0	0	0	1	0	0	0	0	0	1	1	1	0	0	0	0	0	0	0	0	0	0	0	0	0	0	0	0	0
2	0	0	0	0	0	0	0	0	0	0	0	0	4	0	0	0	0	2	3	0	0	0	0	0	0	0	0	0	1	0	0	0	0	0	2	0	0	2
3	0	0	0	0	1	0	0	0	0	2	0	0	3	0	0	0	3	1	3	0	0	0	0	0	0	0	0	0	0	0	0	0	0	0	9	0	0	10
4	0	0	0	0	0	0	0	0	0	1	0	0		0	0	0	2	0	1	0	0	0	0	0	0	0	0	0	0	0	0	0	0	0	14	0	0	18
5	0	0	0	0	1	0	0	1	0	0	0	0	3	0	0	0	1	0	1	0	0	0	0	0	0	0	0	0	0	0	0	0	0	0	26	0	0	54
6	0	0	0	0	0	0	0	0	0	0	0	0	1	0	0	0	19	0	1	0	0	0	0	0	0	0	0	0	0	1	0	0	0	0	17	0	0	51
7	0	0	0	0	1	0	0	0	0	0	0	0	7	0	0	0	16	7	0	0	0	0	0	0	0	0	0	0	1	0	0	0	0	0	18	0	0	40
8	0	0	0	0	0	0	0	2	0	0	0	0	8	0	0	0	4	0	0	0	0	0	0	0	0	0	0	0	0	0	0	0	0	0	17	0	0	11
9	0	0	0	0	0	0	0	1	0	3	0	0	5	0	0	0	15	1	2	0	0	0	0	0	0	3	0	0	0	0	0	0	0	1	7	0	3	34
10	0	0	0	1	0	0	0	0	0	2	0	0	9	0	1	0	9	7	0	0	0	0	1	0	0	2	0	1	0	0	0	0	0	0	16	0	0	41
11	0	0	0	0	0	0	0	0	0	4	0	1	10	0	0	0	11	17	0	0	0	1	0	0	0	1	0	1	0	0	1	0	0	0	25	0	3	34
12	0	0	0	0	0	0	0	2	0	0	0	0	9	0	0	0	8	10	0	0	0	0	0	0	0	2	0	1	0	0	0	0	2	0	35	0	3	38
13	0	0	0	0	1	0	1	0	0	0	0	0	3	0	0	0	4	1	0	0	0	0	0	0	0	0	0	2	0	0	1	0	0	0	11	0	5	20
14	0	0	0	0	0	0	0	0	0	0	2	0	11	0	0	1	14	9	0	0	0	0	0	0	0	1	0	3	1	0	0	0	0	0	25	1	9	19
15	0	0	0	0	0	0	2	1	0	0	0	0	6	0	0	0	5	5	0	0	0	0	0	1	0	1	0	2	0	0	0	0	0	0	25	0	11	10
16	0	0	0	1	0	0	0	0	0	1	0	1	10	0	0	0	6	0	0	0	0	0	0	0	0	3	0	4	0	0	1	0	0	0	18	0	8	10
17	0	0	0	0	1	0	0	2	0	0	0	0	3	0	0	0	5	2	0	0	0	0	0	0	0	1	0	0	0	0	0	0	0	0	6	0	2	8
18	0	0	0	0	0	0	0	3	0	1	1	0	3	0	1	0	8	16	0	0	0	0	0	0	0	9	0	4	0	0	0	0	0	0	27	6	3	21
19	0	0	0	0	0	0	0	3	0	3	0	0	5	0	2	0	6	0	0	0	0	0	0	0	4	8	0	3	0	0	0	0	0	0	9	0	3	11
20	0	0	0	1	2	0	1	1	0	1	1	1	3	1	0	0	4	0	0	0	0	0	0	0	1	2	1	2	0	0	0	1	0	0	8	1	0	5
21	0	0	0	2	0	0	0	1	0	0	0	0	1	0	1	0	2	0	0	0	0	0	0	0	3	6	0	3	2	0	0	0	0	0	6	0	0	0
22	0	0	0	0	5	0	1	1	0	0	0	0	4	0	0	0	2	0	0	0	0	0	0	0	3	8	0	0	1	1	1	0	0	0	8	1	0	1

continued over

Liang Nabulei Lisa: Faunal Data continued

SPIT	*DASYURUS ALBOPUNCTATUS*	CF *SMINTHOPSIS* SP.	*ISOODON MACROURUS*	PERORYCTIDAE	UNIDENTIFIED BANDICOOT	*DORCOPSIS* SP.	*THYLOGALE STIGMATICA*	*THYLOGALE BRUNII*	*MACROPUS AGILIS*	*SPILOCUSCUS MACULATUS*	*PHALANGER GYMNOTIS*	*PHALANGER MIMICUS*	*PHALANGER* SP.	*DACTYLOPSILA TRIVIRGATA*	*UROMYS CAUDIMACULATUS*	SMALL MURID	PTEROPODIDAE	MICROCHIROPTERA	SUIDAE	CERVIDAE	CANIDAE	FROG	BIRD	CROCODILE	CHELUID TURTLE	BOIDAE	COLUBROIDEA	UNIDENTIFIED SNAKE	VARANIDAE	AGAMIDAE	ARIIDAE	PLOTOSIDAE	LUTJANIDAE	LABRIDAE	UNIDENTIFIED FISH	PORTUNIDAE TYPE A	PORTUNIDAE TYPE B	XANTHIDAE
23	0	0	0	0	3	1	0	5	0	0	0	0	8	0	1	0	0	0	0	0	0	0	0	0	0	3	0	7	3	0	3	1	0	0	10	1	0	1
24	0	0	0	0	2	0	1	2	0	0	0	0	5	0	1	0	0	0	0	0	0	0	0	0	1	3	0	1	2	0	1	0	0	0	13	0	0	0
25	0	0	0	1	3	0	0	7	0	0	0	0	11	0	0	0	2	0	0	0	0	0	0	0	3	7	0	2	5	1	0	0	0	0	19	0	0	0
26	0	0	1	0	1	0	4	0	0	1	0	0	4	0	2	0	1	0	0	0	0	0	0	0	0	7	1	3	0	1	3	1	0	0	7	1	0	0
27	0	0	0	0	1	0	0	6	1	2	1	1	5	0	1	0	3	0	0	0	0	0	0	0	0	4	0	2	5	0	5	0	0	0	6	0	0	0
28	0	0	3	0	0	0	6	11	2	2	5	0	14	1	0	0	2	12	0	0	0	0	0	0	0	23	3	3	2	1	16	0	4	0	65	1	0	1
29	0	0	0	0	1	0	2	7	5	1	0	4	5	0	0	1	4	22	0	0	0	0	0	0	0	25	4	7	3	2	8	0	0	0	30	1	0	0
30	0	0	2	1	1	0	5	3	4	1	1	2	11	1	1	0	6	1	0	0	0	0	0	0	0	29	0	7	3	3	2	0	0	0	8	0	0	0
31	0	0	0	0	3	1	2	0	4	1	0	0	8	1	0	0	5	14	0	0	0	0	0	0	0	42	3	16	0	2	2	0	0	0	20	1	0	0
32	0	1	0	0	6	2	8	1	11	0	0	0	8	0	1	0	3	7	0	0	0	0	0	0	0	53	1	12	1	0	1	0	0	0	23	3	0	0
33	0	0	1	0	9	0	8	3	1	5	0	0	7	0	1	0	2	1	0	0	0	0	0	0	0	13	0	4	0	0	0	0	0	0	1	0	0	0
34	0	0	10	3	5	1	14	4	14	7	1	0	6	0	0	0	9	4	0	0	0	0	0	0	0	54	2	5	0	0	0	0	0	0	10	0	0	0
35	0	0	0	2	4	1	10	11	11	3	2	0	1	0	0	0	4	0	0	0	0	0	0	0	0	44	0	7	3	0	0	0	0	0	8	0	0	0
36	0	0	1	3	4	0	15	2	4	3	0	0	2	0	0	0	2	4	0	0	0	0	0	0	0	26	0	4	0	2	0	0	0	0	4	0	0	0
37	1	0	1	0	6	1	20	4	6	3	0	0	3	0	0	0	1	0	0	0	0	0	0	0	0	39	0	0	2	1	0	0	0	0	2	0	0	0
38	0	0	0	10	0	0	9	3	8	0	1	1	0	0	0	0	3	2	0	0	0	0	0	0	0	39	0	2	1	0	0	0	0	0		0	0	0
39	0	0	0	1	2	0	12	4	2	3	0	0	2	0	0	0	2	1	0	0	0	0	0	0	0	23	0	1	10	0	0	0	0	0	2	0	0	0
40	0	0	0	1	2	0	7	0	1	0	0	0	0	0	0	0	0	0	0	0	0	0	1	0	0	2	0	0	0	0	0	0	0	0	0	0	0	0
41	0	0	0	0	2	0	9	1	3	1	1	0	1	0	0	0	4	1	0	0	0	0	0	0	0	5	0	1	0	0	0	0	0	0	0	0	0	0
42	0	0	0	0	1	1	5	0	0	0	0	0	0	0	0	0	4	16	0	0	0	0	0	0	0	1	0	0	0	0	0	0	0	0	0	0	0	0
43	0	0	0	0	1	2	0	0	0	0	0	0	1	0	0	0	6	59	0	0	0	0	0	0	0	3	1	0	0	0	0	0	0	0	0	0	0	0

NB: the values are not adjusted for excavated weight/volume

Weight (g) of Bone for each Identified Taxonomic Group and Weight of Bone in Each Burning Category by Spit

SPIT	TOTAL UNBURNT BONE	TOTAL LIGHTLY BURNT BONE	TOTAL BURNT BONE	TOTAL CALCINED BONE	TOTAL ALL BONE	TACHYGLOSSIDAE	DASYURIDAE	PERAMELOIDEA	MACROPODIDAE	PHALANGERIDAE	PETAURIDAE	MURIDAE	CHIROPTERA	SUIDAE	CERVIDAE	CANIDAE	FROG	BIRD	CROCODILE	CHELUID TURTLE	SNAKE	VARANIDAE	AGAMIDAE	FISH	UNIDENTIFIED BONE
1	1.2	1.0	0	8.0	10.1	0	0	0	0	0.6	0	0	0	0	0.1	0.3	0	0	0	0	0	0	0	0	9.2
2	2.5	3.3	0.7	16.8	23.3	0	0	0	0	0.7	0	0	0.1	1.8	0	0	0	0	0	0	0	0.3	0	0.2	20.2
3	3.9	4.0	0.5	8.5	16.9	0	0	0.3	0.6	1.3	0	0	0.4	2.8	0	0	0	0	0	0	0	0	0	0.8	10.9
4	8.0	1.0	0.5	2.8	12.2	0	0	0	0.7	0.2	0	0	0.2	2.2	0	0	0	0	0	0	0	0	0	2.3	6.7
5	8.9	4.4	1.0	2.8	17.0	0	0	0.2	0.1	0.3	0	0	0.2	0.4	0	0	0	0	0	0	0	0	0	1.7	14.2
6	5.1	2.6	0.7	0.7	9.0	0	0	0	0	0.1	0	0	2.4	0.8	0	0	0	0	0	0	0	0	0.1	2.1	3.7
7	7.0	1.4	0.6	3.1	12.2	0	0	0.3	0	1.0	0	0	3.7	0	0	0	0	0	0	0	0	0.3	0	1.2	5.8
8	9.7	3.6	0.6	1.1	14.9	0	0	0	1.5	1.9	0	0	0.5	0	0	0	0	0	0	0	0	0	0	3.3	7.8
9	10.5	4.9	1.0	1.4	17.7	0	0	0	2.8	2.3	0	0	1.5	2.8	0	0	0	0	0	0	1.5	0	0	3.4	3.5
10	11.8	5.0	3.8	1.3	21.9	0	0	0.1	0.2	2.6	0	0.7	1.5	0	0	0	0	1.2	0	0	0.8	0	0	2.5	12.3
11	10.0	3.1	8.1	2.2	23.4	0	0	0	0.5	6.7	0	0	1.9	0	0	0	0.1	0	0	0	0.3	0	0	3.8	10.1
12	10.6	3.5	2.5	2.9	19.5	0	0	0	1.7	1.5	0	0	1.9	0	0	0	0	0	0	0	0.2	0	0	5.9	8.4
13	6.1	5.6	1.5	1.1	14.2	0	0	0.1	0.5	0.9	0	0	0.4	0	0	0	0	0	0	0	0.1	0	0	1.6	10.7
14	15.4	6.6	2.6	0.6	25.1	0	0	0	1.2	7.2	0	0.1	1.9	0	0	0	0	0	0	0	0.3	0.4	0	5.3	8.8
15	14.2	3.3	1.3	4.2	23.0	0	0	0	3.1	2.2	0	0	0.8	0	0	0	0	0	3.2	0	0.5	0	0	4.3	8.9
16	20.8	9.0	2.5	0.8	33.1	0	0.1	0.1	0.5	3.7	0	0	1.6	0	0	0	0	0	0	0	3.7	0	0	7.1	16.3
17	9.5	3.8	1.9	0.3	15.5	0	0	1.1	0.3	2.4	0	0	1.6	0	0	0	0	0	0	0	0.6	0	0	1.1	8.4
18	21.7	16.8	4.6	0.4	43.5	0	0	0	2.9	5.2	0	0.3	2.5	0	0	0	0	0	0	0	4.6	0	0	5.6	22.3
19	31.5	7.6	5.2	1.1	45.3	0	0	0	3.4	7.0	0	0.3	1.1	0	0	0	0	0	0	5.8	6.6	0	0	1.2	19.9
20	27.3	10.3	2.5	2.7	42.7	0	0	1.3	4.3	8.4	0.3	0	0.6	0	0	0	0	0	0	0.7	1.8	0	0	2.3	23.1
21	23.3	10.6	3.7	0.1	37.7	0	0	1.3	3.6	0.8	0	0.7	0.4	0	0	0	0	0	0	3.3	4.6	0.6	0	1.4	21.1
22	15.9	10.9	5.7	3.1	35.6	0	0	1.1	1.7	2.8	0	0	1.0	0	0	0	0	0	0	0	4.5	0.3	0.2	3.0	20.9
23	47.4	10.3	4.1	1.3	63.1	0	0	1.9	6.0	5.6	0	1.3	0	0	0	0	0	0	0	2.2	3.5	0.7	0	3.9	38.1
24	33.3	17.4	3.5	1.4	55.6	0	0	0.7	7.7	2.7	0	0	0	0	0	0	0	0	0	0	3.6	0.4	0	4.9	35.7
25	48.1	20.6	6.8	2.4	77.9	0	0	2.6	15.8	3.9	0	0	0.5	0	0	0	0	0	0	0.6	5.5	1.5	0.2	2.3	45.1
26	32.0	19.6	14.5	2.7	68.8	0	0	0.6	8.4	6.7	0	0.8	0.1	0	0	0	0	0	0	1.3	5.3	0	0.2	4.4	41.1

continued over

Weight (g) of Bone continued

SPIT	TOTAL UNBURNT BONE	TOTAL LIGHTLY BURNT BONE	TOTAL BURNT BONE	TOTAL CALCINED BONE	TOTAL ALL BONE	TACHYGLOSSIDAE	DASYURIDAE	PERAMELOIDEA	MACROPODIDAE	PHALANGERIDAE	PETAURIDAE	MURIDAE	CHIROPTERA	SUIDAE	CERVIDAE	CANIDAE	FROG	BIRD	CROCODILE	CHELUID TURTLE	SNAKE	VARANIDAE	AGAMIDAE	FISH	UNIDENTIFIED BONE
27	33.1	11.8	6.9	3.0	54.9	0	0	0.3	6.0	7.7	0.2	0.7	0.7	0	0	0	0	0	0	0	2.2	2.8	0	3.4	31.0
28	66.9	35.8	14.3	23.4	140.3	0	0	0.3	20.1	8.9	1.0	0	0.4	0	0	0	0	0	0	0	11.0	0.5	0.1	9.1	88.9
29	43.6	22.6	12.8	14.3	93.3	0	0	0	13.6	2.8	0	0.2	1.0	0	0	0	0	0	0	0	6.5	0.9	0.2	4.3	63.8
30	73.3	52.6	18.3	9.0	153.1	0	0	1.4	16.7	9.9	0	0.3	1.7	0	0	0	0	0	0	0	14.5	2.0	0.4	1.9	104.5
31	66.5	54.0	17.1	20.1	157.5	0	0	0.6	14.8	3.8	0.2	0	2.0	0	0	0	0	0	0	0	16.4	0	0.6	2.3	117.0
32	75.1	56.3	16.0	22.7	170.0	0	0.1	1.1	13.3	1.9	0	0.8	0.9	0	0	0	0	0	0	0	19.6	0.1	0	1.8	130.6
33	123.5	54.3	15.1	18.6	211.4	0	0	4.2	21.4	6.8	0	0.2	0.8	0	0	0	0	0	0	0	2.9	0	0	0.2	174.9
34	163.5	60.3	16.2	14.3	254.3	0	0	8.0	48.1	9.9	0	0	3.6	0	0	0	0	0	0	0	19.1	0	0	0.8	164.7
35	157.3	55.7	39.6	12.9	265.4	0.5	0	2.4	41.0	5.1	0	0	1.0	0	0	0	0	0	0	0	15.9	1.9	0	0.8	197.4
36	140.7	30.2	11.0	6.3	188.2	0	0	2.1	18.2	6.3	0	0	0.8	0	0	0	0	0	0	0	7.3	0	0.9	0.3	152.5
37	126.7	28.9	15.0	9.6	180.3	0	0.3	2.5	27.1	2.7	0	0	0.2	0	0	0	0	0	0	0	13.5	0.6	0.2	0.3	132.9
38	181.1	45.6	10.0	13.7	250.4	0	0	7.2	38.9	1.2	0	0	0.8	0	0	0	0	0	0	0	18.0	0.4	0	0	183.7
39	103.3	14.8	3.2	7.2	128.6	0	0	0.8	10.6	2.8	0	0	1.1	0	0	0	0	0	0	0	9.7	9.8	0	0.3	93.4
40	126.4	7.1	3.1	2.2	138.7	0	0	1.6	9.5	0	0	0	0	0	0	0	0	0.4	0	0	0.3	0	0	0	126.9
41	75.5	7.1	5.4	5.1	93.1	0	0	1.8	14.2	0.6	0	0	0.9	0	0	0	0	0	0	0	1.6	0	0	0	73.9
42	61.9	6.9	1.1	4.5	74.4	0	0	0.5	8.7	0	0	0	1.7	0	0	0	0	0	0	0	0.4	0	0	0	63.1
43	5.9	2.1	0.9	0.1	9.0	0	0	0.1	0.6	0.1	0	0	2.1	0	0	0	0	0	0	0	0.4	0	0	0	5.7

8

Human Remains from Liang Nabulei Lisa, Aru Islands

David Bulbeck

School of Archaeology and Anthropology, The Australian National University, Canberra, ACT, Australia

Introduction

Fragments of human skeletal material were recovered from the Liang Nabulei Lisa excavation. They had already been washed and cleaned when brought to the author for study on two occasions, by Sue O'Connor in late 1997 and Juliette Pasveer on 17 May 2001. Their condition could be described as semi-fossilized, whether their appearance is unburnt (the majority) or burnt. I identified the fragments by anatomical element and sought joins between them and other evidence of the minimum number of individuals represented.

With respect to the age of the remains, O'Connor et al. (Chapter 7, this volume) detail the early Holocene age of the dated sample from Spit 23, and the predominantly terminal Pleistocene age (16,200–10,200 cal BP) for spits below Spit 25. Certain patterns in the faunal material from these spits are also interpreted to reflect the Pleistocene to Holocene transition. The observation that human remains have been buried into these spits, as documented in this paper, may indicate that the archaeological evidence for the Pleistocene–Holocene transition would be even clearer were it not for the disturbance associated with the burial of the human material. As for dating the Liang Nabulei Lisa human remains, an early Holocene estimate would seem best for the adult material distributed between Spits 23 and 39, if a single individual is in fact represented. The remains of the younger (Spits 29–35) and older child (Spits 33–36) may also be early Holocene in age, but they could equally date to the terminal Pleistocene in view of the fact that they are distributed in levels which date to the terminal Pleistocene. This interpretation is based on the fact that any burial event would have to be contemporary with, or certainly no older than, the most recent material whose disturbance might be due to the burial event. However, spits above 20 have considerable quantities of marine/estuarine shellfish and there is little or no marine/estuarine shellfish in spits below 23. The lack of marine/estuarine shellfish in the spits where the skeletal material occurs may be taken to indicate that even the adult material was not buried from much higher in the profile than Spit 23.

The author effected measurement of tooth diameters and cranial vault thickness with a Mitotoyu electronic calliper accurate to 0.05mm, and phalanx lengths were taken according to Martin's system (Martin and Saller 1957:554, 589) with a Stalon sliding calliper accurate to the nearest 0.5mm. Dental morphological traits were recorded in terms of the grades established by the Arizona State University (ASU) system, whenever possible with reference to the standard casts illustrating these grades of expression (Hillson 1996:85–102; Scott and Turner 1997: Chapter 2).

The fragments weigh 70.1g in all (see Table 8.1) and came from possibly four individuals: two juveniles, an older adolescent or young adult, and a mature adult. They were encountered between Spits 23 and 41, and many fragments joined across different spits, including one evident join between fragments in Spits 23 and 37, as part of a partial calvarium whose constituent parts were found in eight separate spits as far down as Spit 39 (Fig. 8.1). The depth difference between Spits 23 and 39 is about 32cm, which is over twice the average height of a human cranium (cf. Howells 1989:123). This is indicative of burial or post-depositional factors that led to some vertical dispersion of the human fragments in the site's deposit. A clear dichotomy emerges between the teeth, which are generally splintered and almost always show signs of having been burnt, and the bone fragments which appear unburnt except for a femur fragment from Spit 23.

Table 8.1 Liang Nabulei Lisa: distribution of human material through the sequence

SPIT	ELEMENT	WEIGHT (G)	CONDITION	COMMENTS (REJOINS SHOWN DOWNWARDS)
23	Calvarium	2.7	Unburnt	Rejoins with a Spit 37 fragment
23	Femur	8.2	Well burnt	3 rejoining fragments
27	Pelvis	2.7	Unburnt	Same pelvis as Spit 37 fragment (?)
29	Deciduous tooth	0.2	Burnt	3–6 year old
32	Calvarium	0.7	Unburnt	Rejoins with Spit 37/38 fragments
33	Teeth	1.2	1 burnt	Burnt tooth incorporates an enamel fragment from Spit 34
33	Manual phalanx	0.3	Unburnt	Fused epiphysis
34	Teeth	0.9	Burnt	Tooth enamel fragments that rejoin with Spit 35 crown fragments
34	Zygomatic arch	0.6	Unburnt	
34	Phalanges	3.9	Unburnt	4 manual + 1 pedal
35	Calvarium	2.2	Unburnt	Rejoins with Spit 37/38 fragments
35	Teeth	1.8	Most burnt	1 molar cap rejoins a Spit 37 root
35	Manual phalanges	0.9	Unburnt	
35	Pelvis	2.2	Unburnt	
36	Cranium	1.6	Unburnt	
36	Teeth	2.6	Most burnt	
36	Manual phalanges	2.1	Unburnt	Perforation from excavation damage
37	Calvarium	20.9	Unburnt	Rejoins with Spit 38/39 fragments
37	Teeth	1.6	Burnt	
37	Pelvis	2.3	Unburnt	
38	Calvarium	8.0	Unburnt	
39	Calvarium	2.6	Fractured	
41	Tooth enamel	0.1	Fractured	Spall

Description of the Teeth

Spit 29 yielded a burnt spall of enamel fragment which could not be convincingly matched up with any other teeth from the excavation. The same spit produced a deciduous upper incisor with Smith's (1984) wear stage 3, suggestive of a person who was between three and six years old at the time of death, depending on the rapidity of the rate of occlusal wear. Diameters are 4.5mm (mesio-distal) and 3.85mm (bucco-lingual), lingual shovelling is trace (ASU 1), but there is no labial shovelling, incisor interruption grooves, or signs of caries or macroscopic enamel hypoplasia. Tuberculum dentale development is moderate. The same person is probably represented by a deciduous right lower canine from Spit 35 with Smith's (1984) stage 2 wear. Mesio-distal and bucco-lingual diameters are 6mm and 5.8mm respectively, shovelling is absent, and no traces of caries or macroscopic enamel hypoplasia were observed. Both deciduous teeth would refer to a younger person than any of the permanent Nabulei Lisa teeth do, even though, as with most of the latter, they appear burnt.

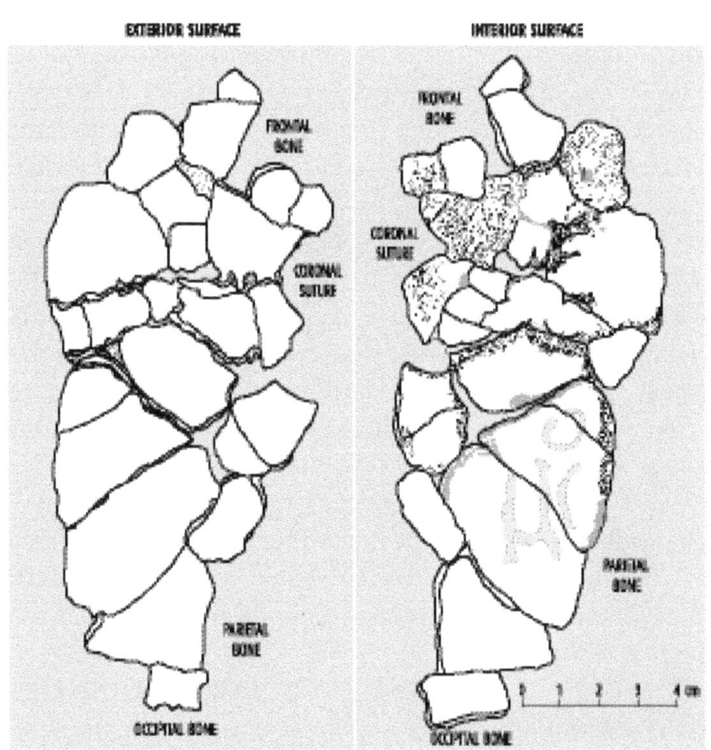

Figure 8.1 Liang Nabulei Lisa: some of the cranial bone from which formed a partial calvarium

A child of approximately seven to ten years of age at death is represented by two upper incisors with light occlusal wear and three unerupted premolars with incompletely formed roots. Even though wear is slightly greater on the right I^2 (Smith 2) than the right I^1 (Smith 1), and the latter alone shows the strong brown staining characteristic of the burnt and fractured cheek teeth, this would not provide sufficient grounds to assign them to separate individuals under a Minimum Number of Individuals model. Morphologically they are similar as both show slight lingual shovelling (ASU 3) and no interruption grooves. Additionally, neither displays any macroscopic enamel hypoplasia and although linear enamel hypoplasia (LEH) is discernible on the lower crown of both unerupted premolars represented by complete crowns, the latter would correspond to an arrest in enamel development after about five years old, by which stage the incisor crowns would have been completely formed (cf. Hillson 1996:144, 175). All four teeth with complete crowns are well preserved, in contrast to the typically fragmented status of the other permanent teeth from the site.

Table 8.2 gives details of provenance and crown diameters of the teeth of the seven to ten year old child. All of the mesio-distal diameters exceed the corresponding means of the large-toothed Walpiri males of central Australia, whereas all of the bucco-lingual diameters essentially match the respective mean values of Walpiri females (cf. Bulbeck 1981:29). The person's youthful status and lack of interstitial tooth wear explain the relatively big mesio-distal diameters, and so tooth size can be considered equivalent to that of central Australian females.

Table 8.2 Liang Nabulei Lisa: teeth assigned to a seven to ten-year-old

TOOTH	SPIT	MAXIMUM CROWN DIAMETERS (MM)		CERVICO-ENAMEL JUNCTION DIAMETERS (MM)	
		MESIO-DISTAL	BUCCO-LINGUAL	MESIO-DISTAL	BUCCO-LINGUAL
Right I^1	36	9.7	7.5	7.7	6.9
Right I^2	35	7.8	6.5	5.9	6.4
P^2 (side?)	33	7.8	10.2	5.9	9.9
P occlusal fragment	34				
Right P_1	35	7.9	8.3	5.5	8.1

The right I^1 lacks any labial shovelling and has a medium tuberculum dentale, while the right I^2 displays 'normal' development, trace labial shovelling (ASU 1) and a small tuberculum dentale. The upper premolar lacks any odontome or accessory marginal tubercle but displays marked accessory ridges on both the mesial and distal margins of the crown. The right P_1 also has an accessory ridge (buccally) and no trace of an odontome, along with absence of any multiple lingual cusps (ASU 0).

The remaining teeth (see Table 8.3) were characterized by fracture lines along the enamel, which had often led to enamel fragments spalling off the crown, and other evidence of burning such as a brown, slightly shiny appearance. They could all well have come from the same adult person. We can be confident that the three second and third molars belong to the same person because the right M^2 and M_2 have perfectly matching occlusal surfaces, and the right M^3 nestles neatly against the M^2 along the margin that would have corresponded to their shared interstitial border. The occlusal wear on the teeth (see Table 8.3) is consistent with derivation from the same individual, as are other observations on them detailed below.

Linear enamel hypoplasia is macroscopically detectable only on the right M^1 and M^3 among the teeth and fragments considered here, in both cases on the cervical third of the crown. The two indicated interruptions to enamel growth would respectively correspond to developmental stages when:

1) only the occlusal quarter of the canines (in this case, subsequently lost through attrition) were being formed; and
2) after all the other tooth crowns had been completely formed (Hillson 1996:175).

Accordingly, we would not expect signs of linear enamel hypoplasia on the other teeth even if they had all come from the same person. Crown diameters can be measured only on:

1) the canines, with values similar to the averages for Walpiri males; and
2) the cheek teeth, with values more commensurate with the average diameters of Walpiri females and / or Melanesian, Bougainville Island males (cf. Bulbeck 1981:29).

Again, this finding is compatible with all of the teeth having come from the same individual.

A moderate degree (cf. Patterson 1984) of interproximal caries can be observed on the right lower canine from Spit 33, and the heavily worn upper premolar from Spit 36 has a small carious lesion low on its distal crown. The extant root of the premolar further bears a dark red stain, suggesting it had been exposed during life (stained during mastication) and, by inference, that the gums had experienced a considerable degree of resorption.

The canine from Spit 37 and canine fragment from Spit 35 both have trace (ASU 1) shovelling, whereas any shovelling is absent from the other two canines. The only other observable,

Table 8.3 Liang Nabulei Lisa: fractured teeth

TOOTH	SPIT	WEAR (SMITH'S CLASSES)	MAXIMUM CROWN DIAMETERS (MM)		CERVICO-ENAMEL JUNCTION DIAMETERS (MM)	
			MESIO-DISTAL	BUCCO-LINGUAL	MESIO-DISTAL	BUCCO-LINGUAL
Right $\underline{I}$ fragment	34	4				
Right lower C	33	4	≥8.0	8.5		
C fragment	35	?				
Right $\underline{C}$	35	4	8.5	9.0	6.2	~8.8
Left $\underline{C}$ fragment	36	2				
Left $\underline{C}$	37	5				
P^2 (?)	36	6	6.8	10.1	5.2	8.4
M_1 (?) fragment	36					
Right M^2	35	3	10.6	12.1	8.6	12.0
Right M^3	35	3	9.0	12.3	8.1	11.3
Right M_2	35	3	11.1		10.3	
Right M_3	36	4	≥9.2			

canine morphological trait is the single-rooted condition of the Spit 37 canine. The upper premolar in Spit 36 is also single-rooted, this being its sole extant morphological trait. The right M^1 displays a clear hypoconulid (ASU 4), a Y-groove pattern, a small (ASU 3) protostylid and two roots. The right M^2 and M^3 are both three-rooted and lack any parastyle, Carabelli's anomaly, or enamel extension. The M^2 has a full hypocone (ASU 4) and the M^3 preserves the trace of some degree of edge-tubercle development.

Scott and Turner (1997) present charts illustrating the frequency of expression of certain key morphological traits among Sino-American populations (divided here between Jomon and other Sino-Americans), Sunda-Pacific (Southeast Asian, Micronesian and Polynesian), and Sahul-Pacific populations. Five of their key traits may be observed on the Nabulei Lisa teeth (see Table 8.4). Although the incisor lingual shovelling would be more typical of Sino-Americans rather than any other circum-Pacific populations, the other expressions are more typical of Sunda-Pacific and Sahul-Pacific groups, and overall these would be the most likely affinities.

Table 8.4 Liang Nabulei Lisa: observed expressions on teeth in relation to circum-Pacific populations (after Scott and Turner 1997:Chapter 6)

MORPHOLOGICAL TRAIT	JOMON	SINO-AMERICAN	SUNDA-PACIFIC	SAHUL-PACIFIC
$\underline{I}$ lingual shovelling (≥ ASU 3)	+/-	+	+/-	-
No $\underline{I}$ labial shovelling (≥ ASU 2)	+	+/-	+	+
$\underline{I}$ lack interruption grooves	-	+/-	+	+
4-cusped M^2	+	+/-	+	+
$\underline{M}$s lack enamel extension	+	+/-	+	+
2-rooted M_1	+	+/-	+/-	+
Overall + or -	3+	1 +	4 +	4 +

+ = expression typical of the comparative populations

+/- = ambiguous expression

- = expression atypical of the comparative populations

Description of the Cranial Bone

Cranial bone was recovered from Spits 23–39, and on anatomical grounds there would be no reason not to assign all fragments to the same individual. Most of the fragments join into a single partial skullcap (see Table 8.1) that starts at the frontal slightly anterior of bregma and the right coronal suture, which it crosses to incorporate much of the right upper parietal and a segment of the right lambdoid suture. An inferior parietal fragment that abuts the (open) temperomastoid suture, and a left supraorbital fragment, both from Spit 37, constitute two calvarial fragments that cannot be joined to the remainder of the skullcap. Spit 34 additionally yielded the zygomatic root of the right temporal bone, anteriorly as far as the zygotemporal suture (which is unfused), and from Spit 36 came the fragment of a malar bone near the zygomaxillary suture.

All sutures were unfused including at those locations along the coronal suture where the sutural teeth of adjoining frontal and parietal fragments could be slotted together (Fig. 8.1). Lack of suture closure would be consistent with a sub-adult status but on its own it is a very unreliable indicator (Brothwell 1981:43–5). Other observed traits would be consistent with a juvenile individual although an adult female status cannot be ruled out. The supraorbital fragment indicates a modest but distinct superciliary ridge, the malar fragment indicates minimal development of the malar tuberosity, while the temporal crest is 'slight' to the point of being indistinct on this specimen (cf. Larnach and Macintosh 1966:14, 16, 33). If the Nabulei Lisa adult teeth are female (and so would represent an individual with large teeth like those of Australian Aborigines) then they could be related to the partial cranium.

No trace of a median frontal ridge was observed at the small portion of the extant frontal that crosses the midline. The parietal boss is 'slight', the obelionic depression is 'medium', there is no trace of an angular torus, and a parietal foramen is present as is a supraorbital foramen (cf. Larnach and Macintosh 1966:17, 19, 47, 52–3). No trace of *cribra orbitalia* could be observed on the tiny available portion of orbital roof.

Some of the frontal fragments, including those from Spits 32, 37 and 38, have lost the inner table, exposing the diploe on their endocranial aspect. Further evidence of post-depositional degradation of the endocranial surface comes from a set of interlinked, curvilinear indentations, inside of the obelionic depression, which are located too high on the vault to correspond to any middle meningeal artery vessels. These lines resemble root growth marks but may also reflect insect boring activity. The skullcap is remarkably thick in this region, measuring 8.2mm near euryon, compared to 4.4mm to ~7mm at other places on the parietal, and merely 4.6mm on the frontal close to bregma. By the standards of Australian Aboriginal adults, we would expect the euryon and bregma thicknesses to be reversed, while by the standards of Aboriginal and Caucasian teenagers, we would expect thickness at euryon to vary between merely 2.6mm and 4.4mm (cf. Brown et al. 1979:64–5). The exaggerated skull thickness at euryon is due to localised thickening of the diploe which measures 5.6mm here, compared to a thickness about the same as that of the outer table wherever the cranial bone is thinner. However, pathological thickening through congenital thalassaemia (cf. Tayles 1997) would be an unlikely cause as the diploe lack the tell-tale 'hair on end' morphology, and the thickening appears localized. Most likely the euryonic thickening represents normal anatomical variation within the adult range of skull thicknesses.

Description of the Postcranial Bone

The postcranial material comprises a burnt femoral shaft fragment from Spit 23, and then from Spits 27–37, three pelvic fragments and ten phalanges which are unburnt and quite possibly represent the same person. The eight phalanges whose lengths could be measured or reasonably estimated (see Table 8.5) are consistently short by Australian male Aboriginal standards (Rao 1966:41–3, 108), but fairly average by male north Chinese standards (Von Bonin 1931, 1932), suggestive of derivation from the same individual. The phalanges would have reached their adult length because the epiphyses are fused in all cases with the relevant portion intact, but this need not imply an adult status because phalanx epiphyses can fuse during the teens as well as early adulthood (Brothwell 1981:66). However, if the phalanges came from the same person as the fragment of a left pubic symphysis in Spit 27, then an adult status would be indicated. Component I of the symphysis shows stage 1 development by male standards and stage 2 development by female standards, Component II corresponds to stage 2 whether male or female, and Component III shows stage 1 and stage 2 development by male and female standards respectively (cf. Brothwell 1981:69–70). If masculine the fragment would indicate an age at death of approximately

Table 8.5 Liang Nabulei Lisa: length of phalanges (mm) and comparative male ranges

SPIT	PHALANX	LENGTH	AUSTRALIAN RANGE	CHINESE MEAN AND RANGE
33	Right 2nd manual distal	16.2	16-23	17.0 (15-19)
34	Left 2nd manual medial	21.0	21-32	22.5 (18-27)
34	Left 2nd manual distal	16.6	16-23	17.0 (15-19)
34	Left 5th manual medial	16.1	17-24	18.0 (12-23)
34	Right 1st pedal proximal	~30	27-39	28.0 (20-34)
35	Left 3rd manual distal	15.6	16-22	17.7 (16-20)
35	Right 5th manual distal	15.5	15-20	16.4 (14-19)
36	Right 1st manual proximal	31.1	27-35	28.9 (26-33)

21 years, whereas if feminine, any age at death between 22 and 40 years old would be possible, with 30 a modal estimate.

The two phalanges whose length could not be reliably recorded are a left fifth proximal manual phalanx from Spit 34, and a left first proximal manual phalanx from Spit 36. Including the phalanges listed in Table 8.5, nine of the 10 recovered phalanges are manual, and one pedal. As well as the pubic fragment mentioned above, pelvic material includes a fragment 11.1mm thick which ends at a crest and is tentatively identified as iliac crest (Spit 35), and a fragment from the left superior ramus of the pubis, which is suggestive of a small but robust ramus (Spit 37). Finally, the femoral fragment from Spit 23, made up of three conjoining fragments, has small development of the pilaster and thin cortical bone, and would more likely be female or sub-adult than adult male.

Conclusions

The two youngest individuals from Liang Nabulei Lisa, who had died at about 3–6 and 7–10 years of age, are represented only by their teeth. The teeth further demonstrate the presence of at least one adult, but this individual's relation to the extant bone is not clear. On balance, the most parsimonious assignment would relate the adult teeth, the partial cranium, the pelvic and femoral fragments and the phalanges to a female adult. This woman would have died between 22 and 40 years of age, and could well have had tooth and phalanx dimensions similar to those of recent Australian Aborigines. Nonetheless, the partial calvarium, the phalanges and/or the femoral fragment could — any or all of them — relate to a teenager.

However these osteological skerricks might be assigned, there is minimal evidence of any stratigraphic ordering in their representation. The younger child is confined to Spits 29–35, and the older child to Spits 33–36, whereas remains of the adult (assuming most material belongs to it) would range from Spits 23–39. If we look at represented parts of the skeleton, although cranium tended to be found lower than teeth and especially postcranial bone (see Table 8.1), there is extensive overlap (e.g. cranium between Spits 23 and 39, teeth and fragments between Spits 29 and 41, and postcranial remains between Spits 23 and 36). Essentially, the greater the number of fragments there are that should be assigned to any individual or to any part of the skeleton, the wider the dispersal of those fragments in the excavated deposit.

The commingling of fragments from at least three persons, the variation among the represented elements from a partial skullcap to bones as small as phalanges, the lack of evidence for stratigraphic ordering of the remains, and the indications of burning of the teeth and the femoral fragment, are all consistent with secondary burial. A scenario of at least two burial events would help account for the considerable vertical dispersion of the fragments but other scenarios would also suffice to explain the point. The fragments start in earnest at Spit 32 and continue unabated till Spit 39, so it would seem that the cavity made to receive these remains had been dug from a higher level than Spit 32 and had bottomed out at Spit 39. The fragment of enamel in Spit 41 could be easily accounted for through post-depositional infiltration, while scuffage and post-burial upward movement could account for the presence of fragments as high as Spit 23.

Acknowledgements

Professor Colin Groves provided sound advice on interpreting the endocranial morphology.

References

von Bonin, G. 1931. Preliminary study of the northern Chinese hand. *Anthropologischer Anzeiger* 7:241–56.

von Bonin, G. 1932. Preliminary study of the northern Chinese foot. *Anthropologischer Anzeiger* 9:214–27.

Brothwell, D.R. 1981. *Digging up Bones*. Third edition. Oxford: British Museum (Natural History)/Oxford University Press.

Brown, T., S.K. Pinkerton, and W. Lambert. 1979. Thickness of the cranial vault in Australian Aboriginals. *Archaeology and Physical Anthropology in Oceania* 14:54–71.

Bulbeck, F.D. 1981. Continuities in Southeast Asian Evolution Since the Late Pleistocene. Unpublished M.A. thesis, Department of Archaeology and Anthropology, Australian National University, Canberra.

Hillson, S. 1996. *Dental Anthropology*. Cambridge: Cambridge University Press.

Howells, W.W. 1989. *Skull Shapes and the Map*. Cambridge, Mass.: Harvard University Press.

Larnach, S.L. and N.W.G. Macintosh. 1966. *The Craniology of the Aborigines of Coastal New South Wales*. Sydney: University of Sydney. *Oceania Monographs* 13.

Martin, R. and K. Saller. 1957. *Lehrbuch der Anthropologie*. Fifth edition. Stuttgart: Gustav Fischer Verlag.

Patterson, D.K. jr. 1984. *A Diachronic Study of Dental Paleopathology and Attritional Status of Prehistoric Ontario Pre-Iriquois and Iriquois Populations*. Ottawa: National Museum of Canada.

Rao, P.D.P. 1966. The Anatomy of the Distal Limb Segments of the Aboriginal Skeleton. Unpublished PhD thesis, Department of Anatomy, University of Adelaide, Adelaide.

Scott, G.R. and C.G. Turner II. 1997. *The Anthropology of Modern Human Teeth*. Cambridge: Cambridge University Press.

Smith, B.H. 1984. Patterns of molar wear in hunter-gatherers and agriculturalists. *American Journal of Physical Anthropology* 63:39–56.

Tayles, N. 1997. Anemia, genetic diseases, and malaria in prehistoric mainland Southeast Asia. *American Journal of Physical Anthropology* 101:11–27.

9

Liang Lemdubu: A Pleistocene Cave Site in the Aru Islands

Sue O'Connor[1], Ken Aplin[2], Katherine Szabó[1], Juliette Pasveer[1], Peter Veth[3], and Matthew Spriggs[1]

1. Department of Archaeology and Natural History, Research School of Pacific and Asian Studies, The Australian National University, Canberra, ACT, Australia
2. Sustainable Ecosystems, CSIRO, GPO Box 284, Canberra, ACT 2601, Australia
3. Research Unit, Australian Institute of Aboriginal and Torres Strait Islander Studies, Canberra, ACT, Australia

Introduction

Liang Lemdubu is located in the western interior of Pulau Kobroor in an area of karstic limestone (Fig. 9.1). This large, double-entranced cave was formed when an ancient subterranean river cut a passage through the limestone. It runs in length for 30m, is up to eight metres wide and has an average height of three metres (Figs 9.2, 9.3). To reach it one has to boat to the upper reaches of Sungai Papakulah, followed by a two hour walk inland through rainforest. This is the same *sungai* where Alfred Russell Wallace spent six weeks collecting skins and other specimens in 1857, at the hamlet he called 'Wanumbai'.

Lemdubu is regarded locally as a sacred cave and despite its relative inaccessibility, it is known outside of the Wanumbai area. We first heard of it from people at the village of Ujir whilst surveying the northwest coast during our 1995 field season. Excavation did not begin until the following field season in 1996, after consultation had been carried out with the owner of the land and the *adat* (customary law) leader for the cave, a resident of Papakulah Besar.

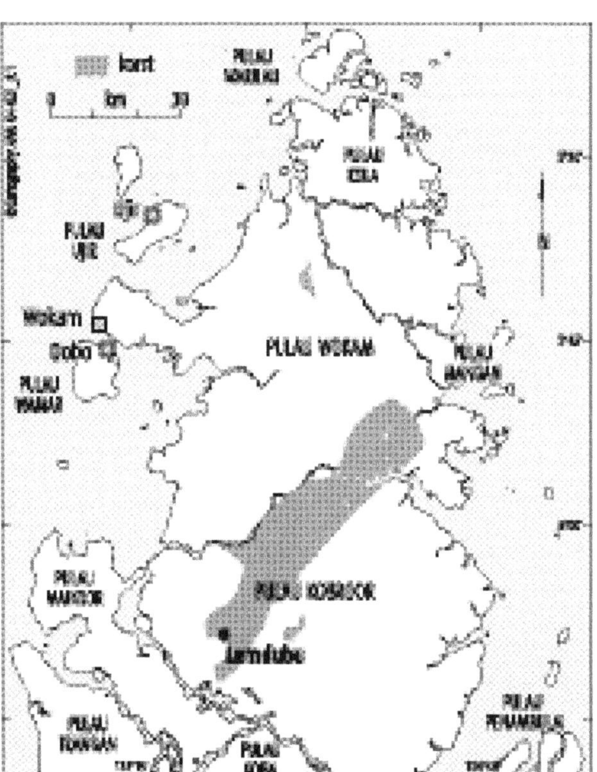

Figure 9.1 Liang Lemdubu: map showing location of the cave and the area of karst limestone in which the cave is located

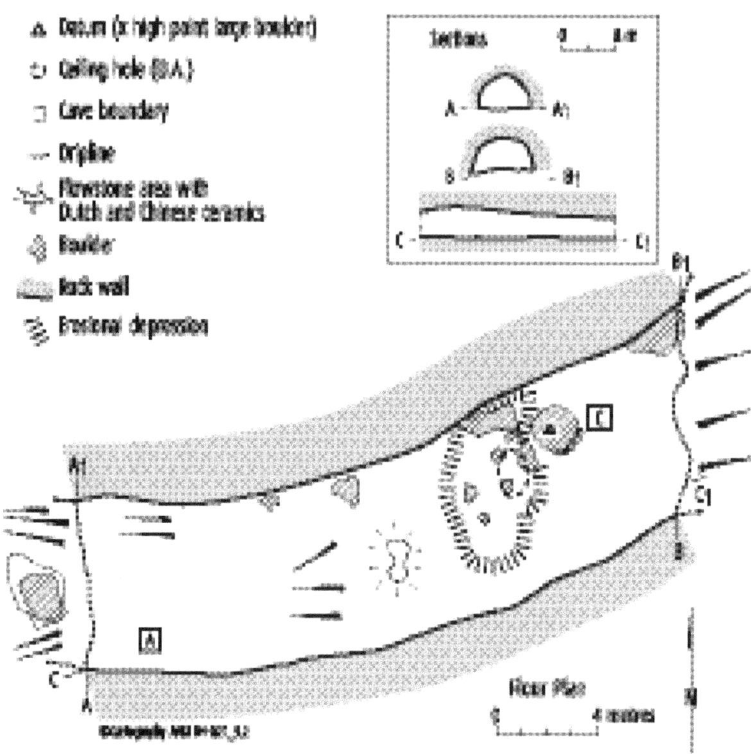

Figure 9.2 Liang Lemdubu: plan of the cave showing location of features discussed in the text and locations of Test Pits A and C

Figure 9.3a Liang Lemdubu: view to west inside the cave with natural flowstone platform with ceramics at mid-centre

Figure 9.3b Liang Lemdubu: view to east entrance

Small stalactite formations occur in the central third of the cave, beneath which a platform of flowstone has accumulated (Fig. 9.3a). The water which drips through the roof at this point is believed to have sacred properties and to imbue the drinker with strength, health and long life; we were told that the cave was still visited periodically to collect the water in times of crisis or ill health. In historic times, Dutch and Chinese ceramics were placed on the flowstone platform and these are now cemented to it (Fig. 9.3a). There is a small hole in the roof in this area through which water and limited sediments enter the cave; this minor collapse appears quite recent.

Lemdubu lies about 25m above sea level and represents a high point in the low-lying local landscape. While other caves were located during our field survey in the surrounding karstic formations, most were low-lying, wet, and unsuitable for human habitation. Lemdubu was the only cave of its size and elevation located during three field seasons, which no doubt accounts for its notoriety.

The cave is surrounded by evergreen rainforest which has a fairly simple structure (Monk et al. 1997:198, 203). Immediately around the cave the rainforest is uncleared but within a few hundred metres to the east it is interrupted by sago swamps and small mixed garden clearings, planted to meet subsistence requirements (Fig. 9.4). At the time of our last visit in 1997 the area was being more intensively cleared for cash crop coffee plantings.

The densest concentrations of cultural material on the extensive sediment floor of Lemdubu are located in the better lit areas at the east and west entrances, near the driplines. Shellfish (*Geloina* sp. and *Terebralia* sp.), pottery and animal bone were noted on the surface, along with pieces of matting and bamboo indicating the contemporary use of the cave by

Figure 9.4 Liang Lemdubu: cleared garden area where our base camp was located, approximately 1.5km from the cave

villagers while on hunting trips or to collect the sacred water. Our initial judgment was that the deposits immediately inside the dripline at each end of the cave were likely to be the deepest and the least disturbed by water action, roots, and major roof fall events. These areas were also more likely to have been the focus of daily occupation than the darker interior of the cave.

The Excavations and Stratigraphy

Two test pits (A and C) were excavated at either end of the cave (Fig. 9.2). Excavation units (spits) averaged approximately five centimetres unless sediment changes were apparent, in which case depths varied to accommodate changes in the stratigraphy. All material was wet sieved through fine mesh (<2mm). Volumes of excavated sediment were recorded prior to wet sieving and an initial sort of cultural residues was carried out at the cave to remove large non-cultural limestone fragments. The remaining material from each excavated unit or 'spit' was then bagged for secondary sorting back at base camp where it was rewashed, thoroughly dried and re-sorted. We found that this method led to the recovery of even small pieces of micro-debitage and bone.

Prior to excavation, it was agreed that the excavated material from Lemdubu would be divided between ourselves and our Indonesian co-workers. All the material and records from Test Pit A were deposited in Puslit Arkenas in Jakarta; to our knowledge, these have not yet been analyzed. The cultural material from Test Pit C was returned to Canberra for analysis. It is this material that forms the basis of this report.

Initially a 1 × 1m pit, Test Pit A, was dug at the western end of the cave (Fig. 9.2). This pit revealed a homogeneous, loose grey-brown to yellowish brown sediment, which changed to a dark yellowish brown mottled clay immediately above the sterile, basal deposit. The upper spits of the grey-brown sediment contained charcoal, terrestrial fauna, earthenware pottery, marine shellfish, stone artefacts, and a fragment of metal. Deeper spits lacked shellfish and pottery and produced fewer stone artefacts, but yielded abundant terrestrial fauna. The basal mottled clay was

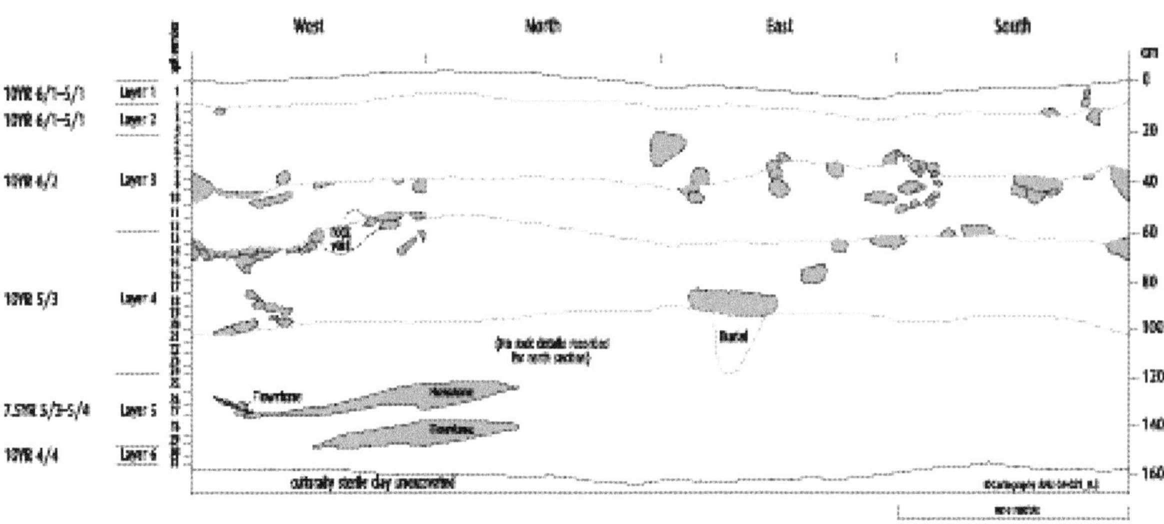

Figure 9.5 Liang Lemdubu: sections of Test Pit C showing spit depths

Figure 9.6 Liang Lemdubu: east section of Test Pit C, showing stone placed over burial

Figure 9.7 Liang Lemdubu: north section of Test Pit C, showing flowstone near base of pit

reached at approximately 50cm below the surface in Test Pit A. This yielded a small quantity of bone but otherwise appeared culturally sterile.

Test Pit C was located near a massive boulder at the eastern end of the shelter (Figs 9.2, 9.3b). This 1 x 1m pit revealed a similar but extended sequence to Test Pit A (Fig. 9.2). Six layers were recognised on the basis of variation in the sediment and cultural materials down the profile. These included: sediment colour; the degree of consolidation of the deposit; differences in texture and/or changes in clay and sand content, and quantities or size of clastic material; as well as changes in the cultural materials, such as presence or absence of shell and degree of cementation of bone. Bulk samples were collected from most spits during excavation of Test Pit C and averaged approximately 200g. Larger samples were not practical for transportation from the field. The sequence described below is based on an examination of the bulk samples and on information recorded on the excavation field sheets. The layers do not always have a one to one correspondence with the divisions as drawn on the sections at completion of the excavation. Figure 9.5 shows Layers 1–6 as well as the unmodified section drawing as it was reproduced in O'Connor et al. (2002). The sediments from the bulk samples are logged in Appendix 9.1. As would be anticipated in a limestone cave, the sediments were alkaline throughout the sequence (pH 8.0–9.0), and bone and shell were well preserved throughout.

Culturally sterile deposits were reached at approximately 150cm below the surface and excavation was discontinued without reaching bedrock at approximately 160cm (Figs 9.5–9.7).

Layer 1 comprises the top spit only: Spit 1. This layer is composed of a grey to greyish brown sediment (Munsell hue 10YR 6/1–5/1). The deposit was unconsolidated and contained large lumps of charcoal. This layer is differentiated from Layer 2 primarily because it was loose and powdery, probably as a result of ongoing disturbance of the surface.

Layer 2 includes Spits 2 through to the base of Spit 4. It is essentially the same as Layer 1 (Munsell 10YR 6/1–5/1), but has been consolidated following burial. It has slightly more fine silts than Layer 1, and the sands are well sorted. It contains less charcoal and the charcoal pieces are much smaller in size.

Layer 3 was recognized as beginning at Spit 5 and continuing down to the base of Spit 12. Although the sediment colour was close in hue to Layer 2 (Munsell 10YR 6/2), this layer was differentiated because it contained significantly less shellfish than the layers above, no visible charcoal, and significantly more bone and small clasts. A particular concentration of rounded, cobble-sized limestone clasts was observed in Spits 8, 9 and 10. The appearance of bone breccia in Spit 10 indicates a zone of carbonate mobilization and it is possible that some clasts are carbonate nodules formed *in situ* as a result of water percolation through the profile. Alternatively, the clasts may represent degraded pieces of roof fall. The field notes indicate that many of the cobbles in Spit 12 were particularly chalky 'as if weathered'. It is possible that they represent a roof fall event following which they lay exposed for some time prior to being covered by sediment.

Layer 4 comprises Spits 13 to 24. It was recognized on the basis of a slight change in sediment colour (Munsell 10YR 5/3) and texture. The sediment is recorded as moister, 'stickier' and slightly lighter or more orange in colour, with a major increase in clay content. The finds from the spits in this layer had to be wet sieved twice as so much fine clay adhered to them. A major decrease in roof fall or nodules was noted as occurring in Spit 21. The human burial occurred in this level under the large rock in Spits 17 and 18.

Layer 5 comprises Spits 25 to 29, and was recognized on the basis of a slight change in sediment colour (Munsell 7.5YR 5/3-5/4) and texture. The sediment becomes much stickier with coarser gritty inclusions. In the northern and northwestern area of the square, two travertine flowstone floors were recorded in Spits 25, 26, and 28 (Fig. 9.7). These formed a partial seal over the underlying deposit which in places was over five centimetres thick and had to be broken up with a crowbar.

Layer 6 begins at approximately 150cm below the surface and comprises Spits 30 and 31. The sediments in this layer are more yellowish in hue (Munsell 10YR 4/4) than those in Layer 5, and have an even higher clay content. This layer contained small bones but no definite cultural material. The fauna in Layer 6 is presumed to predate the first human occupation of the site. Excavation was discontinued in this layer at a maximum depth of 160cm, as the sediments were deemed to be culturally sterile.

Dating the Lemdubu Sequence

Little charcoal was preserved below the upper three spits and we have therefore dated a variety of different materials, using a range of techniques, in an attempt to obtain a chronology for the cave sequence (Table 9.1). Radiocarbon age estimates were obtained on charcoal, marine shellfish, *Celtis* seeds, *Casuarius* eggshell, and a human tooth. All radiocarbon values were calibrated using CALIB 3.4. No ocean reservoir correction has been applied to the marine samples as no standards are available for this equatorial region. ESR was used to estimate the antiquity of the human burial distributed between Spits 18 to 23, and Uranium-Thorium dates were obtained on the travertine

TABLE 9.1 LIANG LEMDUBU: TEST PIT C, RADIOMETRIC DATES [a, b]

Lab. code	Spit	Depth (cm)	Sample type	$\delta^{13}C$	Conventional age (YEARS BP, ±1σ)	Calibrated age (CAL YEARS BP) [c]
ANU-10782	2	5-10	Charcoal	-24.0	1830±60	1574-1916
OZF247	2	5-10	*Casuarius* eggshell	-13.5	2150±50	2000-2308
ANU-10794	3	10-15	Charcoal	-24.0	1100±160	708-1295
ANU-10792	5	25-30	*Geloina* shell	-10.7	11,700±130	13,183-14,057
OZF356	5	20-25	*Celtis* seed	-16.2	9400±50	10,432-11,055
OZF358	7	30-35	*Celtis* seed	-12.4	9280±50	10,242-10,635
OZD701	8	35-40	*Celtis* seed	-16.9	8170±60	9006-9397
OZF357	10	45-50	*Celtis* seed	-15.3	9250±60	10,242-10,577
OZD460	17	85-90	*Geloina* shell	-5.8	16,570±510	18,391-21,019
AA-32848	19	95-100	*Casuarius* eggshell	-10.0	16,770±110	19,321-20,658
OZF248	19	95-100	*Casuarius* eggshell	-11.7	16,850±120	19,402-20,760
OZC776	19	95-100	*Geloina* shell	-5.0	17,750±450	19,835-22,287
OZC777	26	130-135	Charcoal	-24.0 [d]	13,300±300	14,539-16,794
–	26	130-135	Flowstone			25,700±460
–	28	140-145	Flowstone			27,020±290

a In addition to the dates reported here an ESR date of 18,800±2300 years (linear uptake model) was obtained on a tooth representing human remains distributed across excavation layers, Spits 18–23

b All analyses are radiocarbon dates with the exception of two flowstone U-series dates at the base of the sequence

c Minimum - maximum intercepts, ±2σ range

d This sample was too small to measure the delta 13 C

flowstones in Spits 26 and 28. The dates on the human burial are not included in Table 9.1 as they are bone dates and therefore date the burial itself and not the age of the sediments that it was interred within.

Charcoal from Spit 2 returned an age-estimate of 1830±60 (ANU-10782), and from Spit 3 an estimate of 1100±160 (ANU-10794). Thus there is a minor inversion in the charcoal age estimates between Spit 2 and 3. An AMS radiocarbon determination was also obtained on *Casuarius* eggshell from Spit 2. This sample was assayed at 2150±50 BP (OZF247) and confirms the late Holocene age of Spit 2.

We conclude that the upper three spits are Late Holocene in age. The age estimates are consistent with the recovery of pottery and domestic animal remains only from these spits (Table 9.2). Insufficient charcoal was available below Spit 3 for conventional radiocarbon determinations, and small-sized charcoal samples were avoided due to a high risk of vertical displacement within the deposit and of contamination during the process of excavation. Spit 4 remains undated, but as it contains large quantities of shellfish and minimal quantities of Agile wallaby bone (a species that became locally extinct in the early Holocene; see Chapter 7, this volume, and below), we infer that it is likely to also be Late Holocene in age.

Although marine/estuarine molluscs are abundant only in Spits 1–4, they are present in smaller quantities in Spits 5 and 6 (Table 9.2). It was therefore anticipated that Spit 5 would date to the period of sea level stabilization approximately 6000 years ago. However, a single *Geloina coaxans* valve (ANU-10792) from Spit 5 returned an age estimate of 11,700±130 BP, considerably older than predicted. A sample of *Celtis* seed from Spit 5 was also analyzed and returned an age estimate of 9400±50 BP (OZF356). The two dates for Spit 5 indicate that at least some of the cultural material in this unit was deposited during the terminal Pleistocene or earliest Holocene. Two *Celtis* samples from Spits 7 and 10 (OZF358 and OZF357, respectively) yielded similar age estimates to OZF356 from Spit 5. A fourth *Celtis* sample from Spit 8 (OZD701) gave a slightly younger estimate. If the *Celtis* dates provide a generally accurate indication of age, Spits 5–10 accumulated fairly rapidly in the terminal Pleistocene/early Holocene, between 9000 and 11,000 cal BP.

Table 9.2 Liang Lemdubu: Test Pit C, weights (g) of cultural material by spit (this table supersedes an earlier version published in O'Connor et al. 2002)

CONV. AGE BP	SPIT	STONE ARTEFACTS	BONE	MARINE/ ESTUARINE SHELL	*CELTIS* SEEDS	CHARCOAL	CASSOWARY EGGSHELL
	1	54.1	1178.7	2227.9	11.3	57.6	4.4
1830±60	2	11.4	430.5	515.1	7.6	5.5	2.3
1100±60	3	22.0	361.0	526.2	5.3	0.8	0.2
	4	2.8	475.0	286.0	4.6	0.2	2.6
9400±50	5	5.9	617.4	52.6	3.9		0.3
	6	5.7	546.1	23.7	1.1	0.2	
9280±50	7	167.6	1085.2	2.2	0.8		
	8	89.2	1162.9	0.2	0.1		
	9	54.6	2062.1	2.7	0.2	0.8	
9250±60	10	216.7	3482.7	4.1	0.1	0.01	
	11	10.6	1352.6	2.0	0.1		
	12	53.7	1241.7	0.1			
	13	4.5	1168.8	2.4			
	14	26.3	1591.8	1.2			
	15	32.7	1488.2	0.1			
	16	3.2	1658.4	1.7			
16,570±510	17	7.9	1566.3	9.5			0.1
	18	1.9	1421.3	1.5			0.1
16,850±120	19	6.3	2112.9	7.2			1.7
	20	0.5	2400.6				0.2
	21		2433.8				
	22		1567.6				
	23	0.2	1531.9				
	24	2.6	3356.4				
	25	1.7	5665.8				
25,700±460	26		1912.0				
	27		1004.2				
27,020±290	28		640.9				
	29	0.1	207.9				
	30		91.7				
	31		59.3				

The *Geloina* fragment from Spit 17 (OZD460) returned an estimated age of 16,570±520 BP. This value is broadly consistent with the results of two radiocarbon determinations on *Casuarius* eggshell from Spit 19 of 16,770±110 (AA-32848) and 16,850±120 BP (OZF248), and one on *Geloina* shell from Spit 19 of 17,750±450 BP (OZC776). The two *Casuarius* eggshell dates are statistically identical and although the A/I ratios for these samples are slightly different — 0.407±0.001 (AAL 8559C) and 0.390±0.005 (AAL 8559C) — the possibility must be considered that they derive from the same egg but have had slightly different thermal histories (see Chapter 13, this volume). However, even if the *Casuarius* eggshell samples (AA-32848 and OZF248) are not independent ages, the production of close age estimates on the two valves of *Geloina* from Spits 17 and 19 with the *Casuarius* from Spit 19 provides reason for confidence in the inference that Spits 17–19 accumulated between 18,400 and 22,200 cal BP.

As mentioned above, small-sized charcoal samples were not used for radiocarbon analyses as their provenance was uncertain. The exception to this was a small fleck of dark coloured material, tentatively identified as charcoal, which was found adhering to the flowstone from Spit 26. As this part of the sequence clearly had not been disturbed during the period after travertine deposition, and furthermore, the flowstone fragment had not been through the wet sieving process, there seemed little possibility of modern or ancient contamination. However, the sample yielded an anomalously young age estimate of 13,300±300 BP (OZC777), which is at odds with the suite of mutually supportive age estimates from Spits 17–19, and with age estimates obtained from Uranium-Thorium analysis of other pieces of flowstone from the same level (see below). In view of these radically different chronological estimates, we are now inclined to think that the sample was not charcoal but rather some kind of secondary carbonaceous deposit.

Attempts were made to directly date a human burial which occurs predominantly between Spits 18 and 23, using AMS radiocarbon dating of bone collagen and ESR dating of tooth enamel. The stratigraphic position of the burial is shown in Figures 9.5 and 9.6, and the morphological description and analyses are presented fully in Bulbeck (Chapter 12, this volume). The results of the analyses and dating of the burial are reported in some detail here as they are critical to the reliability of the assessment of the Lemdubu burial's age.

Three independent radiocarbon analyses aimed at extracting collagen from the bone produced inconsistent results. Two laboratories were unable to extract any datable material from the bone, while a third laboratory, the Australian Nuclear Science and Technology Organisation (ANSTO), produced a late Holocene determination. A section was cut from the medial diaphysis fragment of the right femur (from Spit 18) for the purpose of getting an AMS radiometric analysis of the bone from ANSTO. This section of femoral bone was divided and the other half sent to Donald Pate's laboratory at Flinder's University, in an attempt to get a stable isotope ratio assay. The section sent to ANSTO (OZD577) was assayed at 3180 BP. However, the reliability of the ANSTO analysis on OZD577 must be evaluated in the light of the failure by Pate to extract any collagen from the bone. This raised the prospect that the ANSTO analysis was not carried out on collagen extant in the bone sample, but rather on some contaminant. A third sample of the same section of femoral bone was then submitted to the AMS dating facilities at Oxford as a further check on the ANSTO determination. The Oxford laboratory was also unable to extract datable material from the bone. On this basis alone — that the extraction of datable material could not be replicated by two high quality laboratories — we conclude that the ANSTO analysis must be regarded as an unreliable estimate of the age of the burial. Furthermore, the ANSTO radiocarbon determination is inconsistent with the stratigraphic context of the burial in relation to all other age estimates presented here, *and* with the ESR analysis obtained for the tooth from the burial, which was recovered from the same depth below surface in the excavation (Spit 18). When ANSTO was approached about the details of the collagen extraction for OZD577 their representative Ugo Zoppi (pers. comm.) stated that:

> OZD577 was first pretreated in October 1998 ... the high C/N ratio and low value of $d^{13}C$ (-26 per mil) for the second attempt at extracting collagen indicated that the extracted collagen still consisted of some humic acid contamination and was not suitable for dating. As a result the age estimate of 3180 BP should be used as a minimum age.

Taking all of these lines of evidence together, OZD577 is regarded as unreliable and is not used in subsequent discussion of the chronology of Lemdubu burial.

The tooth used in the ESR analysis, also from Spit 18, is thought to belong to the same individual as the femur described above. The analyses and dating were undertaken by Rainer Grün at the Australian National University. The ESR analysis was carried out using a single aliquot technique (for experimental details see Grün 1995; for details on ESR age estimation see Grün 1989). The tooth yielded an age estimate of 15,800±1800 years if a model of early Uranium-uptake is employed, and an age of 18,800±2300 years if a model of linear Uranium-uptake is used. The sample has surprisingly high uranium concentrations. In view of the young age of the sample, it is unlikely that the early uptake model (which assumes that the uranium that is measured migrated into the sample in a very short time compared to its age) is applicable. Grün therefore considers an

ESR age of 18,800±2300 years to be the best estimate for the human burial (Grün pers. comm., September 2001). This implies that the human remains are roughly contemporaneous with the deposition of Spit 17 or 18, and were not dug into the deposit from much higher in the profile. The ESR date accords well with the stratigraphic context of the burial which shows a large stone in Spits 17 and 18 capping the burial (Fig. 9.6), and no evidence of vertical displacement of cultural materials found in the Holocene levels into the Pleistocene levels of the deposit.

Uranium-Thorium (Th/U) age estimates were obtained for fragments of speleothems found in Spits 26 and 28. One flowstone formed a partial seal over the deposit beginning at 130cm below the surface in Spits 25 and 26, and a lower flowstone occurred at approximately 150cm below the surface, mostly in Spit 28 (Fig. 9.7). Analytical methods follow that of Ayliffe et al. (1998), and the results are reported in full by O'Connor et al. (2002). The Th/U ages indicate that the lower portion of the cultural deposit, represented by material in Spits 26–28, is approximately 25–28,000 years old.

The Liang Lemdubu Cultural Sequence

Several features of the assemblage were evident during excavation and the on-site sorting of material. The estuarine molluscs found on the surface were restricted to the upper few spits. These levels also produced occasional pottery sherds along with the remains of introduced species such as pig and dog. Other vertebrate faunal remains in these levels were noticeably burnt and fragmented. At greater depth, the vertebrate remains became more abundant and less fragmented, with remains of small to medium-sized wallabies particularly evident. Stone artefacts were present in fairly low numbers throughout the sequence. Most were small and not typologically distinctive. The abundant faunal remains held promise of a detailed record of environmental change and human exploitation of game around the site.

Raw weights for all cultural material are presented in Table 9.2, and weights adjusted for difference in volume of sediment removed in each excavation unit are presented in Table 9.3. The depth of spits as they correspond with the volume of sediment removed can be found in Appendix 9.2. Some shell and bone is cemented with calcium carbonate and sediment, and this will tend to inflate the weights slightly in most levels. In Spits 25 and 26 this problem is exacerbated by the presence of several fragments of bone breccia cemented by travertine.

Organic Remains

Molluscs

Marine/estuarine shellfish

Marine/estuarine shellfish remains are relatively abundant in Spits 1–3. The quantity declines somewhat in Spit 4 and then falls dramatically below Spit 4 (at ca. 20cm below surface level; Table 9.2, Fig. 9.8a). Occasional fragments of marine/estuarine shell occur down to Spit 19.

Species represented include the gastropods *Terebralia* sp. and *Ellobium aurismidae*, which live intertidally amongst mangroves (Coleman 1981:19) and the bivalves *Geloina coaxans*, *Anadara* sp. and *Isognomon* sp. (see Table 9.4, Fig 9.8b). A few cowrie shells (Cypraeidae) were found in Spits 2 and 3. All shellfish found in the site, with the exception of the cowrie shells, probably could be obtained from the *sungai*, a few hours walk from the site.

Two morphologically similar bivalves, *Geloina coaxans* and *Batissa violacea*, are both represented in the samples. The primary way to distinguish between these bivalves is the nature of

Table 9.3 Liang Lemdubu: Test Pit C, distribution and weights (g) of cultural material through the sequence, adjusted for volume of deposit (m^3) removed per spit

CONV. AGE BP	SPIT	STONE ARTEFACTS	BONE	MARINE/ ESTUARINE SHELL	*CELTIS* SEEDS	CHARCOAL	CASSOWARY EGGSHELL	TOTAL VOLUME
	1	54.1	1178.7	2227.9	11.3	57.6	4.4	5.0
1830±60	2	14.3	538.1	643.9	9.5	6.9	2.8	4.0
1100±60	3	36.7	601.7	877.0	8.8	1.3	0.3	3.0
	4	4.7	791.7	476.7	7.6	0.3	4.4	3.0
9400±50	5	8.4	882.0	75.1	5.5		0.5	3.5
	6	9.5	910.2	39.5	1.8	0.3		3.0
9280±50	7	239.4	1550.3	3.1	1.2			3.5
	8	127.4	1661.3	0.3	0.1			3.5
	9	68.3	2577.7	3.4	0.2	1.0		4.0
9250±60	10	270.9	4353.4	5.1	0.1	0.01		4.0
	11	13.3	1690.8	2.5	0.1			4.0
	12	89.5	2069.5	0.2				3.0
	13	7.5	1948.0	4.0				3.0
	14	37.6	2274.0	1.7				3.5
	15	54.5	2480.3	0.2				3.0
	16	5.3	2764.0	2.8				3.0
16,570±510	17	13.2	2610.5	15.8			0.1	3.0
	18	3.2	2368.8	2.5			0.1	3.0
16,850±120	19	10.5	3521.5	12.0			2.8	3.0
	20	0.8	4001.0				0.3	3.0
	21		2897.4					4.2
	22		2612.7					3.0
	23	0.3	1914.9					4.0
	24	3.3	4195.5					4.0
	25	2.0	6745.0					4.2
25,700±460	26		2390.0					4.0
	27		1434.6					3.5
27,020±290	28		712.1					4.5
	29	0.1	231.0					4.5
	30		114.6					4.0
	31		74.1					4.0

the hinge; *Batissa violacea* has transversely serrated or grooved lateral teeth, whereas *Geloina* has smooth lateral teeth. Despite the broken and chalky condition of much of the shell, most of the hinge fragments examined were identified as *Geloina coaxans*. However, positive identifications of *Batissa violacea* were made in Spits 4, 6 and 10. The majority of the valve fragments are probably also from *Geloina,* nevertheless the possibility remains that some *Batissa* has been conflated with the *Geloina*.

Isognomon sp. is an oyster that lives on the roots of mangroves in estuarine environments. It has a very distinctive hinge and was easy to separate from the other bivalves. The bivalves *Geloina* and *Isognomon* sp., and the gastropods *Terebralia* sp. and *Ellobium aurismidae,* would probably have been available in the upper reaches of the Sungai Papakulah, which is the point at which the *sungai* is closest to the cave.

Live specimens of *Geloina coaxans, Terebralia* sp., and *Ellobium aurismidae* were collected in 1997 for comparison with those found in the deposit. The bivalve *Batissa violacea* is found in fresh to brackish water conditions and tolerates pools, creeks, and even fast flowing rivers. The upper reaches of the *sungai* are fed by freshwater streams coming off the higher limestone karst, and at

Table 9.4 Liang Lemdubu: Test Pit C, marine and estuarine shellfish weights (g) and minimum numbers of individuals (MNI) represented by spit

SPIT	*ANADARA* SP.		*BATISSA VIOLACEA*		*ISOGNOMON* SP.		*GELOINA COAXANS*		*TEREBRALIA* SP.		*ELLOBIUM* SP.		*CYPRAEIDAE*		UNIDENTIFIED SHELL	TOTAL SHELL
	(g)	MNI	(g)	MNI	(g)	MNI	(g)	MNI	(g)	MNI	(g)	MNI	(g)	MNI	(g)	(g)
1	17.6	1			3.4	2	1118.4	23	280.0	60	399.2	24			409.3	2227.9
2	31.6	2			8.9	2	167.4	6	98.6	19	128.8	7	0.7	1	79.1	515.1
3	0.9	1			1.0	1	311.6	5	56.3	12	94.6	5	1.2	2	60.6	526.2
4			16.0	2	0.7	1	200.7	10	1.0	1	10.0	1			57.6	286.0
5	1.3	1					15.7	1	0.3	1	2.4	1			32.9	52.6
6			5.0	1			6.8	1	0.3	1	0.8	1			10.8	23.7
7							1.3	1	0.1	1					0.8	2.2
8															0.2	0.2
9							2.0	1	0.7	1						2.7
10			4.1	1												4.1
11							1.3	1							0.7	2.0
12							0.1	1								0.1
13											2.4	1				2.4
14											1.2	1				1.2
15									0.1	1						0.1
16							1.7	1								1.7
17							9.5	1								9.5
18											1.5	1				1.5
19							7.2	1								7.2

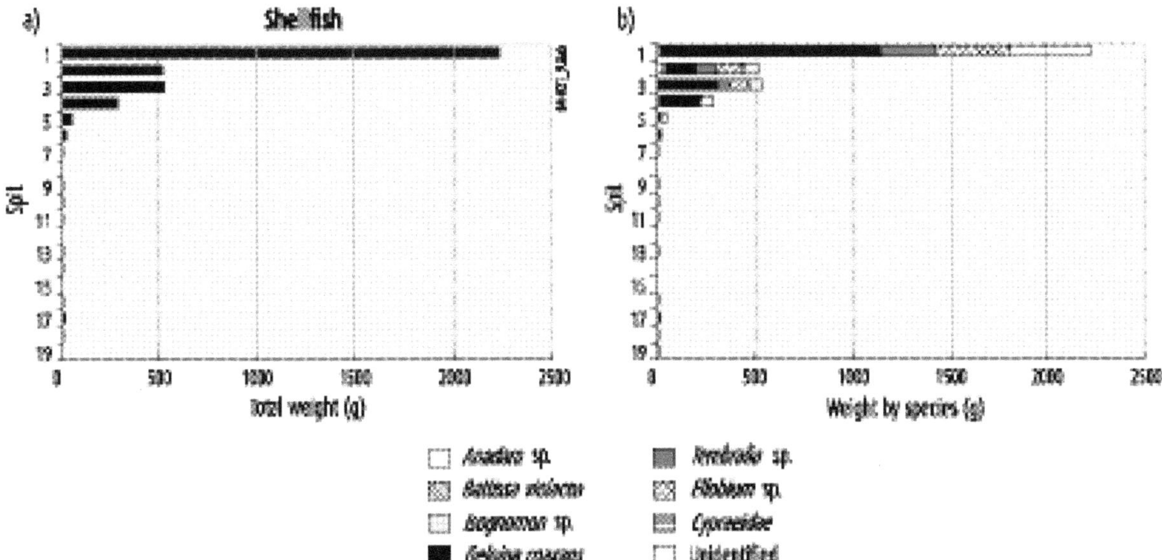

Figure 9.8 Liang Lemdubu: Test Pit C, a) shellfish raw weights (g) per spit and b) weight (g) by species per spit

low tide fresh to brackish water conditions prevail in some areas. *Batissa violacea* has been included with the estuarine molluscs as it may be obtainable in brackish pools at the head of the *sungai*, although none were observed in that habitat.

Small numbers of the marine/estuarine bivalve *Anadara* sp. — a group of species that inhabit sandy/muddy flats of the littoral zone — were recovered in the upper spits.

The few cowries must have been brought from a marine reefal environment and, in view of their small size, may have been transported inland as decorative items. However, none displayed any evidence of modification. Similarly, the *Geloina* fragments found in the lower spits may have been transported to the site for use as artefacts. *Geloina* with evidence of use wear and/or modification have been reported as artefacts from caves elsewhere in Island Southeast Asia. Their use as artefacts has also been confirmed in northern Australian sites where they occur at far greater distances inland (O'Connor 1999).

In terms of weight, the estuarine bivalve *Geloina* is clearly dominant within the shellfish assemblage (Fig. 9.8b). However, when measured by MNI, they are comparable to *Ellobium* but less numerous than *Terebralia* in the upper levels. Both measures of weight and MNI probably under-represent the importance of *Geloina* relative to *Terebralia* and *Ellobium*, as the bivalves tend to fracture along the pallial line, and once broken the valves often split through the hinge and cannot be used for MNI. For this reason it is believed that the weights provide a more accurate estimate of the relative contribution of the different species. Most of the shell in the unidentified category is probably attributable to *Geloina*.

The decrease in shellfish remains with depth is not likely to be due to preservation. Although the shell does become less well preserved with depth, the species recorded in the upper four spits were easily identifiable from the more eroded fragments and identifiable fragments of *Ellobium* and *Geloina* were found down to Spits 18 and 19 respectively. Further, thin-shelled terrestrial snails increase in number at the same time as the marine species begin to decline; an unlikely scenario if preservation was influencing the survival of shell down the profile.

The vertical distribution of shellfish suggests that it is only in the upper three spits that conditions similar to those prevailing in Sungai Papakulah today were fully established. The mangrove-associated species *Terebralia* and *Ellobium* are only present in any numbers in the top three spits. Although *Geloina* occur in some numbers in Spit 4, this species is not strictly mangrove-associated and might be expected to appear prior to *Terebralia* and *Ellobium*. The small quantity of shell below Spit 5 would suggest that it was transported from some distance away.

Terrestrial and freshwater gastropods

The most numerically important of the terrestrial gastropods are *Chloritis gruneri, Chloritis circumdata, Chloritis argillacea, Papuina* sp. cf. *P. pratti, Japonia* sp. and *Cyclotus politus.* A number of so far unidentified species were recorded simply as species A–H. The freshwater gastropods *Melanoides tuberculata,* and *Thiara scabra* also make a minor contribution (Table 9.5). The distribution of terrestrial and freshwater gastropods through time is shown in Table 9.5 and Figure 9.9. All the species recorded are likely to be part of the extant fauna; however, there is no modern day list of species from the Aru Islands.

The freshwater snails are found on rocky substrate in variable conditions from stagnant pools to fast flowing rivers (Haynes 2001). In Lemdubu they are most prevalent in the top two spits but occasional examples are found down to Spit 17 (Table 9.5). The individuals recovered are small in size and few in number and it seems likely that they were scooped up when freshwater was being collected and then brought to the site inadvertently in the water containers. The terrestrial snails are damp forest dwellers and their overall abundance may be taken as a general indication of the prevalence of wet forest in proximity to the cave. Low quantities of land snail are found in spits 28–24, dated to between ca. 27,000 and 23,000 cal BP (Fig. 9.9, Table 9.5). Terrestrial molluscs disappear almost entirely from Spit 22 to 10, probably reflecting drier conditions and less dense vegetation around the

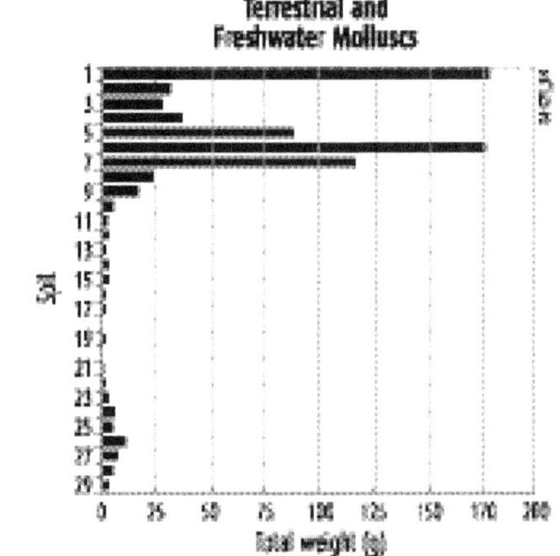

Figure 9.9 Liang Lemdubu: Test Pit C, raw weights (g) of terrestrial and freshwater molluscs

Table 9.5 Liang Lemdubu: Test Pit C, terrestrial and freshwater molluscs weights (g) and minimum numbers of individuals (MNI) represented by spit

SPIT	CYCLOPHORIDAE					THIARIDAE	TROCHOMORPHIDAE			CAMAENIDAE							TO BE IDENTIFIED							UNID.	TOTAL WT.
	CYCLOTUS POLITUS	*JAPONIA SP.*	*LEPTOPOMA MINUS*	*PLATYRAPHE SP.*	*MELANOIDES TUBERCULATA*	*MELANOIDES SP.*	*THIARA SCABRA*	*VIDENA SP. CF. V. BICOLOR*	*CHLORITIS GRUNERI*	*CHLORITIS CIRCUMDATA*	*CHLORITIS ARGILLACEA*	*CHLORITIS SPP.*	*PAPUINA SP. CF. P. PRATTI*	*PAPUINA SP. F. P. BLAINVILLEI*	*PAPUINA PILEUS*	*ALBERSIA TENUIS*	A	B	C	E	F	G	H		
1	16.1	11.9	11.4	0.5	0.7	0.1	0.7	0.4	11.1	39.6	1.1	16.6	4.0	1.3	1.0	2.4	0.1	0.6				0.01		79.2	198.9
2	4.4	2.6	0.1	0.03	0.8	0.1		0.1		2.1		6.2	0.5										0.2	13.8	31.0
3	1.1	0.3		0.04		0.1				1.2		1.0	0.7				0.1	0.04		0.03				23.1	27.8
4	0.4	0.5	0.03		0.1							7.0					0.1							28.7	36.7
5	0.2	0.1	0.2			0.1				0.3	1.3	24.1	0.1		0.4			0.01						61.0	87.8
6	0.1		0.04		0.1					0.4	1.2	56.8									0.02			118.1	176.7
7		0.04	0.1	0.01								39.5												75.9	115.6
8	0.5	0.01			0.1							6.4	0.1											16.2	23.4
9	0.1	0.01										2.4		0.1										14.0	16.6
10				0.06	0.5							0.7			0.03									3.1	4.4
11	0.2	0.1			0.2							0.1		0.3										0.7	1.5
12	0.2									0.04	0.5	0.8	0.3	0.2			0.04							0.5	2.5
13		0.1								0.2		0.3												0.6	1.2
14	0.7	0.1										1.8		0.03										0.2	2.8
15					0.3					0.7		0.3	0.1				0.04							1.0	2.5
16	0.1											0.3	0.02											1.1	1.5
17						0.2						0.1												0.7	1.0
18		0.1										0.2													0.3
19												0.3		0.1										0.8	1.1
20												0.1												0.2	0.2
21												0.2												0.3	0.4
22		0.1								1.0															1.2
23	1.3	0.01										0.4		0.1										1.4	3.2
24	1.1	0.3								0.1		0.6	0.2	0.03					0.01					3.2	5.5
25	0.7	0.1						0.02				0.8						0.01						3.1	4.7

cave through the terminal Pleistocene. From Spit 9 numbers begin to rise again, with a dramatic increase from Spit 7 to the top of the deposit.

The dominant terrestrial snail genus is *Chloritis* spp. Judging from the size of the fragments, most of the pieces identified as *Chloritis* spp. were probably *C. gruneri*, however they were too broken to make identification to species possible. A large proportion of the unidentified snails were also likely to be *C. gruneri*.

The way in which the terrestrial snails entered the cave is open to question. They may have been brought into the cave attached to freshly cut vegetation used by the cave occupants as sitting mats, bedding or for wrapping food. Our field assistants commonly cut palm leaves and placed them on the floor of the cave to sit on while sorting or resting during breaks, or to produce a clean surface to prepare or serve food. The peak in land snails in Spits 7–5 compared with Spits 4–2 may indicate that wetter conditions and denser vegetation prevailed during the early Holocene. Alternatively, it may be that vegetation was reduced in the late Holocene following forest clearance for gardening (represented by Spits 1–4). *Chloritis gruneri* is a large species which could possibly have been brought in as food. If some of the terrestrial molluscs were food species, their decline at this time may indicate their replacement in the diet by estuarine species after the establishment of fully estuarine conditions (reflected in the fauna in Spit 4 and above). Distinguishing between these different scenarios is not possible on the basis of the available data.

Vertebrate fauna

The Liang Lemdubu excavation produced a large quantity of bone, with especially high densities encountered in the lower levels of Test Pit C (Tables 9.2 and 9.3). As observed also in the Liang Nabulei Lisa sequence (Chapter 7, this volume), the vertebrate fauna from the uppermost deposit in Lemdubu contrasts strongly in physical condition and taxonomic composition with that from the lower part of the sequence. Essentially, bone from the upper levels is more heavily burnt and fragmented, and includes a wide range of animal groups but without any overwhelming pattern of dominance. In contrast, bone from the lower levels is less fragmented and less often burned, and is dominated by the remains of only one family, the Macropodidae.

Analytical methods

All samples were washed in a fine-mesh sieve and air dried. Bone artefacts were separated from the remaining bone material at this stage; these are reported by Pasveer in Chapter 11 of this volume.

The analytical methods essentially follow those described for the treatment of the Nabulei Lisa assemblage (see Chapter 7 for details). The critical objectives were as follows:

1) to determine the range of species present;
2) to establish the pattern of distribution of each species through the sequence; and
3) to estimate the relative abundance of the major species, both within each unit (interspecific) and through the sequence (intraspecific).

The physical condition of the assemblage was documented in terms of the proportions of four different burning categories, as described in Chapter 7.

Vertical distribution and preservational state of bone

The vertical distribution of bone is shown in Figure 9.10a and the bone weights adjusted for spit volumes in Figure 9.10b (Table 9.3). Peak values for bone are observed in Spits 24–25; however, as explained above, this is probably an artefact of the heavily cemented condition of bone in these levels. Ignoring this artificial peak, the true maximum values are observed at two points in the sequence: a sharp peak at Spit 10, and a broad peak centred on Spit 20. Relatively smaller quantities of bone were recovered in the uppermost levels of the site, in Spit 6 and above, and at the base of the sequence, below Spit 27.

Three main stratigraphic zones are distinguished by the proportion of bone in each burning class (Fig. 9.11). Bone from the uppermost 11 spits shows a high proportion of burning, with calcined bone accounting for 3–17% of the total bone. The 'lightly burnt' category is particularly prominent in these levels. Between Spits 12 and 26 there is a marked decline in the proportion of the three burnt categories; unburnt bone makes up 60–80% of the total remains in these levels. Below Spit 26 less than 10% of the bone is burnt.

The bone is moderately well preserved throughout the sequence, with little indication of differential degradation. Material from the upper levels of the sequence (in Spit 11 and above) appears more highly fragmented than that from the lower levels. The greater degree of fragmentation and burning in the upper part of the deposit is likely to be causally related. In the lower levels, the bone is often thinly coated with a layer of calcium carbonate and fine sediment. In Spits 25–26, the encrustation is more extensive and there are several chunks of 'bindstone' — made up of densely packed bone fragments, thin layers of travertine, and cemented cave earth.

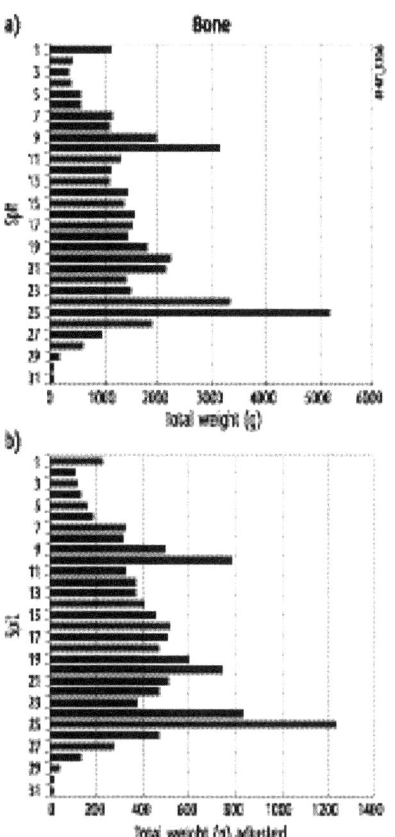

Figure 9.10 Liang Lemdubu: Test Pit C, a) raw weight (g) of bone through the sequence b) adjusted weight (g) of bone through the sequence

Origin of the remains

The preponderance of medium- to large-bodied animals such as macropodids, possums and large reptiles (Fig. 9.12), indicates that the Lemdubu fauna is predominantly derived from human activity, rather than being the product of non-human carnivore or raptor activity. The scarcity of tooth marks on the remains and the lack of rounding of fracture edges on all but a few specimens, also lend support to this view. This inference applies to all spits down to Spits 28 or 29. In contrast, the basal Spits 30 and 31 contain a higher proportion of smaller birds and mammals and may be derived wholly or in part from non-human activity. The fact that the lowest stone artefact was recovered from Spit 29 supports this view.

Material from the lowermost levels of human occupation (Spits 25–28) is noticeably less fragmented than that from the higher levels. In addition, the preserved fragments of 'bindstone' show several examples of anatomical association

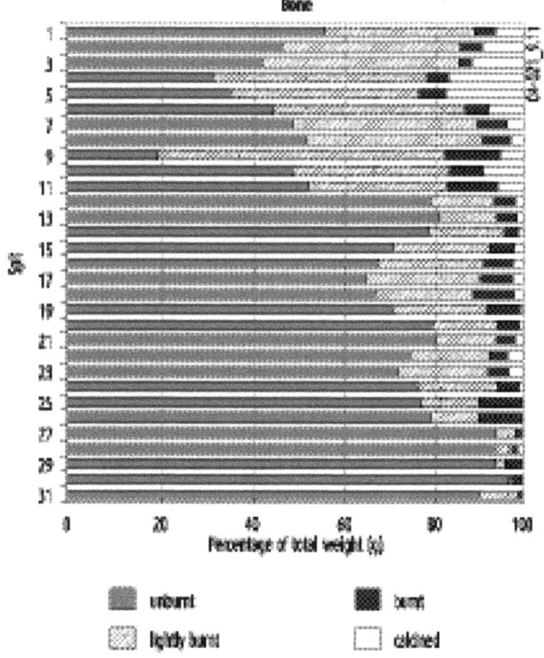

Figure 9.11 Liang Lemdubu: Test Pit C, percentage of total bone weight in each burning class

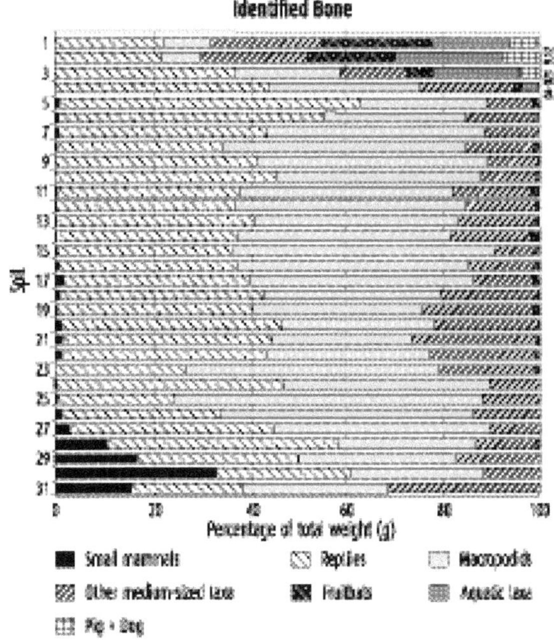

Figure 9.12 Liang Lemdubu: Test Pit C, summary of taxonomic categories (weight %) within the vertebrate faunal remains. Much of the small mammal category is likely to be derived from raptor use of the site. The 'reptile' category is dominated by large goannas and pythons

of skeletal elements, most notably among bones of the lower leg and hindfoot. The articulation of these elements suggests that little effort was being made to extract all available protein from these carcasses, and this in turn, may suggest an abundance of animal foods at that period in the history of cave occupation.

In all levels, some of the smaller mammal remains, including the occasional bones of smaller rodents and bats, might be derived from other sources including the regurgitated pellets of predatory birds roosting in the cave. However, as these are scattered through the sequence (Fig. 9.12), they do not influence the overall composition of the fauna.

Species distributions

The taxonomic composition of the Liang Lemdubu archaeological fauna was reported by O'Connor et al. (2002). NISP and weight data for all identified specimens are presented by spit in Appendix 9.3. Aplin and Pasveer (Chapter 3, this volume) document various subsequent changes in identifications and taxonomic nomenclature. Changes in nomenclature chiefly affect the murid rodents, where recent taxonomic revisions have led to the recognition of some new species, and the reassignment of others into different genera. Changes in identification reflect more detailed study by Aplin of some groups since the previous publication; these principally concern the peroryctid bandicoots and the rodents. The other significant change concerns the phalanges (foot bones) previously reported as belonging to a large 'megafaunal' species of kangaroo, tentatively referred to the genus *Macropus*. Access to better comparative material has now clarified that these specimens are from a species of *Casuarius*, probably *C. casuarius* (see Chapter 3 for details).

The Lemdubu faunal assemblage includes many taxa that are not recorded from the contemporary fauna of the Aru Islands. These include three macropodids (*Macropus agilis*, *Thylogale stigmatica*, and *Dorcopsis* sp.), two or three bandicoots (*Isoodon macrourus*, a previously unknown taxon, and possibly *Echymipera kalubu*), and the Short-beaked Echidna (*Tachyglossus aculeatus*). Other additions are a Native Cat (*Dasyurus albopunctatus*), several small rodents (*Rattus sordidus*, *Pogonomys* sp., *Pseudomys* sp. cf. *P. nanus*, *Melomys* sp. cf. *M. burtoni*), a medium-sized rodent (*Parahydromys asper*) and a small megachiropteran species (*Dobsonia* sp.).

The Lemdubu fauna contains the same four species of macropodids as are recorded in the Nabulei Lisa fauna. Only one of these is found on the Aru Islands today — *Thylogale brunii*, a small, rainforest dwelling pademelon. As reported previously in O'Connor et al. (2002), a second group of *Thylogale* specimens compares most closely as a group with modern specimens of *T. stigmatica*. However, the archaeological sample shows greater size variation than would be expected within a single population and may include two closely related taxa. *Thylogale stigmatica* today is polytypic, with two or more subspecies usually recognized. Unfortunately, as it was not possible to allocate many of the less complete specimens to either the larger or smaller form of *T. stigmatica*, the two groups were not distinguished in the analysis. In Eastern Australia, *Thylogale stigmatica* is an inhabitant of rainforest margins and wet gallery forests. The other macropodids are a true grassland/savannah wallaby, *Macropus agilis*, and an inhabitant of dense rainforest, *Dorcopsis* sp.

The changing proportional representation of the three most important species is illustrated by percentage weight of bone in Figure 9.13, and by NISP in Figure 9.14. Numerically, the two *Thylogale* species together make up the greater part of the macropodid remains throughout the sequence. *Thylogale brunii* shows two peaks in abundance: one centred on Spits 18 to 24, and the other on the uppermost four spits. In contrast, *T. stigmatica* is most abundant in the lowermost part of the deposit and between Spits 17 and 5. *Macropus agilis* also varies in abundance, with the lowest quantities in the upper three spits, the highest quantities between Spits 4–18, and intermediate values in Spit 19 and below. *Dorcopsis* sp. is represented by a single specimen: a very worn lower premolar, from Spit 24. This taxon is too poorly represented to register in the graphs.

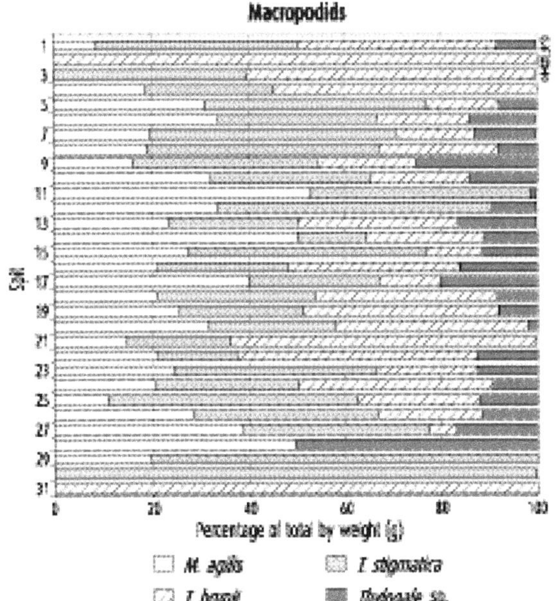

Figure 9.13 Liang Lemdubu: Test Pit C, the changing proportional representation (weight % of bone) of the macropodids through the sequence

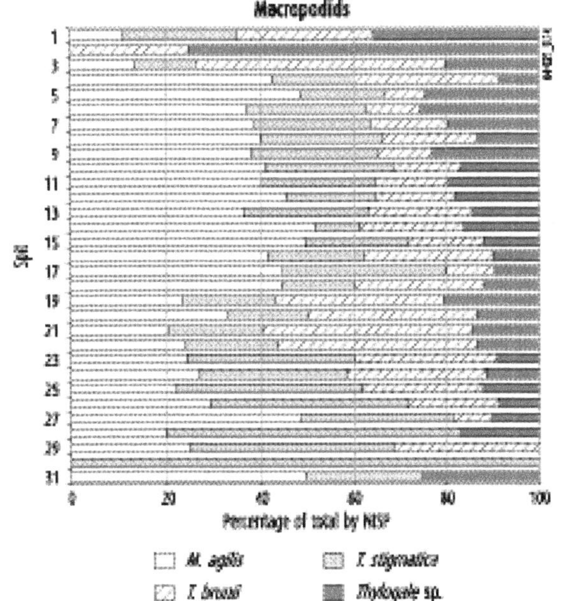

Figure 9.14 Liang Lemdubu: Test Pit C, the changing proportional representation (NISP) of the macropodids through the sequence

The increased quantities of the savannah dwelling *M. agilis* between Spit 18 and Spit 4 suggests drier and more open conditions during this period. This inference is supported by the reduced abundance of *T. brunii* relative to *T. stigmatica* during this period. Where the two species occur in regional sympatry today, in the Trans-Fly region of New Guinea, it appears that *T. brunii* tends to occupy the core rainforest habitats, whereas *T. stigmatica* is perhaps pushed into rainforest margin habitats.

Four species of bandicoots are probably represented in the Lemdubu assemblage, compared with a single species in the modern fauna. The sole surviving taxon, *Echymipera rufescens*, is represented throughout the deposit but is only dominant in the uppermost levels. *Echymipera kalubu* is tentatively identified from Spits 3–4 only. Both species of *Echymipera* occur today in lowland rainforest habitats on the New Guinea mainland. *Isoodon macrourus*, a species that is broadly associated with savannah grassland habitat in New Guinea and northern Australia (Flannery 1995), is present throughout the deposit but with peak values in Spits 17–25 (Fig. 9.15). A fourth bandicoot taxon, an unnamed taxon of uncertain ecological significance, is present in most spits between Spit 18 and Spit 27, with sporadic occurrences in higher levels (Spits 6 and 14). This taxon is also represented in Nabulei Lisa.

Four species of possums are represented in the assemblage. All are part of the contemporary fauna of the Aru Islands. The Spotted Cuscus, *Spilocuscus maculatus*, is present in almost all excavated spits, with the highest quantities in the lower part of the deposit (Spits 18 and below) and in the uppermost levels (Fig. 9.16a). Two smaller cuscuses, *Phalanger gymnotis* and *P. mimicus*, also occur through the sequence. *Phalanger mimicus* shows a similar pattern to that of *S. maculatus*, with greater quantities in the lower part of the deposit (Fig. 9.16b). *Phalanger gymnotis* occurs more sporadically through the deposit and is generally less abundant than the other cuscuses (Fig. 9.16c). The Striped Possum, *Dactylopsila trivirgata*, is poorly represented by comparison, with single fragments in each of Spits 1 and 9. All four species are indicative of forest habitats. *Phalanger gymnotis* has not been recorded outside of rainforest habitats. The remaining species are more adaptable and occur today in a variety of forest types including riparian forests and relatively open woodlands. The decrease in abundance of *S. maculatus* and *P. mimicus* above Spit 19 is compatible with the suggestion that the local vegetation was drier and more open from that time through until the more recent period represented by Spits 1–4.

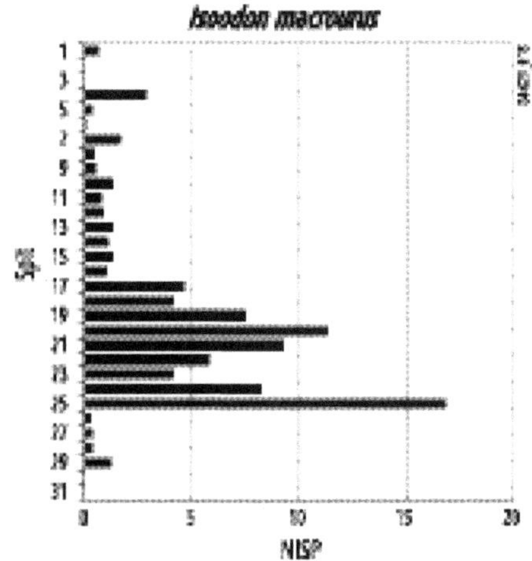

Figure 9.15 Liang Lemdubu: Test Pit C, the changing proportional representation (NISP) of the bandicoot *Isoodon macrourus* through the sequence

Echidna (*Tachyglossus aculeatus*) is represented in most levels from Spits 25 to 5 (Fig. 9.17), with slightly higher quantities below Spit 18 than above (but with a localized peak in Spit 9). This taxon is absent from the Aru Islands today, despite it being present in both northern Australia and southern New Guinea.

The Lemdubu assemblage includes a limited quantity of small mammal remains. These are concentrated below Spit 10 and include examples of six or seven mammal species, such as *Myoictis wallacei*, another smaller dasyurid taxon, and five murid rodents. The murids include: *Parahydromys asper*, a partially

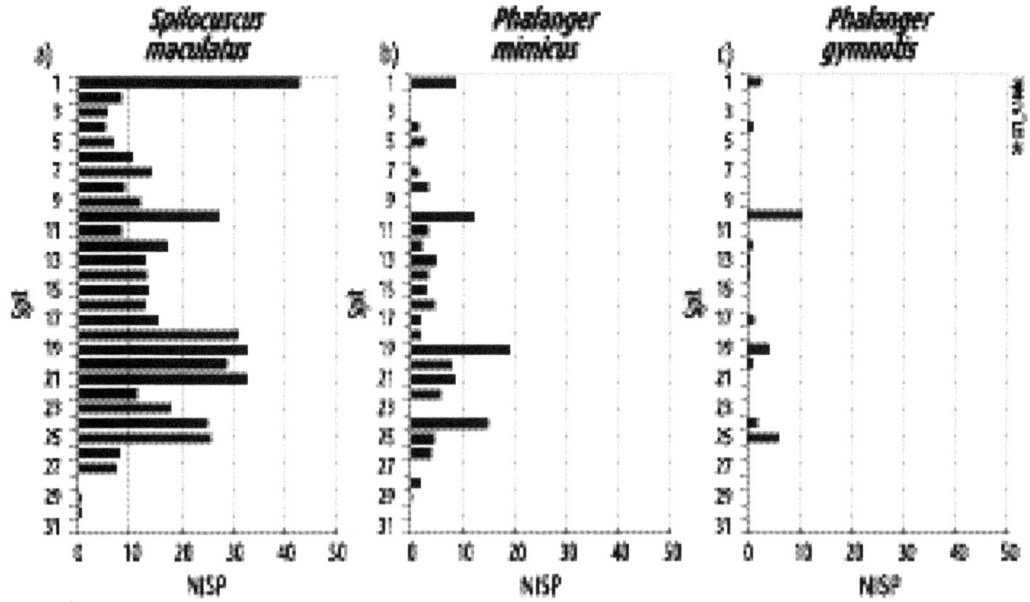

Figure 9.16 Liang Lemdubu: Test Pit C, distribution and proportional representation (NISP) of a) the Spotted Cuscus, *Spilocuscus maculatus* b) *Phalanger mimicus* and c) *Phalanger gymnotis* through the sequence

aquatic species found only in the lowermost part of the site; *Pogonomys* sp., a rainforest dwelling tree mouse found in Spits 30 to 13; *Rattus sordidus*, a tropical grassland taxon found in Spits 28 to 11; and species of *Pseudomys* (cf. *P. gracilicaudatus* group), represented by a few specimens only. The few larger murid specimens are all referrable to *Uromys caudimaculatus*, a highly adaptable species that occurs across a variety of habitat types.

Megachiropteran bats (family Pteropodidae) are present in virtually all samples. They show a minor peak in abundance in the lower levels, culminating in Spit 19 (Fig. 9.18), and a larger peak in Spits 1–3. The bulk of the more diagnostic material is referrable to *Dobsonia moluccensis*. However, at least some of the material is derived from a smaller species of *Dobsonia*. The most likely candidate is *D. viridis*, a species known from the nearby Kei Islands (Aplin and Pasveer, Chapter 3, this volume).

The remains of introduced mammal species are confined to the upper four spits. Pig bones and teeth occur in Spits 2–4, whereas dog is represented exclusively in Spit 2. Although no deer remains were found during excavation, bones and teeth of *Rusa timorensis* were collected from the surface of the site.

Snakes are well-represented throughout the Liang Lemdubu sequence; in most spits they account for around 20% of all bone (Fig. 9.19). Almost all of the snake remains come from moderately large snakes belonging to the Boidae (pythons), with fewer examples of other groups including Colubridae. In view of the high meat weight to bone ratio of these large pythons they must have made a regular and important contribution to the diet. Monitors (*Varanus* spp.) are also represented in most levels, with peak values between Spits 19–25 and in Spit 10 (Fig. 9.20). Most varanid remains are from moderate to large-bodied individuals. Today, the only large *Varanus* found in the Aru Islands is the semi-aquatic *V. salvator*. However, under drier conditions and with land connections through to northern Australia, it is possible that other large-bodied species were represented, including *V. gouldi*, *V. panoptes* and *V. mertensi*.

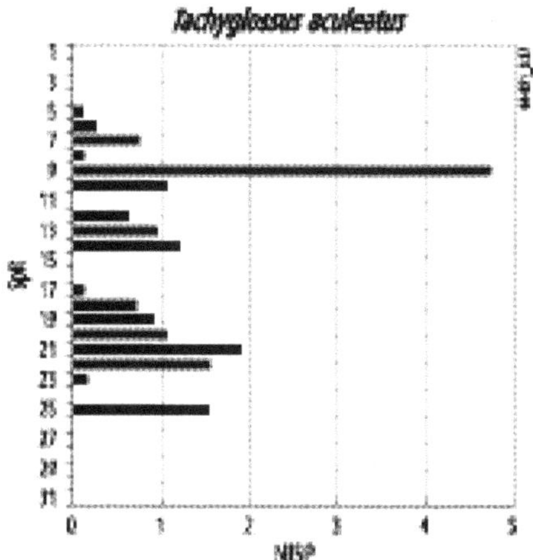

Figure 9.17 Liang Lemdubu: Test Pit C, distribution and proportional representation (NISP) of Echidna (*Tachyglossus aculeatus*) through the sequence. This species is represented in most levels from Spits 25–5

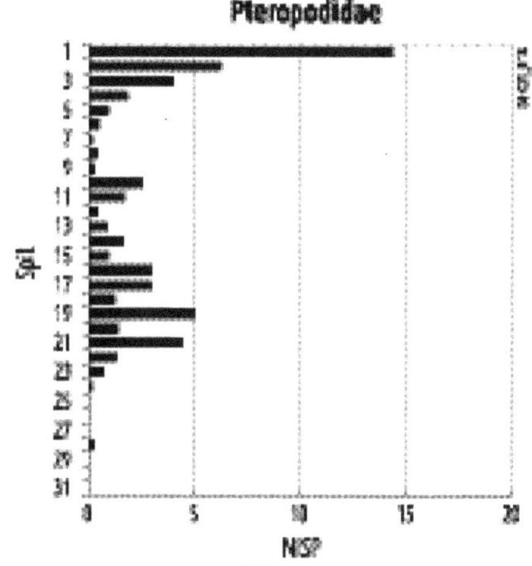

Figure 9.18 Liang Lemdubu: Test Pit C, distribution (NISP) of Pteropodidae bats through the sequence

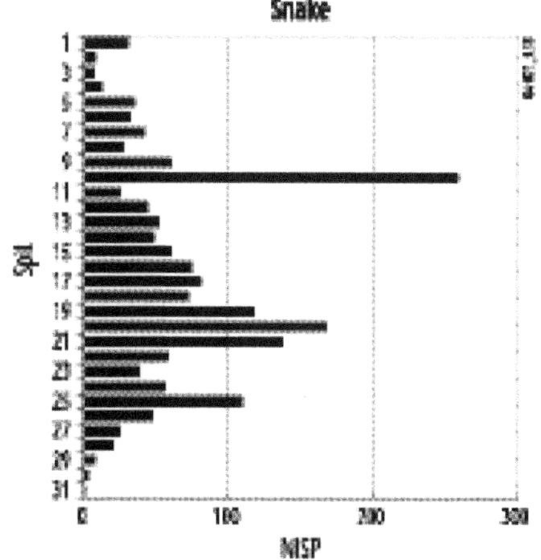

Figure 9.19 Liang Lemdubu: Test Pit C, distribution of snakes through the sequence (NISP)

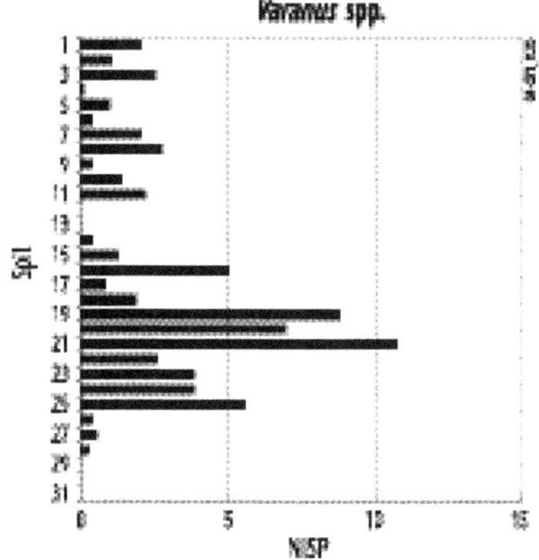

Figure 9.20 Liang Lemdubu: Test Pit C, distribution of Varanid lizards through the sequence (NISP)

Other reptiles represented in the Lemdubu fauna include skinks (Scincidae) and dragons (Agamidae). A dentary fragment from Spit 26 is tentatively identified as *Tiliqua gigas*. The agamid material has not been closely examined. However, the fact that this group peaks in Spits 1–5 and Spits 16–25 suggests a likely predominance of wet forest taxa such as *Goniocephalus* spp. over drier country agamids (e.g. *Amphibolurus* spp., *Chlamydosaurus* sp. and *Lophognathus* spp.).

Turtle bone is present in three spits only: Spits 1, 14 and 29. All fragments probably come from one or more species of freshwater cheluid turtles rather than from any of the larger-bodied marine species. Frog bone is present in small quantities down to Spit 13.

Small quantities of bird bone are scattered through the deposit. This includes recognizable examples of cassowary bones in Spit 3 and Spits 20–21. Although three species of cassowary are found in New Guinea (*C. unappendiculatus*, *C. bennetti*, and *C. casuarius*), only *C. casuarius* subspecies *aruensis* is found in the Aru Islands today. Cassowaries are hunted in the forest around Lemdubu today and the eggs collected for food.

Cassowary eggshell fragments were found in Spits 1–5 and 17–20 of the Lemdubu excavation (see Clarke and Miller, Chapter 13, this volume). Identification of the eggshell from Spits 17–20 as cassowary (*Casuarius* sp.) rather than emu (*Dromaius novaehollandiae*) requires further comment. As Aru was connected to northern Australia in the late Pleistocene, and the other terrestrial fauna from the lower levels of the site suggest savannah grassland conditions prevailed at this time, it is possible that the area supported populations of emu, perhaps living in regional sympatry with one or more cassowary species. Emu and cassowary eggshell are difficult to tell apart on the basis of morphology. Fortunately, eggshell of the two groups differs in the rate of amino acid racemisation and in their carbon stable isotope signals. As described by Clarke and Miller (Chapter 13, this volume), the rate of racemisation in the samples of egg shell from Lemdubu is comparable with that documented in samples from Toé and Kria Caves in the Bird's Head of Indonesian Papua. These sites contain exclusively closed forest fauna, and it is certain that the Bird's Head eggshell is from a species of cassowary (Pasveer 2004). Further, the carbon stable isotope results on the eggshell from Lemdubu indicate a bird whose diet consists of less than 20% tropical grasses (Clarke pers. comm).

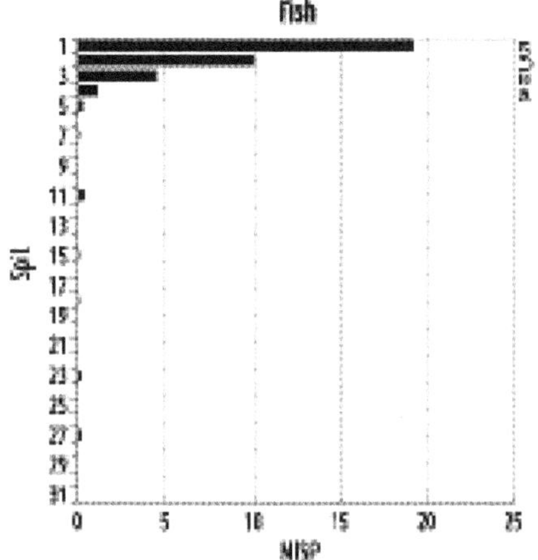

Figure 9.21 Liang Lemdubu: Test Pit C, distribution of fish bone through the sequence (NISP)

All cassowary eggshell in the deposit must derive from eggs brought into the site by people as food. Although no information is available on breeding times of *C. casuarius* in Aru, in north Queensland breeding 'occurs mostly in the dry season' coinciding 'with the average maximum availability of fruit in the forest' (Crome 1975:9, 13). The archaeological eggshell fragments presumably demonstrate use of the site in the dry season. The absence of eggshell fragments between Spit 6–16 and below Spit 20 is noteworthy; coupled with the absence of cassowary bone in the same levels, it suggests a genuine scarcity or absence of remains of this prized game item through much of the occupation of the site.

Fish remains are concentrated in the uppermost four spits, with scattered examples from lower levels (Fig. 9.21). The sample from the upper levels includes both freshwater (e.g. Ariidae) and marine (e.g. Scariidae) taxa.

Plant material

Charcoal was sparse below Spit 2 but occurs in measurable quantities down to Spit 10 (Tables 9.2 and 9.3). Small flecks of what appear to be charcoal were found after wet sieving in all spits, down to the base of the site, but as they were not recovered *in situ* these fragments were considered unreliable for dating. In view of the large quantity of burnt bone and shell in units below Spit 3, the paucity of charcoal is presumed to be due to taphonomic factors leading to the progressive destruction of charcoal over time.

The only seeds preserved were those of *Celtis philippinensis* which were found in Spits 1–11 (Table 9.2). *Celtis* seeds are commonly found in archaeological sites and are usually assumed to enter sites independently of people. They may enter incidentally attached to branches destined for firewood or other purposes. *Celtis* grow close to the entrances of Lemdubu today, however, the faunal data demonstrate that during the Pleistocene vegetation around the cave was much more open. It is significant that *Celtis* seeds were not recovered from the lower spits coinciding with this period of open vegetation.

Palaeoenvironmental Interpretation

The combined molluscan and vertebrate faunal analysis provides a detailed picture of environmental changes and human responses in the vicinity of Liang Lemdubu over the past 28,000 years. The sequence of changes is most conveniently described as a succession of three time periods. However, the exact delineation of these periods should be regarded as somewhat arbitrary.

Spits 31–19 (ca. 28,000–ca. 20,000 cal BP)

The basal two or three spits produced a small quantity of bone and no clear evidence of human activity; these may predate the earliest occupation of the site. However, from Spit 28 on, there is abundant evidence for human activity. From the composition of the vertebrate fauna from this period it is clear that the dominant vegetation community in the vicinity of the site was relatively dry and open vegetation, probably savannah woodland with grassy understorey. This supported a range of species today found in savannah woodland and grasslands of the Trans-Fly and across northern Australia, including *Macropus agilis, Isoodon macrourus* and *Rattus sordidus*. However, the presence in the same levels of many species found today in rainforest or dense gallery forest (i.e. *Thylogale* spp., *Dorcopsis* sp., *Echymipera rufescens, Pogonomys* sp., *Spilocuscus maculatus* and *Phalanger* spp.), also points to the presence in the area of substantial patches of wetter, denser vegetation. These communities presumably occupied topographic lows in the karst landscape, including the major drainage features.

Exactly how much of the area was occupied by each of these vegetation communities is difficult to judge. However, the fact that the two largest of the obligate rainforest animals, namely *Dorcopsis* sp. and *Casuarius* sp., are recorded only sporadically through this period suggests either that the wetter forest communities were of insufficient size and continuity to support viable populations of larger animals, or that these patches were subject to early and intense hunting pressure such that the larger animals were rapidly extirpated. If the latter process took place, then it left no archaeological signature, at least not in the excavated part of Lemdubu.

Spits 18–5 (ca. 20,000–ca. 9000 cal BP)

This zone is characterized by an increase in the relative abundance of the dry community taxa, and a corresponding fall in those taxa associated with wetter, denser habitats. Although the transition point between this zone and the last is set at the boundary between Spits 18 and 19, the transition between the two zones is really a gradual one, with different taxa most likely responding to common stimuli at different times and rates. Thus *T. brunii*, a taxon of deep rainforest habitat, begins to decline in relative abundance from peak values in Spits 20–21, while *T. stigmatica*, a taxon of forest edge habitats, does not increase until after Spit 18. *Macropus agilis*, a true savannah grassland wallaby, is relatively more abundant in Spit 18 and above. The two cuscuses, *S. maculatus* and *P. mimicus*, decrease in abundance after Spit 19, as do varanids and megachiropteran bats. In contrast, cassowary eggshell is present through to Spit 17. A somewhat anomalous trend is the decrease in abundance of *I. macrourus*, a bandicoot of tropical grassland habitats, above Spit 17.

The overall impression, then, is that the rainforest patches probably declined in both extent and quality through this period, perhaps starting from the time Spit 20 was deposited onwards. This may have occurred as a result of climatic deterioration, or through increasing pressure on these habitats as a consequence of hunting and/or general exploitation of forest products. The timing of this change, which corresponds with the peak of the last glaciation, perhaps lends weight in favour of a climatic explanation.

Spits 4–1 (ca. mid-Holocene?–present)

This period is characterized by numerous changes in the faunal assemblage. Most conspicuous is the marked increase in the quantities of shellfish remains and in fish bone, clearly marking the emergence of a marine drainage system within the *sungai* and their tributaries. Other changes include a marked decrease in the relative abundance of wallabies relative to all other groups, an increase in the abundance of *T. brunii* relative to the other macropodids, and a marked increase of both megachiropteran bats and cuscuses. Cassowary bone and eggshell reappear during this period. All of these changes point to an expansion of closed rainforest habitats at the expense of open savannah communities. The addition of pig and dog remains to the assemblage also represents a significant change, indicative of external cultural influence.

The general composition of the vertebrate fauna in this zone is thus consistent with the contemporary habitat of the Aru Islands. In this light, the continued presence of various savannah elements such as *M. agilis* and *I. macrourus* into these levels begs comment. Two possibilities spring to mind. The first is that populations of various savannah dwelling taxa persisted long after the general expansion of rainforests. The second is that the upper levels of Lemdubu are disturbed to the extent that a small quantity of material from the lower levels has moved up into the uppermost spits. One observation that would favour the latter view is the fact that *M. agilis* and *I. macrourus* both disappear before 7700 BP in the extended Nabulei Lisa sequence.

Human Skeletal Material

Human bones which appear to constitute a single burial were recovered from Spits 18–23. The remains are described in detail by Bulbeck (Chapter 12, this volume). The burial is capped by a large flat slab of limestone which occurs in Spits 17 and 18, and which can be seen in the section in Figures 9.5 and 9.6.

The burial is judged to be that of a female. Although the bones are in approximate anatomical position, occasional bones are misplaced or misaligned, and the foot and hand bones are missing altogether. This arrangement suggests a secondary burial; however, it is also possible that it is a primary burial that has been subject to inquest or disturbance after burial.

Dating the Lemdubu burial was essential both to provide an age for the burial itself and in order to ascertain the degree of stratigraphic disturbance within the site. On stratigraphic grounds, it appeared that the body or skeleton had been placed in a hole dug to a depth of approximately 25–30cm from Spit 18 into the surface of Spit 19, and the capping stone placed on top (with subsequent accumulation of the sediment of Spit 18 and 17). The alternative scenario, that the burial and capping stone had been placed at this depth from much higher in the sequence, potentially even from the late Holocene unit, would have major implications for potential mixing of cultural materials in all spits above the burial. However, the clear patterning in the vertebrate and invertebrate faunal remains argues against major disturbance of this kind, as does the evidence for the late Pleistocene age of the burial itself, as indicated by the ESR dating results.

Bone Artefacts

Thirty-seven bone artefacts were recovered from the excavation, of which 34 occurred in Spits 1 to 5, one in Spit 16, and two in Spit 24 (Fig. 9.22). Pasveer (Chapter 11, this volume) provides a full description and analysis of the bone artefact assemblage from Lemdubu. The assemblage comprises unipointed and spatulate artefacts, but within each of these categories there is great variability. Many artefacts are manufactured on fragments of long-bone shaft, such as wallaby fibulae. A high proportion of lightly burnt examples may indicate preparation or intentional selection of this material for bone artefact manufacture. The fact that all specimens found at Lemdubu were 'fragments' makes it likely that the artefacts were used and broken on site. It would also seem likely that maintenance activities, such as replacement or repair, took place on site given that mid sections (or butts) occur. A relatively high incidence of specimens with unpolished and undamaged tips may also indicate that primary manufacture took place at the cave, however, since no half-products or 'unfinished' specimens were found this remains uncertain.

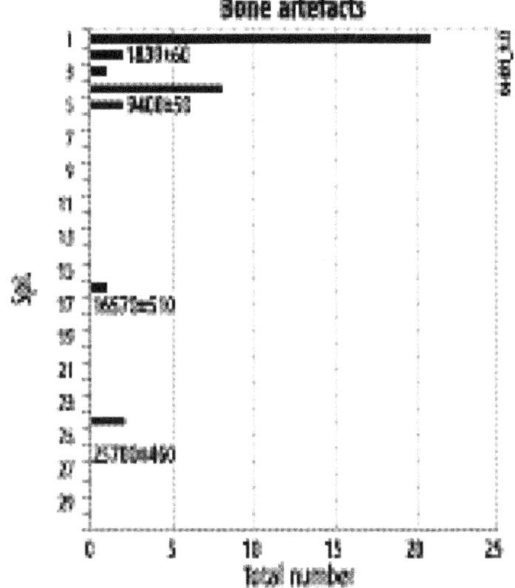

Figure 9.22 Liang Lemdubu: Test Pit C, distribution of bone artefacts through the sequence, also showing selected radiometric dates

Pasveer discusses possible functions for the bone artefacts from Lemdubu based on the use-wear and damage they exhibit, and concludes that while the historical accounts from the Aru Islands emphasize the importance of bows and composite arrows as hunting weapons (Merton 1910:60), the wear patterns on the Lemdubu artefacts do not support their use as projectile tips. The Lemdubu assemblage display various combinations of damage and polish, often of quite high intensity. The presence of polish in general suggests a mode of use including repeated friction, and this is unlikely to accumulate on artefacts that are subjected to high velocity impact such as arrow tips or spear points. Pasveer concludes that the bone artefacts were most likely used for drilling holes or in engraving activities; the actions most likely to generate both polish and damage such as crushing or step fracturing of the tip. A similar conclusion was reached by Pasveer (2004) and Pasveer & Bellwood (2004) for the bone artefacts from the Bird's Head of New Guinea and Northern Maluku, respectively.

Stone Artefacts

Stone artefacts occurred throughout the excavation, generally in low numbers (Tables 9.2 and 9.3). The stone artefacts are described in detail by Hiscock in the following chapter (Chapter 10). The assemblage is essentially composed of small percussion struck flakes (Fig. 9.23), with a minor modified component represented by a few retouched/utilized flakes. An interesting change in dominant lithology occurs within the sequence, with silicified limestone dominant in the upper five spits and cherts present in larger proportion in the lower levels. One interesting and unusual feature of the assemblage is the near absence of both cores and micro-debitage of the kind produced during flake manufacture or retouch. This may indicate that manufacturing took place off site, i.e. that the flakes in the assemblage were brought into the site, ready-made for use. Most artefacts occur between Spits 7 and 10 at the terminal Pleistocene/Holocene boundary. The peak value for stone artefacts in Spit 1 is due to the presence of a single large specimen.

The change in lithology may be due to changes in the local site environment. It is possible that the source of the chert used to produce artefacts in the Pleistocene became inaccessible when present sea level conditions were established (thought to coincide with the deposition of Spit 4). Alternatively, it may simply be that there was a change in site function in the late Holocene, after which time the site was presumably used in much the same way as it is today, by hunter-horticulturalists with metal and bamboo tools. Hunters today use predominantly metal and sharp bamboo knives to skin and butcher their catch. While there is no indication of the appearance of metal in the site, we may presume from the dates for the upper three spits that metal tools were in general circulation by this time.

Figure 9.23 Liang Lemdubu: Test Pit C, typical small chert flake

Pottery

Aside from the historic porcelain and pottery vessels cemented to the natural flowstone platform in the central area of the cave, there was little pottery to be seen on the surface of the cave floor. Three sherds were recovered from the upper two spits in Test Pit C but were returned to Jakarta and were not included in the petrological analysis of the Aru sherds. The field records indicate that these were small body fragments of earthenware pots, and were calcite-quartz tempered.

Conclusions

The lowest stone artefact at Liang Lemdubu is found in Spit 29. The earliest dated level with evidence for occupation is Spit 28, dated at 27,000 BP. As the fauna in Spits 30 and 31 is probably not humanly derived, it seems likely that the date of 27,000 years is close to the real age for initial human occupation at the site.

The initial occupation of Liang Lemdubu is considerably later than that documented from areas elsewhere in Melanesia and in northern Australia (O'Connor and Chappell 2003). This begs the question as to whether evidence for older occupation might be found with more extensive sampling of Lemdubu or elsewhere on the Aru Islands, or alternatively, whether the Aru Plateau may have been unattractive to human occupants of the wider region prior to 27,000 BP. Evidence from elsewhere in the region does suggest that the period prior to 28,000 BP was wetter than subsequently (van der Kaars 1991; van der Kaars et al. 2000), and it is probable that the Aru Plateau would have supported a rainforest community at that time. The Aru Plateau may have become more favourable for human occupation after 27,000 as drier conditions ensued and the vegetation opened up, producing more diverse habitats for an array of mammal fauna.

The Liang Lemdubu faunal sequence beginning 27,000 years ago, documents the presence on the late Pleistocene Kobroor Plateau of open savannah with denser, lusher vegetation present in pockets along watercourses and in other sheltered areas. The mammal fauna present at that time was basically similar to that found today in the Trans-Fly region of New Guinea and in parts of Cape York Peninsula, but included more species than either of these areas has today. People using the site at this time focussed their efforts on the procurement of the large-bodied Agile Wallaby (*Macropus agilis*) and several smaller wallabies (*Thylogale* spp.), with more casual acquisition of various medium-sized animals including cuscuses, bandicoots and pythons. Around 20,000 BP, the faunal assemblage changes slightly, with an increase in savannah elements at the expense of rainforest fauna. This may reflect a deterioration of climatic conditions associated with the glacial maximum or it might be related to a progressive deterioration of the rainforest patches over time.

The terminal Pleistocene saw the inundation of the Carpentarian Plain, the change to insular conditions, and the expansion of rainforest habitats across the Aru Islands. Human occupation of the cave and net sediment accumulation appears to have ceased entirely or been minimal during this time, at least in the area of Test Pit C.

In an earlier paper (O'Connor et al. 2002) we questioned whether widespread human abandonment may have been a response to the spread of rainforest in the early Holocene, and discussed this possibility within the context of hunter/gatherer responses to rainforest elsewhere in the tropical world (e.g. Bailey and Headland 1991; Roosevelt et al. 1996). The disappearance of the savannah species such as the Agile Wallaby, which appear to have been a significant component of the Pleistocene subsistence strategy, led us to question whether Aru may have represented a similar case to southwest Tasmania, where Kiernan et al. (1983) argued that 'recolonization of the region by forest tree species [in the Holocene] reduced the preferred habitats of the game species; game became scarce and humans also left' (see also Porch and Allen 1995:725). The excavation and dating of Liang Nabulei Lisa (Chapter 6, this volume) has demonstrated beyond doubt that Aru was occupied throughout the Holocene. If Liang Lemdubu was indeed abandoned at this time, it was perhaps as a response to local rather than regional changes. The cave may have been too remote from the *sungai* to make regular visitation worthwhile once the rich savannah plains were no longer a hunting drawcard. Alternatively, this chronostratigraphic gap may simply be a product of limited sampling in a large cave where material is unevenly distributed across the floor.

The stone artefacts in Liang Lemdubu show little variation through time, with the exception of a change in dominant lithologies. Silicified limestone dominates the upper five spits, and below Spit 9 around 80-90% of all artefacts are made on chert. It may be that the source of the chert became inaccessible in the mid-late Holocene following sea level rise. As noted earlier, a similar situation has been reported in the southwest of Western Australia where offshore chert sources were drowned by post-glacial sea level rise and cease to be available after 6000 BP, and consequently late Holocene tools are predominantly made on other lithologies (Glover 1975; Pearce 1977). Alternatively, it may simply be that in the late Holocene the site was being used predominantly by 'horticultural' hunters who acquired and used stone on a much more expedient basis and probably also used metal tools.

One interesting and unusual feature of the stone artefact assemblage is the near absence of cores and very small flakes resulting from artefact manufacture or retouch, indicating that manufacturing took place off site, and the flakes in the assemblage were brought into the site for use. The highest numbers of artefacts occur between Spits 7 and 10, whereas bone weights are highest in Spits 24 and 25, following fairly fast on initial occupation of the site. However, the bone above Spit 12 is more heavily burnt and highly reduced, suggesting more intense use of the site and local resources — including stone — and perhaps more intense reduction of the bone to extract marrow.

The late Holocene spits (1–4) indicate a shift in the patterns of resource use and presumably site use. They contain pottery, dog and pig bones, and presumably reflect the arrival of agriculturalists. The non-domesticated fauna indicates a change in the environment around the site as well as hunting strategy. There is an increased use of marine resources obtainable from the *sungai* following post-transgressive sea levels. Specific, targeted hunting of wallabies declines. This may simply reflect species availability following the spread of wetter forests and the loss of the open savannah element, most prominently the Agile Wallaby. The decrease in wallabies is countered by an increased use of riverine resources, such as fish and shellfish, and of various lesser game items such as cuscuses and fruitbats. This phase of cave use may have looked much like the present-day use of the cave, which is predominantly by people with a horticulturally-based economy who use it on hunting trips or when passing through the karst on their way from one area of gardens to another. Wallace's (1869:343) observation of the interior groups of this area contrasts sharply with the faunal deposit from the Pleistocene levels of Liang Lemdubu, but sits more comfortably with the Holocene assemblage:

> Now and then they get wild pig or kangaroo, but too rarely to form anything like a regular part of their diet, which is essentially vegetable ... e.g. plantains, yams, sweet potatoes and raw sago; sugar cane, betel nuts, gambir and tobacco.

References

Ayliffe, L.K., P.C. Marianelli, K.C. Moriarty, R.T. Wells, M.T. McCulloch, G.E. Mortimer, and J.C. Hellstrom. 1998. 500 Ka precipitation record from south-eastern Australia: evidence for interglacial relative aridity. *Geology* 26:147–50.

Bailey, R.C. and T.N Headland. 1991. The tropical rainforest: is it a productive environment for human foragers? *Human Ecology* 19(2):261–85.

Coleman, N. 1981. *What Shell is That?* Sydney: Lansdowne Press.

Crome, F.H.J. 1975. Some observations on the biology of the Cassowary in northern Queensland. *Emu* 76:8–14.

Flannery, T.F. 1995. *Mammals of New Guinea* (revised edition). Sydney: Reed Books.

Glover, J.E. 1975. Aboriginal chert artefacts probably from quarries on the continental shelf, Western Australia. *Search* 6:392–4.

Grün, R. 1989. Electron spin resonance (ESR) dating. *Quaternary International* 1:65–109.

Grün, R. 1995. Semi non-destructive, single aliquot ESR dating. *Ancient TL* 13:3–7.

Haynes, A. 2001. *Freshwater Snails of the Tropical Pacific Islands.* Suva: Institute of Applied Science, University of the South Pacific, Fiji.

van der Kaars, W.A. 1991. Palynology of eastern Indonesian marine piston-cores: a late Quaternary vegetational and climatic record for Australasia. *Palaeogeography, Palaeoclimatology, Palaeoecology* 85:239–302.

van der Kaars, W.A., X. Wang, P. Kershaw, F. Guichard, and D.A. Setiabudi. 2000. A late Quaternary palaeoecological record from the Banda Sea, Indonesia: patterns of vegetation, climate and biomass burning in Indonesia and northern Australia. *Palaeogeography, Palaeoclimatology, Palaeoecology* 155:135–53.

Kiernan, K., R. Jones, and D. Ranson. 1983. New evidence from Fraser Cave for glacial age man in southwest Tasmania. *Nature* 301:28–32.

Merton, H. 1910. *Forschungsreise in den Sudostlichen Molukken (Aru- und Kei Inseln).* Frankfurt am.M.: Senckenbergischen Naturforschenden Geschellschaft.

Monk, K.A., Y. De Fretes, and G. Reksodiharjo-Lilley. 1997. *The Ecology of Nusa Tenggara and Maluku.* Hong Kong: Periplus.

O'Connor, S. 1999. *30,000 Years in the Kimberley: A Prehistory of the Islands of the Buccaneer Archipelago and Adjacent Mainland, West Kimberley, Western Australia.* Canberra: Archaeology and Natural History Publications, Research School of Pacific and Asian Studies, Australian National University. *Terra Australis* 14.

O'Connor, S., K. Aplin, M. Spriggs, P. Veth, and L.A. Ayliffe. 2002. From savannah to rainforest: changing environments and human occupation at Liang Lemdubu, the Aru Islands, Maluku, Indonesia. In A.P. Kershaw, B. David, N. Tapper, D. Penny, and J. Brown (eds), *Bridging Wallace's Line: The Environmental and Cultural History and Dynamics of the Southeast Asian–Australian Region*, pp. 279–306. Reiskirchen: Catena Verlag. *Advances in GeoEcology* 34.

O'Connor, S. and J. Chappell. 2003. Colonization and coastal subsistence in Australia and Papua New Guinea: different timing, different modes. In C. Sand (ed.), *Pacific Archaeology: Assessments and Prospects. Proceedings of the International Conference for the 50th Anniversary of the First Lapita Excavation (July 1952), Koné-Nouméa 2002*, pp. 15–32. Nouméa: Départment Archéologie, Service des Musées et du Patrimoine de Nouvelle-Calédonie. *Le Cahiers de l'Archéologie en Nouvelle-Calédonie* 15.

Pasveer, J.M. 2004. *The Djief Hunters: 26,000 Years of Rainforest Exploitation on the Bird's Head of Papua Indonesia.* Lisse: A.A. Balkema. *Modern Quaternary Research in Southeast Asia* 17.

Pasveer, J.M. and P. Bellwood. 2004. Prehistoric bone artefacts from the northern Moluccas, Indonesia. In S.G. Keates and J.M. Pasveer (eds), *Quaternary Research in Indonesia*, pp. 301–59. Lisse: A.A. Balkema Publishers. *Modern Quaternary Research in Southeast Asia* 18.

Pearce, R.H. 1977. Relationship of chert artefacts at Walyunga in south-west Australia, to Holocene sea levels. *Search* 10:375–7.

Porch, N. and J. Allen. 1995. Tasmania: archaeological and palaeo-ecological perspectives. *Antiquity* 69(265):714–32.

Roosevelt, A.C., M. Lima Da Costa, C. Lopes Machado, M. Michab, N. Mercier, H. Valladas, J. Feathers, W. Barnett, M. Imazo Da Silverira, A. Henderson, J. Silva, B. Chernoff, D.S. Reese, J.A. Holman, N. Toth, and K. Schick. 1996. Paleoindian cave dwellers in the Amazon: the peopling of the Americas. *Science* 272:373–84.

Wallace, A.R. 1869. *The Malay Archipelago: The Land of the Orang-Utan and the Bird of Paradise. A Narrative of Travel, with Studies of Man and Nature.* London: MacMillan.

Appendix 9.1: Liang Lemdubu: Test Pit C, Log of the Sediments from the Bulk Samples by Spit

SPIT	MUNSELL COLOUR	pH	DESCRIPTION
1	Grey: 10YR 6/1-5/1	8.0	Very well sorted medium and fine silts with minor very fine sands (loose unconsolidated powdery with no aggregates). Occasional 4–6mm angular to subangular fine gravels of limestone dispersed. Occasional clasts (<5mm) of travertine. The broken shell and bone component are unweathered
2		8.0	No bulk sample
3	Grey: 10YR 6/1-5/1	8.0	Very well sorted medium and fine silts, with minor very fine sands (loose unconsolidated powdery with no aggregates). Occasional to frequent 10-15mm irregular nodular subrounded concretions of calcrete. Occasional large broken shell and some bone to 35mm
4	Grey: 10YR 6/1-5/1	8.0	Very fine silts. Well sorted to very well sorted. Powdery and loose. Occasional irregular 20–30mm calcrete (?) nodules with pitted exteriors, angular limestone fragments (20–25mm) and broken shell/bone
5		8.5	No bulk sample
6		8.0	No bulk sample
7	Light Brownish Grey to Pale Brown: 10YR 6/2-6/3	8.0–9.0	Very fine to medium silts with minor component of fine sands. < frequency in 2–4mm aggregates (rounded nodular) of silts. < frequency in large calcrete nodules. Frequent clasts of 5–20mm — calcrete or limestone. Some bone
8	Light Brownish Grey: 10YR 6/2	8.5	Very fine to medium silts with minor component of fine sands (well sorted). With occasional poorly sorted inclusions and irregular angular clasts of limestone/calcrete (25–30mm), occasional large broken bone. Minor flecking of 0–5mm white carbonate through matrix. Very minor aggregates
9	Light Brownish Grey: 10YR 6/2	8.5	Very fine to medium silts with minor component of fine sands (well sorted). Numerous 2–4mm subrounded silt aggregates (> with respect to Spit 8). Decrease in % of large limestone clasts although occasional and still irregular clasts (angular to subangular) of limestone 15–30mm. Carbonate adhering to some smaller bones
10	Light Brownish Grey: 10YR 6/2	8.0–9.0	Fine to medium silts, well sorted. Minor fine sands. Minor aggregates (nodular) 2–4mm of silts. < in gravel-sized limestone/calcrete inclusions. Most inclusions 20–40mm are fractured bone
11			No bulk sample
12	Light Brownish Grey to Pale Brown: 10YR 6/2-6/3	8.5	Fine to medium slightly gritty silts. > in 1–3mm pellet aggregates. <1mm spotting of carbonate with loose matrix and ped aggregates. 10–15mm limestone/calcrete clasts (subrounded to subangular). Bone occasional only
13			No bulk sample
14			No bulk sample
15	Brown: 10YR 5/3	8.5	Moderately sorted fine sandy silts. Well developed aggregates (1–3mm, mostly subrounded) of sandy silts. Carbonate flecking (white) <1mm throughout both matrix and aggregates. Infrequent irregular 2-3mm inclusions of reddish — yellow colour (5YR 6/6) — possibly burnt clays/soil peds/Fe-rich
16	Brown: 10YR 5/3	8.0–9.0	Moderately sorted fine sandy medium to fine silts with frequent subrounded to subangular clasts of broken limestone/bone 10–20mm. Numerous aggregates of silty sands/sandy silts in 1–3mm range. Also minor fractured bone typically <10mm. NB: Infrequent particles of Fe-rich nodules/aggregates continue from previous sample (typically 1–2mm, case hardened, with dusty red-brown silty-clay (?) interiors
17			No bulk sample
18	Brown: 10YR 5/3	8.5	Moderately sorted fine sandy medium silts and coarse (1–5mm) sandy silt aggregates. Some aggregates 5–15mm — deposit better aggregated. Comminuted carbonate (1–2mm) in loose matrix and within aggregates. Occasional large (10–15mm) subrounded limestone clasts/calcrete clasts and broken bone (bone has sediment cemented to surface). Dusty red-brown clay-silt pellets 1–3mm continue

continued over

Appendix 9.1: continued

SPIT	MUNSELL COLOUR	pH	DESCRIPTION
19	Greyish Brown to Brown: 10YR 5/2-5/3	8.0-9.0	Moderately sorted fine sandy silts, and 2-5mm aggregates of sandy silts with carbonate bone inclusions. Sediment adheres to broken mammal bone and is within the long bone shafts. Occasional larger 5-12mm fragments irregular partially cemented. Aggregates of charcoal/sandy silts around nucleii of bone
20	Brown: 10YR 5/3	8.0-9.0	Moderately sorted fine to sandy silts. Aggregation increased with sizes 0-5mm to 10mm with amorphous carbonate present in aggregates. Broken bone/shell predominantly <10mm, and breakage in 2-4mm faction very high. Occasional Fe-rich nodules/aggregates of 2-4mm size — 5YR 6/6-6/8 (reddish yellow)
21	Brown: 10YR 5/3	8.5	As for Spit 20 with some occasional larger bone fragments
22		8.0-9.0	No bulk sample
23		8.0-9.0	No bulk sample
24	Brown: 10YR 5/3	8.0-9.0	Moderately sorted sandy silts and sandy silt aggregates. High development of aggregation and partial cementation. Most sediment is aggregates 1-10mm wide size range. Frequent broken bone with partial mineralization of sediment onto exterior and infilling of marrow cavity within long bones with wide range of sediment sizes. Dark specking, possible charcoal 1-3mm?
25	Brown: 7.5YR 5/3-5/4	8.0-9.0	Poorly sorted aggregated sandy slightly gritty silts, possibly with some clay. Stiff cohesive aggregates with 1-3mm flecking of carbonates within silty matrix. Numerous broken fine fragments of bone (?) — larger bone appears to act as sites for matrix. (In situ deposit possibly a 1-2mm subrounded pellet aggregates — with voids, becoming cemented?)
26	Brown: 7.5YR 5/3-5/4	8.0-9.0	Poorly sorted to very poorly sorted. Stiff slightly sandy, gritty clayey silts with numerous 2-6mm limestone grits or flecking throughout. Some 10-15mm subrounded limestone gravels, occasional broken bone, partially encrusted. Occasional subrounded fine gravels (10-15mm) (elongate) of 10YR 7/6 (yellow) sandy marls. Majority of sediment is a matrix supported sandy clayey silt with fine carbonate pellets/ very fine gravels (Cave Earth)
27		8.0-9.0	No bulk sample
28	Brown: 7.5YR 5/3-5/4	8.0-9.0	Poorly sorted to very poorly sorted. A stiff slightly sandy clayey silt matrix supporting subrounded limestone grits/pellets. Again some 10-20mm 7.5YR 7/6-10YR 7/6 (reddish yellow — yellow) subrounded marlstone clasts. Also fragments of irregular travertine and fine carbonate pellets, and travertine/marls/limestone fine gravels (Cave Earth)
29		8.0-9.0	No bulk sample
30		8.0-9.0	No bulk sample
31	Dark Yellowish Brown: 10YR 4/4	8.0-9.0	Poorly sorted stiff sandy silty clays and clayey silts supporting dispersed limestone pellets (subrounded) 1-3mm throughout. Structure, massive. Clasts 8-15mm of limestone pitted/weathered on surface. Occasional marlstone and 2-4mm Fe-rich siltstone fine pellet casts. No bone or shell fragments

Appendix 9.2: Liang Lemdubu: Test Pit C, Depths (cm) of Excavation Units (Spits) and Deposit Volumes (m^3) by Spit

SPIT	NW DEPTH	NE DEPTH	SE DEPTH	SW DEPTH	TOTAL VOLUME
1	10	6	9	9	5.0
2	5	6	5	3	4.0
3	5	5	5	5	3.0
4	5	6	5	4.5	3.0
5	5	5	5	.5	3.5
6	5	6	4	4	3.0
7	5	5	6	5	3.5
8	3	3	4	5	3.5
9	5	4	6	4	4.0
10	7	5	6	6	4.0
11	9	6	4	6	4.0
12	4	6	5	5	3.0
13	5	5	5	5	3.0
14	5	5	5	5	3.5
15	5	5	5	5	3.0
16	5	5	5	5	3.0
17	5	5	5	5	3.0
18	4	5	5	6	3.0
19	6	2	5	4	3.0
20	3	5	5	5	3.0
21	7	8	5	5	4.2
22	5	5	5	5	3.0
23	5	5	5	5	4.0
24	4	5	5	3	4.0
25	9	5	5	7	4.2
26	3	5	5	6	4.0
27	4	5	5	4	3.5
28	9	7	6	8	4.5
29	4	5	6	4	4.5
30	3	6	7	5	4.0
31	6	5	3	3	4.0

Appendix 9.3: Liang Lemdubu: Test Pit C, Faunal Data

NISP Data for all Identified Faunal Specimens by Spit

SPIT	*TACHYGLOSSUS ACULEATUS*	*DASYURUS ALBOPUNCTATUS*	*MYOICTIS WALLACEI*	CF *SMINTHOPSIS* SP.	*ISOODON MACROURUS*	PERORYCTIDAE	UNIDENTIFIED BANDICOOT	*DORCOPSIS* SP.	*THYLOGALE STIGMATICA*	*THYLOGALE BRUNII*	*THYLOGALE* SP. *(BRUNII OR STIGMATICA)*	*MACROPUS AGILIS*	*SPILOCUSCUS MACULATUS*	*PHALANGER GYMNOTIS*	*PHALANGER MIMICUS*	*PHALANGER* SP. *(GYMNOTIS OR MIMICUS)*	*DACTYLOPSILA TRIVIRGATA*	*UROMYS CAUDIMACULATUS*	*PARAHYDROMYS ASPER*	*MELOMYS* SP. CF. *M. BURTONI*	*PARAMELOMYS NASO*	*POGONOMYS* SP.	*PSEUDOMYS* SP. CF. *P. NANUS*	*RATTUS SORDIDUS*	SMALL MURID	CHIROPTERA	SUIDAE	CANIDAE	PIG/DEER/DOG	FROG	SMALL BIRD	*CASUARIUS* SP.	CHELUID TURTLE	BOIDAE	COLUBROIDEA	VARANIDAE	AGAMIDAE	SCINCIDAE	UNIDENTIFIED LIZARD	FISH
1	0	0	1	0	1	2	6	0	11	13	16	5	39	4	21	59	1	9	0	0	0	0	0	0	5	103	28	0	15	1	1	1	1	86	0	1	8	1	0	69
2	0	0	0	0	0	4	5	0	0	3	9	0	8	1	0	25	0	4	0	0	0	0	0	0	1	27	11	1	9	1	0	0	0	28	0	1	2	0	0	30
3	0	0	0	0	1	2	0	0	2	8	3	2	5	1	0	1	0	0	0	0	0	0	0	0	1	4	3	0	0	0	0	0	0	21	0	0	1	1	2	12
4	0	0	0	0	3	1	1	0	6	11	3	15	7	1	2	14	0	0	0	0	0	0	0	0	5	2	0	0	0	0	0	0	0	46	0	0	1	0	1	4
5	0	0	0	1	2	1	2	0	8	4	11	22	6	0	4	4	0	0	1	0	0	0	0	0	4	3	0	0	0	0	0	0	0	104	0	1	2	0	0	0
6	0	0	0	0	1	2	3	0	13	6	13	19	7	0	0	19	0	2	0	0	0	0	0	0	0	1	0	0	0	1	1	0	0	93	0	1	0	0	1	0
7	0	0	0	0	2	0	3	0	33	22	26	52	19	0	2	14	0	0	0	0	0	0	0	0	0	1	0	0	0	0	1	0	0	124	0	2	0	0	1	0
8	0	0	0	0	2	0	7	0	31	25	16	49	14	0	6	11	0	0	0	0	0	0	0	0	1	4	0	0	0	0	0	0	0	78	0	2	0	0	0	0
9	4	0	0	0	2	0	9	0	53	23	45	75	9	0	3	28	1	0	0	0	0	0	0	0	3	1	0	0	0	0	0	0	0	164	0	1	0	0	1	0
10	1	0	0	0	7	1	18	0	91	49	56	138	24	5	13	46	0	2	0	0	0	0	0	0	2	8	0	0	0	0	0	0	0	339	1	2	0	0	7	0
11	0	0	0	0	3	0	7	0	28	18	22	46	10	0	3	35	0	0	0	0	0	0	0	1	3	5	0	0	0	0	0	0	0	88	0	4	0	0	3	0
12	1	0	0	0	3	2	5	0	21	19	20	51	16	1	3	5	0	0	0	0	0	0	0	3	0	2	0	0	0	0	0	0	0	83	0	0	0	0	0	0
13	1	0	0	0	3	0	4	0	26	22	14	36	12	1	8	19	0	0	0	0	0	1	0	0	0	3	0	0	0	0	0	0	0	91	0	0	0	0	0	0
14	0	0	0	0	3	3	13	0	12	29	21	67	12	3	6	20	0	1	0	0	0	0	0	2	4	5	0	0	0	0	0	0	1	106	1	0	0	0	1	0
15	0	0	0	0	3	2	1	0	40	30	22	92	12	1	2	11	0	0	0	0	0	1	0	3	5	4	0	0	0	0	0	0	0	118	0	2	0	0	1	1
16	0	0	0	0	3	1	11	0	35	47	17	71	16	0	7	20	0	0	0	0	0	1	0	1	12	5	0	0	0	0	0	0	0	121	0	4	1	0	0	0
17	0	0	0	0	10	3	10	0	63	19	18	82	9	1	3	23	0	0	0	0	1	1	1	2	10	6	0	0	0	0	0	0	0	147	0	1	0	0	1	0
18	1	0	0	0	11	3	18	0	18	33	14	53	15	0	2	22	0	0	0	0	0	0	0	5	7	2	0	0	0	0	1	0	0	126	0	2	0	0	3	0
19	3	0	0	0	21	4	31	0	34	61	35	40	13	3	17	50	0	0	0	0	0	5	0	4	12	6	0	0	0	0	1	0	0	181	0	6	2	0	0	0
20	0	0	0	0	25	5	27	0	26	55	21	51	18	1	7	37	0	0	0	0	0	4	0	2	3	1	0	0	0	1	0	1	0	213	0	3	0	0	2	0

continued over

Appendix 9.3: continued

SPIT	*TACHYGLOSSUS ACULEATUS*	*DASYURUS ALBOPUNCTATUS*	*MYOICTIS WALLACEI*	CF *SMINTHOPSIS* SP.	*ISOODON MACROURUS*	PERORYCTIDAE	UNIDENTIFIED BANDICOOT	*DORCOPSIS* SP.	*THYLOGALE STIGMATICA*	*THYLOGALE BRUNII*	*THYLOGALE* SP. (*BRUNII* OR *STIGMATICA*)	*MACROPUS AGILIS*	*SPILOCUSCUS MACULATUS*	*PHALANGER GYMNOTIS*	*PHALANGER MIMICUS*	*PHALANGER* SP. (*GYMNOTIS* OR *MIMICUS*)	*DACTYLOPSILA TRIVIRGATA*	*UROMYS CAUDIMACULATUS*	*PARAHYDROMYS ASPER*	*MELOMYS* SP. CF. *M. BURTONI*	*PARAMELOMYS NASO*	*POGONOMYS* SP.	*PSEUDOMYS* SP. CF. *P. NANUS*	*RATTUS SORDIDUS*	SMALL MURID	CHIROPTERA	SUIDAE	CANIDAE	PIG/DEER/DOG	FROG	SMALL BIRD	*CASUARIUS* SP.	CHELUID TURTLE	BOIDAE	COLUBROIDEA	VARANIDAE	AGAMIDAE	SCINCIDAE	UNIDENTIFIED LIZARD	FISH
21	0	0	0	0	19	6	46	0	27	59	19	27	19	0	6	35	0	1	0	0	0	4	0	2	14	3	0	0	0	0	0	1	0	182	0	4	2	0	2	0
22	0	0	1	0	8	2	7	0	13	28	9	16	13	0	4	13	0	1	0	0	0	2	0	2	6	2	0	0	0	0	0	0	0	77	0	2	1	0	0	0
23	0	0	0	0	9	4	0	0	35	30	9	24	15	0	0	10	0	1	0	0	0	0	0	0	0	2	0	0	0	0	0	0	0	46	0	2	1	0	0	0
24	0	0	0	0	11	2	17	1	112	108	41	98	23	3	13	35	0	0	0	1	0	1	0	0	4	1	0	0	0	0	0	0	0	104	0	6	0	0	3	0
25	0	0	0	0	21	5	16	0	212	141	66	120	30	4	7	30	0	0	0	0	0	0	0	1	8	0	0	0	0	0	0	0	0	192	0	3	0	0	5	0
26	0	1	0	0	3	0	9	0	62	29	13	44	3	1	6	23	0	2	0	0	1	1	0	1	5	0	0	0	0	0	0	0	0	90	0	0	0	1	1	0
27	0	1	0	0	1	1	4	0	19	5	6	29	5	0	0	0	0	0	0	0	0	1	0	1	1	0	0	0	0	0	0	0	0	53	0	1	0	0	1	0
28	0	0	0	0	1	0	2	0	19	0	5	6	1	0	3	10	0	0	2	0	0	0	0	3	6	1	0	0	0	0	0	0	0	47	0	0	0	0	1	0
29	0	1	0	0	2	0	0	0	7	5	0	4	0	0	1	9	0	0	0	0	0	0	0	0	9	0	0	0	0	0	0	0	0	16	0	0	0	0	0	0
30	0	0	0	0	0	0	1	0	5	0	0	0	1	0	0	0	0	0	0	1	0	1	0	0	3	0	0	0	0	0	1	0	0	5	0	0	0	0	0	0
31	0	0	0	0	0	0	2	0	1	0	1	2	1	0	0	0	0	2	0	0	0	0	0	0	1	0	0	0	0	0	1	0	0	3	0	0	0	0	0	0

Weight (g) of Bone for each Identified Taxonomic Group and Weight of Bone in Each Burning Category by Spit

SPIT	TOTAL UNBURNT BONE	TOTAL LIGHTLY BURNT BONE	TOTAL BURNT BONE	TOTAL CALCINED BONE	TOTAL BONE	TACHYGLOSSIDAE	DASYURIDAE	PERAMELOIDEA	MACROPODIDAE	PHALANGERIDAE	PETAURIDAE	MURIDAE	CHIROPTERA	SUIDAE	CANIDAE	PIG/DEER/DOG	FROG	*CASUARIUS* SP.	SMALL BIRD	CHELUID TURTLE	SNAKE	VARANIDAE	AGAMIDAE	SCINCIDAE	UNIDENTIFIED LIZARD	FISH	UNIDENTIFIED BONE
1	627.1	367.5	50.0	68.2	1112.8	0	0.2	3.7	32.9	69.8	0.2	1.0	14.3	0	0	56.2	0.2	4.4	0.1	4.0	30.0	2.0	2.5	0.04	0.8	19.1	871.6
2	197.5	163.7	20.1	37.7	419.0	0	0	2.4	7.0	17.3	0	0.6	6.2	8.9	0.1	34.9	0.1	0	0.03	0	8.2	1.0	0.4	0	0.1	10.1	321.8
3	145.6	148.7	10.0	38.3	342.5	0	0	2.6	12.7	9.0	0	0.0	3.9	18.1	0	0	0	0	0	0	7.2	2.5	0	0	3.5	4.5	278.4
4	124.6	182.5	19.3	63.7	390.1	0	0	3.1	16.9	10.2	0	0.9	1.8	0.8	0	0	0	0	0	0	12.6	0.1	0	0.01	0.5	1.1	341.8
5	199.1	230.8	32.4	93.9	556.2	0.1	0.1	2.3	35.1	11.7	0	0.6	0.9	0	0	0	0	0	0	0	34.4	1.0	0.3	0	0.3	0.3	469.1
6	249.3	234.6	27.2	42.7	553.7	0.3	0	3.2	74.2	15.5	0	1.2	0.5	0	0	0	0.02	0	0.1	0	31.5	0.4	0	0	0.1	0	426.9
7	560.8	455.1	74.8	42.5	1133.3	0.8	0.2	6.1	140.0	21.3	0	0	0.2	0	0	0	0	0	0.1	0	41.8	2.0	0	0	0.2	0.1	926.4
8	567.8	420.4	64.9	32.7	1085.9	0.1	0	4.1	153.7	14.7	0	0.1	0.4	0	0	0	0	0	0.3	0	26.8	2.7	0	0	0.0	0	886.1
9	389.9	1243.0	240.3	101.1	1974.2	4.7	0	4.7	236.4	23.8	0.02	0.0	0.2	0	0	0	0	0	0	0	59.3	0.4	0	0	0.7	0	1681.5
10	1549.5	1082.6	227.1	278.5	3137.7	1.1	0	12.9	354.7	58.8	0	0.3	2.5	0	0	0	0	0	0	0	259.7	1.4	0	0.02	1.6	0.04	2444.7
11	677.4	390.2	138.4	74.2	1280.2	0	0	3.9	82.8	16.4	0	0.3	1.6	0	0	0	0	0	0	0	24.4	2.2	0	0	0.8	0.3	1154.1
12	878.4	154.2	51.2	20.1	1103.9	0.6	0.1	6.2	126.6	22.5	0	0.3	0.4	0	0	0	0	0	0	0	43.6	0	0	0	0	0	909.6
13	895.8	135.5	48.2	15.8	1095.2	1.0	0	3.8	195.2	22.0	0	0.1	0.9	0	0	0	0.1	0	0	0	50.8	0	0	0	0	0	874.0
14	1122.2	230.2	42.1	18.5	1412.9	1.2	0	12.7	250.9	20.3	0	0.3	1.6	0	0	0	0	0	0	0.9	48.0	0.3	0	0.08	0.3	0	1133.7
15	973.8	289.5	71.0	27.5	1361.7	0	0	2.8	209.1	18.4	0	1.1	0.9	0	0	0	0	0	0	0	59.6	1.2	0	0	0.1	0.2	1099.9
16	1050.4	364.6	98.3	36.3	1549.5	0	0	10.8	189.6	22.7	0	0.7	2.9	0	0	0	0	0	0	0	74.7	5.0	0.2	0	0	0	1257.3
17	987.9	381.4	108.2	34.3	1511.8	0.1	0	15.8	190.0	26.6	0	1.1	2.9	0	0	0	0	0	0	0	80.3	0.8	0.3	0	0.2	0	1198.9
18	951.3	306.0	127.8	26.3	1411.3	0.7	0	23.2	153.5	44.0	0	1.1	1.2	0	0	0	0	0	1.1	0	71.9	1.9	0.03	0	0.5	0.1	1122.3
19	1278.5	374.0	128.7	11.1	1792.4	0.9	0.1	43.6	253.4	64.2	0	1.5	5.0	0	0	0	0	0	3.4	0	117.2	8.7	0	0	0.2	0	1432.9
20	1782.6	312.4	107.1	17.3	2219.5	1.1	0	39.6	295.6	54.9	0	1.2	1.3	0	0	0	0	4.3	0	0	168.1	6.9	0	0	0.6	0	1642.9
21	1746.2	277.6	90.2	37.2	2151.2	1.9	0	54.3	337.7	60.5	0	1.3	4.4	0	0	0	0	4.4	0	0	136.6	10.7	0.4	0	0.5	0	1573.8
22	1057.7	246.5	54.9	47.2	1406.3	1.6	0.2	16.4	113.2	26.1	0	1.6	1.3	0	0	0	0	0	0	0	57.8	2.6	0.1	0	0	0	1174.6
23	1082.6	294.2	69.0	47.3	1493.0	0.2	0.0	16.6	137.3	26.7	0	1.3	1.1	0	0	0	0	0	0	0	38.2	3.8	0.4	0	0	0.2	1253.4
24	2557.6	577.1	161.9	30.5	3327.1	0	0.1	23.8	360.8	50.2	0	0.3	0.2	0	0	0	0	0	0	0	55.7	3.8	0	0	0.8	0	2818.6
25	4022.6	644.9	482.1	20.0	5169.5	1.5	0.3	35.5	557.5	47.5	0	0.4	0	0	0	0	0	0	0	0	109.3	5.5	0	0	1.0	0	4399.5
26	1499.4	194.6	176.8	6.0	1876.8	0	0.8	4.4	143.9	14.2	0	0.9	0	0	0	0	0	0	0	0	46.4	0.4	0	0.3	0	0	1664.3
27	886.9	38.1	15.4	1.4	941.8	0	2.0	4.0	109.6	7.7	0	0.4	0	0	0	0	0	0	0	0	24.4	0.5	0	0	0.2	0.2	792.3

continued over

Weight (g) od Bone continued

SPIT	TOTAL UNBURNT BONE	TOTAL LIGHTLY BURNT BONE	TOTAL BURNT BONE	TOTAL CALCINED BONE	TOTAL BONE	TACHYGLOSSIDAE	DASYURIDAE	PERAMELOIDEA	MACROPODIDAE	PHALANGERIDAE	PETAURIDAE	MURIDAE	CHIROPTERA	SUIDAE	CANIDAE	PIG/DEER/DOG	FROG	*CASUARIUS* SP.	SMALL BIRD	CHELUID TURTLE	SNAKE	VARANIDAE	AGAMIDAE	SCINCIDAE	UNIDENTIFIED LIZARD	FISH	UNIDENTIFIED BONE
28	562.6	22.1	8.7	6.4	599.8	0	0	1.1	34.5	3.2	0	1.2	0.3	0	0	0	0	0	0	0	20.0	0.2	0	0	0	0	539.4
29	170.3	3.8	6.3	0.7	181.1	0	1.2	1.2	19.5	1.6	0	0.6	0	0	0	0	0	0	0	1.4	8.6	0	0	0	0	0	146.9
30	47.4	0.4	1.1	0.1	49.0	0	0	0.2	1.4	0.7	0	0.3	0	0	0	0	0	0	0.1	0	3.5	0	0	0	0	0	42.8
31	44.5	4.2	0.6	0	49.3	0	0	0.4	0.8	0.7	0	0.2	0	0	0	0	0	0	0.1	0	1.4	0	0	0	0	0	45.6

10

Artefacts on Aru: Evaluating the Technological Sequences

Peter Hiscock

School of Archaeology and Anthropology, The Australian National University, Canberra, ACT, Australia

Introduction

Cultural sequences from excavations at the two cave sites, Liang Lemdubu and Liang Nabulei Lisa, provide fundamental information about not only ancient cultural activities in this landscape, but also about the environmental history of the region and the nature of human exploitation in the changing ecosystems. In this context, the human use of lithic artefacts, which involved exploitation of rock resources and chronological changes in the procurement and processing of those resources, tells us about the human responses to changing environments. Although these excavations were small and exploratory in nature, their location in different parts of the landscape provides an opportunity to develop initial models of resource exploitation. In this way, the analysis of stone procurement and technology presented here compliments the analysis of vertebrate and invertebrate fauna discussed in Chapters 7 and 9 (this volume).

Chronological Framework

Although the interpretations of Liang Lemdubu and Liang Nabulei Lisa presented in this chapter are consistent with the analyses contained in other chapters in this volume, the particular needs of the lithic investigations have required a somewhat different treatment of chronological evidence. In particular, the emphasis on calculating rates of artefact accumulation required the use of both age estimates expressed in calendar years and the estimation of the antiquity of specific points in the deposits.

Calendrical dates were obtained where required by calibration carried out in appropriate ways. All radiocarbon values were calibrated using CALIB 3.0.3. Procedures for carrying out these calibrations can be summarized as follows: non-marine samples were processed using CALIB's bidecadal atmospheric/inferred atmospheric curve; and, marine samples used CALIB's composite marine and terrestrial carbon curve and the Australian standard ocean reservoir correction was applied. No southern hemisphere correction was applied in any of the calibration calculations.

The estimation of antiquity for specific depths in each deposit was accomplished using age-depth curves. Inferences about the relationship of depth below the current surface of the deposit and samples for which absolute age-estimates have been obtained permitted estimates of the antiquity of sediments at any point in the deposit by reference to their depth. Readers should note two points about these analyses. Firstly, the age-depth relationships were developed statistically using regression statistics, the correlation coefficients being a measure of the predictive value of the inferred relationships. This is an incalculably better approach than impressionistic, non-statistical approaches to identifying age-depth relationships. Secondly, these age-depth relationships are employed only to obtain robust estimates of the age of the boundaries of analytical units. Subsequent uses of these estimated ages do not express variations in deposition rates, or artefact accumulation rates, with the analytical units, but nor do they assume that deposition was constant throughout the sequence. Hence there is no contradiction in employing these age-depth relationships as an heuristic device for the expression of discard rates, while acknowledging that sedimentation rates varied or even ceased at some points during the formation of the deposits.

Liang Lemdubu chronology

A data set consisting of 13 samples, each with a calendrical age estimate and average depth, were employed to construct an age-depth relationship for Liang Lemdubu. For the relationship between age and depth within these data points the Spearman's rho is 0.861 ($p<0.0005$), indicating a positive relationship that is highly unlikely to result from chance. The nature of this relationship was defined using further regression analyses (see Fig. 10.1).

A simple linear regression, forced through origin, provides a strong correlation. This linear regression line can be defined as:

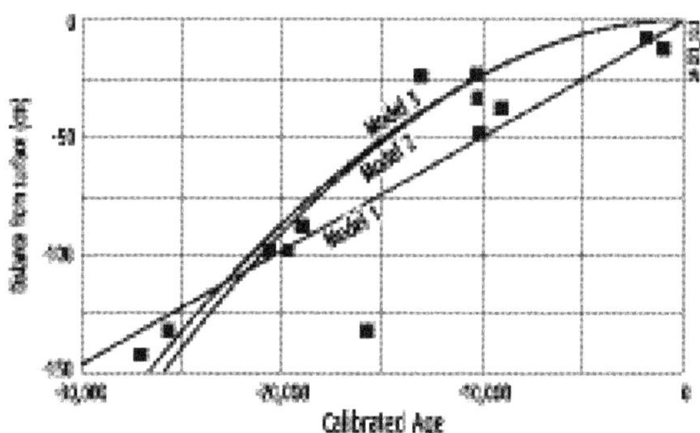

Figure 10.1 Liang Lemdubu: age-depth curves, examining all levels of the deposit

1) *Depth = 0.0049032376 * Age*

where Depth is centimetres below surface (0) and Age is years before 0. Such an equation gives an r^2 value of 0.789 (N=13), indicating that much of the variation in age estimates is explicable in terms of depth of the sample. Being a linear estimate, each five centimetre spit is calculated as representing the same duration (Fig. 10.1, Model 1). In this equation each spit represents approximately 1020 years.

Simple non-linear fitted lines using all data points do not provide estimates of the relationship between age and depth that are as good as the linear model. For instance, non-linear regression (of the form $y=a+bx^2$) can be defined by the equation:

2) *Depth = -0.00000022563473 * Age* ^{2}

where again Depth is centimetres below surface (0) and Age is years before 0.

This equation gives an r^2 value of 0.726 (N=13), and represents a trend to decreased sedimentation rates in the Holocene (Fig. 10.1, Model 2). A single outlier has reduced the calculated coefficient for this model.

In both equations 1 and 2 the charcoal sample OZC777 from Spit 26 constitutes a radical outlier, having a standardized residual value of almost three (i.e. being three standard deviations from the predicted y value). This sample is the lowest charcoal sample dated, and the only one from deep in the deposit. It has yielded a very different age estimate than all other dated materials, and may well have been contaminated. Since this datum point is atypical of the overall age-depth trend there is reason to explore the effect on regression analyses of excluding the sample.

Excluding OZC777 from the simple non-linear $y=a+bx^2$ model gives a dramatically changed depiction of the age-depth relationship, yielding a regression equation:

3) $Depth = -0.00000021298028 * Age^2$

This line of best fit can be seen as an improvement on the previous as the r^2 value has risen to 0.915 (N=12), revealing an impressive capacity to predict depth from age (Fig. 10.1, Model 3). The strength of this coefficient leads me to disregard sample OZC777 from considerations of age estimation in this site, and that the non-linear model given in equation 3 provides the best estimate of the relationship between age and depth in the Lemdubu deposit, when all parts of the deposit are incorporated in a single model. Using this model it is possible to estimate the sedimentation rates during different periods in the formation of the deposit (Table 10.1). These estimates indicate that sedimentation was an order of magnitude higher at the base of the sequence than at the top. Consequently, the levels representing Pleistocene times contain far higher chronological resolution than levels that accumulated during the Holocene.

Table 10.1 Liang Lemdubu: calculated sedimentation rates using model 3

ESTIMATED AGE (USING EQUATION 3)	ESTIMATED SEDIMENTATION RATE (CM/1000 YEARS)
0–10,000	2.12
10,000–15,000	5.30
15,000–20,000	7.42
20,000–25,000	9.54

While model 3 is the best description of age-depth relationships for the deposit as a whole it implies uninterrupted sedimentation throughout the Holocene at a low rate. While this is possible, the radiometric age-estimates that have been obtained do not compel such a presumption to be accepted. For instance, no radiometric sample has yielded an age-estimate between 9000 BP and 2000 BP, and it is possible that sedimentation may have slowed or ceased in that intervening period. Given the possibility that Holocene sedimentation rates may have departed significantly from those implied by model 3, I consider it safest to treat the top five spits as a single unit of Holocene age of low temporal resolution, within which chronological subdivisions and age-depth relationships cannot be precisely defined.

If only the inferred Pleistocene levels of the deposit are considered, involving spits 6 and below, an additional age-depth relationship can be defined. For the Pleistocene portion of the deposit alone, a simple linear regression yields a powerful description of the relationship between age-estimate and depth (again OZC777 is excluded for reasons discussed earlier). This linear regression line can be defined as:

4) $Depth = 34.712072 + (0.0064504317 * Age)$

This equation gives an r^2 value of 0.9267 (N=10), indicating that much of the variation in age estimates is explicable in terms of depth of the sample. Figure 10.2 shows the regression line for this equation. As a linear estimate each five centimetre spit is calculated as representing the same duration (Fig. 10.2). In this equation each spit represents approximately 770 years. The result is an estimate of age for lower levels of the deposit broadly similar to those provided by model 1. Since model 4 does not take into account the reduced sedimentation rates apparently occurring in the Holocene level of the site, as model 3 had, I take it to be a more reliable indication of age-depth relationships for the Pleistocene levels. Consequently, model 4 has been used to estimate ages for Spits 6 and below, while Spits 1–5 have been inferred to represent the last 9–10,000 years.

These age-depth estimates were used to develop a chronological analysis based on the artefactual sequence divided into four zones, labelled I at the top through to IV at the base. Table 10.2 lists the spits attributed to each analytical unit, and the estimated age range of those zones. The rationale for the divisions is based on a combination of dating and stratigraphic considerations.

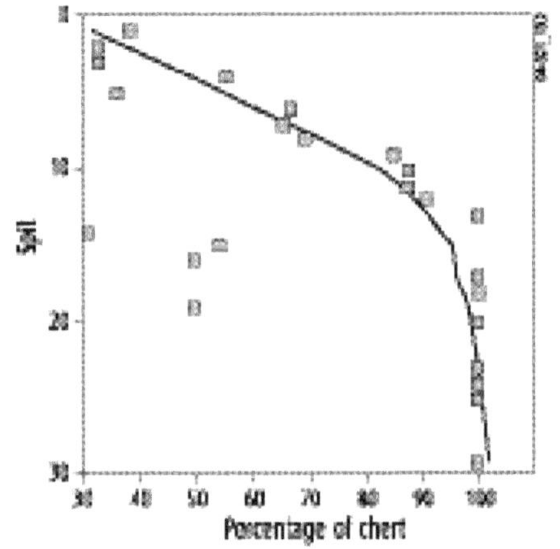

Figure 10.2 Liang Lemdubu: long-term trend in raw material composition as revealed by a Lowess curve fitted to 80% of data points

Zone I represents Spits 1–4, comprising Layers 1 and 2, and is Holocene in age on the basis of radiometric dating and the analysis of archaeo-fauna (see Chapter 9, this volume). Spit 5 is considered to be of uncertain chronological attribution, perhaps being a mixed level, and was excluded from statistical analyses of zones. Faunal evidence suggests that this zone represents a rainforest environment with no grassland areas close to the site (see Chapter 9, this volume).

Zone II contains Spits 6–11, which represents sediments laid down in Layer 3, primarily during the terminal Pleistocene. This zone represents a transitional environment, with the decline of grassland patches.

Zone III consists of a small number of spits (12-16) that are estimated to date from approximately 18,000 to 14,000 BP. These spits lay stratigraphically above the burial that is found in Zone IV. The faunal suite recovered from this zone indicates the existence of extensive tracts of open savannah.

Zone IV comprises those parts of the deposit in and below Spit 17. This combination of spits was selected because the inferred burial pit reported by Bulbeck (Chapter 12, this volume) is likely to have been dug from the surface of the deposit when it was represented by the sediments in Spit 17. Consequently, although the fill of the pit was not differentiated from the *in situ* sediments during excavations, both the pit fill and the pre-existing sediments are combined in this single analytical unit, which therefore dates to an age greater than approximately 18,000 years. The faunal suite recovered from this zone, like that of Zone III, is indicative of extensive tracts of open savannah.

Table 10.2 Liang Lemdubu: analytical divisions of the sequence

ZONE	SPITS (YEARS BP)	APPROXIMATE AGES	DURATION (YEARS)
I	1-5	0-9255	9255
II	6-11	9255-13,910	4655
III	12-16	13,910-17,785	3875
IV	17-9	17,785-28,580	10,795

Nabulei Lisa chronology

The chronology of the Nabulei Lisa sequence has been discussed in Chapter 7 and is used here for interpretation of the lithic sequence. The lithic interpretation centres on the differentiation of two analytical zones as a device for analysis. The rationale and chronology for two zones at Nabulei Lisa can be outlined as follows (see Table 10.3).

Zone I covered Spits 1–29, representing Layers 1–3 and the upper portion of Layer 4 (see Chapter 7, this volume). Radiometric examinations suggest this zone represents the last 10–12,000 years. The faunal assemblage from these levels has been interpreted as indicating the onset of extensive closed rainforest, the loss of grassland habitats, and the subsequent establishment of tidal conditions (see Chapter 7, for full details).

Zone II consisted of Spits 30–38, all of which were removed from Layer 4. Dating of spits from this zone indicates a terminal Pleistocene antiquity, of approximately 16,500–12,000 BP. Faunal assemblages in this zone show high relative abundance of *M. agilis* and the presence of taxa such as *Dorcopsis*, and probably reveal the presence of open grasslands in the vicinity of the site.

Table 10.3 Liang Nabulei Lisa: analytical divisions of the sequence

ZONE	SPITS (YEARS BP)	APPROXIMATE AGES
I	1-29	0-11-12,000
II	30-38	12,000-16,500

Comparison of chronological frameworks

These analytical divisions imposed on each site facilitate comparison between the assemblages. At a broad level Zones I at each site are contemporary, as are the Zone II assemblages, though there is no analogue at Nabulei Lisa for the material represented in Zones III and IV at Lemdubu. However, comparisons of these analytical units can only be made at a general level in recognition of the imprecision of current dating, and that the long time spans represented in each zone mean that the assemblages are 'time-averaged' samples of artefacts discarded during a number of occupational events — a point long recognized in archaeological and palaeontological literature (e.g. Bailey 1983; Behrensmeyer 1982, 1984; Behrensmeyer and Schindel 1983; Flessa et al. 1993; Fursich and Aberhan 1990; Potts 1986). Short-term strategies and variations in foraging and technological activities may not be discernible at the chronological resolution available in these analytical zones, and the following discussions concentrate on pronounced temporal trends in stone-working technology apparent at the two sites.

Table 10.4 Comparison of the Lemdubu and Nabulei Lisa chronology

APPROXIMATE AGES (YEARS BP)	PALAEOCLIMATE	LEMDUBU	NABULEI LISA
<12,000	Entire Holocene	Zone I (Spits 1-4)	Zone I (Spits 1-29)
ca. 12,000-ca. 14-16,000	Terminal Pleistocene	Zone II (Spits 6-11)	Zone II (Spits 30-38)
ca. 14,000-18,000	Final stage of LGM	Zone III (Spits 12-16)	N/A
>18,000	Earlier stage of OIS2	Zone IV (Spits 17-29)	N/A

Key Issues in Artefact Analysis

Regional and chronological comparisons are often said to drive artefact analyses, but in itself such comparisons do not generate the standard analytical frameworks so often applied to archaeological assemblages in Island Southeast Asia. In reality, those typological frameworks derive from an essentialist perspective on variation combined with an interest in the ideas of the artisan (see Hiscock in press, for an extended critique). Such typological perspectives, often with a French aetiology, have been widely applied despite the key notions being increasingly challenged. One effect of the persistence of typological analyses is that many assemblages have been described only in terms of those retouched flakes and cores thought to have been 'tools'. This approach is incapable of describing technology in those localities and regions where prehistoric strategies did not focus on the production of such items, a point that Australian researchers have repeatedly noted. What was immediately apparent from a cursory inspection of these two Aru assemblages is the infrequency of retouched flakes and cores, a characteristic that lends itself to a non-typological technological study using the materialist perspective outlined by Hiscock (in press). Within that framework the key issues to be examined include the analytical method and the chronological resolution available.

Analytic methods

Central to the investigation of the Aru assemblages is the measurement of characteristics about each specimen. The attribute analysis provides information about the range of technological activities evidenced in the assemblage, the contribution of taphonomic processes to the formation of the material, the economic context of the site, and the antiquity of human use of the site. Like many attribute analyses undertaken in archaeology the approach employed here involves measuring a number of interval variables to describe the size and shape of flakes, and a number of nominal variables to describe the treatment to the core (or retouched flake) prior to the production of the flake. The variables used in this study are defined in Table 10.5, and with the exceptions noted these definitions are consistent with those provided by Hiscock (1986a). One way to employ such measurements is as a quantified image of the various actions and products represented in an assemblage, in which the frequency of meaningful characteristics is measured. Applied to the two Aru assemblages, the attribute analysis can characterize the technology represented to describe the reduction system: the frequency of manufacturing patterns (Hiscock 1993:65).

Table 10.5 List of variables measured in the attribute analysis of stone artefacts

NOMINAL VARIABLES	DEFINITION
Amount of cortex	Amount of cortex on the dorsal face, measured in three categories
Artefact characteristics	Presence or absence of: an external initiation for the fracture, a bulb of force, a fracture termination, a platform, or negative scars
Colour	Dominant colour on the standard rock-color chart scale
Crazing	Presence of surface crazing
Crenated	Presence of crenated fractures
Flake termination	Form of the fracture termination on a flake, using HoHo committee terminology (feather, hinge, step, and outrepasse)
Fracture Initiation	The nature of fracture initiation: either Hertzian or bending initiations
Fragment (Breakage)	The portion of a flake represented by the specimen, using the categories discussed by Hiscock (2002)
Overhang removal	Presence of small scars on the dorsal face indicating the removal of platform overhang
Length	Distance from fracture initiation to fracture termination
Platform surface	The condition of the platform surface: cortex, single scar, multiple scars or unknown
Platform thickness	Distance from ventral to dorsal faces, across the platform surface
Platform width	Distance across the platform surface from one lateral margin to the other
Potlidding	Presence of negative or positive potlid scars
Raw material	Category of rock on which the artefact was made (silicified limestone, chert or other)
Retouch	Presence of retouch scars on a flake
Thickness	Distance from ventral to dorsal face, at intersection of length and width
Type	Category of artefact (flake, core or flaked piece), as defined by Hiscock (in press)
Weathering	Category of weathering (Fresh, light Patination, Patination, Heavily Weathered) after Hiscock (1985)
Weight	Weight of the specimens in grams
Width	Distance from one lateral margin to the other, half way along the length

Lithics at Liang Lemdubu

The archaeological sequence from Liang Lemdubu is the longest yet recovered from the Aru Islands. Since stone artefacts are known from most levels of this site it represents an opportunity to characterize the lithic assemblage through time.

Artefact identification

In a site such as Lemdubu, where small numbers of chert and limestone artefacts exist within a deposit containing large quantities of naturally fractured chert and limestone fragments, the issue of accurate artefact identification is paramount. The question of how to differentiate natural from human conchoidal fractures has posed great difficulties for archaeological interpretations. In the archaeological literature, one focus has been on examining situations in which natural mechanisms were available and could conceivably have created fractures. One of the classic studies, by Alfred Barnes (1939), suggested that it might be possible to distinguish natural from human flakes by looking at the angle between the platform and the dorsal face. The notion was that humans controlled fracture by keeping the angle low, whereas natural mechanisms could not regularly duplicate that pattern. So, Barnes concluded, if 75% or more of flakes had acute angles the material could be considered to have been produced by humans. This principle was derived through a study of material in glacial areas. More recently, the range of contexts in which natural hertzian fractures occur, and therefore the diversity of fracture forms, has been recognized as too great to be dealt with using a simple principle like Barnes'. For example, Bryan and Schnurrenberger (1985) discuss the variation in natural mechanisms that can cause fracture. They point out that while fracture produced by static loading in high energy environments (such as during glacial transport) often produces obtuse platform angles, dynamic loading in other environmental situations often produces acute platform angles. For this reason, they argue that the interpretation of fractured rocks as artefacts should be made with regard to their context: 'it must be demonstrated that the type of alteration exhibited by the specimens is anomalous in their reconstructed geomorphic context' (Bryan and Schnurrenberger 1985:139).

In Lemdubu 527 specimens were accepted as having adequate morphological features to indicate unambiguously that they were anomalous within the cave context, and are explicable only as the result of human knapping. Within the site there are no obvious natural mechanisms capable of inducing mechanical fractures, apart from rare roof fall events. Evidence from the deposit is consistent with the rarity of fracture mechanisms: crushing is rare on debris recovered from the sieves; and multiple, step terminated fractures are also rare. The material recovered from the sieves was divided into two groups: non-artefactual fragments (those with no morphological evidence for manufacture, including heat shattered rocks), and artefacts.

The objects identified as artefacts at Lemdubu conform to typical archaeological patterns in similar cave contexts. The assemblage comprises conchoidal flakes with acute platform angles and dorsal scar arrangements that are typically highly patterned. Specimens were only accepted as artefacts if they possessed diagnostic features indicating controlled blows producing conchoidal fracture. The characteristics deemed important in this context were:

1) a platform to which the blow was applied (85% of artefacts displayed this attribute);
2) signs of an external initiation to the fracture surface, such as a ringcrack or cone of force (91% of artefacts);
3) a bulb of force on the ventral surface of a flake (72% of artefacts);
4) a termination to the conchoidal fracture plane (91% of artefacts); and
5) one or more negative scars (92% of artefacts).

These characteristics easily distinguished flaked specimens from the rounded and weathered gravel in which they were lodged. The frequency of these features varied between the raw material, and the percentage of complete specimens identified as artefacts with each feature is summarised in Table 10.6. Many specimens have all, or almost all, of the characteristics. Of 394 complete flakes of chert and limestone, 279 (70.1%) have all five features, a further 103 (26.1%) have four features, and 16 (4.1%) have three features. The reliability of the identification of the specimens as artefactual is enhanced by the presence of multiple characteristics on most of the objects.

Table 10.6 Liang Lemdubu: proportions of characteristics in complete flakes by material

RAW	CHARACTERISTICS PRESENT AS PERCENTAGES OF SAMPLE					
MATERIAL	EXTERNAL INITIATION	PLATFORM	BULB OF FORCE	TERMINATION	NEGATIVE SCARS	N
Chert	302 (100%)	286 (94.7%)	253 (83.8%)	300 (99.3%)	293 (97.0%)	302
Limestone	92 (100%)	83 (90.2%)	54 (58.7%)	91 (98.9%)	79 (85.9%)	92
Total	394 (100%)	369 (93.7%)	307 (77.9%)	391 (99.2%)	372 (94.7%)	394

Raw materials and material acquisition

The 527 artefactual specimens recognized were classified into three raw material categories: chert, limestone, and 'other'. The limestone was a rough-textured, grey rock consistent with an unaltered or partly silicified dolomitic limestone. Cherts were rough-textured cryptocrystalline silica — white, grey and yellow in colour — and consistent with the form of chert that can be obtained in limestone and dolomitic landscapes. 'Other' is a catch-all category for rocks not described in the categories listed above: primarily fine-grained siliceous sedimentary rocks other than chert.

Of the 527 objects recorded 75% was chert, 24.1% was limestone and 0.9% was other materials. In the following sections statistics are only calculated for chert and limestone since only they constitute adequate samples. The excavators did not locate the source(s) of these materials, but it is likely that they were available in the immediate vicinity of the site. Intriguingly, there is a distinct temporal trend in the proportions of raw materials, a pattern that can be expressed in terms of the percentage of chert per spit through the archaeological sequence (see Table 10.7). Expressed by zone, the relative abundance of either chert or limestone is sufficiently different that they can have little chance of arising randomly (Table 10.8).

Figure 10.2 represents the trend in a visually digestible manner, with a Lowess curve fitted to 80% of data points. Two observations can be made about these data. Firstly, the overall trend as represented by the smoothed trend line (i.e. the Lowess curve), is that chert is the primary raw material in the lower half of the sequence, but the proportion of chert declines as it is replaced by limestone, until at the surface chert artefacts constitutes only about one third of the assemblage. A second pattern is an exception to the general trend, with four spits containing half the proportion of chert that would be predicted by the smoothed curve of the general trend (Spits 19, 16, 15, and 14). All four spits fall in Zone III, as defined earlier, dating approximately to the latter stage of the last glacial maximum (LGM). These spits represent outliers which may reflect a period in which material procurement may have been different to that which occurred earlier in the LGM or during the terminal Pleistocene/early Holocene. However, the importance of these proportional changes in raw materials in Zone III is unclear in view of the small numbers of artefacts involved. For instance, it is possible that one or two knapping events involving limestone rather than chert could be responsible for these exceptions to the long-term trend. However, it is also plausible that these dramatic departures from the long-term trend represent some shift in raw material procurement

Table 10.7 Liang Lemdubu: vertical changes in artefact abundance by raw material

SPIT	CHERT	LIMESTONE	OTHER	TOTAL	%CHERT
1	5	8	0	13	38.5
2	2	4	0	6	33.3
3	3	6	0	9	33.3
4	5	4	0	9	55.5
5	4	7	0	11	36.4
6	12	6	0	18	66.7
7	48	24	1	73	65.8
8	45	19	1	65	69.2
9	74	13	0	87	85.1
10	123	17	0	140	87.9
11	28	2	2	32	87.5
12	10	0	1	11	90.9
13	1	0	0	1	100.0
14	4	9	0	13	30.8
15	6	5	0	11	54.6
16	2	2	0	4	50
17	8	0	0	8	100
18	5	0	0	5	100
19	1	1	0	2	50
20	1	0	0	1	100
21	0	0	0	0	
22	0	0	0	0	
23	1	0	0	1	100
24	4	0	0	4	100
25	2	0	0	2	100
26	0	0	0	0	
27	0	0	0	0	
28	0	0	0	0	
29	1	0	0	1	100
Total	395	127	5	527	75.0
	(%)	(75.0%)	(24.1%)	(0.9%)	

Table 10.8 Liang Lemdubu: comparison of raw material abundance by Zone (Zone IV excluded because of zero cells)

ZONE	CHERT	LIMESTONE	TOTAL
I	15	22	37
II	330	81	411
III	23	16	39
Total	368	119	487

$\chi^2 = 35.369$, d.f. = 2, $p < 0.001$

strategies during the LGM. Complicating any such interpretation is the question of whether artefacts were made at Lemdubu or simply transported here, in which case procurement took place at some other point in the landscape. I return to this issue later.

With these observations it is possible to characterize the use of raw material in each of the four zones (Table 10.9). The base of the archaeological sequence represents a period in which only chert was being procured for artefact manufacture. This may be interpreted as a highly selective but regular strategy for tool production in place during the early portion of Oxygen Isotope Stage 2 (OIS2); perhaps linked to a comparatively mobile or wide ranging foraging strategy capable of obtaining chert from a variety of localities.

During the later portion of the LGM, represented by Zone III, adjoining spits contain very different raw material proportions, a pattern which may well reveal different patterns of movement/foraging/procurement. In contrast to the preceding period, these differences in Zone III might reveal the existence of variable settlement systems or strategy switching during the harshest part of the LGM. An obvious explanation for these variable raw material compositions is the existence of embedded procurement within mobile foraging economies, that have changed spatial emphasis through time.

The terminal Pleistocene and Holocene, represented by Zones II and I contain a progressive transition from tool production strategies, emphasising the procurement and use of chert — perhaps obtained at some distance from Lemdubu — to strategies focussing on the flaking of limestone. In the absence of more specific information about raw material source distributions the most plausible hypothesis is that in the last 10–12,000 years there was a reduction in the radius of foraging and/or reduction in accessibility of chert sources, with a concomitant switch to the use of local material. Alternatively, or additionally, reduction in the reliance on stone artefacts may be related to a decline in the use of stone artefacts, and a switch from using relatively expensive material (chert) to a locally abundant and relatively inexpensive material (limestone).

Table 10.9 Liang Lemdubu: summary of changes in raw material by zone

ZONE	SPITS	RAW MATERIAL COMPOSITION
I	1-4	Limestone is the most common material on which flakes are made
II	6-11	Chert is consistently the dominant material being employed, but during Zone II it displays a progressive reduction in the level of dominance
III	12-16	Spit contents are radically varied, either containing all or almost all artefacts made on chert, or else having relatively little chert (<55%)
IV	17-29	With the exception of one artefact, in Spit 19, chert is the only raw material used for artefact manufacture

Trends in density

Chronological changes in artefact abundance are observable in the Lemdubu excavation. Figure 10.3 plots raw artefact counts by spit, and because spits are a uniform volume these plots effectively display vertical changes in artefact density within the deposit. If no taphonomic processes can be invoked to explain this pattern these density changes can be interpreted as a clear chronological trend in artefact accumulation. A pronounced unimodal curve is displayed in Figure 10.3, revealing low quantities of artefacts accumulating both early and late in the occupational sequence, separated by a period of comparatively high levels of artefact loss. The most

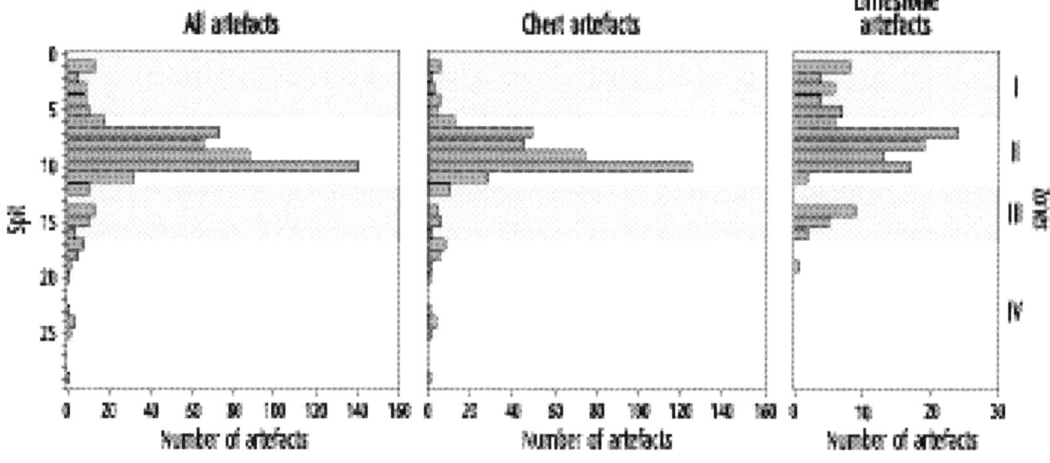

Figure 10.3 Liang Lemdubu: vertical changes in artefact numbers

pronounced rates of artefact accumulation occur in Spits 6–12: the late Pleistocene levels designated 'Zone II'. This chronological trend is apparent in both chert and limestone specimens, although more pronounced in the chert component of the assemblage.

By re-expressing artefact numbers per square metre in terms of the duration of each zone, using the chronological estimates discussed above, it is possible to construct an image of chronological changes in the artefact accumulation rates in this portion of Lemdubu (see Fig. 10.4). These calculations indicate that during the terminal Pleistocene, represented by Zone II, artefact discard was approximately an order of magnitude higher than at any other period during human occupation of the locality. During the occupational sequence discard rates were extremely low prior to 20–18,000 BP; increased substantially during the latter part of LGM; increased substantially again immediately following the LGM; and decreased to a low level during the Holocene.

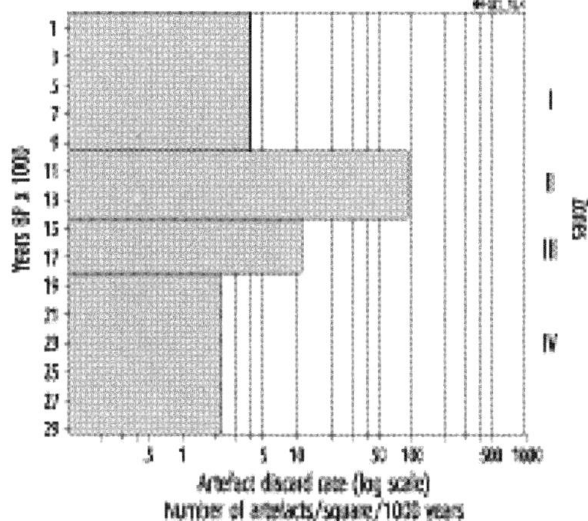

Figure 10.4 Liang Lemdubu: estimated discard rate by analytical zone

Interpreting this directional long-term trend is difficult for several reasons. For instance, this sequence derives from only one square metre (Test Pit C) and may reveal occupational patterns in only one part of the site. If preferred discard locations within the cave varied through time the changing accumulation rate in this test pit might reflect different discard behaviour rather than an overall shift in the level of artefact discard in the site. Without excavation and analysis of test pits from other parts of Liang Lemdubu this possibility cannot be excluded.

Another factor constraining interpretation is the complex issue of the extent to which variation in artefact numbers reflects variation in the intensity of occupation or change in the nature of cave use. Changes in the rate with which artefacts have accumulated may be signalling temporal variations in the frequency or nature of knapping, rather than changes in the level of all activities that took place during an occupation. This possibility was examined by looking at the degree of covariation between artefacts and faunal material. Weight of artefacts per spit or zone was used as the measure of artefact abundance and compared to selected categories of faunal material drawn from the data recorded by Aplin (Chapter 9, this volume). The relationship between the abundance of artefacts and faunal remains was examined using Spearman's correlations for the 24 spits containing artefacts. The results are listed in Table 10.10. The most noteworthy result in this table is the extremely poor relationship between the weights of artefacts and bones ($r = 0.145$, $p = 0.499$, $n = 24$; $r_s = -0.063$, $p = 0.768$, $n = 24$). Some spits with less than 10 artefacts have less than 200g of bone, while in other spits with similar artefact numbers there is more than five kilograms of bone. Table 10.10 also shows the coefficients for the relationship between artefacts and sub-groups of the faunal assemblage. These were calculated because at least a proportion of the bone is likely to derive from non-archaeological sources, and these sub-groupings are considered to be dominated by archaeological fauna. All bivariate comparisons reveal negligible covariation between artefact weights and the abundance of any of the categories of faunal material.

Table 10.10 Liang Lemdubu: correlations between weight of stone artefacts (g) and the quantity of bone using 24 spits

	WEIGHT OF ALL BONE	WEIGHT OF MAMMAL	WEIGHT OF THYLOGALE/PETROGALE	WEIGHT OF M.AGILIS	WEIGHT OF PHALANGER
Spearman's rank correlation	-0.063	-0.060	0.178	0.067	-0.008
(p value)	(0.768)	(0.781)	(0.405)	(0.756)	(0.971)

The reason for this non-correspondence of bone and stone is obvious in the visual comparison given in Figure 10.5, which expresses change by zone. Spits from the lower levels of the sequence, representing Zone IV, contain very few artefacts but generally have large quantities of bones. The earliest phase of occupation was one in which very large quantities of bone were deposited without much evidence of artefact use or discard. During later occupation, represented by Zones I–III, artefact discard is apparently more balanced with the quantity of fauna that was processed. The intriguing result of this analysis is a change in the relationship of artefacts and fauna at the end of Zone IV and the start of Zone III. In Zone IV there are very few artefacts at all, and large quantities of bone that vary independently of the artefacts. In Zones I to III artefacts are not only far more abundant and bones less abundant but artefacts and bone appears to covary by spit in a far stronger way (r = 0.668, p = 0.005, n = 16; rs = 0.438, p = 0.09, n = 16). This alteration in the relationship of bone and artefact discard is distinct and may well mark either a change in the function of the cave or a change in the discard patterns within the cave. In either case the final stage of the LGM marks an alteration in human behaviour at Liang Lemdubu.

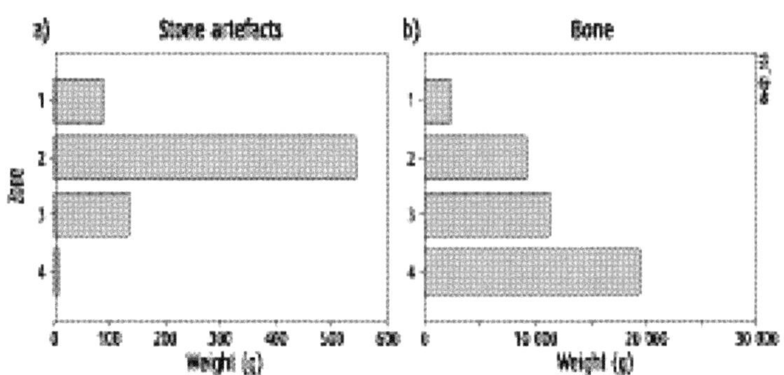

Figure 10.5 Liang Lemdubu: graphical comparison of temporal trends in the weight of a) stone artefacts and b) bone by analytical zone

Taphonomic processes

Changes in abundance of archaeological material should always be interpreted in light of a study of taphonomic processes. Stone artefacts are not immune to the sorts of taphonomic processes that effect other classes of archaeological material (Hiscock 1985). In the Australasian region two processes are frequently documented from limestone caves and rockshelters: shattering of stone through exposure to heat, and weathering of stone in seasonally wet deposits (see Hiscock 1988). Both of these processes are frequent in the Lemdubu assemblage, and need to be examined in some detail.

Artefact fragmentation

Fragmentation of rocks in this assemblage is likely to have occurred for a number of reasons, including exposure to fire, the knapping process itself, and post-depositional mechanical damage. Of the 518 flake fragments recognized, 23% were broken (Table 10.11). One consequence of this fragmentation is that the actual number of flakes represented may be less than a simple count of the fragments. As a result, calculations of artefact abundance are necessary.

Table 10.11 Liang Lemdubu: flake breakage by raw material

	COMPLETE*	PROXIMAL	MEDIAL	DISTAL	LCS	TOTAL
Chert	302	27	5	25	31	390
Limestone	92	6	0	10	16	124
Other	4	0	0	0	0	4
Total	398	33	5	35	47	518

* One specimen was encrusted and material could not be determined. It was excluded from this table

A simple estimate of the original number of flakes in this assemblage is provided in Table 10.12. This is achieved by counting only those flake fragments with platforms, since this is one indication of the number of blows represented by flake fragments in the collection. This kind of procedure is widely advocated in the literature (see Andrefsky 1998). In this estimation complete flakes, proximal fragments, and longitudinal cone-split fragments (LCS) have been employed to estimate the number of flakes that originally existed.

Table 10.12 Liang Lemdubu: flake breakage by raw material

	COMPLETE	PROXIMAL	LCS	ESTIMATED FLAKING EVENTS	%
Chert	302	27	31	360	75.3
Limestone	92	6	16	114	23.9
Other	4	0	0	4	0.8
Total	398	33	37	478	

A more sophisticated estimate of minimum numbers of flakes (MNF) can be obtained using Hiscock's (2002) procedure involving the equation $MNF = C + T + L$, where C is the number of complete flakes, T is the largest category of transverse fragments excluding medial fragments (i.e. the greater of the number of proximal fragments or distal fragments), and L is a count of longitudinal fragments. For chert this MNF value is 350 (= 302 + 27 + 21) or 74% of the assemblage, for limestone the calculated MNF value is 117 (= 92 + 10 + 15) or 25% of the assemblage, and for other materials it is 4 or 1% of the assemblage. Hence, the total MNF value for the assemblage (calculated from $MNF_{chert} + MNF_{limestone} + MNF_{other}$) is 471.

Of course, this estimate is a minimum one. In addition to the cores and flake fragments there were eight flaked pieces that must have derived from shattered cores and/or flakes. Furthermore, it is possible that some artefacts were heat shattered to such an extent that the fragments can no longer be recognized, and are not represented by artefactual fragments. Hence the minimum estimate of 459 may well represent up to 500 artefacts.

One thing that is obvious from these counts is the low intensity of artefact use, and perhaps occupation throughout the archaeological sequence. Over a period of perhaps 29,000 years, even 500 artefacts per square metre represents only 17 artefacts/1000 years/square metre. Given that many of these artefacts are very small (see below) it is likely that many are production debris that represent minimal activity beyond maintaining a few tools. As a very rough indication of the level of activities that may be involved here, Hayden (1979:166) estimated that at Walukaritji and Ngarulurutja, two sites in the Western Desert, the debris created by tool production and maintenance was 6.7 artefacts/person/week and 28–57 artefacts/person/week respectively. Acknowledging the difference in environmental context and tool form, this kind of ethnographic measure suggests that the artefactual debris may only reflect a few people visiting the site for a day or two every few years. These calculations should not be taken literally, as many factors including different site functions may make a recent Australian analogue inappropriate, but they can be used to reinforce the impression of this site as the location of occasional occupation by small groups.

Fire

Approximately one in eight artefacts (11.4%) display evidence of heat damage in the form of crenation, potlid scars, or surface crazing. Table 10.13 records the proportions of these categories of heat damage by raw material category. There appear to be differences in the frequency of thermal damage between raw materials, with chert having a far higher rate than limestone. Non-random differences between chert and limestone are confirmed by chi-squared statistics (Table 10.14), even when Zone II alone is examined to remove the effects of any chronological change (Table 10.15). These differences probably reflect the resilience of each material to heat. Consequently, any attempt to measure chronological changes in the abundance of heat damage will need to examine each rock type separately.

Table 10.13 Liang Lemdubu: thermal damage by raw material

	% CHERT (N=395)	% LIMESTONE (N=127)	% OTHER (N=5)	% TOTAL (N=527)
Crenation	4.8	3.9	20.0	4.7
Potlid	9.6	3.9	0	8.2
Crazing	1.0	1.6	0	1.1
Total damage*	13.4	4.8	20.0	11.4

* Total is not a column sum because some specimens have more than one kind of damage

Table 10.14 Liang Lemdubu: thermal damage by raw material

	CHERT	LIMESTONE	TOTAL
Unheated	342	120	462
Heated	53	6	59
Total	395	126	521

χ^2 = 6.291, d.f. = 1, p = 0.012, V = 0.117

Table 10.15 Liang Lemdubu: thermal damage by raw material for Zone II

	CHERT	LIMESTONE	TOTAL
Unheated	287	77	364
Heated	39	3	42
Total	326	80	406

χ^2 = 3.828, d.f. = 1, p = 0.05, V = 0.107

Temporal changes in thermal damage to chert flakes are described by the data listed in Table 10.16. Upper portions of the artefactual sequence, represented by Zones I and II, have roughly 13% of artefacts thermally damaged, whereas the lower Zones III and IV have more than 20% of specimens damaged. It is tempting to interpret this vertical change in the relative abundance of thermal damage as an indication that heat sources, such as fires, may have been more frequent or intense during the earlier parts of the Lemdubu sequence. However, such a conclusion is unwarranted, since the abundance of heat damage is likely to reflect a number of other factors in addition to heat sources. For instance, the rate of thermal shattering is likely to be related to sedimentation rates, since the length of time artefacts are exposed on or near the ground surface will be positively related to the probability of damage being sustained (see Hiscock 1985). Sedimentation rates in Lemdubu were higher in Zones III and II than earlier or later in the sequence, a pattern that parallels far higher accumulation rates for heat shattered specimens in Zones II and III (Spearman's r = 0.8, N=4). The conjunction of sedimentation and heating rates is the opposite of what would be predicted if thermal damage was proportional to the stability of the cave surface, possibly indicating that exposure of artefacts to heat sources was greatest during the LGM and terminal Pleistocene (see Fig. 10.6). However, the abundance of heat affected artefacts in the Lemdubu sequence is probably caused by variations in sample size. Impressively strong correlations exist between

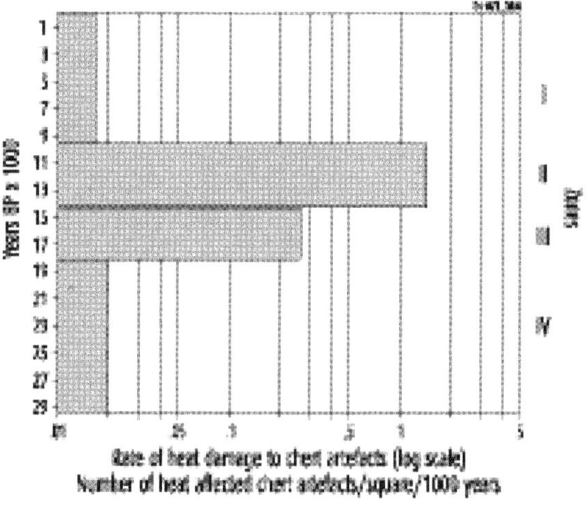

Figure 10.6 Liang Lemdubu: calculated accumulation rates for thermally affected chert artefacts by zone

the number of chert artefacts per spit and the number of artefacts with crenations (r = 0.95), with potlid scars (r = 0.88), and with crazing (r = 0.71). All of these correlations are significant at the p = 0.001 level. These statistics are best interpreted as indicating that the numbers of heat shattered fragments vary in response to changing artefact abundance; and perhaps when artefacts are more frequent they are more often exposed to heat sources, even when the abundance and nature of heat sources remains unchanged. Consequently, it is not possible to interpret heat shattering in Lemdubu as revealing temporal differences in site use. Regardless of this conclusion, the changing artefact density described above demands explanation.

Table 10.16 Liang Lemdubu: thermal damage by zone for chert flakes

ZONE	CRAZING	CRENATION	POTLIDDING	TOTAL THERMALLY DAMAGED*	% FLAKES DAMAGED	TOTAL ARTEFACTS
I	0	2	0	2	13.3	15
II	3	12	33	41	12.4	330
III	0	3	5	8	21.6	37
IV	1	2	0	2	22.2	9
Total	4	19	38	53	13.6	391
	(1.1%)	(4.8%)	(9.6%)			

* Total is not the sum of crazing, crenation and potlidding because some specimens have more than one kind of damage

Weathering

One characteristic of the Lemdubu chert artefacts that is immediately obvious is that they vary in colour. More interestingly, the colours change systematically through the deposit. These changes were quantified by recording the colour of each artefact using the Rock-color Chart distributed by the Geological Society of America. Table 10.17 presents the percentage of chert artefacts in each of 22 colour categories represented in the assemblage. Common colours include white (N9), light grey (N7-8), medium grey (N5), pinkish grey (5YR 8/1), light brownish grey (5YR 6/1), and pale yellowish brown (10YR 6/2). Some of these colour classes probably reflect the colours of chert being knapped, but the changes in the frequency of each colour class through the deposit are also likely to reflect alteration of the colour through processes such as weathering. This can be examined by characterising the colour frequencies for each zone.

Changes in the colour of chert artefacts at different depths in the deposit were quantified by zone. Interpreting these changes is complicated by the variation in sample sizes between the zones. This is shown by the strong Pearson's correlation between number of colour categories and number of chert artefacts per zone (r = 0.94, r2 = 0.87, p = 0.07), and a similarly strong Spearman's rank coefficient ($r_S = 1.0$, $p < 0.0001$). Zones I, III, and IV have a small range of colours compared to Zone II, and while this pattern may have other causes it is consistent with their low sample sizes.

Table 10.17 Liang Lemdubu: colours of chert artefacts (N=395)

		CHROMA (SATURATION)											
		HUE 5YR				HUE 10YR			HUE 5Y				N
		/1	/2	/4	/6	/2	/4	/6	/1	/2	/4	/6	/0
Value (Lightness)	9/												11.6
	8/	12.4		0.8		2.0		0.3	2.5				10.1
	7/		0.5				1.3						9.6
	6/	17.5		2.0		6.1			1.5		0.3		6.1
	5/		1.5				0.3						6.8
	4/	2.3											3.5
	3/												0.5

However, the differences in the frequency of colours between zones is not easily explained in this way. Trends from pinkish greys, brownish greys, and yellowish browns towards whites and greys, and from darker to lighter, can be observed from the surface to the base of the deposit. These trends are illustrated in Figure 10.7, which graphically depicts an increase in greys/whites and of lighter shades with increasing depth.

These vertical trends in the colour of chert artefacts through the sequence display a relationship with the erosion and weathering of the chert. The measurement of weathering here follows the approach developed by Hiscock (1985) in his description of the dolomitic chert artefacts from the small limestone rockshelter at Colless Creek in northern Australia. Although weathering is probably a continuous process four categories were distinguished as a means of quantifying the changes in the Lemdubu chert artefacts:

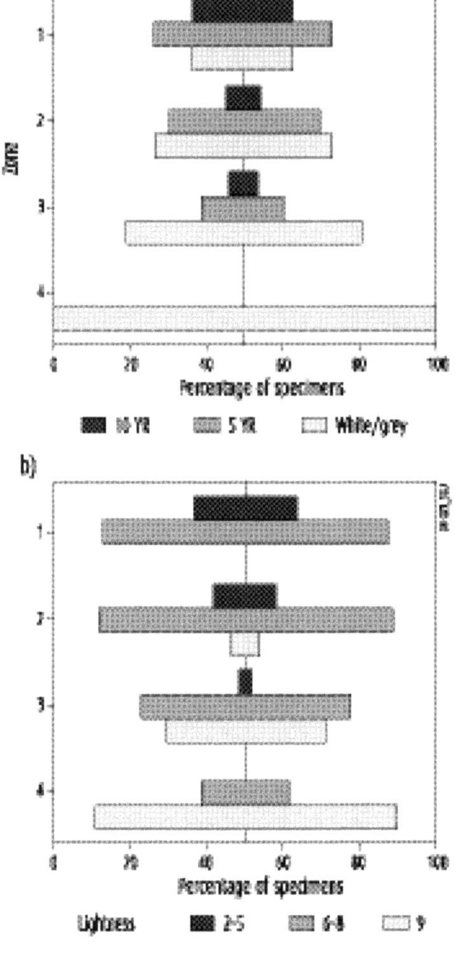

Figure 10.7 Liang Lemdubu: changes to the colour of chert artefacts in a) hue and chroma, and b) value (i.e. lightness)

1) fresh — in which the fracture surfaces of the chert are hard, lustrous, and the same as the interior of the artefact;
2) light patination — where the surface appears to have a dull film, and may be mottled, some areas having the appearance of fresh chert and others displaying a patina;
3) patinated — where the texture of the surface has become dull and rough. Broken specimens reveal that while the weathering is not confined to the surface it need not occur throughout the entire artefact; and
4) heavily weathered — where the artefact is porous, and has become crumbly and powdery. Broken artefacts show that this degree of weathering occurs uniformly throughout the entire artefact.

Using these categories it is possible to quantify the relationship between aspects of colour and the extent of weathering. Table 10.18 shows that fresh chert is dominated by darker values, heavily weathered chert specimens are never dark and are often extremely light, with intermediate weathering categories being dominated by values of intermediate lightness. On the basis of this pattern it is likely that variation in colour in the Lemdubu assemblage is largely a consequence of different levels of weathering. Consequently, the vertical changes in chert colour within the deposit probably reflect changes in the levels of artefact weathering quantified in Table 10.19.

Variations through the deposit in the relative frequencies of these weathering categories appear to be independent of the frequency of heat damage. Table 10.20 documents this for chert flakes in Zone II, revealing that differences in the frequency of heat damage between the three weathering classes frequently represented in that zone may simply be due to chance. The independence of weathering and heat damage is not surprising in Lemdubu since it has already been demonstrated that there are no chronological changes in heating frequency that cannot be explained in terms of sample size. The chronological changes in weathering classes are clearly patterned in a different way.

Table 10.18 Liang Lemdubu: percentage of chert specimens in each weathering category by lightness category

LIGHTNESS	FRESH	LIGHT PATINATION	PATINATION	HEAVILY WEATHERED
9/	0	0.7	3.4	41.7
6-8/	36.3	75.7	83.6	58.3
2-5/	63.7	24.6	13.0	0

Table 10.19 Liang Lemdubu: relative abundance of weathering categories on chert artefacts

	LIGHT		HEAVILY	TOTAL	
SPIT	FRESH	PATINATION	PATINATED	WEATHERED	NUMBER
1	3	1	1	0	5
2	1	1	0	0	2
3	0	3	0	0	3
4	3	1	1	0	5
5	0	0	4	0	4
6	3	6	3	0	12
7	1	20	21	6	48
8	0	28	13	4	45
9	0	52	19	3	74
10	0	25	61	37	123
11	0	1	16	11	28
12	0	0	6	4	10
13	0	0	0	1	1
14	0	0	1	3	4
15	0	0	0	6	6
16	0	0	0	2	2
17	0	0	2	6	8
18	0	0	1	4	5
19	0	0	0	1	1
20	0	0	0	1	1
21	0	0	0	0	0
22	0	0	0	0	0
23	0	0	0	1	1
24	0	0	0	4	4
25	0	0	0	2	2
26	0	0	0	0	0
27	0	0	0	0	0
28	0	0	0	0	0
29	0	0	0	1	1
Overall	11	138	149	97	395
Assemblage	(2.8%)	(34.9%)	(37.7%)	(24.6%)	

Table 10.20 Liang Lemdubu: relationship between heat damage and weathering categories for chert flakes in Zone II

	HEAT DAMAGE		TOTAL
	ABSENT	PRESENT	
Light patination	111	19	130
Patination	115	16	131
Heavily weathered	57	4	61
Total	283	39	322

χ^2 = 2.535, d.f. = 2, p = 0.282, V = 0.089

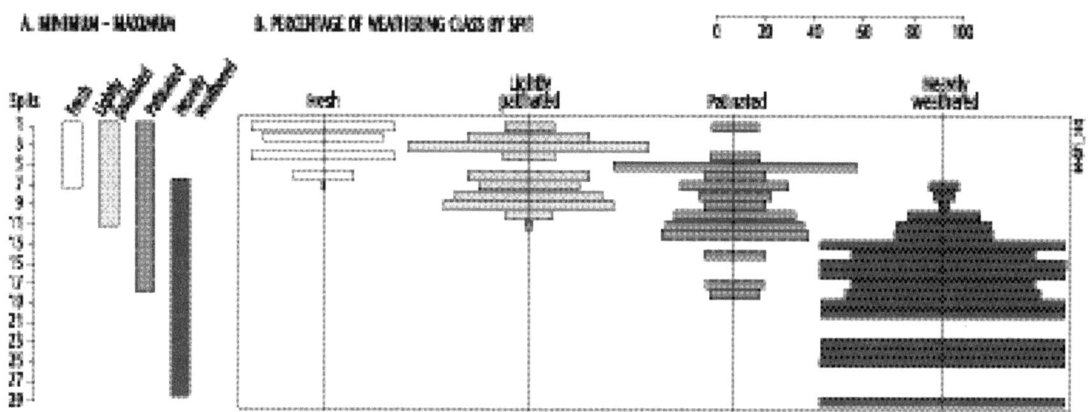

Figure 10.8 Liang Lemdubu: changes in weathering through the sequence

As shown in Figure 10.8, the proportion of artefacts in each weathering class varies vertically in a manner consistent with increased intensity of weathering at greater depth in the deposit. Departures from smooth battleship curves are directly related to spits with only one, two or three artefacts. Fresh chert artefacts extend down only six spits. Lightly patinated artefacts do not become common until Spit 6 but extend down only to Spit 11. Patinated artefacts are numerically dominant in Spits 10–12, although they extend down to Spit 18. Heavily weathered artefacts are not common until Spit 13, but below that point in the deposit almost all artefacts are highly altered by weathering. In the lower spits all chert artefacts are heavily weathered.

Several inferences can be drawn from these data on the distribution of weathering categories within the deposit:

1) the patterns are consistent with a decay of chert over time, with all chert artefacts being deposited in a fresh state and becoming progressively more weathered as they lay buried in the deposit. Hence the longer the artefacts have lain buried in the deposit, the more altered they are;
2) the rate of chert weathering can be broadly established by reference to the radiometric dates available for the cave. For instance, no artefacts remained in a fresh state for as long as 8000 years, and after 16–18,000 years have elapsed all artefacts had been altered to a point where they were patinated or heavily weathered; and
3) the absence of fresh or lightly patinated artefacts from the lower levels of the deposit should be interpreted as evidence that the deposit has not been homogenised by vertical movement of objects, and that the four zones defined earlier are a useful representation of chronologically different assemblages. Zone I is characterized by frequent fresh artefacts, Zone II by many lightly patinated and patinated artefacts, Zone III by patinated and heavily weathered specimens, and Zone IV contains only heavily weathered artefacts. These weathering patterns provide independent evidence of chronological differences between the artefacts in these analytical zones, thereby validating the interpretation of inter-zonal differences as a chronological sequence. Assemblage changes through time can therefore by recognized in the Lemdubu material.

Technological Interpretations

Artefact classes

A consistent pattern throughout the Liang Lemdubu sequence is the absence of cores. The artefact assemblage is dominated by flakes — only a few of which are retouched (see below) — and a few 'flaked pieces' (fragmentary specimens with negative scars unable to be classified as either flakes or cores). The relationship between artefact type and raw material is listed in Table 10.21. Based on these data it can be emphasised that cores are too infrequent to account for the flakes and flake fragments. The likely explanation for this pattern is one of three mechanisms, working individually or in combination:

1) flakes may have been made elsewhere and transported to this locality without cores;
2) cores might have been preferentially removed from the site; and
3) flakes may have been produced by knapping retouched flakes rather than cores.

These models will be considered in light of more detailed information about flake sizes.

Table 10.21 Liang Lemdubu: counts of artefacts by raw material

	FLAKES	FLAKED PIECES	TOTAL	(%)
Chert	390	5	395	(75.0)
Limestone	124	3	127	(24.1)
Other	5	0	5	(0.9)
Total	519	8	527	(100)
(%)	(98.5)	(1.5)	(100)	

Artefact sizes and shapes

The characteristics of these artefacts can be evaluated using a number of standard measures. Complete flakes have been used to indicate the characteristics of flaking in this assemblage. Descriptive statistics for flake size and shape are provided in Table 10.22. Variation between raw chert and limestone is apparent in these data, with the platforms of chert flakes being distinctly smaller than those of limestone flakes. However, the size and shape of chert and limestone flakes are remarkably similar in other traits. Taking flakes of all materials it is clear that the assemblage is dominated by small, squat flakes.

Table 10.22 Liang Lemdubu: descriptive statistics for the size and shape of complete flakes by raw material

VARIABLES	ALL MATERIALS	CHERT	LIMESTONE	DIFFERENCE BETWEEN CHERT AND LIMESTONE	IS THIS DIFFERENCE DUE TO CHANCE?
Length	14.1±7.3 (N=400)	14.2±7.5 (N=303)	13.7±5.8 (N=92)	t = 0.69 p = 0.485	Very likely
Width	14.5±7.2 (N=400)	14.1±7.1 (N=303)	15.7±7.4 (N=92)	t = -1.85 p = 0.065	Fairly unlikely
Thickness	3.3±2.3 (N=399)	3.2±2.3 (N=302)	3.4±1.8 (N=92)	t = 0.83 p = 0.406	Very likely
Platform width	9.1±8.1 (N=341)	8.3±5.8 (N=259)	11.4±5.9 (N=78)	t = -4.14 p = 0.001	Extremely unlikely
Platform thickness	2.4±2.0 (N=338)	2.1±1.9 (N=256)	3.2±2.1 (N=78)	t = -4.33 p = 0.001	Extremely unlikely
Elongation	1.0±0.4 (N=400)	1.1±0.4 (N=303)	0.9±0.4 (N=92)	t = 2.41 p = 0.017	Very unlikely
Area (mm^2)	241.9±258.5 (N=400)	238.5±255.9 (N=304)	242.5±218.9 (N=92)	t = -0.11 p = 0.913	Extremely likely
Weight (g)	1.5±3.5 (N=399)	1.5±3.6 (N=302)	1.4±2.1 (N=92)	t = 0.32 p = 0.748	Extremely likely

These patterns of flake size are not, of themselves, diagnostic of either particular forms of technology or of particular stages in a reduction process. However, the following statements are useful in typifying the bulk of the assemblage:

1) these generally small flakes are unlikely to have derived from early-stage reduction, including decortication. This inference is supported by the rarity of decortication flakes (see below);
2) reduction involves production of regular flakes but does not reveal frequent production of elongate flakes (sometimes called 'blades'); and
3) the majority of flakes are likely to have been removed from either large retouched flakes and/or small cores.

Change through time in these characteristics of flake size can be observed in the data presented in Table 10.23. The primary trend is a progressive increase in flake dimensions, especially flake width and platform width and thickness. The composite effect of increases in these dimensions is the progressive and marked increase in flake weight through time. The increase in width through time is more pronounced than the increase in flake length, and consequently the frequency of elongate flakes declines through time. For example, the percentage of complete chert flakes with a length more than twice their width was highest in the terminal Pleistocene (16.8% in Zone III) and declined to less than one per cent in Zones I–II. This decline in the relative abundance of elongate flakes represents subtle shifts in flake production and need not be construed as indicating a change in the overall technological strategy. However, it does demonstrate that there is no evidence from this site for Holocene blade technologies.

Table 10.23 Liang Lemdubu: descriptive statistics for the size and shape of complete chert flakes

VARIABLES		ZONE I (N=11)	ZONE II (N=257)	ZONE III	ZONE IV (N=14)
Length	Mean±Std.	15.6±7.4	14.2±7.6	14.1±6.4	13.7±7.7
	median (IQR)	12.6 (13.3)	12.2 (8.6)	12.6 (8.3)	13.7 (11.5)
Width	Mean±Std.	19.0±14.3	14.1±6.7	13.1±7.6	13.3±6.2
	median (IQR)	15.7 (8.5)	12.8 (9.1)	12.0 (7.9)	11.8 (10.1)
Thickness	Mean±Std.	3.9±4.2	3.1±2.1	4.0±4.3	3.4±2.1
	median (IQR)	3.0 (3.2)	2.5 (2.2)	2.9 (2.5)	3.0 (3.2)
Platform width	Mean±Std.	14.2±17.8	8.0±4.9	10.5±5.9	6.5±5.3
	median (IQR)	8.2 (6.1)	6.8 (6.0)	7.7 (10.2)	5.1 (3.3)
Platform thickness	Mean±Std.	4.8±6.9	2.1±1.5	2.6±1.5	1.4±0.8
	median (IQR)	2.0 (2.8)	1.6 (1.7)	2.5 (2.6)	1.3 (0.7)
Elongation	Mean±Std.	0.9±0.3	1.1±0.4	1.2±0.6	1.0±0.4
	median (IQR)	0.9 (0.6)	1.0 (0.5)	1.1 (1.0)	0.8 (0.7)
Area (mm^2)	Mean±Std.	373.8±475.8	238.3±250.5	215.2±223.6	208.7±167.4
	median (IQR)	231.6 (310.6)	156.1 (225.1)	152.1 (153.6)	159.1 (330.1)
Weight (g)	Mean±Std.	4.6±11.8	1.4±2.8	1.7±4.3	0.8±0.8
	median (IQR)	0.6 (1.6)	0.4 (1.3)	0.4 (1.0)	0.3 (1.6)

The location of knapping

The absence of cores and extensively retouched flakes, indeed, the rarity of any retouched flakes, perhaps suggests that either knapping was carried out on this part of the site and cores/retouched flakes have been preferentially removed, or that the flakes were made elsewhere and transported to this locality without the items from which they are struck. One test of these alternative models involves examining the sizes of flakes. During knapping large quantities of small flakes are produced for each larger flake, and these small flakes are left behind in the sediments at or near the spot where knapping took place. A larger number of archaeologists have concluded, on the basis of experiments, that small flakes will be produced at a far higher rate than large flakes during knapping (e.g. Amick and Mauldin 1989; Kluskens 1995; Newcomer 1971; Schick 1986). Consequently, in an intact knapping floor we would expect very small flakes to be more numerous than large ones by an order of magnitude or more. Where an artefact assemblage contains large flakes but does not contain small ones this may indicate that knapping was done elsewhere and flakes carried in to the site. In contrast, an assemblage containing a high proportion of small flakes may indicate that knapping was done at this locality and cores/retouched flakes carried away. These alternatives can be evaluated by inspecting flake size at Lemdubu for all time periods simultaneously to give a long-term image of behaviour at the site. What emerges is an intriguing pattern.

Artefacts in Lemdubu are generally small, and some are very small (see Table 10.24). For example, complete flakes have percussion lengths ranging from 2.7mm to 45.4mm, and widths ranging from 1.9mm to 58.2mm. At first glance these statistics suggest the presence of small flakes, a pattern that might indicate *in situ* knapping. However, a more detailed examination of these size data indicates that very small flakes — less than 5–6mm — are extremely rare. Three-quarters of the flakes are longer and wider than 8.5mm. Only two per cent of flakes have a length less than five millimetres, while five per cent of specimens have a length less than six millimetres. Similarly, only two per cent of complete flakes have widths less than five millimetres; 4.3% of specimens are less than six millimetres in width.

Table 10.24 Liang Lemdubu: descriptive statistics for complete flakes (in mm)

	MINIMUM	MAXIMUM	MEAN± STD.DEV.	MEDIUM (IQR)	LOWER QUARTILE	UPPER QUARTILE	N
Length	2.7	45.4	14.2±7.4	12.3 (8.7)	8.7	17.4	302
Width	1.9	58.2	14.1±7.2	12.6 (8.8)	8.9	17.7	302

Since artefacts greater than two millimetres would have been retained in the sieves the rarity of specimens between two millimetres and 5–6mm is curious. This rarity of flakes less than 5–6mm in length or width is illustrated graphically in Figure 10.9, which shows the frequency of complete flakes in size classes above two millimetres for both length and width. In this figure the grey band represents those size classes that *could* be retrieved using the two millimetres sieve mesh that was employed during excavation of Lemdubu, but which were rarely found. This pattern suggests that knapping was not frequently carried out at this locality. This conclusion is even more strongly evidenced by an examination of the similarity in this pattern for both flake width and length.

A scatter plot of chert flake sizes is illustrated in Figure 10.10, which plots lengths and widths for complete chert flakes from all levels. Although the two millimetres sieve mesh in conjunction with the careful wet sieving and sorting procedures employed, were capable of recovering specimens 2–6mm in both dimensions, no such specimens were recovered. The greyed block in Figure 10.10 illustrates the size of specimens that could have been recovered, but below the dimensions of specimens actually retrieved. Not a single chert flake with both a length and width of 2–5mm was obtained. An identical pattern is found when limestone flakes

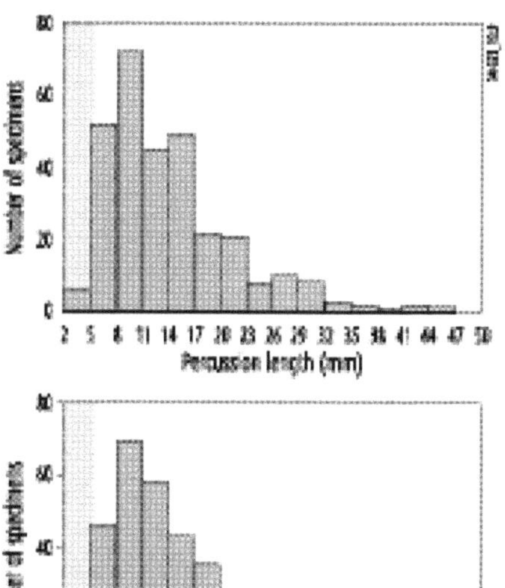

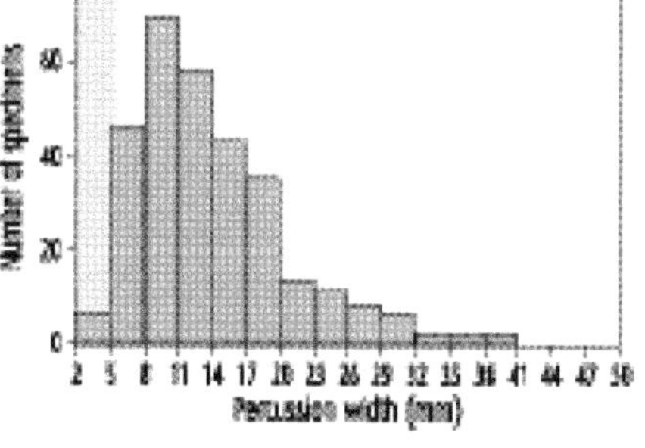

Figure 10.9 Liang Lemdubu: distribution of the frequency of complete flakes in size classes above 2mm. Grey portion represents those size classes that could be retrieved using the sieve mesh but which were rarely recovered

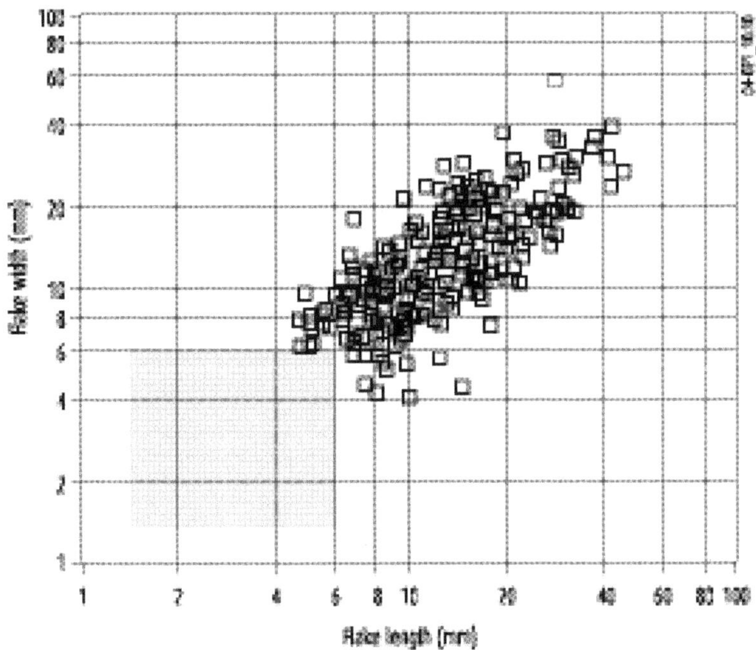

Figure 10.10 Liang Lemdubu: scatter plot of length (log scale) and width (log scale) for complete chert flakes. Grey portion represents those size classes that could be retrieved using the sieve mesh but which were rarely recovered

are plotted in the same manner, revealing that this pattern cannot be explained merely in terms of the mechanics of knapping the chert material.

The absence of flakes 2–5mm in either length or width cannot be explained by invoking erosional processes capable of removing rocks of that size, since the 2mm sieve retained large amounts of gravel of that size. Furthermore, the faunal analysis demonstrates an abundance of light bone fragments only a few millimetres long. It is therefore necessary to hypothesise that small flakes were never deposited in this area. Hence it can be concluded that at least in this portion of Lemdubu, people brought in flakes they manufactured elsewhere, used and lightly retouched them, and discarded those retouched flakes and the small resharpening flakes they removed. Flaking, including extensive retouching of flakes, may have happened elsewhere within the cave but appears always to have been rare in the vicinity of Test Pit C.

Because the data used in Figures 10.9 and 10.10 consist of all chert flakes recovered from the excavation, from all spits, this pattern can be viewed as being a consistent treatment/process throughout the history of occupation. Given the chronological shifts in raw material proportions and the likelihood that at least some of this material is available near the site, this constant tool provisioning strategy may indicate short term visitation by highly mobile foragers. If such a pattern has persisted despite changes in climate, rock procurement and diet it probably indicates that the interior location of this shelter has meant that it remained on the periphery of foraging ranges throughout the late Pleistocene and early Holocene. This model would account for the inferred high mobility, flake-based tool transport strategy, low tool discard rates, and minimal dietary debris. If this model explicates the artefact assemblage, what remains is to describe the patterns that were involved in retouching the flakes brought into the site. This can be accomplished by examining the small flakes removed during retouching as well as the retouched flakes themselves.

Platform characteristics

Platform characteristics are often some of the most revealing characteristics of flakes, reflecting the preparation of platform surfaces and core faces. For instance, Table 10.25 lists observations of platform surfaces on chert flakes from Lemdubu. The pattern is broadly consistent in all levels of the site, with conchoidal platforms dominating at all times. Most of these flakes are consistent with specimens removed from retouched flakes by blows to the ventral surface, although a few may have been removed from cores. The largest flakes in the assemblage, including the retouched ones (see below) have probably been struck from cores, although as argued above, this was probably done at another locality. While the absence of platforms with multiple scars in Zone IV and the presence of cortical platforms in Zone II only may represent different technical patterns of knapping, it is more likely that those variations merely represent differences in sample size. Consequently, these data are interpreted as indicating that platforms with multiple scars or cortex remain at similar relative frequencies throughout the sequence. The source of flakes with cortical platforms could be small cores but there is no need to propose such an explanation since the weight (1.8±2.3 vs 1.2±2.6, t=0.726, d.f.=328, p=0.468), length (15.3±4.8 vs 13.8±7.2, t=0.745, d.f.=326, p=0.457), and platform thickness (2.2±1.4 vs 2.1±1.6, t=0.166, d.f.=259, p=0.868) of flakes with cortical and other platform surfaces are not statistically different. In other words, flakes with cortical platforms have the same dimensions as other flakes — being on average 14–15mm long and about two millimetres thick at the platform — and could have been removed either from large retouched flakes or from small cores. In view of the absence of cores and the presence of large retouched flakes (see below) it is perhaps likely that almost all the flakes in the assemblage were struck from the dorsal face of retouched flakes, but that some were struck from the margin or ventral face of retouched flakes.

Table 10.25 Liang Lemdubu: summary of platform surface characteristics on chert flakes

ZONE	CONCHOIDAL	CORTEX	MULTIPLE SCARS	TOTAL	PERCENTAGE CONCHOIDAL
I	9	0	1	10	90
II	224	13	23	260	87
III	22	0	3	25	88
IV	8	0	0	8	100
TOTAL	263	13	27	303	87

A small but persistent proportion of unretouched flakes have other evidence of preparation. More than one in 10 artefacts display overhang removal. In Zone II the frequency of this feature varies between materials, being higher on chert flakes (13.2%) than on limestone flakes (7.5%). However, this difference is not statistically significant, as documented in Table 10.26, (=1.460, d.f.=1, p=0.227, V=0.069), and hence is not strong evidence that knappers treated these two materials differently. Nevertheless, chronological change in the frequency of overhang removal is best measured using chert flakes alone, as shown in Table 10.27. Data presented in this table indicates an extremely similar frequency of overhang removal in Zones II–IV, with a slight and statistically insignificant decline in Zone I. This reinforces the image of a consistent technological pattern throughout the archaeological sequence.

Table 10.26 Liang Lemdubu: frequency of overhang removal by raw material for Zone II

	NONE	OVERHANG REMOVAL	TOTAL
Chert	283	43	326
Limestone	74	6	80
TOTAL	357	49	406

χ^2 = 1.460, d.f. = 1, p = 0.227, V = 0.069

Table 10.27 Liang Lemdubu: frequency of overhang removal on chert flakes by zone

ZONE	NONE	OVERHANG REMOVAL	TOTAL	%OVERHANG REMOVAL
I	14	1	15	6.7
II	283	43	326	13.2
III	19	3	22	13.6
IV	20	3	23	13.0
Total	336	50	386	13.0

χ^2 = 0.551, d.f. = 3, p = 0.907, V = 0.38

Flake retouching

Only four retouched flakes were recovered from Test Pit C at Lemdubu. Of the four retouched flakes three are made on chert and one on limestone. As calculated in Table 10.28, the relative frequency of retouching is similar on both chert and limestone flakes, and is extremely rare on either material at an assemblage wide level. However, two of the four retouched flakes were obtained from Spit 15, which had only 11 artefacts, and hence the relative frequency of retouching for that spit alone is high. This evidence suggest consistent, low level accumulation of retouched flakes, but at variable rates.

Table 10.28 Liang Lemdubu: the frequency and location of retouched flakes

	UNRETOUCHED	RETOUCHED	% FLAKES RETOUCHED	SPITS CONTAINING RETOUCHED FLAKES
Chert (N=390)	387	3	0.8	7, 10, 15
Limestone (N=124)	123	1	0.8	15
Other (N=4)	4	0	0	
Total (N=518)	514	4	0.8	

Table 10.29 summarizes information about retouched flakes at Lemdubu. The following points are noted about these specimens:

1) the specimen from Spit 7 is technically retouched but has only one small retouch scar;
2) the specimen from Spit 10 had three burin spalls removing the platform — all scars abruptly terminated and originated from the same direction. The longest scar was 16.4mm in length;
3) the chert specimen in Spit 15 possessed a continuous series of retouch scars onto the ventral face at the distal end and right lateral margin. The left margin also had a continuous set of scars, but this time on the dorsal face. Scars were up to 8.1mm in length but most scars were 2–3mm long. The majority of scars were abruptly terminated; and
4) the limestone specimen from Spit 15 has retouch onto the dorsal face at the distal end. All visible retouch scars are less than five millimetres long. However, as this specimen is both heavily heat shattered and weathered the description of the retouch is limited.

Table10.29 Liang Lemdubu: summary of information about retouched flakes

	RAW MATERIAL	FRAGMENT	LENGTH (MM)	WIDTH (MM)	WEIGHT (G)	DESCRIPTION	MAX. SCAR LENGTH (MM)
Spit 7 (#594)	Chert	Complete	7.86	10.32	0.2	Irregular	5.0
Spit 10 (#210)	Chert	Complete	27.98	36.50	9.8	Burinate	16.4
Spit 15 (#95)	Limestone	Distal	22.02	30.01	3.9	Irregular	5.0
Spit 15 (#96)	Chert	Complete	29.86	29.62	18.2	Irregular	8.1
Statistics			21.9±10.0	26.6±11.3	8.1±7.9		

Discussion of technology at Liang Lemdubu

This analysis has demonstrated minimal changes in flake dimensions, shape and reduction characteristics through the Liang Lemdubu archaeological sequence. In conjunction with evidence of size classes these features have been interpreted as a relatively unchanging tool provisioning strategy, that may reflect short-term visitation to this site on the periphery of foraging ranges by highly mobile foragers.

Knapping at Liang Nabulei Lisa

Although the Liang Nabulei Lisa sequence complements the one from Liang Lemdubu by providing greater chronological resolution of Holocene change, the description of technological change during that period is limited by the small number of artefacts that were recovered from the test pit. As listed in Table 10.30, only 42 stone artefacts were identified from the site. Approximately one third of these artefacts were made from chert, while nearly two thirds were made from limestone. As at Lemdubu, most of the artefacts were small flakes.

Table 10.30 Liang Nabulei Lisa: frequency of artefact types by raw material

	CHERT	LIMESTONE	TOTAL
Flake	15 (93.8%)	25 (96.2%)	40 (95.2%)
Core	1 (6.3%)	0	1 (2.4%)
Flaked Piece	0	1 (3.8%)	1 (2.4%)
Total	16 (38.1%)	26 (61.9%)	42

Using the estimated antiquity for Zone I (Spits 1–29) and Zone II (Spits 30–38), as given above, Table 10.31 provides estimates for artefact discard in Nabulei Lisa. These data reveal a marked decline in artefact discard during the Holocene (Zone I) compared to the terminal Pleistocene (Zone II). This trend becomes exaggerated in the latter part of the sequence, with no stone artefacts being recovered from the uppermost six spits. While this final decline may be explicable in terms of radical techno-economic change, including the advent of agriculture and ceramic and metal tools, it may also be understood as part of a longer term trend.

Table 10.31 Liang Nabulei Lisa: analytical divisions of the sequence

ZONE	SPITS	ELAPSED YEARS (CAL BP)	NUMBER OF ARTEFACTS	ESTIMATED DISCARD RATE (#/1000 YEARS)
I	1-29	12,000	20	1.7
II	30-38	4500	22	4.9
All	1-38	16,500	42	2.6

Patterns in changing raw material usage are sufficiently strong in the Nabulei Lisa chronological sequence that they are apparent despite the small assemblage size. Table 10.32 lists the frequency of chert and limestone artefacts by spit. The pattern that exists is as follows: no stone artefacts at all were recovered from the upper six spits; limestone is the main material on which artefacts are made in Spits 7–29; and chert is the dominant artefactual material in Spit 30 and below (see Table 10.33). The shift in raw material emphasis at about Spit 30 in the deposit is dramatic, with the pattern of raw material abundance between Spits 7–29 and 30–38 being significantly different (= 15.155, d.f. = 1, $p < 0.001$). Hence, it is argued that the change from a chert dominated assemblage to a limestone dominated one in Spits 29–30 is extremely unlikely to be randomly produced, and is best explained as an alteration in the procurement of material about 12,000 years ago. As discussed below, this trend is broadly similar with that inferred from Lemdubu.

Another point of similarity with the Lemdubu assemblage is the rate of weathering of chert artefacts. Applying the same weathering classification as was employed earlier to the 14 chert artefacts retrieved from Nabulei Lisa below Spit 30 produced the following result: two (14.3%) were classified as fresh; nine (64.3%) as lightly patinated; and three (21.4%) as patinated. No heavily weathered artefacts were recovered. These weathering patterns at Nabulei Lisa are consistent with the artefact assemblage being largely *in situ*, with specimens in Spits 30–38 having levels of weathering congruent with a Pleistocene age. A similar pattern is found in Spits 6–9 at Lemdubu,

Table 10.32 Liang Nabulei Lisa: changes in raw material through the sequence

SPIT	CHERT	LIMESTONE	TOTAL	% CHERT
1	0	0	0	-
2	0	0	0	-
3	0	0	0	-
4	0	0	0	-
5	0	0	0	-
6	0	0	0	-
7	1	1	2	50
8	0	1	1	0
9	0	1	1	0
10	0	2	2	0
11	0	0	0	-
12	0	1	1	0
13	0	0	0	-
14	0	1	1	0
15	0	0	0	-
16	0	1	1	0
17	0	0	0	-
18	0	0	0	-
19	0	0	0	-
20	0	0	0	-
21	0	1	1	0
22	0	2	2	0
23	0	1	1	0
24	0	1	1	0
25	0	2	2	0
26	0	2	2	0
27	0	0	0	-
28	0	1	1	0
29	0	1	1	0
30	1	1	2	50
31	3	1	4	75
32	3	1	4	75
33	2	0	2	100
34	3	3	6	50
35	2	0	2	100
36	0	0	0	-
37	1	0	1	100
38	0	1	1	0
Total	16	26	42	75.0
(Percentage)	(38.1%)	(61.9%)		

Table 10.33 Liang Nabulei Lisa: raw material frequencies by groups of spits

SPITS	CHERT	LIMESTONE	TOTAL	% CHERT
1-6	0	0	0	-
7-29	1	19	20	5.0
>29	15	7	22	68.2
Total	16	26	42	38.1

levels that are also inferred to date to the terminal Pleistocene and early Holocene. This broad similarity in weathering within the two chert assemblages, despite the micro-environmental differences at the two sites, supports the use of these weathering classes as a rough indication of assemblage antiquity.

Artefact sizes are typically small at Nabulei Lisa and limestone flakes are often slightly larger than chert ones (Table 10.34). Although the samples are small, significance tests reveal that the differences are unlikely to be randomly produced. Minor technological differences between the knapping of the two materials might be responsible for the different sizes and shapes of flakes on each. For instance, the transportation and retouching of slightly smaller chert flakes would perhaps be sufficient to explain the size contrasts between artefacts made from the two materials. Such size differences may reflect a contrast between local and non-local sources, although in the absence of further geological information that possibility is speculative.

Table 10.34 Liang Nabulei Lisa: descriptive statistics for the size and shape of complete flakes by raw material

VARIABLES	CHERT	LIMESTONE	DIFFERENCE BETWEEN CHERT AND LIMESTONE	IS THIS DIFFERENCE DUE TO CHANCE?
Length	16.7±6.8 (N= 12)	22.7±7.9 (N= 19)	t = -2.19 p = 0.036	Fairly unlikely
Width	17.1±5.3 (N= 12)	27.4±14.5 (N= 19)	t = -2.83 p = 0.009	Very unlikely
Thickness	3.1±1.6 (N= 12)	5.4±2.5 (N= 19)	t = -2.85 p = 0.008	Very unlikely
Platform width	9.6±4.2 (N = 12)	16.1±10.0 (N= 19)	t = -2.50 p = 0.019	Very unlikely
Platform thickness	2.2±1.3 (N= 12)	3.3±3.3 (N= 19)	t = -1.16 p = 0.257	Fairly likely
Elongation	0.9±0.3 (N= 12)	0.9±0.3 (N= 19)	t = 0.591 p = 0.559	Very likely
Area (mm^2)	308.9±180.3 (N= 12)	695.9±545.8 (N= 19)	t = -2.85 p = 0.009	Very unlikely
Weight (g)	1.5±1.2 (N= 12)	6.9±8.3 (N= 19)	t = -2.84 p = 0.010	Very unlikely

Artefacts on Aru

It must be acknowledged that archaeological exploration of the Aru Islands is in its pioneering stage and consequently our ability to comprehend the patterns observed at Liang Lemdubu and Liang Nabulei Lisa is limited by two factors. First is the excavation of only one small area in each site. This recovery strategy is justified in terms of the exploratory nature of the project, but has the consequence of yielding very small artefact sample sizes and preventing any understanding of spatial patterns of artefact manufacture and discard within the shelters. A second factor inhibiting more detailed models is the lack of contextual environmental data with which economic and technological statements could be framed. The most obvious need is for information about the abundance, size, shape and distance of the sources of rock that were procured and transported to each site. Without these data our ability to identify and explain spatial and chronological variations in human behaviour remains imperfect.

However, in view of the exploratory nature of investigations on Aru, the archaeological data is surprisingly highly patterned. Despite their different landscape positions the two archaeological sites discussed in this paper display distinctly similar assemblages of stone artefacts, and by inference similar knapping technologies, throughout the Stone Age occupation of the region. These similarities offer us baseline descriptions of the uniformity and change in stone assemblages on Aru.

The chronological trends identified at Lemdubu and Nabulei Lisa are summarized in Table 10.35. At both sites there was a noticeable reduction in the rate of artefact discard during the Holocene, a pattern hypothesized to reflect the reduction of open and patchy vegetation systems, and a shift in the economic focus of foraging groups. At Lemdubu, which has the benefit of a longer archaeological sequence, the evidence points to increasing occupation and tool using activity in the terminal Pleistocene. At both sites the reduction in artefact discard is broadly coincident with a switch from chert dominated assemblages to limestone dominated ones, revealing that changes in the intensity of knapping and tool use were linked to alterations in the procurement and transportation of stone materials, and by implication forager landuse and/or mobility. Furthermore, the similarities in the archaeological assemblages indicate that a relatively uniform technological strategy may have been in place at both sites and throughout much of the late Pleistocene and early Holocene. As shown in Table 10.36 the size of chert flakes is extremely similar between the two sites, while limestone flakes are larger at Nabulei Lisa than at Lemdubu. This pattern may reflect difference in the form, availability, or cost of raw materials at each site, but what is remarkable is the strong concurrence of archaeological assemblages and chronological trends at both sites.

Table 10.35 Liang Lemdubu and Liang Nabulei Lisa: comparison of chert and limestone complete flakes (mean±std.)

	RELATIVE DISCARD RATES		DOMINANT RAW MATERIAL	
	LEMDUBU	NABULEI LISA	LEMDUBU	NABULEI LISA
Zone I	Low (3-4/1kyr)	Low (<2/1kyr)	Limestone	Limestone
Zone II	High (80/1kyr)	Medium (5/1kyr)	Chert	Chert
Zone III	Medium (10+/1kyr)	-	Varied	-
Zone IV	Low (2-3/1kyr)	-	Chert	-

Table 10.36 Liang Lemdubu and Liang Nabulei Lisa: comparison of chert and limestone complete flakes (mean±std.)

	CHERT		LIMESTONE	
	LEMDUBU ZONE I (N = 11)	NABULEI LISA (N = 12)	LEMDUBU ZONE I (N = 14)	NABULEI LISA (N = 19)
Length	15.6±7.4	16.7±6.8	14.8±8.6	22.7±7.9
Width	19.0±14.3	17.1±5.3	15.7±8.9	27.4±14.5
Area (mm^2)	373.8±475.8	308.9±180.3	279.7±333.2	695.9±545.8

The broad correspondence in the raw material usage, pattern of knapping and tool production, and changes in artefact density and raw material procurement between the two sites described here, suggests that many of the patterns identified may be regional in scale rather than site-specific. This is intriguing because in many areas of both mainland and Island Southeast Asia depictions of archaeological trends have often focused on changes in technology and assemblage composition, with assertions that change was substantial. Such a pattern is not in evidence in the sites on the Aru Islands. For instance, over the last 30,000 years on Aru there is no sign of the Hoabhinian pattern involving large flaked cobbles, and no evidence for the advent of different technologies emphasizing blade production. Instead, the archaeological observations document transportation and knapping of small retouched flakes and cores, even when changes to foraging range stimulate an alteration in raw material procurement patterns. In some ways this technology is similar to that reported from comparable limestone landscapes in Australia (see Hiscock 1988), but broad similarity in assemblages across the lowlands of Northern Sahul cannot be interpreted as a reflection of cultural affinity, and is better viewed as representing broadly similar technological and foraging strategies responding to similar stone resources. The data offered in this chapter offers a baseline description of the nature of, and chronological changes in stone artefacts on Aru, together with intriguing hints of technological adjustments in an ecologically dynamic landscape. The detailed understanding of those adjustments awaits future researchers.

Acknowledgements

To Erica Lindgren, who assisted with much of the analysis and data entry, many thanks. Thanks also to Sue O'Connor and Ken Aplin for helpful discussions on the material presented here. The analysis of both assemblages was carried out at the School of Archaeology and Anthropology, The Australian National University, Canberra.

References

Amick, D. and R. Mauldin. 1989. *Experiments in Lithic Technology*. Oxford: British Archaeological Reports. *BAR International Series* S528.

Andrefsky, W. 1998. *Lithics: Macroscopic Approaches To Analysis*. Cambridge: Cambridge University Press.

Bailey, G.N. 1983. Concepts of time in Quaternary prehistory. *Annual Review of Anthropology* 12:165–92.

Barnes, A.S. 1939. The difference between natural and human flaking on prehistoric flint implements. *American Anthropologist* 41:99–112.

Behrensmeyer, A.K. 1982. Time resolution in fluvial vertebrate assemblages. *Paleobiology* 8:211–27.

Behrensmeyer, A.K. 1984. Time sampling intervals in the vertebrate fossil record. In G.E.G. Westermann (ed.), *Jurassic-Cretaceous Biochronology and Paleogeography of North America: The Proceedings of a Symposium Held in Honour of Ralph W. Imlay and George W. Jeletzky at the 3rd North American Paleontological Convention in Montreal, Quebec, August 6th, 1982*, pp. 41–5. St. John's, Nfld.: Geological Association of Canada, Dept. of Geology, Memorial University of Newfoundland. *Geological Association of Canada Special Paper* 27.

Behrensmeyer, A.K. 1991. Terrestrial vertebrate accumulation. In P.A. Allison and D.E.G. Briggs (eds), *Taphonomy: Releasing the Data Locked in the Fossil Record*, pp. 291–335. New York: Plenum Press. *Topics in GeoBiology* 9.

Behrensmeyer, A.K. and D. Schindel. 1983. Resolving time in paleobiology. *Paleobiology* 9:1-8.

Bryan, A.L. and D. Schnurrenberger. 1985. A contribution to the study of the naturefact/artifact controversy. In M.G. Plew, J.C. Woods, and M.G. Pavesic (eds), *Stone Tool Analysis: Essays in Honor of Don E. Crabtree*, pp. 133–59. Albuquerque: University of New Mexico Press.

Flessa, K.W., A.H. Cutler, and K.H. Meldahl. 1993. Time and taphonomy: quantitative estimates of time-averaging and stratigraphic disorder in a shallow marine habitat. *Paleobiology* 19(2):266–86.

Fursich, F.T. and M. Aberhan. 1990. Significance of time-averaging for paleocommunity analysis. *Lethaia* 23:143–52.

Hayden, B. 1979. *Palaeolithic Reflections: Lithic Technology and Ethnographic Excavation Among Australian Aborigines*. Canberra: Australian Institute of Aboriginal Studies. *AIAS New Series* 5.

Hiscock, P. 1985. The need for a taphonomic perspective in stone artefact analysis. *Queensland Archaeological Research* 2:82–95.

Hiscock, P. 1986a. Technological change in the Hunter River Valley and the interpretation of Late Holocene change in Australia. *Archaeology in Oceania* 21(1):40–50.

Hiscock, P. 1988. Prehistoric Settlement Patterns and Artefact Manufacture at Lawn Hill, Northwest Queensland. Unpublished PhD thesis, University of Queensland, Brisbane.

Hiscock, P. 1993. Bondaian technology in the Hunter Valley, New South Wales. *Archaeology in Oceania* 28(2):64–75.

Hiscock, P. 2001. Sizing up prehistory: sample size and composition of artefact assemblages. *Australian Aboriginal Studies* 1:48–62.

Hiscock, P. 2002. Quantifying the size of artefact assemblages. *Journal of Archaeological Science* 29:251–8.

Hiscock, P. in press. Looking the other way: a materialist/technological approach to classifying tools and implements, cores and retouched flakes. In S. McPherron and J. Lindley (eds), *Tools or Cores? The Identification and Study of Alternative Core Technology in Lithic Assemblages*. Pennsylvania: University of Pennsylvania Museum.

Kluskens, S. L. 1995. Archaeological taphonomy of Combe-Capelle Bas from artefact orientation and density analysis. In H.L. Dibble and M. Lenoir (eds), *The Middle Paleolithic Site of Combe-Capelle Bas (France)*, pp.199–243. Philadelphia: University Museum Press.

Newcomer, M. 1971. Some quantitative experiments in handaxe manufacture. *World Archaeology* 3:85–94.

Potts, R.B. 1986. Temporal span of bone accumulations at Olduvai Gorge and implications for early Hominid foraging behavior. *Paleobiology* 12:25–31.

Schick, K. 1986. *Stone Age Sites in the Making: Experiments in the Formation and Transformation of Archaeological Occurrences*. Oxford: British Archaeological Reports. *BAR International Series* 319.

11

Bone Artefacts from Liang Lemdubu and Liang Nabulei Lisa, Aru Islands

Juliette Pasveer

Department of Archaeology and Natural History, Research School of Pacific and Asian Studies, The Australian National University, Canberra, ACT, Australia

Introduction

Bone artefacts in the form of small bipoints, slender unipointed specimens and spatulae, have been found in many sites throughout Australasia and Oceania. They were more common during the Holocene, but certainly also occurred during Late Pleistocene times. Due to their perishable nature and often limited modification, many may have been lost or gone unrecognised in existing assemblages. In some instances, the manufacture and use of bone artefacts through time may have been as common as that of stone tools (Webb and Allen 1990).

Systematic studies on bone points from this region have been carried out only occasionally (e.g. Lampert 1966, 1971; Olsen and Glover 2004; Pasveer 2004; Pasveer and Bellwood 2004; Pickering 1979; Webb 1987). Most individual assemblages are too small to make such analyses worthwhile. However, the few systematic studies have shown the potential of these artefacts to provide insight into their specific function and the mode of occupation of the particular site or region.

The cave sites Liang Lemdubu and Liang Nabulei Lisa produced small and highly variable bone artefact assemblages which are discussed here. The compositional similarities to assemblages from neighbouring areas offer possibilities for wider regional comparisons.

The Context

The geographical context of the two sites has been described by O'Connor et al. (Chapters 6 and 8, this volume). Lemdubu was inhabited during the period of the Last Glacial Maximum, as well as through the subsequent period of sea level transgression that ultimately formed the islands as they were cut off from New Guinea and Australia. Analysis of the faunal remains from both sites has

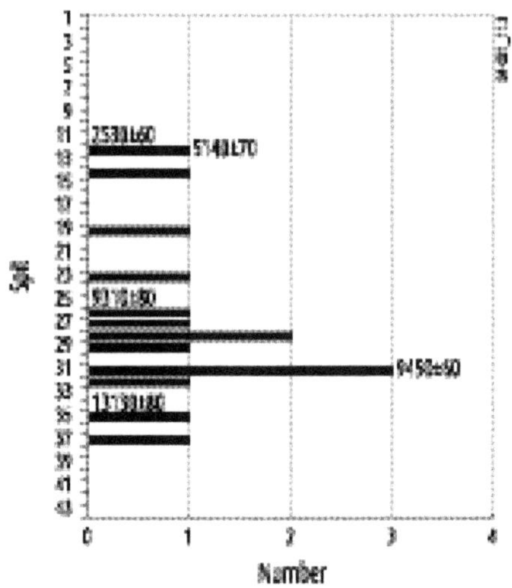

Figure 11.1 Liang Nabulei Lisa: distribution of bone artefacts through the deposit

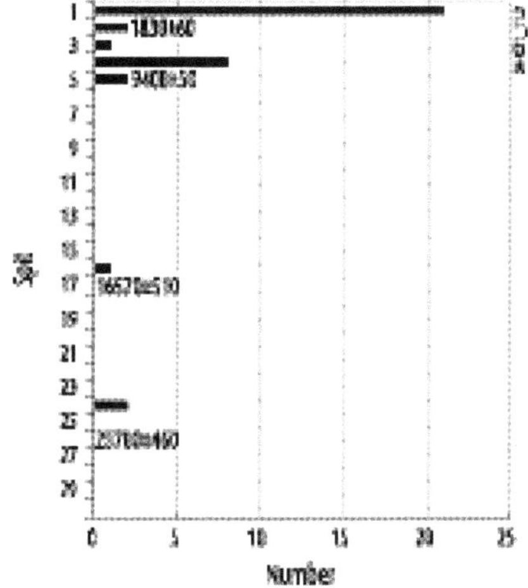

Figure 11.2 Liang Lemdubu: distribution of bone artefacts through the deposit

provided a detailed picture of environmental changes and the pattern of exploitation of animal resources through time (see Chapters 3, 7 and 9, this volume).

In Nabulei Lisa (see Chapter 7, this volume), bone artefacts were found in small numbers but consistently between Spit 12 and Spit 37. There are a total of 15 specimens, with a peak occurrence in Spit 28 and Spit 31 (see Fig. 11.1). The first 10 spits in this cave probably represent the last 1000 years. Spits 11–23 produced dates between ca. 7000 and 2500 BP (uncalibrated), and the remainder of the deposit is dated between 13,000 and 9000 BP. Eleven out of the 15 artefacts in Nabulei Lisa are thus dated roughly between 13,000 and 9000 BP.

In total, 37 bone implements were recovered from Lemdubu. The specimens were found predominantly in the top five spits (see Fig. 11.2). The majority (N=21) come from Spit 1, i.e. the first five centimetres. The numbers fall progressively in lower levels, with a slight return in Spit 4. Interestingly, virtually no modified bone was found below Spit 5, except for one specimen in Spit 16 and two artefacts in Spit 24.

As described by O'Connor et al. (Chapter 9, this volume), the first three spits of Lemdubu are dated roughly to the last 2000 years (uncalibrated). Spits 5–10 produced a number of dates between ca. 12,000 and 8000 BP. However, faunal analysis shows that Spit 5 shares broad similarities to the upper four spits, including the presence of pig bone, suggesting that some mixing of younger and older material has probably occurred in this spit. Spits 17–26 date roughly around 17,000 BP, with a flowstone in Spit 26 of ca. 27,000–26,000 years old; the artefact from Spit 16 is presumably younger than 17,000 BP. The bone artefacts from Spit 24 may be assumed to date to around 18,000–17,000 BP.

The three specimens found in these deeper levels in Lemdubu seem somewhat anomalous. However, they are probably not very much older than some of the lowermost examples from Nabulei Lisa. Moreover, while the majority of bone implements reported from the wider Australasian and New Guinean region are of latest Pleistocene and Holocene age, small numbers of bone points have been found in much older contexts e.g. Devil's Lair in Western Australia (Dortch 1984:59–60), Bone Cave in south Tasmania (Webb and Allen 1990:75), and Niah Cave in Sarawak (Majid 1982). In this wider context, the presence of bone artefacts in these spits is not so extraordinary. Indeed, what is more surprising is that they are absent from the remainder of the sequence, prior to the latest Holocene.

Methods

In several recent analyses of bone artefacts from sites in northern Maluku (Pasveer and Bellwood 2004) and the Bird's Head of Papua (Pasveer 2004), I have employed a uniform approach to describe variation in raw material, manufacture and evidence for use of these often neglected classes of artefacts. The methods are similar to those employed by many lithic analysts, and emphasize aspects of raw material selection, methods of modification, basic metric attributes, the morphology of functional edges or points and patterns of use-wear and damage. To increase comparability, the same methods were followed for the two Aru collections, although not all aspects could be analysed due to the high degree of variability of these assemblages.

Although I have tried to avoid a strictly typological approach in favour of one that emphasizes aspects of technology and function, I have nonetheless found it useful to distinguish several 'classes' of bone artefacts within the assemblages, based on their basic morphology.

Descriptive terminology

In this study, a bone artefact is defined as a piece of bone showing evidence of human modification other than simple breakage. The following attributes were recorded for each artefact:

Shape

Three broad categories were distinguished on the basis of location and type of modification together with evidence of use. Elongate artefacts with an attenuate point at one end only are classed as 'attenuate unipoints'. 'Bipoints' are attenuate and taper to points at both ends. A third, clearly recognisable class is 'spatulae', distinguished by their broad, rounded tip. Spatulae are generally modified at one end only and thus might also be viewed as a subclass of unipoints.

A fourth, loosely defined 'class' consists of what might be termed 'expedient' tools (after Pickering 1979); these show evidence of use but only minimal or no modification prior to use. Expedient tools can include unipointed or bipointed examples, or fragments thereof. Specimens that might be regarded as 'unfinished', recognisable from their limited modification and no evidence of use, are absent from the Aru assemblages.

Breakage

Fragments of bone artefacts were classified as broken bipoints if they showed obvious signs of tapering at both ends. However, short fragments with no sign of distal tapering at the other end (usually short isolated tips) might be either fragments of attenuate unipoints or bipoints broken at or before their midpoint. These fragments were scored as 'broken uni- or bipoints'. Fragments that are clearly modified and/or used but have lost both ends, and show no tapering towards the broken ends are classified as midsections (despite the fact that one end could potentially be the original butt). All breaks were recorded as either pre- or post-excavation in origin, based on the nature of the fracture surface (stained or encrusted versus fresh).

Raw material

Two types of bone were used for artefact manufacture — 'cortical': splinters of cortical bone derived from larger long bones of medium-sized to large mammals; or 'shaft': sections of small, narrow shaft bones that retain an intact (or partially intact) medullary canal (e.g. fibula, radius, wing elements of bats, typically bones from smaller mammals).

Burning state of the raw material

Many of the artefacts are manufactured from bone that has been subjected to some degree of heating or burning. Four states are recognized, drawing on previous classifications by Ubelaker (1978), Shipman et al. (1984), and Pearce and Luff (1994):

1) Unburnt (bone is pale, yellow to light brown and porous);
2) Lightly burnt (bone is light brown to dark brown and more dense in texture; this is usually the result of cooking of the bone inside a fleshed carcass rather than direct contact with flames);
3) Burnt (bone is very dark brown or dark grey to black and very dense, usually resulting from direct contact with flame); and
4) Calcined (bone is grey to white, very dense and sometimes crazed or warped; all organic material has been lost, resulting in shrinkage and increased brittleness).

Method of manufacture

Three main techniques can be distinguished. Some artefacts show evidence of more than one method:

1) Cutting (presumably with a stone flake; resulting in wide, flat surfaces with few striations);
2) Shaving (presumably with a stone flake or retouched flake; resulting in semi-regular, linear striations, generally oriented in one direction but with complex patterns of intersection and overlay);
3) Grinding (presumably on a fine-grained sedimentary or metamorphic rock; resulting in flat facets with fine, parallel and generally non-intersecting striations).

Use polish

Many specimens bear localised polish at one or both of their pointed ends. In other cases the polish is more generalized and occurs as a light gloss over much of the bone surface. Four 'degrees' of polish were recorded: no polish, light polish, medium polish, and high polish. The degree of polish present was recorded separately for each end of a bipoint.

Tip damage

This refers to localised damage to the tip of an artefact, and is distinguished from an actual break. At least some of the tip damage probably results from use of the artefacts, although some damage might also have occurred following discard. Five categories of damage were recorded for each tip:

1) Intact (i.e. no damage);
2) Snap fracture (usually transverse);
3) Step fracture (directed along the length of the artefact and often hinged at its termination);
4) Crushing; and
5) 'Complex' (usually ragged, possibly multiple step fractures or a combination of step and snap fractures).

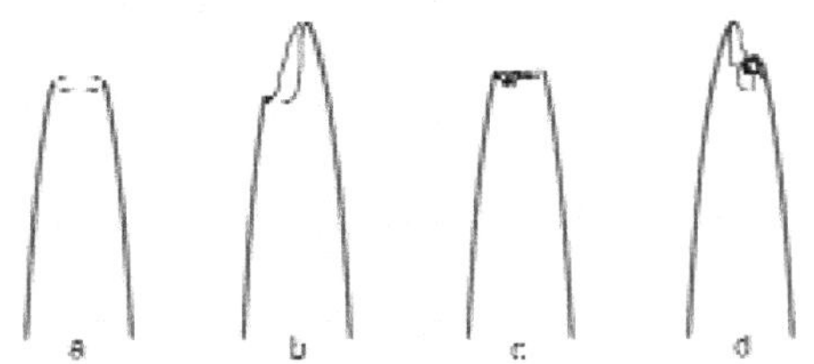

Figure 11.3 Types of damage found at the tip of bone artefacts: a) snap-fracture b) step-fracture c) crushing and d) multiple types of damage ('complex')

Each category is exemplified in Figure 11.3. Similar kinds of damage have been described on the tips of bone and antler artefacts by other researchers (e.g. Arndt and Newcomer 1986; Campana 1989; Johnson 1985; Olsen 1984).

Bone collections inevitably suffer some damage during excavation and subsequent storage. This is easily recognized by the lighter colour of the fractured surface and by the lack of soil or calcium carbonate attached to this surface. However, damage that occurs during manufacture or use cannot be distinguished from post-depositional damage. Breakage of bone artefacts after discard or loss, for example by trampling by the occupants of the cave or by other taphonomic processes, can strongly bias the breakage frequency caused by manufacturing or actual use. This problem will be discussed where necessary in this paper.

Additional modification

A small number of specimens from the northern Maluku and Bird's Head sites were clearly burnt after manufacture; this has not been observed on the Aru artefacts.

Although the bone artefacts studied here were collected by the editors of this volume and by their excavation team, as well as by the author during subsequent sorting of the faunal assemblages, it is possible that fragments such as isolated tips may have been missed. However, it is believed that the majority of the bone artefacts were recovered.

Measurements

The Aru bone artefacts have been measured following the system used for the northern Maluku and Bird's Head specimens. However, due to the highly variable nature of the assemblages, there is little value in a metrical or statistical analysis. The raw data of the artefacts are presented in Tables 11.8 and 11.9.

The following measurements (see Fig. 11.4) were taken on all bone artefacts with a vernier calliper, to a precision of 0.1mm:

1) Maximum length: no attempt was made to correct for minor damage that has affected the tip of many otherwise complete specimens. This damage has removed no more than an estimated 1–2mm of the artefact.
2) Width and thickness: taken perpendicular to each other and at the same position on the artefact. The width and the thickness of each artefact were defined in relation to the greatest width of the tip. For attenuate unipoints the width and thickness were measured at the base of the point/modified area. However, in some heavily modified specimens the boundary between the point and the shaft of the artefact is unclear; in such cases the measurements were taken at the widest or thickest point of the artefact. For most specimens, the width exceeded the thickness, but the opposite was true for some nearly circular shaft bones. For bipoints the width and thickness were measured at the widest point of the artefact.
3) Point length: with the 'point' defined as the zone of modification or, in specimens showing general modification, as the distance from the tip to the widest point on the artefact. For intact bipoints, point length was measured for the primary end (the end with the most polish and/or damage), with the length of the secondary end being obtained by subtraction from the maximum length. If the point had broken through the zone of modification, the point length would be the same as the maximum length of the fragment, although the original point length of the artefact is likely to have been longer.

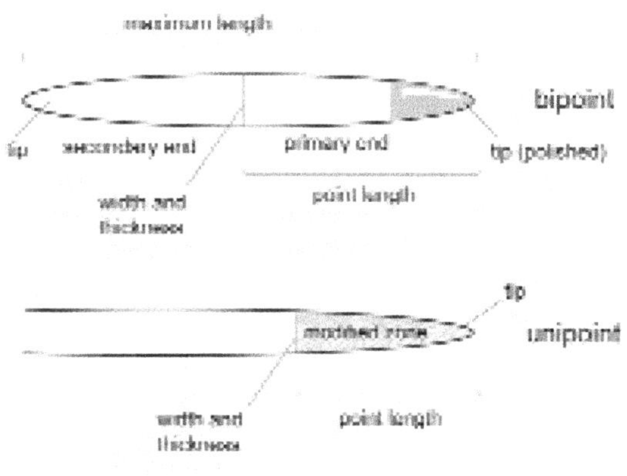

Figure 11.4 Liang Lemdubu and Liang Nabulei Lisa: descriptive terminology and measurements of bone artefacts

Description of the Artefacts

A total of 52 bone artefacts were found in the two cave sites on Aru: 37 in Liang Lemdubu and 15 in Liang Nabulei Lisa (see Figs 11.5 and 11.6 for examples from each assemblage). Both sites produced highly variable assemblages, containing various unipointed artefacts and spatulae, or fragments thereof. Only one bipointed artefact was found, from Nabulei Lisa.

Liang Lemdubu

Liang Lemdubu did not provide any complete bipointed specimens, but there are 21 short unipointed fragments that are parts of broken uni- or bipoints. Only two artefacts could be classified as attenuate unipoints with some confidence considering their length, narrow width and lack of tapering towards the butt. Three specimens have a broad, rounded tip and are classified as spatulae. Five specimens that have lost one or both ends, but which show clear modification marks, form the midsection of attenuate unipoints, bipoints or spatulae. The assemblage also includes six fragments (again midsections) of bone from Spit 1 with varying degrees of polish suggestive of use. Because these specimens show no clear indications of modification, they are classified as parts of potential 'expedient tools'. However, the incomplete state of these artefacts is a cause for doubt as to their true nature.

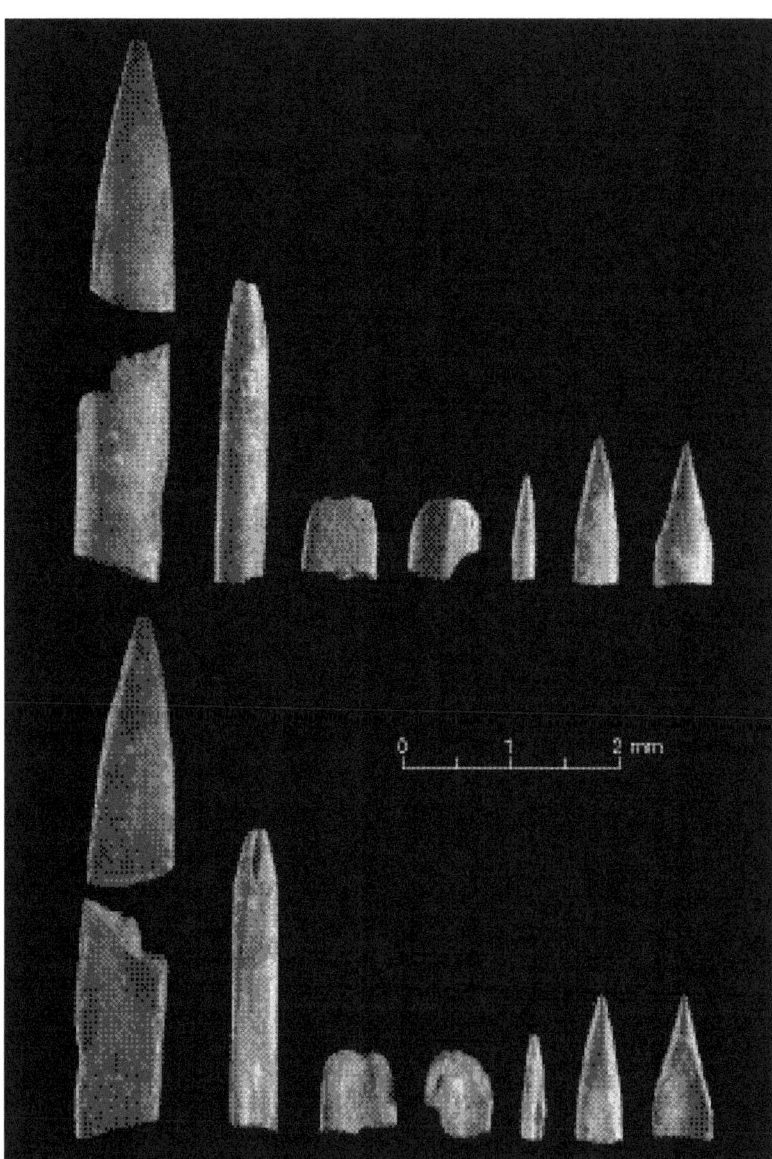

Figure 11.5 Liang Lemdubu: examples of bone artefacts. From left to right: specimen numbers LL4h (broken uni- or bipoint); LC2a (unipoint); LC1c (spatula fragment); LC1d (spatula fragment); LC1i (broken uni- or bipoint); LC1b (broken uni- or bipoint); LC5b (broken uni- or bipoint)

Almost three-quarters (70%) of the artefacts were made from fragments of small shaft bones (Table 11.1). Several of these are recognisable as the central and distal sections of wallaby fibulae, including both *Thylogale* sp. and *Macropus agilis* (Agile Wallaby). The remaining artefacts, including broken uni- or bipoints and one spatulate tool, were made of fragments of cortical bone of various unidentified mammals.

A large proportion (54%) of the raw material that was used for artefact manufacture consisted of lightly burnt bone (Table 11.2); 27% of the artefacts were made of unburnt bone, and eight per cent of burnt bone. Four specimens are calcined, but show no sign of warping or other distortion. Even though it cannot be excluded that they were made originally from calcined bone, it seems more likely that they have become calcined after discard. In general, intense heating or burning of bone has no advantages for bone modification, as the material becomes increasingly brittle (Campana 1989). None of the artefacts showed secondary burn marks, such as were observed on some bone artefacts from Kria Cave on the Bird's Head Peninsula of Papua (Pasveer 2004:152, 167).

Most of the artefacts showed the finely striated, regular facets produced by grinding (Table 11.3). In some cases they were cut or shaved before being ground into their present shape. Although cut and shaving marks are in some cases somewhat obscured by the subsequent grinding, the earlier phase of modification is usually recognisable from the deeper, irregular striations produced by a stone tool, or by a straight cutting plane. However, it cannot be ruled out that cutting planes, shaving marks, or even grinding facets may have been obliterated by subsequent modification or use.

Shaft artefacts: attenuate unipoints

One of the two artefacts that were classified as a potential attenuate unipoints shows a slight gloss over its entire surface, but it is otherwise unpolished. The tip was damaged during or after excavation. The butt was evidently snapped off at some stage in antiquity. The length of the artefact is 27.8mm but it may have once been longer. The point length is 6.3mm; its width is five millimetres and its thickness is 3.2mm (see Table 11.8). It was made of the central part of a *Thylogale* fibula; the medullary canal is visible at one side of the tip (specimen LC2a, Fig. 11.5).

The other attenuate unipoint is unpolished and has an undamaged tip. It is 28.7mm long, 4.2mm wide, and 2.7mm thick, with a point length of 14.2mm. It was ground into its present shape and was also made from the central part of a *Thylogale* fibula.

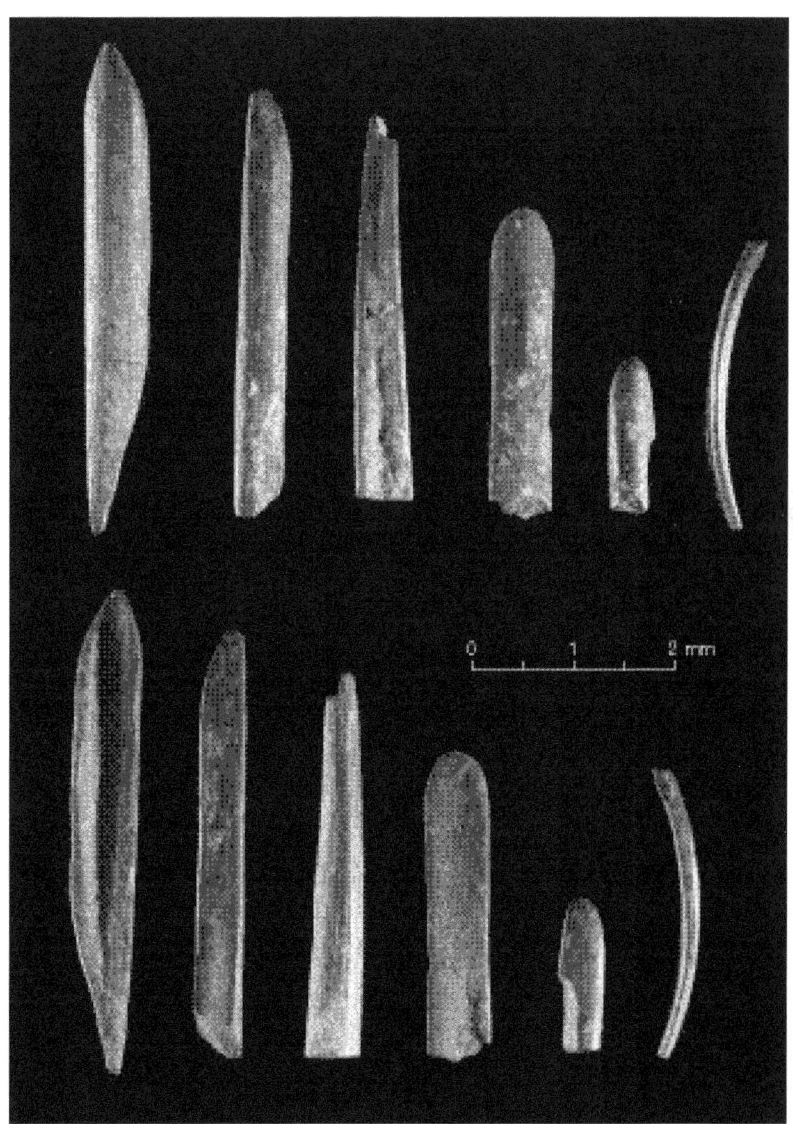

Figure 11.6 Liang Nabulei Lisa: examples of bone artefacts. From left to right: specimen numbers NL/I/29a (bipoint); NL/I/37a (unipoint); NL/I/27a (unipoint); NL/I/23a (spatula); NL/I/14a (spatula fragment); NL/I/28a (expedient tool)

Table 11.1 Liang Lemdubu and Liang Nabulei Lisa: type of raw material used for the various bone artefacts

	LEMDUBU			NABULEI LISA		
	SHAFT	CORTICAL	TOTAL	SHAFT	CORTICAL	TOTAL
Attenuate unipoints	2	-	2	2	-	2
Bipoints	-	-	-	1	-	1
Broken uni- or bipoints	11	10	21	5	3	8
Spatulae	2	1	3	2	-	2
Midsections	5	-	5	1	-	1
Expedient tools?	6	-	6	1	-	1
Total	26	11	37	12	3	15

Table 11.2 Liang Lemdubu and Liang Nabulei Lisa: degree of burning of raw material used for bone artefact manufacture (c=cortical; s=shaft)

	LEMDUBU										NABULEI LISA							
	UNBURNT		LIGHTLY BURNT		BURNT		CALCINED		TOTAL		UNBURNT		LIGHTLY BURNT		BURNT		TOTAL	
	c	s	c	s	c	s	c	s	c	s	c	s	c	s	c	s	c	s
Attenuate unipoints	1	1	-	1	-	-	-	-	-	2	-	1	-	1	-	-	-	2
Bipoints	-	-	-	-	-	-	-	-	-	-	-	1	-	-	-	-	-	1
Broken uni- or bipoints	3	5	5	3	1	-	1	3	10	11	2	-	-	4	1	1	3	5
Spatulae	1	-	-	2	-	-	-	-	1	2	-	-	-	2	-	-	-	2
Midsections	-	-	-	4	-	1	-	-	-	5	-	-	-	-	-	1	-	1
Expedient tools?	-	-	-	5	-	1	-	-	-	6	-	1	-	-	-	-	-	1
Total	4	6	5	15	1	2	1	3	11	26	2	3	-	7	1	2	3	12

Table 11.3 Liang Lemdubu and Liang Nabulei Lisa: manufacturing techniques used in bone artefact production (c=cortical; s=shaft)

	LEMDUBU								NABULEI LISA											
	GROUND		SHAVED THEN GROUND		CUT THEN GROUND		TOTAL		GROUND		SHAVED, THEN GROUND		CUT, THEN GROUND		SHAVED		UNKNOWN*		TOTAL	
	c	s	c	s	c	s	c	s	c	s	c	s	c	s	c	s	c	s	c	s
Attenuate unipoints	-	1	-	1	-	-	-	2	-	1	-	1	-	-	-	-	-	-	-	2
Bipoints	-	-	-	-	-	-	-	-	-	-	-	1	-	-	-	-	-	-	-	1
Broken uni- or bipoints	6	8	2	2	-	1	8	11	-	1	1	3	-	1	1	-	1	-	3	5
Spatulae	1	2	-	-	-	-	1	2	-	2	-	-	-	-	-	-	-	-	-	2
Midsections	-	3	-	2	-	-	-	5	-	-	-	1	-	-	-	-	-	-	-	1
Total	7	14	2	5	-	1	9	20	-	4	1	6	-	1	1	-	1	-	3	11

*On one very small broken uni- or bipoint from Nabulei Lisa no modification marks were visible

NB: six artefacts in Liang Lemdubu, and one artefact in Liang Nabulei Lisa are classified as expedient tools, i.e. used but unmodified. Two artefacts from Liang Lemdubu are encrusted and modification marks are unclear

Shaft artefacts: broken uni- or bipoints

Eleven artefacts made of shaft bone were classified as either broken attenuate unipoints or broken bipoints. An intact tip is present at one end, but the lack of tapering at the broken end inhibits any further identification.

Seven out of 11 specimens show a light to high polish (Table 11.4), either localised at the tip or extending over the entire surface. Four artefacts show no polish at all; some merely have an overall light gloss. The majority of tips are undamaged (Table 11.5); two are somewhat crushed or blunted in antiquity and one was slightly damaged after excavation. In two-thirds of cases the broken end shows a snap fracture (Table 11.6); three artefacts showed a less specific breakage, and one has a recent break. The length of these artefacts is highly variable and ranges from 4.1–22.4mm. Some specimens are modified over their entire surface down to the point of breakage, hence the point length may originally have been longer.

Shaft artefacts: midsections and expedient tools

Eleven shaft fragments of artefacts were found which lack the tip, and possibly the butt as well, and were classified as midsections. Six of these show no signs of modification but are clearly polished, albeit with varying intensity. These artefacts are therefore assumed to have been part of expedient tools — artefacts that were simply used because of their convenient shape. The length of these artefacts ranges from 6.3–13.7mm. Three artefacts show snap fractures at both ends; in the other three cases step fractures were found at one end of the artefact, with the other end snapped off. In all cases the breakage occurred at some stage in antiquity.

The remaining five midsections show evidence of modification. All but one of these are also polished. The ends are either snapped off or show more complex fractures; one specimen has a step fracture at one end and less specific breakage at the other. Their length varies between 10.7–18.1mm.

Shaft artefacts: spatulae

Two 'shaft' spatulae were found in Liang Lemdubu. Both were made from the distal part of *Thylogale* fibulae and both are small fragments of the broad rounded tip (see for one example specimen LC1d, Fig. 11.5). One is highly polished at the tip, the other shows a light polish over most of its surface. One has an intact tip, the other was damaged some time before excavation and bears a large step fracture. The length, width and thickness of these fragments are very similar (L: 7.8mm and eight millimetres; W: 6.8mm and 6.4mm; T: 2.2mm and 2.3mm, respectively), reflecting the dimensions of the parent bone. Both artefacts were ground into their present shape.

Cortical artefacts: broken uni- or bipoints

The majority of cortical artefacts (10 out of 11) were classified as broken uni- or bipoints. Seven out of these 10 specimens show definite polish to varying intensity (Table 11.4); the others are somewhat glossy, although probably not as a result of use. In four cases the tip was undamaged (Table 11.5). Three of the damaged specimens show a somewhat crushed or blunted tip. The others have a step fracture, a snap fracture and more complex damage. The broken end was in most cases snapped off (Table 11.6); in one artefact a step fracture caused the breakage, and the remaining specimens showed more complex damage. Their length ranges from 6.1–17.2mm; however, one very large specimen (in two parts), with a length of 44.6mm, is also included in this category on account of its exceptional width (specimen LC4h, Fig. 11.5). Width and thickness vary between 3.2–8.0mm (W) and 1.1-3.3mm (T). The point length of the broken uni- or bipoints ranges from 4.9–17.2mm. Some of the points might originally have been longer as the modification marks run across the breakage.

Table 11.4 Liang Lemdubu and Liang Nabulei Lisa: variation in polish found across artefact categories (c=cortical; s=shaft)

	LEMDUBU								NABULEI LISA							
	NO POLISH		LIGHT POLISH		MEDIUM POLISH		HIGH POLISH		NO POLISH		LIGHT POLISH		MEDIUM POLISH		HIGH POLISH	
	c	s	c	s	c	s	c	s	c	s	c	s	c	s	c	s
Attenuate unipoints	-	2	-	-	-	-	-	-	-	2	-	-	-	-	-	1
Bipoints	-	-	-	-	-	-	-	-	-	-	-	1	-	-	-	-
Broken uni- or bipoints	3	4	1	3	3	2	3	2	2	2	-	1	1	-	-	2
Spatulae	-	-	1	1	-	-	-	1	-	-	-	-	-	-	-	2
Midsections	-	1	-	1	-	1	-	2	-	1	-	-	-	-	-	-
Expedient tools?	-	-	-	4	-	-	-	2	-	-	-	-	-	-	-	-
Total	3	7	2	9	3	3	3	7	2	5	-	2	1	-	-	5

Table 11.5 Liang Lemdubu and Liang Nabulei Lisa: type of tip damage found across artefact categories (c=cortical; s=shaft)

	LEMDUBU												NABULEI LISA									
	INTACT		SNAP FRACTURE		STEP FRACTURE		CRUSHED		COMPLEX		POST-EXCAVATION		INTACT		SNAP FRACTURE		STEP FRACTURE		CRUSHED		COMPLEX	
	c	s	c	s	c	s	c	s	c	s	c	s	c	s	c	s	c	s	c	s	c	s
Attenuate unipoints	-	1	-	-	-	-	-	-	-	-	-	1	-	-	-	-	-	-	-	1	-	1
Bipoints	-	-	-	-	-	-	-	-	-	-	-	-	-	1*	-	-	-	-	-	-	-	-
Broken uni- or bipoints	4	8	1	-	1	-	3	2	1	-	-	1	2	4	-	-	-	1	-	-	1	-
Spatulae	-	1	-	-	-	1	-	-	1	-	-	-	-	2	-	-	-	-	-	-	-	-
Expedient tools	-	-	-	-	-	-	-	-	-	-	-	-	-	-	-	1	-	-	-	-	-	-
Total	4	10	1	-	1	1	3	2	2	-	-	2	2	7	-	1	-	1	-	1	1	1

*Both ends intact

Table 11.6 Liang Lemdubu and Liang Nabulei Lisa: type of breakage found across artefact categories (c=cortical; s=shaft)

	LEMDUBU										NABULEI LISA											
	SNAP FRACTURE		STEP FRACTURE		CRUSHED		COMPLEX		POST-EXCAVATION		INTACT		SNAP FRACTURE		STEP FRACTURE		CRUSHED		COMPLEX		POST-EXCAVATION	
	c	s	c	s	c	s	c	s	c	s	c	s	c	s	c	s	c	s	c	s	c	s
Attenuate unipoints	-	1	-	-	-	-	-	1	-	-	-	-	-	1	-	1	-	-	-	-	-	-
Bipoints	-	-	-	-	-	-	-	-	-	-	-	1*	-	-	-	-	-	-	-	-	-	-
Broken uni- or bipoints	5	7	1	-	-	-	3	3	1	1	-	-	1	3	-	2	-	-	1	-	1	-
Spatulae	-	1	-	-	-	-	1	1	-	-	-	-	-	1	-	-	-	-	-	1	-	-
Midsections end 1	-	2	-	1	-	-	-	2	-	-	-	-	-	-	-	-	-	-	-	1	-	-
Midsections end 2	-	2	-	-	-	-	-	3	-	-	-	-	-	-	-	-	-	-	-	1	-	-
Expedient tools? end 1	-	3	-	3	-	-	-	-	-	-	-	-	-	-	-	-	-	-	-	-	-	-
Expedient tools? end 2	-	6	-	-	-	-	-	-	-	-	-	-	-	-	-	-	-	-	-	1	-	-

*Both ends intact

NB: the breakage at the butt-end of the artefact may or may not represent the artefact's original 'end'

Cortical artefacts: the spatula

One spatula made from unidentified cortical bone has a similar morphology to those made of *Thylogale* fibula (specimen LC1c, Fig. 11.5). However, it is slightly wider and thinner than the fibula specimens (7.4mm and 1.9mm respectively), and shows a light polish over its surface. Its rounded tip was slightly damaged in antiquity with a complex fracture. Like the fibula spatulae, it was ground into its present shape.

Liang Nabulei Lisa

The bone artefacts from Liang Nabulei Lisa show a large variation in size and shape (see Fig. 11.6, Table 11.9). A total of 15 specimens were found, all but one of which were definitely modified. The one exception is a bone that bears high polish but otherwise shows no modification and thus is classified as an expedient tool. Two artefacts are classified as attenuate unipoints considering their total length, relatively narrow width and lack of tapering at the butt. There is only one bipoint in this collection, and also only one midsection. Eight artefacts are classified as broken uni- or bipoints because their short length and lack of tapering at the broken end precludes more precise identification. The remaining two artefacts have the typical rounded tips of spatulae. The majority of the artefacts were made of fragments of small mammalian shaft bones, most of which could not be further identified to taxon. However, recognisable *Thylogale* fibula fragments and a snake rib are included among them.

Almost half of the artefacts were made of lightly burnt bone (Table 11.2); five were made of unburnt bone and three of burnt bone. Calcined artefacts were not found. None of the artefacts showed secondary burn marks, which would have indicated burning after discard.

Seven of the 14 modified artefacts were first shaved and then ground into shape, and one was cut and then ground (Table 11.3). This is a larger proportion than present in the assemblage from Liang Lemdubu. Four artefacts were ground only, and one was shaved only. As for Lemdubu, grinding facets were evident on many of the artefacts. Earlier shaving marks were recognised as irregular striations, often somewhat obscured by subsequent grinding. Again, in all cases, cutting planes, shaving marks, or even grinding facets may have been obliterated by subsequent modification or use. One tiny isolated tip fragment proved too small to determine its mode of manufacturing.

Shaft artefacts: attenuate unipoints

Three attenuate unipoints were found at the site; one of these is classified as an expedient tool, which will be discussed below. The other two specimens are 34.3mm and 38mm in length, measuring 5.1mm and 4.6mm in width, and 2.9mm and 2.5mm in thickness, respectively. The longer unipoint (specimen NL/I/37a, Fig. 11.6) has a point length of 5.8mm; the shorter unipoint (specimen NL/I/27a, Fig. 11.6) is modified all over its surface so the boundary of the tip is difficult to establish. The tip of NL/I/27a shows some complex damage, and the butt was snapped off. Specimen NL/I/37a has a rather blunted tip and a large step fracture at the butt. Both artefacts showed only very light polish, probably caused by handling rather than use.

Table 11.7 Liang Lemdubu and Liang Nabulei Lisa: relationship between damage and polish. Specimens showing post-excavation damage are excluded (shaft and cortical bone combined)

	LEMDUBU				
	NO DAMAGE	SNAP FRACTURE	STEP FRACTURE	CRUSHING	COMPLEX
No polish	5	1		3	
Light polish	3	3	3	1	1
Medium polish	3	1	1		
High polish	3	1	2	1	3
	NABULEI LISA				
	NO DAMAGE	SNAP FRACTURE	STEP FRACTURE	CRUSHING	COMPLEX
No polish	2		1	1	3
Light polish	2				
Medium polish	1				
High polish	4	1			

Table 11.8 Liang Lemdubu: bone artefacts raw data

SPECIMEN	SPIT	CATEGORY	TYPE OF BONE	BURNING	POLISH - DEGREE	POLISH - LOCATION*	LENGTH	WIDTH	POINT LENGTH	TIP DAMAGE*	BREAKAGE*	MANUFACTURING	TECHNIQUE	SPECIES
LC1a	1	mid	shaft	lb	light	one end	14.1	7.8	4.5		snap fr	snap fr	sh/gr	mammal
LC1b	1	1/2b	cort	lb	high	tip	13.6	4.4	2.3	13.6	complex	snap fr	gr	mammal
LC1c	1	spat	cort	u	light	ent surf	7.7	7.4	1.9	7.7	complex	complex	gr	mammal
LC1d	1	spat	shaft	lb	high	tip	7.8	6.8	2.2	4.8	intact	complex	gr	*Thylogale* distal fibula
LC1e	1	1/2b	cort	lb	high	tip	9.7	4.5	1.1	9.7	crushed	snap fr	sh/gr	mammal
LC1f	1	1/2b	cort	lb	med	ent surf	16.3	4.4	2.4	16.3	snap fr	step fr	gr	mammal
LC1g	1	mid	shaft	b	high	one end	18.1	4.1	2.9		complex	complex	gr	*Thylogale* mid part fibula
LC1h	1	mid	shaft	lb	med	ent surf	11.1	3.2	1.8		step fr	complex	sh/gr	mammal
LC1i	1	1/2b	shaft	u	no		9.7	2.2	1.6	9.7	intact	post-exc	gr	mammal
LC1j	1	1/2b	shaft	u	high	ent surf	8.3	2.6	1.9	8.3	intact	snap fr	gr	mammal
LC1k	1	1/2b	shaft	u	med	ent surf	–	2.8	2.7	–	post-exc	complex	gr	mammal
LC1l	1	mid	shaft	lb	high	ent surf	11.7	2.1	2.3		complex	complex	gr	mammal
LC1m	1	spat	shaft	lb	light	ent surf	8.0	6.4	2.3	8.0	step fr	snap fr	gr	*Thylogale* distal fibula
LC1n	1	exp*	shaft	lb	high	one end	13.7	4.7	1.8		snap fr	snap fr	-	*Thylogale* distal fibula
LC1o	1	exp*	shaft	lb	light	ent surf	6.3	5.5	1.8		step fr	snap fr	-	*Thylogale* distal fibula
LC1p	1	exp*	shaft	b	light	ent surf	22.1	3.4	2.5		snap fr	snap fr	-	*Thylogale* mid part fibula
LC1q	1	exp*	shaft	lb	light	ent surf	9.8	3.7	2.3		snap fr	snap fr	-	mammal
LC1r	1	exp*	shaft	lb	light	ent surf	8.9	3.0	2.7		step fr	snap fr	-	mammal
LC1s	1	exp*	shaft	lb	high	ent surf	7.6	3.2	1.3		step fr	snap fr	-	mammal
LC1t	1	1/2b	cort	u	no		8.9	5.0	1.6	8.9	intact	complex	?	mammal
LC1u	1	1/2b	cort	u	no		9.3	4.5	1.6	9.3	intact	complex	?	mammal
LC2a	2	1	shaft	lb	no		27.8	5.0	3.2	6.3	post-exc	snap fr	sh/gr	*Thylogale* mid part fibula
LC2b	2	1/2b	shaft	calc	light	ent surf	16.1	4.6	2.6	5.5	intact	snap fr	sh/gr	*Thylogale* mid part fibula
LC3a	3	1/2b	shaft	lb	med	tip	11.9	3.5	3.9	6.6	intact	complex	sh/gr	mammal
LC4a	4	1/2b	shaft	lb	light	ent surf	10.2	5.9	3.1	10.2	intact	snap fr	gr	Agile Wallaby distal fibula
LC4b	4	1/2b	cort	b	med	ent surf	6.1	3.2	1.1	4.9	intact	post-exc	gr	mammal
LC4c	4	1/2b	cort	u	no		10.1	3.9	1.8	10.1	crushed	snap fr	gr	mammal
LC4d	4	1/2b	shaft	u	no		10.0	2.0	1.8	7.0	crushed	complex	ct/gr	mammal
LC4e	4	1/2b	cort	lb	high	tip	11.7	-	1.8	-	step fr	complex	gr	mammal
LC4f	4	1/2b	shaft	calc	no		18.7	4.4	3.4	7.8	intact	snap fr	gr	*Thylogale* mid part fibula
LC4g	4	1/2b	shaft	calc	no		22.4	7.6	3.7	22.4	crushed	snap fr	gr	Agile Wallaby distal fibula
LC4h	4	1/2b	cort	lb	med	tip	44.6	8.0	3.3	14.5	intact	snap fr	sh/gr	mammal
LC5a	5	1/2b	cort	calc	light	ent surf	17.2	6.1	2.6	17.2	crushed	snap fr	gr	mammal
LC5b	5	1/2b	shaft	lb	high	tip	13.2	5.7	2.2	10.9	intact	snap fr	gr	*Thylogale* distal fibula
LC16a	16	mid	shaft	lb	no		10.7	5.6	3.2		snap fr	snap fr	gr	*Thylogale* distal fibula
LC24a	24	1	shaft	u	no		28.7	4.2	2.7	14.2	intact	complex	gr	*Thylogale* mid part fibula
LC24b	24	1/2b	shaft	u	light	ent surf	4.1	1.4	0.8	4.1	intact	snap fr	gr	mammal

NB: for midsections, 'tip damage' and 'breakage' are both 'type of breakage' at either end

*Legend: 1=unipoint; 2=bipoint; 1/2b=broken uni- or bipoint; spat=spatula; mid=midsection; cort=cortical; u=unburnt; lb=lightly burnt; b=burnt; calc=calcined; med=medium; ent surf= entire surface; snap fr=snap fracture; step fr=step fracture; post-exc=post-excavation; gr=ground; sh/gr= shaved then ground; exp=expedient tool (*all midsections); ct/gr=cut then ground

*Measurements are in mm

Table 11.9 Liang Nabulei Lisa: bone artefacts raw data

SAMPLE	SPIT	CATEGORY	TYPE OF BONE	BURNING	POLISH - DEGREE	POLISH - LOCATION*	LENGTH	WIDTH	POINT LENGTH	TIP DAMAGE*	BREAKAGE*	MANUFACTURING	TECHNIQUE	SPECIES
NL/I/12a	12	1/2b	cort	u	no		16	4.4	2.4	16	complex	complex	sh	mammal
NL/I/14a	14	spat	shaft	lb	high	ent surf	13.8	4.5	2.9	13.8	intact	snap fr	gr	mammal
NL/I/19a	19	1/2b	shaft	lb	no		25	5.2	3.1	11.1	step fr	step fr	ct/gr	mammal
NL/I/23a	23	spat	shaft	lb	high	ent surf	27.8	6.1	2	5.9	intact	complex	gr	*Thylogale* distal fibula
NL/I/26a	26	1/2b	shaft	lb	light	ent surf	20	4.1	2.2	5.5	intact	snap fr	sh/gr	mammal
NL/I/27a	27	1	shaft	lb	no		34.3	5.1	2.9	34.3	complex	snap fr	sh/gr	*Thylogale* central fibula
NL/I/28a	28	1/2b	shaft	lb	high	tip	14.7	4.5	3.6	14.7	intact	step fr	sh/gr	
NL/I/28b	28	exp*	shaft	u	high	ent surf	25.9	1.7	1.9	25.9	snap fr	complex	-	snake rib
NL/I/29a	29	2	shaft	u	light	ent surf	43.1	5.9	3.2	14	intact	intact	sh/gr	mammal
NL/I/31a	31	mid	shaft	b	no		15.8	6.2	3.4		complex	complex	sh/gr	mammal
NL/I/31b	31	1/2b	shaft	b	no		12.8	5.4	2.7	12.8	intact	snap fr	sh/gr	mammal
NL/I/31c	31	1/2b	shaft	lb	high	tip	14.8	3.8	3.2	5.5	intact	snap fr	gr	mammal
NL/I/32a	32	1/2b	cort	b	med	tip	12	4.5	1.5	12	intact	snap fr	sh/gr	mammal
NL/I/35a	35	1/2b	cort	u	no		4.5	2.4	1.3	4.5	intact	post-exc	?	mammal
NL/I/37a	37	1	shaft	u	no		38	4.6	2.5	5.8	crushed	step fr	gr	*Thylogale* central fibula

NB: for midsections, 'tip damage' and 'breakage' are both 'type of breakage' at either end

*Legend: 1=unipoint; 2=bipoint; 1/2b=broken uni- or bipoint; spat=spatula; mid=midsection; cort=cortical; u=unburnt; lb=lightly burnt; b=burnt; calc=calcined; med=medium; ent surf= entire surface; snap fr=snap fracture; step fr=step fracture; post-exc=post-excavation; gr=ground; sh/gr= shaved then ground; exp=expedient tool (*unipoint); ct/gr=cut then ground

*Measurements are in mm

Shaft artefacts: the bipoint

The only bipointed specimen that was found during the Nabulei Lisa excavations is an asymmetric artefact made of a split long bone, perhaps a tibia or femur of a small or young animal (specimen NL/I/29a, see Fig. 11.6). It has a total length of 43.1mm, the long tip measuring 14mm and the short tip 7.2mm. Both tips are intact and the artefact is lightly polished over its entire surface. The width of the artefact is 5.9mm and the thickness is 3.2mm, the latter constituting about half the original thickness of the parent bone.

Shaft artefacts: broken uni- or bipoints

Five artefacts made of shaft bone were classified as broken uni- or bipoints. Four of these have undamaged tips; one tip bears a step fracture. The butts of these specimens are either snapped off or show step fractures. Two of the undamaged tips show a high polish, the others light to medium or only a very light polish. The artefacts range in length from 12.8–25mm; the width from 3.8–5.4mm. The thickness ranges from 2.2–3.6mm. The point length is variable and ranges from 5.5–14.7mm; this includes two specimens that are modified over their entire surface, so the actual point length may have been longer.

Shaft artefacts: midsections

Only one midsection was found in Nabulei Lisa; it is a rather large fragment, perhaps from a rib of a mammal, and it bears clear modification marks. It is 15.8mm long, 6.2mm wide and 3.4mm thick. It is slightly glossy over its entire surface (probably from handling) and is broken at both ends. There are no other artefacts that bear any close resemblance to this fragment.

Shaft artefacts: spatulae

Two artefacts have the typical morphology of spatulae: one is a wide artefact with a broad, rounded tip (specimen NL/I/23a, Fig. 11.6), the other is narrower but with an equally smooth, rounded tip (NL/I/14a, Fig. 11.6). The wider specimen was made of the distal part of a *Thylogale* fibula, the other of an unidentified mammal bone. Both are highly polished and their tips are intact. The fragments are 13.8mm and 27.8mm long, 4.5mm and 6.1mm wide, and 2.9mm and two millimetres thick, respectively. The shorter artefact is polished to such an extent that it has obliterated most modification marks, making it difficult to establish the point length. The point section of the longer specimen measures 5.9mm.

Shaft artefacts: the expedient tool

A thin, curved bone, identifiable as part of a snake rib, bears high polish over its entire surface but otherwise shows no modification marks (specimen NL/I/28b, Fig. 11.6). Although it is classified as an expedient tool, it clearly functioned as an attenuate unipoint. The end of the tip has snapped off. It is 25.9mm long, 1.7mm wide and 1.9mm thick.

Cortical artefacts: broken uni- or bipoints

Three artefact fragments made of cortical bone could be parts of either unipoints or bipoints. One of these is the very end of a tip and shows no polish. It is only 4.5mm long, 2.4mm wide and 1.3mm thick. The tip itself is intact, but the fragment was broken off some time during or after excavation. The remainder of the artefact has not been located and may be unrecognised amongst the faunal remains.

The other two broken uni- or bipoints are 16mm and 12mm long, 4.4mm and 4.5mm wide, and 2.4mm and 1.5mm thick, respectively. The shorter one has medium polish at its intact tip; the other specimen is unpolished and has its tip broken off. In both cases, the modification marks go beyond the point of breakage, so the original point length could not be established.

Morphological Comparison and Discussion

Each of the bone artefact assemblages from the Aru sites is highly variable. Because of this, and also because of the relatively small sample size, metrical analysis fails to provide a meaningful basis for comparison. Nevertheless, there are some noteworthy features that need to be discussed, both within and between the assemblages, and between the Aru assemblages and others in the region.

Both sites produced small numbers of attenuate unipoints and spatulae, and larger numbers of artefact fragments, both tips and midsections (or butts). Nabulei Lisa produced the only artefact that could be classified as a bipoint.

Shaft bone was the preferred material for artefact production in both Aru sites, although Nabulei Lisa contained a higher proportion (80%) of shaft artefacts than Lemdubu (70%). The majority of cortical artefacts, in both sites, are classified as broken uni- or bipoints, the only exception being a spatula from Lemdubu. In the Kria Cave assemblage, from the Bird's Head of Papua, there is a clear distinction in the use of raw material between unipoints and bipoints: bipoints were almost exclusively made of cortical splinters of bone, while attenuate unipoints were mostly made of shaft fragments (Pasveer 2004:175). The same distinction is observed in the two largest samples from the investigated sites in northern Maluku (Siti Nafisah and Golo Cave). Here too, the vast majority of bipoints are made from cortical bone (Pasveer and Bellwood 2004:Table 3), while attenuate unipoints, although fewer in number, are primarily made from shaft fragments. An obvious possibility in regard to the Aru assemblages is that the broken cortical specimens are primarily parts of originally bipointed artefacts. This possibility is explored further below.

Lemdubu produced bone artefacts that were in most cases (72.4%, against 28.6% in Nabulei Lisa) ground into their present shape, while those of Nabulei Lisa were mostly first shaved and then ground (50%, against 24% in Lemdubu). However, in both sites the same techniques were applied, albeit in varying combinations, and it is possible that the differences may be explained by the subsequent obliteration of shaving marks on the Lemdubu specimens through excessive grinding.

Around 50% of the artefacts in both Aru sites were made of lightly burnt bone. Twenty-seven per cent and 33% of the artefacts in Lemdubu and Nabulei Lisa, respectively, was made of unburnt bone. Nabulei Lisa contained a higher proportion of specimens made of burnt bone (20%) than Lemdubu (eight per cent). However, the latter site had some calcined artefacts that were, most likely, burnt after deposition, therefore obscuring their original state.

Lightly burnt bone (a state which is usually the result of cooking of the bone) is also the dominant raw material of bone artefacts in Golo Cave in the northern Maluku Province. However, in the absence of information on the burning condition of the wider assemblage, it remains uncertain whether this was due to deliberate selection or simply reflected the availability of raw material at the site (Pasveer and Bellwood 2004). For the Aru sites, we can be more certain that deliberate selection has occurred because, in both sites, unburnt bone was present in higher proportions than lightly burnt bone. The top five spits in Lemdubu (where the majority of bone artefacts were found) contained ca. 43% unburnt and ca. 41% lightly burnt bone. In Nabulei Lisa, for the whole deposit (the artefacts were scattered throughout the sequence), these proportions are ca. 57% and 26%, respectively. These comparisons suggest some moderate preference for lightly burnt bone as raw material for bone artefact production in this area.

Various authors have reported on the qualities of unburnt versus burnt bone for artefact manufacture and use (e.g. Bird and Beeck 1980; Campana 1989; Evans 1973; Guthrie 1983; Knecht 1997; Olsen 1984). Opinions vary somewhat over what constitutes the best kind of bone for this purpose. In general, unburnt or 'green' bone is a hard but flexible raw material but it is said to be difficult to modify. Slightly desiccated bone is said to be better for bone point manufacturing (Bird and Beeck 1980:169). Heating of bone will initially make bone denser and harder; however, excessive heating and burning of bone destroys the organic part of the matrix and renders the bone increasingly brittle (Campana 1989:36).

For the Kria Cave assemblage it was observed that tip-bearing shaft fragments were more consistent in length than shaft midsections (Pasveer 2004:170–1). From this analysis it was concluded that the tip-bearing fragments resulted from breakage during use, rather than through random damage after discard. Because the original artefacts varied in length, the remainder of the tool (i.e. the midsection, which could also simply be the butt of the artefact) also tend to be more variable. The Lemdubu shaft artefacts appear to show the reverse pattern. The shaft midsections (or butts) appear relatively uniform in length, peaking between 7.5–12.5mm, while the tip-bearing fragments are more variable in length, although the majority also measure between 7.5–12.5mm. Unfortunately, the sample size is too small to support a statistical analysis and it is not possible to justify any particular conclusion in regard to the breakage pattern.

The presence of predominantly broken specimens at both Aru sites makes it likely that the composite artefacts in which the points were hafted, were subject to maintenance on site, such as replacement or repair. A relatively high incidence of specimens with unpolished and undamaged tips also points to the likely manufacture of bone artefacts on site, leaving behind those that broke during this process. However, the sites produced no obvious examples of unfinished artefacts, such as the cortical splinters with fairly coarsely produced tips and unmodified butts found at Kria and Golo Caves.

The Nabulei Lisa assemblage shows an interesting dichotomy among the tip-bearing artefacts between those with polished and intact tips, and those with unpolished but damaged tips (see Table 11.7). In the Lemdubu assemblage, there is no comparable dichotomy between polished and damaged tips (i.e. many artefacts are polished and damaged). The dichotomy between 'no polish — damage' and 'polish — no damage' in the Nabulei Lisa assemblage might be taken as evidence for two different modes of use: one that produced polish but with little risk of damage, and another that carried a risk of damage but did not produce polish. Alternatively, the dichotomy could be between artefacts that either sustained damage shortly after they were brought into use, and others that managed to sustain the rigours of use for long enough to develop polish. With larger samples, it might be possible to test these alternative hypotheses by metrical comparison between the various damage/polish classes.

For the bone artefact assemblages from Kria and Golo Caves, a strong case was made that the bipointed artefacts were hafted as components of composite tools (Pasveer 2004:177–8; Pasveer and Bellwood 2004:130–1). One reason was that many were simply too small to be hand-held (some of the Kria Cave bipoints were only 16mm long; those from Golo Cave as short as 19mm). However, other, no less important evidence came from their polish and breakage patterns. Kria Cave bipoints predominantly bear polish on only one end, despite the fact that, without exception, they are neatly pointed at both ends. This indicates that they were nearly always oriented the same way during repeated use, an outcome that is difficult to reconcile with hand-held use. Furthermore, major breakage was most often found at the secondary end (i.e. the end that showed the least use-wear) of both Kria and Golo bipoints. With hand-held use, breakage is more likely to occur at the end that is under direct pressure (the functional end). In contrast, experimental use of hafted bipoints has shown more consistent breakage at the secondary end where the artefact is under strain within the haft. In combination, these observations support the conclusion that the bipointed artefacts from the sites were frequently hafted for use.

Given this evidence of a regional tradition of bipoint production and composite tool use, it is especially noteworthy that complete or broken bipoints are absent or extremely rare in the Aru sites. Apart from the one complete bipoint from Nabulei Lisa, the only possible evidence for this class of artefacts are fragments classified as 'broken uni- or bipoints'. If originally bipointed, these specimens all snapped at positions before their midpoints and the remaining portion was discarded elsewhere. Moreover, if we assume that the broken uni- or bipoints from Lemdubu (the largest sample) were originally parts of hafted bipoints, then in two-thirds of the 21 cases, it was the functional (polished) end that broke off, rather than the unpolished, hafted end. This observation is the reverse of the pattern observed in both Kria and Golo Cave, where the ends that broke off tend to lack polish or damage. The obvious conclusion is that hafted bipoints of the kind produced in the northern Maluku and Bird's Head sites were not in common use in the Aru Islands through the Late Pleistocene and Holocene. This is not to say that the unipointed artefacts found in the Aru sites were not similarly hafted for use in composite tools. However, there is no direct evidence either for or against this possibility.

The potential function of the bone implements from this region has been extensively discussed in the literature (see for example Lampert 1966; Pasveer 2004; Pasveer and Bellwood 2004; Pickering 1979; Webb 1987). Numerous suggestions have been put forward, based on, or supported by, ethnographic accounts and some by experiments (e.g. Bird and Beeck 1980; Webb 1987). The most frequently described functions are use as arrow or spear tips (e.g. Jones and Johnson 1985:60; Lampert 1966, 1971; McCarthy 1940; Schrire 1982), or as fishing gorges (e.g. Anell 1955; Codrington 1969[1891]:316; Hale and Tindale 1930; Massola 1956:4–5; Mulvaney 1960:77). Other functions, such as *ad hoc* usage including removing splinters, lancing boils (Blackwood 1950:32), piercing, engraving, or personal adornment (fastening cloaks, nose bones, hairpins) have also been mentioned.

Pasveer (2004) and Pasveer and Bellwood (2004) have discussed the possible function of bone artefacts from the Bird's Head and the northern Maluku Province, drawing on their observations from use-wear (polish) and damage. The presence of high polish on many of the specimens, comparable with that observed on many artefacts from the Aru sites, along with damage types such as step fractures, virtually rules out a function as a fish gorge. Step fractures are also unlikely to occur on barbs, since these parts of composite tools usually do not receive any direct impact or pressure on the tip (except perhaps when pulled out, in which case they are more likely to snap). The presence of polish in general suggests a mode of use including repeated friction, and this is unlikely to accumulate on artefacts that are subjected to high velocity impact such as arrow tips or spear points — unless the projectile always hits its target, only penetrates the softer parts of it, and is returned to its owner undamaged (an unlikely scenario). For the Bird's Head and the northern Maluku sites it was concluded that the bone artefacts were most likely used for drilling holes or in engraving activities, the only actions that might generate both polish and damage such as crushing or step fracturing of the tip. This conclusion was strongly supported by a detailed account from the Wola of the Southern Highlands of Papua New Guinea (Sillitoe 1988:64), who use hafted bone points and animal incisors in activities of this kind. Wallaby incisors with obvious use-related damage are present in the Kria Cave assemblage (Pasveer 2004:171–5). A sample of approximately 50 isolated Agile Wallaby incisors from Lemdubu was examined, but none was found to show any convincing sign of use. Wallaby incisors from the faunal assemblage from Golo Cave have not been examined. A more detailed analysis of wallaby and other mammal incisors from all three regions may yield interesting results.

Historical accounts from the Aru Islands indicate that bows and arrows were the main hunting weapons of the Aru people (Merton 1910:60); according to one early observer, they were 'masters of the art' (von Rosenberg 1867:21). Spears were of minor importance. Arrow tips were mostly made of hardwood or iron, although cassowary bone was also used (von Rosenberg 1867:21). These arrows were employed to hunt wild boars and kangaroos. Tips of bamboo were used to hunt for stingrays, and triangular arrows with barbs for fishing (Merton 1910:61). Special blunt tips were used to shoot birds of paradise, so as to catch them alive and undamaged. Leaf veins of sago palms were specifically used to produce small, light arrows with very sharp tips, mostly used by young boys to kill birds. The possible use of bone artefacts as arrowheads in the past therefore warrants further consideration. As mentioned before, the Nabulei Lisa assemblage includes a number of artefacts with unpolished yet damaged tips. This pattern of use wear is consistent with the use of the artefacts as projectile tips. However, more than half of the specimens show no damage at the tips, while others especially in the Lemdubu assemblage, show various combinations of damage and polish, often of quite high intensity. As argued for the northern Maluku and Bird's Head assemblages, the overall pattern of use-wear and damage in the Aru sites, even though based on smaller samples, is more consistent with the option that most specimens were used for drilling or engraving purposes. Obviously, this does not rule out the possibility that some or even many bone artefacts were used for more than one purpose during their functional life.

From available site reports and other publications, it appears that morphologically unspecialised bone artefacts of the kind found in Lemdubu and Nabulei Lisa, are widely distributed through the Indo–Pacific region, from Tasmania, through southeastern, western and northern Australia, across Melanesia (including at least the Bismarck Archipelago, Papua New Guinea and Papua), and west into Indonesia (including northern Maluku, Sulawesi, and Java), the Philippines and mainland Southeast Asia (see, for a review of sites with bone artefacts in Southeast Asia, Olsen and Glover 2004).

Bone artefacts were not only used widely throughout the region but also for a prolonged period of prehistory. Artefacts of this kind have been used from at least ca. 30,000 BP, e.g. Bone Cave in south Tasmania (Webb and Allen 1990) and Niah Cave in Sarawak (Majid 1982). However, most examples come from sites of Late Pleistocene and early Holocene age onwards. In sites where larger numbers of bone artefacts were found, reports mention no change in morphology or parent bone through time (see, for example, Olsen and Glover 2004; Pasveer 2004).

Liang Lemdubu produced twice as many bone artefacts as Liang Nabulei Lisa in approximately the same period of time. Similarly contrasting rates of bone artefact discard between geographically and temporally related sites seem to be no rarity in this region. For example, Golo Cave on Gebe Island produced 130 bone artefacts, as opposed to one example from another coastal cave, Um Kapat Papo, located 10–15kms to the east. Kria Cave on the Bird's Head produced 92 specimens against a total of three bone artefacts in contemporary Toé Cave, 12km to the southwest. On New Ireland, the inland site of Balof Shelter produced numerous bone artefacts, while contemporaneous coastal sites on the island lack bone artefacts altogether (Downie and White 1978:777–9). Other examples of highly variable discard rates come from sites in the Gunung Sewu area of Central Java (Simanjuntak 2004), and in Victoria, southeastern Australia (Pickering 1979). The significance of these striking contrasts needs to be carefully investigated in each context before any general conclusions can be drawn.

The contrasting sample sizes in the northern Maluku and Bird's Head sites are explained in terms of the function of the site related to the local environment, or the nature of the visiting groups and/or intensity of occupation (Pasveer 2004; Pasveer and Bellwood 2004). Both Aru sites contained vast quantities of faunal remains (although Nabulei Lisa less so than Lemdubu) and its continuing presence throughout the deposit demonstrate that the small sample size of the bone artefact assemblages is neither a matter of preservation nor of infrequent occupation of the sites.

Conclusion

In general terms, the bone artefacts found at Liang Lemdubu and Liang Nabulei Lisa are similar to those described recently from elsewhere in the eastern Indonesian region (Pasveer 2004; Pasveer and Bellwood 2004). While the Aru sites produced many fragments of unipoints or bipoints and spatulae, complete specimens are extremely rare. The morphology of the Aru bone artefacts seems more variable than those from sites in northern Maluku and Papua provinces, although this may in part reflect the small sample size of the Aru assemblages. Most artefacts were made of sections of small shaft bones, with a more or less intact medullary canal. A smaller proportion was made of splinters of cortical bone, originating from larger long bones. Their manufacturers had a preference for lightly burnt bone, presumably because of its stronger properties compared to fresh, burnt or calcined bone. Grinding was the most frequently applied manufacturing technique, often preceded by shaving.

Due to the relatively low numbers of artefacts, a statistical analysis of metrical attributes was not attempted, however, the distribution and association of use-related polish and damage provided some insights into the potential function of the artefacts, particularly in comparison to the assemblages from Golo Cave and Kria Cave. These comparisons are greatly assisted through application of the same analytical methods in all three studies (Pasveer 2004; Pasveer and Bellwood 2004).

While bone artefacts from Liang Lemdubu show various combinations of polish and damage, those from Liang Nabulei Lisa appear to show a dichotomy between unpolished but damaged specimens and specimens with polish but little or no damage. This could simply be because the intact, polished specimens were higher quality artefacts. However, it is also possible that it is related to a difference in function between the two groups of artefacts. For example, projectile points are unlikely to accumulate polish but might become damaged as a result of high-velocity impacts, whereas those used as drills or engravers are likely to sustain polish rather than damage. Ethnographic sources indicate that the Aru people, at least in historical times, were highly skilled archers (von Rosenberg 1867); this observation is clearly consistent with the possibility that some bone artefacts might have been used as projectile points.

As noted above, drilling or engraving activities are more likely to produce polished tips as a result of repeated friction. Bone artefacts used in this way may or may not receive damage, such as step fractures or crushing, to the tip. The occurrence of artefacts with similar polish and damage patterns in Golo and Kria Caves, in combination with Sillitoe's (1988:64) detailed account of the Wola in Papua New Guinea using hafted bone artefacts and teeth for drilling or engraving activities, supports the notion that similar activities were carried out in either of the Aru sites. However, wallaby incisors with use-related damage, such as were found in Kria Cave, were not noted during analysis of the Lemdubu fauna. Nabulei Lisa's incisor collection was not examined for this purpose.

An intriguing observation from the Aru bone artefact assemblages is that virtually no complete artefacts were found. The vast majority of specimens in both sites are fragments of artefacts. This probably means that the artefacts were used (and broken) on site. We might assume that repair and replacement were also carried out on site, given that midsections (or butts) also occur. Although undamaged and unpolished specimens were recovered from both sites, it remains uncertain whether actual manufacture took place, since no half-products or 'unfinished' specimens were found.

Another important contrast with the Bird's Head and northern Maluku assemblages is that bipoints are extremely rare in both Aru sites. Only one complete specimen was found, a peculiar artefact from Liang Nabulei Lisa that has the appearance of a bipointed spatula and is unlike any artefact seen in the northern Maluku and Bird's Head collections. In addition, the Aru sites produced no specimens that could be identified as broken bipoints. Of course it is possible that the basal portion of any broken bipoint was meticulously removed from the sites — but is it likely that every single broken bipoint was taken away? Why were the broken unipoints or spatulae not removed? Virtually every other site in the region has produced bipoints, either complete or in broken form. In this light, perhaps the only sensible conclusion is that the occupants of the Aru sites did not regularly manufacture and use bipoints. This (tentative) conclusion that bipointed specimens were not part of the regular bone artefact assemblage in use at Liang Lemdubu and Liang Nabulei Lisa may set the Aru Islands outside of a Late Pleistocene to mid-Holocene cultural area that included the Bird's Head and the northern Maluku Province.

References

Anell, B. 1955. *Contribution to the History of Fishing in the Southern Seas.* Uppsala: Almqvist and Wiksells Boktryckeri Ab. *Studia Ethnographica Upsaliensia* IX.

Arndt, S. and M. Newcomer. 1986. Breakage patterns on prehistoric bone points: an experimental study. In D.A. Roe (ed), *Studies in the Upper Palaeolithic of Britain and Northwest Europe*, pp. 165–73. *BAR International Series* 296.

Bird, C. and C. Beeck. 1980. Bone points and spatulae: salvage ethnography in southwest Australia. *Archaeology and Physical Anthropology in Oceania* 15:168–71.

Blackwood, B. 1950. *The Technology of a Modern Stone Age People in New Guinea.* Oxford: Oxford University Press. *Occasional Papers on Technology* 3.

Campana, D.V. 1989. *Natufian and Protoneolithic Bone Tools: The Manufacture and Use of Bone Implements in the Zagros and the Levant.* Oxford: B.A.R. *BAR International Series* 494.

Codrington, R.H. 1969[1891]. *The Melanesians. Studies in their Anthropology and Folklore.* Oxford: Clarendon Press.

Dortch, C.E. 1984. *Devil's Lair, a Study in Prehistory.* Perth: Western Australian Museum.

Downie, J.E. and J.P. White. 1978. Balof Shelter, New Ireland — Report on a small excavation. *Records of the Australian Museum* 31:762–802.

Evans, F.G. 1973. *Mechanical properties of bone.* Springfield: Charles C. Thomas.

Guthrie, R.D. 1983. Osseous projectile points: biological considerations affecting raw material selection and design among Paleolithic and Paleoindian peoples. In J. Clutton-Brock and C. Grigson (eds), *Animals and Archaeology. 1. Hunters and Their Prey*, pp. 273–94. *BAR International Series* 163.

Hale, H.M. and N.B. Tindale. 1930. Notes on some human remains in the Lower Murray Valley. *Records of the South Australian Museum* 4:145–218.

Johnson, E. 1985. Current developments in bone technology. In M.B. Schiffer (ed.), *Advances in Archaeological Method and Theory*, 8:157–235. New York: Academic Press.

Jones, R. and I. Johnson. 1985. Rockshelter excavations: Nourlangie and Mt Brockman Massifs. In R. Jones (ed.), *Archaeological Research in Kakadu National Park*, pp. 39–76. Canberra: Australian National Parks and Wildlife Service. *Special Publication* 13.

Knecht, H. 1997. Projectile points of bone, antler, and stone. Experimental explorations of manufacture and use. In H. Knecht (ed.), *Projectile Technology*, pp. 191–212. New York: Plenum Press.

Lampert, R.J. 1966. An excavation at Durras North, New South Wales. *Archaeology and Physical Anthropology in Oceania* 1:83–118.

Lampert, R.J. 1971. *Burrill Lake and Currarong: Coastal Sites in Southern New South Wales*. Canberra: Department of Prehistory, Research School of Pacific Studies and Asian Studies, Australian National University. *Terra Australis* 1.

Majid, Z. 1982. The west mouth, Niah, in the prehistory of Southeast Asia. *Sarawak Museum Journal (N.S.)* 31:1–200. *Special Monograph* 3.

Massola, A. 1956. Australian fish hooks and their distribution. *National Museum of Victoria, Memoirs* 22:1–16. *Anthropology Series* 1.

McCarthy, F.D. 1940. The bone point, known as *Muduk*, in eastern Australia. *Records of the Australian Museum* 20:313–9.

Merton, H. 1910. *Forschungsreise in den Sudostlichen Molukken (Aru- und Kei Inseln)*. Frankfurt am.M.: Senckenbergischen Naturforschenden Geschellschaft.

Mulvaney, D.J. 1960. Archaeological excavations at Fromm's Landing on the lower Murray Valley, South Australia. *Proceedings of the Royal Society of Victoria* 72:53–85.

Olsen, S.L. 1984. Analytical Approaches to the Manufacture and Use of Bone Artifacts in Prehistory. Unpublished PhD thesis, University of London, London.

Olsen, S.L. and I.C. Glover. 2004. The bone industry of Ulu Leang 1 and Leang Burung 1 rockshelters, Sulawesi, Indonesia, in its regional context. In S.G. Keates and J.M. Pasveer (eds), *Quaternary Research in Indonesia*, pp. 273–99. Leiden: A.A. Balkema Publishers. *Modern Quaternary Research in Southeast Asia* 18.

Pasveer, J.M. 2004. *The Djief Hunters: 26,000 Years of Rainforest Exploitation on the Bird's Head of Papua, Indonesia*. Lisse: A.A. Balkema. *Modern Quaternary Research in Southeast Asia* 17.

Pasveer, J.M. and P. Bellwood. 2004. Prehistoric bone artefacts from the northern Moluccas, Indonesia. In S.G. Keates and J.M. Pasveer (eds), *Quaternary Research in Indonesia*, pp. 301–59. Lisse: A.A. Balkema Publishers. *Modern Quaternary Research in Southeast Asia* 18.

Pearce, J. and R. Luff. 1994. The taphonomy of cooked bone. In R. Luff and P. Rowley-Conwy (eds), *Whither Environmental Archaeology?*, pp. 51–6. Oxford: Oxbow Books. *Oxbow Monograph* 38.

Pickering, M.P. 1979. Aboriginal Bone Tools from Victoria. Unpublished B.A. Honours thesis, La Trobe University, Melbourne.

von Rosenberg, C.B.H. 1867. *Reis Naar de Zuidoostereilanden Gedaan in 1865 op last der Regering van Nederlandsch-Indie*. 's-Gravenhage: Martinus Nijhoff.

Schrire, C. 1982. *The Alligator Rivers: Prehistory and Ecology in Western Arnhem Land*. Canberra: Department of Prehistory, Research School of Pacific Studies and Asian Studies, Australian National University. *Terra Australis* 7.

Shipman, P., G. Foster, and M. Schoeninger. 1984. Burnt bones and teeth: an experimental study of color, morphology, crystal structure and shrinkage. *Journal of Archaeological Science* 11:307–25.

Sillitoe, P. 1988. *Made in Niugini: Technology in the Highlands of Papua New Guinea*. London: British Museum Publications.

Simanjuntak, T. 2004. New insight on the prehistoric chronology of Gunung Sewu, Indonesia. In S.G. Keates and J.M. Pasveer (eds), *Quaternary Research in Indonesia*, pp. 9–30. Leiden: A.A. Balkema Publishers. *Modern Quaternary Research in Southeast Asia* 18.

Ubelaker, D.H. 1978. *Human Skeletal Remains*. Chicago: Aldine Publishing Co.

Webb, C. 1987. Use-Wear on Bone Tools: An Experimental Program and Three Case-Studies from South-East Australia. Unpublished Honours thesis, La Trobe University, Melbourne.

Webb, C. and J. Allen. 1990. A functional analysis of Pleistocene bone tools from two sites in Southwest Tasmania. *Archaeology in Oceania* 25:75–8.

12

The Last Glacial Maximum Human Burial from Liang Lemdubu in Northern Sahulland

David Bulbeck

School of Archaeology and Anthropology, The Australian National University, Canberra, ACT, Australia

Introduction

The one metre square test pit (Test Pit C) excavated by O'Connor, Spriggs and Veth at the Liang Lemdubu site, Aru, recovered a semi-complete human skeleton. When alive, the individual ('Lemdubu Woman') had been a tall woman of around 166cm in height, with a rugged skull and quite large teeth by female standards (Fig. 12.1). Age at death is estimated at around 30 years old based on the morphology of the pubic symphysis and stage of tooth wear. The vertebral discs, right tibia and right clavicle present a series of holes which are suggestive of metastatic lesions. All parts of the skeleton are definitely represented except the fingers and toes. The bulk of the material was recovered within the cramped depth of 30cm between Spits 18 and 23, and the remains include tilted and vertically inverted elements. These observations are incompatible with a standard primary burial and, in the most likely scenario, the corpse had decomposed to a state of bones and connective tissue which had then been buried in bundles.

As discussed in Chapter 9 (this volume), the age of the burial would be placed at around 16,000–18,000 years ago based on its stratigraphic context and ESR dating of its tooth from Spit 19, but we also have a conflicting, middle Holocene chronometric determination on the bone. Although for the reasons outlined in Chapter 9 the bone date has been dismissed as unreliable, it was thought that for the sake of completeness Lemdubu Woman should be compared with both Pleistocene and Holocene aged skeletal materials.

The two very different estimates of the skeleton's age would imply either a similarity with terminal Pleistocene Australian female specimens, such as those from Coobool Creek in southeast Australia, or an affinity with middle Holocene Nusatenggara female specimens such as Leang Toge (see Fig. 12.2). Few morphological comparisons support the latter alternative and, instead, a diagnostic likeness clearly emerges with ancient Australians. The Lemdubu burial should therefore be considered representative of the Last Glacial Maximum inhabitants of the northwestern rim of the

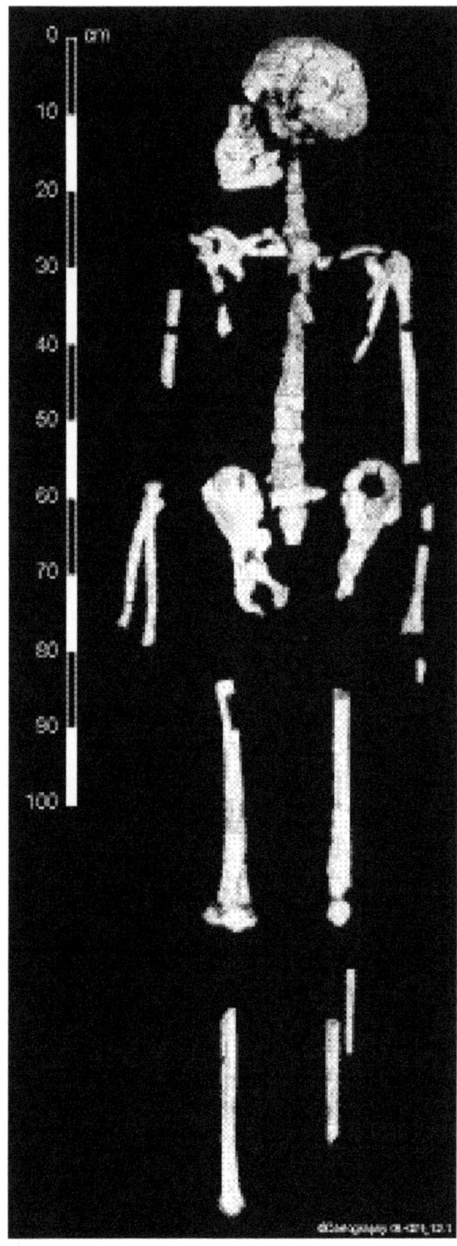

Figure 12.1 Liang Lemdubu: reconstruction of the semi-complete skeleton

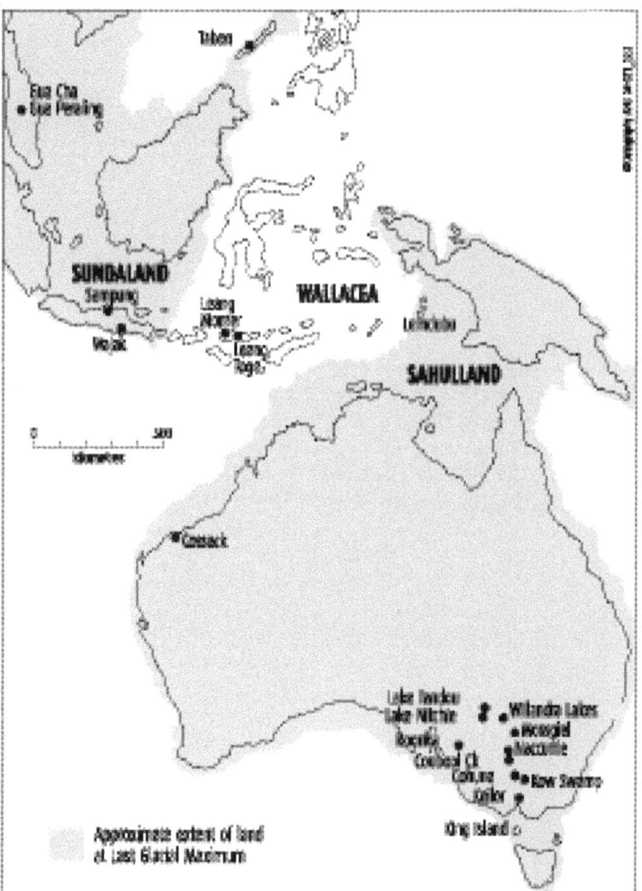

Figure 12.2 Map indicating fossil sites mentioned in the text (Lambert Azimuthal Equal-Area Projection)

vast, former continent of Sahulland. While there certainly are differences with penecontemporary southeastern Sahulland burials, these may be attributed to chronological and/or geographical variation.

Treatment and Disposition of the Material

The author received approximately 400 fragments of suspected human material in over 50 plastic bags whose contents ranged from a single fragment to associations that weighed over 500g (Table 12.1). Most had been identified as human bone during the excavation, supplemented with further fragments when Ken Aplin separated the faunal and the human material. A small number of fragments proved not to be human, and a similar number are human but evidently do not belong to Lemdubu Woman. Because none of the material had been cleaned, the author undertook this labour by brushing off the loose adhering sediments, and employing fine, stainless-steel instruments (as used

Table 12.1 Liang Lemdubu: distribution of human material from the excavation

SPIT	WEIGHT (g)	NO. FRAGS	CONTENTS
1	0.5	2	Distal pedal phalanx, tooth enamel fragment*
6	0.1	1	Molar fragment*
7	4.7	2	Sphenoid body, right lunate*
10	0.8	1	Proximal manual phalanx*
11	0.3	1	Left second distal pedal phalanx~
12	2.1	2	Femur*, calcaneus~
14	0.5	1	Femur*
15	1.3	1	Basicranium~
16	0.5	1	Right lower first incisor
17	15.9	2	Right femur epicondyle
18	188.9	29	Right femur, right tibia, right humerus, left ulna, calvarial fragments
19	946.7	80	Left humerus, left radius, right ulna, calvarium, face, mandible, teeth, cervical & upper thoracic vertebrae, right lunate, rib & scapula fragments#
20	450.0	79	Right femur, right tibia, left femur, left tibia, right fibula, calvarial fragments, right upper third molar, cervical & thoracic vertebrae, lower lumbar & upper sacral vertebrae, rib & scapula fragments, right & left pelvic iliac fragments, metacarpal fragment
21	451.3	142	Right tibia, right humerus, left ulna, left humerus, right ulna, left femur, right radius, left fibula, 2 teeth, calvarial frags, lower thoracic & upper lumbar vertebrae, ribs, right & left scapulae, right & left partial clavicles, sternum frag, right pelvic iliac fragments
22	285.0	39	Right tibia, left femur, left humerus, right radius, left fibula, right I_1, rib & sacral fragments, right & left clavicle frags, sternum frags, right & left pelvic iliac & pubic fragments, right talus
23	97.3	11	Right & left patellae, right pelvic iliac, ischial & pubic fragments, left pelvic ischial & pubic fragments, right talus
25	1.1	1	Rib fragment+
TOTAL	2447.0	394	

NB: *well-burnt and light in weight; ~unburnt but not clearly Lemdubu Woman; #the remains further include one forearm and two humerus fragments, all burnt, evidently not Lemdubu Woman (47.3 g); +only possibly human

in anatomical sectioning) to remove the thin calcreted skin which coated most of the fragments. Great care was taken to reveal the underlying surface morphology without damage to the original bone. Washing and chemical methods of cleaning were avoided to ensure there would be no ionic contamination of the fossilized tissue. During the cleaning, five samples of the loose adhering sediment (in the bags marked 200, 234, 235, 236, and 248) were collected and stored in plastic bags. These were passed onto Matthew Spriggs in June 2000 to assist Rainer Grün's efforts in dating the skeleton through Electron Spin Resonance.

The osteological material is at an advanced stage of semi-fossilization and its condition appears no different from that of the faunal fragments seen by the author. None of the fragments assignable to Lemdubu Woman show signs of heat exposure. However, the distal diaphysis of her right humerus exhibited four parallel, horizontal cutmarks on its dorsal face and three angled parallel cutmarks on its ventral face, while a deep, sharp cutmark was observed on the proximal fragment of her right ulna. These incisions could suggest that some dismemberment of the corpse had been necessary to help cram the remains into the bounds of the grave cavity. Three cutmarks were also noted posterior to the acetabulum of one of the pelves, but the incisions appeared fresh and could be damage from the excavators' trowels.

After cleaning, the fragments were weighed, identified to their skeletal element, and glued with Tarzan's Grip™ as far as possible into complete elements. Red modelling plasticene was sometimes used to simulate missing portions of bone and to hold fragments together along unstable joins. Information on the excavated context of the fragments was recorded in notes and laboratory sketches of the reconstructed elements during reconstruction. I concurrently recorded metrical and morphological features which are more easily observed on fragments than on complete or re-assembled specimens (thickness of the cranial bone, its diploe and inner and outer tables; morphology and thicknesses of the medullary cavity and the cortical walls of the limb bone shafts; and so forth). These measurements, and other small-scale measurements like tooth diameters, were made with a Mitutoyo electronic calliper accurate to 0.01mm. The remainder of my measurements were performed with a GPM spreading calliper, Stalon sliding calliper, Stalon coordinate calliper, GPM protractor (angulometer), and the ANU Biological Anthropology Laboratory's mandible board, according to the specifications in the measurement definitions sourced in due course below.

Following reconstruction and photography, Lemdubu Woman was repatriated to the National Research Centre of Archaeology, Jakarta, in late 2000. This photographed and remitted material (Fig. 12.1) excludes a residue of the extremity and other fragments which were finally identified as human in 2001 and passed onto the author. Further, prior to remittance, three samples were extracted from the skeleton and sacrificed to assist in dating it. One of these specimens is the lower left third molar, which had been retrieved as a loose tooth from Spit 19. In addition, a section was cut from the medial diaphysis fragment of the right femur (retrieved from Spit 18) for the purposes of the AMS date from AINSE, and Donald Pate's attempted stable isotope ratio assay. Another sample of femoral bone was later submitted to the AMS dating facilities at Oxford as a check on the AINSE determination.

The distribution of the human material is detailed in Table 12.1. Ninety-nine per cent of the remains, by weight, was recorded between Spits 18 and 22. Within this band, the elements' distribution is not random, and roughly proceeds from the skull and limb bones higher up, to the vertebrae, ribs and scapulae, then the clavicles, pelves and sternum, and the patellae at the bottom. Hand and foot bones are scarce, and comprise merely a single right carpal (the lunate) and metacarpal fragment identified at an intermediate level, and three right talus fragments observed among the most deeply buried remains. The recorded depths of fragments from the same skeletal element indicate that the left femur, left humerus, right radius, left ulna, pelves and most of the vertebral column had been oriented or, more probably, slanted right way up at the time of excavation, whereas the right femur, right tibia and right ulna had sat (or been tilted) upside down. The uppermost skull fragments belong to the left calotte; slightly beneath them were the superior calotte fragments, face and jaws; and the deepest fragments pertain to the right posterior calvarium — as though the skull had leaned behind the right shoulder at the time of burial. The vertebral discs from the fourth lumbar to the second sacral vertebral positions were recovered as a single block cemented together at the discs (Fig. 12.3).

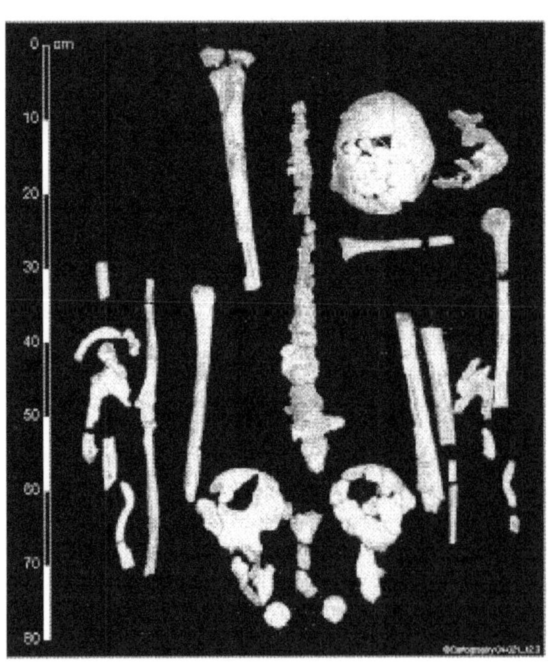

Figure 12.3 Liang Lemdubu: approximate distribution of the elements of Lemdubu Woman in the test pit, with the vertical scale exaggerated about 2.5 times, and elements represented in vertical orientation

Moreover, 65% of the human material by weight came from Spits 18 to 20 where the excavators noted a boulder which partly covered the burial, but with the bone fragments often protruding along the sides of the boulder. Only the right radius, left fibula, clavicles, sternum, and patellae completely underlay the boulder (see Table 12.1). It seems likely that the boulder had originally been placed to cover the burial, but sank into the deposits and displaced many of the fragments upwards. Further upward movement of the right lower first incisor (which clearly belongs to Lemdubu Woman) to Spit 16, and three basicranial and extremity fragments (which may belong to the burial) to Spits 11 to 15, could have occurred through subsequent scuffage. These observations permit three possible scenarios.

Lemdubu Woman could have been a primary burial seated in a tightly curled hocker position after the hands and feet (except the parts closest to the articulation with the limbs) had been removed. At a later stage, following decomposition of the corpse, the mourners could have exposed the skeleton, handled three of the limb bones, and then replaced them upside down, at the same time disturbing other bones. Perhaps the burial had been covered by loose grave fill as the corpse decomposed, and the boulder was placed to seal the grave after the bones had been handled. Alternatively, the boulder could have covered the corpse while it decomposed, and then been re-positioned at final burial. Raath's (1996:17, 87) study of ethnographic burial practices among Western Australian Aborigines would account for this scenario in terms of incapacitating the deceased through wreaking intentional damage to the manual extremities, followed by the 'inquest' when the grave is re-opened, and the defleshed bones are inspected to identify the culprits responsible for the death. Raath (1996:100) further noted instances where the corpse had been jumped or stood upon to make it fit into a grave no more than two feet (65cm) deep, and a practice like this could account for the compression of a primary burial into the restricted space where most of the bones belonging to Lemdubu Woman were found.

Two further scenarios may be entertained, and in both of them the boulder would have been placed on top of the burial at the end of the mortuary ceremony. In the second possible scenario, the hands and legs might have been severed from the corpse, the feet from the legs, and the left leg or both legs separated into thigh and calf. The intentions could have been to disable the deceased and/or fit the body parts into a restricted cavity (cf. Raath 1996:100). The torso with its attached skull and arms would have been thrust into the grave, and the legs fitted in with the knee joints at the bottom, either with the thigh and calf as separate parts (applicable at least to the left leg), or tightly flexed with the knee oriented downwards (possibly applicable to the right leg).

In the third scenario, which is the most parsimonious and plausible, the corpse had been largely defleshed through exposure to the elements (cf. Raath 1996:120–3) or preliminary burial, but still partly held together by ligaments when the act of secondary burial occurred. The mourners would have overlooked most of the hands and feet when they collected the body parts for secondary burial, then redeposited the remainder of the corpse in bundles similar to those suggested for the second scenario. The approximately upright orientation of most of Lemdubu Woman's skeleton could have resulted from residual preservation of some connective tissue at the time of secondary burial, or the detail of the mortuary procedure.

The minuscule assemblage of human remains that are burnt (Table 12.1) represent the deposition of human scraps unrelated to the main burial event. We may infer this because the tooth fragments and lunate in the upper spits, and the burnt arm bone fragments found in Spit 19, duplicate osteological elements that are unambiguously attributed to Lemdubu Woman. The Spit 19 fragments mentioned here may have been deposited as part of the grave fill, or may have lain at the same level with the burial in a different part of the test pit. However, the burnt fragments from the upper spits must have postdated the burial.

The unburnt pedal bone from Spits 11 and 12, and the Spit 15 basicranial fragment, may or may not relate to Lemdubu Woman. Their unburnt status is not diagnostic of their mode of deposition because post-depositional processes (e.g. incorporation in the walls of a hearth scooped into the deposits) are responsible for most cases of burnt archaeological bone. These fragments are compatible with all three burial scenarios. They could have dropped onto the shelter floor during a secondary burial, or, if a manipulated primary burial had occurred, the pedal bones might have been detached during dismemberment of the corpse's extremities. While it could be argued that these three unburnt fragments would allow for the grave to have been cut from a level as high as Spit 11, the burial would still be marginally Pleistocene because, as noted elsewhere in this volume, the Pleistocene-Holocene boundary is placed at around Spit 10. Further to the point, they could have derived from Lemdubu Woman and still not rule out cutting of the grave from much lower in the deposits, e.g. Spit 17 where the human remains begin in earnest (Table 12.1). This is because, if they had been detached from the main skeleton at the time of burial, they could have been scuffed upwards as further deposits accumulated, or been moved upwards through localized disturbance such as construction of a hearth. Thus the human scraps in the higher spits do not constitute evidence against the burial of Lemdubu Woman from Spit 17 (dated to about 17,000 radiocarbon years ago), because none of them need relate to that individual and, even if any do, they would have been susceptible to upward post-depositional disturbance.

In summary, the mortuary ceremony for Lemdubu Woman most probably occurred at around 17,000 radiocarbon years ago. It was neither a simple primary burial nor the secondary disposal of completely disarticulated bones and fragments, but lay somewhere in between. The cutmarks observed on the right humerus and ulna provide direct evidence for the scenario which invokes dismemberment of the corpse, but similar cutmarks could also have been effected at some point in either of the other two possibilities, the inquest and secondary burial scenarios. Whatever the precise detail, the burial displays similarities with ethnographic practices recorded among Western Australian Aborigines (Raath 1996:139–42).

Sex and Age Assessment

The adult status of the burial is clear from the fully fused status of all of the extant epiphyses, the fused basilar synchondrosis, and the occluded status of all teeth including the third molars. The morphology of the pelvis (Fig. 12.4) demonstrates the specimen's female status (cf. Brothwell 1981:62–3). The right, greater sciatic notch is very wide, measuring 87°, high within the female range found among humans generally (~60–95°), and above the male range (~30–65°). The left side (but not the right) shows a well-developed pre-auricular sulcus, another female marker. In relation to the sexually dimorphic, innominate measurements recorded on Australian Aborigines (Davivongs 1963a), the Lemdubu values compare well with those of female Australians (Table 12.2). Only on ischial length and coxal index are the Lemdubu values masculine trending, though still within the female range. Elsewhere, Lemdubu falls outside the male range on three indicators, and barely scrapes in the male range on several others (the female status of the Leang Toge innominates, included in Table 12.2 for comparative purposes, is even clearer than is the case with Lemdubu Woman). The gracile status of Lemdubu Woman's clavicles, especially the height at the mid-point (eight millimetres right, 7.5mm left) which falls below the male Aboriginal range, and is low

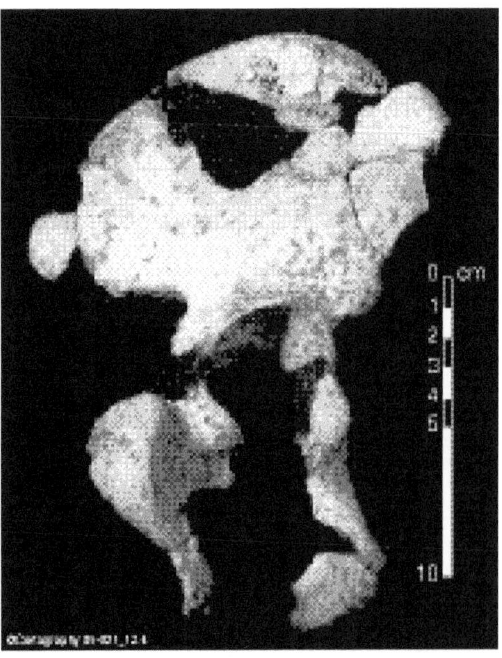

Figure 12.4 Liang Lemdubu: the Lemdubu Woman right innominate

within the female range (Ray 1959:219), further indicates a female status. Most other observations on the postcranial skeleton are consistent with this assessment.

If the skull alone had been present it would certainly have been (mis-) classified as male (Table 12.3). Lemdubu Woman scores at least 15 on the seven sex discrimination traits of Larnach and Freedman (1964), and 14 in Brown's (1989:19–20) revised system, and so would lie in the male range as has been determined for both recent Australian Aborigines and for the markedly rugged, terminal Pleistocene crania from Coobool Creek in the Murray Valley (Brown 1989:19–25). However, it need not follow that Lemdubu Woman's population was morphologically more rugged than the population to which Coobool Creek belonged, as she may represent the zone of male-female overlap that is to be expected in any population.

Lemdubu Woman had evidently died before reaching middle age. Some closure of the ectocranial aspect of the coronal, sagittal and lambdoid sutures would usually be expected by the thirties (Szilvássy 1988:430), but there is no sign of this on the Lemdubu skull. The first, second and third lower molars all show tooth wear that closely matches the average expression for Anglo-Saxon individuals of about 25 years of age; as the gradient of tooth wear closely matches this Anglo-Saxon standard, the rate of occlusal wear must have been similar to the Anglo-Saxon average and, accordingly, Lemdubu Woman could not have died at an age very different from 25 (Miles 1963). However, the morphology of the pubic symphysis suggests an older individual. A ventral rampart can be observed in an active stage of formation on both the left and right faces,

Table 12.2 Liang Lemdubu and Leang Toge innominate measurements compared to Australians

MEASUREMENT	LEMDUBU	L. TOGE	AUSTRALIAN FEMALE MEAN	AUSTRALIAN MALE RANGE
Maximum innominate length	188 (R), ≥190 (L)	180 (L)	182.0±7.3	178-221
Iliac breadth	≥139 (R)	143 (L)	142.2±7.2	133-167
Coxal Index	≥73.9 (R)	79.4 (L)	78.0±2.8	70.1-80.9
Length of pubic symphysis	32 (R), 33 (L)	-	34.5±3.1	27-44
Acetabulum vertical diameter*	44 (R, L)	43 (R)	45.9±2.0	45-58
Acetabulum horizontal diameter	46.5 (R)	43 (L)	45.5±1.9	45-57
Pubic length*	74 (R)	-	69.2±5.1	54-73
Ischial length	82 (R)	-	74.7±3.6	74-91
Ischium-pubis index*	90.2 (R)	-	92.7±6.0	70.9-86.8
Greater sciatic notch greatest width	≤52 (R)	47 (L)	50.9±3.8	37-55
Greater sciatic notch greatest depth	~23 (R)	17 (L)	26.1±2.7	18-31
Greater sciatic notch index	~44.2 (R)	36.2 (L)	51.4±5.5	37.5-77.5

NB: measurements in mm; (R) indicates right side, and (L) indicates left side. Australian data from Davivongs (1963a), where the measurements are also defined. Leang Toge measurements from Jacob (1967:87). Lemdubu measurements fall outside the Australian male range on the asterisked measurements and index

Table 12.3 Liang Lemdubu: sex assessment of the skull by Australian standards

TRAIT	EXPRESSION	BROWN'S (1989:19-20) SCORE	LARNACH AND FREEDMAN'S (1964) SCORE
Glabella development	Martin 5	3	3
Superciliary ridges	Medium	2	2
Zygomatic trigone	Medium	2	2
(Right) malar tuberosity	Slight	1	1
(Left) mastoid process size	~122 (very large)	3	3
Palate size module	41.4	2	3
Nuchal musculature	Not extant	1-3	1-3
All seven traits		14-16	15-17

NB: see section on cranial morphology below for further background flanked by a largely planed surface on both sides of the rampart on the left pubis, and a slightly more billowed surface on the right pubis. These features correspond to median ages in the 30s, and age ranges whose minimum value often exceeds 27 or 28 years old, for Components I to III as identified by Gilbert and McKern (1973) for female pubic bones (Table 12.4). Further, in terms of the Suchey-Brooks scheme for female pubic age determination, both of Lemdubu Woman's surfaces would correspond to phase IV, whose mean age is 38.2 and 95% range is 26–70 years old (Brooks and Suchey 1990). An age at death of approximately 30 years old strikes a balance between the various indications.

Table 12.4 Liang Lemdubu: morphology of Lemdubu Woman's pubic surfaces (Gilbert & McKern criteria)

SIDE	COMPONENT	STAGE	AGE MEAN AND RANGE
Right	I	4	40.8 (28-59)
Right	II	3	38.8 (27-57)
Right	III	4	39.9 (21-58)
Left	I	3	31.0 (22-40)
Left	II	3	38.8 (27-57)
Left	III	3	35.6 (22-57)

Teeth

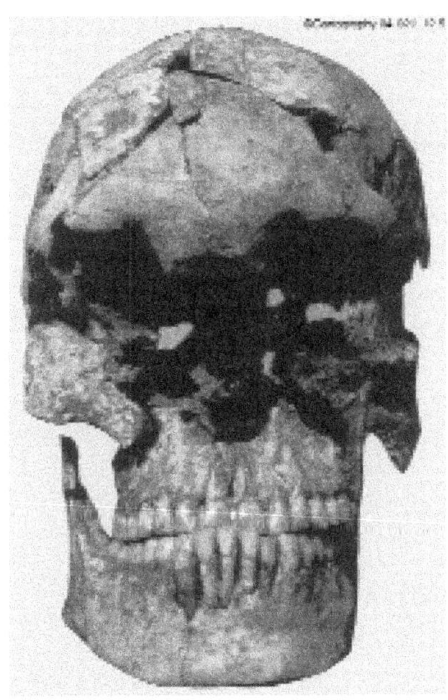

Figure 12.5 Liang Lemdubu: frontal view of the skull

Lemdubu Woman's occlusal wear is modest by hunter-gatherer standards. It almost always falls between the early stages of enamel polishing, especially on the upper third molars, and the exposure of small pools of dentine on the cusps, i.e. grades 2 or 3 wear in terms of Smith's scale (cf. Hillson 1996:232). More advanced wear was observed only on two of the first molars, in the form of an early stage of Smith's stage 4, involving slightly larger dentine pools on the buccal cusps. Interproximal wear on the teeth is slight but the individual's bite had nonetheless reached an edge-to-edge stage by the time of death (Fig. 12.5).

One of the second molars was evidently free of calculus, but otherwise slight calculus formation was observed on all of the teeth, and always at a coronal location (reflecting minimal resorption of the gums). Slight blunting resorption was noted at 15 of the tooth sites, involving all of the tooth classes between the incisors and the second molars. Slight buccal dehiscences were recorded at the sites of both lateral maxillary incisors, both maxillary canines, both first maxillary molars, and three of the premolars. Small interproximal septa were recorded at the site of the left lower canine, and in between the right upper premolars, the right lower premolars, and the lower left second premolar and first molar. Otherwise the extant alveolar bone looks in excellent condition, and no traces of caries were evident. At the time of her demise, Lemdubu Woman had had a sound and fully functional dentition.

The mesio-distal lengths and bucco-lingual breadths of the teeth were measured twice, in the first instance before they had been replaced in the jaws, and in the second instance (without reference to the original measurements) as members of the restored dentition. The mesio-distal measurements usually varied between the two occasions, with a discrepancy of up to 0.7mm, whereas the bucco-lingual diameters were identical on approximately half of the measurements, and, where they differed, did so by less than 0.2mm. The greater reliability of the bucco-lingual measurements thus provides another reason, in addition to their reduced alteration through interproximal wear (e.g. Brown 1992), to prefer them over mesio-distal diameters in drawing comparisons with neighbouring populations.

The size of the teeth of Lemdubu Woman (Table 12.5) may be regarded as approximately the same as the size of the mid-Holocene Flores male teeth. In the comparison with Leang Toge, which also is female, Lemdubu has larger mesio-distal lengths in 9/13 cases, and larger bucco-lingual breadths in 11/16 instances (Table 12.5). In the comparison with the 'other Flores' teeth, which are predominantly male — as most of the specimens with teeth are sexed as male and the others are unsexed (Jacob 1967:96–113) — any size discrepancy diminishes. The 'other Flores' teeth are larger on 6/16 breadths (the more reliable comparison) and 8/16 lengths. If we compare cross-sectional tooth area (Brace and Hinton 1981), notwithstanding the uncertainty of relying on mesio-distal diameters, the value for Lemdubu Woman of 1353mm^2 is essentially indistinguishable from the value of 1358mm^2 for 'other Flores'. As demonstrated elsewhere, the middle Holocene Flores teeth are overall smaller than those of (mixed-sex) recent Australian Aborigines (Bulbeck 1981:Fig. 4–8).

Lemdubu Woman's tooth size falls broadly in between Australia's terminal Pleistocene (Coobool Creek/Kow Swamp) and recent average female tendencies, albeit showing the idiosyncratic variation to be expected of any individual. Seven of the teeth (in the premolar/upper first molar region) have breadths that exceed the averages in any comparative Australian series, contrasting with eight other teeth that have breadths beneath any comparative Australian average (Table 12.6). The overall slightly smaller tooth size than the values recorded for terminal Pleistocene Murray Valley Aboriginals could reflect individual, chronological and/or geographic variation.

Morphological traits were recorded on the Lemdubu teeth according to the grades of the Arizona State University (ASU) system, with reference to the casts illustrating the standards for the various grades of expression wherever possible (Hillson 1996:85–102; Scott and Turner 1997:Chapter 2). Dental morphology is of limited value in determining an individual's affinities,

Table 12.5 Liang Lemdubu: diameters (mm) of the burial's teeth (prior to replacement in the jaws) compared to mid-Holocene Flores average diameters (from Jacob 1967:82, 103)

	MESIO-DISTAL LENGTHS				BUCCO-LINGUAL BREADTHS			
	LEMDUBU LEFT	LEMDUBU RIGHT	LEANG TOGE	OTHER FLORES	LEMDUBU LEFT	LEMDUBU RIGHT	LEANG TOGE	OTHER FLORES
Upper central incisor	9.1	8.7	—	8.4	7.3	7.4	7.1	**7.7**
Upper lateral incisor	6.5	6.4	—	**6.9**	6.8	6.8	**7.0**	**7.1**
Upper canine	8.3	8.8	8.1	8.4	8.7	8.7	8.55	**9.1**
Upper first premolar	7.4	7.5	7.1	**7.5**	10.4	10.6	9.85	10.1
Upper second premolar	7.3	7.6	6.7	**7.5**	10.5	10.7	10.15	10.1
Upper first molar	11.6	11.5	10.2	10.9	13.2	13.3	11.65	12.1
Upper second molar	9.8	9.3	**9.9**	**10.0**	12.8	12.6	11.95	11.9
Upper third molar	8.7	8.5	8.5	**10.1**	11.9	11.8	11.85	11.7
Lower central incisor	5.6	6.2	5.5	5.7	6.4	6.3	6.0	6.3
Lower lateral incisor	5.6	7.0	**6.5**	6.1	6.1	6.4	**6.4**	**6.7**
Lower canine	6.8	6.9	**7.05**	**7.4**	8.3	8.0	7.75	8.1
Lower first premolar	7.8	7.6	7.3	7.2	8.7	8.9	8.6	8.5
Lower second premolar	7.5	7.1	**7.6**	**7.4**	8.4	9.0	**9.2**	**8.8**
Lower first molar	12.3	12.0	—	12.0	11.8	11.9	11.45	11.1
Lower second molar	11.9	10.8	11.25	11.4	11.0	10.8	**11.45**	10.7
Lower third molar	10.3	10.1	10.45	**11.8**	10.2	10.3	**10.8**	**10.9**

NB: Flores diameters larger than the Lemdubu average are shown in bold face particularly as Pleistocene Australians have not (to my knowledge) been studied in this regard, and the differences between recent Australians and Southeast Asians in dental morphology are merely subtle (Bulbeck 2000a:Figs 4 and 5; Scott and Turner 1997:Fig. 7.5). The Aru individual's observations are presented here (Table 12.7) in the hope of contributing to a sample of comparable fossils as may become available at a future time.

Further observations include: slight bilateral winging of the upper central incisors but no winging of the lower central incisors; absence of any mesial ridging on the upper canines, or any

Table 12.6 Liang Lemdubu: tooth breadths compared to Australian Aboriginal female averages

SIZE OF TOOTH	TEETH INVOLVED	NO.
Above both the Pleistocene and recent Australian averages, but still within the recent range	Both P^1, both P^2, both M^1, R P_1	7
Equal to Pleistocene average, greater than recent averages	R lower C, R P_2	2
Equal to Pleistocene and recent Australian averages which themselves barely differ	Both C, both I_1, R I_2, L P_1, both M_1	8
Above recent averages but below Pleistocene average	Both I^2, both M^2	4
Within range of recent averages, smaller than Pleistocene average	Both M^3, L lower C	3
Less than all Australian averages, sometimes beneath Pleistocene range (incisors) but always within recent range	Both I^1, L I_2, L P_2, both M_2, both M_3	8

NB: comparative data from Brown (1989:144–157) with reference to samples having at least five measurements for the tooth concerned. The Pleistocene sample is Kow Swamp and Coobool Creek combined. R denotes right and L denotes left

Table 12.7 Liang Lemdubu: various dental morphological traits of Lemdubu Woman (ASU system)

TRAIT	POSITION	LEFT	RIGHT	POSITION	LEFT	RIGHT
Upper incisor shovel	Central	Trace (1)	Trace (2)	Lateral	Absent (0)	Trace (1)
Upper I double shovel	Central	Trace (1)	Trace (1)	Lateral	Absent (0)	Absent (0)
Upper I curvature	Central	(2)	(3)	Lateral	(3)	(4)
I tuberculum dentale	Central	(3)	(3)	Lateral	(3)	(2)
I interruption groove	Central	Lateral	Lateral	Lateral	Lateral	Absent
Lower incisor shovel	Central	Absent (0)	Absent (0)	Lateral	Absent (0)	Absent (0)
Lower I curvature	Central	(1)	(2)	Lateral	(2)	(3)
Canine shovelling	Upper	Absent (0)	Absent (0)	Lower	Trace (1)	Trace (1)
Distal accessory ridge	Upper	Absent (0)	Absent (0)	Lower	Absent (0)	Absent (0)
C tuberculum dentale	Upper	(3)	(3)	Lower	(3)	(2)
Premolar odontome	P^1	Absent (0)	Absent (0)	P^2	Absent (0)	Absent (0)
Premolar odontome	P_1	Absent (0)	Absent (0)	P_2	Absent (0)	Absent (0)
P accessory ridges	P^1	Absent (0)	Absent (0)	P^2	Absent (0)	Absent (0)
P accessory ridges	P_1	Absent (0)	Absent (0)	P_2	Absent (0)	Absent (0)
Premolar accessory marginal tubercles	P^1	Absent (0)	Absent (0)	P^2	Absent (0)	Absent (0)
P lingual cusps	P_1	Single	Single	P_2	Double	Double
Upper M metacone	First	Full (5)	Full (5)	Second	Full (4)	Full (4)
Upper M hypocone	First	Full (5)	Full (5)	Second	Full (4)	Full (4)
Upper M metaconule	First	Absent (0)	Absent (0)	Second	Trace (1)	Absent (0)
M Carabelli's trait	First	Absent (0)	Absent (0)	Second	Absent (0)	Absent (0)
Upper M parastyle	First	Absent (0)	Absent (0)	Second	Cingulum	Cingulum
M enamel extension	First	Absent (0)	Absent (0)	Second	Absent (0)	Absent (0)
Upper molar roots	First	Three	Three	Second	Two	?
Lower molar cusp 5	First	Present (3)	Present (3)	Second	?	?
Lower M cusps 6 & 7	First	Absent (0)	Absent (0)	Second	Absent (0)	Absent (0)
Dryopithecus pattern	First	Y	Y	Second	X	X
M enamel extension	First	Absent (0)	Absent (0)	Second	Absent (0)	Absent (0)
Lower M protostylid	First	Absent (0)	Absent (0)	Second	Absent (0)	Absent (0)

distosagittal ridge on the first upper premolars, or size and shape diminution of the upper lateral incisors; and the single-rooted status of the lower canine and first lower premolar (both observed only on the right side). The upper third molars show slight metacone reduction (ASU 3) and considerable hypocone reduction (ASU 2 and 3), threshold expression of Carabelli's trait (ASU 1), no enamel extension but a unilateral (right) enamel pearl on the distal root, unilateral (left) trace presence of the metaconule, unilateral (right) expression of the parastyle as a faint cingulum, and a single root (observable only on the left side). The lower third molars have very large fourth cusps but no evidence of supernumerary cusps apart from a metaconulid on the right side. They also display an X *Dryopithecus* pattern bilaterally, absence of the anterior fovea or enamel extension, a unilateral (right) protostylid (ASU 3), and two roots on the left side (the only lower molar whose number of roots could be observed).

Of the observed traits, the upper incisor winging may be the most interesting as it tends to occur more commonly among East Asians (and Micronesians) than elsewhere in the world, especially compared to Australian and New Guinea people (Scott and Turner 1997:Fig. 5.2). However, it is hardly diagnostic, and all the other observations, including the tendency to mild shovelling on the anterior teeth, could be equally comfortably fitted within a southwest Pacific or Southeast Asian population affinity (cf. Scott and Turner 1997:Chapter 5).

Mildly expressed, single grooves and pitted lines of macroscopic enamel hypoplasia were noted on eight of the teeth (Table 12.8). The heights of the hypoplasic lines above the cervico-enamel junction of the crown were related to the enamel-defect matching system of Hillson (1996:Table 6.3). These observations provide sufficient evidence to recognise only one disruption to the individual's development that had resulted in interruption to enamel formation. That event, involving the first molars and central incisors, would be best interpreted as a Hillson 'C' event, and involve a stage of dental development that would correspond to an approximate age of three to four years old. Mild physiological disruption associated with weaning, when the individual had to develop her own antibodies rather than rely on those from lactation, would provide a plausible explanation for these observations.

Table 12.8 Liang Lemdubu: macroscopic enamel hypoplasia observed on Lemdubu Woman

TOOTH	SEVERITY	HEIGHT (MM)	CROWN HEIGHT (MM)	POSITION
Left M_1	Slight	2.5	~7.1	Intermediate
Right M_1	Slight	2.2	~7.0	Cervical
Left M^1	Slight	2.5	~8.0	Cervical
Left I^1	Moderate	2.5	10.8	Cervical
Right I^1	Slight	3.3	10.5	Low intermediate
Left I_1	Slight	1.5	8.2	Cervical
Right I_1	Slight	2.5	8.7	Cervical
Left M_3	Slight	1.8	6.3	Cervical

Cranial Morphology

Observations on the cranial morphology of Lemdubu Woman were made predominantly following the system of Larnach and Macintosh (1966), as presented in Tables 12.3 and 12.9. Supplementary semi-discrete cranial traits were noted, where possible, according to the inventories listed by Kellock and Parsons (1971), Berry (1974), and Brothwell (1981:95), and are included in the textual description. Most of the utilized cranial measures are those employed by Pietrusewsky (1984:55), including those in Martin's system (Martin and Saller 1957:453–81), which are denoted with an 'M' in brackets in Table 12.10. Other measurements come from Howells

Table 12.9 Liang Lemdubu: craniomorphological observations of Lemdubu Woman following Larnach and Macintosh (1966)

TRAIT	EXPRESSION	TRAIT	EXPRESSION
Cranial index	Mesocranic	Cranial contour	Ovoid
Brow ridge type	Divided	Maximum supraborbital breadth	Large
Supraglabellar fossae	Medium	Ophrionic grooves	Medium
Temporal crests	Slight	Median frontal ridge	Absent
Supraorbital notches	Marked	Supraorbital foramina	Absent
Frontal recession	Slight	Naso-frontal articulation width	Very broad
Anterior nasal spine shape	Pointed	Anterior nasal spine size	Between Broca 1 & 2
(R) infra-orbital fossa depth	8mm (deep)	Anterior narial margins	Type 2 (non-anthropine)
Subnasal prognathism	Large	Orbital border of malar bones	Rounded
Size of right malar bone	Large	Inferior margin of zygomatic process of (R) maxilla	Markedly concave
(L) auditory exostoses	Absent	(L) external auditory meatus	Martin 3
(R) tympanic bone thickness at meatus	Thick	Glenoid fossa depth	7.5mm (R); 8mm (L)
(L) suprameatal ridge	Marked	(R) postglenoid tubercle	Large
(L) mastoid crest	Marked	(R) foramen of Huschke	Absent
(L) digastric fossa	Medium	(L) occipito-mastoid crest	Large
(L) angular torus	Absent	(L) supramastoid crest	Slight
Sagittal keeling	Trace	Pterion region articulation	Spheno-parietal
Parietal bosses	Large	Parietal foramina	Absent
Obelionic depressions	Slight	Occipital bun	Large
Inca bone	Absent	Supra-iniac fossa	Very small
Sulcus supratoralis	Absent	Transverse occipital torus	Trace ridge
(L) *foramen ovale* development	Complete	*Foramen spinosum* development & confluence with *f. ovale*	Complete; no confluence
(L) palatine torus	Large ridge	(L) transverse palatine suture direction	Anterior
Palate shape	Borderline mesuranic	Palate shape	Parabolic (L); elliptical (R)

NB: seven further traits are presented in Table 12.3. (R) indicates right side, and (L) indicates left side

Table 12.10 Liang Lemdubu: cranial measurements (mm) and main derivative expressions of Lemdubu Woman

Maximum cranial length (M1)*	179.0	Nasi-occipital length (M1d)	172.5
Maximum cranial breadth (M8)*	140.0	Basion-bregma cranial height (M17)*	133.5
Basion-nasion length (M5)*	89.0	Bi-auricular breadth (M11b)*	120.0
Bi-asterionic breadth (M12)	107.0	Maximum frontal breadth (M10)	111.0
Minimum frontal breadth (M9)	95.0	Bi-stephanic breadth (M10b)	108.0
Minimum cranial breadth (M14) (S)	~70.0	Minimum cranial breadth (WCB) (S)	~66.0
Nasion-bregma chord (M29)*	107.0	Frontal subtense (FRS, LM)	29.0
Frontal fraction (FRF)	40.0	Bregma-lambda chord (M30)*	117.0
Parietal subtense (PAS)	24.0	Parietal fraction (PAF)	56.0
Mastoid height (MDH)*	29.0	Mastoid breadth (MDB)	14.0
Mastoid antero-posterior diam. (LM)	30.0	Nasofrontal articulation width (LM)	23.0
Glabella subtense (GLS)	6.0	Supraorbital subtense (SOS)	8.5
Max. supraorbital diameter (M43)*	111.0	Fronto-malar breadth (FMB)	103.0
Nasio-frontal subtense (NAS)	12.0	Nasal breadth (M54)*	26.0
Bimaxillary breadth (M46) (S)	~97.0	Zygo-maxillary breadth (ZMB) (S)	~100.0
Cheek height (M48(4)) (R)	21.5	Cheek height (WMH) (R)	21.0
Palate length (M60)	60.0	Palate breadth (M61)*	69.0
Palate module (M60 x M61/100)	41.4	Palate index (100M61/M60)	115.0
Palate depth (LM)	13.0	Frontal index (100FRS/M29)	27.1
Mastoid process module (LM)	121.8	Cranial index (100M8/M1)	78.2

NB: (S) indicates that symmetry of the cranium was assumed to make the resulting approximate measurement. (R) indicates measurement on the right side; otherwise, the left side was used for unilateral variables. Asterisked measurements appear in the FORDISC 2.0 analysis (below)

(1973:163–83; marked by their three-letter acronym), and Larnach and Macintosh (1966:82–3; denoted 'LM' in Table 12.10).

The skull's masculine appearance stems from the strong development of the glabella, superciliary ridges and zygomatic trigone, the large diameter across the supraorbital region, the very large mastoid process whose module of ca. 122 is obtained from multiplying its three diameters, and the large palate (Figs 12.5, 12.6; Tables 12.3, 12.9, 12.10). The brow-ridge morphology arises from the bilaterally large frontal and nasal sinuses, covered by thin bone. The frontal sinuses are approximately 18mm deep antero-posteriorly, and around 15–24mm wide. The slightly asymmetric, left-skewed shape of the brows is also evident in the sinuses, so that the left nasal sinus articulates with the left frontal sinus, and its antimere lies under the nasal saddle rather than on the right side. Slight metopism is present in the form of a remnant frontal suture running from nasion to a point 20mm supero-posterior of glabella. Frontal foramen and frontal groove / notch are absent.

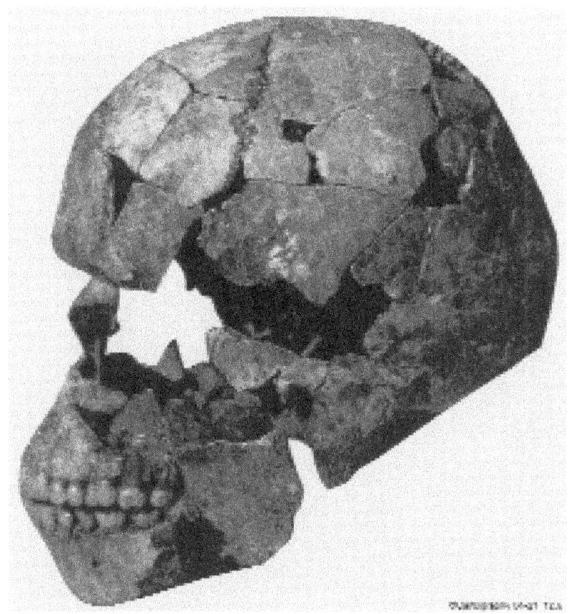

Figure 12.6 Liang Lemdubu: left lateral view of the skull

The frontal bone is well-vaulted, as shown by its curvature index of 27.1, but also angled in lateral view, owing to a flattened plane immediately anterior of bregma. The contour of the posterior braincase is even more sharply angled, owing to a steeply dropping occipital plane immediately posterior to the most bulging point along the parietal midline, and the large occipital bun. Poor preservation of the bone beneath the weakly developed, transverse occipital torus prevents any observation on the external occipital protuberance or the nuchal markings. However, absence of a highest nuchal line can be recorded on the left side, at least, and the inion region lacks any emissary foramen.

In superior view the cranium has a moderately short, ovoid shape, as the parietal bosses cover a large area but are not especially prominent. In contrast to the open ectocranial status of the coronal, sagittal and lambdoid sutures, the occipito-mastoid suture shows incipient obliteration. Parietal foramina, sagittal ossicles and a bregmatic bone are all absent. Medially, the lambdoid sutures are simple, without any signs of ossicles at lambda or an Inca bone. Laterally, however, these sutures become complicated, leading to the expression of single lambdoid ossicles 17mm medially of the asteria, and on the left side (which is observable), a biasterionic suture 20mm long, an asterionic bone, and occipito-mastoid wormian bones. The left mastoid region is extant and shows a moderately rugged morphology (see Table 12.9), a mastoid groove, mastoid notch, and a mastoid foramen which does not however occupy an extra-sutural position. The glenoid fossa has a normal morphology bilaterally (cf. Richards and Brown 1981) and, at least on the right side, is of normal form without any tympanic dehiscence. Other traits observable on the right include the single and unbridged hypoglossal canal, the single condylar facet, and the absence of any paracondylar process, precondylar tubercle, or intermediate condylar canal. On the left side, the *foramen spinosum* is closed without any accessory expression of this foramen or confluence with the *spinosum laterale*.

When the face is joined to the calvarium, it is clearly short and prognathic, with broad orbits and nasal aperture, even if few facial measurements can be accurately taken. As shown on the right side, the malar bone has a rough lower masseteric border and a single zygomatico-facial foramen, there are no maxillary hyperostoses on the buccal aspect of the alveolar arcade, and *cribra orbitalia* is present as a weak, trabecular development. This condition of partly healed *cribra orbitalia* would represent a probably mild bout of anaemia during childhood, most likely associated with physiological insult suffered at the time of weaning (cf. Webb 1995:93-9). Small maxillary hyperostoses can be observed bilaterally on the lingual aspect of the palate above the second molar. Finally, the left middle meningeal artery on the endocranial surface would be classified as Type 1 in Giuffrida-Ruggeri's system, whereas the right middle meningeal artery would more probably register as Type 2 (cf. von Bonin 1963:47–8). These Type 1 and 2 patterns appear to be the most common variants among recent East Asian and Pacific populations, with the possible exception of Polynesians (Bulbeck 1981:342).

The cranial bone is thin with a very thin inner table which is generally about half the thickness of the outer table, the latter 30–60% of the thickness of the diploe. Thicknesses at landmarks include 10.1mm at nasion, 11.3mm at glabella, 6.3mm at bregma, 5.6mm at right euryon, 5.1mm at left euryon, and about 6.0mm at the frontal bosses. These euryon, bregma and frontal thicknesses barely differ from those of Lake Mungo 1 (Willandra Lakes 1, WL1) which is renowned in the annals of Australian palaeoanthropology for its thin cranial bone (e.g. Brown 1987:49). Lemdubu Woman's skull bone thicknesses are consistently smaller than those of WL3, WL130, and especially WL19 (cf. Webb 1989:24), which are all fossil crania of small size (Bulbeck 2001:Figs 4 and 5) but which have moderate to thick cranial bone by Willandra Lake standards. Even by recent, female Aboriginal standards (Brown et al. 1979), the Lemdubu braincase registers very low nasion and bregma thicknesses, although euryon thickness is high. Its combination of thin cranial bone and relatively rugged morphology disputes the relationship between robustness and cranial bone thickness proposed by Thorne (1977) and Webb (1989:74) for Pleistocene Sahulland people.

Cranial Size

During her PhD studies at the Australian National University, Catherine Willis (1998) developed a technique to gauge cranial size, subsequently refined by the author (Bulbeck 2001). Only female crania will be considered here, but the technique would be the same for males. On any compared measurement, a cranium is classified either as very small (scoring 1), small (scoring 2), large (scoring 3), or very large (scoring 4), in comparison to recent Australian Aborigines. A measurement is 'very small' when it is smaller than the smallest value two standard deviations below the mean recorded by either Pietrusewsky (1984) or Brown (1989) on each and every mainland Australian series. 'Small' means a measurement between that value and the grand Australian mean as found by either Pietrusewsky or Brown (as appropriate). 'Large' means a measurement above the grand Australian mean, but not exceeding the mean of all the Australian series by more than two standard deviations, while 'very large' means greater than two standard deviations beyond any recorded mainland Australian mean. At least three measurements must be available for a specimen to be included. The cranium's scores, between 1 and 4, are tallied and divided by the number of measurements to produce an overall assessment of cranial size; Lemdubu Woman for instance scores 45/15 or 3.0 (Table 12.11).

The distribution of recent Australian, female cranial size is obtained by assessing all 382 adult female crania with three or more measurements published by Hrdlička (1928). Cranial size ranges between approximately 1.8 and 3.3, with an average (as expected) at about 2.5; the modal class coincides with the average as would be expected of a normal curve, which the distribution resembles albeit with some irregularities (Fig. 12.7). As previously established (Bulbeck 2001), all Late Pleistocene to early Holocene Australian crania — both male and female — differ from recent Australians in being larger, with their size lying above the recent mean, and the largest individuals lying either at the highest extreme of the Australian range or, very occasionally, beyond it.

Table 12.11 Liang Lemdubu: Lemdubu Woman in relation to boundary values for very small (below <2 SD), small (<2 SD to Mean), large (Mean to >2 SD), and very large (over >2 SD) Australian female crania

MEASUREMENT	<2 SD	MEAN	>2 SD	LEMDUBU (MM)	LEMDUBU SCORE
Maximum cranial length (P)	161.7	178.0	193.0	179	3
Maximum cranial breadth (P)	112.1	125.4	136.1	140	4
Basion-bregma height (P)	114.7	127.3	137.2	133.5	3
Basion-nasion length (P)	88.9	96.2	107.7	89	2
Basion-prosthion length (M40) (B)	88.9	100.2	111.5	-	-
Bi-auricular breadth (P)	101.3	112.1	122.8	120	3
Bi-asterionic breadth (P)	90.9	102.2	114.9	107	3
Minimum frontal breadth (P)	84.1	93.1	105.0	95	3
Bi-stephanic breadth (P)	87.2	100.2	113.8	108	3
Nasion-bregma chord (P)	96.3	106.7	121.2	107	3
Bregma-lambda chord (P)	98.9	111.3	125.5	117	3
Lambda-opisthion chord (M31) (P)	80.6	90.9	103.9	-	-
Max. supraorbital diameter (P)	95.5	103.1	112.2	111	3
Bi-orbital breadth (EKB) (P)	89.6	96.7	104.9	-	-
Bimaxillary breadth (M46) (P)	76.8	89.5	103.1	97	3
Bizygomatic breadth (M45) (B)	116.5	126.8	138.1	-	-
Nasion-prosthion (M48) (P)	52.4	62.2	71.7	-	-
Nasal height (M55) (P)	40.1	47.7	53.7	-	-
Nasal breadth (P)	21.3	25.4	30.2	26	3
Orbital breadth (M51a) (B)	39.0	42.2	45.6	-	-
Orbital height (M52) (P)	27.3	32.7	38.1	-	-
Palate (alveolar) length (B)	52.6	58.6	65.6	60	3
Palate (alveolar) breadth (P)	49.7	62.4	70.3	69	3

NB: comparative Australian Aboriginal size ranges from Pietrusewsky (1984:Tables 7, 9), indicated (P) except where unavailable, in which case size ranges are from Brown's (1989) series, indicated (B), where the sample size of measurements is greater than 14

Accordingly, if Lemdubu Woman was a Late Pleistocene inhabitant of Sahulland age, its size should be comparable to the size of Late Pleistocene or early Holocene, female Australian crania. On the other hand, a middle Holocene antiquity for the Lemdubu burial would be confirmed if it is found to resemble Leang Toge in cranial size.

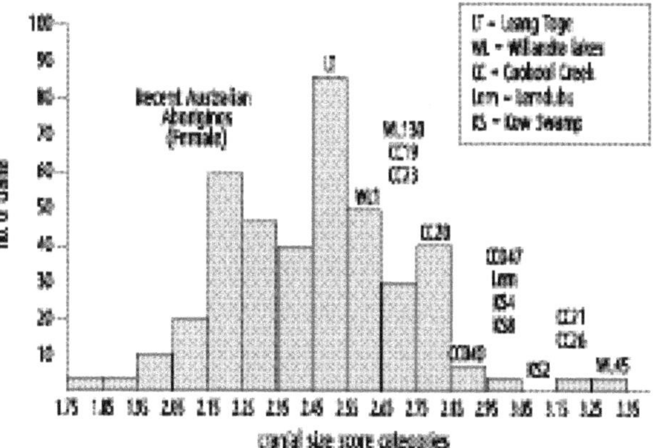

Figure 12.7 Liang Lemdubu: cranial size of Leang Toge, Lemdubu and Australian female fossils compared to recent Australian Aborigines

In this comparison, Leang Toge's measurements are taken from Jacob (1967:97–8), except for alveolar length, which is given by Storm (1995:178). For fossil Australians, preference is given to Pietrusewsky's and Brown's measurements where possible, as their measurements are used in establishing size-assessment boundaries. Pietrusewsky's measurements (reproduced in Willis 1998:20–35) are used for Kow Swamp females (sexes given in Thorne 1975:A79). Measurements on individual Coobool Creek females are taken from Brown (2001), despite the potential risk of using data privately published via the internet. The measurements for WL3 also come from Brown (1989:46–7), but for the other Willandra Lake females (WL45 and WL130), we need to turn to Webb (1989:45).

Note that this comparison excludes Lake Mungo 3 (WL3), notwithstanding Brown's (2000) doubts over the male status conventionally assigned to this burial. The fact that its ulna length of 297mm lies near the top of the recent Aboriginal male range and well above the female range (Brown 2000:747; Rao 1966:267) will be accepted here as demonstrating the burial's male status. Brown argues that regression formulae developed on black South African ulnae would produce an estimated stature for WL3 barely greater than the recent Aboriginal male average, and within the Late Pleistocene female range. However, even assuming that these regression formulae are appropriate for Australians, it is well known that least-squares regression estimates made from the dependent to the independent variable, stature in this case, are biased in systematically dragging the estimates back towards the reference population's mean value (Formicola 1993). Note also that the King Island burial is excluded regardless of whether it is female (Brown 1994, 1995) or male (Thorne and Sim 1994). Several of the measurements given by Sim and Thorne (1990) are obviously unreliable: the combination of an extremely long nasion-bregma chord (130mm) with an anomalously short bregma-lambda chord (94mm) (cf. Table 12.11); and fibula mid-shaft measurements which would minimally lead to a diameter of 82mm, 13 standard deviations above the male Australian mean (cf. Rao 1966:272). Whether the cause for these anomalies is the very brief period of three hours available to inspect the burial (Brown 1994), poor proof reading, or remarkably deviant skeletal morphology, Sim and Thorne's published measurements are difficult to use with confidence.

Lemdubu Woman's score of 3 on overall cranial size is very typical of early Australian fossils, whereas Leang Toge's score of 2.55 approximates the recent Australian female average, and is smaller than the result found for any early Australian female (Fig. 12.7). Accordingly, the similarity in cranial size that would be expected if the Lemdubu and Leang Toge crania were of the same middle Holocene age is disproved, and instead we conclude that Lemdubu Woman had the large cranial size expected of a Pleistocene Sahulland inhabitant.

Cranial Comparisons

Craniometric comparisons are made here to the worldwide coverage of recent populations by Howells (1973:193–238), as mediated through FORDISC 2.0 (Ousley and Jantz 1996). Eleven measurements from the Lemdubu skull may be used in this analysis, as asterisked in 12.10. As the Lemdubu cranial measurements regularly exceed the recent Australian female average (Table 12.11), they should arguably be compared with recent male as well as female craniometrics as a check that any identified similarities are not dominated by size effects. Leang Momer E, a middle Holocene male skull from Flores, is included in this analysis along with Leang Toge. Eighteen measurements are available for both Leang Momer E and Leang Toge, preferentially from Jacob (1967:80, 97–8) but otherwise from Storm (1995:169, 178–9). Our expectation is that Lemdubu should affiliate with Howells' southwest Pacific populations if the chronological determination making it a Pleistocene inhabitant of Sahulland is correct. If that result is obtained, and the compared Flores specimens do not resemble Howells' southwest Pacific populations, then the case is further strengthened for assigning Lemdubu Woman and the inhabitants of middle Holocene Flores to chronologically distinct populations.

FORDISC 2.0 usefully provides both 'typicality' and 'posterior' probabilities. Typicality essentially registers the likelihood of a specimen with the said measurements belonging to any given comparative population, while posterior probability estimates are based on the assumption that the specimen must belong somewhere among the recent comparative series. The typicality probabilities need not delay us long as they are always low. Leang Momer E has the highest, with a 5.0% probability of being Hawaiian, 4.4% of being South Japanese, 3.4% of being a Teita, and lower probabilities otherwise. Lemdubu would have a 1.4% probability of being a Tasmanian male, and a 0.1% to 0.5% probability of being a male Tolai, !Kung, Zulu, South Australian or Andaman Islander. Lemdubu (and Leang Toge) registers 0.0% probabilities of belonging to any of Howells's recent female series, confirming its large cranial size by recent female standards.

With the posterior probabilities, Lemdubu is much more similar to Tasmanians than to any other of Howells' populations, although the Tolai from New Britian and southern African !Kung emerge as remote affinities (see Table 12.12). This result is consistent with a terminal Pleistocene Sahulland status for Lemdubu Woman, given that Pietrusewsky (1984:Fig. 4) similarly found a remote craniometric relationship between Kow Swamp and Tasmanians.

The suggested affinities of the Flores crania are less clear. Both find their nearest match with 'Mongoloid' groups, Polynesians (and Japanese) in the case of Leang Momer E, and Eskimos in the case of Leang Toge (Table 12.12). But there would be little to choose between Eskimos, South Australians, and Melanesians in identifying Leang Toge's closest resemblance. This latter point is the only craniometric result that lends any support at all to Jacob's (1967:114) claim for a Melanesian element in the mid-Holocene inhabitants of Flores. The Aru specimen on the other hand is definitely closer to southwest Pacific populations than any others in its craniometrics, reinforcing its status as a representive of the Pleistocene population of Sahulland. A further feature that reinforces the same impression is the angular contour of Lemdubu Woman's braincase, a trait shared with most Coobool Creek and related ancient crania from southeastern Australia (Brown 1982:202–4; Webb 1989:Fig. 12.1), in contrast to the more rounded countours of Leang Momer E and Leang Toge (Storm 1995:Figs 23 and 25).

Comparisons involving relevant selections of Larnach and Macintosh's 'race discrimination traits' reiterate the same conclusion. For these comparisons, Queensland Aboriginal males are taken from a photocopy of Larnach's original records (see Larnach and Macintosh 1970). Melanesians include Johan Kamminga's observations on New Caledonia males and the author's observations on Solomon Island crania, while the Java/Malay all-male sample was recorded by Kamminga in the British Museum of Natural History (see Bulbeck 1981:278). Kamminga's observations on Leang Momer E and Leang Toge (reported in Bulbeck 1981:325–40) are also included here.

The first comparison involves glabella prominence, superciliary ridge development, zygomatic trigone size, palate size, frontal recession, maximum supra-orbital breadth, and cranial index, employing the grade boundaries and scoring system of Larnach and Macintosh (1966:82–3). The justification for this choice of traits is that Brown (1982:Appendix 3) recorded them on Coobool Creek and Murray Valley (including Swanport) Aborigines. Two male Kow Swamp crania, KS1 and KS5, are also recorded on all seven traits (Thorne 1975:189–90, A79). However, females need to be treated in this analysis separately from males as most of the traits show marked sexual dimorphism. Characteristically Australian (masculine) expressions score 3, non-Australian expressions score 1, and ambiguous expressions score 2, so that when the individual specimens'

Table 12.12 Posterior probabilities greater than 10% (in bold face) comparing the Liang Lemdubu and Flores fossil crania with Howells's recent populations

RECENT SERIES	LEMDUBU (CF. FEMALES)	LEMDUBU (CF. MALES)	LEANG MOMER E	LEANG TOGE
Tasmanians	**0.556**	**0.588**	0.001	0.000
Eskimos	0.000	0.000	0.072	**0.328**
South Australians	0.014	0.006	0.000	**0.282**
Tolai	**0.158**	**0.151**	0.049	**0.257**
Hawaiians	0.000	0.000	**0.244**	0.000
South Japanese	0.005	0.002	**0.192**	0.000
Zulu	0.042	0.030	0.020	**0.127**
San !Kung	**0.105**	**0.120**	0.023	0.000
Teita	0.000	0.000	**0.113**	0.002

scores are added across the traits, Australian Aborigines tend to score higher than Melanesians who in turn score higher than Indonesians (Fig. 12.8).

All the fossil Australian crania fall within the top half of the recent Australian range, bar one Coobool Creek female. The same generalisation would also apply to the Lemdubu cranium which, indeed, lies above the recorded Melanesian range. Leang Momer E and Leang Toge, by contrast, fall comfortably within the Melanesian range, which is the same result that I have found when assessing other pre-Neolithic to Iron Age, Indonesian and Malaysian crania in terms of Larnach and Macintosh's traits (Bulbeck 1981:Figs 7–3 to 7–10). These results confirm the making of a clear distinction between Lemdubu Woman — who should be thought of simply as an ancient Australian — and the Flores specimens, which behave in the same way as other prehistoric Southeast Asian crania located to the west of the Sahul shelf.

The second comparison focuses on those traits with little or no sexual dimorphism: cranial index, parietal bossing, transverse occipital torus development, sagittal keeling, median frontal ridge expression, frontal recession, naso-frontal articulation width, malar orbital boder rounding, anterior nasal spine morphology, subnasal prognathism and palatine torus expression. In some of those traits, Larnach and Macintosh accord '0' to non-Australian expressions and '1' to ambiguous developments; otherwise, methodology is the same as in the previous comparison. In this case, Melanesian males and females do not seem to differ appreciably, suggesting that sex has been nullified as a relevant factor (Fig. 12.9). The expanded array of traits disqualifies Kow Swamp, Leang Momer, and Brown's observations from inclusion; otherwise, the same sources are availed as in the first comparison.

Figure 12.9 produces the sort of result typically found for prehistoric Southeast Asians (Bulbeck 1981:Figs 7–3 to 7–10), with Lemdubu Woman and Leang Toge both lying near the midpoint of the recent Melanesian range (and, in this instance, above the Java/Malay range). The Lemdubu and Leang Toge specimens behave similarly here, in contrast to their marked separation in the first comparison, because these specimens' differences are concentrated on sexually dimorphic traits — those that involve size and related robustness. When ca. 10,000 year old Murray Valley Aborigines are compared with their recent (and presumably descendant) counterparts, their cranial differences are also predominantly a function of size and robustness (Brown 1987). By analogy, it may also be suggested that Lemdubu Woman could represent the population broadly ancestral to the middle Holocene population represented by the Flores crania.

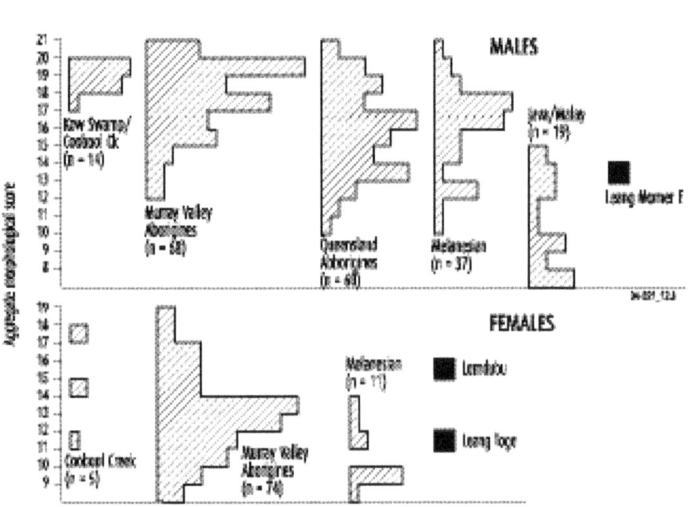

Figure 12.8 Australasian recent crania and prehistoric fossils compared on seven morphological traits

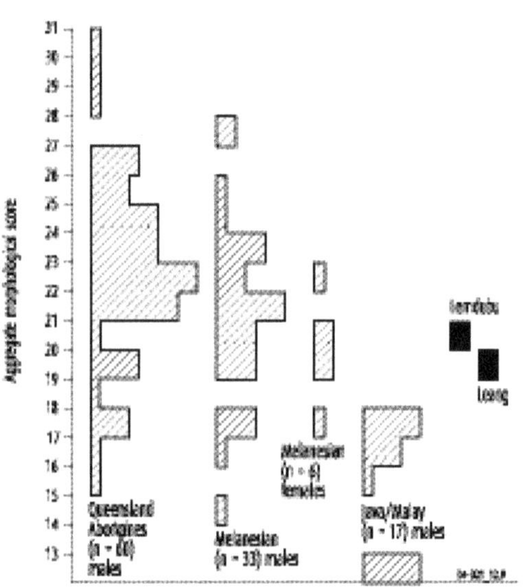

Figure 12.9 Australasian recent crania and prehistoric fossils compared on less sexually dimorphic characters

Mandibular Morphology

The Lemdubu mandible (see Fig. 12.10 and Table 12.13) is of masculine morphology by recent Australasian standards, to follow Larnach and Macintosh's (1971:31) standards for sexing mandibles. In addition to the large bigonial breadth and minimum ramus breadth (scoring 3 each), and the medium symphysis height (2), Lemdubu has a large *planum triangulare* area and everted gonia (3 each), though its anterior marginal tubercle is merely slight on the left side and medium on the right (1.5), and the *sulcus intertoralis* is bilaterally slight (1). Even if the Lemdubu mandible is given a score of 1 for the four Larnach and Macintosh traits which are not extant on this specimen, its resulting score of 20.5 would lie comfortably above the lower boundary of 19 recognised by Larnach and Macintosh (1971:33) and Bulbeck (1981:489) for male Australasian mandibles.

The following morphological traits on the Lemdubu mandible were also recorded in terms of Larnach and Macintosh's (1971) grades. On the right side, the *sulcus extramolaris* is slight, the lateral prominence is marked, and the posterior marginal tubercle is prominent. The superior lateral torus and marginal torus show medium development bilaterally, while the single mental foramen lies beneath the second molar on both sides. The chin region includes a large *trigonum mentale* but nonetheless has negative projection owing to the medium decline of the *planum alveolare* and the medium anterior mandibular incurvature. There is a slight submental notch, a slight *trigonum basale* and a faint *sulcus praedigastricus,* but no trace of any superior transverse torus, and the *fossae mentalis* are bilaterally slight. Genial pit is absent whereas the genial spines are large. Moving posteriorly we remark bilaterally marked digastric fossae and submaxillary fossae, but the absence of any sublingual fossae. The mylohyoid ridge is large bilaterally but there is no sign of a mandibular torus. At the rear of the dental arcade, the bilaterally trace *crista pharyngea* couples with precoronoid fossae of medium depth. On the left side we may note the marked mylohyoid groove, trace lingula, slight *sulcus colli* and marked *crista endocoronoidea* on the medial surface of the ramus. The lateral face of the ramus exhibits a more or less flat *fossa masseterica,* and a marked *torus triangularis.*

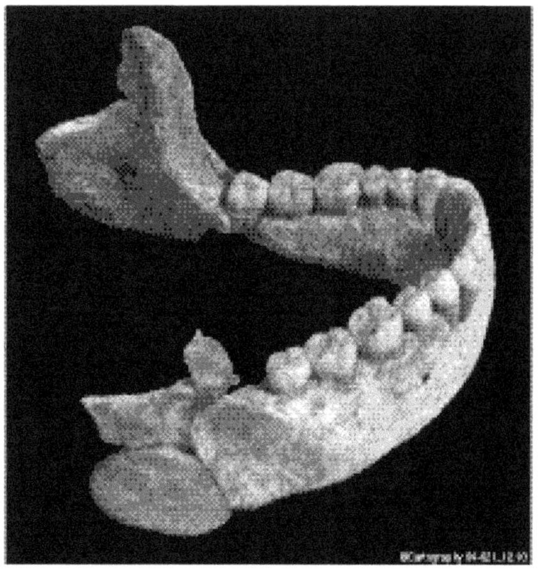

Figure 12.10 Liang Lemdubu: the mandible in oblique superior view

Table 12.13 Liang Lemdubu: mandibular measurements (mm)

Measurement	mm	Measurement	mm
Bigonial breadth (M66, w2)*	99.5	Bigonial width ($g_o g_o$)	96.0
Bicoronoid breadth (M65(1), $c_r c_r$) (S)	~88.0	Corpus length (M68, cpl) (S)	~94.0
Chin height (M69, h1)*	29.0	Symphysis height (LM)	30.5
Bimental breadth (zz)	45.5	Interobliqual breadth (Jacob)	81.0
Corpus height at mental foramen (M69 (1))	30.5	Corpus breadth at mental foramen (M69 (3))	12.0
Corpus height between first and second molar (Olivier) (R)*	26.5	Corpus thickness between first and second molar (Olivier) (R)*	15.0
Molar-premolar chord ($m_2 p_1$)	25.0	Gnathion-gonion length (gngo)	90.0
Minimum ramus breadth (M71, rb')*	37.5	Coronion height (M70, crh)	67.0

NB: (S) indicates that symmetry of the mandible was assumed to estimate the measurement. (R) indicates measurement on the right side; otherwise, the left side was used. Asterisked measurements appear in the Penrose size and shape analysis (below). Where a measurement definition comes from Martin and Saller (1957:481–2), it is marked with M and the relevant number in their system. Alphanumerically tagged measurements are defined by Cleaver (1937); LM means the source is Larnach and Macintosh (1971:28–30); and other measurement definitions are from Jacob (1967: 61), and Olivier et al. (1966)

A combination of features such as this is more characteristic of southwest Pacific than East Asian mandibles. Eleven of the 12 'race discrimination' characters in Larnach and Macintosh (1971:30) are extant, and Lemdubu's score of 21 / 33 would fall within the range of overlap between Australian (20–32), Melanesian (20–32), and Iron Age to recent Indonesian mandibles (16.5–25), but above the recorded Northeast Asian range of 14–20 (Bulbeck 1981:Table 8–10). On the 11 characters used by the author (Bulbeck 1981:359) to distinguish Melanesian mandibles (range, 18-29) from their Indonesian counterparts (range, 14.5–23), the Lemdubu specimen scores 24. Lemdubu thus lies outside the recorded Indo-Malaysian range, even when we consider the reported, preceramic specimens from the Philippines (Tabon), Java (Wajak 2), and Malaysia (Gua Cha 1, Gua Peraling) whose range is 20.5–22 (Bulbeck 2004: Fig. 1). Males and females may be pooled in these comparisons as sexual dimorphism among Australasian mandibles seems to be insignificant here (Bulbeck 1981:359, 380).

For more detailed comparisons, we turn to Storm's (1995:235–6) description of nine anatomical features in Larnach and Macintosh's (1971) system based on casts of the WL3, Kow Swamp 1, and Kow Swamp 5 mandibles, and the originals of Leang Toge, Leang Momer E, Wajak 2, and Sampung (preceramic Java). Based on these data, the Lemdubu mandible most frequently matches Wajak 2 and Sampung in its morphology, followed by a reasonable similarity with the WL3 and Kow Swamp mandibles, and pronounced differences from Leang Toge and Leang Momer E (Table 12.14). Further, because I had earlier reported Wajak 2, based on a cast, it is possible to check comparability between Storm's observations and mine. Our observations disagree on four features, but all differences involve merely one step (Table 12.14), suggesting that differences between our observations may be considered definite when they are two steps removed. In that case, four of the nine features definitely differ between Lemdubu and Leang Momer E, and 3/9 definitely differ from Leang Toge, whereas the definite differences from Kow Swamp 5 (3/9), Wajak (2/9), Sampung (1/8), WL3 (1/8) and Kow Swamp 1 (0/9) are less (Table 12.14). There seems little doubt that Lemdubu's mandibular morphology is particularly dissimilar from that of the Flores middle Holocene specimens.

Various traits not considered by Larnach and Macintosh (1971) may be noted on the Lemdubu mandible. The lower border of the posterior corpus does not display the pronounced convexity found on rocker jaws, which occur at rates of approximately 70–90% across East Asia, Australia, and the Pacific (Pietrusewsky 1984:99, 104–6). The mental foramina are directed posteriorly and superiorly, as is the usual condition among Indonesian, Australian and other Pacific mandibles (Bulbeck 1981:370). The genial spines coalesce into a common median spine — type G of de Villiers (1968:Fig. 55) — which is evidently a rare variant (cf. Bulbeck 1981:356, 373),

Table 12.14 Liang Lemdubu: mandibular anatomical comparisons

FEATURE	LEMDUBU	WL3	KS1	KS5	LEANG TOGE	LEANG MOMER	WAJAK 2	SAMPUNG
Trigone	marked	medium	medium	slight	medium	slight	medium*	-
Incurvature	medium	-	medium	medium	slight	medium	medium*	medium
Chin	-ve	-ve	neutral	-ve	-ve	+ve	-ve	neutral
Planum alveolare	medium/large	slight	slight	medium/large	slight	slight	slight	medium/large
Mylohyoid	marked	marked	med.	slight	slight	medium	marked*	marked
Sulcus extramolaris	slight	marked	med.	slight	medium	slight	marked	medium
Prominence	marked	medium	marked	slight	slight	slight	marked	marked
Precoronoid	medium	medium	deep	shallow	medium	shallow	medium	shallow
triangulare	large	medium	large	medium	small	small	large	small
Agreement	N/A	3/8	3/9	4/9	2/9	2/9	6/9	4/8

NB: features are respectively mental trigone development, anterior mandibular incurvature, chin projection (-ve = negative, +ve = positive), *planum alveolare* decline, mylohyoid ridge development, *sulcus extramolaris* development, lateral prominence development, precoronoid fossa depth, and *planum triangulare* area. The last row shows the ratio of features shared between Lemdubu and the other mandible. KS = Kow Swamp. Comparative observations from Storm (1995:235–7); asterisked Wajak 2 observations show where his observations disagree with those made by myself (Bulbeck 1981:393), in all cases by one step and is associated with an absence of genial grooves in the Lemdubu case. Finally, there is no trace of a mylohyoid bridge (Lundy 1980), a feature that occurs at about 3-30% rates among Pacific and Pacific Rim mandibles (Bulbeck 1981:375).

Five measurements, asterisked in Table 12.13, have been recorded in common on the Coobool Creek, Lemdubu and Leang Toge mandibles, as well as a useful spread of recent female populations in the region. Coobool Creek, Murray Valley, and Swanport data come from Brown (1989); Javanese data come from combining the measurements in Snell (1938:68–106) and Storm (1995:184–8); and my measurements on Papua New Guinea mandibles housed at the Australian Museum in Sydney are produced in Table 12.15. Storm (1995:184–5) gives the height and thickness of the Leang Toge corpus in the M_1/M_2 region, otherwise, Jacob's (1967:85) measurements are used.

The preferred statistic employed here is Penrose's (1954) size and shape statistic, as it usefully distinguishes between these two main components of overall metrical distance. The statistical formulae produce squared distances, so, to scale them back to Euclidean space, the square roots of the calculated distances are used here. Indeed, the square roots of the size differences obey the properties of one-dimensional Euclidean geometry, so size distinctions can be expressed as the square root of the distance from Papua New Guinea females, who proved to have the smallest mandibles. Thus the greater size of the Coobool Creek (1.91), Leang Toge (1.49), and Lemdubu (1.02) mandibles, compared to Papua New Guineans, is approximately two to four times the size difference of any recent sample — Murray Valley (0.58), Swanport (0.50), and Javanese (0.23) — compared to Papua New Guinea mandibles. Note also that the large size of the Leang Toge mandible contrasts with the situation in southeast Australia where, according to Brown's (1989:171–2; 1992:42) analysis, reduction in mandibular size to recent standards had been completed by the middle Holocene.

The shape distance square roots presented in Table 12.16 cluster (using the average-linkage algorithm) into the hierarchical dendrogram illustrated in Figure 12.11. The dendrogram is seriated in the way that ensures that, as far as possible, the greater the juxtaposition of any two samples, the smaller the shape distance between them, while samples spaced far apart from each other in the dendrogram differ markedly in their shape distances. Thus the smallest distances in Table 12.16 lie along the diagonal, and the greatest distances lie farthest from the diagonal. In a perfect seriation, each step away from the diagonal would encounter an equal or greater distance. This ideal is closely approached in Table 12.16 and, to be precise, its goodness of fit in comparison to a perfect seriation is 92.2% (for procedural details, see Bulbeck 1992:Appendix A; 1993; 1997; 2000b). So, all of the samples and specimens slot along a single main axis of variation with the Coobool Creek mandibles at one extreme, and the Lemdubu and Leang Toge mandibles at the other extreme (Fig. 12.11). In its shape, the Lemdubu mandible is very similar to the average Swanport mandible, but also quite similar to Papua New Guinea and Leang Toge.

Inspection of the original measurements reveals a major distinction between the Coobool Creek and Murray Valley mandibles, whose recorded average thickness at the M_1/M_2 region is small relative to their average height at the symphysis and the M_1/M_2 region, compared to the other samples and specimens where the opposite applies. This can be shown by constructing indices involving these measurements, where the relatively tall, slender shape of the Coobool Creek and Murray Valley mandibular corpora is quite clear (Table 12.17). However, no consistent pattern is observable when thickness at the M_1/M_2 region is compared to bigonial width or

Table 12.15 The author's measurements on female Papua New Guinea mandibles

	w2	h1	M_1/M_2 HEIGHT	M_1/M_2 THICKNESS	rb'
No. observations	25	21	25	24	25
Mean	89.46	28.33	24.80	14.21	32.68
Standard deviation	4.80	2.34	2.03	1.71	3.16

NB: acronyms for the measurements are explained in Table 12.13

Table 12.16 Liang Lemdubu: seriated square roots of Penrose shape distances for five mandibular measurements (females)

	CC	MV	JAVANESE	PNG	SPT	LEMDUBU	L. TOGE
Coobool Creek (CC)	-	0.457	1.143	1.177	1.368	1.494	1.188
Murray Valley (MV)		-	0.751	0.770	0.975	1.180	0.961
Javanese			-	0.464	0.767	0.976	1.099
Papua New Guinea (PNG)				-	0.345	0.617	0.701
Swanport (Spt)					-	0.425	0.683
Lemdubu						-	0.758
Leang Toge (L. Toge)							-

Table 12.17 Liang Lemdubu: mandibular indices relating average measurements (females)

	COOBOOL CREEK	MURRAY VALLEY	JAVA	PNG	SWAN-PORT	LEMDUBU	LEANG TOGE
M1/M2 T:M1/M2 H	47.2	45.5	55.6	57.3	58.8	56.6	58.8
M1/M2 T:h1	39.8	43.4	51.7	50.2	50.2	51.7	46.7
M1/M2 T:w2	14.3	15.3	16.9	15.9	15.8	15.1	14.7
M1/M2 T:rb′	41.8	43.5	46.9	43.4	41.4	40.0	42.8
w2:M1/M2 H + T	224.2	203.8	211.0	229.5	234.5	239.8	252.4
rb′:M1/M2 H + T	76.7	71.8	76.3	83.8	89.4	90.4	86.5
rb′:w2	34.2	35.3	36.1	36.5	38.1	37.7	34.3

NB: indices are constructed from thickness (M1/M2 T) and height (M1/M2 H) of the corpus at the interval between the first and second molars, symphysis height (h1), bigonial width (w2) and minimum ramus breadth (rb′)

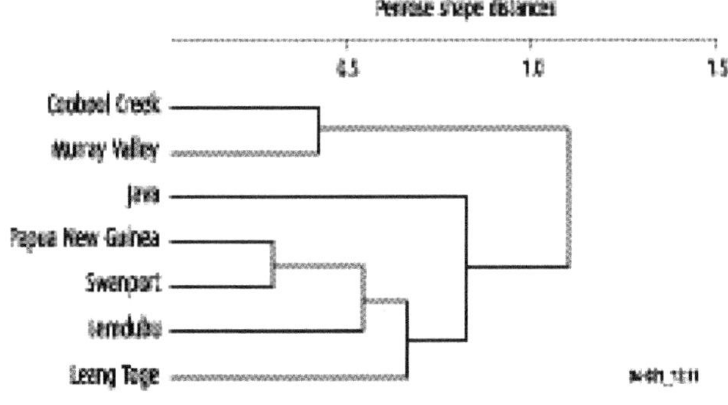

Figure 12.11 Seriated average-linkage dendrogram of female mandible shape distances (bigonial width, symphysis height, ramus breadth, corpus diameters at M_1/M_2). Goodness of fit 92.2%

minimum ramus breadth; instead, the latter two measurements appear to be specifically large as a common feature of the Swanport, Lemdubu and Leang Toge mandibles. This can be shown by expressing these two measurements as an index relative to the sum of the height and the thickness at the M_1/M_2 region, yielding highest values for Swanport, Lemdubu and Leang Toge (Table 12.17). On the other hand, Leang Toge has a relatively small minimum ramus breadth compared to bigonial width, a feature it specifically shares with the Coobool Creek and Murray Valley mandibles, as reflected in a small rb′:w_2 index (Table 12.17). This may explain why Leang Toge has slightly smaller shape distances from Coobool Creek and Murray Valley than Swanport and Lemdubu do (Table 12.16), a detail which is not reflected in the seriation, and which would indeed explain most of 7.8% discrepancy (100% minus 92.2%) from a perfectly seriated order.

To summarize, the Lemdubu mandible is tolerably close to Leang Toge in both size and shape, but its shape is particularly reminiscent of Swanport (Australian) mandibles, even if it is much larger than the Swanport average. It differs considerably from Coobool Creek (and Murray Valley) mandibles in its squatter corpus and relatively broad ramus and bigonial width. These metrical comparisons differ somewhat from the analysis using anatomical features where, as noted above, Lemdubu differs sharply from Leang Toge (and Leang Momer E), and instead shows an overall resemblance to recent Melanesians, Australian Aborigines both past and present, and preceramic mandibles from Java.

Postcranial Description

The Lemdubu individual (Fig. 12.1) shows a tall, linear build, and long distal members compared to proximal limb bone lengths. Muscular development would appear to have been moderate to strong, to judge by the related osseous features. The morphology of the limb bones is slender, apart from the femora, which show a masculine degree of thickness ('robustness') that is presumably related to the individual's considerable stature (around 166cm) when alive. In contrast, the Leang Toge individual was evidently less muscular, much shorter in stature, and less linear in build. A notable feature of Lemdubu Woman is her thick cortical bone on the humerus and femur, to a degree usually found among Neandertals and other archaic hominins, and which is not shared by the Kow Swamp skeletons (at least, on the femur). Comparisons between Lemdubu Woman and the Lake Nitchie male, a huge individual of around 187.5cm stature who lived approximately 7000 years ago in western New South Wales (Macintosh 1971), demonstrate the less linear build of the latter skeleton, as detailed below. Lemdubu Woman's more linear build, which also holds true in relation to recent southeast Australian Aborigines, would be an expected concomitant of her tropical lowland habitat, even during the Last Glacial Maximum.

Postcranial axial skeleton

Reconstruction of the vertebral column was based on the discs' anatomical features and measurements, and my best attempts to articulate the extant cranial and caudal disc surfaces (Fig. 12.12). Very rarely was it possible to relate any of the discs to the other vertebral fragments. The axis appeared to be represented only by its right superior articular surface and pedicle, the atlas by its left and right superior articular facets, the sixth and seventh cervical vertebrae by a single nondescript fragment, and the fifth and sixth thoracic vertebral discs by small fragments. Otherwise measurements could be made on all of the discs, including the first sacral disc, which was anchored to the second sacral disc but not fused to it. Such 'lumbarisation' of the S1 segment more commonly affects females than males, at rates of up to about 10% of women, according to Aufderheide and Rodrígues-Martín (1998:66).

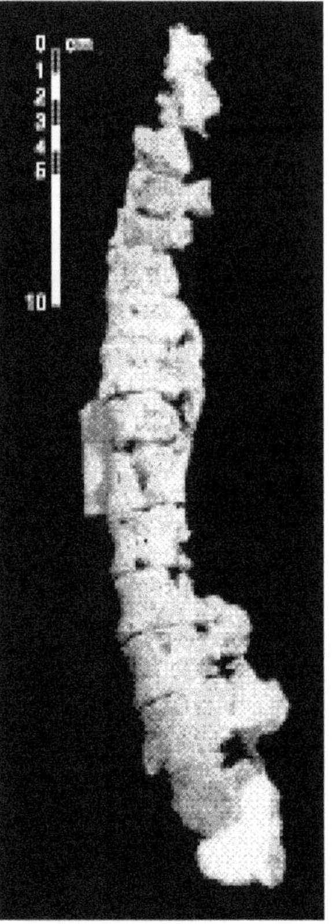

Figure 12.12 Liang Lemdubu: left lateral view of the reconstructed vertebral column of Lemdubu Woman

Pathological pitting, with a 'punched out' appearance to the larger holes, was consistently noted on the Lemdubu vertebral discs except the sacral, third thoracic and upper cervical discs (Fig. 12.12). It took the form of a single puncture at the middle level of the disc on the sixth (or seventh) cervical, the first thoracic, and the second thoracic discs. This pitting affected the dorsal surface in the first two cases and the ventral surface in the third case. The fourth thoracic disc appears internally eroded, while the sixth thoracic disc has a nine millimetre deep hole on its right side. The seventh to ninth thoracic discs are pitted with 10 to 14 small holes on their left side (right side not well enough preserved for definitive observations), while the 10th thoracic disc is bilaterally pitted with 10 holes of various sizes. The 11th and 12th thoracic discs have two main punctures bilaterally expressed on the ventral face, accompanied by approximately a dozen smaller holes on both discs. The first, second and fourth lumbar discs could show a similar expression, but either the left or the right side is poorly preserved, even while the better preserved side exhibits a main hole. Large bilateral holes can be observed on the fifth lumbar disc, but the third lumbar disc is much less affected, with none of the holes larger than two millimetres in diameter.

The bone of the discs sometimes appears eroded from within, as is characteristic of multiple myelomic lesions (Rothschild et al. 1998). However, multiple myeloma is so rare among people aged less than 40 years that, when diagnosed for a younger person, it has probably been confused with a metastatic carcinoma (Aufderheide and Rodrígues-Martín 1998:351–3). Further, even though the vertebrae would be the prime site of myelomic lesions, they should still be widely distributed around the skeleton. This is not the case with Lemdubu Woman, where comparable lesions were noted at only two other parts of the skeleton, to wit, the medio-dorsal epiphysis of the right tibia, with a 22mm deep hole of 8–8.5mm diameter, and the right clavicle, with an oval pit 11.5mm long by 4.5mm wide and five millimetres deep on the cranial surface near the rhomboid impression. The focus of the lesions on the vertebral column does however rule out myelocytic leukaemia as the cause, when most of the skeleton should have been affected, as well as syphilis, yaws or trepanamotosis, which characteristically affect the cranium and the tibiae moreso than the vertebrae (cf. Rothschild et al. 1998). Further, Aufderheide and Rodrígues-Martín (1998:388) note that 30–50% of breast cancers may metastasise as lesions to the vertebrae, and other cancers may do so at lower frequencies. Accordingly, a metastatic cancerous lesion at an early stage of development is the most likely diagnosis for Lemdubu Woman's palaeopathological condition.

Aufderheide and Rodrígues-Martín (1998:388) further note that metastases commonly lead to vertebral collapse, and this may be related to the unusually small dorsal heights of Lemdubu Woman's vertebral discs. These heights are usually less than the ventral heights on the same disc (Table 12.18), in contrast to recent South Australian Aborigines whose dorsal disc heights usually exceed the ventral heights except on the lowest two lumbar vertebrae (Tulsi 1972). Impressionistically speaking, any vertebral collapse would seem to have had only minor effects on the Lemdubu disc heights, especially on their ventral aspect (Fig. 12.12). So the similarity between Lemdubu Woman and South Australian females in their summed ventral height of those discs that can be compared — 263mm for Lemdubu, compared to the female Australian average of 260.08mm (Tulsi 1972) — can be taken to reflect a similar length of the vertebral column regardless of any effects of pathology. By the same token, Lemdubu Woman would have had a short column compared to recent Japanese and American white females, because Tulsi (1972) found the Australian ventral disc heights to be consistently shorter, on average, than those of Japanese and American whites of the same sex.

The Lemdubu and Leang Toge vertebrae can be compared on 12 measurements, as asterisked in Table 12.18. The only systematic difference is the consistently greater dorsal disc heights of Leang Toge, which may however reflect pathological shortening of Lemdubu Woman's dorsal disc heights. On the other hand, the Leang Toge disc heights also exceed the South Australian averages, except for the dorsal height on the first lumbar vertebra (cf. Tulsi 1972:131). These comparisons may suggest that the much shorter long bones of Leang Toge compared to Lemdubu, as discussed below, were to some degree compensated by Leang Toge's longer vertebral column. It may also be noted that the summed height of the ventral discs of the Lake Nitchie burial is around 34% greater than the South Australian male average, and the pattern is consistent on every vertebral disc (Macintosh 1971:51; cf. Tulsi 1972:131, 133), showing that Lake Nitchie did not have a short vertebral column, compared to its stature, by recent South Australian standards.

Three joining fragments of the sternum, including a complete manubrium were identified. Length of the manubrium is 41.5mm, its maximum and minimum breadths are 48mm and 21mm respectively, and its maximum thickness is 9.5mm (M1, 4, 6 and 7, according to Martin and Saller 1957:571). These dimensions correspond to a fairly small sternum, in accord with the individual's sex. The potential area to see if there is a sternal foramen (Brothwell 1981:97) is not preserved.

Table 12.18 Liang Lemdubu: measurements and estimates of the vertebral discs (to nearest 0.5mm)

VERTEBRAL DISC	HEIGHTS (M1-2)		CRANIAL DIAMETERS (M4-5)		CAUDAL DIAMETERS (M7-8)	
	VENTRAL	DORSAL	SAGITTAL	TRANSVERSE	SAGITTAL	TRANSVERSE
3rd cervical	9.0	9.5	11.5	~20.0	13.0	16.5
4th cervical	**12.0**	**11.0**	13.0	21.0	12.0	17.0
5th cervical	10.0	**11.0**	13.0	24.5	~14.0	25.0
1st thoracic	**14.0**	13.0	13.0	26.5	14.0	26.5
2nd thoracic	~14.0	-	-	~25.5	-	~26.5
3rd thoracic	14.0	15.0	13.0	23.0	13.0	23.0
4th thoracic	-	15.0	-	~25.0	-	-
7th thoracic	-	-	-	-	~17.0	~26.0
8th thoracic	16.0	~15.5	~21.5	~29.0	~21.0	~32.0
9th thoracic	17.0	-	-	-	-	-
10th thoracic	18.5	18.0	26.0	~30.0	28.0	~32.0
11th thoracic	**21.0**	18.0	23.0	26.0	22.0	28.0
12th thoracic	**21.5**	_*22.0_	22.5	*27.5	~23.5	32.0
1st lumbar	-	_*~21.0_	-	~35.0	-	-
2nd lumbar	**~24.0**	_*~21.0_	~26.0	~33.0	~29.0	~33.0
3rd lumbar	**24.0**	_*23.0_	28.0	~36.0	32.0	~34.0
4th lumbar	**_*23.0_**	_*~21.0_	*~31.0	_*~40.0_	*34.0	*45.0
5th lumbar	**25.0**	_*~21.0_	32.0	44.5	29.0	~44.0
1st sacral	27.0	~23.0	27.0	44.5	24.0	29.0

NB: measurements in bold exceed Tulsi's (1972) female Australian Aboriginal averages; asterisked measurements are those that can be compared with Leang Toge (Jacob 1967:92); italicized measurements indicate that Leang Toge has the larger measurements

Shoulder girdle

The Leang Toge remains do not include the clavicle (Jacob 1967:79), so we shall restrict comparisons to Australians. The Lemdubu measurements (Table 12.19) always fall within the female Australian range (Ray 1959:219), although the minimum width is located much farther from the inner end of the clavicle than is the usual case for Aborigines, and the inner segment length slightly exceeds the corresponding Australian average (a shape difference related to the greater torsion of the Lemdubu clavicle at the outer angle). In other respects, Lemdubu lies slightly below the recorded Australian average (Table 12.19). Based on the estimated, maximum humerus length of 313mm for Lemdubu Woman, and her maximum clavicle length of about 119mm, her claviculo-humeral index would be approximately 38.0. This value would fall towards the bottom of the recent Australian range, even though Australian Aborigines exceed most other recent

Table 12.19 Liang Lembudu: right clavicle measurements (Lem.) and female Australian (Aus.) means

MEASUREMENT	LEM.	AUS.	MEASUREMENT	LEM.	AUS.
Maximum length	≥119	123.5	Sternal-acromial distance	≥116	120.6
Inner angle	~150	149.3	Outer angle	~147	140.8
Inner segment length	41	36.1	Middle segment length	54	63.7
Outer segment length	23	26.6	Mid-point circumference	31	32.1
Inner end width	17	18.6	Inner angle width	10.5	10.9
Minimum width	9	9.8	Inner end-minimum width distance	79	30.9
Width at conoid	11	14.0	Minimum height at outer end	7.5	7.6
Height at conoid	8	9.9	Thickness index	≤26.1	26.0
Mid-point height	8	10.1	Mid-point width (M4)	10	-

NB: all measurements in mm except the angles (in degrees). Thickness index is 100 x mid-point circumference/maximum length. Left clavicle measurements also available for the mid-point circumference (30mm), width and height at conoid tubercle (10.5 and 7.5mm respectively), and midpoint width and height (10.5 and 7.5mm respectively) populations in the shortness of their clavicle compared to their humerus length, as one aspect of their linear build (Ray 1959:221). The very low claviculo-humeral index of Lemdubu Woman highlights her linear build.

The pathological hole near the rhomboid impression on the right clavicle makes it hard to define the development of anatomical features in this area, but fortunately the left Lemdubu clavicle preserves these features well (Table 12.20). In addition to the traits itemised in Table 12.20, no accessory perforations were noted, here following the usual Australian condition (Ray 1959:222); the impression for the first rib is a shallow furrow, and the trapezoid ligament has left a shallow oval impression, so its apparently large size may reflect differences in definitions between Ray's and mine. To be sure, Ray's categories are not sufficiently well defined to guarantee accurate comparisons, so the comparisons in Table 12.20 serve mainly to confirm the visual impression that the Lemdubu clavicles are generally rather gracile, in accord with the skeleton's female status (cf. Ray 1959:225). In contrast, the Lake Nitchie clavicles have more rugged muscular markings, as per their male status, and the length measurements lie near the top of the recent Australian range, in accord with the individual's great size (Macintosh 1971:52). Similarly, the clavicle from the Lake Tandou male, buried about 15,000 years ago near Lake Nitchie, has a diameter close to the top of the recent Australian range (Freedman and Lofgren 1983; Ray 1959:219).

The Lemdubu scapulae are poorly preserved, with only the lateral border, glenoid cavity, acromion and coracoid process present to any degree. The dimensions are rather large compared to those of other female skeletons in the vicinity. Coraco-acromial breadth and glenoid fossa diameters fall within the range of overlap between recent male and female Australians (van Dongen 1963:482–3; see also Table 12.21, this volume), while the glenoid fossa diameters and acromial dimensions are larger than those of Leang Toge (Table 12.21). Yet her glenoid fossa diameters measure 6–8mm less than those of the robustly built Lake Nitchie male (cf. Macintosh 1971:52). Two further measurements may be taken on the right scapula of Lemdubu Woman: maximum length of the coracoid process (M11), which measures 38mm; and depth of the glenoid fossa (M14), which measures approximately 4.5mm.

These Lemdubu scapulae show complete absence of the following semi-discrete traits illustrated by Brothwell (1981:97, 99): suprascapular foramen, rectangular acromion, acromial articular facet, and glenoid extensions. Bilaterally, there is no trace of a suprascapular notch, as also

Table 12.20 Liang Lembudu: percentages of female Australians (% Aus.) sharing the Lemdubu clavicular non-metric trait expression (based on Ray 1959:222-5)

LEMDUBU WOMAN'S CONDITION	% AUS.	LEMDUBU WOMAN'S CONDITION	% AUS.
Small rhomboid impression (L)	24	Small impression for first rib (L)	34
Nutrient foramen a single large pit (L)	42	Nutrient foramen not patent (R)	4
Irregular inner end shape (R)	24	Absent sternocleidomastoid impression (L, R)	29
Small *pectoralis major* impression (R)	37	Absent deltoid impression (R)	1
Medium subclavian groove (L)	30	Small subclavian groove (R)	42
Large conoid tubercle (R)	18	Medium trapezoid ligament (R)	35

Table 12.21 Liang Lembudu: scapula measurements (mm) compared to Leang Toge and recent Australians

MEASUREMENT	LEMDUBU	L. TOGE	AUSTRALIAN ♀	AUSTRALIAN ♂
Coraco-acromial breadth	67 (R)	-	60.3±3.2	68.8±5.1
Vertical glenoid diameter (M12)	34 (R), ~33 (L)	29 (R), 28 (L)	30.9±1.8	35.3±2.3
Transverse glenoid diameter (M13)	22 (L, R)	22 (R), 21 (L)	21.7±1.3	24.8±1.8
Acromial breadth (M9)	≥39 (R)	36.5 (R)	-	-
Acromial length (M10)	51 (R)	41 (R)	-	-

NB: Leang Toge measurements from Jacob (1967:85). Recent Australian measurements from van Dongen (1963:479). Measurements defined by Martin and Saller (1957:530-1) are indicated with an M noted on approximately fifty percent of Australian Aborigines (van Dongen 1963:477) and, reading between the lines, on Leang Toge (Jacob 1967:85). The axillary borders are strongly developed and show extensive 'dorsal inclination', a feature more common among male than female Australians (van Dongen 1963:477) and also displayed by Leang Toge (Jacob 1967:85). The circumflex groove of Lemdubu Woman is slight on the left scapula and large on the right; presence of this groove occurs on less than half the recorded Australian scapulae, but is observed on Leang Toge (Jacob 1967:85; van Dongen 1963:478). The bilaterally piriform shape of the Lemdubu glenoid cavity is the most common condition among all people, including Australians and Leang Toge (Jacob 1967:85; van Dongen 1963:478). Further similarities with the Leang Toge scapulae include the triangular shape of the acromial extremities, well-developed markings where the *teres minor* muscles inserted, and general rugosity by usual female standards.

The arms

Only the left Lemdubu humerus is considered here because it is much better preserved than the right antimere. Its maximum length is estimated from its measured lengths of 33mm for segment 1 (Steele 1970; Steele and McKern 1969), 54mm and 192mm respectively for segments 2 and 3 (Steele and McKern 1969), and 246mm for segment 2 (Steele 1970). These measurements indicate a maximum length of around 313mm (Table 12.22) whether we employ the regression formulae for Mesoamerican females (Steele and McKern 1969 — 311.3±3.7mm), American Whites (312.6±3.0mm), or Afro-Americans (313.2±3.0mm) (Steele 1970). The Lemdubu value lies slightly above the maximum humerus lengths of 305mm to 310mm estimated by Webb (1989:47) for female humeri from the Willandra Lakes.

Other measurements may be taken directly and are compared with Leang Toge and recent Australian females in Table 12.22. These measurements show little in the way of noteworthy differences. For instance, platybrachy, or a flattish humerus mid-shaft with a diaphyseal index less than 76.5 (Jacob 1967:86), characterizes all of the comparisons. Being longer than the average female Australian humerus, and much longer than the Leang Toge humerus, the Lemdubu humerus has a lower calibre index than either of the latter (Table 12.22), further demonstration of its female status (cf. van Dongen 1963:472–3). In contrast, the calibre index of the Willandra Lake humeri is consistently estimated to be larger, between 17.5 and 22.8, and their mid-shaft shape rounder, with a diaphyseal index greater than 76.5 in 17 of the 18 recorded cases (Webb 1989:47). Relatively round mid-shafts are also registered for the Lake Tandou, Lake Nitchie and Cossack humerus diaphyseal indices, which all lie between 76.2 and 84.0 (Freedman and Lofgren 1979:291; Freedman and Lofgren 1983:103; Macintosh 1971:52).

Table 12.22 Liang Lemdubu: left humerus measurements (mm) compared to Leang Toge (Jacob 1967:86) and Australian females (van Dongen 1963:471)

MEASUREMENT	LEMDUBU	LEANG TOGE	AUSTRALIANS
Maximum length (M1)	~313	273 (R)	302.4±14.1
Upper epiphysis breadth (M3)	41	~42 (R)	-
Humerus head circumference (M8)	113	-	111.5±5.4
Humerus head transverse diameter (M9)	~34.5	32 (R)	34.2±1.9
Humerus head vertical diameter (M10)	34	38 (R)	36.3±2.3
Major diameter at shaft mid-point (M5)	16.5	18 (L), 17 (R)	17.3±1.8
Minor diameter at shaft mid-point (M6)	12	13 (L, R)	12.9±1.5
Diaphyseal index (100xM6/M5)	72.7	72.2 (L), 76.5 (R)	75.3±5.8
Mid-shaft circumference (M8)	50	48 (L), 49 (R)	48.5±4.4
Calibre Index (100xM8/M1)	~16.0	17.9	16.1±1.4

NB: for mid-shaft circumference, the exact measurements provided are sub-deltoid circumference for Leang Toge and minimum circumference for Australians. M: Martin and Saller (1957:532-3)

In accord with its slender shape, muscular relief on the Lemdubu humerus is modest. Examples include its very weak (almost imperceptible) deltoid tuberosity, moderately developed *pectoralis major* crista, and the broad and shallow intertubercular groove. The Lemdubu and Leang Toge humeri are specifically similar in the morphology of their intertubercular groove, and the ovoid shape of their diaphysis in cross-section (cf. Jacob 1967:86).

The Lemdubu radii are represented by the head and proximal shaft on the right, and the distal shaft and epiphysis on the left. Both radii are very long and slender. As the medio-distal shaft is present on both sides, we may appose the two extant segments and infer an approximate length of 270mm (Table 12.23). This value would lie beyond the recent female Australian range and above the recent male Australian average (Rao 1966:265), and would approximate the maximum length of 276mm measured on the Lake Nitchie right radius (Macintosh 1971:52). The remarkably long Lemdubu radius is also apparent when related to the circumference of the shaft (as reflected in a low calibre index) and to maximum humerus length. Note that, in both these respects, Leang Toge provides a closer match to Lemdubu Woman than recent Australians do, notwithstanding the much greater length of the Lemdubu radius compared to Leang Toge's (Table 12.23).

Jacob (1967:87) remarks on the gracile morphology of the Leang Toge radii, but this would be less true of the Lemdubu radii. The right side shows a very strongly developed interosseous fossa, a dull radial tuberosity of moderate size, and a long, well-developed groove for the *abductor pollicis longus* muscle. Asymmetric development is apparent with the groove for the *extensor pollicis brevis* muscle (moderately developed on the left, but barely noticeable on the right), and with the inferior groove for the *flexor pollicis longus* muscle (well-developed on the left but not on the right). The distal radius is gracile as shown by its shallow fossa for the attachment of the *pronator quadratus* muscle, the undetectable attachment area for the *pronator teres* muscle, and the small inferior epiphysis breadth of 30mm (M5[6]). Additional measurements not included in Table 12.23 for the right radius, according to Martin and Saller's (1957:536–7) definitions, are: transverse and sagittal diameters of the head, 19.5mm and 19mm respectively (M4[1] and M5[1]); head circumference, 62mm (M5[3]); neck sagittal diameter, 10.5mm (M5[2]); neck circumference, 35mm (M5[4]); and mid-shaft circumference, 36mm (M5[5]).

The Lemdubu ulnae consist of the proximal epiphysis and shaft on the right side, as well as a portion of the right distal shaft, and a couple of fragments from the left proximal shaft. The extant shaft is thick relative to female Australian Aborigines or Leang Toge, whereas the upper epiphysis measurements compare well with female Australian averages but usually exceed those measured on Leang Toge (Table 12.24). An exception is that Lemdubu does not share the marked olecranon depth of Leang Toge, which Jacob (1967:87) observes to be a rare feature. The right Lemdubu ulna presents very sharp supinator and interosseous crests, a robust coronoid process, strong development of the furrow for the *extensor pollicis longus* muscle and the ulna's anterior border, a well-defined if shallow area for the insertion of the *anconeus* muscle, and a slightly developed furrow for the *extensor indicis* muscle. Overall, the Lemdubu ulna appears rugged relative to its radius. Other available measurements on the right ulna, following Martin and Saller's (1957:540–1) definitions, are as follows: height of the proximal facet and humerus facet (M5[1] and M5[2]), 34mm and 22mm respectively; upper ulna breadth (M6[1]), 28mm; anterior and posterior breadth of the radial notch (M9 and M10), 11.5mm and 8.5mm respectively; and dorso-volar and transverse diameters of the shaft (M11 and M12), 13mm and 11mm respectively.

The innominate bones

The demonstrably female status of the Lemdubu (and Leang Toge) innominate bones was noted above. The Lemdubu innominates could be considered as being of typically Australian shape but of above average size (Table 12.2). This description could equally apply to the Lake Nitchie innominates, whose pubic length, ischial length and greatest depth of the sciatic notch lie close to the recent male Australian maxima, while its sciatic notch greatest width lies close to the recent male Australian mean (cf. Davivongs 1963a:448 and Macintosh 1971:51). Leang Toge shows a slightly greater iliac breadth than Lemdubu and consequently a much larger coxal index, but its other measurements as indicated in Table 12.2 are 1–10mm less than their Lemdubu counterparts. Two further measurements of the innominate can be compared (see Jacob 1967:89) and these indicate considerable differences in the shape of the iliae. Specifically, Lemdubu's minimum iliac breadths (66mm left, 68mm right) are much larger than Leang Toge's measurement of 57mm (M13), while the Lemdubu iliac height (112mm left) is considerably less than the Leang Toge values of 121mm and 122mm (M9). Some further measurements, as defined by Martin and Saller (1957:550–9) and/or Arsuaga and Carretero (1994), are listed in Table 12.25.

The Lemdubu innominates display intermediate robustness (Fig. 12.4). The iliac crest is moderately developed, with a well-developed tubercle on both sides, a large anterior superior iliac spine (at least, on the left), and a sharp if small anterior inferior iliac spine. The iliac fossae are

Table 12.23 Liang Lemdubu: radius measurements (mm) compared to Leang Toge (Jacob 1967:88) and Australian females (Rao 1966:265–6)

MEASUREMENT	LEMDUBU	LEANG TOGE	AUSTRALIANS
Maximum length (M1)	~270	223 (L)	235.8±12.1
Radio-humeral index (maximum lengths)	~86.3	81.7	~77.8
Least circumference, distal half (M3)	35 (R)	30 (L, R)	35.0±3.0
Calibre Index (100xM3/M1)	~13.0	13.5	15.5±1.3
Shaft transverse diameter (M4)	12.5 (R)	-	12.8±1.5
Mid-shaft transverse diameter (M4a)	12 (R)	10 (L), 11 (R)	-
Shaft sagittal diameter (M5)	10 (R)	-	10.1±0.9
Mid-shaft sagittal diameter (M5a)	10 (R)	9 (L, R)	-
Diaphyseal index (100xM5/M4)	80.0 (R)	75.0 (L)	78.8±7.7
Neck transverse diameter (M4(2))	10 (R)	10 (L)	-
Collo-diaphyseal angle (M7)	160° (R)	162° (L)	164°±2.9

NB: as Rao (1966:266) used physiological lengths in deriving the Australian radio-humeral index, the Australian value in Table 12.23 is estimated from the average maximum lengths for the radius and humerus (cf. Table 12.22). M: Martin and Saller (1957:535–8)

Table 12.24 Liang Lemdubu: right ulna measurements (mm) compared to Leang Toge (Jacob 1967:88) and Australian females (Rao 1966:267–8)

MEASUREMENT	LEMDUBU	LEANG TOGE	AUSTRALIANS
Minimum circumference (M3)	~34	30 (L), 31 (R)	30.3±2.4
Height of olecranon cap (M5)	4	3 (L, R)	4.3±1.1
Olecranon breadth (M6)	21	19 (L), 18.5 (R)	21.3±1.7
Olecranon depth (M7)	15	21 (L, R)	16.7±1.1
Olecranon-coronoid distance (M7(1))	24.5	23 (L)	-
Upper transverse diameter (M13)	20	16.5 (L), 16 (R)	-
Upper sagittal diameter (M14)	17.5	14.5 (L), 15 (R)	-

NB: M: Martin and Saller (1957:539–41)

Table 12.25 Liang Lemdubu: further measurements (mm) of the right innominate

MARTIN	A & C	VALUE	MARTIN	A & C	VALUE	MARTIN	A & C	VALUE
3	22	~145	4	1	~108	10	-	98
14	-	~94	-	16	46	21	-	~55
28	-	94	29	-	~106	30	-	107

NB: Martin's measurement No.10 (Martin & Saller 1957:556) is 102mm on the left side, and A & C measurement No.16 (Arsuaga and Carretero 1994) is 46.5mm on the left side rather deep and the bone here often appears paper thin, as thin as 0.3mm in places. The arcuate line is weakly expressed on the right side and very weak on the left. The ischial tuberosity is a solid, swollen structure bilaterally. The gluteal lines are not visible on either side, nor is there an acetabular crease, but the arterial impressions are visible on the right side.

The legs

The extant Lemdubu femora convey the visual impression of impressive length, as confirmed by my attempt to estimate their maximum length. Segment 3 of Steele and McKern (1969) and Steele (1970) measures approximately 77mm on the right member, which would lead to length estimates of the complete bone of 444.9±16.7mm (based on the female Mesoamerican formula in Steele and McKern 1969), 464.1±26.0mm and 476.5±20.7mm (based, respectively, on the female American White and Afro-American formulae in Steele 1970). This range of estimates essentially matches the maximum lengths of 444–470mm that lie more than one standard deviation above the average as measured on recent female Australian femora (Davivongs 1963b:459). Thus, the length of the Lemdubu femora would have lain at the top of the recent female Australian range. Similarly, Webb (1989:49) provides maximum length estimates of 435–463mm for the female femora from the Willandra Lakes, while the Lake Nitchie femoral lengths lie more than two standard deviations above the recent Australian average (cf. Davivongs 1963b:459 and Macintosh 1971:52). The Lemdubu femora would certainly have been much longer than is the case with Leang Toge whose left femur has a maximum length of merely 380mm (Jacob 1967:90).

Other measurements and indices available on the Lemdubu femora include several that fall beyond the recent female Australian range and indeed appear hyper-masculine, including pilastric index (reflecting the strongly developed *linea aspera*), popliteal index, and transverse condylar breadth (Table 12.26). However, Lemdubu falls among good company: both male and female Willandra Lake femora have instances of transverse mid-shaft diameters and pilastric indices that fall above the range of the same-sexed recent Australian femora; the transverse condylar breadth of Lake Nitchie falls well beyond the recent Australian range; and Cossack has mid-shaft diameters that lie at the extreme of the recent Australian range (Table 12.26). Only the Kow Swamp femora cannot be distinguished from recent Australians in these regards. Therefore the male-like shape and size of the Lemdubu femora (Fig. 12.13) essentially reflects its ancient Sahulland status. In all these same respects, the gracile Leang Toge femur resembles recent Australian female femora, even if its shorter length (43.6mm shorter than the female Australian average) means that it is comparatively less slender.

In contrast to the large size of the femora, the Lemdubu patellae are patently small (measurement definitions taken from Martin and Saller 1957:570–1). The Lemdubu dimensions are consistently similar to those of the Leang Toge (right) patella (Table 12.27), and 6–10mm less than the Lake Nitchie patella on height, breadth and thickness (cf. Macintosh 1971:52). The Lemdubu patellae do not show a vastus notch, though their outline is concave here, nor a bipartite morphology or emarginate form (cf. Brothwell 1981:97, 99).

Maximum length of the right Lemdubu tibia can be estimated from its lengths of segments 3 and 4 (~173mm and ~111mm respectively) as defined by Steele (1970; Steele and McKern 1969). Based on these estimates, tibia length would be 367.1±5.1mm, 394.8±9.9mm and 390.7±9.8mm, using the Mesoamerican, American white and Afro-American formulae respectively (Steele 1970; Steele and McKern 1969). The resulting range of 368–395mm closely matches the range measured by Rao (1966:269) for Australian female tibiae longer than the mean (364–402mm), so the Lemdubu tibia would be of above average length by recent female Australian standards. As the same would apply to Lemdubu Woman's femur, her relationship between femoral and tibia length would probably be similar to the usual situation among recent Australians. This point would certainly apply to both Lake Nitchie and Leang Toge, notwithstanding their great differences in body size.

Table 12.26 Specimens and series arranged from most to least masculine in their femoral measurements (mm)

SPECIMEN/ SERIES	M6	M7	100X M7/M6	M8	M11	M12	100XM11/ M12	M21
Lake Nitchie ♂	32	28	114.3	-	-	-	-	89.5
Cossack ♂	35	28	125	-	-	-	-	-
Willandra Lake ♂	32.3	28.8	114.1	-	-	-	-	-
	(31-35)	(25-33)	(103-140)					
Lemdubu ♀	30.5	24	127.1	84	28	32	87.5	≥71 (R)
	(R,L)	(R)	(R)	(R)	(R)	(R)	(R)	
Kow Swamp	-	-	~114	-	-	-	~72	-
Willandra Lake ♀	29.6	27.5	108	-	-	-	-	-
	(28-31)	(26-31)	(94-119)					
Australian ♂	27.6	24.7	112.0	82.5	26.9	36.9	73.4	69.9
	(21-37)	(21-29)	(85-135)	(70-105)	(22-34)	(31-45)	(61-91)	(60-84)
Australian ♀	23.9	22.4	106.6	72.8	22.9	34.0	67.4	61.3
	(18-30)	(19-26)	(86-132)	(61-84)	(19-28)	(27-44)	(56-82)	(54-67)
Leang Toge ♀	22	23.5	93.6	71	24	36	66.7	59

NB: M6 = sagittal mid-shaft diameter; M7 = transverse mid-shaft diameter; 100xM7/M6 = pilastric index; M8 = mid-shaft circumference; M11 = sagittal supracondylar diameter; M12 = transverse supracondylar diameter; 100xM11/M12 = popliteal index; M21 = transverse condylar breadth (Martin and Saller 1957:563-4). Cossack data from Freedman and Lofgren (1979:291). Willandra Lake data from Webb (1989:49), excluding estimated values. Kow Swamp values estimated from Kennedy (1984:Fig. 1), and include five males and one female. Recent Australian data from Davivongs (1963b:459). Leang Toge data from Jacob (1967:90)

Table 12.27 Liang Lemdubu: patella measurements (mm) compared to those of Leang Toge

MEASUREMENT	RIGHT	LEFT	LEANG TOGE	MEASUREMENT	RIGHT	LEFT	LEANG TOGE
Greatest height (M1)	35	36	35	Greatest breadth (M2)	38	38.5	36
Greatest thickness (M3)	17	17	18	Articular surface height (M4)	7	9	7.5
Medial articular surface height (M5)	17	16	16	Lateral articular surface breadth (M6)	24	25	20

Their tibio-femoral indices of 80.5 (Macintosh 1971:52) and 80.3 (Jacob 1967:91), respectively, closely match the averages of 80.5 and 80.6 recorded on Australian males and females (Rao 1966:270). It may also be noted that the Lemdubu tibia would have been longer than the single Willandra Lakes, female tibia which is complete enough for Webb (1989:51) to venture an estimate of its maximum length (360mm).

The remaining Lemdubu tibia measurements are similar to the average values for female Australians (Table 12.28), apart from the flatter shape of the Lemdubu tibia at the nutrient foramen, and the low retroversion and inclination angles which reflect a straightish tibia shape, similar to the typical European condition (cf. Rao 1966:62). Lemdubu's platycnemia departs from the generally rounder tibiae at Willandra Lakes (average 66.1; Webb 1989:51) and Lake Nitchie (65.5; Macintosh 1971:52), so this is one feature where Lemdubu resembles Leang Toge (Jacob 1967:91) more so than Australian skeletons. However, the Leang Toge tibia is dissimilar from

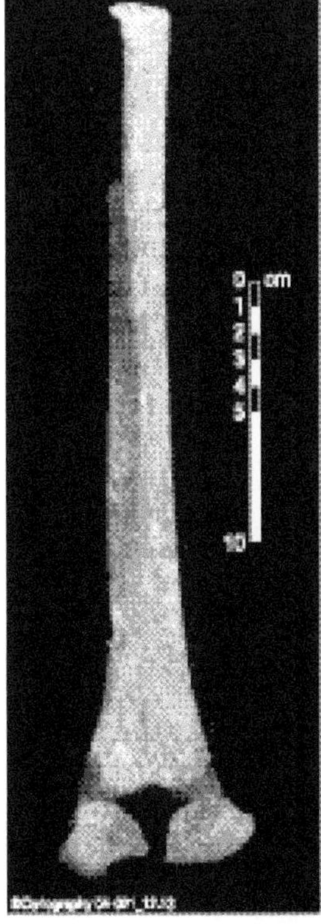

Figure 12.13 Liang Lemdubu: posterior view of the right femur (note the portion cut from the shaft for AMS dating and attempted stable isotope ratio analysis)

Australian tibiae on other criteria too, such as its higher calibre index, and remarkably large retroversion and inclination angles as reported (Table 12.28).

The Lemdubu tibiae have a long shape at their mid-shaft and a hollowed lateral surface — i.e. Hrdlička's Type 3 — while Leang Toge has a long oval shape — Hrdlička's Type 6 (Jacob 1967:91). The Type 3 form would be quite common among Australian Aborigines, especially the males, whereas the Type 6 morphology is rare among Australian males and even rarer among Australian females (cf. Rao 1966:61). The right Lemdubu tibia displays an ilio-tibial or lateral squatting facet, as found on Leang Toge (Jacob 1967:91) and around 80% of Australians (Rao 1966:67); preservation is inadequate to tell whether a medial squatting facet is also expressed. As noted previously, the distal shaft of the right tibia bears a hole attributable to metastatic carcinoma (the corresponding area of the left tibia is not extant).

The left fibula of Lemdubu Woman is rugged, with marked furrows for the attachment of the *soleus* and *peroneus longus* muscles, and for the origins of the *flexor hallucis longus* and *tibialis posterior* muscles. It is also remarkably slender, with a minimum circumference recorded as 21mm, compared to a corresponding value of 28mm on the extant right fibula fragments. The left-side value falls slightly below the recorded Australian range, while the right-side estimate equals the female Australian average (Rao 1966:272) and falls just beneath Leang Toge's value of 29mm (Jacob 1967:92). The right-side maximum and minimum fibula diameters are respectively 10.5mm and 8.5mm on the extant fragments, slightly less than Leang Toge's values of 14.5mm and nine millimetres as recorded at the mid-shaft (Jacob 1967:92). A slender fibula shape, noted to be a feature of Leang Toge (Jacob 1967:92) and Australian Aborigines (Rao 1966:75), would seem to be particularly a feature of Lemdubu Woman.

Table 12.28 Liang Lemdubu: tibia measurements (mm) compared to Leang Toge and Australian females

MEASUREMENT	LEMDUBU	L. TOGE	AUSTRALIANS
Sagittal diameter at nutrient foramen level (M8a)	32 (R)	-	29.4±2.8
Transverse diameter at nutrient foramen level (M9a)	19 (R)	-	19.8±1.9
Circumference at nutrient foramen level (M10a)	82 (R)	-	-
Maximum diameter at mid-shaft (M8)	27 (R), 28 (L)	24.5 (R), 24 (L)	25.6±2.5
Transverse diameter at mid-shaft (M9)	17 (R), 18 (L)	16.5 (R), 18 (L)	18.6±1.8
Circumference at mid-shaft (M10)	76 (R), 78 (L)	66 (R), 65 (L)	72.0±5.9
Platycnemic index of Rao (M9ax100/M8a)	59.4 (R)	<63.0	67.6±5.5
Platycnemic index of Jacob (M9x100/M8)	63.0 (R), 64.3 (L)	67.4 (R), 75.0 (L)	-
Calibre index	~19	20.3 (R)	17.6±1.1
Sagittal diameter of distal epiphysis (M7)	~33 (R)	-	32.4±1.7
Retroversion angle	~11° (R)	30° (R)	18.0°±4.1
Inclination angle	~9° (R)	21° (R)	14.1°±3.8

NB: Leang Toge from Jacob (1967:91) and Australian Aborigines from Rao (1966:269–71). Calibre index is minimum circumference x 100 divided by physiological length; the estimate for the Lembubu skeleton is indicative only. M: Martin and Saller (1957:573–4)

The extremities

As noted in in the discussion above on the disposition of the bones, the majority of the extremity bones excavated at Lemdubu would not appear to relate to Lemdubu Woman. The distal pedal phalanx from Spit 1 is adult, as indicated by its fused epiphyses, and short at 14.5mm in length, which might point to a female status. It is burnt, as is the right fifth proximal manual phalanx from Spit 10, which also has fused epiphyses. Its phalanx length of 29mm falls at the bottom of the male Australian range recorded by Rao (1966:43). The distal pedal phalanx (second digit) from Spit 11 measures 12mm in length, which falls within the range of 8–21mm recorded by Rao (1966:108) on recent male Australians. It is adult and could conceivably have derived from Lemdubu Woman, as could the small calcaneus fragment from Spit 12. A proximal fragment from a left fourth metacarpal, recovered from Spit 20, is of a size that would be consistent with a tallish individual like Lemdubu Woman. The talus fragments from the base of the excavation are too incomplete to allow any anatomically useful observations. Finally, two right lunate bones are present, a small burnt specimen from Spit 7 (which could relate to the other extremity bones from Spits 1 and 10) and a larger, unburnt specimen from Spit 19. Their measurements are given in Table 12.29.

Table 12.29 Liang Lemdubu: measurements (mm) of the two right lunate bones

SPECIMEN	M1	M2	M3	M4	M5	M6	M7	M8	M9	M10	M11	M12
Spit 7	21	17	13	13	10	13	10	10.5	10	8	7	1.5
Spit 19	21.5	21	15.5	15	18	16.5	11	12	5	14	7.5	3

NB: M: Martin and Saller (1957:544–5)

Stature and postcranial robustness

The two maximum limb bone lengths of Lemdubu Woman that allow a useful estimate of her stature during life are the left humerus length of around 313mm, and right tibia length of 365-400mm. The most suitable regression formulae to estimate stature would be those which both use maximum limb bone lengths for the humerus and tibia, and are derived from female skeletons of a population in the same region. Only the study by Bergman and The (1955) on Javanese corpses fits the bill. However, because they estimated corpse length rather than stature, two centimetres should be subtracted from the resulting estimate (Snell 1949:358). The humerus would therefore lead to an estimated stature of 165.9±4.5cm, likewise the tibia an estimate of 162–173±3.9cm (Bergman and The 1955:200) or 167.5cm as a middling estimate. The relatively short vertebral discs and, therefore, short vertebral column of Lemdubu Woman (given her long limbs by female standards) might suggest an accommodatory reduction of her estimated stature. However, the appropriate degree of reduction would be difficult to stipulate, especially as her tall cranium (taller even than the recent male Australian average) would suggest the contrary accommodation, and, as noted above, least-squares regression estimates of a tall individual's stature from that individual's limb-bone lengths would tend to produce conservative results. Hence, the humerus-based estimate of 166cm for Lemdubu Woman's stature is probably the best available.

In contrast, Leang Toge's stature estimates would be 143.0cm (left femur), 143.9cm (right tibia), 149.3cm (right humerus), 151.5cm (left radius), and 152.5–155.2cm (ulnae) with reference to female Javanese regression formulae, employing Jacob's measurements of the particular limb bone length definitions given by Bergman and The (1955:198). These stature estimates compare well with Jacob's (1967:94) own estimate of 148.4cm. The stature of Leang Toge would therefore have been 11–23cm less than that of Lemdubu Woman, or 17cm as a middling estimate.

Lemdubu Woman's stature of around 166cm would be very similar to the average male stature found among recent Australian Aborigines and, accordingly, around 10cm taller than the recent female Australian average (cf. Kirk 1981:91–4). This tall stature is in accord with the large size of other documented Sahulland skeletons of Pleistocene age, as reflected by the ulna length of Lake Mungo 3, which lies at the top of the recent Australian male range, and the large stature of the Coobool Creek and Nacurrie males as estimated from their cranial dimensions (Brown 2000:747). It is also in accord with the stature estimates of the ancient Willandra Lake skeletal collections studied by Webb (1989:92–142), whether we use Webb's estimates using Afro-American regression formulae (Webb 1989:20), or estimates based on Javanese formulae regressed against maximum limb-bone lengths (Table 12.30). Estimates for males range from the recent Australian average to a value around 15cm higher, while estimates for females fall within a tighter range between the recent Australian average and the estimated stature of Lemdubu Woman. The huge stature of the virtually complete Lake Nitchie male, placed reliably at 187.7cm (Macintosh 1971:51), has already been alluded to.

As discussed above, when considered in terms of muscular markings, the postcranial robustness of Lemdubu Woman is not particularly marked, lying more or less between the average conditions that would pertain to recent male and female Australians. Pronounced postcranial robustness is evident, however, when considered in terms of the thickness of the shaft bone. At the cross-sections exposed by breakages in the bones near the mid-shaft of the femur and humerus, the combined thicknesses of the cortical bone always exceeded the thickness of the medullary cavity along the same axis, and was sometimes thicker on just one of the sides. In the case of the humerus, the relative thickness of Lemdubu Woman's cortical bone is very similar to that of a Willandra Lake humerus that Webb (1989:48) singled out as having the thickest cortical bone in the series (Table 12.31). With regard to the femur, the percentage of Lemdubu Woman's medio-lateral axis that is cortical bone is very similar to the average values recorded for other specimens of *Homo sapiens*, including those in Australia, but in the antero-posterior axis, Lemdubu Woman approximates the average recorded for *H. erectus*. Even here, however, the variation among *H. sapiens* (including recent Australians) is so wide that the Lemdubu value would comfortably fall within the sapient range (Table 12.31).

At Lemdubu Woman's femoral mid-section, the medullary area is circa 85mm^2, cortical area 366mm^2, and total cross-sectional area 451mm^2. A breakage approximately 35% along the femoral shaft from its distal epiphysis naturally displayed thinner cortical bone, but even here the cortex is thick, with an estimated area of 338mm^2, compared to total cross-sectional area of 546mm^2, and medullary area of 208mm^2. The estimated values at the humerus mid-section are 23mm^2 for the medullary area, 145mm^2 for cortical area, and 168mm^2 for total cross-sectional area. When the estimated cortical area is expressed as a percentage of the total cross-sectional area, thickness of the bone approximates the condition observed among Neandertals, and lies well above the recent *Homo sapiens* average (Table 12.32). This does not however reflect a Neandertal-like shape of the femoral and humerus cross-sections; in particular, Lemdubu Woman has the strongly developed pilaster of early, anatomically modern *H. sapiens* rather than the round femora of the Neandertals (Pearson 1999:241; cf. Ruff et al. 1993:Fig. 1) or, for that matter, *H. erectus* (Kennedy 1984:166). Rather, it emphasises the relatively great thickness of the cortical bone of Lemdubu Woman.

Discussion and Conclusion

As well as discussing the terminal Pleistocene age of the fragments assignable to Lemdubu Woman, this paper shows that the biological affinities confirm the burial's Late Pleistocene Sahulland status. It is only in the comparison with ancient Australians that Lemdubu Woman registers a higher frequency of matches (11) compared to mismatches (6). This strong agreement specifically reflects the common features of large size (tall stature, long limb bones, large cranium) and robust cranial anatomy (Table 12.33). At the detailed level, some differences do emerge between Lemdubu Woman and penecontemporary fossils to the south, as in mandibular anatomy (Table 12.14), and various divergences from the Kow Swamp and Coobool Creek morphological pattern summarized by Brown (1989:169–74). For example, the Lemdubu mandible does not have the particularly tall corpus noted for the ancient Murray Valley mandibles, the lateral maxillary incisors are not particularly robust, and the cranium is not markedly (not at all) dolichocranic or characterized by thick vault bone. Further Late Pleistocene burials from northern Sahulland would be required to assess whether these differences reflect individual, geographic or chronological variation.

Even in those cases where a distinction may be noted between the anatomy of Lemdubu Woman and ancient Australian fossils to the south, a similarity with the osteology of recent Australians usually emerges (Table 12.33), reinforcing the burial's affinity with southwest Pacific populations. Thickness of the limbs' cortical bone is the sole aspect where Lemdubu Woman's

Table 12.30 Ancient Willandra Lake burials estimated statures (cm) (from Webb 1989:92–142)

Males Specimen	Stature	Indeterminate Specimen	Stature	Females Specimen	Stature
WL67	177–180 [171–177]	WL117 (if ♂)	169	WL25	161–165 [162]
WL107	170	WL117 (if ♀)	166	WL72	159–162 [160]
WL106	164–173 [162–171]	WL6 (if ♂)	158 [156]	WL45	159–160 [162.5]
WL110	164 [162]	WL6 (if ♀)	153 [152]		

NB: ancient status determined either by advanced mineralization (WL6, WL25, WL110), or carbonate encrustation (WL45, WL67, WL106, WL107, WL117), or both (WL72). Webb offers both male and female stature estimates for several of these burials; both estimates are shown here when he considered the burial's sex to be indeterminate. Estimates in square brackets are derived from Javanese regression formulae (Bergman and The 1955:200); these however cannot be used when the femur is the limb bone allowing a stature estimate, as Bergman and The measured femoral length in natural position, while Webb's estimates are maximum lengths of the limb bone

Table 12.31 Liang Lemdubu: compared on percentage of mid-shaft diameter made up of cortical bone

SPECIMEN/SERIES	FEMUR MEDIO-LATERAL	FEMUR ANTERO-POSTERIOR	HUMERUS MEDIO-LATERAL	HUMERUS ANTERO-POSTERIOR
Lemdubu Woman	~57.6	~61.5	~68.3	~53.6
Willandra Lakes	~37.8	~51.5	~55.1, ~63.2	~61.0, ~60.4
Kow Swamp	41.7-68.2	37.5-50.9	-	-
Murray Valley males	58.3±6.3	54.6±5.7	-	-
Murray Valley females	54.2±7.2	50.5±8.9	-	-
Tasmanian males	53.3±9.9	51.8±13.8	-	-
Tasmanian females	59.2±19.5	57.5±11.2	-	-
Romano-British males	57.6±7.8	58.1±7.6	-	-
Romano-British females	55.3±11.1	55.2±7.5	-	-
Homo erectus	62.3±5.0	62.8±7.3	-	-

NB: Willandra Lake values estimated from photographs of the femur of WL107 (Webb 1989:Plate 1) and the the humeri of WL110 (Webb 1989:Plate 16). Other comparative data from Kennedy (1984)

Table 12.32 Liang Lemdubu: compared cortical area as a percentage of total cross-sectional area on the femur and humerus

	LEMDUBU WOMAN	NEANDERTALS	EARLY MODERN *H. SAPIENS*	RECENT *H. SAPIENS*
Distal femur (~35% along shaft length)	~61.9%	~66%	~55%	~55%
Medial femur (~50% along shaft length)	~81.2%	~78%	~79%	~70%
Medial humerus (~50% along shaft length)	~86.3%	78.6%	-	67.6%

NB: averages for Neandertals, early modern *Homo sapiens*, and recent *Homo sapiens* estimated from Ruff et al. (1993:Figure 2) or taken from Ruff et al. (1993:37)

skeletal morphology clearly departs from both ancient and recent Australians' usual condition (as currently documented). And in at least some cases where Lemdubu Woman could not be claimed to be similar to either ancient or recent Australians (+/– in Table 12.33), this reflects the skeleton's 'hyper-Australian' attributes. For instance, her body build was more linear than is the case with the ancient Australian from Lake Nitchie, or with most recent Australians, but as detailed in the post cranial description above, linearity of body build — elongated distal limbs compared to proximal limb-bone lengths, long limb bones compared to the length of the vertebral column, and gracile epiphyses compared to limb-bone lengths — is a distinguishing trait of Australian Aborigines compared to most other recent populations. Where Lemdubu Woman differs most clearly from recent Australians is in her larger body size and greater cranial robustness, two general attributes that also distinguish ancient southeast Australian fossils from recent Australians (Brown 1987; 1989:172).

Lemdubu Woman rarely agrees with the morphological attributes of the middle Holocene Flores' specimens (Table 12.33), as best represented by the Leang Toge skeleton. Size and robustness distinctions dominate the differences, along with the far more linear build of the Aru

12.33 Liang Lemdubu: summary of Lemdubu Woman and Leang Toge skeletal comparisons

	LEMDUBU WOMAN			LEANG TOGE		
SKELETAL ASPECT	AA	RA	FL	AA	RA	LM
Tooth size	+	+	-	-	-	-
Cranial size	++	-	-	-	+	-
Craniometrics	+	-	-	-	+	-
Cranial anatomy	++	-	-	-	+	-
Mandibular anatomy	+/-	+	-	+/-	+	-
Mandibular size	+/-	-	+	+	-	+
Mandibular shape	-	+	+	+/-	+/-	+
Vertebral disc dimensions	?	+/-	-	?	-	-
Clavicle	-	+	?	?	?	?
Scapula size	+	-	-	-	+	-
Scapula anatomy	?	-	+	?	-	+
Humerus length	+	-	-	-	-	-
Humerus shape	-	+	+	-	+	+
Radius length	+	-	-	-	+/-	-
Radius shape	?	+/-	+/-	?	+/-	+/-
Ulna	?	+	-	?	-	-
Innominates	+	+/-	-	-	+	-
Femur size	+	-	-	-	-	-
Femur robustness	+	-	-	-	+	-
Small patella	-	?	+	-	?	+
Tibia shape	-	+	+/-	-	-	+/-
Slender fibula	?	+	+	?	+	+
Proximal/distal limb bone relationship	+/-	+/-	+/-	+	+	+/-
Linearity of build	+/-	+/-	-	+	+	-
Stature	+	-	-	-	-	-
Thick cortex (limb bones)	-	-	?	?	?	?
Total matches/mismatches	11+/++, 4+/-, 6-	8+/++, 5+/-, 12-	6+, 3+/-, 15-	3+, 2+/-, 14-	11+, 3+/-, 9-	6+, 3+/-, 15-

NB: AA = ancient Australians, RA = recent Australians, FL = Flores, LM = Lemdubu Woman; ++ = strong agreement, + = agreement, +/- = ambiguous, - = disagreement, ? = comparison unavailable

skeleton, but there are also other divergences as in the detail of the mandibular morphology (Table 12.14). However, while the Leang Toge and Lemdubu skeletons clearly represent different populations, it is far less apparent that Leang Toge could be osteologically distinguished from recent Australian Aborigines. Storm (1995:98) noted that 'Liang Toge shows a combination of some characters resembling the morphology often found in recent female Australian skulls'. This conclusion is reinforced here in cranial size (Fig. 12.7), craniometrics (Table 12.12), overall cranial anatomy (Figs 12.8 and 12.9), and, notwithstanding Leang Toge's small stature, proximal-distal limb bone proportions and many shape details of the limb bones (Table 12.33). To think of Lemdubu Woman as ancient Australian (Sahulland), and Leang Toge as similar to recent Australians, would certainly allow us to propose deriving, at least in part, the ancestry of the middle Holocene inhabitants of Flores from the Pleistocene inhabitants of northern Sahulland.

Accepting the Pleistocene Sahulland status of Lemdubu Woman, we should consider how this new find reflects on the much-vaunted (and debated) distinction between 'robust' and 'gracile', ancient Australians (Brown 1987; Bulbeck 2001; Thorne 1977; Webb 1989:73–6). Thick bone on the cranial vault is one debated component of the so-called robust morphology (Brown 1987:48–50, 61; Thorne 1977:191), and in this respect Lemdubu Woman would be decidedly 'gracile'. The flat, receding frontal bone of certain Murray Valley specimens has also been invoked as a component of the robust morphology, although this feature is now convincingly related to cranial deformation (Antón and Weinsten 1999; Brown 1981). The naturally receding frontal of the very robust WL50 specimen (Hawks et al. 2000) may help to rehabilitate the claimed assocation, but in that case, Lemdubu's rounded frontal would make it truly gracile. A third component is the distinction between huge (robust) and relatively small (gracile) crania at Willandra Lakes, which can be attributed to the enormous elapse of time represented by those specimens, even if the chronological details are not as yet entirely clear (Bulbeck 2001:98; see Fig. 12.7, this paper). Lemdubu would fit into neither of these categories as its cranial size fits centrally in the terminal Pleistocene Sahulland range. Fourth is the greater size and robustness (but also variations in angularity in the parietal region unrelated to cranial deformation). Lemdubu Woman would be considered robust on this criterion but, as emphasised by Brown (1987:61), so would the Keilor specimen from terminal Pleistocene Victoria, a specimen frequently held up as gracile. Once differences that could be attributed to sex are removed, the main difference between Lemdubu and Keilor may lie in the greater angulation of the Lemdubu cranium's parietal contour (cf. Weidenreich 1945), and so Lemdubu could be considered more robust on those terms.

From the above, it would seem that the 'robust' and 'gracile' categories, despite their continued retention as objective classifications in some recent studies (e.g. Adcock et al. 2000), are poorly defined in the terminal Pleistocene Sahulland context. These morphological categories are based on components which often appear contradictory rather than correlated, and so attempting to classify a specimen as either robust or gracile may hinder our appreciation of that specimen's overall morphology. The Lemdubu skeleton does not fit with the view of these two 'morphologies' as espoused, for instance, by Thorne (e.g. Adcock et al. 2000; Sim and Thorne 1990; Thorne 1977, 1980; Thorne and Wilson 1977). It may be more productive, instead, to try and understand spatial and chronological variation among Sahulland's occupants in terms of modern evolutionary theory. For instance, while this paper is not the place for an extended discussion, it may be suggested that Lemdubu Woman's combination of thick cortical limb bone, robust femora compared to gracile arm bones, and markedly linear build reflects in part retention of early modern *Homo sapiens*' features and, in part, adaptation to a tropical environment during a period when temperatures generally were dropping (Pearson 1999; cf. Ruff et al. 1993).

In summary, this article certifies the terminal Pleistocene status of the human burial excavated at the Lemdubu site in the Aru Islands, and concurrently, shows its two unique credentials. It is the only terminal Pleistocene Sahulland specimen whose postcranial skeleton has been published in any detail, and it is the only described, terminal Pleistocene representative of the tropical belt of Sahulland.

Acknowledgments

I would like to thank Matthew Spriggs and Sue O'Connor for giving me the opportunity to work on the Lemdubu human remains and for their discussions and advice on issues of stratigraphic association, chronology and likely burial practices. Thanks are also due to Frédérique Valentin who provided many useful comments as peer reviewer for the article.

References

Adcock, G.J., E.S. Dennis, S. Easteal, G.A. Huttley, L.S. Jermlin, W.J. Peacock, and A. Thorne. 2001. Mitochondrial DNA sequences in ancient Australians: implications for modern human origins. *Proceedings of the National Academy of Sciences* 98(2):537–42.

Antón, S.C. and K.J. Weinstein. 1999. Artificial cranial deformation and fossil Australians revisited. *Journal of Human Evolution* 36:195–209.

Arsuaga, J.L. and J.M. Carretero. 1994. Multivariate analysis of the sexual dimorphism of the hip bone in a modern human population and in early hominids. *American Journal of Physical Anthropology* 93:241–57.

Aufderheide, A.C. and C. Rodríguez-Martín. 1998. *The Cambridge Encyclopedia of Human Paleopathology*. Cambridge: Cambridge University Press.

Bergman, R.A.M. and T.H. The. 1955. The length of the body and long bones of the Javanese. *Documenta de Medecina Geographica et Tropica* 7:197–214.

Berry, A.C. 1974. The use of non-metrical variations of the cranium in the study of Scandinavian population movements. *American Journal of Physical Anthropology* 40:345–58.

von Bonin, G. 1963. *The Evolution of the Human Brain*. Chicago: University of Chicago Press.

Brace, C.L. and R.J. Hinton. 1981. Oceanic tooth-size variations as a reflection of biological and cultural mixing. *Current Anthropology* 22:549–69.

Brooks, S. and J.M. Suchey. 1990. Skeletal age determination based on the os pubis: a comparison of the Acsádi-Nemeskéri and Suchey-Brooks methods. *Journal of Human Evolution* 5:227–38.

Brothwell, D.R. 1981. *Digging up Bones*. Third edition. Oxford: British Museum (Natural History)/Oxford University Press.

Brown, P. 1981. Artificial cranial deformation: a component in the variation in Pleistocene Australian Aboriginal crania. *Archaeology in Oceania* 16:156–67.

Brown, P.J. 1982. Coobool Creek: A Prehistoric Australian Hominid Population. Unpublished PhD thesis, The Australian National University, Canberra.

Brown, P. 1987. Pleistocene homogeneity and Holocene size reduction: the Australian human skeletal evidence. *Archaeology in Oceania* 22:41–67.

Brown, P. 1989. *Coobool Creek*. Canberra: The Australian National University, *Terra Australis* 13.

Brown, P. 1992. Pleistocene change in Australian Aboriginal tooth size: dental reduction or relative expansion? In T. Brown and S. Molnar (eds), *Craniofacial Variation in Pacific Populations: Papers Presented at a Symposium Honolulu, Hawaii, May 30, 1991*, pp. 33–51. Adelaide: The University of Adelaide.

Brown, P. 1994. A flawed vision: sex and robusticity on King Island. *Australian Archaeology* 38:1–7.

Brown, P. 1995. Still flawed: a reply to Pardoe (1994) and Sim and Thorne [*sic!*] (1994). *Australian Archaeology* 41:26–9.

Brown, P. 2000. Australian Pleistocene variation and the sex of Lake Mungo 3. *Journal of Human Evolution* 38:743–9.

Brown, P. 2001. Peter Brown's Australian Palaeoanthropology. URL: http://metz.une.edu.au/~pbrown3/ausindex.html.

Brown, T., S.K. Pinkerton, and W. Lambert. 1979. Thickness of the cranial vault in Australian Aboriginals. *Archaeology and Physical Anthropology in Oceania* 14:54–71.

Bulbeck, F.D. 1981. Continuities in Southeast Asian Evolution Since the Late Pleistocene. Unpublished M.A. thesis, The Australian National University, Canberra.

Bulbeck, F.D. 1992. A Tale of Two Kingdoms: The Historical Archaeology of Gowa and Tallok, South Sulawesi, Indonesia. Unpublished PhD thesis, The Australian National University, Canberra.

Bulbeck, F.D. 1993. Report on the human osteological remains from Tanjung Pinang, Morotai Island, Maluku Utara, Indonesia. In Archaeological Survey and Excavation in the Halmahera Island Group, Maluku Utara, Indonesia. Unpublished report for the Australasian Indonesian project.

Bulbeck, D. 1997. Seriated dendrograms (Appendix B). In A. Flavel, Sa-Huynh-Kalanay? Analysis of the Prehistoric Decorated Earthenware of South Sulawesi in an Island Southeast Asian Context, pp. 212–25. Unpublished B.Sc. Hons subthesis, University of Western Australia, Perth.

Bulbeck, D. 2000a. Dental morphology at Gua Cha, West Malaysia, and the implications for 'Sundadonty'. *Indo–Pacific Prehistory Association Bulletin* 19:17–41.

Bulbeck, D. 2000b. Multivariate statistical analysis of the Gua Peraling 4 cranium (Appendix 7). In Adi bin Haji Taha, Archaeological Investigations in Ulu Kelantan, Peninsular Malaysia, unpaginated. Unpublished PhD thesis, The Australian National University, Canberra.

Bulbeck, F.D. 2001. Robust and gracile Australian crania: the tale of the Willandra Lakes. In T. Simanjuntak, B. Prasetyo, and R. Handini (eds), *Sangiran: Man, Culture and Environment in Pleistocene Times*, pp. 60–106. Jakarta: Yayasan Obor Indonesia/The National Research Centre of Archaeology/École Française d'Extrême-Orient.

Bulbeck, D. 2004. Appendix 1: Human remains from Kria Cava and Toé Cave, Papua, Indonesia. In J.M. Pasveer, *The Djief Hunters: 26,000 Years of Rainforest Exploitation on the Bird's Head of Papua, Indonesia*, pp. 379–98. Modern Quaternary Research in Southeast Asia 17. Leiden: A.A. Balkema.

Davivongs, V. 1963a. The pelvic girdle of the Australian Aborigine; sex differences and sex determination. *American Journal of Physical Anthropology* 21:443–55.

Davivongs, V. 1963b. The femur of the Australian Aborigine. *American Journal of Physical Anthropology* 21:457–67.

van Dongen, R. 1963. The shoulder girdle and humerus of the Australian Aborigine. *American Journal of Physical Anthropology* 29:469–88.

Formicola, V. 1993. Stature reconstruction from long bones in ancient population samples: an approach to the problem of its reliability. *American Journal of Physical Anthropology* 90:351–8.

Freedman, L. and M. Lofgren. 1979. Human skeletal remains from Cossack, Western Australia. *Journal of Human Evolution* 8:283–99.

Freedman, L. and M. Lofgren. 1983. Human skeletal remains from Lake Tandou, New South Wales. *Archaeology in Oceania* 18:98–105.

Gilbert, B.M. and T.W. McKern. 1973. A method for ageing the female *os pubis*. *American Journal of Physical Anthropology* 38:31–8.

Hawks, J., S. Oh, K. Hunley, S. Dobson, G. Cabana, P. Dayula, and M.H. Wolpoff. 2000. An Australasian test of the recent African origin theory using the WLH–50 calvarium. *Journal of Human Evolution* 39:1–22.

Hillson, S. 1996. *Dental Anthropology*. Cambridge: Cambridge University Press.

Howells, W.W. 1973. *Cranial Variation in Man*. Cambridge, Mass.: Harvard University Press.

Hrdlička, A. 1928. Catalogue of human crania in the United States National Museum collections. *Proceedings of the U.S. National Museum* 71:1–140.

Jacob, T. 1967. *Some Problems Pertaining to the Racial History of the Indonesian Region*. Utrecht: Netherlands Bureau for Technical Assistance.

Kellock, W.L. and P.A. Parsons. 1971. A comparison of the incidence of minor nonmetrical cranial variants in Australian Aborigines with those of Melanesia and Polynesia. *American Journal of Physical Anthropology* 33:235–40.

Kennedy, G.E. 1984. Are the Kow Swamp hominids 'archaic'? *American Journal of Physical Anthropology* 65:163–8.

Kirk, R.L. 1981. *Aboriginal Man Adapting*. Oxford: Clarendon Press.

Larnach, S.L. and L. Freedman. 1964. Sex determination of crania from coastal New South Wales. *Records of the Australian Museum* 26:295–308.

Larnach, S.L. and N.W.G. Macintosh. 1966. *The Craniology of the Aborigines of Coastal New South Wales*. Sydney: University of Sydney. *Oceania Monographs* 13.

Larnach, S.L. and N.W.G. Macintosh. 1970. *The Craniology of the Aborigines of Queensland*. Sydney: University of Sydney. *Oceania Monographs* 15.

Larnach, S.L. and N.W.G. Macintosh. 1971. *The Mandible in Eastern Australian Aborigines*. Sydney: University of Sydney. *Oceania Monographs* 17.

Lundy, J.K. 1980. The mylohyoid bridge in the Khoisan of southern Africa and its unsuitability as a Mongoloid genetic marker. *American Journal of Physical Anthropology* 53:43–8.

Macintosh, N.W.G. 1971. Analysis of an Aboriginal skeleton and a pierced tooth necklace from Lake Nitchie. *Anthropologie* 9(1):49–62.

Martin, R and K. Saller. 1957. *Lehrbuch der Anthropologie. Band I.* Fifth edition. Stuttgart: Gustav Fischer Verlag.

Miles, A.E.W. 1963. The dentition in the assessment of individual age in skeletal material. In D.R. Brothwell (ed.), *Dental Anthropology*, pp. 191–209. London: Pergamon Press.

Ousley, S.D. and R.L. Jantz. 1996. *Fordisc 2.0: Personal Computer Forensic Discriminant Functions*. Knoxville: University of Tennessee.

Pearson, O.M. 1999. Postcranial remains and the origin of modern humans. *Evolutionary Anthropology* 9:229–47.

Penrose, L.S. 1954. Distance, size and shape. *Annals of Eugenics* 18:337–43.

Pietrusewsky, M. 1984. *Metric and Non-metric Cranial Variation in Australian Aboriginal Populations Compared with Populations from the Pacific and Asia*. Canberra: Australian Institute of Aboriginal Studies. *Occasional Papers in Human Biology* 3.

Raath, P. 1996. A Grave Look at Western Australian Prehistory. Unpublished B.Sc. Hons subthesis, University of Western Australia, Perth.

Rao, P.D.P. 1966. The Anatomy of the Distal Limb Segments of the Aboriginal Skeleton. Unpublished PhD thesis, University of Adelaide, Adelaide.

Ray, L.J. 1959. Metrical and non–metrical features of the clavicle of the Australian Aboriginal. *American Journal of Physical Anthropology* 17:217–26.

Richards, L.C. and T. Brown. 1981. Dental attrition and degenerative arthritis of the temporomandibular joint. *Journal of Oral Rehabilitation* 8:293–307.

Rothschild, B.M., I. Hershkovitz, and O. Dutour. 1998. Clues potentially distinguishing lytic lesions of multiple myeloma from those of metastatic carcinoma. *American Journal of Physical Anthropology* 105:241–50.

Ruff, C.B., E. Trinkaus, A. Walker, and C.S. Larsen. 1993. Postcranial robusticity in *Homo*. I: temporal trends and mechanical interpretation. *Journal of Physical Anthropology* 91:21–53.

Scott, G.R. and C.G. Turner II. 1997. *The Anthropology of Modern Human Teeth*. Cambridge: Cambridge University Press.

Sim, R. and A. Thorne. 1990. Pleistocene human remains from King Island, southeastern Australia. *Australian Archaeology* 31:44–51.

Snell, C.A.R.D. 1938. *Menschelijke Skeletresten uit de Duinfromatie van Java's Zuidkust nabij Poeger (z-Banjoewangi)*. Surabaya: G. Kolff.

Snell, C.A.R.D. 1949. Human skeletal remains from Gol Ba'it, Sungai Siput, Perak, Malay Peninsula. *Acta Neerlandica Morphologicae et Pathologicae* 6:353–77.

Steele, D.G. 1970. Estimation of stature from fragments of limb bones. In T.D. Stewart (ed.), *Personal Identification in Mass Disasters*, pp. 85–97. Washington: National Museum of Natural History, Smithsonian Institute.

Steele, D.G. and T.W. McKern. 1969. A method for assessment of maximum long bone length and living stature from fragmentary long bones. *American Journal of Physical Anthropology* 31:215–28.

Storm, P. 1995. *The Evolutionary Significance of the Wajak Skulls*. Leiden: National Natuurhistorisch Museum. *Scripta Geologica* 110.

Szilvássy, J. 1988. Altersdiagnose am Skelett. In R. Knußman (ed.), *Wesen und Methoden der Anthropologie, 1. Teil, Wissenschafttheorie, Geschichte, morphologischen Methoden*, pp. 421–42. Stuttgart: Gustav Fischer Verlag.

Thorne, A.G. 1975. Kow Swamp and Lake Mungo: Toward a Craniology of Early Man in Australia. Unpublished PhD thesis, University of Sydney, Sydney.

Thorne, A.G. 1977. Morphological contrasts in Pleistocene Australians. In J. Allen, J. Golson, and R. Jones (eds), *Sunda and Sahul*, pp. 187–204. London: Academic Press.

Thorne, A.G. 1980. The longest link: human evolution in southeast Asia and the settlement of Australia. In J. Fox, R. Garnaut, P. McCawley, and J. Mackie (eds), *Indonesia: Australian Perspectives*, pp. 35–43. Canberra: The Australian National University.

Thorne A. and. R. Sim 1994. The gracile male skeleton from late Pleistocene King Island, Australia. *Australian Archaeology* 38:8–10.

Thorne, A.G. and S.R. Wilson. 1977. Pleistocene and recent Australians: a multivariate comparison. *Journal of Human Evolution* 6:393–402.

Tulsi, R.S. 1972. Vertebral column of the Australian aborigine: selected morphological and metrical features. *Zeitschrift für Morphologie und Anthropologie* 64:117–44.

de Villiers, H. 1968. *The Skull of the South African Negro: A Biometrical and Morphological Study*. Johannesburg: Witwatersrand University Press.

Webb, S.G. 1989. *The Willandra Lakes Hominids*. Canberra: The Australian National University.

Webb, S.G. 1995. *Palaeopathology of Aboriginal Australians: Health and Disease Across a Hunter-Gatherer Continent*. Cambridge: Cambridge University Press.

Weidenreich, F. 1945. The Keilor skull: a Wadjak type from southeast Australia. *American Journal of Physical Anthropology*.

Willis, C.J. 1998. 'The Dome of Thought, the Palace of the Soul': Interpreting the Craniological Morphology of Ancient and Near-contemporary Australian Aborigines. Unpublished PhD thesis, Department of Archaeology and Anthropology, The Australian National University, Canberra.

13

Isoleucine Epimerization in *Casuarius* Eggshells from Archaeological Sites in the Aru Islands, Liang Lemdubu and Liang Nabulei Lisa

Simon J. Clarke[1] and Gifford H. Miller[2]

1. School of Earth and Environmental Sciences, University of Wollongong, Wollongong, NSW, Australia
2. Center for Geochronological Research, Institute of Arctic and Alpine Research and Department of Geological Sciences, University of Colorado, Boulder, U.S.A.

Introduction

The epimerization of the amino acid isoleucine in avian eggshells has been used to determine the timing of a variety of events throughout the Late Quaternary. Epimerization is a chemical reaction that interconverts L-isoleucine into its epimer D-alloisoleucine. Geochronological investigations based on isoleucine epimerization in avian eggshells have been used to help assess the timing of the extinction of a member of the Australian megafauna, *Genyornis*, a large flightless bird (Miller et al. 1999a). Isoleucine epimerization in *Genyornis* and water bird eggshells have been used to confine the timing of lacustrine episodes beyond the limit of radiocarbon dating in central Australia (Magee and Miller 1998). Ages derived from isoleucine epimerization in *Struthio* eggshells in African archaeological sites have been important in refining the chronology for the evolution of modern humans (Brooks et al. 1990; Miller et al. 1999b). Recently, the extent of isoleucine epimerization in *Casuarius* eggshells was used to support a radiocarbon chronology attesting to a Pleistocene antiquity for the occupation of Papuan rainforest (Pasveer et al. 2002).

The spatial interaction of eggshell proteins and carbonate produces a microenvironment that is well suited to the preservation of indigenous protein residues over geological time. It is hypothesized that during calcification eggshell proteins form an organic matrix around which crystals precipitate producing a population of intracrystalline proteins (Hincke et al. 1999; *sensu* Sykes et al. 1995). This microenvironment approximates a closed system during diagenesis, thereby restricting the diffusion of protein residues from the eggshell structure (Brooks et al. 1990; Miller et al. 2000). This characteristic makes avian eggshells excellent candidates for biogeochemical analyses in applications such as amino acid racemization-based geochronology and palaeo-thermometry (e.g. Miller et al. 1997).

The aim of the present study is to evaluate the potential of isoleucine epimerization in *Casuarius* eggshells for age estimation, and to provide an independent age assessment for the Aru

Islands' archaeological sites Liang Nabulei Lisa and Liang Lemdubu (for a location map see Chapters 7 and 9, this volume). It is suggested that the Aru Islands archaeological sites are highly suitable for the application of isoleucine epimerization geochronology for two reasons. First, because the rate of epimerization is temperature-sensitive the reaction proceeds rapidly in warm tropical locations, effectively maximizing the ability of the technique to distinguish specimens of different ages. Second, the effects of diurnal temperature fluctuations are expected to be dampened in cave and rockshelter sites such as Lemdubu and Nabulei Lisa, thereby eliminating problems that are encountered at sites with complex thermal regimes (Pillans 1982).

There are three extant species of cassowary: the Dwarf Cassowary (*Casuarius unappendiculatus*), Bennet's Cassowary (*C. bennetti*), and the Southern Cassowary (*C. casuarius*). All three species inhabit New Guinea but only the subspecies *C. casuarius johnsonii* is found in Australia. *C. casuarius aruensis* is the subspecies that inhabits the Aru Islands at present (Grzimek 1972). The presence of this large flightless frugivore on the Aru Islands is presumably the result of dispersal from New Guinea over a former land bridge, however, it is also possible that the bird was introduced to the archipelago by people. *C. casuarius* stands approximately 1.5–1.7m tall and can weigh over 55kg, with females being slightly larger than males (Crome 1975; Marchant and Higgins 1990). A female will commonly lay a clutch of three or four eggs per season that are incubated by the male. The eggs are approximately 135mm long by 95mm wide, and feature a pea-green 'embossed' surface texture on a pale green background (Beruldsen 1980; Marchant and Higgins 1990).

It is assumed that fragments of *Casuarius* eggshell accumulate in rockshelter and cave deposits as the remnants of meals consumed by people. During historic times the people inhabiting the rainforests of tropical Australasia harvested *Casuarius* eggs as part of their traditional subsistence regimes (Harris 1978; Pernetta 1989). The presence of *Casuarius* eggshell in archaeological deposits throughout New Guinea suggests that this practice has been taking place for thousands of years (Gillieson and Mountain 1982; Jelsma 1998; Pasveer and Aplin 1998; Pernetta 1989).

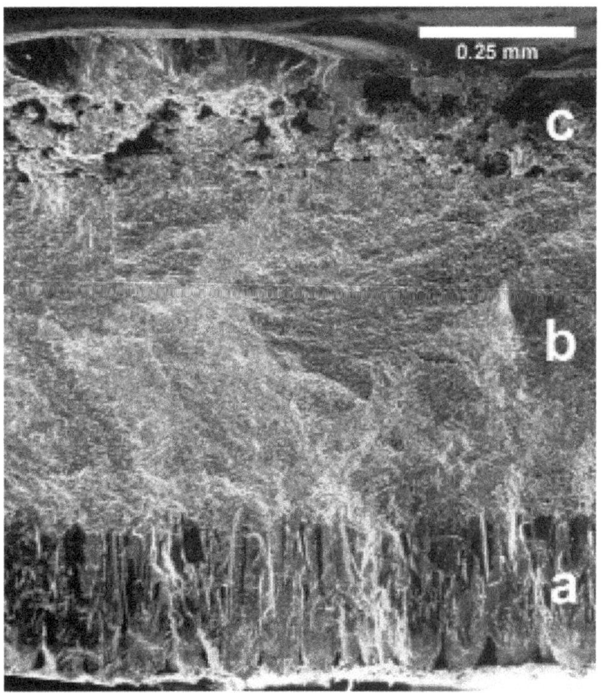

Figure 13.1 Scanning electron microscope image of modern *C. casuarius johnsonii* eggshell. The image is orientated with the outer surface of the eggshell at the top. The eggshell mammillary layers a) squamatic zone b) cavernous outer prismatic layer and c) outer surface are clearly evident

Casuarius eggshell is primarily calcite and consists of four morphological layers: the mammillary layer, squamatic zone, cavernous outer layer, and textured outer surface (Fig. 13.1). Pores interrupt the lateral homogeneity of the eggshell structure. Eggshell membranes present during incubation are not preserved over geological time. The squamatic zone is isolated for biogeochemical analyses because the protein and amino acid composition of ratite eggshells vary between the structural phases (Miller et al. 2000). Consistent analysis of squamatic zone amino acids circumvents the possible introduction of uncertainties relating to intra-sample differences in the extent of isoleucine epimerization.

Materials and Methods

Casuarius eggshells were recovered during excavation from the two Aru Islands cave sites, Liang Lemdubu and Liang Nabulei Lisa (see O'Connor et al., Chapters 7 and 9, this volume). To examine the relationship between the extent of isoleucine epimerization and time, eight fragments of *Casuarius* eggshells (three from Lemdubu and five from Nabulei Lisa) were submitted for radiocarbon dating. In general, eggshells with the lowest A/I of those excavated from similar depths were submitted for radiocarbon dating. Conventional radiocarbon ages (BP) are reported corrected for isotopic fractionation and converted to calendar years (cal BP) using CALIB 4.3 (Stuiver and Reimer 1993; Stuiver et al. 1998). Where multiple calibrated ages were obtained a unique solution was defined as the median of the 2s range. This method of defining unique calendar ages has been used previously (e.g. Kaufman 2003; Oches et al. 1996).

The methods used to determine the extent of isoleucine epimerization in *Casuarius* eggshells follow those of Miller et al. (2000). To isolate the protein residues of the squamatic layer, the outer surface of samples (including the cavernous layer) was removed with a rotary drill. To remove potential contaminant amino acids from the eggshell surface and within the pores 33% of the calcium carbonate was dissolved with 2N HCl. Cleaned samples were dissolved in vials with 7N HCl (0.02ml/mg), capped under nitrogen gas, and placed in an oven at 110°C for 22 hours to hydrolyze peptide bonds. To determine the extent of isoleucine epimerization in naturally hydrolysed (i.e. free) amino acids, this hydrolysis step was eliminated. The resulting solution was dried in a heating module set at 80°C under a flow of nitrogen gas. Prior to analysis, samples were rehydrated with 0.01N HCl then loaded into an autosampler for high performance ion-exchange liquid chromatographic separation of amino acids. A fluorescence detector identified amino acids after post-column derivatization with o-phthalaldehyde. The extent of isoleucine epimerization is the ratio of the relative abundance of D-alloisoleucine to L-isoleucine (A/I) calculated using peak areas on electronically integrated chromatograms. A correction based on peak width at half peak height was applied to the peak area data to account for possible differences in the geometry of the two peaks such that:

$$A/I = A_{area}/I_{area} \times A_{width}/I_{width} \qquad \text{Eqn. 1}$$

Typically, the D-alloisoleucine and L-isoleucine peaks are congruent so the correction produces an A/I value only slightly different (within two standard deviations) from that calculated for the more commonly used peak height data. To correct for batch effects the A/I values have been normalized to an internal series of A/I values.

To simulate the diagenesis of protein residues at environmental temperatures over thousands of years, fragments of a modern *C. casuarius johnsonii* eggshell from a wildlife park near Cairns, Australia, were heated for a series of discrete time intervals at 143°C. The high temperature enables chemical reactions such as epimerization, peptide bond hydrolysis, and amino acid decomposition to reach the same extent over a period of weeks as would be attained over thousands of years at environmental temperatures. Following the method of Miller et al. (2000) fragments of eggshell weighing approximately 50mg were embedded in two grams of sterilized quartz sand moistened with 0.5ml deionized water, sealed within a pyrex test tube under normal atmosphere, heated at 143°C, then prepared for analysis as described above.

Isoleucine epimerization at high temperature

In Figure 13.2 it is observed that the extent of isoleucine epimerization in *Casuarius* eggshell increases from an initial A/I of 0.025 in modern eggshell towards values in excess of A/I = 1.20.

The pattern of isoleucine epimerization at high temperature in *Casuarius* eggshell conforms to the model described by Kriausakul and Mitterer (1980) that identifies two phases during which the reaction approximates first-order kinetics. First-order kinetics are observed where the relationship between A/I values transformed using the logarithm term of the integrated rate equation and time is linear. The integrated rate equation relates the extent of isoleucine epimerization to time:

$$\ln [(1 + A/I)/(1 - K'A/I)] = (1 + K')\, k_1 t + c \qquad \text{Eqn. 2}$$

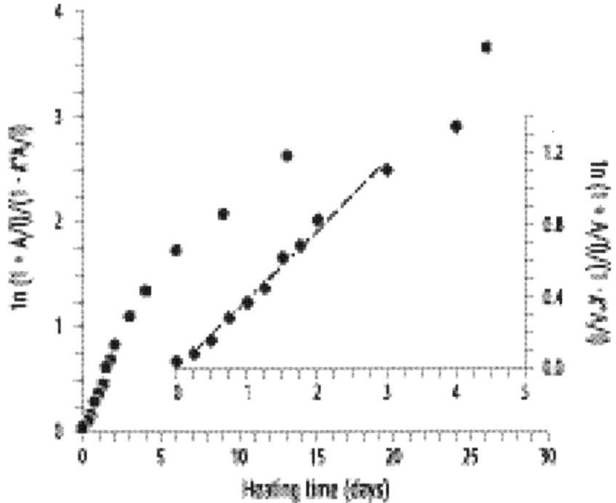

Figure 13.2 The extent of isoleucine epimerization in the hydrolyzate of modern *C. casuarius johnsonii* eggshell heated at 143°C. A/I values are transformed using the logarithm term of the integrated rate equation. Results obtained over the initial phase of rapid epimerization are shown in the inset. Also highlighted is the range over which the reaction is observed to obey first-order kinetics

where K' is the reciprocal of the equilibrium A/I (0.77), k_1 is the forward reaction rate (years^{-1}), t is time measured in years, and c is a constant derived by solving the left-hand side of the equation for the extent of laboratory-induced epimerization at $t = 0$, obtained by analyzing modern eggshell. Inputting the above-mentioned initial A/I, a value of 0.044 for c is obtained. In *Casuarius* eggshell there is an initial phase of rapid epimerization (average $k_1 = 66.9$ yr^{-1}) separated from a phase of markedly slower epimerization by a transition zone of intermediate reaction rates. The rate of isoleucine epimerization in *Casuarius* eggshell at 143°C is similar to that observed in *Dromaius* eggshell under the same experimental conditions ($k_1 = 69.3$ yr^{-1}) by Miller et al. (2000:Fig. 13–5d). However, the slow non-linear reaction rate observed by these authors in *Dromaius* eggshell at the onset of epimerization is not evident in *Casuarius* eggshell. These authors provided evidence indicating that this non-linear phase lasts no more than a decade in warm (>20°C mean annual temperature) settings and, if it were to be applicable to epimerization in *Casuarius* eggshell, is negligible at the temporal scale under investigation in this research.

At 143°C the initial phase of isoleucine epimerization in *Casuarius* eggshells deviates from first-order linear kinetics at an A/I of approximately 0.7. According to Miller et al. (1991) the duration of this phase of first-order kinetics shortens as temperature decreases. It is suggested at environmental temperatures isoleucine epimerization in *Casuarius* eggshell will deviate from first-order kinetics at an A/I less than 0.7. The integrated rate equation can therefore be used to relate an A/I less than 0.7 to derive age estimates on *Casuarius* eggshells. The age of eggshells with an A/I approaching or greater than 0.7 will be underestimated.

Isoleucine epimerization in archaeological contexts

Casuarius eggshell A/I values and radiocarbon ages are presented in Tables 13.1 and 13.2, corresponding to the Lemdubu and Nabulei Lisa excavations, respectively. The oldest radiocarbon ages were obtained on eggshells from Spit 19 of Lemdubu Test Pit C. Two separate eggshell

Table 13.1 Liang Lemdubu: radiocarbon ages and A/I values of *Casuarius* eggshells

SPIT	DEPTH (CM)[a]	LAB. CODE	RADIOCARBON AGE[b]	$\delta^{13}C$ (‰, PDB)	RADIOCARBON AGE[c]	AAL[d]	A/I (± 1SD) Hydrolyzate	Free
1	7.8					8553A	0.173±0.001	0.356±0.009
1	7.8					8553B	0.115±0.006	
1	7.8					8553C	1.221±0.020	1.204±0.007
1	7.8					8553D	0.728±0.001	0.998±0.042
2	12.5	OZF247	2150±50	-13.5	2310–1990 (2150)	8554A	0.102±0.004	0.289±0.025
2	12.5					8554B	0.581±0.008	1.109±0.024
4	22.6					8713A	1.239±0.028	1.180±0.001
4	22.6					8713B	1.219±0.023	1.156±0.014
17	88.3					8557A	0.695±0.006	1.032±0.006
19	97.5					8559A		0.734±0.006
19	97.5	AA-32848	16770±110	-10.0	20,670–19,320 (19,980)	8559B	0.538±0.005	0.735±0.001
19	97.5	OZF248	16850±120	-11.7	20,770–19,400 (20,070)	8559C	0.523±0.008	0.719±0.001
20	102.0					8560A	0.742±0.002	1.119±0.001
20	102.0					8560B	0.630±0.005	1.030±0.007

a Mean of depths recorded at the four corners of the excavated unit
b Years BP, ±1σ range
c Calendar years BP, maximum-minimum 2s range (unique age)
d Center for Geochronological Research Amino Acid Laboratory code

Table 13.2 Liang Nabulei Lisa: radiocarbon ages and A/I values of *Casuarius* eggshells

SPIT	DEPTH (CM)	LAB. CODE	RADIOCARBON AGE	$\delta^{13}C$ (‰, PDB)	RADIOCARBON AGE	AAL	A/I (± 1SD) Hydrolyzate	Free
9	24.5					8784A	0.266±0.001	0.442±0.003
9	24.5					8784B	0.711±0.002	0.992±0.001
11	30.5	OZF249	2530±60	-13.6	2760–2360 (2710)	8785A	0.151±0.004	0.336±0.013
19	50.2					10078A	0.405±0.002	
25	68.5	OZF250	9310±80	-16.1	10,730–10,240 (10,490)	8786A	0.384±0.001	0.621±0.001
26	71.0	AA-32849	10460±75	-16.0	12,890–11,950 (12,420)	8787A	0.421±0.005	
27	72.5					10079A	0.396±0.001	
28	76.0					10080A	0.520±0.001	
28	76.0					10081A	0.673±0.11	
32	86.2	OZF848	10340±60	-15.9	12,800–11,770 (12,280)	8788A	0.717±0.002	1.161±0.007

fragments from this excavation unit had ages of about 20,000 cal BP. Late Holocene age estimates were obtained from both Lemdubu and Nabulei Lisa eggshells. The radiocarbon ages on *Casuarius* eggshell from Nabulei Lisa range from late Pleistocene to late Holocene.

Overall, there is good agreement between the eggshell radiocarbon ages for the Lemdubu and Nabulei Lisa sequences and the respective chronologies of these sites (Figs 13.3, 13.4). At Lemdubu the two similar radiocarbon ages obtained (by different labs) on *Casuarius* eggshells from approximately one metre depth are in close agreement with that of a marine estuarine shell recovered 10cm higher in the profile. The eggshell fragment from the top of the excavation also features a radiocarbon content comparable with charcoal fragments recovered from the same depths. The three Nabulei Lisa eggshells recovered from ca. 65–85cm depth have radiocarbon ages similar to *Celtis* seeds and marine estuarine shells from the same section of the profile. The eggshell from ca. 90cm depth has the oldest radiocarbon age in the profile and this is explicable in terms of its location towards the base of the sequence. While there are no samples with radiocarbon ages similar to that of the eggshell from ca. 30cm depth this specimen is situated between charcoal and mollusc shells with radiocarbon ages that bracket that of the eggshell.

Figure 13.3 shows the extent of isoleucine epimerization in *Casuarius* eggshells versus excavation depth at Lemdubu. The *Casuarius* eggshells analyzed form a bimodal distribution within the profile because they are concentrated in the upper 25cm and between 85cm and 100cm depth. The range of A/I values within the less deeply buried samples is approximately 1.150. The range of A/I values within the group of eggshells excavated from greater depth is approximately 0.220. As expected of such highly variable A/I values, there appears to be little correlation between the radiocarbon chronology for Lemdubu and the amino acid results.

Figure 13.4 shows the extent of isoleucine epimerization in *Casuarius* eggshells versus excavation depth at Nabulei Lisa. There is not a well-defined increase in the extent of isoleucine

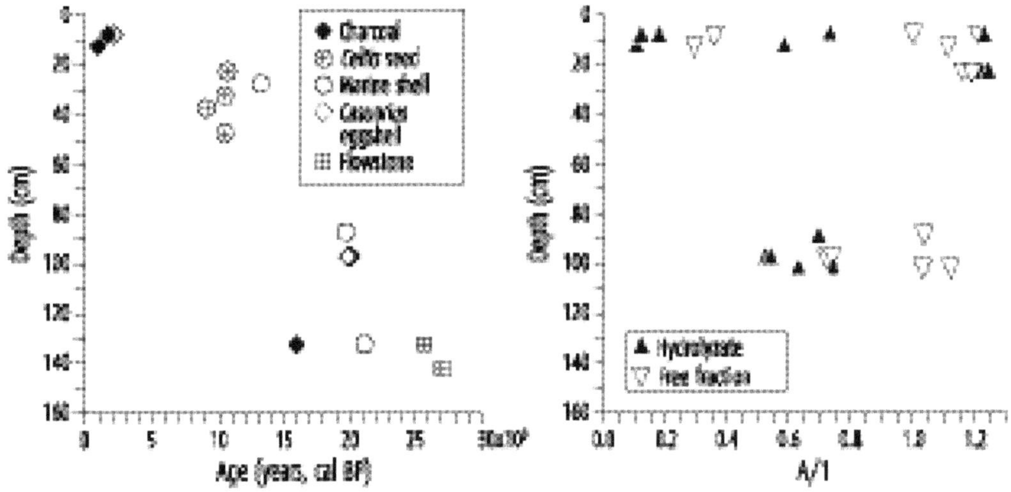

Figure 13.3 Liang Lemdubu: comparison of numeric age control and *Casuarius* eggshell A/I values. Values for the extent of isoleucine epimerization in both the hydrolyzate and free amino acids are shown. Radiocarbon ages on eggshells are listed in Table 13.2 while ages on other sample types are from O'Connor et al. (Chapter 9, this volume)

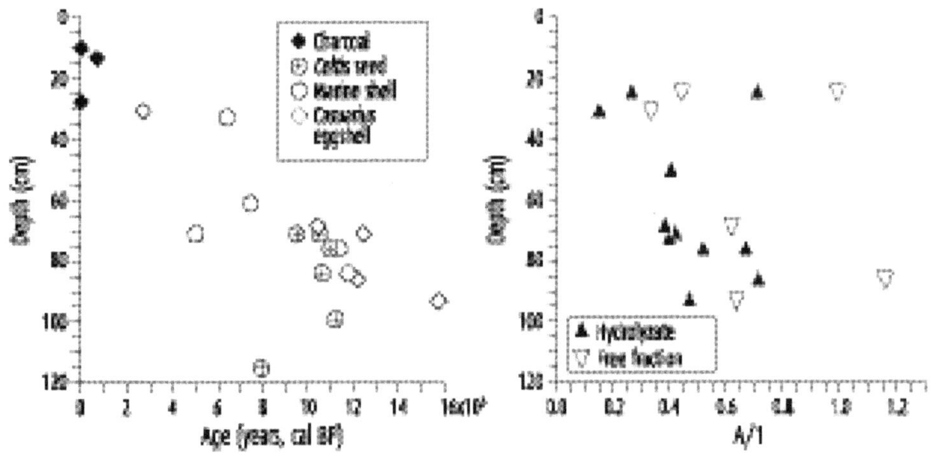

Figure 13.4 Liang Nabulei Lisa: comparison of radiocarbon ages and *Casuarius* eggshell A/I values. Values for the extent of isoleucine epimerization in both the hydrolyzate and free amino acids are shown. Radiocarbon ages on eggshells are listed in Table 13.2 while ages on other sample types are from O'Connor et al. (Chapter 7, this volume)

epimerization with respect to depth. The range in A/I amongst eggshells excavated from similar depths is as high as 0.560 (units 9 and 11) and as low as 0.037 (units 25 to 27). Despite the noise the A/I values in both the hydrolyzate and free amino acids bear some resemblance to the radiocarbon chronology. The A/I values from ca. 70–100cm depth tend to be greater than those from ca. 20–30cm depth, and these depth intervals have terminal Pleistocene and Holocene radiocarbon ages, respectively. At both Lemdubu and Nabulei Lisa free amino acid A/I values essentially mirror the results obtained for the hydrolyzate.

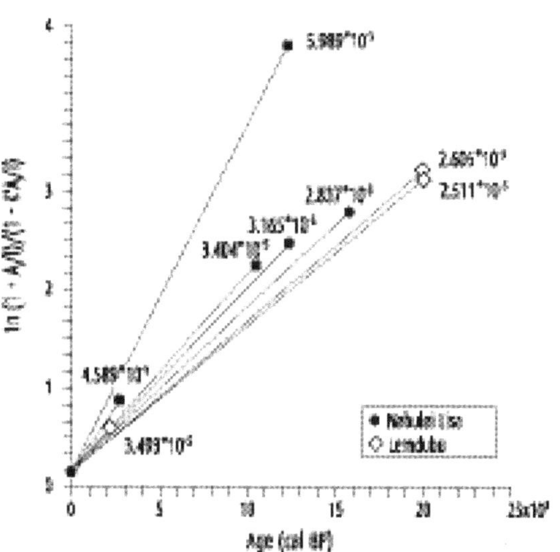

Figure 13.5 Liang Lemdubu and Liang Nabulei Lisa: *In situ* rate constants for isoleucine epimerization in *Casuarius* eggshells. A/I values are transformed using the logarithm term of the integrated rate equation. Rate constants (k_1, yr^{-1}) are indicated next to their corresponding data points

In situ reaction rates calculated by solving the integrated rate equation for k_1 using *Casuarius* eggshell A/I values and radiocarbon ages are presented in Figure 13.5. The majority of values fall within the range $2.5*10^{-5} < k_1 < 4.6*10^{-5}$ yr^{-1} but there is an outlier for which $k_1 = 6.0*10^{-5}$ yr^{-1}. Amongst the majority of the k_1 values there appears to be a systematic negative correlation between the reaction rate and eggshell age. Although this could be a statistical artefact of the small dataset it potentially represents depression of the reaction rate by cooler temperatures during the Pleistocene. Further work is necessary to gauge the temperature sensitivity of the isoleucine epimerization in *Casuarius* eggshells in order to explore the implications of the observed trends in terms of palaeotemperatures.

Discussion

Ancient *Casuarius* eggshells, unlike those of several other large flightless birds (*Dromaius, Struthio,* and *Genyornis*) studied for isoleucine epimerization geochronology, have only been obtained from archaeological sites. *Casuarius* nests are thin mattresses of vegetative matter (Beruldsen 1980) that are not constructed in settings conducive to the preservation of eggshells over geological time. The association with archaeological sites means that heating in or near hearths will always pose a potential problem to studies of isoleucine epimerization in *Casuarius* eggshell. Such transient heating events are problematic because they accelerate the rate of isoleucine epimerization to produce elevated and highly variable A/I values (Ellis et al. 1996; Goodfriend and Ellis 2000; Miller et al. 1992; Murray-Wallace and Colley 1997).

Exposure of *Casuarius* eggshells to high temperature is a likely explanation for the wide range of A/I values observed within excavation units and the absence of a well-defined down-profile increase in A/I at Lemdubu and Nabulei Lisa. For example, several eggshells from the upper excavation units of Lemdubu feature A/I values of approximately 1.2, close to the value expected at equilibrium (A/I = 1.3, Williams and Smith 1977). The simplest explanation for such high A/I values is an anomalously high integrated thermal history such as that produced by short-term exposure to the high temperatures of hearth flames or coals. Mixing within a site could bring older samples (high A/I) upward through the profile to be recovered amongst younger specimens (low A/I), while downward mixing would have the opposite effect. In the absence of objective criteria for the identification of exposure to high temperature such processes cannot be ruled out.

Overall, however, the radiocarbon ages and sharply defined boundaries that mark changes through time in other cultural materials suggest a high degree of stratigraphic integrity, at least at Lemdubu.

The relationship between the extent of isoleucine epimerization in the hydrolyzate and free amino acids of *Casuarius* eggshells is in accord with the idea that the excellent preservation of amino acids in avian eggshells promotes the systematic diagenesis of these molecules. The A/I values observed in the hydrolyzate of *Casuarius* eggshells from Lemdubu and Nabulei Lisa are plotted against the corresponding A/I values of free amino acids in Figure 13.6. There is a linear relationship between these two sets of A/I values where the reaction extent amongst free amino acids is less than A/I = 0.8. Across this range the A/I values in free amino acids are approximately 30% higher than that observed in the hydrolyzate. This systematic trend is explicable in terms of the retention of both high and low molecular weight protein residues. Typically, amino acids in low molecular weight residues (e.g. free amino acids) are preferentially lost from the fossil matrix. This is significant because (as apparent in Fig. 13.6) these amino acids have a characteristically high extent of isoleucine epimerization. If the retention of the low molecular weight residues of *Casuarius* eggshells during diagenesis is variable then their contribution to the A/I value of the hydrolyzate would be variable, thereby introducing noise into the relationship between the extent of isoleucine epimerization in free amino acids and the hydrolyzate.

While amino acid diagenesis in *Casuarius* eggshells may take place in a systematic fashion where A/I values are low, the correlation between A/I values in the hydrolyzate and free amino acids deteriorates where A/I > 0.8 in the latter fraction. Because the eggshells that feature anomalous results in Figure 13.6 also exhibit anomalously high A/I values in the contexts of Figures 13.3 and 13.4, confidence in ascribing their spurious nature to the effects of campfire heating events is increased. However, it is not clear from the available data what geochemical mechanisms lead to the deterioration of the relationship between hydrolyzate and free amino acid A/I values. Normally, the rate of epimerization in free amino acids is governed by the epimerization of amino acids at the terminal positions of polypeptides and their subsequent release from the chain by hydrolysis. Perhaps the rate of epimerization in the free pool is particularly responsive to the high temperatures of campfire heating events, forcing these A/I values higher than would normally be attained by the hydrolytic release of terminal amino acids.

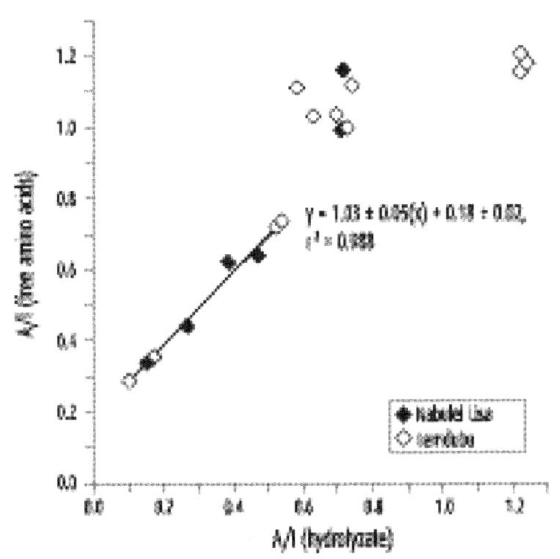

Figure 13.6 Relationship between the extent of isoleucine epimerization in the hydrolyzate and free amino acids of *Casuarius* eggshells. Results for the linear regression where A/I < 0.8 amongst free amino acids are presented

Like their influence on the extent of isoleucine epimerization, it may be difficult to account for the effect of short duration, high temperature events on the radiocarbon content of eggshells. As observed in other biominerals (e.g. Haas and Banewicz 1980), high temperatures can release carbon dioxide from carbonates such as eggshell calcite and produce residual calcium oxide. Calcium oxide will react with CO_2 and water producing secondary carbonate and calcium hydroxide, respectively. The exchange of CO_2 between the biomineral and the environment promoted by the formation of secondary carbonates is of concern because it will introduce ^{14}C that is not contemporaneous with the radiocarbon content of the indigenous calcite. However, it is unlikely that eggshells featuring a large amount of calcium hydroxide will be recovered from geological sequences because the formation of this mineral destroys a specimen's mechanical integrity (SJC pers. observ.). Also of concern are the observations of Williams (1981) and Vogel et al. (2001) of radiocarbon age estimates on modern ratite eggshells that suggest the samples are hundreds of years old (see also Higham 1994). These results contrast with those of Miller et al. (1999a) that demonstrate the radiocarbon activity of modern *Dromaius* eggshells to be equivalent to that of the contemporaneous atmosphere. As the results of these studies fail to demonstrate the existence of a consistent ratite eggshell radiocarbon anomaly, and in the absence of similar research on *Casuarius* eggshell, a correction has not been applied to the radiocarbon ages presented here. The resulting uncertainty is negligible in terms of the temporal scale of environmental and cultural change under investigation in the Aru Islands archaeological sites.

One of the major advantages of amino acid racemization as a geochronological tool is the ability to determine the timing of events beyond the limits of radiocarbon dating (ca. 50,000 years BP). The epimerization of isoleucine in *Casuarius* eggshells is no exception to this observation. However, the warm temperatures of the bird's tropical habitat and the range of A/I values over which the reaction was observed to obey reversible first-order kinetics, impose limits to this application. Using the mean of the rate constants in Figure 13.5 (excluding the anomalously high data point) as an example, isoleucine epimerization in *Casuarius* eggshell ceases to obey reversible first-order kinetics after approximately 21,000 years. Under these conditions, in eggshells older than 21,000 years A/I will be greater than 0.7 and the integrated rate equation will systematically underestimate specimen age. This problem may be reconciled by the mathematical transformation of amino acid data. For example, Murray-Wallace and Kimber (1993), and Hearty and Kaufman (2000) observed that the D/L values of field samples could be accurately related to time by describing the decrease in the reaction rate as a parabolic function of time (Mitterer and Kriausakul 1989).

Setting uncertainties in deriving numeric ages aside, isoleucine epimerization in *Casuarius* eggshells will provide a reliable index of relative age for samples with similar thermal histories. Furthermore, when supported by a radiocarbon chronology, the A/I values can be used to estimate numeric age. The results from the Aru Islands combined with those from the Ayamaru Plateau, Papua (Pasveer et al. 2002; Clarke and Miller unpublished data) constitute a substantial set of paired *Casuarius* eggshell A/I values and radiocarbon ages spanning the last 30,000 years (Fig. 13.7). Importantly for studies of long-term environmental and cultural change, the Holocene can be distinguished from the Pleistocene at an A/I of approximately 0.3. Late Holocene eggshells can be distinguished from those of the early Holocene, and an A/I of approximately 0.15 is expected of mid-Holocene eggshells. From the oldest eggshells in the dataset, although limited by few data points and the variability in those available, an A/I greater than 0.5 may provide a useful means of identifying eggshells greater than 20,000 years old. In

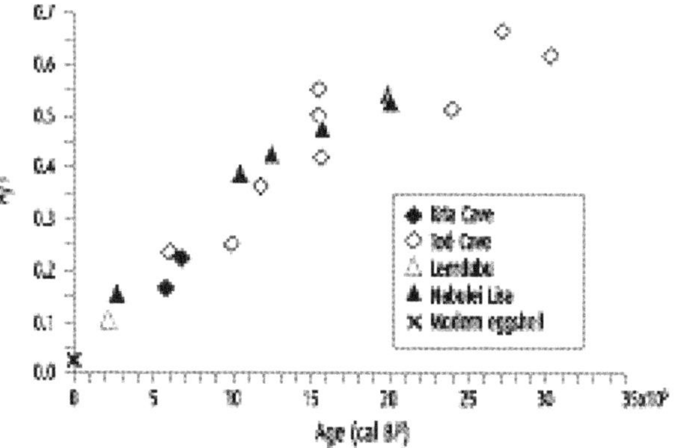

Figure 13.7 Extent of isoleucine epimerization in radiocarbon dated *Casuarius* eggshells from archaeological sites in the Aru Islands (Liang Lemdubu and Liang Nabulei Lisa) and the Ayamaru Plateau, Papua (Kria and Toé Caves). Data points represent mean A/I values and calibrated radiocarbon ages. An anomalously high data point from Liang Nabulei Lisa has been omitted from the plot. Ayamaru Plateau data from Pasveer et al. (2002) and Clarke and Miller (unpublished data)

summary, the combined Aru Islands and Ayamaru Plateau datasets offer a simple index for ascribing an age to a *Casuarius* eggshell based on its A/I value; a method applicable to other lowland archaeological sites occupied over the last 30,000 years where this sample type is encountered. It should be noted that in both relative and numeric chronologic applications the geochronological use of A/I will be most confident in archaeological sites where *Casuarius* eggshells are abundant. Multiple analyses permits rigorous assessment of within-excavation unit variability and identification of the expected down-profile increase in A/I, two trends that aid in the identification of anomalous A/I values resulting from effects such as exposure to campfire heating events.

Conclusions

Eggshells of *Casuarius* are well preserved in archaeological sites on the Aru Islands. Laboratory experiments indicate isoleucine epimerization within this eggshell type follows linear first-order kinetics to an A/I of 0.7, permitting interpretation of the extent of the reaction in terms of numeric age. The eggshells are also suitable for radiocarbon dating. A close correlation between paired A/I values and ages has been demonstrated. However, isoleucine epimerization shows substantial variability in many excavation units and this is attributable to transient heating by hearths. By selecting the eggshells with the lowest A/I values from each unit it is possible to reduce the likelihood of extracting erroneous inferences from amino acids influenced by such transient heating events. Radiocarbon ages and A/I values from *Casuarius* eggshells indicate initial occupation of Liang Lemdubu and Liang Nabulei Lisa during the late Pleistocene and further occupation during the Holocene. Combined with previous work on isoleucine epimerization in *Casuarius* eggshells, the results from the Aru Islands archaeological sites provide a basis for which an approximate age can be assigned to a *Casuarius* eggshell based on its A/I value in future work.

Acknowledgements

Michael O'Brien of the Wildworld wildlife park, Cairns, Queensland, Australia, provided the modern *C. casuarius johnsonii* eggshell. Charles P. Hart and Steve DeVogel (University of Colorado) are thanked for their help with the isoleucine epimerization laboratory analyses. Amino acid analyses at the University of Colorado were supported by NSF grant ATM-9709806. Radiocarbon age estimates were obtained at ANSTO funded by AINSE grant 01/107. The scanning electron microscope image was produced with the expert assistance of David Carrie (University of Wollongong) and Sean Maguire. Colin Murray-Wallace (UOW) and Sue O'Connor (Australian National University) are thanked for their comments and encouragement. This work has benefited from the constructive comments of Brad Pillans (ANU) for which he is thanked.

References

Beruldsen, G. 1980. *A Field Guide to Nests and Eggs of Australian Birds*. Adelaide: Rigby.

Brooks, A.S., P.E. Hare, J.E. Kokis, G.H. Miller, R.D. Ernst, and F. Wendorf. 1990. Dating Pleistocene archaeological sites by protein diagenesis in ostrich eggshell. *Science* 248:60–4.

Crome, F.H.J. 1975. Some observations on the biology of the cassowary in northern Queensland. *Emu* 76:8–14.

Ellis, G.L., G.A. Goodfriend, J.T. Abbott, P.E. Hare, and D.W. von Endt. 1996. Assessment of integrity and geochronology of archaeological sites using amino acid racemization in land snail shells: examples from central Texas. *Geoarchaeology* 11:189–213.

Gillieson, D. and M.-J. Mountain. 1982. Environmental history of Nombe rock-shelter, Papua New Guinea highlands. *Archaeology in Oceania* 20:37–9.

Goodfriend, G.A. and G.L. Ellis. 2000. Stable carbon isotope record of middle to late Holocene climate changes from land snail shells at Hinds Cave, Texas. *Quaternary International* 67:47–60.

Grzimek, D.H.C. 1972. *Grzimek's Animal Life Encyclopaedia*. New York: Van Nostrand Reinhold Co.

Haas, H. and J. Banewicz. 1980. Radiocarbon dating of bone apatite using thermal release of CO_2. *Radiocarbon* 22:537–44.

Harris, D.R. 1978. Adaptation to a tropical rain-forest environment: Aboriginal subsistence in northeastern Queensland. In N.G. Blurton-Jones and V. Reynolds (eds), *Human Behaviour and Adaptation*, pp. 113–34. London: Taylor and Francis.

Hearty, P.J. and D.S. Kaufman. 2000. Whole-rock aminostratigraphy and Quaternary sea-level history of the Bahamas. *Quaternary Research* 54:163–73.

Higham, T. 1994. Radiocarbon dating New Zealand prehistory with moa eggshell: some preliminary results. *Quaternary Geochronology (Quaternary Science Reviews)* 13:163–9.

Hincke, M.T., M. St Maurice, Y. Nys, J. Gautron, M. Panheleux, C.P.W. Tsang, M.M. Bain, S.E. Solomon, and M.D. McKee. 1999. Eggshell proteins and shell strength: molecular biology of eggshell matrix proteins and industry applications. In J.S. Sim, S. Nakai, and W. Guenter (eds), *Egg Nutrition and Biotechnology*, pp. 447–61. Wellingford: CABI Publishing.

Jelsma, J. 1998. Room with a view: an excavation in Toé cave, Ayamaru district, Bird's Head, Irian Jaya. In G.-J. Bartstra (ed.), *Bird's Head Approaches: Irian Jaya Studies, A Programme For Interdisciplinary Research*, pp. 41–65. Rotterdam: A.A. Balkema. *Modern Quaternary Studies in Southeast Asia* 15.

Kaufman, D.S. 2003. Amino acid paleothermometry of Quaternary ostracodes from the Bonneville Basin, Utah. *Quaternary Science Reviews* 22:899–914.

Kriausakul, N. and R.M. Mitterer. 1980. Some factors affecting the epimerization of isoleucine in peptides and proteins. In P.E. Hare, T.C. Hoering, and K. King, Jr (eds), *Biogeochemistry of Amino Acids*, pp. 283–96. New York: John Wiley & Sons.

Magee, J.W. and G.H. Miller. 1998. Lake Eyre palaeohydrology from 60 ka to the present: beach ridges and glacial maximum aridity. *Palaeogeography, Palaeoclimatology, Palaeoecology* 144:307–29.

Marchant, S. and P.J. Higgins. 1990. *Handbook of Australian, New Zealand and Antarctic Birds* (vol. 1, ratites to ducks). Oxford: Oxford University Press.

Miller, G.H., F. Wendorf, R.D. Ernst, R. Schild, A.E. Close, I. Friedman, and H.P. Schwarcz. 1991. Dating lacustrine episodes in the eastern Sahara by the epimerization of isoleucine in ostrich eggshells. *Palaeogeography, Palaeoclimatology, Palaeoecology* 84:175–89.

Miller, G.H., P.B. Beaumont, A.J.T. Jull, and B. Johnson. 1992. Pleistocene geochronology and palaeothermometry from protein diagenesis in ostrich eggshells: implications for the evolution of modern humans. *Philosophical Transactions of the Royal Society of London, B* 337:149–57.

Miller, G.H., J.W. Magee, and A.J.T. Jull. 1997. Low–latitude glacial cooling in the southern hemisphere from amino-acid racemization in emu eggshells. *Nature* 385:241–4.

Miller, G.H., J.W. Magee, B.J. Johnson, M.L. Fogel, N.A. Spooner, M.T. McCulloch, and L.K. Ayliffe. 1999a. Pleistocene extinction of *Genyornis newtoni*: human impact on Australian megafauna. *Science* 283:205–8.

Miller, G.H., P.B. Beaumont, H.J. Deacon, A.S. Brooks, P.E. Hare, and A.J.T. Jull. 1999b. Earliest modern humans in southern Africa dated by isoleucine epimerization in ostrich eggshell. *Quaternary Science Reviews* 18:1537–48.

Miller, G.H., C.P. Hart, E.B. Roark, and B.J. Johnson. 2000. Isoleucine epimerization in eggshells of the flightless Australian birds *Genyornis* and *Dromaius*. In G.A. Goodfriend, M.J. Collins, M.L. Fogel, S.A. Macko, and J.F. Wehmiller (eds), *Perspectives in Amino Acid and Protein Geochemistry*, pp. 161–81. New York: Oxford University Press.

Mitterer, R.M. and N. Kriausakul. 1989. Calculation of amino acid racemization ages based on apparent parabolic kinetics. *Quaternary Science Reviews* 8:353–7.

Murray-Wallace, C.V. and R.W.L. Kimber. 1993. Further evidence for apparent 'parabolic' racemization kinetics in Quaternary molluscs. *Australian Journal of Earth Sciences* 40:313–7.

Murray-Wallace, C.V. and S.M. Colley. 1997. Amino acid racemisation and radiocarbon dating of a contact period midden, Greenglade rockshelter, New South Wales. *Archaeology in Oceania* 32:163–9.

Oches, E.A., W.D. McCoy, and P.U. Clark. 1996. Amino acid estimates of latitudinal temperature gradients and geochronology of loess deposition during the last glaciation, Mississippi Valley, United States. *GSA Bulletin* 108:892–903.

Pasveer, J.M. and K.P. Aplin. 1998. Late Pleistocene to modern vertebrate faunal succession and environmental change in lowland New Guinea: evidence from the Bird's Head of Irian Jaya, Indonesia. In J. Miedema, C. Odé, and R.A.C. Dam (eds), *Perspectives on the Bird's Head of Irian Jaya, Indonesia: Proceedings of the Conference, Leiden, 13–17 October 1997*, pp. 891–930. Amsterdam: Rodopi.

Pasveer, J.M., S.J. Clarke, and G.H. Miller. 2002. Late Pleistocene occupation of inland rainforest, Bird's Head, Papua. *Archaeology in Oceania* 37:92–5.

Pernetta, J.C. 1989. Analysis of faunal remains from the archaeological sites. In P.P. Gorecki and D.S. Gillieson (eds), *A Crack in the Spine: Prehistory and Ecology of the Jimi-Yuat Valley, Papua New Guinea*, pp. 191–208. Townsville: James Cook University of North Queensland.

Pillans, B. 1982. Amino acid racemisation dating: a review. In W. Ambrose and P. Duerden (eds), *Archaeometry: An Australasian Perspective*, pp. 228–35. Canberra: Department of Prehistory, Research School of Pacific Studies, Australian National University.

Stuiver, M. and P.J. Reimer. 1993. Extended 14C database and revised CALIB radiocarbon calibration program. *Radiocarbon* 35:215–30.

Stuiver, M., P.J. Reimer, E. Bard, J.W. Beck, G.S. Burr, K.A. Hughen, B. Kromer, F.G. McCormac, J. van der Plicht, and M. Spurk. 1998. INTCAL98 Radiocarbon age calibration 24,000–0 cal BP. *Radiocarbon* 40:1041–83.

Sykes, G.A., M.J. Collins, and D.I. Walton. 1995. The significance of a geochemically isolated intracrystalline organic fraction within biominerals. *Organic Geochemistry* 23:1059–65.

Vogel, J.C., E. Visser, and A. Fuls. 2001. Suitability of ostrich eggshell for radiocarbon dating. *Radiocarbon* 43:133–7.

Williams, D.L.G. 1981. *Genyornis* eggshell (Dromornithidae; Aves) from the Late Pleistocene of South Australia. *Alcheringa* 5:133–40.

Williams, K.M. and G.G. Smith. 1977. A critical evaluation of the application of amino acid racemization to geochronology and geothermometry. *Origins of Life* 8:91–144.

14

On the Cultural History of the Aru Islands: Some Conclusions

Sue O'Connor[1], Matthew Spriggs[1], and Peter Veth[2]

1. Department of Archaeology and Natural History, Research School of Pacific and Asian Studies, The Australian National University, Canberra, ACT, Australia
2. Research Unit, Australian Institute of Aboriginal and Torres Strait Islander Studies, Canberra, ACT, Australia

> My expedition to the Aru Islands had been eminently successful…I brought away with me more than nine thousand specimens of natural objects, of about sixteen hundred distinct species. I had made the acquaintance of a strange and little-known race of men; I had become familiar with the traders of the far East; I had revelled in the delights of exploring a new fauna and flora, one of the most remarkable and least-known in the world; and I had succeeded in the main object for which I had undertaken the journey — namely, to obtain fine specimens of the magnificent birds of paradise, and to be enabled to observe them in their native forests. By this success I was stimulated to continue my researches in the Moluccas and New Guinea for nearly five years longer, and it is still the portion of my travels to which I look back with the most complete satisfaction.
>
> Wallace 1869:486

In the introduction to this volume (Chapter 1) we discussed the specific objectives of the Aru Islands research project and how these were framed within the context of broader regional themes and issues that have directed, and continue to direct, archaeological enquiry within Island Southeast Asia, Australia, and elsewhere in Oceania. Here we review the results of our field work and analysis in the context of these broad research questions.

Specifically we had hoped to find archaeological evidence in the Aru Islands that would throw light on the following issues:

1) the nature and rate of maritime colonization and island settlement by early *H. sapiens sapiens* in the Pleistocene, and the subsequent impact of such settlement on the 'pristine' landscapes of previously unoccupied islands;
2) the extent of inter-island connectivity or isolation, and contact and exchange in the Pleistocene and early Holocene, as demonstrated by the evidence relating to the translocation of animal species, plants and exotic stone;

3) the origins and timing of the introduction of agriculture and domestic animals, and the impetus for the development and/or adoption of agriculture by pre-agricultural communities or hunter-horticulturalists;
4) the interaction between indigenous groups and incoming Austronesian settlers and/or traders; and
5) the involvement of Aru as a supplier of bird of paradise feathers and other forest and marine products to world markets over the last 2000 years or so.

As is often the case when research is initiated in a previously unexplored area, our endeavours met with mixed success: positive results in some areas which were unanticipated and little information about other issues or periods of time that we thought would almost certainly be productive. These are reviewed in chronological succession.

The Timing and Nature of Maritime Colonization, Island Settlement and Evidence for Inter-Island Connectivity in the Pleistocene and Early Holocene

As discussed in Chapter 1, the dates for the first peopling of Sahul or Greater Australia have now been pushed back to about 55,000 to 65,000 years ago. These dates result from the application of techniques such as TL, OSL, and ESR, which are capable of dating materials that are well beyond the range of radiocarbon chronology. Using these techniques, early dates have now been obtained from open and shelter site types in both northern and southern Australia (see O'Connor and Chappell 2003 for a summary of results and the debate). For a variety of reasons, however, some researchers are still reluctant to accept these early dates and prefer to rely on the radiocarbon chronology (Allen and O'Connell 2003). However, even if we rely exclusively on the radiocarbon chronology, an arrival date of ca. 50,000 BP seems overly conservative, in view of the fact that radiocarbon dates of the order of 47,000 BP have been obtained for early occupation levels in the southwest of the continent (Turney et al. 2001). Occupation of what is now northeastern New Guinea occurred at least 40,000 years ago (references in O'Connor and Chappell 2003), and the islands to the east of New Guinea requiring further water crossings were also first settled by at least 40,000 BP (Leavesley and Chappell 2004).

In Island Southeast Asia beyond the Sunda Shelf the oldest dates published for modern human occupation so far are those from Lene Hara cave in East Timor at 35,000 years (O'Connor et al. 2002). In Halmahera and Sulawesi earliest occupation dates are between 28,000 and 31,000 years BP (Bellwood et al. 1998; Glover 1981). The remarkable discoveries in Flores relate to a much earlier mid-Pleistocene settlement, seemingly by *Homo erectus* populations who may later have evolved into the diminutive *Homo floresiensis* (Brown et al. 2004; Morwood et al. 1998, 1999, 2004). Early occupation of that island by *Homo sapiens* is very likely but as yet undocumented.

The combined evidence available to us in 1995 suggested that evidence of modern human settlement in Wallacea in the order of at least 40,000 to 45,000 years BP should be forthcoming, and Aru seemed like a good candidate for discovering early settlement.

As already mentioned, the Aru Islands looked to be a logical field target for investigating initial and subsequent maritime colonizations into Sahul. First, their location on the edge of the Sahul shelf appeared optimal in terms of detecting initial Pleistocene colonization (Chapter 1:Figure 1.1; cf. Birdsell 1977). Secondly, the narrow water channel between the southeastern Moluccan islands and the edge of the Sahul shelf at this point (the Aru Plateau) would also have facilitated two-way voyaging. Given the steeply shelving submarine profile to the west, there seemed a good chance that Pleistocene/early Holocene archaeological sites would be found not far inland from the present coast, in limestone caves with well preserved faunal and botanical remains that would enable us to track faunal translocation and extinction events.

The field survey carried out in 1995 demonstrated that suitable limestone caves were not to be found on the west coast. This meant that we had no promising sample points in the areas assessed to have greatest potential for uncovering initial colonization. We then turned our attention to the inland karst limestone areas, which produced a wealth of caves, and the two most promising were selected for excavation in the subsequent field seasons: Liang Lemdubu in 1996 and Liang Nabulei Lisa in 1997.

The 1995–97 investigations provide no support for colonization onto the Sahul Shelf by early maritime colonists making their way through the island chain around 50,000 years ago or earlier (Birdsell's (1977) route 2A). As discussed in Chapter 9, the excavation at Liang Lemdubu produced a rich Pleistocene record of human occupation, but one confined to the past 28,000 years, with little evidence available for the period after the beginning of the Holocene. Occupation at Liang Nabulei Lisa begins about 16,000 years ago and fills in the terminal Pleistocene and early Holocene picture which is missing in Liang Lemdubu. The cave faunas are rich and well preserved, and provide an excellent record of changes in species distributions through time. Changes that occur during the late Pleistocene and early Holocene appear to reflect changes in the vegetation structure of the surrounding site environment, rather than to relate to human agency such as translocation of wild animals, changing predation patterns, or hunting pressure. Perhaps the principal contribution of the Aru faunal record is as a proxy for past vegetation change and inferred climate change on the Aru Plateau in the late Pleistocene and early Holocene.

As discussed in Chapter 2, most of the vegetation records in this region are based on pollen and charcoal recorded in marine and terrestrial cores. The catchments for these records are broad and subject to a variety of influences. It is thus often difficult to apply the data obtained from them at the local scale. The complex relationships between land mass, altitude, wind circulation patterns, and sea surface temperature also make it difficult to model the impact of climate change at the local level. For this reason, there is disagreement amongst specialists about the severity and impact of cooling and aridity at different latitudes and altitudes during the LGM. It is at the local scale that change may be most influential in terms of human choices about whether or not occupation of a region is sustainable.

The composition of the vertebrate fauna in the earliest human occupation levels at Lemdubu suggests that the dominant vegetation in the vicinity of the cave was relatively dry and open, probably savannah woodland with a grassy understorey. This supported a range of species found today in the Trans-Fly area of New Guinea and across northern Australia, including *Macropus agilis*, *Isoodon macrourus*, and *Rattus sordidus*. However, in the same levels, a smaller but significant contribution is made by species which inhabit rainforest or dense gallery forest (i.e. *Thylogale* spp., *Dorcopsis* sp., *Echymipera rufescens*, *Poponomys* sp., *Spilocuscus maculatus* and *Phalanger* spp.), indicating that substantial patches of wetter, denser vegetation were still to be found in the vicinity of the site. Presumably these wetter plant communities were located along drainage lines and in topographic lows in the karst landscape.

Grassland-associated taxa increase and wet closed forest associated species decrease after this time, with a peak in open grassland species occurring about 20,000–17,000 years ago. The faunal evidence for extensive and sustained savannah grassland from 28,000 years ago until the terminal Pleistocene/early Holocene at both Lemdubu and Nabulei Lisa tends to support the palaeoenvironmental models that propose more extreme cooling and reductions in precipitation at low altitude in this tropical region, with drops in temperature of up to 5–6 degrees during the glacial maximum, rather than the more conservative estimates (see Hope 2001:143). In general, the Aru faunal data fit well with the broad vegetation and inferred climate change derived from the most recently obtained palaeobotanical records (Hope et al. 2004; Kershaw et al. 2002).

Although it is easy to see why the drier conditions associated with the onset of the LGM would have created favourable habitats for a range of human prey species on the Plateau, it is more difficult to understand why it was that Lemdubu was not occupied, even intermittently, prior to 28,000 years ago. It was suggested in Chapter 9 that slightly wetter conditions and more closed vegetation communities may have prevailed prior to this time, and that the Aru Plateau may have been a less bountiful environment for human occupation than subsequently, when savannah grassland was more extensive. Although this is no doubt the case, there is little evidence in the Banda core or other regional records to support the contention that rainforest would have been sufficiently dense to have acted as a barrier to human exploitation of the area surrounding Lemdubu in the 10,000 years preceding its first settlement (see Kershaw et al. 2002).

At this stage it must remain an open question whether or not hunter-gatherers were on the Aru Plateau prior to 28,000 years ago. It seems likely that the Aru dates reflect limited regional sampling of sites or of the extensive cave deposits of the island group. Discussion of other aspects of human occupation such as exchange or technology is hampered by the limited number of stone and bone artefacts in Lemdubu and Nabulei Lisa. Neither site provides any indication of changing technology prior to the introduction of pottery in the late Holocene. It is salutary to contemplate what we would have made of these two important cave sites if we had not had the excellently preserved faunal remains. We would no doubt have come to the conclusion that the caves were only occupied on a very fleeting basis during the late Pleistocene and the Holocene.

One find from Lemdubu may well give us a picture of what the earliest modern humans to reach northern Sahul would have looked like. This was the 18,000 BP burial of a female discussed in detail in Chapter 12. Lemdubu Woman is the earliest northern Sahulland skeleton, albeit dating from a time long after first human settlement of the region. The skeleton therefore probably displays evolution in body form from the initial inhabitants, currently best represented by the Mungo 1 and 3 skeletons from western New South Wales that date to in excess of 40,000 BP (Bowler et al. 2003, Thorne et al. 1999). The completeness of the Lemdubu skeleton, especially the pelvis, allowed its identification as a woman although the robustness of the skull would on its own have suggested the skeleton to be male. The discovery, when compared with other Sahul skeletons of approximately the same period, suggests that at the end of the LGM the inhabitants continent-wide were already characterized by a distinctive suite of 'Australoid' features. They differed from modern Australian Aborigines in having a larger, more robust cranium. Most individuals, however, would have combined robust and more gracile traits. This suggests that the classic distinction made between robust and gracile populations within Pleistocene Sahul (Thorne 1980, 1989) is a false one, and that there was basically a single population evolving through time, with extensive gene flow between north and south.

East to West or West to East? The Origins and Timing of the Introduction of Agriculture and Domestic Animals in Southeastern Maluku, and Interaction Between Indigenous Groups and Incoming Austronesian Settlers

At the time we began this project there were two major competing hypotheses relevant to a consideration of the origins of horticulture in this region. The orthodox view had domesticated crops and animals — pigs, dogs and chickens — brought by Austronesian language speakers who also introduced pottery technology, approximately 3500 years ago. There was evidence to support this migration and diffusion from other areas of Island Southeast Asia, including Halmahera (updated references are provided by Bellwood 1997, Bellwood et al. 1998). The alternative view, gaining strength recently with the work of Denham and his colleagues at Kuk in the New Guinea Highlands (Denham 2003; Denham et al. 2003), stresses the independent development of agriculture in the New

Guinea region and the spread to the west into Island Southeast Asia, as well as to the east into the Pacific, of a range of locally domesticated tuber and tree crops (cf. Spriggs 1996).

Related to this issue and also central to our investigation were the claims for the introduction of pigs into New Guinea sometime between 9000 and 6000 years ago, and a mid-Holocene date for the first appearance of pottery in Papua New Guinea (Bulmer 1985, 1991; Gorecki 1992; Gorecki et al. 1991; Swadling et al. 1989, 1991). These claims have been criticized on the basis that the finds are vertically displaced from higher in the profile, and because several of the sites for which the early finds are claimed are poorly published and inadequately dated (Spriggs 1996, 2001). However, they are worthy of discussion because they accord with the possibility of pre-Austronesian interaction between New Guinea and islands to the west. If crops dispersed from New Guinea into Southeast Asia in the early to mid-Holocene, then why could not pigs have been translocated in the other direction at the same date?

Unfortunately, the Aru Islands archaeological record is almost mute on this score. Pollen is not preserved in the cave sites of Lemdubu and Nabulei Lisa, nor in the Wangil Midden. Other palaeobotanical remains are rare. We therefore have no subsistence information about plant foods to complement the faunal sequences. Evidence for the introduction of domestic animals such as pig and dog, and by proxy the introduction of an agricultural economy, appears only in the last thousand years at Liang Nabulei Lisa and Wangil Midden. A putative indication of horticulture in the Aru Islands record is given by indirect evidence obtained from the Wangil swamp pollen core (Zone WGL 2: see Chapter 2). This sequence shows a distinct increase in charcoal perhaps indicating an increase in disturbance by fire and vegetation clearing at an inferred age of approximately 4400–3600 cal BP. Weed indicators such as some ferns, grass, and daisies also become more common in the core above this point. There is, however, nothing registered in the pollen record to demonstrate that this increased clearing is related to agriculture. It may simply reflect more intensive human activity near the site at a time when it was in the process of being removed from direct coastal influence and becoming less swampy.

The arrival of the Southeast Asian Neolithic as signalized by the introduction of pottery and/or domestic animals is barely registered in the archaeological record of Aru to date, and where it is, it occurs very late in the sequence. Pottery is confined to the last thousand years at the Wangil Midden and at Liang Nabulei Lisa. Three nondescript small body sherds in the Liang Lemdubu sequence may be slightly earlier, although in view of the size of the pottery sample, the fragment size, and the range for the dates in the upper three spits at Lemdubu, it would be foolhardy to argue for early pottery at this site.

The Involvement of Aru as a Supplier of Bird of Paradise Feathers and Other Forest and Marine Products to World Markets Over the Last 2000 Years: the Metal Age, Pre-colonial, and Colonial Periods

Perhaps the most unanticipated outcome of the Aru field program was the richness of the pre-colonial and colonial archaeological records. We began the systematic survey with the expectation that the control of the region by the Dutch East India Company during the historic period assured a good documentary coverage of the cultural record during this period. We discovered however, that at least for the later period (18th and 19th Centuries) — represented by sites such as Sirlasi and Jambu Air Lama in the southeast of the islands — the extent and scale of trade is poorly reflected in the historic records, which are either incomplete or absent. The presence of Indonesian Metal Age style pottery at midden/village sites such as Wangil, the considerable number of recent middens containing quantities of prestige goods such as European liquor bottles and Chinese porcelain, and the remarkable architecture of the Ujir ruins all attest to a vigorous exchange network at a scale that is largely otherwise undocumented. Some of these findings are summarized in Veth et al. (2000) and in revised form in Chapter 5, in Chapter 4 detailing the sites located during our survey of the Aru Islands, and in Chapter 6 on the Wangil Midden with its late Metal Age sequence.

We think it is likely that the Islamic-influenced structures of Ujir, situated adjacent to a protected deep water harbour, likely served as an entrepôt for the trade in birds of paradise, marine produce, and sago. The historic evidence for trade in other parts of Maluku, suggests that the original settlement could have been established by the late 15th century. This would fit well with the style of the numerous sherds of Chinese trade ware found scattered around the ruins. Whoever made the structures, it is clear that a settlement of this permanence and extent implies an involvement in regional, if not global, trading systems. The degree of Aru's involvement in these early trading systems has been historically neglected, due in part to the dominance of the north Moluccan and Bandanese trade-polities of the 15th and 16th centuries.

Lape (2000a, b) has documented a pre-colonial trade network centred in Banda. The presence of red slipped pottery from Banda in the early levels of the Wangil Midden demonstrates trade between the two islands as early as 500–800 BP (see Chapter 6 for further details). Three Dutch garrisons (and several churches) were established on Aru in the mid–late 17th century in an effort to control regional trade.

During our surveys around the Aru Islands, particularly on the east coast, we recorded a number of mounded and linear middens, some of considerable extent. Only one of these coastal sites has been excavated and analysed (Wangil Midden on Wamar Island — see Chapter 3). Many of the coastal middens were noted to contain both plain and decorated pottery and from the presence of imported ceramics were certainly used well into the 19th century. This was shown by the presence of glass bottles eroding from upper units that could be dated to the early to 19th century. The location of large village sites dating from about ca. 1800 AD adjacent to the extensive reef systems on the east coast of Aru suggests a much greater involvement of this area with the wider trading world than is commonly appreciated, or than would be anticipated from the historic records relating to this later period. Yet, if we read Wallace's and other 19th century accounts carefully, we can see that Europeans were aware of the significance of this part of the archipelago. Wallace (1869:439) wrote:

> ... on the east coast are a great number of islands extending some miles beyond the mainland, and forming the 'blakang tana' or 'back country,' of the traders, being the principal seat of the pearl, tripang, and tortoise-shell fisheries.

Kolff (1840:175–6) gives an account of the scale of activity on the pearl banks in 1824 (cf. Spyer 2000:20-22). Oral history suggests that the large village sites we found in that area were decimated by a smallpox epidemic that passed through the region in the mid- to late-1800s and the communities then split their settlements into a number of smaller villages.

Conclusions

During the project we failed to find evidence of the probable earliest settlement of the Aru Plateau of Sahul, although with the burial of Lemdubu Woman — the earliest yet found in northern Sahul — we can get some idea of the appearance of the region's slightly later Pleistocene inhabitants. The stone artefacts from the early sites were particularly undiagnostic and unchanging over time, and provide little clue as to the cultural connections of the Pleistocene inhabitants of Aru. The fauna from the sites, on the other hand, gave a particularly rich picture of changing environments as Aru entered the drier period of the LGM, and then underwent climatic amelioration and the expansion of rainforest in the Holocene. Rising sea levels are also reflected in the freshwater and marine faunal record as the Aru Plateau became an island group cut off from its Sahulland roots by about 11,500 BP. We detected little or no trace of the spread of the Island Southeast Asian Neolithic and can attest to introduced animals such as pig, dog and deer only very late in our cultural sequences. We did, however, pick up a strong signal of the scale and importance of immediately pre-colonial and colonial period trading networks, including pre-1620s pottery imports from the Banda Islands. There is clearly much further potential for detailed work on the historical archaeology of Aru. Further research may also throw light both on the earliest period of occupation of what was then a low plateau on the edge of a continent and on the timing and impact of the spread of the Island Southeast Asian Neolithic in what by then was an archipelago. Without any doubt, Aru remains as fascinating — but hopefully not quite as mysterious — as it appeared to Alfred Russell Wallace on that January day in 1857.

References

Allen, J., and J.F. O'Connell. 2003. The long and the short of it: archaeological approaches to determining when humans first colonized Australia and New Guinea. *Australian Archaeology* 57:5–19.

Bellwood, P. 1997. *Prehistory of the Indo-Malaysian Archipelago*. 2nd Edition. Honolulu: University of Hawaii Press.

Bellwood, P., G. Nitihaminoto, G. Irwin, Gunadi, A. Waluyo, and D. Tanudirjo. 1998. 35,000 years of prehistory in the northern Moluccas. In G.-J. Bartstra (ed.), *Bird's Head Approaches: Irian Jaya Studies, A Programme for Interdisciplinary Research*, pp. 233–75. Rotterdam: A.A. Balkema. *Modern Quaternary Studies in Southeast Asia* 15.

Birdsell, J.B. 1977. The recalibration of a paradigm for the first peopling of Greater Australia. In J. Allen, J. Golson, and R. Jones (eds), *Sunda and Sahul: Prehistoric Studies in Southeast Asia, Melanesia and Australia*, pp. 113–67. London: Academic Press.

Bowler, J.M., H. Johnston, J.M. Olley, J.R. Prescott, R.G. Roberts, W. Shawcross and N.A. Spooner. 2003. New ages for human occupation and climatic change at Lake Mungo, Australia. *Nature* 421:837–840.

Brown, P., T. Sutikna, M.J. Morwood, R.P. Seojono, Jatmiko, E.W. Saptomo, and R.A. Due. 2004. A new small-bodied hominin from the Late Pleistocene of Flores, Indonesia. *Nature* 431: 1055–61.

Bulmer, S. 1985. Papuan pottery — an archaeological consideration. *Bulletin of the Indo-Pacific Prehistory Association* 6:123–32.

Bulmer, S. 1991. Variation and change in stone tools in the highlands of Papua New Guinea: the witness of Wanelek. In A. Pawley (ed.), *Man and a Half: Essays in Pacific Anthropology and Ethnobiology in Honour of Ralph Bulmer*, pp. 470–8. Auckland: The Polynesian Society.

Denham, T.P. 2003. The Kuk Morass: Multi-Disciplinary Investigations of Early to Mid Holocene Plant Exploitation at Kuk Swamp, Wahgi Valley, Papua New Guinea. Unpublished PhD thesis, Australian National University, Canberra.

Denham, T.P., S.G. Haberle, C. Lentfer, R. Fullagar, J. Field, M. Therin, N. Porch, and B. Winsborough. 2003. Origins of agriculture at Kuk Swamp in the Highlands of New Guinea. *Science* 301:189–93.

Glover, I. 1981. C Leang Burung 2 south Sulawesi. *Modern Quaternary Research in SE Asia* 6:1–38.

Gorecki, P. 1992. A Lapita smoke screen? In J.-C. Galipaud (ed.), *Poterie Lapita et Peuplement: Actes du Colloque Lapita, Noumea, Nouvelle-Caledonie, Janvier 1992*, pp. 27–47. Noumea: ORSTOM.

Gorecki, P., M. Mabin, and J. Campbell. 1991. Archaeology and geomorphology of the Vanimo coast, Papua New Guinea: preliminary results. *Archaeology in Oceania* 26:119–22.

Hope, G.S. 2001. Environmental change in the Late Pleistocene and later Holocene at Wanda Site, Soroako, South Sulawesi, Indonesia. *Journal of Palaeogeography, Palaeoclimatology, Palaeoecology* 17:129–45.

Hope, G.S., X. Sun, P.-M. Liew, A.P. Kershaw, W.A. van der Kaars, H. Takahara, M. McGlone, L.E. Heusser, and N. Miyoshi. 2004. History of vegetation and habitat change from the PEP II transect. *Quaternary International* 118–119:103–26.

Kershaw, A.P., S. van der Kaars, P. Moss, and X. Wang. 2002. Quaternary records of vegetation, biomass burning, climate and possible human impact in the Indonesian–Northern Australian region. In A.P. Kershaw, B. David, N. Tapper, D. Penny, and J. Brown (eds), *Bridging Wallace's Line: The Environmental and Cultural History and Dynamics of the Southeast Asian–Australian Region*, pp. 97–118. Reiskirchen: Catena Verlag. *Advances in GeoEcology* 34.

Kolff, D.H. 1840. *Voyages of the Dutch Brig of War 'Dourga' through the Southern and Little Known Parts of the Moluccan Archipelago ... during the Years 1825 and 1826*. London: James Madden.

Lape, P.V. 2000a. Contact and Conflict in the Banda Islands, Eastern Indonesia, 11th to 17th Centuries. Unpublished PhD thesis, Brown University, Rhode Island.

Lape, P.V. 2000b. Political dynamics and religious change in the late pre-colonial Banda Islands, Eastern Indonesia. *World Archaeology* 32(1):138–55.

Leavesley, M.G. and J. Chappell. 2004. Buang Merabak: additional early radiocarbon evidence of the colonisation of the Bismarck Archipelago, Papua New Guinea. *Antiquity* 78(301). URL: http://antiquity.ac.uk/ProjGall/leavesley/index.html

Morwood, M.J., P. O'Sullivan, F. Aziz, and A. Raza. 1998. Fission track age of stone tools and fossils on the east Indonesian island of Flores. *Nature* 392:173–76.

Morwood, M.J., F. Aziz, P. O'Sullivan, Nasruddin, D.R. Hobbs, and A. Raza. 1999. Archaeological and palaeontological research in central Flores, East Indonesia: results of fieldwork 1997–98. *Antiquity* 73:273–86.

Morwood, M.J., R.P. Seojono, R.G. Roberts, T. Sutikna, C.S.M. Turney, K.E. Westaway, W.J. Rink, J.-x. Zhao, G.D. van den Bergh, R.A. Due, D.R. Hobbs, M.W. Moore, M.I. Bird, and L.K. Fifield. 2004. Archaeology and age of a new hominin from Flores in Eastern Indonesia. *Nature* 431:1087–91.

O'Connor, S., M. Spriggs, and P. Veth. 2002. Excavation at Lene Hara establishes occupation in East Timor at least 30,000–35,000 years on: results of recent fieldwork. *Antiquity* 76:45–50.

O'Connor, S. and J. Chappell. 2003. Colonization and coastal subsistence in Australia and Papua New Guinea: different timing, different modes. In C. Sand (ed.), *Pacific Archaeology: Assessments and Prospects. Proceedings of the International Conference for the 50th Anniversary of the First Lapita Excavation (July 1952), Koné-Nouméa 2002*, pp. 15–32. Nouméa: Départment Archéologie, Service des Musées et du Patrimoine de Nouvelle-Calédonie. *Le Cahiers de l'Archéologie en Nouvelle-Calédonie* 15.

Spriggs, M. 1996. What is Southeast Asian about Lapita? In T. Akazawa and E. Szathmary (eds), *Prehistoric Mongoloid Dispersals*, pp. 324–48. Oxford: Clarendon Press.

Spriggs, M. 2001. Who cares what time it is? The importance of chronology in Pacific archaeology. In A. Anderson, I. Lilley and S. O'Connor (eds), *Histories of Old Ages: Essays in Honour of Rhys Jones*, pp. 237–49. Canberra: Pandanus Books, Australian National University.

Spyer, P. 2000. *The Memory of Trade: Modernity's Entanglements on an Eastern Indonesian Island*. Durham and London: Duke University Press.

Swadling, P., J. Chappell, G. Francis, N. Araho, and B. Ivuyo. 1989. A late Quaternary inland sea and early pottery in Papua New Guinea. *Archaeology in Oceania* 24:106–9.

Swadling, P., N. Araho, and B. Ivuyo. 1991. Settlements associated with the inland Sepik-Ramu Sea. *Bulletin of the Indo–Pacific Prehistory Association* 11:92–110.

Thorne, A.G. 1980. The longest link: human evolution in southeast Asia and the settlement of Australia. In J. Fox, R. Garnaut, P. McCawley and J. Mackie (eds), *Indonesia: Australian Perspectives*, pp. 35–43. Canberra: The Australian National University.

Thorne, A.G. 1989. The emergence of the Pacific peoples, in L.H. Schmitt, L. Freedman and N.W. Bruce (eds), *The Growing Scope of Human Biology*, pp. 103–111. Perth: Australasian Society for Human Biology.

Thorne, A., R. Grün, G. Mortimer, N.A. Spooner, J.J. Simpson, M. Mcculloch, L. Taylor and D. Curnoe. 1999. Australia's oldest human remains: age of the Lake Mungo 3 skeleton. *Journal of Human Evolution* 36:591–612.

Turney, C.S.M., M.I. Bird, L.K. Fifield, R.G. Roberts, M.A. Smith, C.E. Dortch, R. Grun, E. Lawson, L.K. Ayliffe, G.H. Miller, J. Dortch, and R.G. Cresswell. 2001. Early human occupation at Devil's Lair, southwestern Australia 50,000 years ago. *Quaternary Research* 55:3–13.

Veth, P., S. O'Connor, M. Spriggs, W. Nayati, A. Jatmiko, and H. Mohammad. 2000. The mystery of the Ujir site: insights into early historic settlement in the Aru Islands, Maluku. *The Bulletin of the Australian Institute for Maritime Archaeology* 24:125–32.

Wallace, A.R. 1869. *The Malay Archipelago: The Land of the Orang-Utan and the Bird of Paradise. A Narrative of Travel, with Studies of Man and Nature*. London: MacMillan.

www.ingramcontent.com/pod-product-compliance
Lightning Source LLC
Chambersburg PA
CBHW061306270326
41935CB00028B/1849

* 9 7 8 1 7 4 0 7 6 1 1 3 0 *